KT-567-460

SPSS 16 MADE SIMPLE

PAUL R. KINNEAR
COLIN D. GRAY

School of Psychology,
University of Aberdeen

Ψ Psychology Press
Taylor & Francis Group

First published 2009 by Psychology Press
27 Church Road, Hove, East Sussex BN3 2FA

Simultaneously published in the USA and Canada
by Psychology Press 270 Madison Avenue, New York NY 10016

Psychology Press is an imprint of the Taylor & Francis Group, an informa business

Copyright © 2009 Psychology Press

Printed and bound in Great Britain by TJ International Ltd, Padstow, Cornwall, from pdf files
supplied by the authors. Cover design by Hybert Design.

All rights reserved. No part of this book may be reprinted or reproduced or utilised in any form
or by any electronic, mechanical, or other means, now known or hereafter invented, including
photocopying and recording, or in any information storage or retrieval system, without permission
in writing from the publishers.

This book is not sponsored or approved by SPSS, and any errors are in no way the responsibility
of SPSS. SPSS is a registered trademark and the other product names are trademarks of SPSS Inc.
SPSS Screen Images © SPSS Inc. SPSS UK Ltd, First Floor St Andrew's House, West Street,
Woking, Surrey, GU21 1EB, UK.

Windows is a registered trademark of Microsoft Corporation. For further information, contact:
Microsoft Corporation, One Microsoft Way, Redmond, WA 98052-6399, USA.

This publication has been produced with paper manufactured to strict environmental
standards and with pulp derived from sustainable forests.

British Library Cataloguing in Publication Data

A catalogue record for this book is available from the British Library.

Library of Congress Cataloging-in-Publication Data

Kinnear, Paul R.
  SPSS 16 made simple / Paul R. Kinnear, Colin D. Gray.-- 1st ed.
      p. cm.
  Includes bibliographical references and index.
  ISBN 978-1-84169-729-1 (pbk.)
  1. SPSS (Computer file) 2. Social sciences--Statistical methods--Computer programs.
      I. Gray, Colin D. II. Title.

  HA32.K553 2008
  005.5'5--dc22
                                        2008025409
  ISBN 978-1-84169-729-1

Contents

CHAPTER 2   Getting started with SPSS 16 *25*

CHAPTER 3   Editing and manipulating files *44*

CHAPTER 7   The one-way ANOVA *217*

CHAPTER 8   Between subjects factorial experiments *271*

CHAPTER 9   Within subjects experiments *316*

CHAPTER 10   Mixed factorial experiments *354*

CHAPTER 11   Measuring statistical association *394*

CHAPTER 12   Regression *436*

CHAPTER 13   Analyses of multiway frequency tables & multiple response sets *484*

Preface

In preparing this book, *SPSS 16 Made Simple*, the latest in our *SPSS Made Simple* series, we have endeavoured to retain the practical and informal character of our previous books. No previous knowledge of SPSS is assumed. Throughout the book, we have made extensive use of annotated screen snapshots of SPSS output, windows and dialog boxes to clarify the text. As in *SPSS 15 Made Simple*, we have used numbered call-outs, which not only improve the clarity of the demonstrations, but also help to communicate the correct sequencing. The gratifyingly positive responses to our previous book from our readers and students suggest that we have been successful in providing clear and useful advice, both for those who wish to get started with SPSS and for the more experienced researcher. In our latest book, as always, the presentation has been updated to reflect the improvements embodied in the current version of SPSS.

Like its predecessors, however, *SPSS 16 Made Simple* is far from being merely a cookbook. Certainly, our book was always intended to be a student's (and researcher's) practical guide to SPSS, rather than a statistical textbook. The reader, nevertheless, will find advice on the selection of appropriate statistical tests, as well as an informal revision of certain aspects of statistics that tend to be perennial stumbling blocks. In addition to instructions on the implementation of each technique, the reader will find a clear explanation of its rationale. The assumptions made by the underlying model are described and, where necessary, there is advice on how to proceed if the data do not meet the model's requirements. Over the years, in response to requests from our readers, we have expanded our coverage to include the most relevant aspects of regression theory, dummy variables, reliability, partial and semipartial correlation, odds ratios, the rationale of factor analysis and many other important topics. In this edition, there is a substantial section on the analysis of multiple responses. As in several recent editions, there is a glossary of key terms. At the end of some chapters, there are suggestions for further reading.

An understanding of logarithms is essential for several techniques, especially loglinear analysis and logistic regression. Since many of our readers have admitted to being rather rusty on this topic and told us that some revision of the topic would be welcome, there is now a short appendix on logarithms.

As well as showing the reader how to use of SPSS 16 to run the various statistical analyses, we have also provided guidance, in line with APA recommendations, on how the results of each test should be presented in scientific papers and practical reports.

Our previous books have always contained many practice examples, both for the benefit of the reader studying the subject on an individual basis and for use by the instructor. The examples are of two kinds. Some are designed to consolidate the material of a specific chapter and are clearly labelled as such. Others, however, are intended to give the reader practice in deciding upon a research strategy that is appropriate for a data set that might well require techniques from more than one chapter. There are six Revision Exercises, each of which requires the reader to analyse a data set without the cueing that a chapter context would provide and are intended to help promote a sense of strategy in data analysis. We have always wanted to provide more supplementary material of this kind, but have been prevented from doing so by considerations of space. For this edition, therefore, we have transferred the examples to our website at www.psypress.com/spss-made-simple. There, the reader will find a variety of supplementary materials, including not only examples of the two types we have just described, but also PowerPoint presentations of selected topics and multiple-choice questions.

In this book, as in earlier editions, the emphasis is upon accessing SPSS through windows and dialog boxes. In our view, however, the next step is to acquire a working knowledge of Syntax, the SPSS control language. In the first place, not all the procedures that the researcher requires are available through dialog boxes. For example, in the ANOVA dialogs, there is no opportunity for the user to select tests for simple effects. Simple effects analysis, however, can readily be implemented by writing appropriate syntax commands and the procedure for doing this is fully described in the chapters on analysis of variance. Syntax is also required for the running of a factor analysis with a correlation matrix (rather than the raw data) as the input. The procedure is described in Chapter 15.

There is another good reason for acquiring SPSS syntax. Control language also provides an excellent way of deepening one's understanding of the fundamentals of statistics. Operations such as matrix multiplication, for example, can readily be run with SPSS and an understanding of such methods is essential for further progress in techniques such as factor analysis. We show how this is done in Chapter 15. The properties of key distributions can be investigated by running Monte Carlo sampling experiments from the appropriate syntax.

Throughout the preparation of this book, as with previous editions, we have been most fortunate in having the advice, encouragement and SPSS expertise of John Lemon, Senior Computing Adviser at Aberdeen University's Directorate of Information Systems and Services. We are also very grateful to Caroline Green, Senior Teaching Fellow, for her most helpful observations on the Exercises and her reports of our students' progress with them in the practical classes. We very much appreciate the unfailing support that Martin Fraser, IT Support Officer, and our Chief Technician, Peter Bates, have always given us and the encouragement we have received from Dr Peter McGeorge, Head of the School of Psychology in the College of Life Sciences and Medicine at the University of Aberdeen. Finally, we would like to express our gratitude to all those who, though too numerous to mention individually, have helped us in some way to produce this book.

Colin Gray and Paul Kinnear

May, 2008

CHAPTER 1

Introduction

1.1   MEASUREMENTS AND DATA

Since this book is about the analysis of data, we shall begin with a survey of the kinds of data that result from research and introduce some key terms.

1.1.1   Variables: quantitative and qualitative

A **variable** is a characteristic or property of a person, an object or a situation, comprising a set of different values or categories. Height is a variable, as are weight, blood type and gender. **Quantitative variables**, such as height, weight or age, are possessed in **degree** and so can sometimes be measured in units on an independent scale. In contrast, **qualitative** variables, such as sex, blood group or nationality, are possessed only in **kind**: they cannot be expressed in units on a scale. With qualitative variables, we can only make counts of the cases falling into the various categories, as when we might record that a theatre audience comprises 100 men and 300 women.

1.1.2   Levels of measurement: scale, ordinal and nominal data

A **data set** is a collection of numerical observations of variables. In this book, we shall use the term **measurement** to refer to the making of numerical records of any characteristic, whether quantitative or qualitative. The numbers in a data set can carry varying amounts of information about what is being recorded. Sometimes, as records of category membership, they serve merely as labels; but often, as with heights or weights, they are units on an independent scale. It is useful to identify three **levels of measurement**:

1. At the highest level, **scale data** are measurements of quantity in units on an independent scale. Heights and weights are obvious examples. So also are performance scores, such as the number of times a participant hits a target, as well as IQs, responses to questionnaires and other psychometric data. In such a data set, each individual score or **datum** carries information independently of the other data.

2. At the next level, **ordinal** data are also records of quantitative variables; but these data take the form of ranks, or sequencing information. For example, if two judges rank 10 similar objects according to their perceived weight, assigning the rank 1 to the heaviest and 10 to the lightest, the data set will consist of 10 pairs of ranks, one pair for each object. If the judges cannot say which of several objects is the heaviest, and are allowed to assign the same rank to more than one object, the data set will contain **tied ranks**. Ranks are classified at a lower level of measurement than scale data, because there has been no independent measurement on a scale with units and, in that sense, a rank has no independent meaning.

3. At the lowest level, **nominal** data relate to qualitative variables or attributes, such as gender or blood group, and are merely records of category membership, rather than true measurements. Nominal data, that is, are merely **labels**: they are numbers, but these numbers do not express the degree to which any characteristic is possessed: they are arbitrary code numbers representing, say, different blood groups, genders or nationalities. Any other numbers (as long as they vary between categories) will serve the purpose just as well.

1.1.3   A grey area: ratings

Psychologists, market researchers and political pollsters frequently ask respondents to **rate** objects or people by assigning each to one of a set of ordered categories. There has been much debate about whether, from a statistical point of view, sets of ratings can be treated as scale data. Some argue that, unlike a rank, an individual rating carries information independently of the rest of the data. They do so on the grounds that raters are given reference or **anchor points** at the ends of the scale and are asked to express their judgements in relation to these. Others, however, would say that if 100 participants in a research project are asked to rate, say, 30 objects by placing each object in one of seven ordered categories, where 1 is very good and 7 is very bad, the operation will result in 100 sets of **ranks with ties**: that is, ratings are merely ordinal data and should be treated as such in the statistical analysis. In our view, the decision about which statistics to use should follow consideration of several factors, including the distribution of the data and the number of points on the rating scale.

Sometimes the term **categorical data** is used to include both purely nominal assignments and assignments to ordered categories. This term straddles our distinction between nominal and ordinal data and obscures the difference between ranks and ratings.

1.2   EXPERIMENTAL VERSUS CORRELATIONAL RESEARCH

In this section, we shall consider a distinction which has important implications for the sorts of statistics the researcher will choose to describe and summarise a data set and to confirm the findings with statistical inference.

1.2.1   True experiments

An **experiment** is the collection of comparative data under controlled conditions. In a true experiment, one variable, known as the **independent variable (IV)** is manipulated by the investigator in order to demonstrate that it has a causal effect upon another variable, which is known as the **dependent variable (DV)**. For example, a hypothesis that a drug affects performance could be tested by comparing the performance of a sample of people who have taken the drug with that of a comparison, or **control**, group who have not. (It is usual to improve the comparability of the two groups by presenting the controls with a **placebo**, that is, a neutral medium ideally identical with that in which the drug was presented in the **experimental** condition.) Here the IV is presence/absence of the drug and the DV is performance.

The IV is controlled by the investigator, and its values are determined before the experiment is carried out. This is achieved either by **random assignment** of the participants to the pre-set conditions or by testing each participant under all conditions, if that is feasible. The DV, on the other hand, is measured during the course of the investigation.

In the planning of an experiment, the researcher applies the **rule of one variable**: that is, the conditions under which participants in the different groups are tested must differ only with respect to the independent variable. In a poorly designed experiment, variables other than the independent variable may have a causal effect upon the dependent variable. In a well designed experiment, such **extraneous variables** are neutralised, or subject to **experimental control**. The rule of one variable is one of the most important principles in experimental design. Random assignment to conditions is intended to ensure that any individual differences in ability between the experimental and control groups tend to average out, so that the two groups are comparable in this regard. There are other methods of controlling extraneous variables, such as testing the same participants under all conditions, thus controlling for individual differences. In fact, good experiments are often run with only a single participant. The strategy the researcher should adopt depends on many factors, including the nature of the research question, the local situation and the resources available.

1.2.2   Correlational research

In an experiment, the IV, unlike gender, blood group, or nationality, is not an intrinsic property of the participants: the participants are assigned at random to the experimental and control groups. Such random assignment to different conditions confers upon the experiment a great advantage: should a difference be found between the groups in their performance, the researcher may draw the inference that the active experimental treatment has had a causal effect upon the dependent variable.

Suppose, however, that, with a view to understanding the extent to which a person's earning power depends upon level of education, a research gathers data on both variables. The researcher hopes to find that those with more education tend to have higher final salaries, that is, that salary is positively **correlated** with education. Such research is therefore known as **correlational research**.

In this second research scenario, as in the first, the research was motivated by the hypothesis that one variable has a causal effect upon another: in the drug example, the ingestion of Drug X improves memory; in the second, education improves earning power. There is an important difference between the two situations, however: in the second scenario, neither variable was manipulated by the experimenter: both salary and education are measured as they occur in the participants.

When interpreting the results of correlational research, we should bear in mind the dictum that **correlation does not imply causation**. The researcher may believe that income is, to at least some extent, causally determined by education. Other variables, however, such as IQ, socio-economic status and parental attitude to education, may be the true determinants of final salary. There are situations, in fact, where the direction of causality itself may itself be in doubt: violent people may watch violent television and films; but has viewing screen violence over the years made the viewers violent or are such programmes merely the preferred entertainment of those with violent disposition?

1.2.3   Quasi-experiments

Does smoking shorten one's life? Researchers have conducted many studies comparing the longevity of smokers and non-smokers. In such research, those in the smoking and non-smoking groups are matched with respect to as many possible confounding variables as possible, such as socio-economic status, education, lifestyle and so on. In this way, it is hoped to achieve a comparison between two groups of people who differ only in their smoking category. A difference in longevity between smokers and non-smokers is taken as evidence for the hypothesis that smoking shortens life.

In a quasi-experiment, as in a true experiment, the researcher attempts to control extraneous variables, so that the groups compared differ only with respect to the supposed causal variable. As in correlational research, however, the variables are properties of the participants: there is no random assignment to the smoking and non-smoking conditions. However careful the researchers have been to control the influence of extraneous variables, therefore, there remains the possibility that the groups may yet differ on some other crucial characteristic, such as personality or physical type. Arguably, the quasi-experiment is essentially a refinement of the correlational approach, where **statistical control** is used as an imperfect substitute for true **experimental control**.

1.3   SOME STATISTICAL TERMS AND CONCEPTS

This book, though not a statistics text, is concerned, nevertheless, with the analysis of data. While we must assume that the reader is already familiar with statistics to at least some extent, a review of some key terms and concepts may not go amiss at this point. At the end of the chapter, we make some recommendations for further reading.

1.3.1   Samples and populations

In many disciplines, the units of study (people, plants, coelacanths) vary with respect to what is being studied. When the units of study vary, it is dangerous to generalise about *all* people, *all* animals, *all* trees, *all* coelacanths) on the basis of knowledge about only *some* of them. This is why researchers in such disciplines must make use of the methods of statistics.

A **sample** is a selection of observations (often assumed to be random) from a reference set, or **population**, of possible observations that might be made. By analogy with a lottery, it may be helpful to think of a population as the numbers being churned around in the barrel at a lottery, and the sample as those numbers actually drawn. Selections of numbers picked at random from the same barrel show considerable variation: sampling implies **sampling variability**. It follows that a random sample is not necessarily **representative**: it may have very different characteristics (e.g. mean and standard deviation) from those of the population from which it has been drawn.

When we measure the reaction speeds of 100 participants, we invariably do so because we want to make inferences about the reaction speeds of people in general: it is the **population** that is of primary interest, not the **sample**: the 100 reaction speeds we have obtained are merely a sample from the population of reaction speeds. But to make an inductive inference about *all* people on the basis of data from just *some* people is to risk error. (In statistics, the term **error** denotes the extent to which the properties of a sample deviate from the corresponding values in the population.)

1.3.2 Parameters and statistics

Measures of the characteristics of a sample (such as its mean and standard deviation) are known as **statistics**. The corresponding characteristics in the population are known as **parameters**. Our research question is invariably about parameters, not statistics. **Statistical inference** is a set of methods for making inductive (and hence error-prone) inferences about parameters from the values of statistics.

Conventionally, sample and population characteristics are denoted by the use of Greek and Arabic letters, respectively (Table 1).

Table 1 Notation for parameters and statistics
Greek and Roman letters are used to denote the characteristics of **populations** and **samples** (i.e. parameters and statistics), respectively.
The mean and standard deviation of a **population** are denoted by the symbols μ and σ, respectively.
The mean and standard deviation of a **sample** are denoted by the symbols M and s, respectively.

1.3.3 Description or confirmation?

We turn to the discipline of statistics when:

1. We want to **describe and summarise** the data as a whole.

2. We want to **confirm** that other researchers repeating our study would obtain a similar result.

It is in connection with the second requirement that the need for formal **statistical tests** arises. The researcher may find a theoretically important pattern in a set of data; but is this merely the result of sampling variability or is it an important discovery, which would emerge again if the project were to be repeated?

1.3.4   Statistical inference

We shall consider two kinds of statistical inference:
1. **Estimation of parameters**.
2. **Hypothesis testing**, which we shall consider later.

Since statistical inference, being inductive, is subject to error, all inferences must be qualified by statements of probability or confidence. These two terms are not synonymous. A **probability** arises in the context of an experiment of chance and is a measure of likelihood ranging from 0 (for an impossible outcome) to 1 (a certainty). A **confidence** is a retrospective measure of how sure one ought to be that a parameter lies within a certain range, given that the statistics of a sample have certain values (see below).

Point estimation and interval estimation

The sample mean is said to be a **point estimate** of the population mean: e.g. M is an estimate of μ; and s is an estimate of σ. Our sample mean, however, may be wide of the mark as an estimate of the population mean. From the statistics of a sample, however, it is also possible to specify a range of values, known as a **confidence interval**, within which one can say, with a specified level of certainty, or 'confidence', that the true population mean lies. A confidence interval is an **interval estimate** of the value of a parameter.

Formal statistical tests: hypothesis testing

Data are not gathered just for the sake of it. Research is driven by the desire to test a provisional supposition about nature known as a **hypothesis**. Often, a scientific hypothesis states that there is a causal relationship between two variables: it is an assertion that one variable influences or helps to determine another.

Does a supposedly memory-preserving drug X improve the working memory capacities of those suffering from the early stages of dementia? Two comparable groups of 20 patients are selected: one group is treated with X; the other is a comparison group, which receives a neutral saline solution (a **placebo**) from which the drug is absent. After receiving either a solution containing X or a placebo, the patients attempt a test of memory consisting of 20 questions, so that each patient receives a score in the range from 0 to 20. Suppose that the means and standard deviations of the scores for the X and placebo groups are 12.3 (SD = 2.8) and 9.7 (SD = 3.1), respectively.

The scientific hypothesis is that the presence of X results in better memory performance than when X is absent. While these results appear to support the scientific hypothesis, it is necessary to make formal statistical tests to confirm that the findings are unlikely to have resulted from sampling variability.

Statistical hypotheses

A statistical hypothesis is a statement about a population or populations. The scores of the 20 participants in the Placebo condition are a sample from the population of such scores; likewise the 20 scores of the group who received X are also a sample from a population of scores.

In statistics, the **null hypothesis (H_0)** is the hypothesis of 'no effect': it is the negation of the scientific hypothesis. According to the null hypothesis, the mean performance levels of patients of this kind under drug and placebo conditions are the same. We can write this as follows:

$$H_0: \mu_1 = \mu_2$$

where μ_1 and μ_2 are the means of the populations of scores under the placebo and drug conditions, respectively. Because of sampling variability, of course, the two sample means are very unlikely to have exactly the same value.

In traditional significance testing, there was a preparedness to reject the null hypothesis, but a reluctance to accept it. This is because it was recognised that, because H_0 is unlikely to be exactly true, a test of H_0 would inevitably show significance, provided the sample was large enough (see Chapter 6, Section 6.3.1).

See Section 6.3.1

Critics of significance testing, however, pointed out that its advocates, in focusing exclusively upon the null hypothesis, failed to acknowledge that in order to specify a critical region of values that will lead to rejection of the null hypothesis, attention must be paid to the **alternative hypothesis (H_1)**, that is, the statistical equivalent of the scientific hypothesis. Otherwise, there is no basis for claiming that the critical region should lie in the tails of the distribution of the test statistic, as opposed to a narrower band of more frequently occurring values anywhere else within the range of possible values.

In the system of Neyman and Pearson, the problem of hypothesis testing was re-conceived in terms of a choice or decision between the **null hypothesis (H_0)** and the **alternative hypothesis (H_1)**, against which H_0 is tested. In their view, the null hypothesis could be accepted as well as rejected.

Returning to the drug experiment, the alternative hypothesis (H_1) states that the means of the Placebo and Drug populations are not equal. The alternative hypothesis may be written as follows:

$$H_1: \mu_1 \neq \mu_2$$

The two statistical hypotheses, H_0 and H_1, are complementary, that is, they exhaust the possibilities: in this case, for instance, either the population means are equal or they are not.

Testing the hypotheses

As statements about hypothetical populations, statistical hypotheses must be tested by using the values of sample characteristics, that is, statistics. Special statistics, known as **test statistics**, such as t, F and χ^2, are used to test statistical hypotheses. A test statistic must have a known **sampling distribution**, so that we can determine the probability of obtaining values within a specified range.

In hypothesis testing, it is not the scientific hypothesis that is tested directly, but the null hypothesis. A small, fixed probability known as a **significance level** is decided upon before the data are gathered. Conventionally, the significance level is set at .05 or (less commonly) .01.

Percentiles

The **xth percentile** is the value in a distribution below which x% of values lie. So the 50th percentile is the median, because the latter is the value below (or above) which 50% of values lie. The 97.5th percentile (Figure 1) is the value below which 97.5% of values lie; but it is also the value above which 2.5% of values lie. The 2.5th percentile is the value below which 2.5% of values lie, so 2.5 + 2.5 = 5% of values lie in the tails of a distribution, below the 2.5th percentile and above the 97.5th percentile.

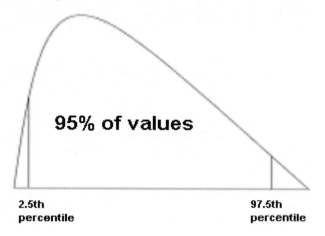

2.5th   **97.5th**
percentile   **percentile**

Figure 1. Distribution showing 5% of values lie in the tails of a distribution, above the 97.5th percentile and below the 2.5th percentile.

The critical region

Once the significance level has been decided upon, a **critical region** is chosen, that is, a range of atypical values for the test statistic under the null hypothesis such that the probability of a value in the range is equal to the significance level. The critical region is taken to lie in one or both **tails** of the distribution, where values of the test statistic would be least commonly found if the null hypothesis is true. If the significance level has been set at .05, and the alternative hypothesis is that the means are not equal, the critical region is divided equally between the two tails of the distribution of the test statistic: in the upper tail, the critical region will lie above the 97.5th percentile; in the lower tail, it will lie below the 2.5th percentile.

Statistical 'significance': the p-value

If the value of the test statistic falls within the critical (tail) region, the result is said to be **significant**, the null hypothesis is rejected and the alternative (scientific) hypothesis is supported.

The **p-value** of a test statistic is the probability, under the null hypothesis, of obtaining a value at least as extreme (as far out in the tails of the distribution) as the one obtained. A statistical test is said to show **significance** if the p-value is less than the significance level, which means that the value of the test statistic has fallen within the critical region.

Directional hypotheses: one-tailed and two-tailed tests

Suppose that two supposedly equivalent forms of a test, A and B, have been prepared and that 50 people take each form. A large difference between the mean scores in either direction (A > B or B > A) is evidence against the null hypothesis that in the population there is no difference between the means for A and B. If the significance level is set at .05, the critical region is therefore divided equally between the two tails of the sampling distribution of the test statistic, that is, the top .025 and bottom .025 of the distribution of the test statistic. When the critical region is distributed symmetrically in this way, we are said to be making a **two-tailed test.**

Often, however, the experimental hypothesis specifies the direction of the difference: Group A might be expected to perform better than Group B. The negation of this **directional** hypothesis is the null hypothesis that, in the population, the mean score under condition A is **not** better than the mean score under condition B, including the possibility that it may be worse. Some argue that, since only a large difference **in favour of Group A** will count as evidence against the null hypothesis, the entire region of rejection can be located in the upper tail of the distribution: that is, we can reject the null hypothesis if the value of the test statistic falls in the top .05 of the distribution, rather than the top .025. If we follow this approach, we are said to be making a **one-tailed test**. Clearly, if you obtain a difference in the expected direction, you are twice as likely to reject the null hypothesis on a one-tailed test as you are on a two-tailed test.

The difficulty with being prepared to reject the null hypothesis when you obtain a less extreme result in the expected direction is that, were the direction of the obtained difference to be opposite to that predicted, however large that difference might be, you would still have to accept the null hypothesis, which now states merely that the mean for condition A is not greater than the mean for condition B. Suppose that the value of t is below the 2.5^{th} percentile and that you decide to reject the null hypothesis. That practice would enlarge the critical region to 5% + 2.5% = 7.5% of the distribution, which is arguably too high. For this reason, some are opposed to the use of one-tailed tests. By default, SPSS gives the results of two-tailed tests of significance in the output.

Journal editors vary in their views on one-tailed and two-tailed tests. Their decision in a particular case is likely to depend partly upon non-statistical considerations, such as the cogency of the scientific hypothesis. For instance, one would hardly expect brain damage to result in an improvement in performance on cognitive tests. It makes a difference whether a specified directional difference is predicted from a coherent theory, rather than having emerged as a result of *ex post facto* data-snooping.

When reporting the results of the test, the researcher must provide:
1. Full information about the statistics.
2. p-values.
3. Whether the p-values are 2-tailed or 1-tailed.

Errors in hypothesis testing

All statistical inference, being inductive, is subject to error. Suppose that the calculated value of a test statistic falls within the critical region and the null hypothesis is rejected. Such a value however, though unlikely under H_0, is still possible. If H_0 is actually true, we shall have made an error in rejecting it. This is known as a **Type I error**.

Suppose that the value of our test statistic falls outside the critical region, so that H_0 is accepted. This is the correct decision if H_0 is really true; however, it may not be true. Suppose that H_1, a directional hypothesis, is true and states that the population mean has a value above the value stated by H_0. The test statistic has a distribution of values under H_1, and the two distributions are likely to overlap, perhaps to a considerable extent. Should the value of the test statistical fall below the 95th percentile of the distribution under H_0, the researcher will decide, wrongly, to accept H_0; whereas, actually, H_1 is true. The decision to accept H_0 when H_1 is true is known as a **Type II error**.

In summary:
1. We may reject the null hypothesis when it is true, thus making a **Type I error**.
2. We may accept the null hypothesis when it is false, thus making a **Type II error**.

The **probability of a Type I error** is denoted by the Greek symbol **alpha α**, which is the significance level (.05 or .01). The **probability of a Type II error** is denoted by the Greek symbol **beta β**. The **Power (P)** of a statistical test is the probability that the null hypothesis, if false, will be rejected. Since one must either accept or reject the null hypothesis and the two events are complementary (i.e. they exhaust the possibilities), the power of a statistical test is $1 - $ (Type II error rate) i.e. **P = 1 − β**. The decisions made in hypothesis testing are set out in Table 2.

Table 2. Correct decisions and errors in hypothesis testing: Type I and Type II errors and power (P)			
		Experimenter's Decision	
		Accept H_0	**Accept H_1**
State of Nature	**H_0 is true**	Correct decision	**Type I error** Probability = α
	H_1 is true	**Type II error** Probability = β	Correct decision Power P = 1 − β

Figure 2 shows the relationships among the Type I and Type II error rates and power for a one-tailed test of the null hypothesis (H_0) that the mean of a population has a specified value (μ_0)

against the alternative hypothesis (H_1) that the population mean is μ_1. The test statistic is the sample mean and the curves are the sampling distributions of the mean under H_0 and H_1. Since the test is one-tailed, the entire critical region is located in the upper tail of the sampling distribution of the mean. With a two-tailed test, values in the critical region would have a probability of $\alpha /2$ under H_0.

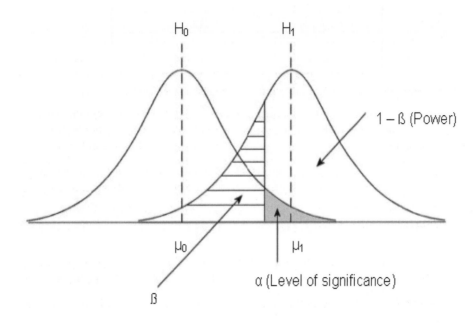

Figure 2. Relations among **Type I** and **Type II error** rates and power

1.3.5 Effect size

An important consideration when you plan to test the significance of, say, a difference between two means for significance is the size of the effect. For the simple two-group between subjects experiment, Cohen (1988) has suggested as a measure of effect size the statistic d, where

$$d = \frac{\mu_1 - \mu_2}{\sigma}$$

Cohen's measure expresses the difference between the two population means as so-many standard deviations. In practice, the parameters μ_1, μ_2 and σ would be estimated from the means of the two samples and an estimate of the supposedly homogeneous population standard deviation. Suppose, for example, that in a drug experiment, the group who had ingested the drug had a mean score of 12, whereas the controls had a mean score of 10. The average standard deviation of the scores in the two groups was 2. According to Cohen's measure, the strength of the effect is $(12-10)/2 = 1$.

On the basis of a study of a considerable body of published literature, Cohen (1988) has suggested a categorisation of effect size as shown in Table 3:

Table 3. Cohen's categories of effect size	
Effect size (d)	**Size of Effect**
$0.2 \leq d < 0.5$	Small
$0.5 < d < 0.8$	Medium
$d \geq 0.8$	Large

The drug experiment, therefore, found that the drug had a 'large' effect upon performance.

Cohen's measure d is much used in **meta-analysis**, that is, the combination of statistics from several independent studies with a view to integrating all the evidence into a coherent body of empirical knowledge.

Many journal editors now insist that reports of the results of statistical tests should include measures of effect size as well as the statistics, the p-value and the confidence interval.

1.4   CHOOSING A STATISTICAL TEST: SOME GUIDELINES

It is common for authors of statistical texts to offer advice on choosing statistical tests in the form of a flow chart, decision tree or similar diagram. The numerous schemes that have been proposed vary considerably, and sometimes seem to contradict one another. Almost any system of classification tends to break down when the user encounters cases that straddle category boundaries. In this area, moreover, the correct choice of statistical technique for certain types of data has been hotly disputed.

On one matter at least, there is general agreement: there is no such thing as a decision tree that will automatically lead the investigator to the correct choice of a statistical test in all circumstances. Some of the later chapters contain illustrations of the penalties that an automated, scheme-reliant approach can incur. At best, a decision tree can serve only as a rough guideline. Ultimately, a safe decision requires careful reflection upon one's own research aims and a thorough preliminary exploration of the data. GET TO KNOW YOUR DATA BEFORE YOU PROCEED TO MAKE ANY FORMAL STATISTICAL TESTS.

1.4.1   Considerations in choosing a statistical test

The choice of a statistical test depends upon several considerations, including:
1.   Your **research question**.
2.   The **plan**, or **design**, of your research.
3.   The **nature of the data** that you wish to analyse.

This list is by no means comprehensive; nor do we intend to imply that any fixed ordering of these three considerations is appropriate in all situations or that they are independent issues.

In general, an important consideration in deciding upon a statistical analysis is whether the research is experimental or correlational. The experimenter is usually interested in **making comparisons** between the average performance level of participants tested under different conditions. Statistical methods such as t-tests and analysis of variance (ANOVA) were designed for the purpose of making comparisons. The correlational researcher typically seeks **statistical associations** among the variables in the study, with a view to imputing causality to theoretically important variables. Correlation and regression are suitable techniques for that purpose.

Five common research situations

We shall identify five basic research situations in which formal statistical tests can be applied (Figure 3). In this book, the techniques appropriate for various situations will be discussed more fully in the sections indicated in the figure.

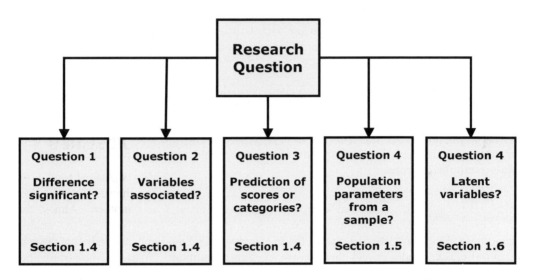

Figure 3. Five types of research situation

The questions are as follows:
1. Is a difference (between averages) significant? For example, is resting heart rate the same before and after a fitness course? (Sections 1.4.2 to 1.4.4)
2. How strongly are variables associated? For example, do tall parents tend to have tall children? (Sections 1.4.5 to 1.4.8)
3. Can scores on a target variable (or category membership, if the variable is qualitative) be predicted from data on other variables? For example, can university performance be predicted by scores on aptitude tests? (Sections 1.4.9 to 1.4.13)
4. From a single sample of data, what can be said about the population? For example, if we know the vocabulary test scores of 100 children, what can we infer about the scores of the entire population of children in the same age group? (Section 1.5)
5. The user has a multivariate data set, perhaps people's scores on a battery of ability tests. Can these scores be accounted for (or classified) in terms of a smaller number of hypothetical latent variables or **factors**? For

example, can performance in a variety of intellectual pursuits be accounted for in terms of general intelligence? (Section 1.6)

1.4.2   Testing a difference between means for significance

The question of whether two or more means are significantly different is one that arises naturally in the context of experimental or quasi-experimental research, where the performance of the participants under different conditions is being compared.

Suppose that in a drug experiment, performance under two different conditions (experimental and control) has been measured and that the means have somewhat different values. This may seem to support the experimenter's hypothesis; but would a similar difference be found if the experiment were to be repeated? Could the obtained difference merely be the result of sampling variability? Here the researcher wishes to test the **statistical significance** of the difference, that is, to establish that the difference is too large to have been merely a chance occurrence.

1.4.3   The design of the experiment: independent versus related samples

Of crucial importance in the choice of an appropriate statistical test for comparing levels of performance is the question of whether the experiment would have resulted in **independent** or **related samples** of scores.

Independent samples

Suppose we select, say, 100 participants for an experiment and randomly assign half of them to an experimental condition and the rest to a control condition. With this procedure, the assignment of one person to a particular group has no effect upon the group to which another is assigned. The two **independent samples** of participants thus selected will produce two independent samples of scores, each consisting of 50 values. A useful criterion for deciding whether you have independent samples of data is that there must be **no basis for pairing the scores in one sample with those in the other**. An experiment in which independent samples of participants are tested under different conditions is known as a **between subjects experiment**.

Related samples

Suppose that each of fifty participants shoots ten times at a triangular target and ten times at a square target of the same area. For each target, each participant will have a score ranging from 0 (ten misses) to 10 (ten hits). As in the previous example, there will be two samples of 50 scores. This time, however, each score in either sample can be paired with the same participant's score with the other target. We have here two **related samples** of scores, or a set of **paired data**. The scores in two related samples are likely to be substantially correlated, because the better shots will tend to have higher scores with either target than will the poorer shots. An experiment like this, in which each participant is tested under both (or all) conditions, is known as a **within subjects experiment**. Within subjects experiments are also said to have **repeated measures** on the IV (the shape of the target).

There are other ways of obtaining paired data. Suppose that in the current example, the participants were pairs of identical or fraternal twins: each participant shoots at only one target and the twin shoots at the other. This experiment will also result in two related samples of scores, because, as in the repeated measures experiment, there is a basis for pairing the data. Different statistical tests are appropriate for use with independent and related samples of data.

1.4.4 Flow chart for selecting a suitable test for differences between means

Figure 4 outlines *some* of the considerations leading to a choice of a statistical test of the significance of differences between means (or frequencies, if one has nominal data). If there are more than two conditions or groups, an analysis of variance (ANOVA) may be applicable. In this section, we shall consider only the comparison between two groups or conditions, such as male versus female, or experimental group versus control group.

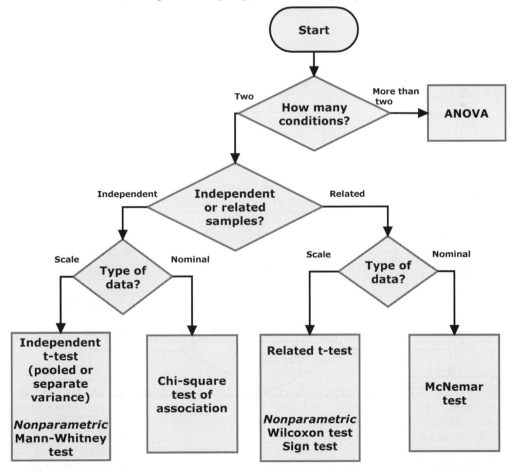

Figure 4. Flow chart showing the selection of a suitable test for differences between means

To use the chart, begin at the START box and consider how many conditions there are in the experiment. If there are two conditions, proceed down the chart to the next stage. The next questions are whether the samples are independent or related and whether the data are **scale data** or **nominal data** (see Section 1.1.2). The appropriate test is shown in the bottom box.

The tests for comparing scores under **two** conditions (t-tests and their nonparametric equivalents) will be described in Chapter 6.

| See Chap. 6 |

The tests for making comparisons among scores obtained under three or more conditions will be discussed in Chapters 7-10, which are concerned with analysis of variance (ANOVA).

| See Chaps 7-10 |

1.4.5   Measuring strength of association between variables

Do tall fathers tend to have tall sons, short fathers to have short sons and fathers of medium height to have sons of medium height? This question is one of a **statistical association** between the two variables *Father's Height* and *Son's Height*. To answer the question, you would need a data set comprising the heights of a substantial sample of fathers and those of their (first) sons.

1.4.6   Flow chart for selecting a suitable test for association

Figure 5 outlines the questions one needs to answer in order to make a decision about an appropriate measure of association.

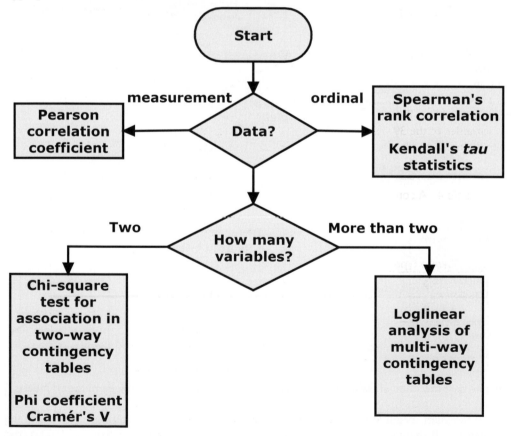

Figure 5. Flow chart showing measures of association

Begin at the START box and consider whether the data are scalar or ordinal. If the two variables are in the form of measurements, a **Pearson correlation** should be considered. However, as we shall see in Chapter 11, there are circumstances in which the Pearson correlation can be highly misleading. **It is essential to examine the data first before proceeding to obtain the Pearson correlation coefficient.**

See Chap. 11

Measuring association in ordinal data

Now suppose we ask two judges to rank twenty paintings in order of preference. We shall have a data set consisting of twenty pairs of ranks. Do the judges agree? Again, our question is one of a statistical association. However, since the data are ordinal, a **rank correlation** is an appropriate statistic to use. The two most common kinds of rank correlation are:

See Chap. 11

    1.   **Spearman's rank correlation**;
    2.   **Kendall tau** statistics.

Both are considered more fully in Chapter 11.

1.4.7   Measuring association in nominal data: Contingency tables

A medical researcher suspects that the incidence of an antibody may be higher in patients of tissue type X, compared with its incidence in patients of tissue types, A, B and C. Seventy-nine patients are tissue-typed and tested for the presence of the antibody. Such an exercise will result in a set of nominal data on two qualitative variables or attributes, *tissue type* (A, B, C, X) and *presence* (Yes, No). Here the scientific hypothesis is that there is an association between the two variables. Table 4 is a **contingency table**, which shows the joint classification on the two variables of the 39 patients in the study. The expected association is indeed evident in the table: there is a much higher incidence of the antibody in patients of tissue type X.

Table 4. A contingency table showing the incidence of an antibody in patients with four different types of tissue		
	Presence	
Tissue type	**No**	**Yes**
A	14	8
B	11	7
C	5	7
X	6	21

The presence of an association can be confirmed by using a **chi-square test** (see Chapter 11). Since the value of the chi-square statistic depends partly upon the sample size, however, it is unsuitable as a measure of the *strength* of the association between two qualitative variables. Figure 5 identifies two statistics

See Chap. 11

that measure strength of association between qualitative variables: **Cramér's V** and the **phi coefficient**. Both measures are discussed in Chapter 11.

1.4.8 Multi-way contingency tables

In recent years, there have been dramatic developments in the analysis of nominal data in the form of multi-way contingency tables. Previously, tables with three or more attributes were often 'collapsed' to produce two-way tables. The usual chi-square test could then be applied. Such 'collapsing', however, is fraught with risk, and the tests may give highly misleading results. The advent of modern **loglinear analysis** has made it possible to tease out the relationships among the attributes in a way that was not possible before (see Chapter 13).

See Chap. 13

1.4.9 Predicting scores or category membership

If there is an association between variables, it is natural to ask whether this can be exploited to predict scores on one variable from knowledge of those on another. For example, in some American universities, students take aptitude tests at matriculation and received an academic grade point average (GPA) at the end of their first year of study. Can students' GPAs be predicted from their earlier scores on the aptitude tests? Such prediction is indeed possible, and the methods by which this is achieved will be briefly reviewed in this section.

There are also circumstances in which one would wish to predict not scores on a target or criterion variable, but membership of a category of a qualitative variable. For example, it is of medical and actuarial interest to be able to assign individuals to an 'at risk' category on the basis of their smoking and drinking habits. Statistical techniques have been specially devised for this purpose also.

The purpose of the methods reviewed here is to predict a target, or **criterion** variable (the term **dependent variable** is also used in this context) from scores on other variables, known variously (depending on the context) as **regressors**, **predictors**, **independent variables**, and **covariates**. The predictors need not always be quantitative variables: qualitative variables, such as gender and blood group, are often included among the predictor variables in research of this kind.

1.4.10 Flow chart for selecting the appropriate procedure for predicting a score or category membership

To use the flow chart (Figure 6) for selecting the appropriate prediction procedure, begin at the START box and consider whether the target variable is qualitative (e.g. a set of categories such as *Pass* and *Fail*) or quantitative (e.g. examination scores, which are scale data).

Begin at the START box and consider the purpose of the test. If it is to test for goodness-of-fit, move down the left-hand side of the chart. If it is to estimate the population mean or its probable range, move down the right-hand side. The next consideration is the nature of the data: different types of data require different tests. If the target variable is quantitative, a **regression** method should be considered. In **simple regression**, there is one predictor; in **multiple regression**, there are two or more (Chapter 12). If the criterion variable is qualitative, the techniques of **discriminant analysis** and **logistic regression** should be considered (Chapter 14).

See Chaps. 12 & 14

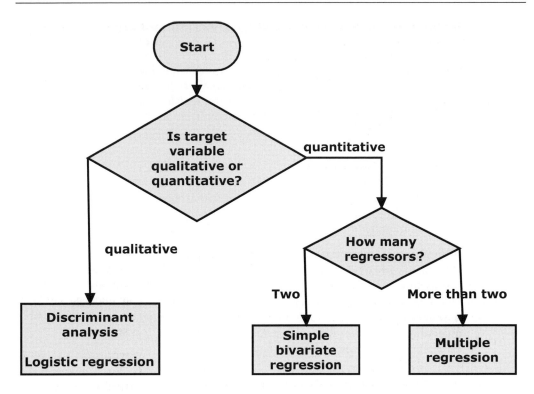

Figure 6. Flow chart showing procedures for prediction

1.4.11   Simple regression

In **simple regression**, a target or criterion variable is predicted from **one** predictor or regressor.

Suppose that, given a student's verbal aptitude score at matriculation, we want to predict the same student's grade point average a year later from the verbal aptitude score alone. This is a problem in **simple regression**, and the method is described in Chapter 12.

See Chap. 12

1.4.12   Multiple regression

A student's grade point average may be associated not only with verbal aptitude, but also with numerical ability. Can grade point average be predicted even more accurately when both verbal ability and numerical ability are taken into account? This is a problem in **multiple regression**. If grade point average is correlated with both verbal and numerical aptitude, multiple regression will produce (provided certain conditions are met) a more accurate prediction of a student's grade point average than will a simple regression upon either of the two regressors considered separately.

See Chap. 12

1.4.13   Predicting category membership: Discriminant analysis and logistic regression

Two statistical techniques designed to help the user make predictions of category membership are **discriminant analysis** and **logistic regression** (both of which are discussed in Chapter 14). In recent years, logistic regression, being a somewhat more robust technique than discriminant analysis, has become the preferred method.

See Chap. 14

1.5   ONE-SAMPLE TESTS

Much psychological research involves the collection of two or more samples of data. This is by no means always true, however: sometimes the researcher draws a **single** sample of observations in order to study just **one** population.

The situations in which one might use a one-sample test are of two main kinds:
1. One may wish to compare a sample distribution with a hypothetical distribution, such as the normal. This is a question of **goodness-of-fit**.
2. One may wish to make **inferences about the parameters of a single population** from the statistics of a sample, either for the purpose of ascertaining whether the sample is from a known population or estimating the parameters of an unknown population.

1.5.1   Flow chart for selecting the appropriate one-sample test

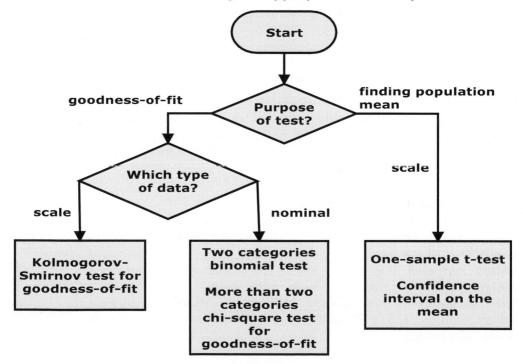

Figure 7. Flow chart of one-sample tests

Figure 7 summarises the circumstances in which a researcher might make various kinds of one-sample tests. The tests reviewed in this section are more fully considered in Chapter 6.

Begin at the START box and consider the purpose of the test. If it is to test for goodness-of-fit, move down the left-hand side of the chart. If it is to estimate the population mean or its probable range, move down the right-hand side. The next consideration is the level of measurement: data at different levels require different tests.

1.5.2   Goodness-of-fit: scale data

A question about a single population may be one of **goodness-of-fit**: has the sample been drawn from a population with a specified distribution shape? Suppose, for example, that one has a sample of measurements and wishes to ascertain whether these have been drawn from a normal population. Figure 7 shows that the **Kolmogorov-Smirnov test** is appropriate for this purpose.

See Chap. 6

1.5.3   Goodness-of-fit: nominal data

Suppose a researcher wants to know whether 5-year-old children of a certain age show a preference for one of two toys (A or B). The choices of one hundred 5-year-olds are noted. Here the population comprises the choices (A or B) of 5-year-olds in general. Of the hundred children in the study, 60 choose toy A and 40 choose toy B. The null hypothesis states that the probability of choosing A (or B) is 0.5: more formally, it states that we have sampled 100 times from a Bernoulli distribution with $p = 0.5$. Does this theoretical distribution fit our data? Figure 7 indicates that a **binomial test** can be used to test this hypothesis.

See Chap. 6

If, in the foregoing situation, there were three or more toys to choose from, the **chi-square test for goodness-of-fit** can be used to test the null hypothesis that the children have no preference for any particular toy.

1.5.4   Inferences about the mean of a single population

Suppose we want to know whether the performance of a group of schoolchildren on a standardised test is typical of those in their age group. Figure 7 shows that a **one-sample *t* test** can be used to test the null hypothesis that a sample has been drawn from a population with a mean of a specified value. Often, however, as when the researcher is working with a non-standardised test, it may not be possible to specify any null hypothesis. Suppose that a lecturer wishes to ascertain the typical reaction speed of first-year university students within a certain age group. The lecturer may have data on, say, two hundred first-year students; but the research question, being about the reaction speeds of first-year students in general, concerns the population of reaction times. The sample mean is a **point estimate** of the unknown population mean. The *t* distribution can also be used to build a **confidence interval** on the sample mean, so that the researcher has a range of values within which the true population mean can, with a specified degree of 'confidence', be assumed to lie.

See Chap. 6

The one-sample *t* test can also be used to test the difference between the means of two related samples of scores. If the difference between scores under the two conditions is found for each participant, we shall have a single sample of differences. If the null hypothesis is correct, the mean difference in the population is zero, which is equivalent to stating that, in the population, the mean scores under the two conditions have equal values. The related-samples t test and the one-sample t test, in fact, are exact equivalents and will produce exactly the same result.

1.5.5   Nominal data: Testing a coin for fairness

When we toss a coin a large number of times to ascertain its fairness, we obtain a sample from the (infinite) population of such tosses. We might find that the coin turned up heads on 58 out of 100 tosses. Is the coin 'fair', that is, in the population, are the relative frequencies of heads and tails both 0.5? (Here, when we speak of the 'population', we refer to a hypothetical experiment in which the coin is tossed an infinite number of times. We should certainly not expect exactly 50 heads in every 100 tosses of the coin.)

The **binomial test** can be used to test the hypothesis that the population proportion is ½ (or, indeed, that it is any other specified proportion). A **confidence interval** can also be constructed on the sample proportion to give a range of values within which we can be confident to a required degree that the true population proportion lies.

> See
> Chap.
> 6

1.6   FINDING LATENT VARIABLES: FACTOR ANALYSIS AND CANONICAL CORRELATION

Suppose that 500 people are measured on twenty tests of ability and that the correlations between each test and every other test are arrayed in a square array known as a **correlation matrix (R-matrix)**. It is likely that, since those who are good at one thing tend also to be good at others, there will be substantial positive correlations among the tests in the battery.

Factor analysis (see Chapter 15) is a set of techniques which, on the basis of the correlations in an R-matrix, classify all the tests in a battery in terms of relatively few underlying (or **latent**) dimensions or **factors**. (The term factor has more than one meaning in statistics. In analysis of variance [ANOVA], a factor is an independent variable, that is, a set of related treatments or categories.) In **exploratory factor analysis**, the object is to find the minimum number of **factors** necessary to account for the correlations among the psychological tests. In **confirmatory factor analysis**, specified models are compared to see which of them gives the best account of the data.

> See
> Chap.
> 15

While factors are hypothetical underlying dimensions, they are estimated, essentially, by sums of participants' scores on all the tests in the battery. Thus, in addition to scores on the tests, each person also receives one or more **factor scores**, each of which represents that person's endowment with the latent variable in question.

Other statistical techniques, such as **canonical correlation**, have also been devised for the purpose of identifying latent variables (Section 15.4).

1.6.1   Multivariate statistics

Factor analysis and canonical correlation belong to a set of techniques collectively known as **multivariate statistics**. While these methods arise naturally in the context of correlational research, however, they are also applicable to certain kinds of experimental data.

In Section 1.2, in which we considered experimental research, we spoke of the dependent variable (DV), which was measured during the course of the experiment and the independent variable (IV), which was manipulated by the experimenter with a view to showing that it had the power to affect the DV.

The DV in an experiment is often, in a sense, a representative or proxy variable. In a test of maze-learning proficiency, for instance, we may use the speed at which participants draw lines through the maze. Arguably, however, another consideration, number of errors, also reflects maze-learning skill; indeed, in some situations there may be several reasonable potential dependent variables, any one of which could be taken as representative of proficiency. Statistical methods relating to a single DV are called **univariate**.

Multivariate statistics are methods designed for the analysis of data sets in which there are two or more DVs. In this context, however, the terms independent and dependent variable tend to be applied more generally to any research, whether experimental or correlational, in which some variables (the IVs) are thought to have a causal influence upon others (the DVs).

In experimental and quasi-experimental research, the t-tests and ANOVA are generalised to multivariate analysis of variance (**MANOVA**). In correlational research, factor analysis and canonical correlation are thought of as explaining associations among the observed variables (the DVs) in terms of latent 'causal' variables (i.e. factors or canonical variables), which are, essentially, sums of the observed variables.

1.7   A FINAL COMMENT

In this chapter, we have offered some advice about using formal statistical tests to support the researcher's claim that what is true of a particular data set is likely to be true in the population. At this point, however, a word of warning is appropriate.

Formal tests, statistical models and their assumptions

The making of a formal statistical test of significance always presupposes the applicability of a statistical **model**, that is, an interpretation (usually in the form of an equation) of the data set as having been generated in a specified manner. The model underlying the one-sample t test, for example, assumes that the data are from a normal population. To some extent, statistical tests have been shown to be **robust** to moderate violations of the assumptions of the models upon which they are based, that is, the actual error rates do not rise above acceptable levels. But there are limits to this robustness, and there are circumstances in which a result, declared by an incautious user to be significant beyond, say, the 0.05 level, may actually have been considerably more probable than that. There is no way of avoiding this pitfall other than by getting to know your data first (see Chapters 4 and 5) to ascertain their suitability for specified formal tests.

See
Chaps
4 & 5

Recommended reading

Terms and ideas in research design

There are available many excellent textbooks on research methodology. We have considered only those terms and principles that we consider to be essential for the purposes of data analysis with SPSS. (SPSS uses many of the terms we have introduced in this chapter.)

Field, A., & Hole, G. (2003). *How to design and report experiments*. London: Sage.

Chapter 1 discusses many of the methodological terms and issues touched upon in this chapter in greater depth and considers some more general issues in methodology.

Readable statistics texts

The reader with a limited mathematical background who is looking for a text on basic statistics is faced with a bewildering array of choices. We suggest the following book:

Sani, F., & Todman, J. (2006). *Experimental design and statistics for psychology: A first course*. Oxford: Blackwell.

For the reader who is more comfortable with algebraic notation, we suggest

Howell, D. C. (2007). *Statistical methods for psychology (6th ed.)*. Belmont, CA: Thomson/Wadsworth.

A useful dictionary of statistical terms

The following is a very useful reference book, with clear definitions.

Nelson, D. (2004). *The Penguin dictionary of statistics*. London: Penguin Books.

CHAPTER 2

Getting started with SPSS 16

2.1   OUTLINE OF AN SPSS SESSION

There are three stages in the use of SPSS:
1.   The data are entered into the **Data Editor**.
2.   Descriptive and statistical procedures are selected from the **drop-down menus**.
3.   The output is examined and edited in the **SPSS Viewer**.

2.1.1   Entering the data

There are several ways of placing data in the **Data Editor**. They can be typed in directly or read in from SPSS data files that have already been created. SPSS can also read data from files produced by other applications, such as EXCEL and STATISTICA, as well as text files.

Once the data are in the **Data Editor**, the user has available a wide variety of editorial functions. Not only can the data be amended in various ways, but also selections from the original set can be targeted for subsequent analysis.

In this chapter, we shall give considerable attention to the **Data Editor**, because it enables the user to control important features of the output (such as the labelling of variables) which can make the results of a statistical analysis easier to interpret.

The user can also access important editing functions from an array of **drop-down menus** at the top of the screen.

2.1.2   Selecting the exploratory and statistical procedures

It is also from the drop-down menus that the user selects statistical procedures. The user is advised to explore the data thoroughly before making any formal statistical tests. SPSS offers many graphical methods described in Chapters 4 and 5 of displaying a data set, which are of great assistance when you are getting to know your data.

2.1.3   Examining the output

The results of the analysis appear in the **SPSS Viewer**. In addition to the selection and trimming of items, the SPSS **Viewer** also offers facilities for more radical editing. The appearance of tables and other output can be dramatically transformed to tailor them to the purposes of the user.

From the SPSS **Viewer**, material can readily be transferred to files produced by other applications, such as Word, or printed out in hard copy.

2.1.4   A simple experiment

In this chapter, we shall illustrate the stages in a typical SPSS session by entering the results of a fictional experiment into the **Data Editor**, describing the data by choosing some statistics from the menu and examining the output. At this stage, we shall concentrate on the general procedure, leaving the details for later consideration.

Table 1 shows the results of an experiment designed to show the effects of a drug upon skilled performance.

Table 1. Results of an experiment designed to show whether a drug improves skilled performance							
Group							
Placebo				**Drug**			
Case	**Score**	**Case**	**Score**	**Case**	**Score**	**Case**	**Score**
1	6	6	3	11	8	16	8
2	5	7	2	12	6	17	6
3	5	8	4	13	6	18	7
4	1	9	5	14	7	19	5
5	2	10	1	15	6	20	10

The experiment was of simple, two-group between subjects design, in which twenty participants attempted a test of skill. Ten participants (cases) were assigned at random to one of two conditions:

1. A *Placebo* condition, in which the participant ingested a harmless saline solution;
2. A *Drug* condition, in which the participant ingested a small dose of a drug.

The dependent variable was the participant's score on the skilled task. The independent variable was the condition to which the participant was assigned: *Drug* or *Placebo*. The experimental hypothesis was that the group that had been assigned to the *Drug* condition would outperform the group assigned to the *Placebo* condition.

We shall shortly show how these data can be placed in the **SPSS Data Editor** and the results summarised with a few statistics.

2.1.5   Preparing data for SPSS

The data shown in Table 1 are not in a form that the SPSS **Data Editor** will accept. In an SPSS data set, **each row must represent only one case** (equivalent terms are **'participant'** and **'subject'**) and each column represents a variable or characteristic on which that case has been measured. In other words, **each row of an SPSS data set must contain data on just one case or participant**. The data in Table 1 do not conform to this requirement: the first row of entries contains data from four different participants.

To make them suitable for analysis with SPSS, the data in Table 1 must be rearranged in a new format. In Table 2, the data in Table 1 have been re-tabulated, so that each row now contains data on only one participant.

Table 2. The data set of Table 1, recast in a form suitable for entry into SPSS

Participant	Condition	Participant's Score
1	1	6
2	1	5
3	1	5
4	1	1
5	1	2
6	1	3
7	1	2
8	1	4
9	1	5
10	1	1
11	2	8
12	2	6
13	2	6
14	2	7
15	2	6
16	2	8
17	2	6
18	2	7
19	2	5
20	2	10

In Table 2, the *Condition* variable identifies the group to which each participant belongs by means of an arbitrary code number, in this case *1* (for the *Placebo* condition) or *2* (for the *Drug* condition). Unlike the numbers in the *Score* column, which express level of performance, the code numbers in the *Condition* column **serve merely as category labels**: the

Condition variable is a special kind of **categorical variable** known as a **grouping variable** (see Chapter 1).

2.2   OPENING SPSS

There are several ways of beginning a session with SPSS, depending upon whether you intend to build a new file or access an old one. When SPSS is opened for the first time by clicking the SPSS icon, an introductory dialog box will appear with the title **SPSS 16.0 for Windows**.

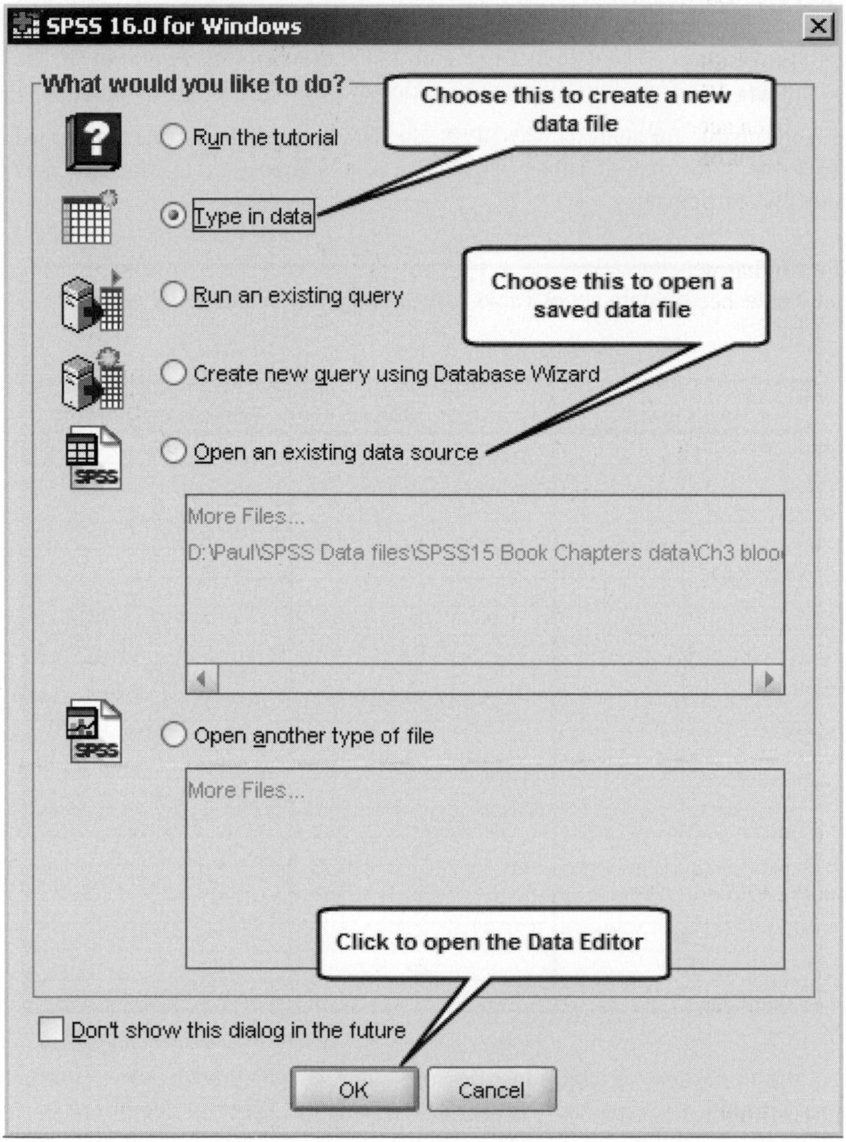

Figure 1. The **SPSS 16.0 for Windows** opening dialog box

Underneath the title is the question: *What would you like to do?* Make your choice by clicking one of the six small radio buttons and then **OK** (Figure 1). Here we shall assume that you wish to enter data for the first time, in which case click the button labelled **Type in data**. When you click **OK**, the **Data Editor** will appear on the screen.

At a later stage, you may wish to omit the introductory dialog box, in which case click the square labelled **Don't show this dialog in the future** in the bottom left corner of the dialog box.

2.3   THE SPSS DATA EDITOR

The SPSS **Data Editor** provides two alternative spreadsheet-like arrays:
1.   **Data View**, into which the user can enter new data or (if an old file has been accessed) view whatever data the file contains.
2.   **Variable View**, which contains the names and details of the variables in the data set.

When you are creating a file for the first time, it is advisable to lay the foundations in **Variable View** first, so that when you come to enter data in **Data View**, the columns in the spreadsheet will already have been labelled, reducing the risk of transcription errors.

A notational convention

In this book, we shall use *italics* to indicate variable names and values. We shall use a **bold** typeface for the names of menus, the names of dialog boxes and the items therein. Emboldening will also be used for emphasis and for technical terms.

2.3.1   Working in Variable View

When the **Data Editor** appears, you may find that you are in **Data View**. If so, click the tab labelled **Variable View** at the bottom left-hand side of the window and you will access **Variable View** (Figure 2).

When the **Data Editor** first appears, the caption in the title bar reads, '**Untitled1 [DataSet0] – SPSS Data Editor**'. Any additional data sets (SPSS 16 allows more than one data set to be available during an SPSS session) would be numbered DataSet1, DataSet 2 and so on. When you finish entering your data (or preferably during data entry as a protection against losing data should the system crash), you can supply a name for the file by selecting the **Save As...** item from the **File** drop-down menu and entering a suitable name in the **File Name** box. After you have done this, the title bar will display your new name for the file.

Recent Releases of SPSS allow more than one data file to be available on the screen though only one of them can be active and is marked with a green cross superimposed on the icon of a grid 🔲 at the left-hand end of the title bar. A file is activated by clicking anywhere within its window.

The word **Untitled** in the title bar is a warning to the user that the file has not yet been given a name and saved.

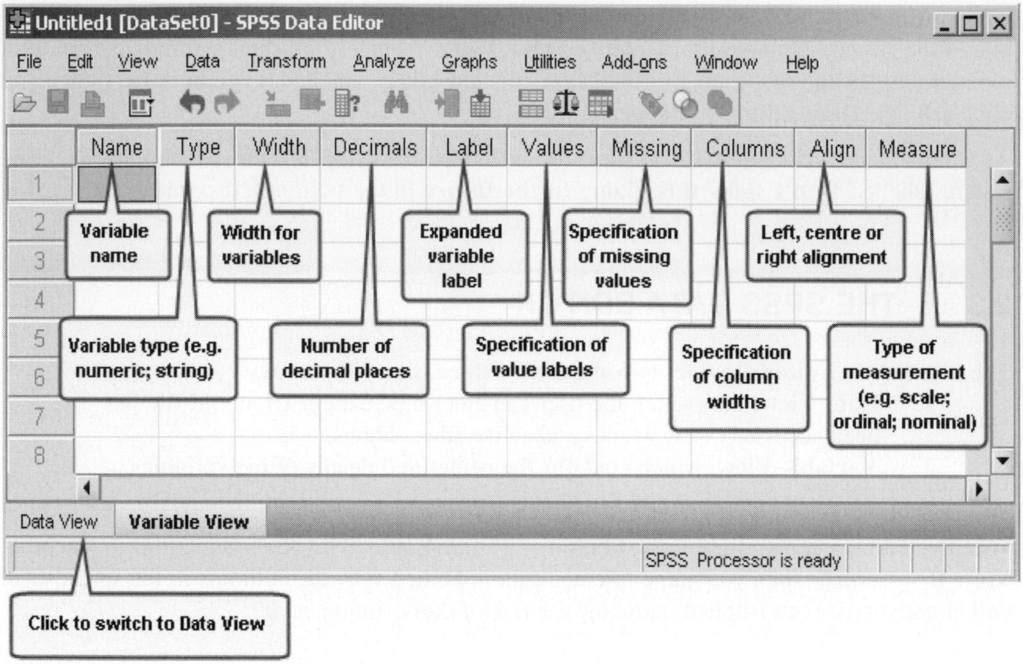

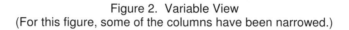

Figure 2. Variable View
(For this figure, some of the columns have been narrowed.)

Notation for selecting from a menu

We shall adopt a notation for selecting items from a drop-down menu by which the sequence of selections is shown by arrows (➜). For example, selection of the **Copy** item from the **Edit** drop-down menu will be written as **Edit➜Copy**.

*The **Name** and **Labels** columns*

Some of the column headings in **Variable View** (such as number of places of decimals) are self-explanatory. The **Name** and **Labels** columns, however, require some explanation. The **name** of a variable is a string of characters (normally letters and spaces but it can include digits) which will appear at the head of a column in **Data View**, but not in the output. In other words, a variable name is a convenient shortened name for use only within **Data View**. There is a set of rules for naming variables. This can readily be accessed by entering SPSS's **Help** menu and choosing **Help➜Topics➜Index➜Variable names**.

The main message is that a variable name must be a **continuous** sequence (no spaces) of up to 64 characters (though long variable names are not recommended), **the first of which must be a letter**. It can be defined with any mixture of upper and lower case characters, and case is preserved for display purposes (e.g. *TimeofDay*). Although certain punctuation marks are permitted, it is simpler merely to remember to use letters and digits only.

*Making entries in **Variable View***

- To name the variables *Case*, *Group* and *Score*, first check that there is a thickened border around the top leftmost cell (see Figure 2). If it is not there, move the cursor there and click with the mouse.
- Type *Case* and press the ↓ cursor key to move the highlighting down to the cell below to complete the entry of *Case* in the cell above. (Entry of information into a cell is only complete when the cursor is moved away by clicking on another cell.)
- Type *Group* into the second cell with a thickened border and press the ↓ cursor key to move the highlighting down to the next row, completing the entry of *Group* in the cell above.
- Use the same procedure to enter the variable name *Score*.

SPSS will accept eight different **types** of variable, two of the most important being **numeric** (numerals with a decimal point) and **string** (e.g. names of participants, cities or other non-numerical material). Initially, some of the format specifications of a variable are set by default, and the pre-set values will be seen as soon as the variable name has been typed and control transferred from the **Name** cell. Unless you specify otherwise, **it will be assumed that the variable is of the numeric type.**

The number of places of decimals that will be displayed in **Data View** is pre-set at 2. Since the scores in Table 2 are all integers, it would be tedious to read entries such as *46.00*, *34.00* and *54.00*, as opposed to *46*, *34* and *54*. It is better to suppress the display of decimals in **Data View** by clicking on the **Decimals** column to obtain the following display

By clicking twice on the downward-pointing arrow, you can replace the number *2* already in the cell with zero (see Figure 3). Note that this countermanding of the default specification will apply **only to the variable concerned**. Rather than over-riding the default specifications piecemeal in this way, you can reset the decimal display to zero for every numeric variable in the data set by choosing **Edit➔Options...➔Data** and resetting the number of decimal places to zero. See Chapter 3 for details.

See Chap. 3

The **Label**, which should be a meaningful phrase, with spaces between the words, is the description of the variable that will appear **in the output**. In order to make the output as clear as possible, therefore, it is important to devise **meaningful** labels for all the variables in the data set. The labels shown in Figure 3, *Case Number* and *Experimental Condition*, are more informative than the corresponding variable names *Case* and *Group*, respectively, which are adequate for use within the **Data Editor**.

File	Edit	View	Data	Transform	Analyze	Graphs	Utilities	Add-ons	Window	Help

	Name	Type	Width	Decimals	Label	Values	Missing	
1	Case	Numeric	8	0	Case Number	None	None	8
2	Group	Numeric	8	0	Experimental Condition	None	None	8
3	Score	Numeric	8	0	Score	None	None	8

Figure 3. Part of **Variable View**, with entries specifying the names and details of the three variables

The **Values** column is for use with **grouping variables**. By clicking on **Values**, the user can supply a key to the meanings of the code numbers. In this case, the grouping variable is *Experimental Condition* and we can arbitrarily decide that *1 = Placebo* and *2 = Drug*. Click the first cell of the Values column to obtain the following display:

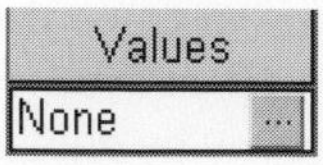

Note the grey area on the right with the three dots (…). Clicking this grey area will produce the **Values** dialog box (see Figure 4).

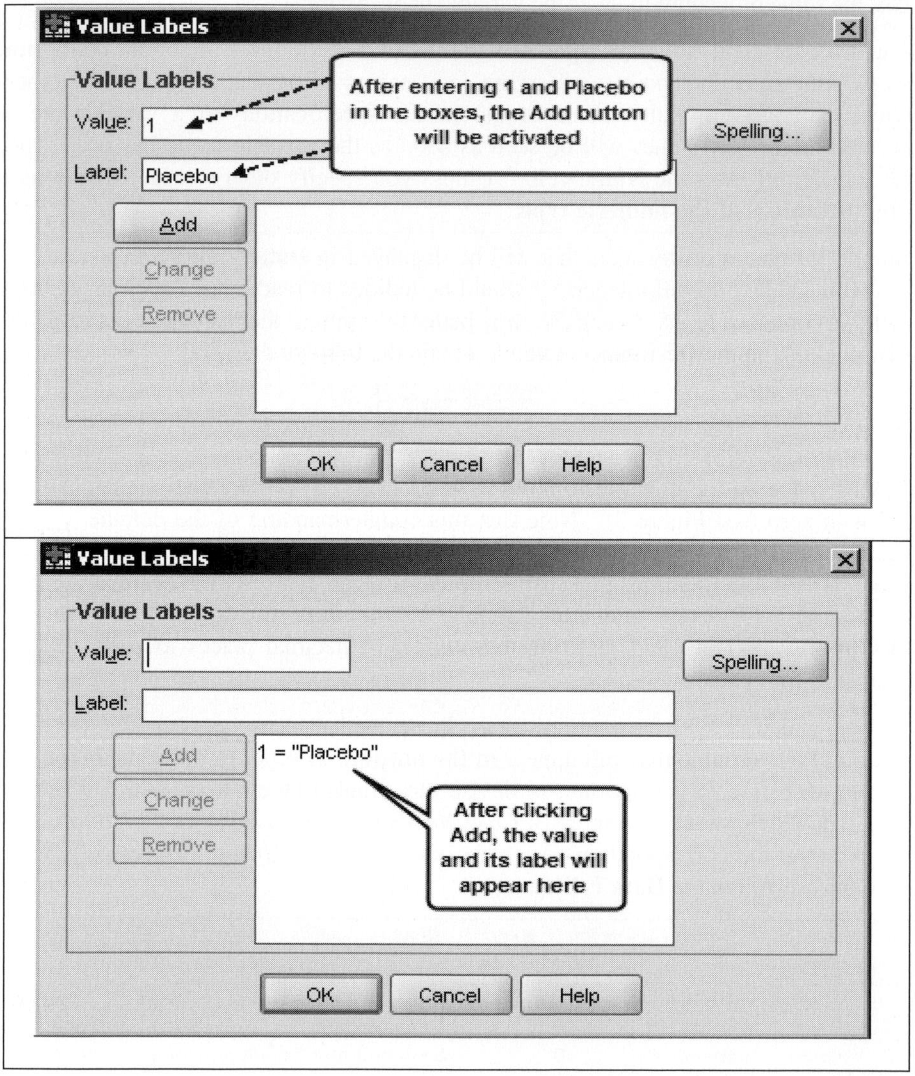

Figure 4. How to enter value labels which, in the output, will replace the code numbers making up a grouping variable. The procedure is repeated for each value label e.g. 2 = "Drug"

Figure 4 shows how to fill in the **Values** dialog box so that, in the output, the code numbers *1* will be replaced by the more informative value label *Placebo*. The same procedure is used to add *Drug* for value *2*. In addition, as you type 1 or 2 in **Data View**, the value labels will appear provided either **Value Labels** within the **View** drop-down menu is ticked or by clicking the icon in the toolbar.

*The **Width** column*

With string variables, the **Width** column controls the maximum length (in number of characters) of the string you will be allowed to enter when you are working in **Data View**. (The setting in Width has no effect upon the number of characters you can type in when working with a numeric variable.)

The default setting for Width is *8*, but this can be changed by choosing **Edit➜Options➜Data** and changing the **Width** setting there. For more details, see Chapter 3. If a string is too long for the set width, you will find that you can no longer type in the excess letters in **Data View**.

> See
> Chap.
> 3

*The **Columns** column*

The cells of this column display the actual widths, for all the variables in the data set, of the columns that will appear in **Data View**. Initially, the cells in **Columns** will show the same setting as the **Width** column: *8*. Were you to create a new numeric variable with a name whose length exceeded the preset width, only part of the name would be displayed in the **Name** column of **Variable View**. Moreover, in **Data View**, only part of the variable name would be visible at the head of the column for that variable.

To specify wider columns for a variable in **Data View** while working in **Variable View**, click the appropriate cell in **Columns** and adjust the setting there.

*The **Align** column*

This determines whether the data are **Left**, **Right** or **Centre** aligned. The default setting is **Right**.

*The **Measure** column*

This enables the user to declare whether the data are **Scale** (i.e. measurements), **Ordinal** or **Nominal** (see Section 1.1.2 *Levels of measurement: scale, ordinal and nominal data*). The default measure is **Scale**. It is important to declare categorical variables such as sex or blood group as **Nominal** and categorical variables such as rating scales as **Ordinal** especially if a graphic (e.g. an item from **Chart Builder**) is going to be used. For our example, *Case* and *Score* would be **Scale** and *Group* would be **Nominal**.

> See
> Section
> 1.1.2

Copying settings

Values in the cells of **Variable View** can be copied and pasted to other cells using the standard Windows methods (see Section 2.3.3). For example, having adjusted the **Columns** setting to, say, *15* characters for one variable of the data set, the new setting can be applied to other variables by copying and pasting the contents of the cell with the entry *15* into the cells for the other variables.

Modified settings can also be copied to **Columns** from the **Width** Column. Having adjusted an entry in the **Width** column to, say, *16*, the new setting can be copied and pasted into **Columns** in the usual way. The effect will be to widen the columns in **Data View** for the variables to which the new **Columns** setting has been copied.

2.3.2   Working in Data View

Once the appropriate specifications have been entered in **Variable View**, click the **Data View** tab at the bottom of the **Variable View** window to enter **Data View** (Figure 5). When **Data View** is accessed, the variable names *Case*, *Group* and *Score* will be seen at the heads of the first three columns as specified in **Variable View**. The default name *var*, which appears in the third, fourth and fifth columns, indicates that those columns have yet to be assigned to specified variables.

Running along the bottom of the **Data View** window is a horizontal band, in which various messages appear from time to time. When SPSS is accessed, the message reads: **SPSS Processor is ready**. The horizontal band is known as the **Status Bar**, because it reports not only whether SPSS is ready to begin, but also on the stage that a procedure has reached. If, for example, a large data set is being read from a file, progress is continually monitored, case by case, in the status bar.

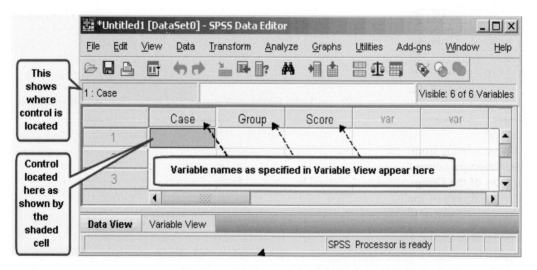

Figure 5.   Part of **Data View**, showing the variable names and active cell

2.3.3   Entering the data

Figure 6 shows a section of **Data View**, in which the data in Table 1 have been entered.

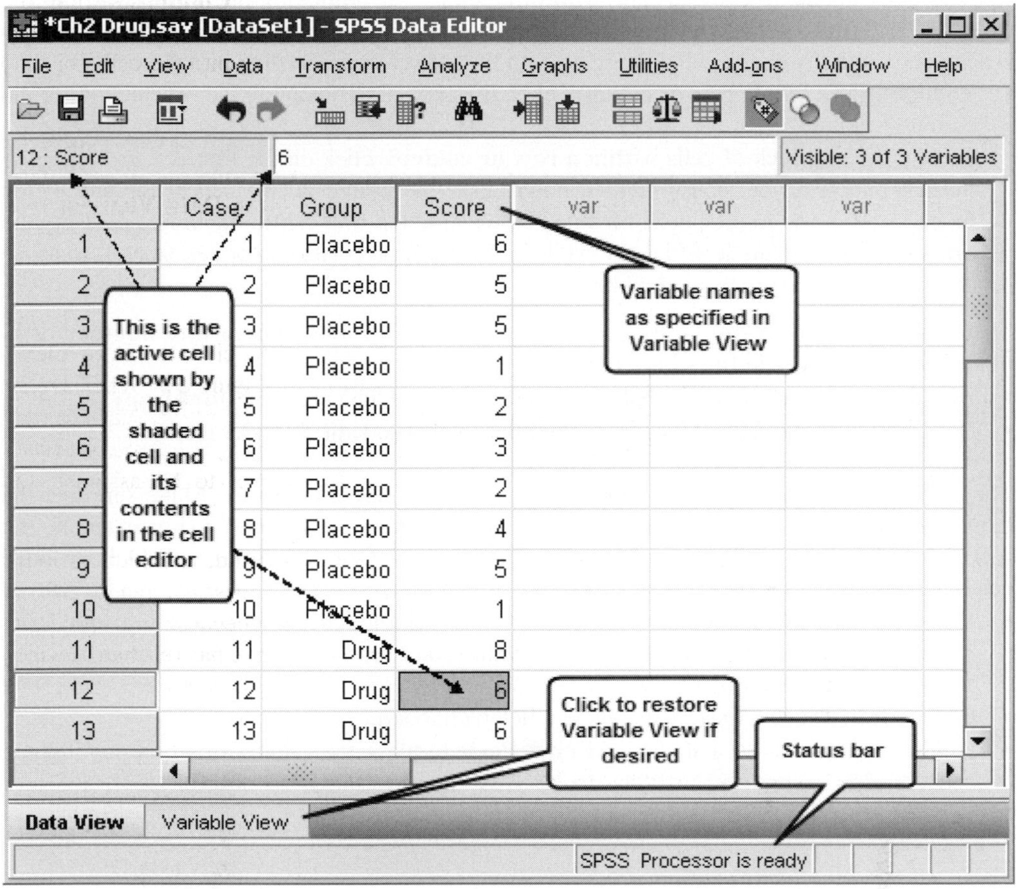

Figure 6. Part of **Data View** after the results in Table 1 have been entered

The first variable, *Case*, represents the case number of the participants. Enter the number of each participant from *1* to *20*. The second variable *Group*, identifies the condition under which each participant performed the task: *1 = Placebo*; *2 = Drug*. Enter ten *1*'s into the first ten rows of the *Group* variable, followed by ten *2*'s. In the first ten cells of the *Score* column, enter the scores of the ten participants who performed the task under the *Placebo* condition, followed by those of the ten participants who performed under the *Drug* condition.

Notice that in Figure 6, location of control is indicated by the shaded cell in the 12th row of the second column. The value in this cell is 6. The contents of this cell are also displayed in a white area known as the **cell editor** just above the column headings. The value in the **cell editor** (and the cell itself) can be changed by clicking in the **cell editor**, selecting the present value, typing a new one and pressing ⏎. The new value will appear in the grid.

Blocking, copying and pasting

Initially, only one cell in **Data View** is highlighted. However, it is possible to highlight a whole block of cells, or even an entire row or column. This **blocking** operation (when all the cells appear in **inverse video**, with the characters printed in white against a black background) is achieved either by clicking and dragging with the mouse or proceeding as follows:

- To **highlight a whole row or column**, click the grey box containing the row number or the column heading.
- To highlight a **block of cells within a row or column**, click on the first cell and (keeping the left button of the mouse pressed down) drag the pointer to the cell at the end of the block. The same result can be obtained by clicking the first cell in the block, pressing the **Shift** key and keeping it held down while using the appropriate cursor key (↑ or ↓) to move the highlighting along the entire block.

The blocking operation can be used to **copy the values in one column into another** or to **place them elsewhere in the same column**.

- Highlight a column of values that you wish to copy and then choose **Edit➔Copy**.
- Next, highlight the cells of the target column and choose **Edit➔Paste**.

The values in the source column will now appear in the target column. (Make sure that the number of highlighted target cells is equal to the number of cells copied.) For example, the successions of *1*'s and *2*'s identifying the *Placebo* and *Drug* conditions could have been entered as follows.

- Place the value *1* in the topmost cell of the *Group* column. Move the black rectangle away from the cell to complete the entry of the value and return the highlight to the cell, which will now contain the value *1*.
- Choose **Edit➔Copy** to store the value *1* in the clipboard.
- Highlight cells *2* to *10* and choose **Edit➔Paste** to place the value *1* in all the highlighted cells.

Using key combinations to copy and paste

Copying and pasting can also be carried out by using the key combinations **Ctrl + C** (that is, by holding the **Ctrl** key down while pressing C) and **Ctrl + V**, respectively.

Deletion of values

Whether you are working in **Variable View** or in **Data View**, entries can be removed by selecting the target items in the manner described above and pressing the **Delete** key.

*Switching between **Data View** and **Variable View***

You can switch from one **Data Editor** display to the other at any point. While in **Data View**, for instance, you might want to return to **Variable View** to name further variables or add further details about existing ones. Just click the **Variable View** tab. When you have finished the new work in **Variable View**, click **Data View** to continue entering your data.

*Creating more space for entries in **Data View***

While the widths of the columns in **Data View** can be controlled from **Variable View** in the manner described above, you can also control column width while working in **Data View**. To widen a column, click on the grey cell containing the variable name at the top of the column and click and drag the right-hand border to the right.

*Displaying value labels in **Data View***

The values assigned to the numerical values of a grouping variable can be displayed in **Data View** by clicking the icon  in the toolbar or by choosing **View➜Value Labels**.

Should the *Group* column in **Data View** not be sufficiently wide to show the value labels completely, create more space by placing the cursor in the grey cell at the head of the column containing the label *Group* and click and drag the right-hand border of the cell to the right.

*Using the display of values in the **Data Editor** as a guide when entering data*

Having specified the variable type as *numeric* when in **Variable View**, you will find that **Data View** will accept, in the first instance, only numerical entries. You can arrange, however, for the first numerical entry, say *1*, to be displayed as the value label by clicking the icon  in the toolbar or by choosing **View➜Value Labels**.

Although you typed in *1*, you will now see the label *Placebo* in the cell. Moreover, you can copy and paste this label to the other nine cases in the *Placebo* group. When you come to the *Drug* group, however, you will need to type in *2* which, when you click another cell, will then appear as the value *Drug*. **Data View will not accept the word *Drug* typed in directly**. You can then copy and paste the second numerical label to the remaining cases in the Drug group. This procedure can be useful if, momentarily, as when your SPSS session has been interrupted, you have forgotten the number-label pairings you assigned in **Variable View**. It also helps you to avoid transcription errors when transferring your data from response sheets.

Saving the data file

When you finish entering your data (but preferably during data entry at intervals in case the system crashes), you can supply a name for the data file by choosing the **Save As...** item from the **File** drop-down menu, selecting an appropriate drive and/or folder and then entering a suitable name in the **File Name** box. After you have done this, the title bar will display your new name for the file. Note that if you do not do this, you will be prompted to supply a name for the data file when you wish to terminate your SPSS session and close down SPSS.

SPSS tutorials

For an animated step-by-step tutorial on entering data into SPSS, readers can work through the tutorial provided by SPSS. Click the **Help** drop-down menu, select **Tutorial** and then **Using the Data Editor**. The arrow buttons in the right-hand bottom corner of each page of the tutorial enable the user to navigate forward and

backward through the tutorial.

2.4   A STATISTICAL ANALYSIS

2.4.1   An example: Computing means

In this section, we shall use SPSS to summarise the results of the experiment by obtaining some descriptive statistics such as the mean and standard deviation of the scores for each treatment group (Placebo and Drug).

• From the drop-down **Analyze** menu, choose **Compare Means➔Means ...** as shown in Figure 7.

• Click **Means...** to access the **Means** dialog box (Figure 8).

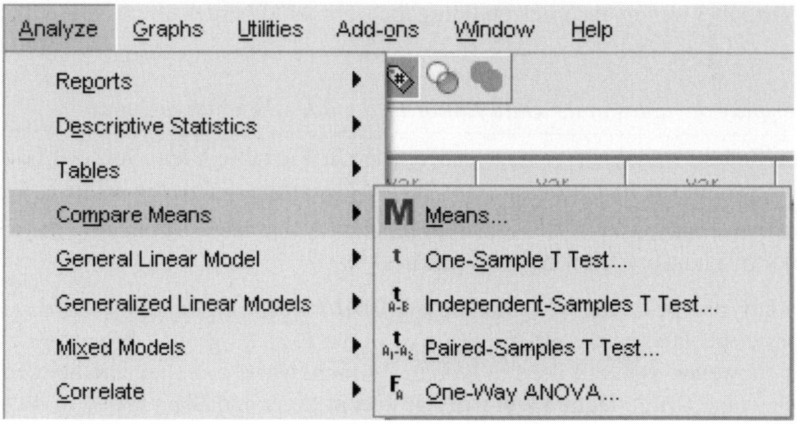

Figure 7. Finding the **Means** menu

Initially, in the left-hand panel the variable names are obscured; but you can view the entire label by touching it with the screen pointer.

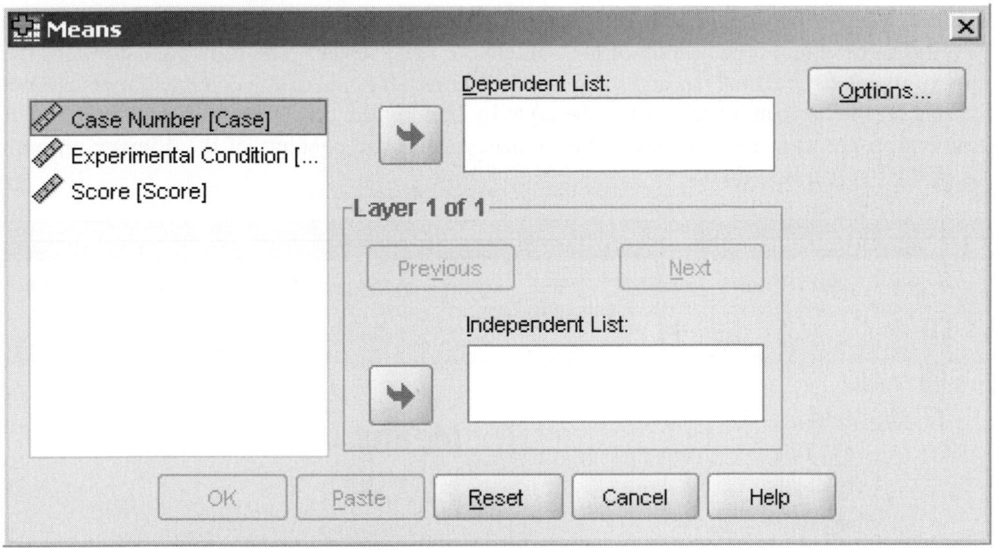

Figure 8. The **Means** dialog box showing the three variables in the data set

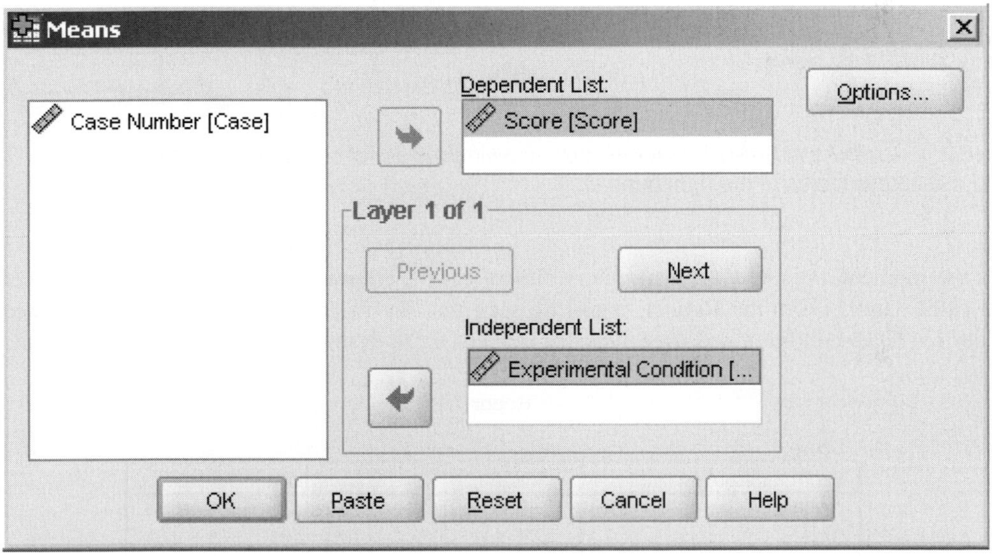

Figure 9. The completed **Means** dialog box for computing the mean scores for the two experimental conditions

- Click on *Score* to highlight it and then on the arrow pointing to the **Dependent List** box. The variable name and label will then be transferred to the Dependent List box.
- In a similar manner transfer the variable *Experimental Condition* to the **Independent List** box (see Figure 9).
- Click **OK** to run the analysis. The results will appear in a new window called the **SPSS Viewer**, a section of which is shown in Output 1.

The SPSS **Viewer** window is divided into two 'panes' by a vertical grey bar. The left pane shows the hierarchical organisation of the contents of the **Viewer**. The right pane contains the results of the statistical analysis and various other items. If some of the contents labels are not fully visible, the bar can be dragged to the right by moving the cursor on to it, pressing the left cursor button and dragging the bar as far as necessary. The contents of the **Viewer** on both sides of the bar can be edited.

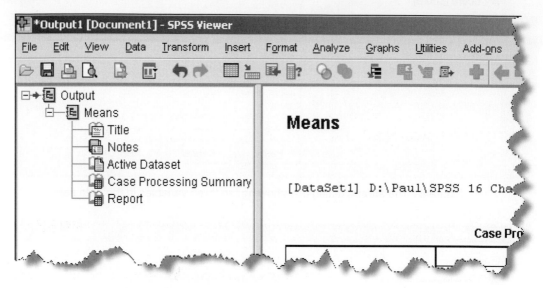

Output 1. Part of the **SPSS Viewer** window showing the list of output items in the left pane and the output tables in the right pane

For the moment, however, the main item of interest is the **Report** (Output 2), which appears in the right pane. From the **Report**, it can be seen that the mean performance of those tested under the *Drug* condition was over twice the level of those tested under the *Placebo* condition.

Report

Score

Experimental Condition	Mean	N	Std. Deviation
Placebo	3.40	10	1.838
Drug	6.90	10	1.449
Total	5.15	20	2.412

Output 2. The **Report** table showing the mean, number of scores and standard deviation in each of the two groups

It would seem, therefore, that the results of the experiment support the hypothesis. This, however, is insufficient: formal tests are necessary to confirm the appearance of the data. It should be noted, however, that before the researcher makes any formal statistical tests, the data should first be thoroughly explored. SPSS has an exploratory data analysis procedure, **Explore**, which offers a wide range of useful statistics. **Explore** can be run by choosing **Analyze➜Descriptive Statistics➜Explore…**.

We shall consider **Explore** more fully in Chapter 4.

See
Chap.
4

Editing the output in SPSS Viewer

The **SPSS Viewer** offers powerful editing facilities, some of which can radically alter the appearance of a default table such as that shown in Output 3. Many of the tables in the output are **pivot tables**, that is, tables in which the columns and rows can be transposed and to which other radical alterations can be made.

Report

Variables Score ▼

Experimental Condition	Mean	N	Std. Deviation
Placebo	3.40	10	1.838
Drug	6.90	10	1.449
Total	5.15	20	2.412

Output 3. An item which has been prepared for editing. On double-clicking the item, a dotted border appears around it

Suppose, for example, like the editors of many scientific journals, you would prefer the experimental conditions *Placebo* and *Drug* to be column headings and the group means, standard deviations and *N*'s to be below them. If you double-click the **Report**, a dotted border will appear around the table (Output 3).

You will notice that, along the drop-down menus at the top of the **Viewer** window, a new menu, **Pivot**, has appeared.

*Output1 [Document1] - SPSS Viewer

File   Edit   View   Insert   Pivot   Format   Analyze   Graphs   Utilities

Output
  Means
    Title
    Notes
    Active Dat
    Case Processing Summary
    Report

Reorder Categories   ▶
Transpose Rows and Columns
Pivoting Trays
Go to Layers...

[DataSet1]

Figure 10. The **Pivot** drop-down menu with **Transpose Rows and Columns** selected

• Choose **Pivot➔Transpose Rows and Columns** (Figure 10).

The effect (see Output 4) is dramatic! The descriptive statistics now occupy the rows and the experimental conditions the columns.

The **Pivot** menu can be used to edit complex tables with three, four or more dimensions of classification. Such manipulation can be of great assistance in bringing out the most important features of your results.

Report

Score

	Experimental Condition		
	Placebo	Drug	Total
Mean	3.40	6.90	5.15
N	10	10	20
Std. Deviation	1.838	1.449	2.412

Output 4. The transposed **Report** table

2.4.2   Keeping more than one application open

One useful feature of Windows is that the user can keep several applications open simultaneously. It is therefore quite possible to be writing a document in **Word** while at the same time running **SPSS** and importing output such as the **Report** in the previous section. If more than one application is open, the user can move from one to another by clicking on the appropriate button on the **Taskbar** (usually located at the foot of the screen). Alternatively, you can hold down the **Alt** key and press the **Tab** key repeatedly to cycle control through whatever applications may be open.

2.5   CLOSING SPSS

SPSS is closed by choosing **Exit** from the **File** menu. If you have not yet saved the data or the output at any point, a default dialog box will appear with the question: **Save contents of data editor to untitled?** or **Save contents of output viewer to Output 1?** You must then click the **Yes**, **No** or **Cancel** button. If you choose **Yes**, you will be given a final opportunity to name the file you wish to save. Beware of saving unselected output files because they can become very large in terms of computer storage, especially if they contain graphics.

2.6   RESUMING WORK ON A SAVED DATA SET

There are several ways of resuming work on a saved data set. After opening SPSS and obtaining the introductory **SPSS 16 for Windows dialog box**, you can click the radio button **Open an existing data source** (Figure 1). A list of saved files with the extension *.sav* will appear in the upper **More Files** window. Select the appropriate file and click **OK**. The data file will then appear in **Data View**. Other kinds of file, such as SPSS output files, can be retrieved from the lower **More Files** window by clicking on the radio button labelled **Open another kind of file**.

While you in the **Data Editor**, it is always possible to access files by choosing **Open** from the **File** menu. A quicker method of accessing an SPSS data file is to double-click its icon. The data will immediately appear in **Data View**.

Exercises

Exercise 1 *Some simple operations with SPSS 16* and Exercise 2 *Questionnaire data* are available in www.psypress.com/spss-made-simple and click on Exercises.

CHAPTER 3

Editing and manipulating files

3.1   More about the SPSS Data Editor

3.2   More on the SPSS Viewer

3.3   Selecting from and manipulating data files

3.4   Importing and exporting data

3.5   Printing from SPSS

3.1   MORE ABOUT THE SPSS DATA EDITOR

3.1.1   Working in Variable View

In Section 2.2, we introduced the **Data Editor**, with its two alternative displays, **Variable View** and **Data View**. Here we describe some additional features of **Variable View** (see Section 2.3.1).

> See
> Section
> 2.3.1

*Inserting new variables among those already in **Variable View***

An additional variable can be inserted in **Variable View** by highlighting any row (click the grey cell on the left), and choosing **Data➜Insert Variable**.

The new variable, with a default name such as VAR00004 (i.e. the next free name), will appear **above** the row that has been highlighted.

In **Data View,** the new variable will appear in a new column **to the left** of the variable that was highlighted in **Variable View**.

*Rearranging the order of variables in **Variable View***

In Figure 1, is a section from **Variable View**, in which the top-to-bottom ordering of the variables determines their left-to-right order of appearance in **Data View**, which is *Case*, *Group*, then *Score*.

	Name	Type	Width	Decimals
1	Case	Numeric	8	0
2	Group	Numeric	8	0
3	Score	Numeric	8	0

Figure 1. The arrangement of the variables in **Variable View** determines their order of appearance in **Data View**

Suppose that you want to change the sequence of the variables in **Data View**: you want *Score* to appear to the left of *Group*. In **Variable View**, click the grey box to the left of the *Score* variable to highlight the whole row. Holding the left mouse button down, drag the screen pointer upwards. A red line will appear above the *Group* row. On releasing the mouse button, the variable *Score* will appear immediately under *Case* (Figure 2). In **Data View**, the variable *Score* will now appear to the left of the variable *Group*.

	Name	Type	Width	Decimals
1	Case	Numeric	8	0
2	Score	Numeric	8	0
3	Group	Numeric	8	0

Figure 2. The arrangement of variables after moving *Score* above *Group*

Large data sets: the advantages of numbering the cases

In the small data set we considered in Chapter 2, each row had a number and could be taken as representing one particular case or person. Suppose, however, that we had a much larger data set, containing thousands of cases. Suppose also that, from time to time, cases were to be removed from the data set or the data were sorted and re-sorted on different criteria. As a result, any particular row in the data set, say the 99th, may not always contain data on the same person throughout the exercise.

With a large data set like this, especially one that is continually changing, it is good practice to create, as the first variable, one with a name such as *Case*, which records each participant's original case number: 1, 2, ..., and so on. The advantage of doing this is that, even though a given person's data may occupy different rows at different points in the data-gathering exercise, the researcher always knows which data came from which person.

Should the accuracy of the transcription of a participant's data into SPSS later be called into question, that person's data can always be identified and checked throughout the entire process of data entry.

Suppose you wish to add case numbers to a data set not currently containing such a variable. This is very conveniently done, especially when the data set is large, by using the **Compute Variable** procedure as follows:

- Ensure that the data file is present in the **Data Editor**.
- In **Variable View**, click on the grey cell to the left of the first row to highlight the entire row.
- Choose **Data➜Insert Variable** to create a new empty row above the original first row with the default variable name *VAR00001*.
- Remove the highlighting from the row by clicking elsewhere in the grid. Click on the **Name** cell and type in the variable name *Case*.
- Adjust the **Decimals** setting to zero.
- Enter the label *Case Number* in the **Label** column.
- Choose **Transform➜Compute Variable…** to open the **Compute Variable** dialog box.
- Place the cursor in the **Target Variable** slot and enter the variable name *Case*.

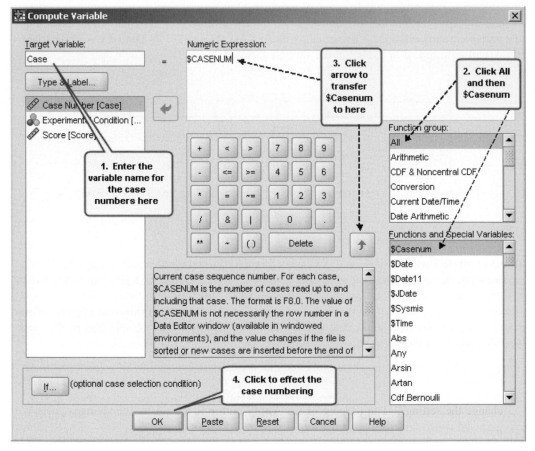

Figure 3. Part of the **Compute Variable** dialog box for generating case numbers

- Follow the instructions shown in Figure 3 and click **OK**.
- A warning box will appear with the question **Change existing variable?** Click **OK**.
- Click the **Data View** tab to confirm that a new variable named *Case* has appeared, containing the counting numbers *1, 2, … .*

Note that this procedure cannot be used for creating case numbers in an empty data file. If it is desired to create case numbers before entering data, then dummy data must be entered (e.g. entering *1* in the first row of the variable *Case* and then copying it down for as many rows as the data set will need) before using *$casenum* in the **Compute Variable** procedure. The warning box with the question **Change existing variable?** will appear as before to which the response is **OK**.

Changing the global default number of decimal places and maximum width for string variables using the Edit menu

The default settings for variable width and the number of places of decimals are *8* and *2*, respectively. If you wish to enter several new variables and display them all as whole numbers (integers), choose **Edit➔Options➔Data** and change the pre-set values. Figure 4 shows the top of the **Options** dialog box.

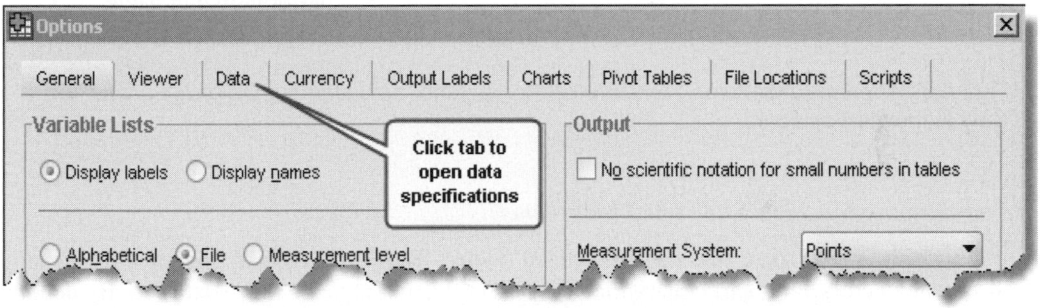

Figure 4. The top of the **Options** dialog box

- Click the tab labelled **Data**. In the new dialog box is an area headed **Display Format for New Numeric Variables** (Figure 5), in which both the width and number of decimal places can be amended.
- In the box containing the number of **Decimal Places**, click the downward arrow on the right until *0* appears. Click **OK** and the **Options** dialog box will close. The changes you have specified will apply only to any **new** numeric variables that you may create. You will find that, even after amending the default settings in **Options**, the appearance of numerical data already in **Data View** is unchanged.
- At the foot of the **Data** dialog box, is a button labelled **Apply**, which is activated when you change the settings. The purpose of the **Apply** button is to register the changes you have made **without closing the dialog box**. You can then click other tabs and make whatever changes you wish to make in those before leaving **Options** by clicking on **OK**.

If you are working on a networked computer where the software and settings are held on a central server, any changes you may make by changing the entries in **Options** may apply only for the duration of your own session: when you log off, the system will restore the original default values.

Options

| General | Viewer | Data | Currency | Output Labels | Charts | Piv |

Transformation and Merge Options

◉ Calculate values immediately

○ Calculate values before used

> Click this tab if it is desired to change the appearance of charts (see Section 5.1.3)

Display Format for New Numeric Variables

Width: 8   Decimal Places: 2

Example: 12345.67

> Change the number of decimal places by amending this value

Figure 5. The **Options** dialog box showing the panel for adjusting the **Display Format for New Numeric Variables**

*Changing the type of variable (the **Type** column)*

In **Variable View**, there is a column headed **Type**. The **Type** column specifies the general form that an entry for a particular variable will take when it appears in the data set. By default, the variable type is assumed to be **numeric**, but seven other types can be specified in SPSS.

A **string** is a sequence of characters, such as a person's name, which is treated as a qualitative variable (not as a numeric variable) by the system. Had we entered, in the variable *Name*, the names of all the participants taking part in the drug experiment, *Name* would have been a **string variable**.

To create a string variable, proceed as follows:
- After typing in the name of the variable, highlight the cell in the **Type** column thus

- Click the grey area with the three dots to the right of **Numeric** to open the **Variable Type** dialog box (Figure 6).
- In the dialog box is a list of eight variable types, each with a radio button. Initially, the **Numeric** button will be marked.
- Descriptions of the different types of variable will be found by clicking the **Help** button in the dialog box.

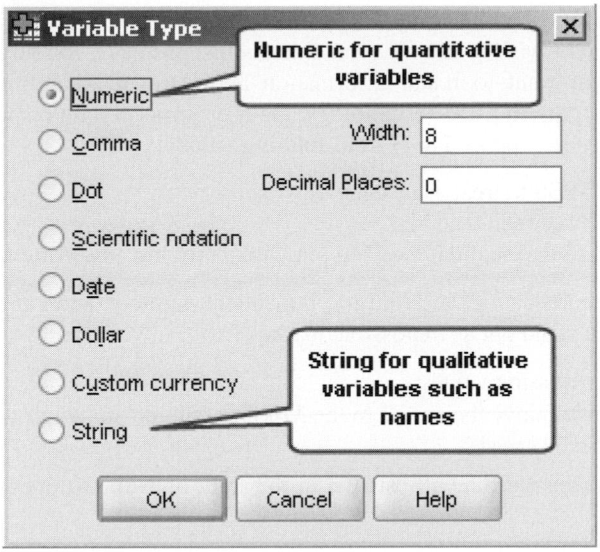

Figure 6. The **Variable Type** dialog box

- Click the **String** radio button at the foot of the list. The **Width** and **Decimal Places** boxes will immediately be replaced by a box labelled **Characters**.
- Change the default value *8* in the **Characters** box to some larger number such as *20* to accommodate the longest likely name. Do this by moving the cursor into the number box, selecting the *8* and typing in *20*.
- Click **OK**. In **Variable View**, the variable type *String* will now appear in the **Type** column and the cell for the *Name* variable in the **Width** column will now show *20*.
- Click the **Width** column and copy the specifications either by choosing **Copy** from the **Edit** menu or with the key combination **Ctrl + C**.
- Click on **Columns** and paste the new **Width** specification *(20)* there either by choosing **Paste** from the **Edit** menu or with the key combination **Ctrl + V**. The effect of this move will be to make sufficient space available in **Data View** to see the longest name in the data set. Alternatively, in **Data View**, the right-hand edge of the box containing the variable *Name* can be dragged to the right by holding down the left mouse button and dragging it as far as desired.

*Missing values (the **Missing** column)*

SPSS assumes that all data sets are complete (i.e. that the cells in every row and every column have something in them). The user, however, may not have entries for every case on every variable in the data set (e.g. a participant's age might not have been recordcd). Such missing entries are marked by SPSS with what is known as a **system-missing** value, which is indicated in the **Data Editor** by a full stop. SPSS will exclude system-missing values from its calculations of means, standard deviations and other statistics.

It may be, however, that for some purposes the user wishes SPSS to treat certain responses actually present in the data set as missing data. For example, suppose that, in an examination, some candidates either walked out the moment they saw the paper or, having attempted at least some of the examination, earned only a nominal mark (say 20% or less) from the examiner. In either case, you might wish to treat the candidate's response as a missing value, but for some purposes you might want to retain information about the relative frequencies of the two responses in the output. In SPSS terminology, the user wants certain responses to be treated as **user-missing** values (as opposed to **system-missing** values).

Suppose you want SPSS to treat as missing:
   1.   Any marks between *0* and *20*.
   2.   Cases where the candidate walked out without giving any written response at all.

A walk-out could be coded as an arbitrary, but salient, number, such as -9: the negative sign helps the number to stand out as impossible mark.

To define such user-missing values:
*   In **Variable View**, move the cursor to the **Missing** column and click on the appropriate cell for the variable concerned.
*   Click the grey area with the ellipsis [...] to the right of **None** to open the **Missing Values** dialog box.
*   Initially, the **No missing values** radio button is marked. The three text boxes underneath give the user the opportunity to specify up to three **Discrete Missing Values**, referred to in SPSS as *missing (1)*, *missing (2)*, and *missing (3)*. These may either be numerical, as with a grouping variable, or short string variables (up to 8 characters in length), but they must be consistent with the original variable type. In the case of a string variable, the procedure is case sensitive. The other options in the dialog box are for scale (quantitative) variables: the user may define a missing value as one falling within a specified range, or one that falls either within a specified range or within a specified category.
*   Click the **Range plus one discrete missing value** button. Enter the values *0* and *20* into the **Low** and **High** boxes, respectively, and *-9* into the **Discrete value** box. The completed dialog box is shown in Figure 7.
*   Click **OK** and the values will appear in the **Missing** column cell.

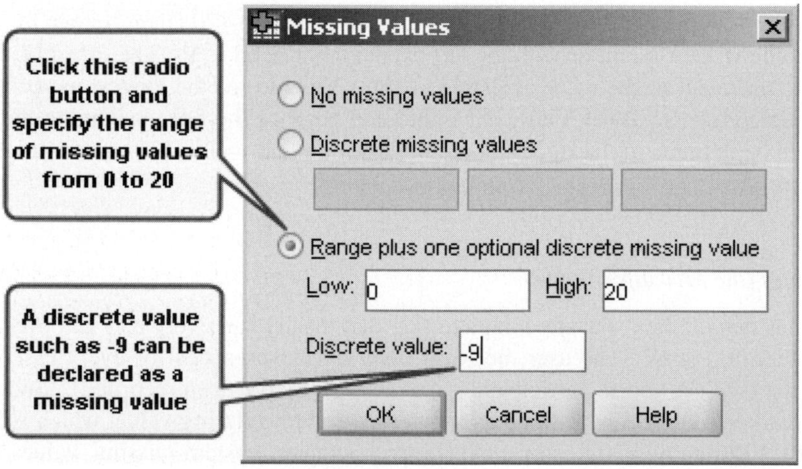

Figure 7. The completed **Missing Values** dialog box showing a range of missing values between *0* and *20* and a discrete value of -9

As with the attributes of number of decimals places and width, missing value specifications can be copied to other variables by pasting them into the appropriate cells.

*Data alignment (the **Align** column)*

In **Data View**, by default, numbers are right-aligned and strings are left-aligned. These settings can be changed by clicking on the appropriate cell in the **Align** column and choosing **Left**, **Right** or **Center**.

*Measurement level (the **Measure** column)*

The default measurement level is **Scale** for numeric variables and **Nominal** for **String** variables. Although a grouping variable refers to a set of qualitative categories, its representation in SPSS is still numeric, because it is a set of code numbers for the groups or conditions; it should be specified as **Nominal** within the **Measure** column in **Variable View**. In most chart-drawing and table-producing procedures, it is imperative that category variables are specified as **Nominal**.

3.1.2   Working in Data View

In Sections 2.3.2 and 2.3.3, the entry of data in **Data View** was briefly considered. Here we shall describe some additional features of **Data View**.

See
Sections
2.3.2 &
2.3.3

Reading in SPSS files

- When the opening SPSS window appears, select **Open an existing data source**.
- Select the appropriate file. (If you are working on a networked computer, you may have to click **More files ...** and locate the file or folder containing the file.)
- Click **OK** to load the data file into **Data View**.

Alternatively, one of the following methods can be used:

- Click the radio button of the opening SPSS window labelled **Type in data** and then **OK** to bring **Data View** to the screen.
- Select **File➔Open➔Data** to show the **Open File** dialog box. The target file can then be specified.
- If SPSS has not yet been opened, you can use the Windows **Find** menu or **My Computer** to locate the file, which should open SPSS with the data loaded in **Data View** (or the variables loaded in **Variable View**) when the file name is double-clicked. Sometimes, especially with networked computers, it may be necessary to open SPSS first. While data are being read into **Data View** from a file, the hour-glass will appear and messages will appear in the **Status Bar** at various stages in the operation. The message **SPSS Processor is ready** signals the end of the reading process.

*Entering data into **Data View** before specifying variables in **Variable View***

Although we strongly recommend that you lay the foundations in **Variable View** before actually entering the data in **Data View**, it is possible to begin immediately to enter data into

Data View. It is also possible to copy blocks of data directly into **Data View**, which can be useful when you are importing data from another application which does not have one of the many data formats recognised by SPSS. The details of the variables can be added in **Variable View** later.

- Choose **File➜New** to create an empty SPSS data file.
- Enter **Data View** and type the value *23* into the cell in the second row of the fourth column. **Data View** will now appear as in Figure 8.

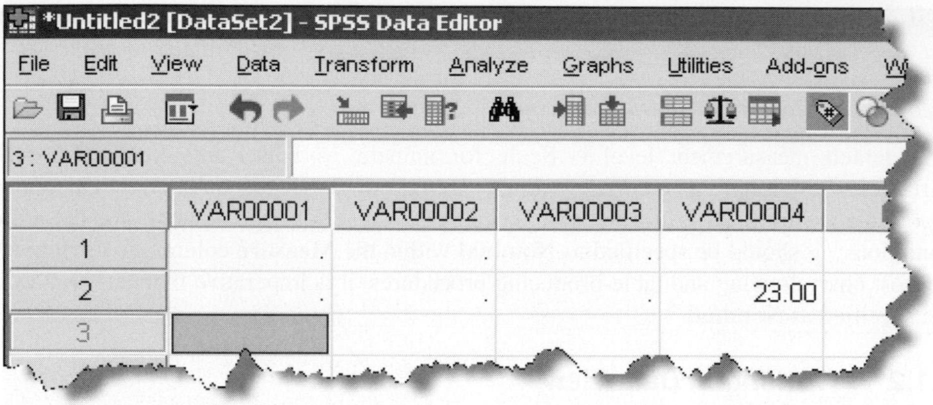

Figure 8. The appearance of **Data View** after entering a datum without previously naming variables in **Variable View**

The fourth variable has now been given the default name *VAR00004*. Notice that SPSS has assumed that we have a 2 × 4 matrix of data and filled in the blank cells with the system-missing symbol. Should you type values into cells to the right of the fourth column, more default variable names will appear as SPSS expands the supposed data matrix to include the new column and row. If you click on a cell underneath the lowest row of dots, more rows of dots will appear, the lowest of which contains the cell you have just clicked.

To assign meaningful names and labels to the default variables visible in **Data View**, switch to **Variable View** and assign the specifications there. You can either enter **Variable View** in the usual way by clicking the **Variable View** tab at the bottom of **Data View** or double-click the default heading of the variable you wish to name. Either way, when you enter **Variable View**, you will see that the default variable names have been entered there. In other words, the two display modes of the **Data Editor** are interchangeable in the order in which they are completed.

Inserting additional variables while working in **Data View**

To add a new variable **to the right of those already in Data View**, you have only to type a value into a cell to the right of the present matrix of data. To add a new column **between two of those within the present data set**,

- Highlight the variable **to the right of** the intended position of the new variable.
- Choose **Data➜Insert Variable** to create a new, empty, variable to the left of the variable you have highlighted.

Rearranging the variables in **Data View**

Suppose that in **Data View**, the order of the variables is *Case*, *Group* and *Score*, and you want to change the order to *Case*, *Score* and *Group*. We recommend that you do this in **Variable View** (see Section 3.1.1), but the following procedure works in **Data View**.

- Create a new, empty variable to the left of *Group* in the manner described above.
- Click on the grey cell at the head of the *Score* column to highlight the whole column.
- Choose **Edit➔Cut** to remove the *Score* variable and place it in the clipboard.
- Click the grey cell at the head of the new, empty variable to highlight the whole column.
- Use **Edit** and **Paste** to move the *Score* variable including its data and definitions into its new position to the left of *Group*.

Adding new cases

Columns can be lengthened by choosing **Data➔Insert cases** which will have the effect of adding new empty rows underneath the existing columns.

There are occasions, however, when you may want to place rows for additional cases in the middle of the data set. Suppose that, in the drug experiment, you want to add data on an additional participant who has been tested under the *Placebo* condition. Proceed as follows.

- Click the grey cell on the left of the row of data **above** which you want to insert the new case. (This will be the row of data for the first participant who performed under the Drug condition.) The row will now be highlighted.
- Choose **Data➔Insert Cases** to create a new empty row above the one you highlighted.

You can now type in the data from the additional placebo participant.

Validation of data

When entering data into a data file, especially a large file, it is possible to mistype a value (e.g. 100 for 10) or when adding more data, to duplicate a case number. In this subsection we look at a way of checking for aberrant data and in the next subsection a way for detecting duplicate values.

SPSS provides a means of checking out the validity of data within the **Validation** item of the **Data** menu where various rules can be specified either for individual variables or across all variables. The procedure is in two parts: the first part consists of defining as many rules as desired, the second part of applying these rules to specified variables. For example, suppose we wish to check that no case number greater than 50 and no score greater than 20 have been entered into our data set.

- From the drop-down **Data** menu, choose **Validation➔Define Rules...** (Figure 9) to access the **Define Validation Rules** dialog box (Figure 10).

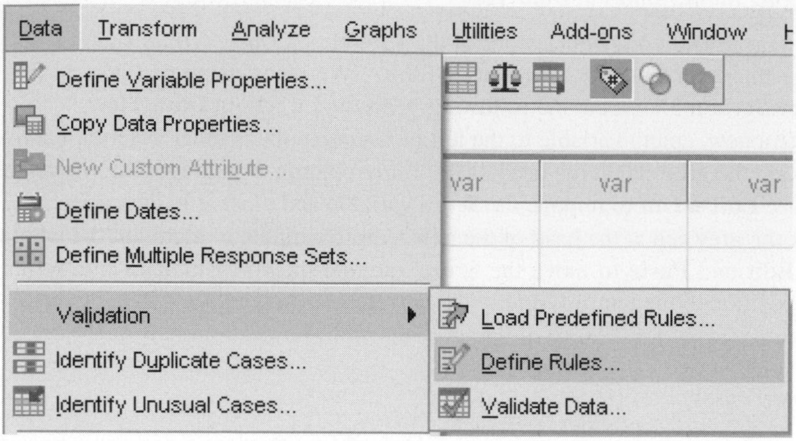

Figure 9. The **Validation** menu

- Within the **Rule Definition** window, change the **Name** *SingleVarRule1* to *Range of Case Numbers*, enter the values 1 and 50 into the **Minimum** and **Maximum** boxes respectively.
- Click **New** and then repeat the procedure but this time replacing *SingleVarRule1* with *Range of Scores* and enter the values 1 and 20 into the **Minimum** and **Maximum** boxes respectively. The names of the rules are arbitrary. Additional rules can be added as desired.
- Finally click **OK**.

Having defined the rules, the next step is to validate the desired variables in the data set by applying the appropriate rules. For illustration, imagine that three more cases have been entered in the data file, one with a case number of 21 and a score of 15, another with a case number of 22 and a score of 30 (this is outside the range of scores) and another with a case number of 200 (this is outside the range of case numbers) and a score of 8.

The next stage is to identify which variables are to be validated because there may be some variables in the data set that are not being validated (for example, *Experimental Condition*).

- From the drop-down **Data** menu (Figure 9), choose **Validation**➜**Validate Data...** to access the **Validate Data** dialog box.
- Select the variable *Score* in the **Variables** box and click the arrow to transfer it to the **Analysis Variables** box. Do likewise with *Case Number* (Figure 11) and then click the **Single-Variable Rules** tab to open the **Single-Variables Rules** dialog box (Figure 12).
- Click the variable names and the check boxes as shown in Figure 12 and then **OK**.

The final stage is applying the appropriate rule(s) to the appropriate variables.

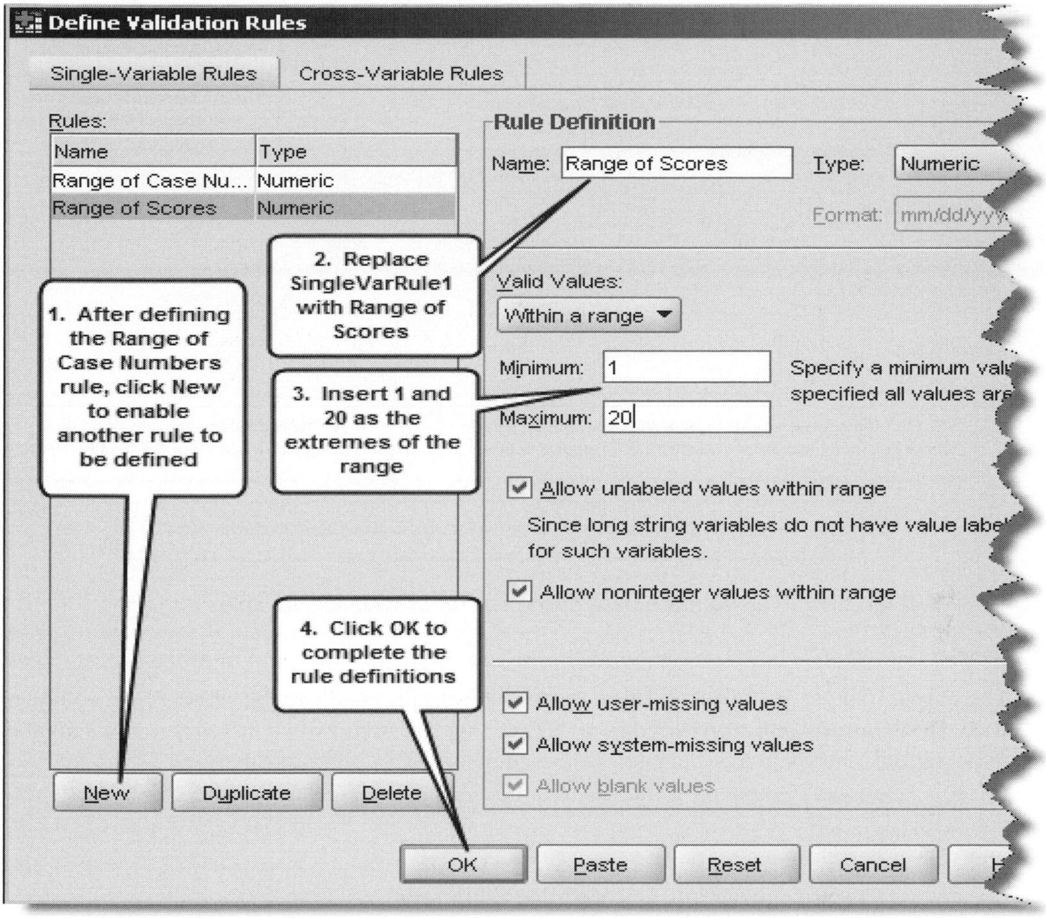

Figure 10. The **Define Validation Rules** dialog box with two rules defined

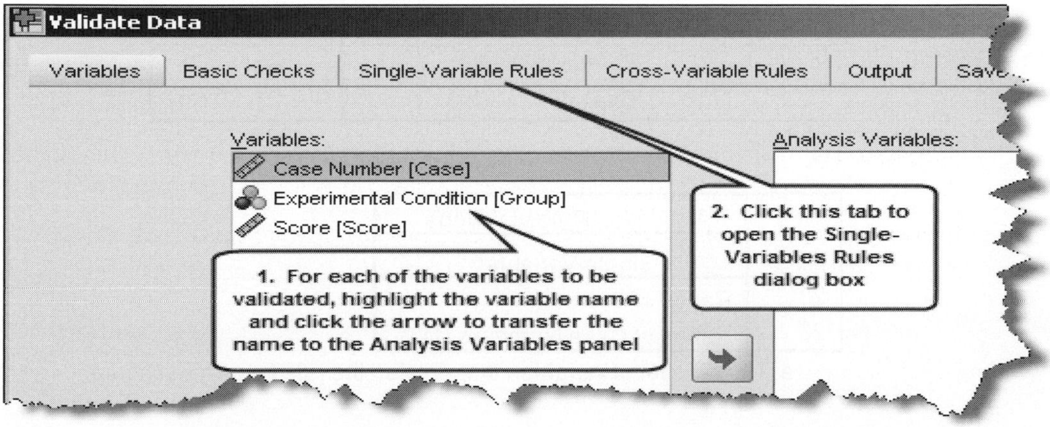

Figure 11. Part of the **Validate Data** dialog box showing the transfer of variable names of variables to be validated

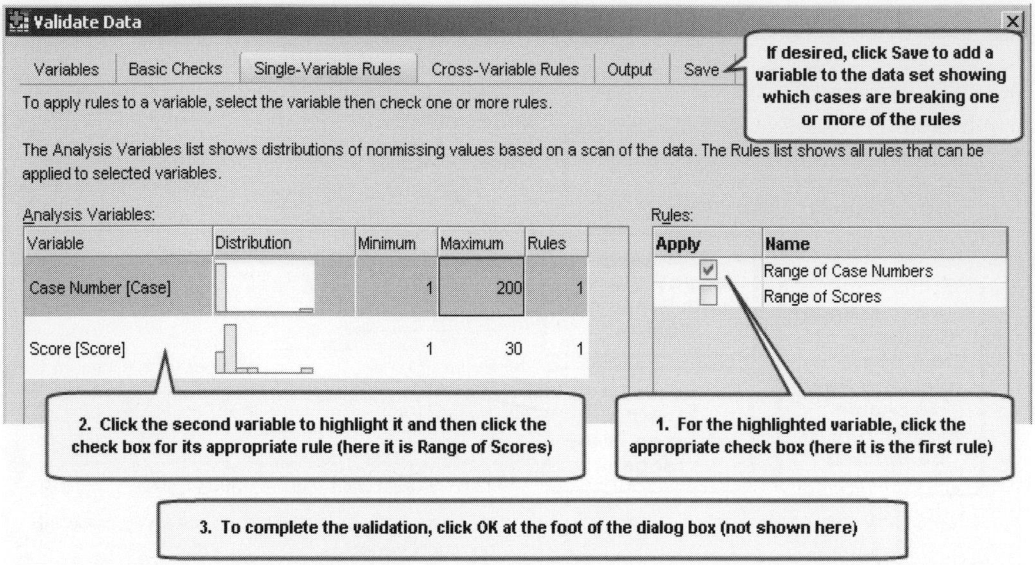

Figure 12. The **Validate Data** dialog box for associating variables and rules

The output (Output 1) of the validation starts with warnings and variable checks, and a table of **Rule Descriptions** (not reproduced here). These are followed by two tables listing the number of violations and their row numbers in the data set (SPSS refers to these as Case) for each variable analysed (Output 1). One invalid *Case Number* and one invalid *Score* have been detected.

Variable Summary

	Rule	Number of Violations
Case Number	Range of Case Numbers	1
	Total	1
Score	Range of Scores	1
	Total	1

Case Report

	Validation Rule Violations
Case	Single-Variable[a]
22	Range of Scores (1)
23	Range of Case Numbers (1)

a. The number of variables that violated the rule follows each rule.

Output 1. Two of the tables in the output showing that one *Case Number* and one *Score* were invalid. The Case Report identifies the row number (Case) with the invalid *Score* and the row number with the invalid *Case Number*

Identifying duplicate cases

Sometimes, especially when incrementing a data set with fresh cases, it is useful to ensure that the same case number is not duplicated. SPSS provides a routine for checking out possible duplications in any variable.

* From the drop-down **Data** menu, choose **Identify Duplicates Cases ...** (Figure 9) to access the **Identify Duplicate Cases** dialog box (Figure 13). Click the variable name *Case Number* and transfer it to the **Define matching cases by** window.
* Assuming that later cases with the same case numbers have been incorrectly numbered, click the radio button **First case in each group is primary** to replace the default option that the **Last case in each group is primary**.
* Click **OK**.

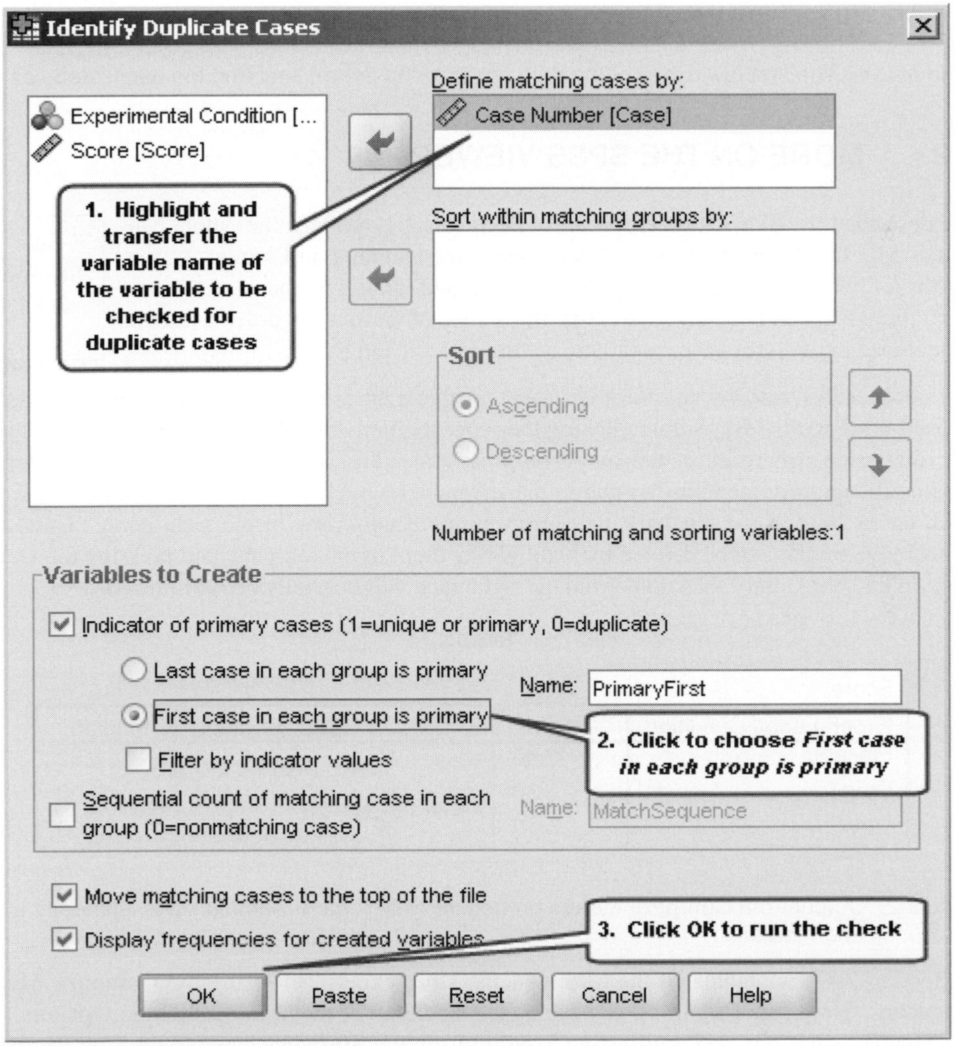

Figure 13. The **Identify Duplicate Cases** dialog box with the variable *Case Number* and the **First Case in each group is primary** option selected

For illustration, assume that another case has been added to the file with a case number of 20. After clicking **OK** in the **Identify Duplicate Cases** dialog box, the data file would appear with the duplicated cases at the top (Figure 14). The case in row 1 is the original case, the most recently added case in row 2 is the one with the duplicate case number. The **SPSS Viewer** also contains tables (not reproduced) showing how many duplicated cases there are.

	Case	Group	Score	PrimaryFirst
1	20	Drug	10	Primary Case
2	20	Placebo	8	Duplicate Case
3	1	Placebo	6	Primary Case
4	2	Placebo	5	Primary Case

Figure 14. The first few cases of the data set showing the original and the duplicated cases

3.2   MORE ON THE SPSS VIEWER

We described the **SPSS Viewer** in part of Section 2.4.1 and how the output can be edited. The **Viewer** consists of two panes (see Output 1 in Chapter 2), the widths of which can be adjusted by clicking and dragging the vertical bar separating them. The left pane lists the items of output in order of their appearance in the right pane, each item having an icon and a title.

See Section 2.4.1

The icon shows whether the item is visible in the right pane (open-book icon) or invisible (closed-book icon). By double-clicking the icon, the item can be made visible or invisible in the right pane, where all actual output is presented. The output can also be rearranged by moving the appropriate icons around in the left pane by clicking and dragging them. A single click on an item in the left pane will bring the item into view in the right pane. Unwanted items in the output can be deleted by highlighting them in the left pane and pressing the **Delete** key. In this book, only selections from the right pane will normally be reproduced.

Report

Score

Experimental Condition	Mean	N	Std. Deviation	Median
Placebo	3.40	10	1.838	3.50
Drug	6.90	10	1.449	6.50
Total	5.15	20	2.412	5.50

Output 2. Output from **Compare Means** procedure, with means, sample sizes, standard deviations and medians

In Section 2.4.1 we tabulated the results of the Drug experiment using the **Compare Means** procedure. Here (see Output 2) we have added a column of medians by clicking **Options...** in the **Means** dialog box and transferring **Median** from the **Statistics** panel to the **Cell Statistics** panel. (It is often a good idea, when exploring data, to compare means with medians: if they have similar values, symmetrical distributions are suggested. Here, however, the medians have been included merely to demonstrate some editing in the **Viewer**.)

3.2.1   Editing the output

In Section 2.4.1, we demonstrated that the output in the **SPSS Viewer** could be edited by showing the effect of a pivoting procedure. Here we consider some more ways of improving the appearance of the output.

To edit an item, say a table, in the **Viewer**, double-click it. The table will now be surrounded by a dotted box indicating that you are now in the **Viewer**'s editor. Once a selected item has been surrounded by a dotted box, the following changes can be made:

- To **widen or narrow columns**, move the cursor on to a vertical line in the table and click and drag the line to the left or the right.
- **Items** can be **deleted** by highlighting them and pressing the **Delete** key.
- **Whole columns or rows** can be **deleted** by highlighting them and pressing the **Delete** key (see below for details).
- **Text** can sometimes be altered by double-clicking an item and deleting letters or typing in new ones.
- If values are listed, it is possible to re-specify the number of decimal places shown by highlighting the numbers concerned in a block, pressing the **right-hand** mouse button, selecting **Cell Properties...** and changing the specification in the **Cell Properties** dialog box.

For example, suppose that, in the **Report** table (Output 2), we want to dispense with the third row (*Total*) containing the statistics of all twenty scores in the data set considered as a single group and also the column of **Medians**.

- Click the first value (5.15) in the bottom row so that it is highlighted.
- Press the **Ctrl** button and, keeping it pressed, click the other value cells in the *Total* row so that they are all highlighted (Output 3).
- Press the **Delete** key. If this key does not work, an alternative way of deleting the material is to click the right-hand mouse button and select **Clear** from the drop-down menu. Note that titles of columns and rows disappear if their values are deleted.
- Delete the values in the *Median* column in a similar manner.
- Click outside the shaded border to leave the **Editor**. The **Report** table will now appear as in Output 4.

Report

Variables [Score ▼]

Experimental Condition	Mean	N	Std. Deviation	Median
Placebo	3.40	10	1.838	3.50
Drug	6.90	10	1.449	6.50
Total	5.15	20	2.412	5.50

Output 3. Highlighting material to be deleted

Score

Experimental Condition	Mean	N	Std. Deviation
Placebo	3.40	10	1.838
Drug	6.90	10	1.449

Output 4. The edited **Report** table after removing the *Total* row and *Median* column

3.2.2   More advanced editing

The **Data Editor** offers even more powerful editing facilities, some of which can radically alter the appearance of a default table such as the **Report** table we have been editing. Many of the tables in the output are **pivot tables**, that is, tables in which the columns and rows can be transposed and to which other radical alterations can be made.

In Chapter 2, we showed how, by choosing **Pivot➔Transpose Rows and Columns** we could change the rows of the default **Report** table into columns and vice versa (see Section 2.4.1). Here we illustrate the manipulation of a three-way table of means.

> See
> Section
> 2.4.1

A three-way table of means

It is well known that generally females are better at recalling verbal material and males are better at recalling graphic material. An experiment was carried out recalling verbal or graphic items after either a short, medium or long period of inspection of the items. Male and female participants were each divided into six subgroups looking at verbal or graphic items for the three inspection times.

Coding variables for *Sex*, *Task*, and *Inspection Time* were named in **Variable View** along with *Score* for the number of items recalled. Corresponding **Labels** were specified as *Sex*, *Type of Task*, *Inspection Time* and *Number of Items Recalled*. The **Means...** procedure with *Number of Items Recalled* entered in the **Dependent List** and each of *Sex*, *Type of Task* and *Inspection Time* entered as layers in the **Independent List** generated Output 5 when only **Mean** was selected for the **Cell Statistics** box within **Options**. The rows for Total have been edited out of Output 5 for simplicity.

It is possible to effect a simple transposition of all the rows in Output 5 into columns and vice versa by choosing **Transposing rows and Columns** from the **Pivot** menu. There is little to be gained from this, however, because of the complexity of the table. To improve the clarity of the table, we want to select individual variables for transposition. This finer control is achieved by using the **Pivoting Trays** procedure.

- After highlighting the **Report** table (Output 5) by double-clicking anywhere within it, choose **Pivot➔Pivoting Trays** to obtain the **Pivoting Trays** display shown in Figure 15.

Report

Mean

Sex	Type of Task	Inspection Time	Number of Items Recalled
Male	Verbal	Short	4.00
		Medium	5.00
		Long	5.00
	Graphic	Short	2.67
		Medium	3.67
		Long	4.00
Female	Verbal	Short	5.33
		Medium	5.67
		Long	6.33
	Graphic	Short	1.67
		Medium	2.33
		Long	3.33

Output 5. The output from the **Mean** procedure

The icons and titles show their locations in the **Report** table. The icons can be dragged to other locations and their order can be changed within the same location. The best way to see how the pivoting trays work is to click and drag the icons to other grey borders in the display and observe the resulting changes in the **Report** table of means.

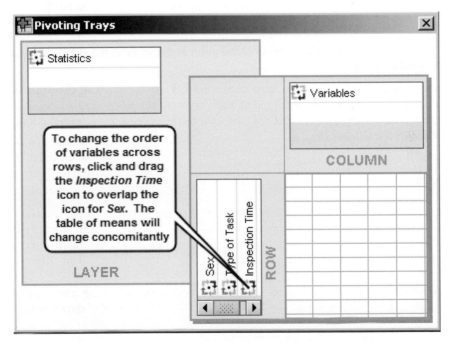

Figure 15. The **Pivoting Trays** dialog box showing what is/are located in layers, rows and columns. The sequence of variables and their locations can be changed by dragging the icons appropriately

From left to right, the three icons in the ROW list represent the variables *Sex*, *Type of Task* and *Inspection Time* respectively, which is the order in which these three dimensions appear in the table. This order can be changed by clicking and dragging an icon to a different position. For example, if we click and drag the present rightmost icon (*Inspection Time*) to the left of the other two icons (Figure 15), that dimension will now appear in the leftmost position in the **Report** table (Output 6).

Report

Mean

Inspection Time	Sex	Type of Task	Number of Items Recalled
Short	Male	Verbal	4.00
		Graphic	2.67
	Female	Verbal	5.33
		Graphic	1.67
Medium	Male	Verbal	5.00
		Graphic	3.67
	Female	Verbal	5.67
		Graphic	2.33
Long	Male	Verbal	5.00
		Graphic	4.00
	Female	Verbal	6.33
		Graphic	3.33

Output 6. The appearance of the table after the order of the icons in the **ROW** list has been changed (compare with Output 5)

In Outputs 5 and 6, the labels of the three factors in the experiment are all in rows. Should we wish to retain the levels of *Sex* and *Type of Task* in rows, but move those of *Inspection Time* into columns, we need only click and drag the icon for *Inspection Time* from the **ROW** list to the **COLUMN** list (Figure 16).

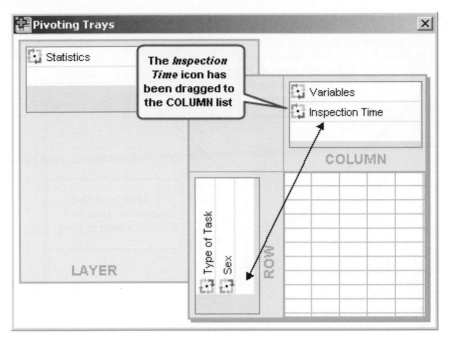

Figure 16. The *Inspection Time* icon has been dragged to the **COLUMN** list

The effect of this manipulation is that, whereas the two types of *Sex* and *Type of Task* will appear in rows as before, the three levels of *Inspection Time* now appear at the heads of three columns (Output 7).

Report

Mean

		Number of Items Recalled		
		Inspection Time		
Sex	Type of Task	Short	Medium	Long
Male	Verbal	4.00	5.00	5.00
	Graphic	2.67	3.67	4.00
Female	Verbal	5.33	5.67	6.33
	Graphic	1.67	2.33	3.33

Output 7. Edited table in which *Inspection Time* has been transposed to columns

The leftmost part of Figure 16 contains the **LAYER** list. A **layer** is a tabulation at one particular level of another factor. In the tables we have looked at so far, all the dimensions have been shown. Suppose, however, that we want to view the two-way table of means for *Type of Task* and *Inspection Time* for each level of *Sex*. Simply click and drag the *Sex* icon from the **ROW** list to the **LAYER** list (Figure 17). The table will now appear as in Output 8.

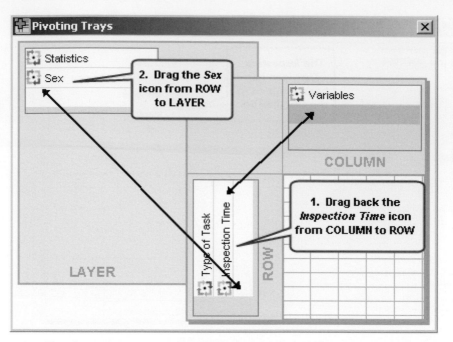

Figure 17. The *Sex* icon has been dragged from ROW to LAYER and *Inspection Time* icon restored from COLUMN to ROW

We can see the means for *Type of Task* and *Inspection Time* only for the Male level of *Sex*. To see the means for Female, simply click on the arrow to the right of Male and select Female.

Report		
Statistics	Mean ▼	
Sex	Male ▼	

Type of Task	Inspection Time	Number of Items Recalled
Verbal	Short	4.00
	Medium	5.00
	Long	5.00
Graphic	Short	2.67
	Medium	3.67
	Long	4.00

Output 8. A layered table, in which the means for *Type of Task* and *Inspection Time* are displayed at only one level of *Sex*. The means for Female can be seen by clicking the arrow to the right of Male and selecting Female

3.2.3   Tutorials in SPSS

The SPSS package now includes some excellent tutorials on various aspects of the system, including the use of the **Viewer** and the manipulation of pivot tables.

To access a tutorial choose **Help➜Tutorial** and double-click to open the tutorial menu. The buttons in the right-hand bottom corner of each page of the tutorial enable the user to see the list of items (magnifier) and to navigate forward and backward through the tutorial (right and left arrows).

3.3   SELECTING FROM AND MANIPULATING DATA FILES

So far, the emphasis has been upon the construction of a complete data set, the saving of that set to a file on disk, and its retrieval from storage. There are occasions, however, on which the user will want to operate selectively on the data. It may be, for instance, that only some of the cases in a data set are of interest (those contributed by the participants in one category alone, perhaps); or the user may wish to exclude participants with outlying values on specified variables. In this section, some of these more specialised manoeuvres will be described.

Transformation and recoding of data will be discussed in Chapter 4.

3.3.1   Selecting cases

Let us assume that, in **Data View**, we have the results of the Drug experiment. In the original data set, there were two variables: *Experimental Condition* and *Score*. Suppose, however, that a *Gender* variable has been added, where *1 = Male* and *2 = Female*, and that we want to examine the data from the female participants only.
- Choose **Data➜Select Cases…** to obtain the **Select Cases** dialog box (see Figure 18).
- Initially, the **All cases** radio button is marked. Click the **Select Cases: If** button and complete the **Select Cases: If** dialog box as shown in Figure 19. Click **Continue** to return to the **Select Cases** dialog box.
- Click **OK** to select only the female participants for analysis.

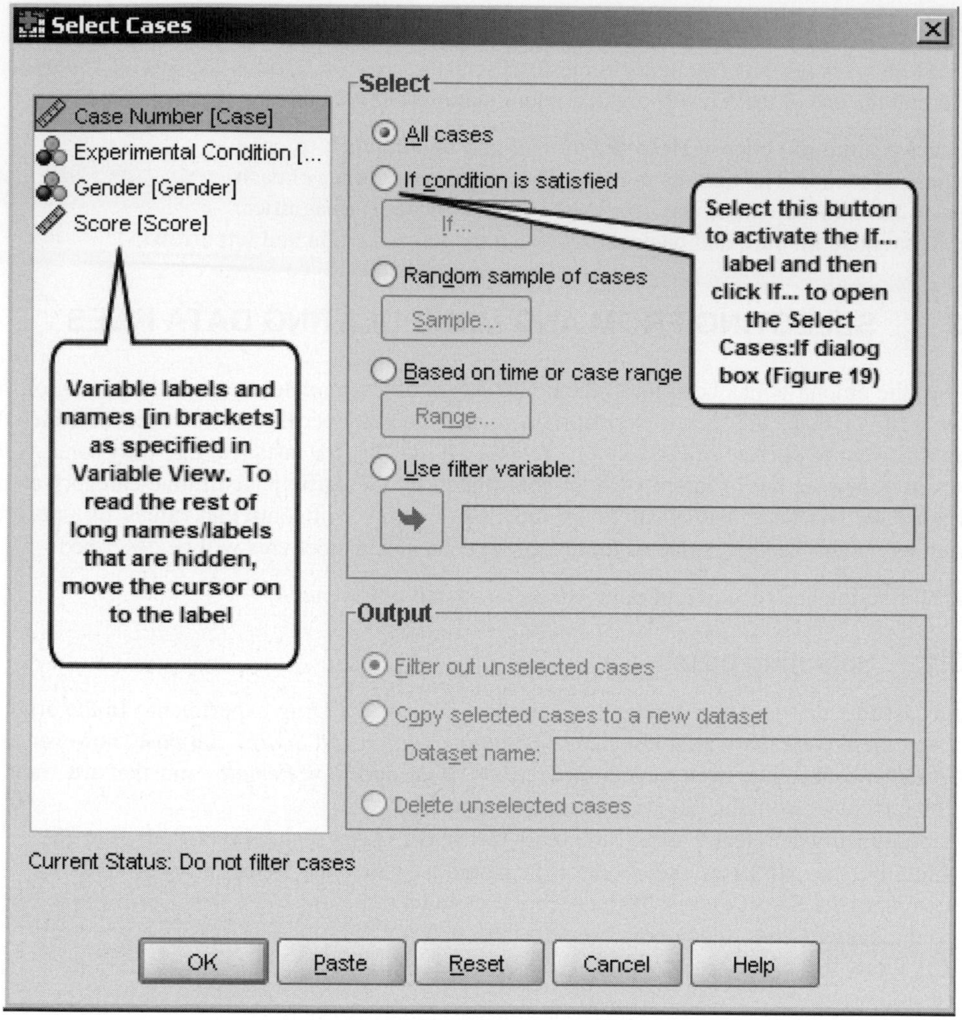

Figure 18. The **Select Cases** dialog box

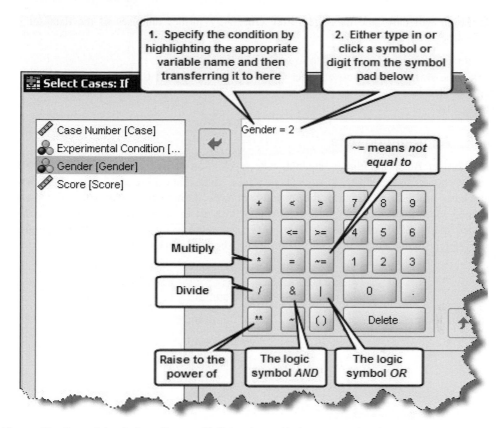

Figure 19. Part of the **Select Cases: If** dialog box with the expression for selecting only Gender 2 (the female participants)

A section of **Data View** is shown in Figure 20. Another column, headed *filter_$*, has now appeared, containing the entries *Not Selected* and *Selected*. Note that, although the name *filter_$* will appear in subsequent dialog boxes, it should not be selected as a variable for analysis because it will only report the number of selected cases.

Case	Case	Group	Gender	Score	filter_$
1	1	Placebo	Male	6	Not Selected
2	2	Placebo	Female	5	Selected
3	3	Placebo	Male	5	Not Selected
4	4	Placebo	Female	1	Selected
5	5	Placebo	Male	2	Not Selected
6	6	Placebo	Female	3	Selected
7	7	Placebo	Male	2	Not Selected

Figure 20. **Data View**, showing that only the scores of the female participants will be included in the analysis. The oblique bars are deselected cases

The row numbers of the unselected cases (the males) have been marked with an oblique bar. This is a useful indicator of **case selection status.** The status bar (if enabled at the foot of

Data View) will carry the message **Filter On**. Any further analyses of the data set will exclude cases where *Gender = 1*.

Case selection can be **cancelled** as follows:
- From the **Data menu**, choose **Select Cases** and (in the **Select Cases** dialog box) click **All cases**.
- Click **OK**.

3.3.2   Aggregating data

In a School of Business Studies, students take a selection of five courses each. (There is a degree of choice, so that different students may take somewhat different selections of courses.) On the basis of their performance, the students are marked on a percentage scale. We shall be concerned with the marks of ten of the students, whose marks on the five courses they took are contained in the SPSS data file *Students marks* and reproduced in www.psypress.com/spss-made-simple. Figure 21 is a section of **Data View**, showing some of their marks.

	Student	Course	Mark
1	Anne	Accountancy	80
2	Rebecca	Accountancy	78
3	Susan	Accountancy	87
4	Anne	Computing	49
5	Fred	Computing	55
6	Rebecca	Computing	65
7	Susan	Computing	56
8	Anne	German	40
9	Fred	German	72
10	Jim	German	73

Figure 21.   Part of the file *Students marks* in **Data View**

*Finding course averages: The **Aggregate** procedure*

Suppose we want to find the mean mark for each of the courses that were taken. SPSS's **Aggregate** procedure groups cases according to the nominal variable specified (e.g. *Course*) and then aggregates the values of the quantitative variable specified (e.g. *Mark*). Various options are available for how the aggregation is done (e.g. mean, median, percentage above a specified value). We shall use the **Aggregate** procedure to group the marks according to course and calculate the mean mark for each course.
- Choose **Data➜Aggregate…** to obtain the **Aggregate Data** dialog box.

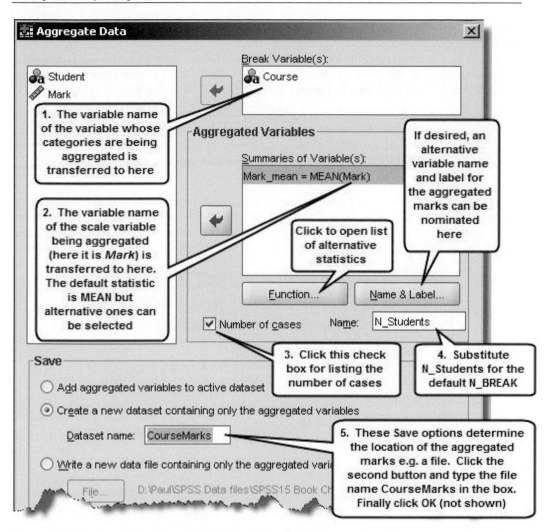

Figure 22. The completed **Aggregate Data** dialog box. The results of the aggregated marks for courses will be saved in the variable *Mark_Mean* within the dataset *CourseMarks* along with the count of cases in the variable *N_Students*

- In the **Aggregate Data** dialog box, the **Break Variable** is the variable on the basis of which the marks are to be grouped (i.e. *Course*).
- The **Aggregated Variable** is the mark that a student received (i.e. *Mark*).
- In case of unintentional actions, it is wiser to create a new dataset or a new file rather than replace the active dataset. A new dataset is created by clicking the radio button **Create a new dataset containing only the aggregated variables** in the **Save** panel of the dialog box. Type in a name for the dataset such as *CourseMarks* – see Figure 22 for the completed dialog box.

Notice that in the **Aggregated Variable(s)** panel is the expression Mark_mean = MEAN(Mark). Unless otherwise instructed, SPSS will calculate the mean mark for each course. You can choose another statistic (such as the Median) by clicking on the **Function...** button and changing the specification. You can also change the variable name and specify a variable label by clicking **Name & Label...** and completing the dialog box.

Since the students had a degree of choice and some courses were more popular than others, the means calculated by the **Aggregate** procedure are based on varying sample sizes. It is therefore wise to request the inclusion of sample sizes by clicking the checkbox **Number of cases** and changing the variable name from *N_Break* to a more meaningful one such as *N_Students*. Finally click **OK**.

To see the results of the aggregation, you need to open the new dataset *CourseMarks* (Figure 23) by clicking *Untitled[CourseMarks]* along the foot of the screen. The dataset shows the mean mark (*Mean*) awarded to the students taking each of the courses that were selected and the size of the sample of marks from which the mean was calculated in the column *N_Students*.

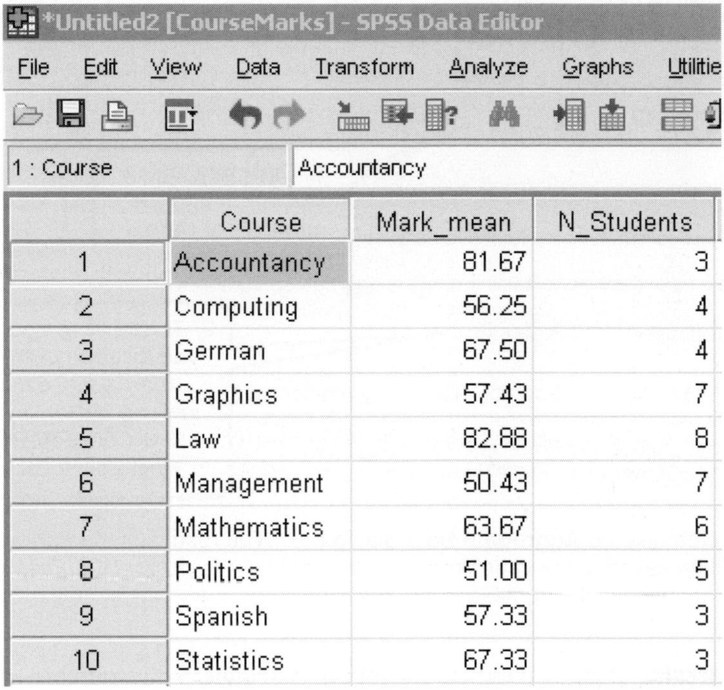

	Course	Mark_mean	N_Students
1	Accountancy	81.67	3
2	Computing	56.25	4
3	German	67.50	4
4	Graphics	57.43	7
5	Law	82.88	8
6	Management	50.43	7
7	Mathematics	63.67	6
8	Politics	51.00	5
9	Spanish	57.33	3
10	Statistics	67.33	3

Figure 23. Mean mark on each of the courses together with the number of students who took each course in the new dataset *CourseMarks*

Note that if the **Add aggregated variables to active dataset** button in Figure 22 had been selected instead of the **Create a new dataset**... button, the mean marks would have appeared in a column alongside the students' actual marks thus allowing a comparison to be made.

3.3.3   Sorting data

Suppose that, in order to appraise the courses, you want to list them in order of the mean marks the students achieved.

- With the data file *CourseMarks* in the **Data Editor**, choose **Data➜Sort Cases...** to obtain the **Sort Cases** dialog box. Figure 24 shows the completed dialog box.

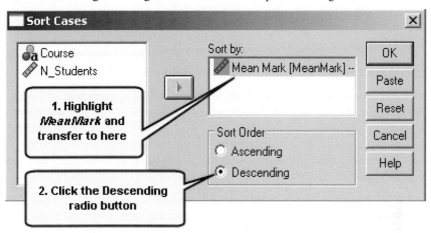

Figure 24. The completed **Sort Cases** dialog box

- Since you will probably want the marks to be arranged with the highest at the top and the lowest at the bottom, we have marked the **Descending** button in **Sort Order**. (Note, however, that in **file merging** – see below – the sort order must be the same as the file to be merged.)
- Click **OK** to see the mean marks listed in descending order of magnitude (Figure 25).

	Course	Mean	N_Students
1	Law	82.88	8
2	Accountancy	81.67	3
3	German	67.50	4
4	Statistics	67.33	3
5	Mathematics	63.67	6
6	Graphics	57.43	7
7	Spanish	57.33	3
8	Computing	56.25	4
9	Politics	51.00	5
10	Management	50.43	7

Figure 25. Results of the sorting procedure. The courses are now listed in descending order of their mean marks

3.3.4   Merging files

SPSS offers a powerful procedure known as **file merging**, which enables the user to import data into a file known as the **working file** from an **external** file. The **File Merge** procedure has two principal uses:

1. You can use it to import extra data (i.e., more cases) on **the same set of variables**.
2. You can use it to import data on **extra variables** that are not already in the working file.

*Using **Merge Files** to import more cases of the same variables from an external file*

In Chapter 2, an experiment was described in which the skilled performance of ten people who had ingested a small quantity of a supposedly performance-enhancing drug was compared with the performance of a placebo group of the same size. The scores of the twenty participants were stored in a file named *Drug Experiment*. Suppose, however, twenty more participants were to be tested under exactly the same conditions (ten under the *Placebo* condition and ten under the *Drug* condition) and the new data stored in a file named *Drug more data*.

The **Merge Files** procedure can be used to import the new data from the file *Drug more data* into the file *Drug Experiment*, so that, instead of having ten scores for each condition we shall have twenty.   The success of this type of file-merging operation requires that **the specifications for the two variables must be exactly the same in both files**. Before attempting the following exercise, check both files in **Variable View** to make sure that the specifications (name, width, type, values) of the variables *Case*, *Group* and *Score* are identical.

Ensure that the file containing the original data *Drug Experiment* is in the **Data Editor**. Then

- Choose **Data➜Merge Files➜Add Cases ...** to obtain the **Add Cases to [dataset name]** dialog box (Figure 26).
- Use **Browse...** to select the file *Drug more data* from wherever it is stored and click **Continue** to obtain the **Add Cases from [dataset name]** dialog box (Figure 27).
- Since both data files contain only the variables *Case*, *Group* and *Score*, the right-hand panel headed **Variables in New Active Dataset** contains *Case*, *Group* and *Score* and no variable names appear in the left-hand panel headed **Unpaired Variables**. Had the external file contained an extra variable (or variables), or a variable specification did not match between the two files, its unmatched name (or names) would have appeared in the left-hand panel.
- Click **OK** to obtain the merged file, a section of which is shown in Figure 28.
- If desired, the cases can be sorted to list all the Drug scores and then all the Placebo scores using **Sort Cases...** in the **Data** menu.

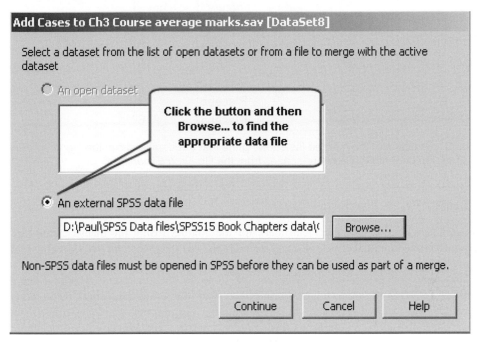

Figure 26. The **Add Cases to...** dialog box

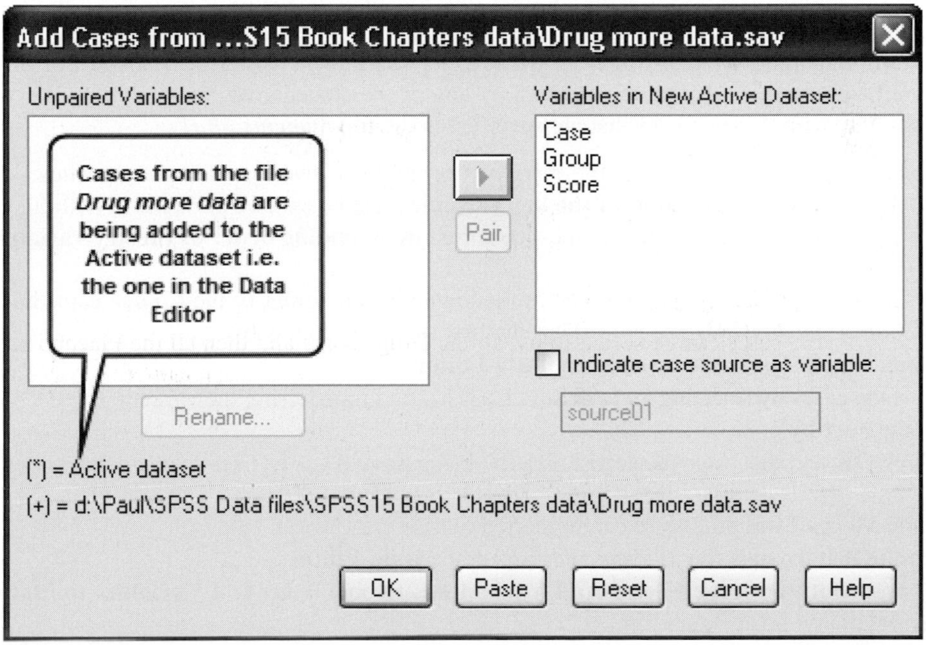

Figure 27. The **Add Cases from ...** dialog box listing the variables existing in both files

	Case	Group	Score
18	18	Drug	7
19	19	Drug	5
20	20	Drug	10
21	1	Placebo	5
22	2	Placebo	3
23	3	Placebo	6

Figure 28. A section of the merged file showing the first three cases from the file *Drug more data* added on beneath the last three cases from the file *Drug Experiment*

Using *Merge Files* to add extra variables

Suppose you wished to add the mean mark for the courses (using the means created by the **Aggregate** procedure in Section 3.4.2 and stored in the file *Course mean marks*) to the table of Students' Marks in the data file *Students marks* so that the students could compare their marks with the mean for their course. This can be done by the procedure **Merge Files Add Variables…**. What we are trying to do, in effect, is to look up in the *Course mean mark* file (Figure 23), the means for all the courses and assign the appropriate mean to each student taking a particular course in the original file *Students marks*. The **Merge Files** procedure uses the common variable (in this case *Course*) as a **key variable**. When matches for cases (in this example *Course*, not students) are found in the external file, the corresponding entries for the target variable *Mean* are imported into the working file.

In the terminology of SPSS, the external file *Course mean marks* is to be used as a **lookup file**, or **keyed table**. We also want **Merge Files** to use the cases of the **key variable** (i.e. *Course*) in the working file, not those in the external file, since there could be (though not in our example) courses there that were not taken by any of the students we are studying. We want matches only with those courses that are specified in the file *Students Marks*.

The success of this second kind of file-merging operation has two essential prerequisites:
1. The **specifications of the key variable** must be exactly the same in both files.
2. The cases in both files must be sorted **in ascending order of the key variable**.

In our example, *Students marks* has been sorted in alphabetic order of the *Course* name but the file of *Course mean marks* has not. Thus the first step is to do this by
- Open the file *Course mean marks* in **Data Editor**.
- Sort the cases by selecting **Data→Sort Cases…** and transferring the variable name *Course* to the **Sort by** box.
- Click **OK** and then save the sorted data file using **Save As…** to *Course mean marks sorted*.

Now the **Merge Files** procedure can be started.
- Ensure that the data file *Students marks* is in the **Data Editor**.
- Choose **Data→Merge Files→Add Variables…** to obtain the **Add Variables to [dataset name]** dialog box (Figure 29).

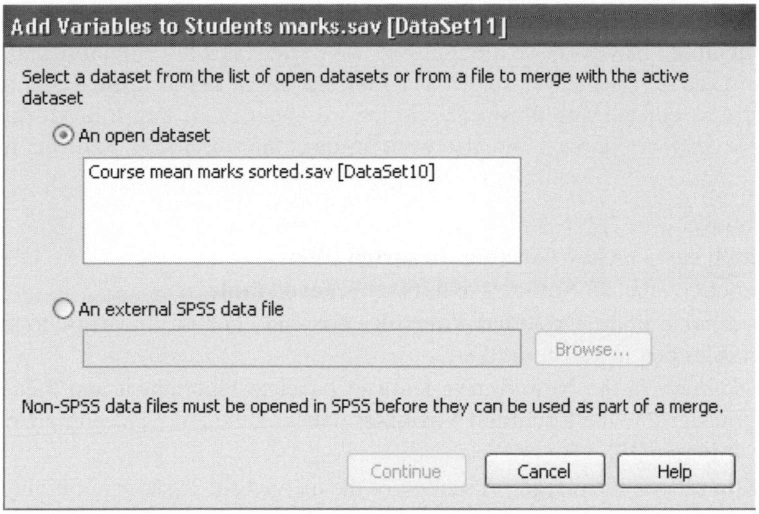

Figure 29. The **Add Variables to** dialog box for selecting the file to which the variables will be added

- Select the required file either from an open dataset (as here) by highlighting it (after which the **Continue** button will become active) or from a saved data file. Click **Continue** to obtain the **Add Variables from [dataset name]** dialog box (Figure 30).

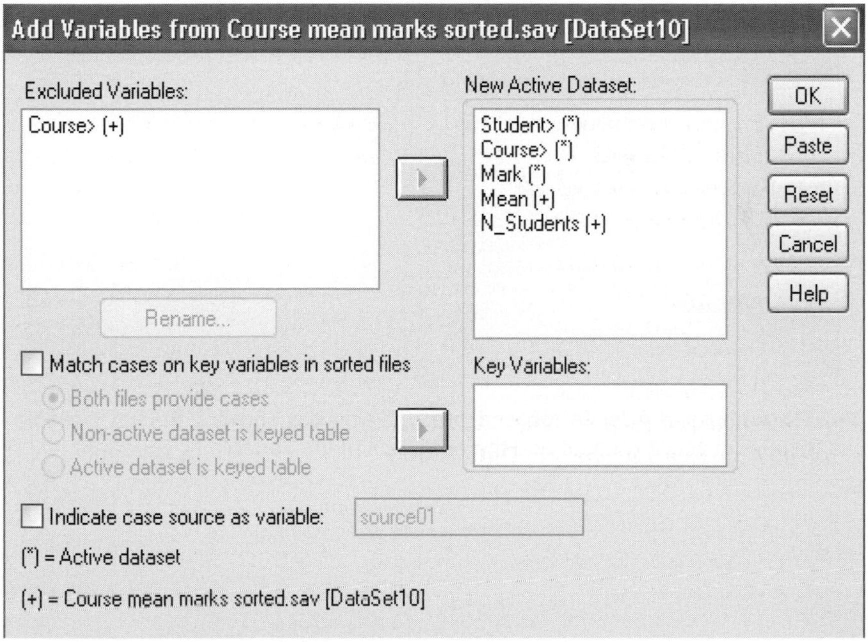

Figure 30. The **Add Variables from** dialog box showing the file from which the variables are coming and the common variables in the merged file

Notice that, for the moment, the common variable *Course* appears in the left-hand panel as an **Excluded Variable**. However, we are going to use *Course* as a **key variable** and use the non-active dataset *Course mean marks sorted* as a **look up file** or **keyed table** to import the means for each course associated with those cases of the variable *Course* that **File Merge** finds in the active data file *Students marks*. We also want to reject the variable *N_Students* from the final data file.

Proceed as follows.

- Click **Match cases on key variables in sorted files**.
- Mark the button labelled **Non-active dataset is keyed table**.
- Highlight *Course* in the **Excluded Variables** box and click on the arrow to the left of the **Key Variables** box to transfer it there.
- Click *N_Students* in the **New Active Dataset** panel to highlight it and then click on the arrow to transfer it to the **Excluded Variables** panel on the left. The completed dialog box is shown in Figure 31.
- Click **OK** to run the file merge. A section of the merged file is shown in Figure 32.

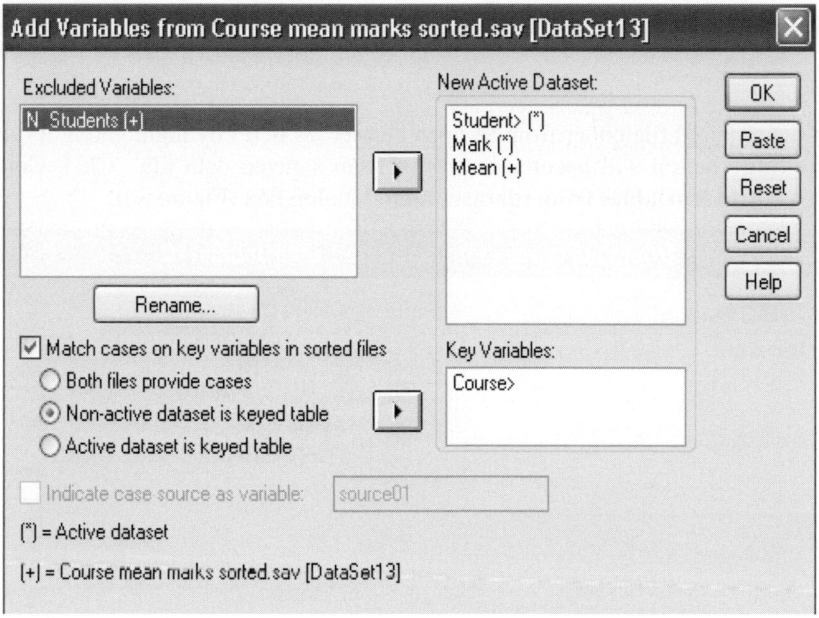

Figure 31. The completed **Add Variables from ...** dialog box showing the key variable as Course as in the non-active dataset and the exclusion of the variable N_Students

	Student	Course	Mark	Mean
1	Anne	Accountancy	80	81.67
2	Rebecca	Accountancy	78	81.67
3	Susan	Accountancy	87	81.67
4	Anne	Computing	49	56.25
5	Fred	Computing	55	56.25
6	Rebecca	Computing	65	56.25
7	Susan	Computing	56	56.25
8	Anne	German	40	67.50
9	Fred	German	72	67.50
10	Jim	German	73	67.50

Figure 32. Part of the merged file, in which the means of the courses have been 'looked up' in the non-active dataset *Course mean marks* sorted and added to the dataset *Students marks*

3.3.5   Transposing the rows and columns of a data set

In an experiment on time estimation, a researcher asks nine participants to make five verbal estimates of each of seven time intervals ranging from 10 to 40 seconds in duration. Each participant, therefore, makes a total of thirty-five judgements.

In the data set shown in Figure 33, the cases represent particular time intervals. For some purposes, such as averaging judgements across participants, we might wish to transform this data set to one in which each row represents a participant and each column represents a time interval.

	Interval	Amy	Fred	Joe	Stephen
1	10	8	120	7	8
2	10	6	10	9	7
3	10	5	20	6	10
4	10	7	5	8	9
5	10	5	10	6	11
6	15	15	25	10	13
7	15	6	8	9	12
8	15	14	12	10	12
9	15	7	8	12	12
10	15	14	10	12	15
11	20	20	60	15	18
12	20	10	18	14	15

Figure 33. A section of **Data View**, showing verbal estimates of the time intervals specified by the first variable, *Interval*

• Choose **Data➔Transpose…** to view the **Transpose** dialog box (Figure 34).

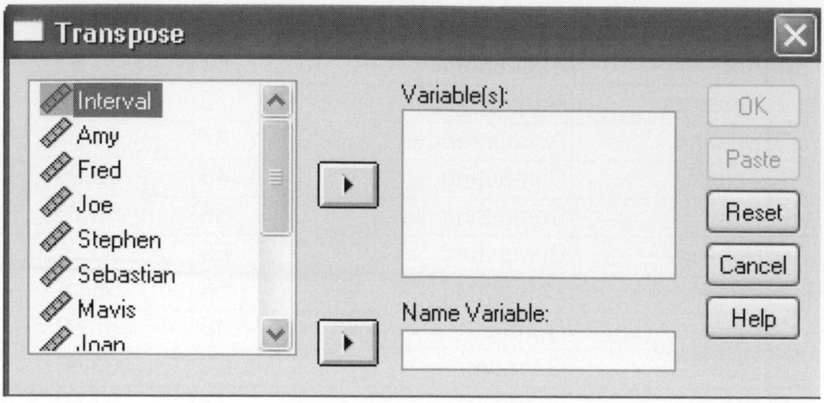

Figure 34. The **Transpose** dialog box

- Select all the variables and transfer them to the **Variable(s)** box on the right by clicking the central black arrow.
- Click **OK** to view the transposed matrix (Figure 35).

It can be seen from Figure 35 that SPSS has created a new variable *CASE_LBL* containing not only the names of the participants but also the *Interval* variable. The row containing the Interval variable should now be deleted and the default names *var001, var002, …*   replaced (in **Variable View**) with names such as *Ten1, Ten2, …, Fifteen1, Fifteen2, …*   remembering that SPSS will not allow duplication of variable names. In addition, the first variable CASE_ LBL should be renamed *Name*. Part of the final transformed data set is shown in Figure 36.

1 : CASE_LBL			Interval		
	CASE_LBL	var001	var002	var003	var004
1	Interval	10	10	10	10
2	Amy	8	6	5	7
3	Fred	120	10	20	5
4	Joe	7	9	6	8
5	Stephen	8	7	10	9
6	Sebastian	6	5	7	6

Figure 35. The transposed data set, in which the data from the participants are now contained in rows

	Name	Ten1	Ten2	Ten3	Ten4	Ten5	Fifteen1	Fifteen2
1	Amy	8	6	5	7	5	15	6
2	Fred	120	10	20	5	10	25	8
3	Joe	7	9	6	8	6	10	9
4	Stephen	8	7	10	9	11	13	12
5	Sebastian	6	5	7	6	5	9	9
6	Mavis	10	8	10	8	10	15	10

Figure 36. Part of the transformed data set in which the columns and rows of the original data set have been transposed

3.4   IMPORTING AND EXPORTING DATA

It is possible to import data into SPSS from other applications or platforms such as Microsoft EXCEL and SPSS for Macintosh. SPSS can also read ASCII tab-delimited or comma-delimited files, with values separated by tabulation symbols or fixed format files with variables recorded in the same column locations for each case. It is also possible to export SPSS data and output into other applications such as word processors and spreadsheets.

3.4.1   Importing data from other applications

Importing EXCEL files

When importing files from EXCEL, the following points should be observed:
1.   If the first row of the EXCEL file does not contain variable/column names or data, then the material may not be read into SPSS properly. Either delete blank rows or amend the **Range** in SPSS's **Opening Excel Data Source** dialog box after selecting the EXCEL file to be read.
2.   Dates must be formatted as *DD-MMM-YYYY in EXCEL.
3.   It may be necessary to have a number of attempts to ensure a satisfactory import. For example, some file types may need changing (e.g. from **String** to **Numeric**) within **Variable View**.

To import the EXCEL file named *test1.xls*, which is stored in the authors' folder *SPSS 16 Book Chapters data*:
*   Choose **File➔Open➔ Data…** to obtain the **Open File** dialog box (Figure 37).
*   Click the directory of file types in the **Files of type:** box and highlight **Excel (*.xls)**.
*   Select the appropriate **Look in** folder.
*   A list of Excel files will then appear in the white panel above. Click the appropriate file and its name will appear in the **File name:** box.

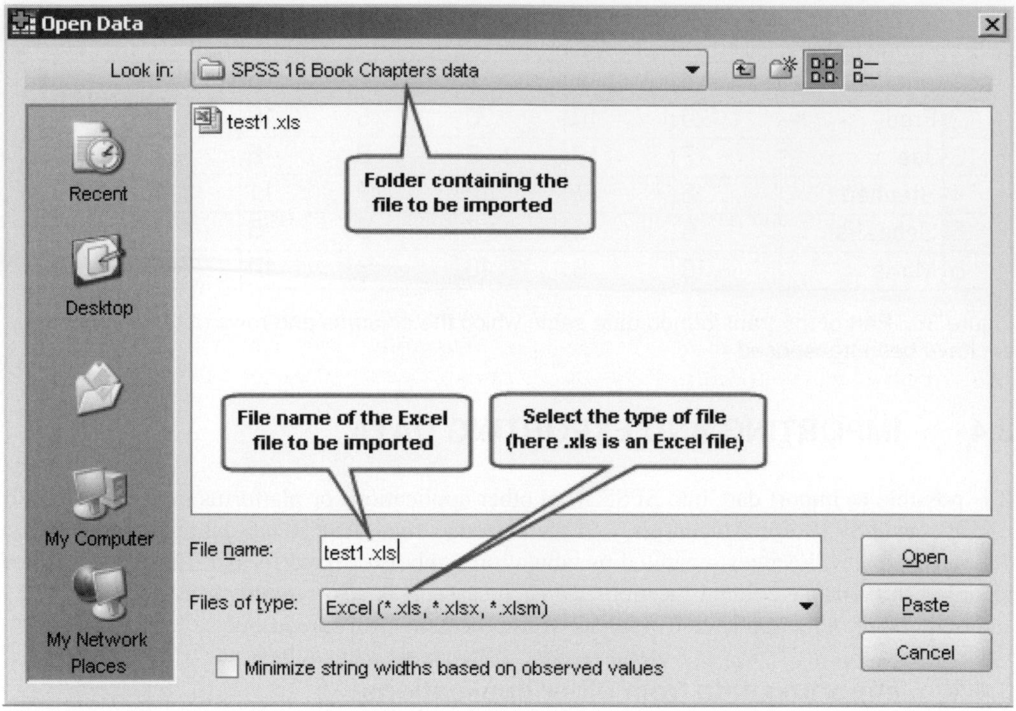

Figure 37. The **Open File** dialog box with Excel [*.xls] selected as the type of file and the file test1 selected from the folder SPSS 16 Book Chapters data

- Click **Open** to open the **Opening File Options** dialog box (Figure 38). Activate the **Read variable names** check box to transfer the EXCEL variable names into the SPSS **Data Editor**.

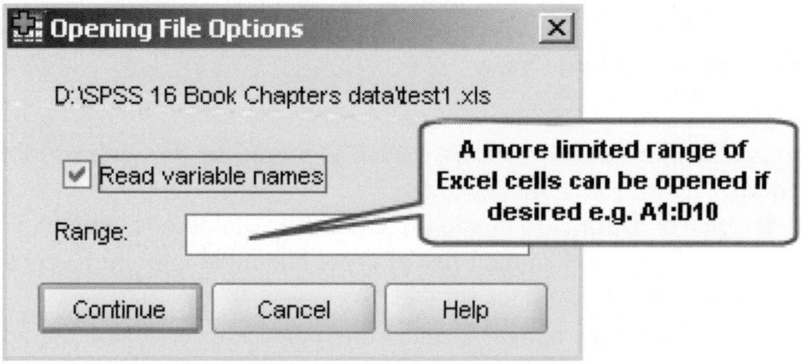

Figure 38. The **Opening File Options** dialog box with **Read variable names** selected

- If the EXCEL file has more than one worksheet, the **Opening File Options** dialog box will contain an extra panel labelled **Worksheet**

  Worksheet: [Sheet1 [A1:N7893]] ⌄ . Different worksheets can then be selected by clicking the directory arrow.
- If an error message appears stating that SPSS cannot load an EXCEL worksheet, it may be necessary to return to EXCEL and re-save the file in the format of a different version of EXCEL, to copy and paste columns of data directly into SPSS **Data View**, or to re-format the cells.
- Click **OK** to transfer the file into SPSS. **Variable View** will list the variable names and their types, and **Data View** will show the transferred data and variable names (Figure 39). It may be necessary to change variable types in **Variable View**. The **SPSS Viewer** will list the names, types and formats of the variables. Note that SPSS Viewer may initially obscure the data file beneath.
- The file can then be saved as an SPSS data file.

	A	B	C	D
1	**Name**	**Sex**	**Age**	**Score**
2	Brown, G	m	25	87
3	Green, F	m	18	78
4	Mason, P	f	23	100
5	Sampson, G	m	24	67
6	Winston, P	f	20	50

	Name	Sex	Age	Score
1	Brown, G	m	25	87
2	Green, F	m	18	78
3	Mason, P	f	23	100
4	Sampson, G	m	24	67
5	Winston, P	f	20	50

Figure 39. Transfer of an EXCEL file (left) to SPSS (right)

It is also possible to copy columns of data from an EXCEL file by highlighting the data (but not the column headings), selecting **Copy** from EXCEL's **Edit** menu and then within SPSS, selecting **Paste** from SPSS's **Edit** menu and pasting the data into **Data View**. (Again, do not include the cell at the head of the SPSS column in the selection.) The variables can then be named in the usual manner within **Variable View**. Should the EXCEL columns contain strings (e.g. names), make sure that, in **Variable View**, you change the **Type** of variable to **String** before pasting. Other types of file can be transferred in a similar manner.

Exporting data from SPSS to EXCEL

The **Save As** procedure allows you to save an SPSS file (or a selection of data) as an EXCEL file. The procedure is entirely straightforward.

SPSS data can also be prepared for export to another application or platform by saving it to a wide range of formats, including **SPSS portable (*.por)**. Full details of importing and exporting files are available in SPSS's **Help** facility.

3.4.2   Copying output

SPSS 16 offers a facility for exporting output. To copy output, proceed as follows:
- Ensure that the item of output in SPSS **Viewer** has a box around it by clicking the cursor anywhere within the table or graphic. If you wish to copy more than one table, then ensure that all the desired tables are boxed by holding down the **Ctrl** key whilst clicking on each table in turn.

- Choose **File➡Export...** (Figure 40) to obtain the **Export Output** dialog box (Figure 41).

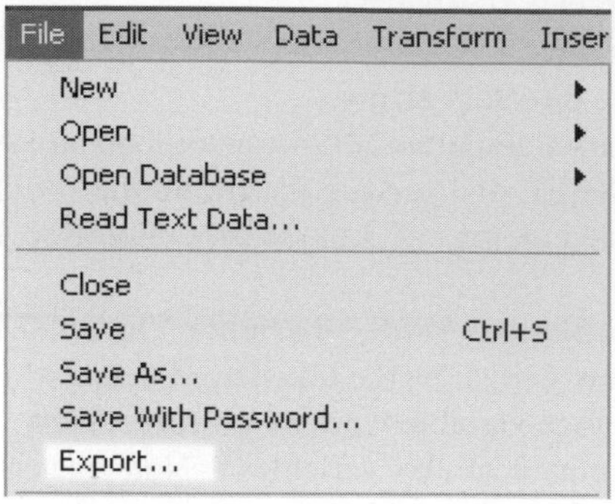

Figure 40. The location of the **Export...** item

- Complete the **Export Output** dialog box (Figure 41) by naming the file to where the output is going and its format (e.g. *.doc for a Word file; *.xls for an Excel file; *.ppt for a Powerpoint file; *.htm for a HTML file). Either type in the file name or use the **Browse...** to locate the appropriate folder (a **Save As** dialog box will appear from which the folder can be selected: insert a file name in the **File Name** panel and click **Save** to return to the **Export Output** dialog box).

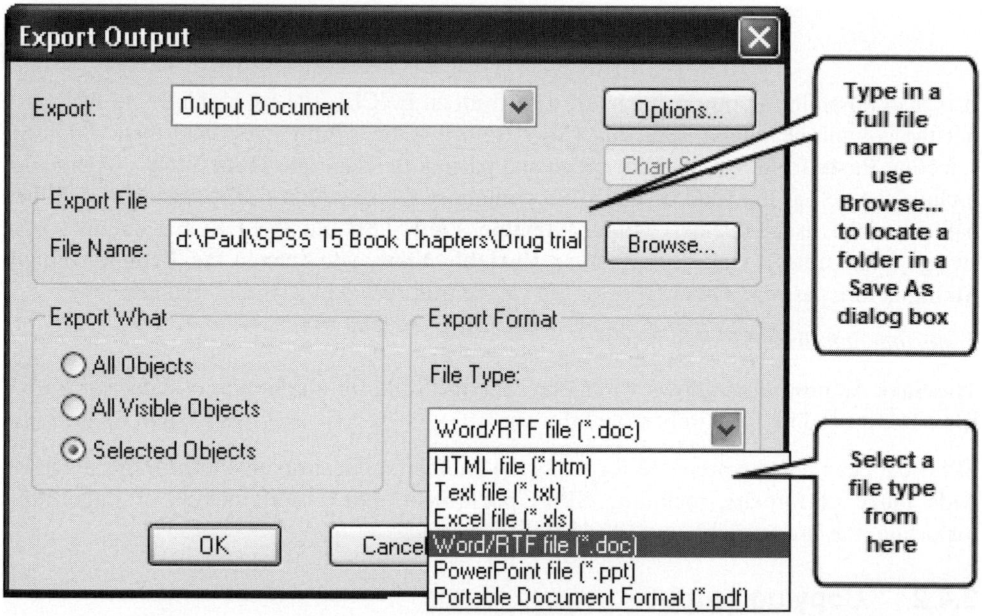

Figure 41. The **Export Output** dialog box for naming the output file and selecting its format

Alternatively, to **copy a table**, proceed as follows:
- Ensure that the table of output in SPSS **Viewer** has a box around it by clicking the cursor anywhere within the table or graphic. If you wish to copy more than one table, then ensure that all the desired tables are boxed by holding down the **Ctrl** key whilst clicking on each table in turn.
- Click **Copy** in the **Edit** menu.
- Switch to the word processor and ensure that the cursor is located at the intended insertion point.
- Select **Paste Special...** in the word processor's **Edit** menu and then **Formatted Text (RTF)** if it is desired to edit or format the table within the word processor.
- Alternatively, select **Paste Special...** in the word processor's **Edit** menu and then **Picture.** The picture can be repositioned and resized within the word processor but it cannot be edited. However the quality of the image is higher than it is when **Paste** is used.

To **copy a graphic**, proceed as follows:
- Ensure that the graphic in the SPSS **Viewer** has a box around it by clicking the cursor anywhere within it. If you wish to copy more than one graphic, ensure that all the desired graphics are boxed by holding down the **Ctrl** key whilst clicking on each chart or graph in turn.
- Click **Copy** in the **Edit** menu.
- Switch to the word processor and ensure that the cursor is located at the insertion point.
- Click **Paste Special...** and select **Bitmap**. The item can then be centred, enlarged or reduced by clicking it so that it acquires a box around it with the usual Windows tabs. To centre the box, click and drag it to the desired position. To enlarge or reduce the size of the graphic, drag one of the tabs in the appropriate direction.

3.5   PRINTING FROM SPSS

It is possible to make extensive use of SPSS without ever printing out either the contents of the **Viewer** or the data in the **Data Editor**. Both data and output can easily be backed up electronically by saving to disk; and important SPSS output is easily exported to the document you actually want to print out. Moreover, SPSS output can be extremely extensive and indiscriminate printing can be very wasteful. In the worst scenario, an inept printing operation could result in dozens of sheets of paper, with a single line of print on each. There are, nevertheless, occasions on which it is both useful and necessary to print out selected items in the **Viewer** window or even a hard copy of the raw data. In this section, we offer some suggestions to help you control and improve printed output from SPSS.

There are differences between printing output from the **SPSS Viewer** and printing data from the **Data Editor**. In either case, however, problems can arise if there has been insufficient editorial control.

3.5.1   Printing output from the Viewer

We shall illustrate some aspects of printing from the **Viewer** with the data from the drug experiment. Suppose that, having entered the data into the **Data Editor**, we run the **Means** procedure, with requests for several optional extras such as medians, range statistics, measures of effect size and one-way ANOVAs to increase the extent of the output.

We strongly recommend that, before you print any output, you should make full use of the **Viewer**'s editing facilities to **remove all irrelevant material**. When using SPSS, one invariably requests output which, at the end of the day, proves to be superfluous. Moreover, as we have seen, radical changes in tables and other output can be made (and great economies in space) by using the **Viewer**'s powerful editing facilities. Since some of the output tables can be very wide, unnecessary columns can be removed. Some pivoting may help not only to make a table more readable but also more manageable for a printing operation.

For some kinds of material, it is better to use **landscape** orientation for the sheet, that is, have the shorter side vertical, rather than the more usual **portrait** orientation. It is easy to make such a specification while working in the **Viewer** before printing anything out. To clarify a batch of printed output, we also recommend that you add explanatory captions, such as *Output for the Drug Experiment*. Otherwise, it is only too easy to accumulate pages of SPSS output, the purpose of which becomes increasingly unclear as time passes. All these things can easily be done while you are working in the **Viewer**. Often, however, even after you have edited and severely pruned the **Viewer**'s contents, you will only be interested in printing out a **selection** of the items.

Using *Print Preview*

- To ascertain the content of each page of the output that will be printed before any selection of items has been made, choose **File➜Print Preview...** to view the content of the first page in the **Viewer (all visible output) box** (Figure 42).
- The contents of the other pages can be viewed by pressing the **PgDn** key as often as you need. Alternatively, you can click on the **Next Page** button in the row of buttons at the top of the dialog box. You will see that, when no item has been selected, the output extends to several pages.

Selecting items for printing

To select two or more items, click the first and, pressing the **Ctrl** key and keeping it held down, click the other items that you wish to select. (You will also need to hold down the **Ctrl** key if you are clicking icons in the left pane to achieve a multiple selection.) The items need not be adjacent. If you now choose **Print Preview**, you will see that it shows only the items you have selected, and it is only those items that will actually be printed.

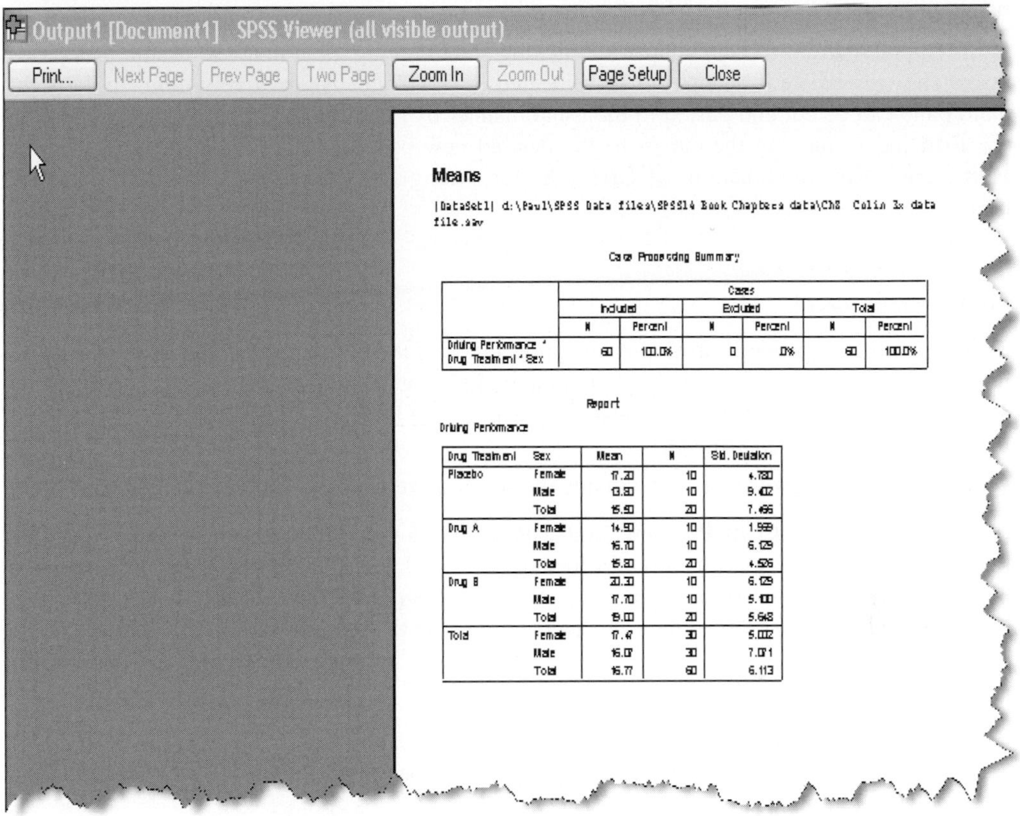

Figure 42. Part of the **Viewer (all visible output)** dialog box for viewing page content when printing from the SPSS **Viewer**

There are two ways of selecting items: you can click the item's icon in the left pane of the **Viewer**; or you can click the item itself in the right pane. Either way, a rectangle with a single continuous border will appear around the item or items concerned. It is, perhaps, easier to click on the items in the right pane directly to make it immediately clear what has been selected.

Try selecting any item in the **Viewer** and choose **Print Preview**, to see the **SPSS Viewer (selected output)** window, which will display only the item you have selected. If you return to the **Print** dialog box, you will see that the **Selection** radio button in the **Print range** panel has now been activated. Were you to click **OK** at this point, only the selected item would be printed.

Deleting items from the **Viewer**

Items are removed from the **Viewer** by selecting them and pressing the **Delete** button. After a multiple selection, pressing the **Delete** button will remove all the selected items.

*Re-arranging the items in the **Viewer***

Items can be rearranged very simply by clicking and dragging them in the left-hand pane, a red arrow showing where the item will be relocated as you drag. Alternatively items in the right-hand pane can be cut and pasted in the usual manner by selecting the item, choosing **Cut** from the **Edit** menu, moving the cursor to the desired new position and choosing **Paste** from the **Edit** menu. Key combinations of **Ctrl + X** for cutting and **Ctrl + V** for pasting can also be used.

Inserting page breaks

You can also exert some control over the appearance of the output in the **Viewer** by creating a **page break** between items that clearly belong to different categories.
- Click the item above which you want to create a page break.
- Choose **Insert➡Page Break**.
- Return to the **Viewer** and click outside the selection rectangle to cancel the selection.

If you now return to **Print Preview**, you will see that a page break has been created and the item you selected is now at the top of a fresh page. Used in conjunction with re-ordering, page breaks can help you to sort the items in the **Viewer**. Bear in mind, however, that creating page breaks always increases the number of sheets of paper in the printed output.

*Changing from portrait to landscape using **Page Setup***

- Click either the **Page Setup** button at the top of the **Print Preview** dialog box or **Page Setup** in the **File** menu to enter the **Page Setup** dialog box (Figure 43).
- In the **Orientation** panel, is the radio button for changing from **Portrait** to **Landscape** orientation. Sometimes, for printing purposes, the landscape orientation can accommodate particularly wide tables that will not fit in portrait orientation.
- Click **OK** to return to the **Viewer**.

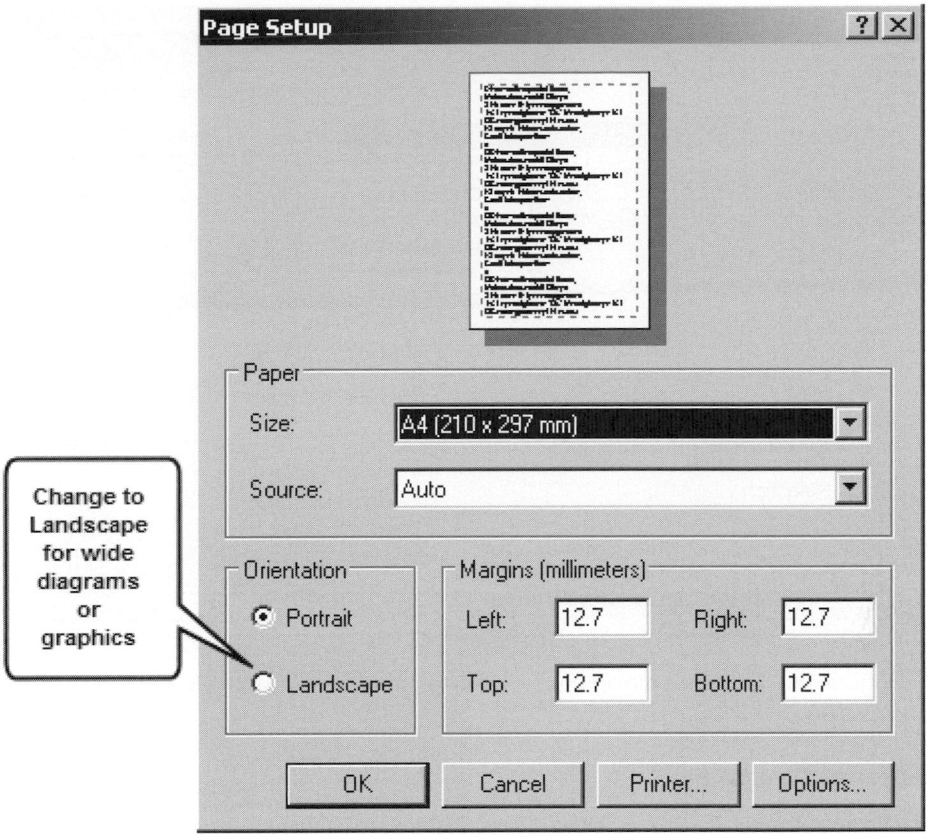

Change to
Landscape
for wide
diagrams
or
graphics

Figure 43. The **Page Setup** dialog box

The Viewer's **Print** *dialog box*
- Access the Viewer's **Print** dialog box (Figure 44) by choosing **File➜Print…**.

Note the **Print Range** section in the lower left area of the box. By default, the radio button labelled **All** is active, which means that pressing **OK** will result in the **entire contents** of the **Viewer** being printed out indiscriminately. The default setting of copies is *1*, but obviously an increase in that value to *2* will double the volume of the printed output.

This **Print** dialog box differs from the dialog you will receive when you print from the **Data Editor**, in which you would be offered the choice of printing either the entire output or the pages within a specified range. It is also possible to print out only the current page. However, no page range is offered in the dialog shown in Figure 44. When you are printing from the **SPSS Viewer**, the radio button marked **Selection** will only become active when a selection from the items in the **Viewer** has been made.

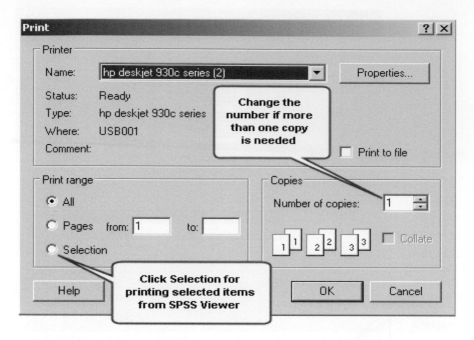

Figure 44.   The **Print** dialog box for printing output from the **SPSS Viewer**

*Printing from the **Data Editor***

It is possible to print out data from **Data View**. There are, however, several problems with this approach. Most notably, if there are too many variables to fit on to one page of printed output and hundreds of cases, it can be difficult to keep track of the output. It sometimes helps to add dummy columns, each cell of which contains a single numerical value, but this can be quite tedious.

To print only selected parts of the data set, use the click-and-drag method to define the target sections by highlighting them to display the material in reverse video. This requires a little practice; but it will be found that when the screen pointer touches the lower border of the window, the latter will scroll down to extend the blackened area to the desired extent. If the pointer touches the right border, the window will scroll to the right across the **Data Editor**. When the **Print** dialog box (Figure 44) appears, the marker will now be on **Selection** (the lowest radio button). Click **OK** to obtain a hard copy of the selected areas.

*Transferring data to the **Viewer** for printing*

An alternative way of obtaining a hard copy of the raw data is to print the data from the **Viewer**.

*   Choose **Analyze➔Reports➔Case Summaries...** to obtain the **Summarize Cases** dialog box (Figure 45).

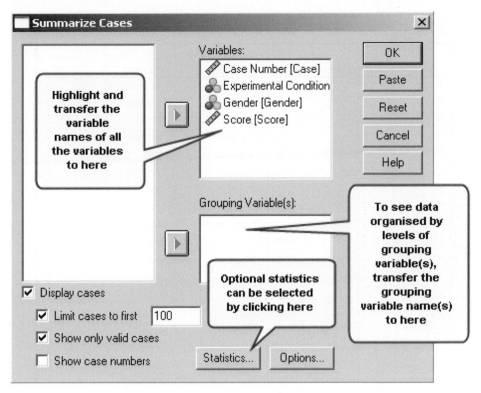

Figure 45. The **Summarize Cases** dialog box

- To see the data arranged as in **Data View**, transfer all the variable names into the **Variables** box. Alternatively, the data can be reorganised by levels of the grouping variables by transferring the grouping variable names to the **Grouping Variable(s)** box. To see all the data, click off the **Limit case to first** check box.
- The **Case Summary** table is shown in Output 9.

Case Summaries

	Case Number	Experimental Condition	Gender	Score
1	1	Placebo	Male	6
2	2	Placebo	Female	5
3	3	Placebo	Male	5
4	4	Placebo	Female	1
5	5	Placebo	Male	2
6	6	Placebo	Female	3
7	7	Placebo	Male	2
8	8	Placebo	Female	4
9	9	Placebo	Male	5
10	10	Placebo	Female	1
11	11	Drug	Male	8
12	12	Drug	Female	6
13	13	Drug	Male	6
14	14	Drug	Female	7
15	15	Drug	Male	6
16	16	Drug	Female	8
17	17	Drug	Male	6
18	18	Drug	Female	7
19	19	Drug	Male	5
20	20	Drug	Female	10
Total N	20	20	20	20

Output 9. The **Case Summaries** of the data from the drug experiment

Exercises

Exercise 3 *Merging files – adding cases & variables* is available in www.psypress.com/spss-made-simple and click on Exercises.

CHAPTER 4

Exploring your data

4.1   INTRODUCTION

In recent years, statisticians have devised a set of statistical methods specially designed for the purpose of examining a data set. Together, they are known as **Exploratory Data Analysis (EDA)**. (For a readable account of EDA, see Howell, 2007, Chapter 2). EDA has now found its way into all good statistical computing packages, including SPSS.

Suppose we have a set of measurements, say the heights in centimetres of a group of children. There are usually three things we want to know about such a data set:

1. The general **level**, or **average value**, of their heights.
2. The **dispersion** of height, i.e. the degree to which the individual scores tend to **vary** around or **deviate** from the average, as opposed to clustering closely around it.
3. The **distribution shape**, i.e. the relative frequencies with which heights are to be found in various regions of the total range of the variable.

We assume that the reader is familiar with the most common measures of level (the **mean**, the **median** and the **mode**) and of dispersion (the **standard deviation** and **quantile range** statistics). We also assume familiarity with terms relating to the distribution of the data set, such as **skewness**, **bimodality** and so on.

Different statistics are appropriate for data of different types: there is little point in finding the mean of a set of ranks, for example, because the resulting average would depend solely upon the number of people (or objects) in the sample. Should the reader be a little rusty on such matters, we strongly recommend reading the relevant chapters of a good textbook on the topic. However before embarking on EDA, it is vital to check the integrity of the data in case there have been date entry errors (e.g. typing 100 instead of 10).

The influence of outliers and asymmetry of distribution

Statistics such as the mean and standard deviation are intended to express, in a single number, some characteristic of the data set as a whole: the former is intended to express the **average**, that is, the general level, typical value, or **central tendency**, of a set of scores; the latter is a measure of their **spread**, or **dispersion**. There are circumstances, however, in which the mean and standard deviation are poor measures of central tendency and dispersion. This can occur when the distribution is markedly skewed, or when extreme cases known as **outliers** exert undue **leverage** upon the values of these statistics.

4.2   SOME USEFUL MENUS

The most important procedures for exploring data are to be found in the **Analyze** and **Graphs** menus. A powerful and complex system such as SPSS can often offer many different approaches to a problem in data analysis. Similar graphics, for instance, can be produced by procedures on either the **Analyze** or the **Graphs** menus. Descriptive statistics are available on several different procedures.

In the **Analyze** menu are **Reports**, **Descriptive Statistics**, **Tables** and **Compare Means**. When the **Reports** or **Descriptive Statistics** are highlighted, the submenus shown in Figure 1 appear.

Reports	Descriptive Statistics
OLAP Cubes...	123 Frequencies...
1,2..n Case Summaries...	Descriptives...
Report Summaries in Rows...	Explore...
Report Summaries in Columns...	Crosstabs...
	1/2 Ratio...

Figure 1. The submenus of **Reports** and **Descriptive Statistics**

The **Reports** submenu (left side of Figure 1) provides facilities for calculating various descriptive statistics of selected quantitative variables subdivided by categories of specified grouping variables. The **OLAP Cubes** (Online Analytical Processing) procedure initially outputs the selected statistics for selected quantitative variables summed across *all* categories of the grouping variables. The initial **OLAP Cubes** table in the output, however, is a pivot table, double-clicking on which brings the **Pivot** menu to view. You can then specify particular categories and combinations of categories by clicking tabs at the top of the table in the usual way (see Chapter 3). The desired combination will then appear as a layer of a multi-way table. As with all pivot tables, the appearance of **OLAP Cubes** can be improved by using the **Viewer**'s editing facilities.

In Chapter 3, we saw that **Case Summaries** provide very useful summaries of data sets, including the raw data themselves. This is ideal for printed records.

The output for **Row Summaries in Rows** or **Report Summaries in Columns** is not tabulated in boxes, is printed in less clear font and is rather difficult to read.

The **Descriptive Statistics** submenu (right side of Figure 1) includes **Frequencies**, **Descriptives**, **Explore**, **Crosstabs** and **Ratio**. All are highly recommended and will be described and illustrated in later sections of this Chapter.

The **Tables** submenu (left side of Figure 2) enables the user to display output in attractive tables, which can be pasted directly into reports of experiments or surveys. The **Multiple Response Sets…** is used to define **Multiple Response Sets** discussed in Chapter 13.

Tables	**Compare Means**	**Transform**
Custom Tables...	M Means...	Compute Variable...
Multiple Response Sets...	t One-Sample T Test...	x? Count Values within Cases...
	t Independent-Samples T Test...	x←x Recode into Same Variables...
	t Paired-Samples T Test...	x←y Recode into Different Variables...
	F One-Way ANOVA...	x←y Automatic Recode...
		Visual Binning...
		Optimal Binning...
		Rank Cases...

Figure 2.   The submenus of **Tables**, **Compare Means** and **Transform**

The **Compare Means** submenu (middle of Figure 2) contains just one item of relevance to exploring data, namely **Means**. This title is misleading because the procedure can only be used for listing the means of variables subdivided by categories of grouping variables: there must be at least one grouping variable present in your data set for the procedure to work. To obtain the means of ungrouped scores, you must turn to **Reports**, **Tables**, or to **Descriptives**, which is found in the **Descriptive Statistics** menu.

Finally, in the **Transform** menu (right of Figure 2) there are several useful procedures, some of which will be described and illustrated at the end of this Chapter.

The **Graphs** menu (not reproduced here) will form the material in Chapter 5, although we shall meet some graphics in this Chapter, since they are options in several of the other exploratory procedures.

4.3   DESCRIBING DATA

To illustrate the data-descriptive procedures, we shall make use of a medical-actuarial data set comprising *Case*, two quantitative variables, *Weight* and *Height*, and two qualitative variables,

Gender and *Blood Group*. Table 1 shows the data set already entered in **Data View** (*Case* has been omitted from the Table for clarity).

4.3.1   Describing nominal and ordinal data

Suppose we want to know the frequencies of cases in the categories in the two grouping variables *Gender* and *Blood Group*. We might also want a graphical display of these frequencies, such as a **bar chart** or **pie chart**. For measurements such as heights or weights, a **histogram** is a useful graph. There are several ways of obtaining such displays.

Table 1. The Blood Group, Sex, Height and Weight data in **Data View**

	Bloodtype	Sex	Height	Weight		Bloodtype	Sex	Height	Weight
1	Group O	Male	178	75	17	Group O	Female	163	60
2	Group O	Male	196	100	18	Group O	Female	142	51
3	Group A	Male	145	60	19	Group A	Female	150	55
4	Group O	Male	170	71	20	Group O	Female	165	64
5	Group B	Male	180	80	21	Group A	Female	160	53
6	Group O	Male	175	69	22	Group O	Female	175	50
7	Group AB	Male	185	78	23	Group O	Female	182	72
8	Group A	Male	190	90	24	Group B	Female	169	65
9	Group O	Male	183	70	25	Group O	Female	162	62
10	Group B	Male	182	85	26	Group B	Female	182	80
11	Group A	Male	170	72	27	Group O	Female	165	67
12	Group O	Male	160	77	28	Group A	Female	171	50
13	Group O	Male	170	95	29	Group O	Female	146	55
14	Group AB	Male	172	68	30	Group AB	Female	151	48
15	Group B	Male	190	120	31	Group O	Female	164	59
16	Group O	Male	180	75	32	Group B	Female	176	71

Custom Tables (on the **Tables** menu), and **Crosstabs** (on the **Descriptive Statistics** menu) provide a convenient two-way contingency table (e.g. rows representing blood groups and columns representing sexes) but **Crosstabs** also supplies a column of totals and statistics such as **chi-square** and various **correlation coefficients**. **Frequencies** (in **Descriptive Statistics**) gives frequency distributions for both nominal and ordinal data, as well as percentages and cumulative percentages. There are options for selecting graphics such as bar charts, pie charts and histograms. A feature of **Custom Tables** is that the user can see in advance the format of the table (i.e. titles of the rows and columns and which counts, statistics or percentages will be computed).

To obtain a table of frequencies with percentages:

- Choose **Analyze➔Tables➔Custom Tables...** to open the **Custom Tables** dialog box (Figure 3). If the warning box about labels appears, click **OK**.
- Highlight and drag the variable name as shown in Figure 4. The cursor with the variable name needs to hover over the Columns or Rows box until the border colours.
- To obtain percentages as well as counts, follow the steps described in Figures 4 and 5.
- Finally click **OK**. The output is shown in Output 1.

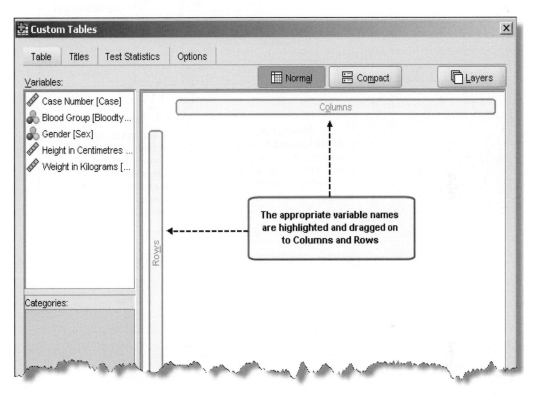

Figure 3. The upper part of the **Custom Tables** dialog box

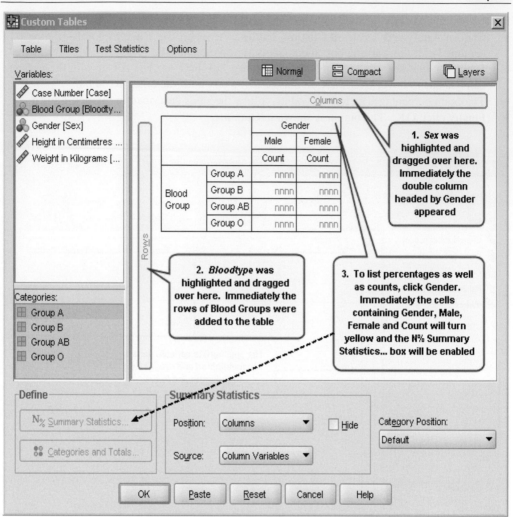

Figure 4. The **Custom Tables** dialog box partially completed by dragging *Gender* and *Blood Group* to **Columns** and **Rows** respectively

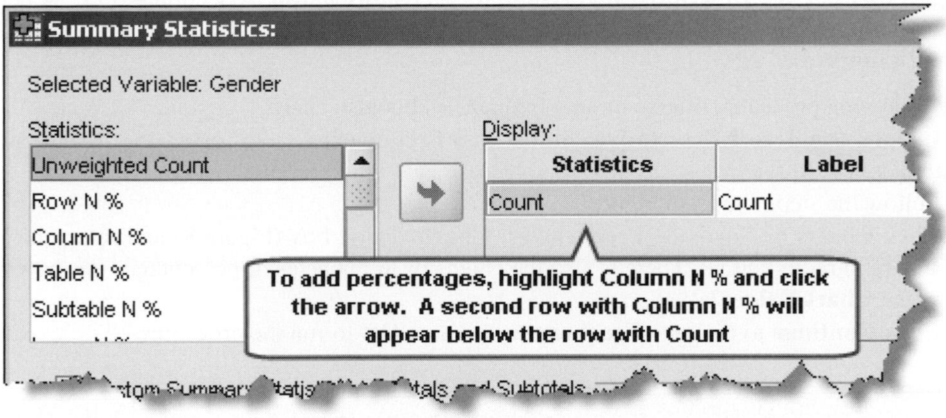

Figure 5. After clicking the **N% Summary Statistics...** button in Figure 4, the **Summary Statistics** dialog box opens (the top half is shown here). Add column percentages as described and then click the **Apply to Selection** button at the foot of the dialog box (not shown) to return to the **Custom Tables** dialog box

		Gender			
		Male		Female	
		Count	Column ...	Count	Column ...
Blood Group	Group A	nnnn	nnnn.n%	nnnn	nnnn.n%
	Group B	nnnn	nnnn.n%	nnnn	nnnn.n%
	Group AB	nnnn	nnnn.n%	nnnn	nnnn.n%
	Group O	nnnn	nnnn.n%	nnnn	nnnn.n%

Figure 6. The appearance of the inner part of **Custom Tables** after adding percentages

Table 1

		Gender			
		Male		Female	
		Count	Column N %	Count	Column N %
Blood Group	Group A	3	18.8%	3	18.8%
	Group B	3	18.8%	3	18.8%
	Group AB	2	12.5%	1	6.2%
	Group O	8	50.0%	9	56.2%

Output 1. Frequencies and percentages of *Blood Group* for each *Gender*

Tables such as that shown in Output 1 quickly show whether the data have been entered correctly by comparing the blood group counts with those in the original data set.   Checks should also be conducted on the other variables (e.g. checking the minimum and maximum heights by using the **Descriptives** procedure for *Height* as shown in Section 4.3.2). A height of over 200 cm or under 100 cm would merit a scrutiny of the data in **Data View** for a possible transcription error.

The following procedure offers not only frequencies but also charts.

- Choose **Analyze➜Descriptive Statistics➜Frequencies...** to open the **Frequencies** dialog box.
- Follow the steps shown in Figure 7.
- Click **Charts** to obtain the **Frequencies: Charts** dialog box (Figure 8) and select the **Bar Chart(s)** radio button. There is also the choice of frequencies or percentages for the y axis in the **Chart Values** box.
- Click **Continue** to return to **Frequencies** and then **OK** to run the procedure.

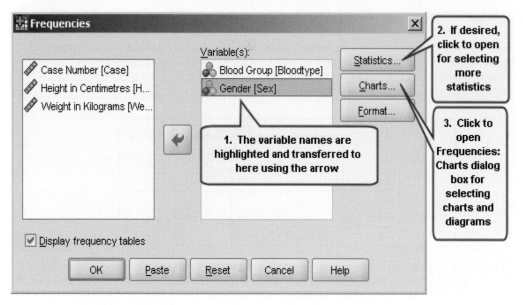

Figure 7. The **Frequencies** dialog box for *Gender* and *Blood Group*

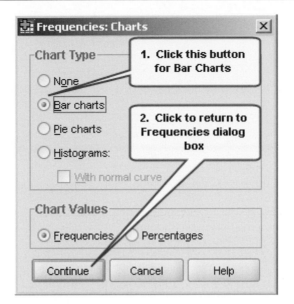

Figure 8. The **Frequencies: Charts** dialog box with **Bar charts** selected

The output consists of a couple of tables (Output 2) and the bar chart for Blood Group is shown in Output 3 (the bar chart for Gender has been omitted). Note that the bar chart can also be requested directly with the **Bar** procedure in the **Graphs** menu. It is possible to edit the bar chart to centre or change the axis labels, the title, the shading of the boxes and other aspects of the graph; more details about editing graphics will be given in the next chapter.

Blood Group

		Frequency	Percent	Valid Percent	Cumulative Percent
Valid	Group A	6	18.8	18.8	18.8
	Group B	6	18.8	18.8	37.5
	Group AB	3	9.4	9.4	46.9
	Group O	17	53.1	53.1	100.0
	Total	32	100.0	100.0	

Gender

		Frequency	Percent	Valid Percent	Cumulative Percent
Valid	Male	16	50.0	50.0	50.0
	Female	16	50.0	50.0	100.0
	Total	32	100.0	100.0	

Output 2. Frequency listings for *Blood Group* and *Gender*

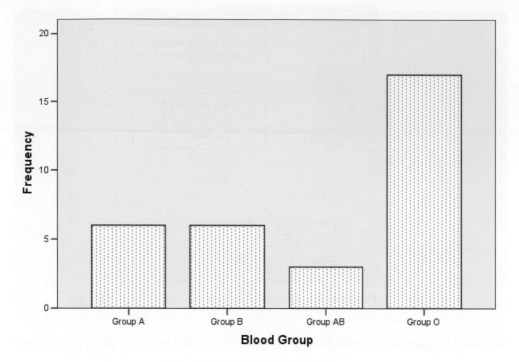

Output 3. Bar Chart for *Blood Group*

- Contingency tables can also be obtained with several procedures. **Crosstabs** generates contingency tables from nominal or ordinal data. Here we illustrate its use with *Blood Group* and *Gender*.
- Choose **Analyze➔Descriptive Statistics➔Crosstabs…** to open the **Crosstabs** dialog box.
- Transfer the variable names as shown in Figure 9 and click **OK**. If one of the variables has more than about four categories, it is better to use it for **Rows** rather than **Columns**, otherwise the output will be too wide for printing on a single page. In this example, a narrower table is produced if *Blood Group* is nominated for **Rows**.
- The output is shown in Output 4.

Crosstabs is only applicable to contingency tables. It should be requested only for nominal or ordinal data (i.e. categories or ranks) and not for measurements such as heights or scores unless they have been recoded into categories (e.g. tall; medium; short).

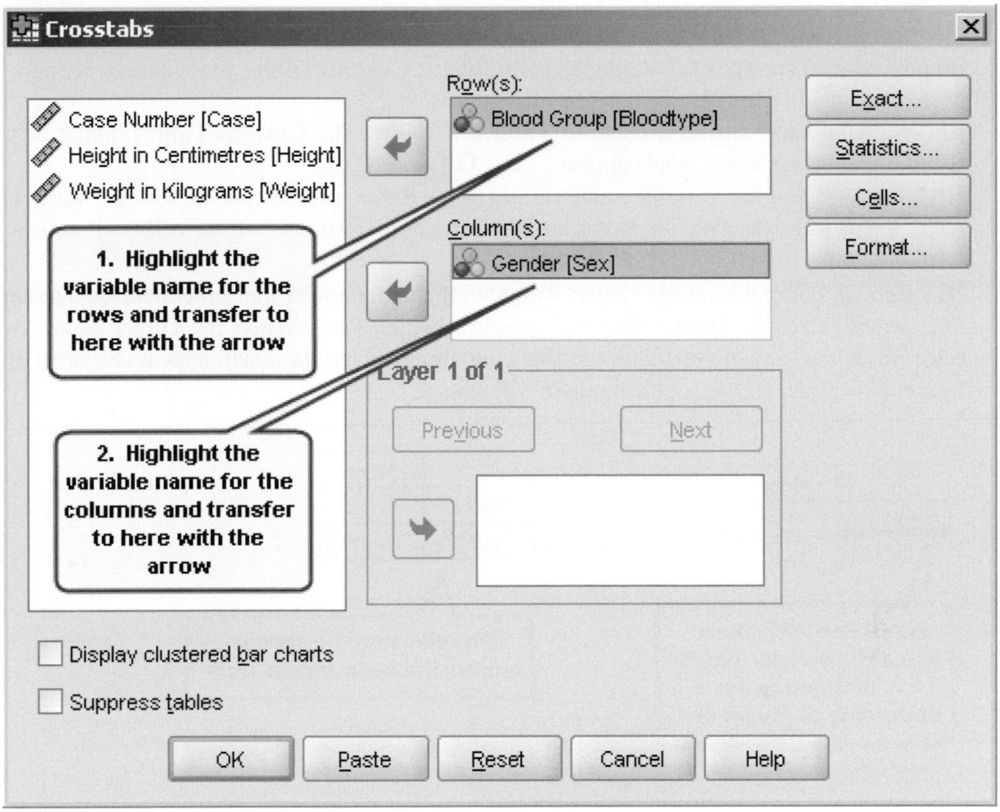

Figure 9. The completed **Crosstabs** dialog box

Blood Group * Gender Crosstabulation

Count

		Gender		Total
		Male	Female	
Blood Group	Group A	3	3	6
	Group B	3	3	6
	Group AB	2	1	3
	Group O	8	9	17
Total		16	16	32

Output 4. Contingency table from **Crosstabs** for *Gender* and *Blood Group*

4.3.2   Describing measurements

There are many procedures for describing and exploring data in the form of measurements.

Exploring variables without subdivision into categories of grouping variables

To compute several statistics for *Height* and *Weight*, the **Custom Tables** procedure described earlier in Section 4.3.1 can also be used for this purpose.

- Choose **Analyze➜Tables➜Custom Tables...** to open the **Custom Tables** dialog box. If the warning box about labels appears, click **OK**.
- Highlight and drag the variable name *Height* to the Rows box (the cursor with the variable name needs to hover over the Rows box until the border colours). Four cells will appear, one containing *Height in...*, another **Mean**.
- Highlight and drag the variable name *Weight* to the underside of the cell containing *Height in...* where a red horizontal line will appear (Figure 10). When the cursor button is released, a new row of cells with the first containing *Weight in...* will appear (Figure 10). four cells with *Height in...* within them will appear.

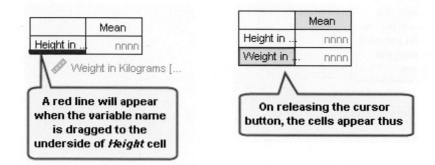

Figure 10. The appearances of the cells in the **Custom Tables** dialog box during and after dragging *Weight* to the underside of *Height* cell

- It now remains to select the statistics for the columns. Follow the procedure described earlier in Figure 5, this time selecting **Mean**, **Median** and **Std. Deviation** for three rows in the **Display** panel of the **Summary Statistics** dialog box. Click the **Apply to All** (not the **Apply to Selection**) box to return to the **Custom Tables** dialog box. The appearance of the cells is shown in Figure 11.
- Finally click **OK**. The output is shown in Output 5.

	Mean	Median	Std. Devi...
Height in ...	nnnn	nnnn	nnnn
Weight in ...	nnnn	nnnn	nnnn

Figure 11. The appearance of the cells in **Custom Tables** dialog box after selecting **Mean**, **Median** and **Std. Deviation**

Table 1

	Mean	Median	Standard Deviation
Height in Centimetres	170	170	14
Weight in Kilograms	70	70	16

Output 5. Output from **Custom Tables** showing the mean, median and standard deviation of *Height* and *Weight*

The same output can be obtained by using the **Descriptives** dialog box in the **Descriptive Statistics** menu.

• Choose **Analyze➔Descriptive Statistics➔Descriptives…** to open the **Descriptives** dialog box.
• Transfer the variable names as shown in Figure 12.
• To obtain percentages as well as counts, follow the steps described in Figures 12 and 13.

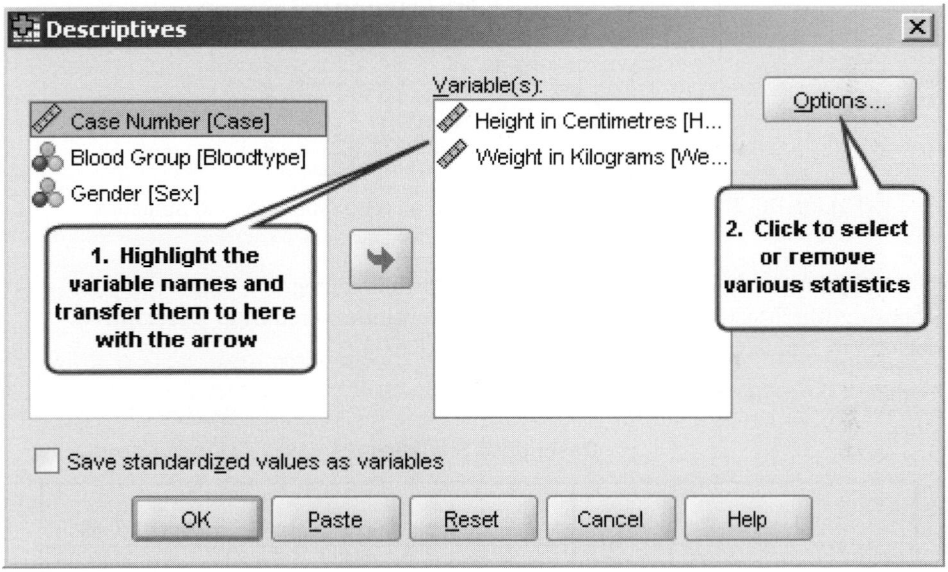

Figure 12. The completed **Descriptives** dialog box

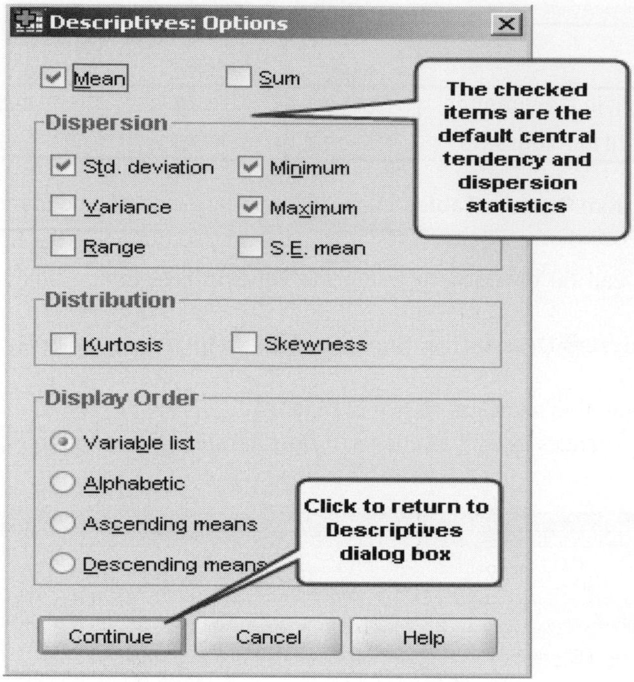

Figure 13. The **Descriptives: Options** dialog box for selecting statistics

- Click **Options…** to open the **Descriptives: Options** dialog box (Figure 13) for
  choosing which statistics are required. Click **Continue** to return to **Descriptives**
  dialog box and then click **OK**.

The output is shown in Output 6.

Descriptive Statistics

	N	Minimum	Maximum	Mean	Std. Deviation
Height in Centimetres	32	142	196	170.28	13.68
Weight in Kilograms	32	48	120	70.22	15.93
Valid N (listwise)	32				

Output 6. Descriptive statistics for *Height* and *Weight*

To obtain percentiles (e.g. quartiles), or to draw various graphics such as boxplots, stem-and-leaf tables or histograms, the appropriate procedures are **Frequencies** and **Explore**.

The next example illustrates the use of **Frequencies** to draw a histogram, compute some descriptive statistics, and display some percentile values for the variable *Height*. Proceed as follows:

- Choose **Analyze➔Descriptive Statistics➔Frequencies…** to open the **Frequencies** dialog box (Figure 7).
- In the **Frequencies** dialog box, enter the variable name Height in Centimetres into the **Variables** box. Check that the **Display frequency tables** checkbox is not showing ✓ , otherwise a full frequency table will be listed. For a large data set, this table could be huge.
- Click **Charts** to open the **Frequencies: Charts** dialog box (Figure 8).
- In the **Chart Type** box, click the **Histograms** radio button, and mark the **With normal curve** box by clicking that also. Click **Continue**.
- Back in the **Frequencies** dialog box, click **Statistics** to open the **Frequencies: Statistics** dialog box and follow the steps shown in Figure 14.
- Click **Continue** to get back to the **Frequencies** dialog box and click **OK**.

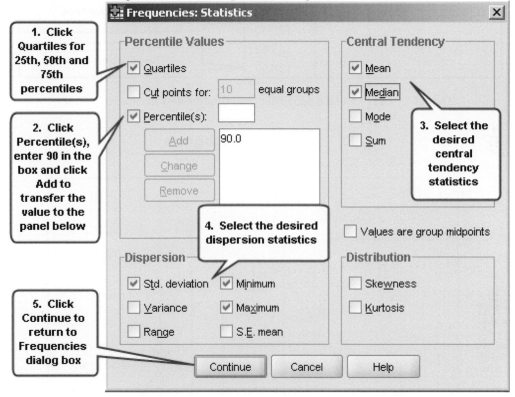

Figure 14. The **Frequencies: Statistics** dialog box with various statistics selected

The statistical output is shown in Output 7 and the edited histogram in Output 8.

Explore also produces stem-and-leaf displays and boxplots.

Statistics

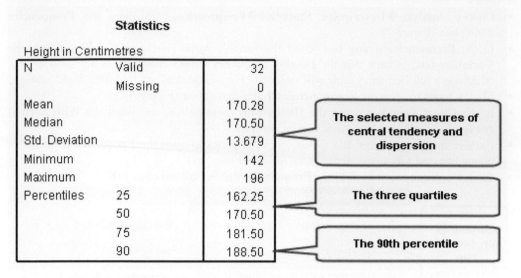

Height in Centimetres

N	Valid	32
	Missing	0
Mean		170.28
Median		170.50
Std. Deviation		13.679
Minimum		142
Maximum		196
Percentiles	25	162.25
	50	170.50
	75	181.50
	90	188.50

The selected measures of central tendency and dispersion

The three quartiles

The 90th percentile

Output 7. The requested percentiles and descriptive statistics for *Height*

Histogram

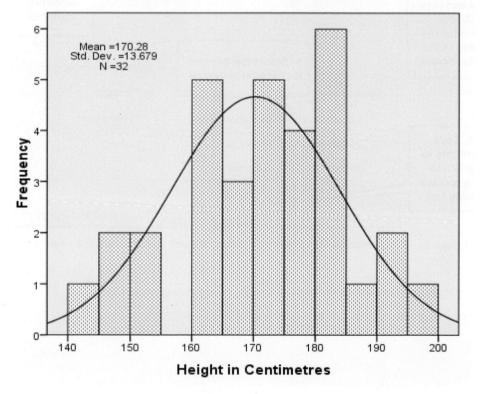

Mean =170.28
Std. Dev. =13.679
N =32

Output 8. Histogram and superimposed normal curve of the distribution of *Height*

Exploring variables with subdivision into categories of grouping variables

When the user wishes to explore quantitative variables subdivided by categories of grouping variables (e.g. the heights of men and women), several procedures are available including **Custom Tables** in the **Tables** menu, **Explore** in the **Descriptive Statistics**, and **Means** in the **Compare Means** menu. There is also the option of a one-way analysis of variance. Note especially that **Means** cannot be used for variables that have not been grouped by another variable: for such variables, **Descriptives** must be used instead. **Explore** in the **Descriptive Statistics** menu contains a large variety of graphs and displays (which are also available directly from the **Graphs** drop-down menu), as well as a variety of statistics.

The first example uses the **Custom Tables** procedure (see Figure 3).

- Highlight and transfer the variable name *Gender* to the **Columns** box and *Blood Group* to the **Rows** box.
- Highlight the variable name *Height* and drag it to the right-hand side of the blood group cells where a red box will appear (Figure 15). When the cursor button is released, four cells with *Height in…* within them will appear.
- Repeat the process with the variable name Weight but this time hover under the cells with height in Centimetres where red lines will appear (Figure 15). When the cursor is released, a cell with *Weight in…* within them will appear under each of the *Height in…* cells.

Figure 15. The appearance of the cells within the Custom Tables dialog box after dragging the variable name Height (left side image) and Weight (right side image) as described in the bullet points

- Whilst the *Height in…* cells are still highlighted, click the now enabled **N% Summary Statistics** button to open the **Summary Statistics** dialog box (see Figure 5). Select **Count** and **Std. Deviation**, each time clicking the arrow to create a new row in the **Display** panel. Note that the order of these statistics can be changed by clicking on the arrows at the right-hand side of the **Display** panel. Click the **Apply to All** button (not **Apply to Selection**) to return to the **Custom Tables** dialog box. The final appearance of the cells is shown in Figure 16.
- Click **OK** to compute the results. The output is shown in Output 9.

			Gender					
			Male			Female		
			Count	Mean	Std. Devi...	Count	Mean	Std. Devi...
Blood Group	Group A	Height in ...	∩∩∩∩	∩∩∩∩	∩∩∩∩	∩∩∩∩	∩∩∩∩	∩∩∩∩
		Weight in ...	∩∩∩∩	∩∩∩∩	∩∩∩∩	∩∩∩∩	∩∩∩∩	∩∩∩∩
	Group B	Height in ...	∩∩∩∩	∩∩∩∩	∩∩∩∩	∩∩∩∩	∩∩∩∩	∩∩∩∩
		Weight in ...	∩∩∩∩	∩∩∩∩	∩∩∩∩	∩∩∩∩	∩∩∩∩	∩∩∩∩
	Group AB	Height in ...	∩∩∩∩	∩∩∩∩	∩∩∩∩	∩∩∩∩	∩∩∩∩	∩∩∩∩
		Weight in ...	∩∩∩∩	∩∩∩∩	∩∩∩∩	∩∩∩∩	∩∩∩∩	∩∩∩∩
	Group O	Height in ...	∩∩∩∩	∩∩∩∩	∩∩∩∩	∩∩∩∩	∩∩∩∩	∩∩∩∩
		Weight in ...	∩∩∩∩	∩∩∩∩	∩∩∩∩	∩∩∩∩	∩∩∩∩	∩∩∩∩

Figure 16. The appearance of the cells in the **Custom Tables** dialog box for computing the counts, means and standard deviations of *Height* and *Weight* subdivided by the levels of *Blood Group* and *Gender*

			Gender					
			Male			Female		
			Count	Mean	Std Deviation	Count	Mean	Std Deviation
Blood Group	Group A	Height in Centimetres	3	168.3	22.5	3	160.3	10.5
		Weight in Kilograms	3	74.0	15.1	3	52.7	2.5
	Group B	Height in Centimetres	3	184.0	5.3	3	175.7	6.5
		Weight in Kilograms	3	95.0	21.8	3	72.0	7.5
	Group AB	Height in Centimetres	2	178.5	9.2	1	160.3	.
		Weight in Kilograms	2	73.0	7.1	1	160.3	.
	Group O	Height in Centimetres	8	176.5	10.7	9	162.7	12.5
		Weight in Kilograms	8	79.0	11.8	9	60.0	7.2

Output 9. Output from **Custom Tables** showing statistics for *Height* and *Weight* across *Blood Group* and *Gender*

The next example shows the use of **Means** to compute statistics such as the mean and standard deviation when one variable has been grouped by categories of another (e.g. height grouped by gender). Proceed as follows:

- Choose **Analyze➜Compare Means➜Means...** to open the **Means** dialog box (the completed version is shown in Figure 17).
- Follow the steps in Figure 17 and click **OK**.

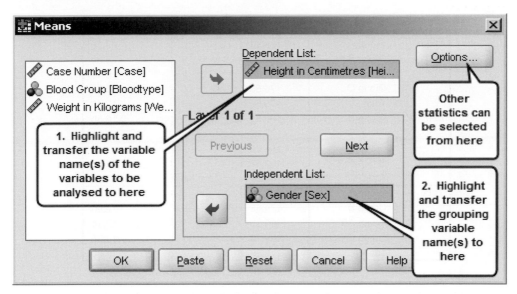

Figure 17. The **Means** dialog box for *Height* categorised by *Gender*. Note that grouping variables can be layered by transferring each in turn and clicking **Next**

The output is listed in Output 10. The **Means** procedure has computed statistics such as the mean and standard deviation for the male and female participants separately.

Height in Centimetres

Gender	Mean	N	Std. Deviation
Male	176.63	16	12.46
Female	163.94	16	12.06
Total	170.28	32	13.68

Output 10. The mean *Height* for each level of *Gender* requested with **Means**

Breaking down the data with two or more classificatory variables: Layering

In Figure 17, notice the centrally located box containing two sub-dialog buttons **Previous** and **Next,** as well as the caption **Layer 1 of 1.** Here a **layer** is a qualitative variable, such as *Sex*. If you click **Next**, you can add another qualitative variable such as Blood Group [*Bloodtype*], so that the data are classified thus:

1st Layer	*Sex*	Male	Female
2nd Layer	*Bloodtype*	A AB B O	A AB B O

The output tabulates the mean *Height*, N and standard deviation for all combinations of *Gender* and *Blood Group* as shown in Output 11.

Height in Centimetres

Gender	Blood Group	Mean	N	Std. Deviation
Male	Group A	168.33	3	22.55
	Group B	184.00	3	5.29
	Group AB	178.50	2	9.19
	Group O	176.50	8	10.66
	Total	176.63	16	12.46
Female	Group A	160.33	3	10.50
	Group B	175.67	3	6.51
	Group AB	151.00	1	.
	Group O	162.67	9	12.47
	Total	163.94	16	12.06
Total	Group A	164.33	6	16.33
	Group B	179.83	6	7.00
	Group AB	169.33	3	17.16
	Group O	169.18	17	13.35
	Total	170.28	32	13.68

Output 11. The use of layering to compute the mean *Height*, N and standard deviation for all combinations of *Gender* and *Blood Group*

Note that if you had not clicked on **Next** before adding the second classificatory variable, the output would have consisted of *Height by Gender* and *Height by Blood Group* separately (i.e. only a single layer would have been used for each analysis).

Explore (in the **Descriptive Statistics** menu) can be regarded as a general exploratory data analysis (EDA) procedure. **Explore** offers many of the facilities already illustrated with other procedures, and (like **Means** and **Compare Means**) allows quantitative variables to be subdivided by the categories of a qualitative variable such as gender. If, for example, a data set contains the heights of 50 men and 50 women collected into a column headed *Height* and (in another column) code numbers making up the grouping variable *Sex*, the procedure **Explore** will produce statistical summaries, graphs and displays either for the 100 height measurements considered as a single group, or the heights of males or females (or both) considered separately.

A useful first step in the analysis of data is to obtain a picture of the data set as a whole. **Explore** offers three kinds of graphs and displays:
1. Histograms.
2. Stem-and-leaf displays.
3. Boxplots.

Readers unfamiliar with these can find, in Howell (2007), clear descriptions of histograms on pp. 19–20, of stem-and-leaf displays on pp. 21–23 and of boxplots on pp. 51-54.

The basis of all three types of graph is a table called a **frequency distribution**, which sets out either (in the case of nominal data) the categories comprising a qualitative variable and gives the frequency of observations in each category or (with measurements) divides the total range of values into arbitrary **class intervals** and gives the frequency of measurements that fall within each interval, that is, have values between the upper and lower **bounds** of the interval concerned. With data on height recorded in centimetres, for example, the total range could be divided into the class intervals (140–149, 150–159, 160–169, ….), and the frequency distribution would give the **frequencies** of heights within each of these ranges.

A **bar graph** (SPSS calls this a 'bar chart': see Output 3) is suitable for qualitative (nominal) data, such as the numbers of people in a sample belonging to the various blood groups. In a bar graph, the bars are separated to clarify the fact that the horizontal axis contains no scale of measurement; in fact, the order of the bars in Output 3 is arbitrary, since the Group AB bar could as well have followed the Group A bar. A **histogram** (see Output 8), on the other hand, is appropriate for measurements. Here the class intervals are stepped out along the horizontal axis and above each interval a bar is drawn whose height represents the number of people whose measurements fell within that interval. *In a histogram, as compared with a bar graph, the bars touch one another.*

To use the **Explore** procedure:
- Choose **Analyze➜Descriptive Statistics➜Explore…** to open the **Explore** dialog box.
- Follow the steps shown in Figure 18.

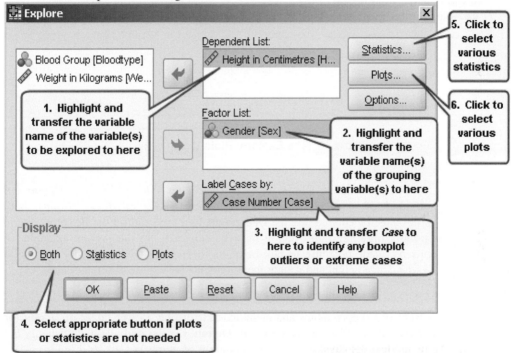

Figure 18. The **Explore** dialog box for *Height* categorised by *Gender*

- If there is a variable identifying the cases (e.g. *Case*), then click *Case* and transfer it with the arrow to the **Label Cases by** box. Outliers or extreme cases (these will be explained later) are identified in boxplots by their row numbers by default or by the identifier in the variable entered in the **Label Cases by** box.
- Click **Plots** to open the **Explore: Plots** dialog box (Figure 19). The default setting for the **Boxplots** is a side-by-side (**Factor levels together**) plot for each level of the factor (i.e. *Female* and *Male*) and **Stem-and-leaf** table. Had we not seen the histogram earlier, we might have clicked the check box for **Histogram**.

- Click **Continue** and then **OK**.

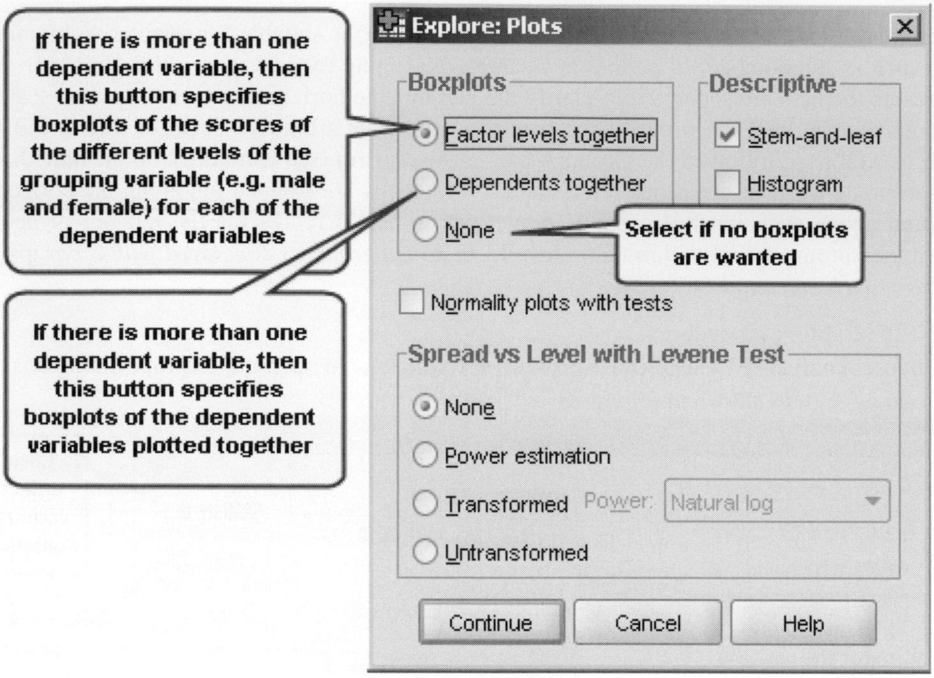

If there is more than one dependent variable, then this button specifies boxplots of the scores of the different levels of the grouping variable (e.g. male and female) for each of the dependent variables

If there is more than one dependent variable, then this button specifies boxplots of the dependent variables plotted together

Explore: Plots

Boxplots
- ⦿ Factor levels together
- ◯ Dependents together
- ◯ None ← Select if no boxplots are wanted

☐ Normality plots with tests

Descriptive
- ☑ Stem-and-leaf
- ☐ Histogram

Spread vs Level with Levene Test
- ⦿ None
- ◯ Power estimation
- ◯ Transformed   Power: Natural log
- ◯ Untransformed

[Continue]   [Cancel]   [Help]

Figure 19. The **Explore: Plots** dialog box

Should you wish to have boxplots of two dependent variables side-by-side (e.g. *Height* and *Weight*) at each level of a classificatory variable (e.g. *Gender* or *Blood Group*), both dependent variables must be entered into the **Dependent List** box, and (in the **Boxplots** dialog box) the **Dependents together** radio button must be selected. In the present example, of course, it would have made no sense to plot boxplots of *Height* and *Weight* side-by-side at each level of *Gender*, since height and weight measurements have quite different scales.

The tables and the boxplots are shown in Outputs 12 and 13.

The descriptive statistics (upper table) and stem-and-leaf display (lower table) of *Height* for Males (one of the levels of *Gender*) is shown in Output 12; the output for Females is not shown. In the **stem-and-leaf display**, the central column of numbers (16, 16, 17, 17, ..., 19), which is the **stem**, represents the leading digit or digits (here they are hundreds and tens of centimetres). The numbers in the column headed **Leaf** are the final digits (centimetres). Each stem denotes the lower bound of the class interval: for example, the first number, 16, represents the lower bound of the class interval from 160 to 164, the second 16 from 165 to 169, the first 17 from 170 to 174 and so on. The column headed **Frequency** lists the number of cases on each stem. In stem 18, for example, there are four cases with heights between 180 and 184 centimetres. They are 180, 180, 182 and 183, since the leaves are listed as 0, 0, 2, 3. In addition, there is one case with a height between 185 and 189, namely 185. The display also shows extreme cases: there is one value equal to or less than 145. The stem-and-leaf display is very useful for displaying information about small data sets, but care should be taken when it is applied to larger databases as it can be ponderous: in this case a histogram is more suitable.

Descriptives

Gender				Statistic	Std. Error
Height in Centimetres	Male	Mean		176.63	3.12
		95% Confidence Interval for Mean	Lower Bound	169.98	
			Upper Bound	183.27	
		5% Trimmed Mean		177.31	
		Median		179.00	
		Variance		155.32	
		Std. Deviation		12.46	
		Minimum		145.00	
		Maximum		196.00	176.63
		Range		51.00	169.98
		Interquartile Range		14.50	183.27
		Skewness		-.95	177.31
		Kurtosis		1.64	179.00

```
Height in Centimetres Stem-and-Leaf Plot for
SEX= Male

 Frequency     Stem &  Leaf

     1.00 Extremes      (=<145)
     1.00         16 .  0
      .00         16 .
     4.00         17 .  0002
     2.00         17 .  58
     4.00         18 .  0023
     1.00         18 .  5
     2.00         19 .  00
     1.00         19 .  6


 Stem width:         10
 Each leaf:        1 case(s)
```

Output 12. Descriptive statistics, and stem-and-leaf display for *Height* categorised by *Gender* (only the output for Males shown here)

The structure of a boxplot is shown in Table 2. The box itself represents that portion of the distribution falling between the 25th and 75th percentiles, i.e. the **lower** and **upper quartiles** (in EDA terminology these are known as **hinges**). The xth percentile is the value below which x% of the distribution lies, so 50% of the heights lie between the 25th and 75th percentiles. The thick horizontal line across the interior of the box represents the median. The vertical lines outside the box, which are known as **whiskers**, connect the largest and smallest values that are not outliers or extreme cases.

Table 2. Structure of a boxplot

✱2	**Extreme case** - more than 3 box-lengths above the box. The number is the identifier, either the row number or from the variable entered in the **Label Cases by** box.
○21	**Outlier** - more than 1.5 box lengths above the box. The number is the identifier.
	Largest value which is not an outlier or an extreme score.
	Top of box: 75th percentile (upper quartile)
	Bar: Median (50th percentile)
	Bottom of box: 25th percentile (lower quartile)
	Smallest value which is not an outlier or an extreme score.
○25	**Outlier** - more than 1.5 box lengths below the box. The numbers are the identifiers.
○26	
✱27	**Extreme case** - more than 3 box-lengths below the box. The number is the identifier.

Whisker ➔

Box   ➔

Whisker ➔

Output 13 shows one **outlier** but no **extreme cases**. An **outlier** (o) is defined as a value more than 1.5 box-lengths away from the box, and an **extreme case** (*) as more than 3 box-lengths away from the box. The number(s) alongside o and * are the case number(s). The case numbers are either the row numbers in **Data View** by default, or the identifiers from the variable entered in the **Label Cases by** box.

Skewness is indicated by an eccentric location of the median in the box. Notice that the distribution of heights for females is much more symmetric than that for males. The o^{3} under the Male boxplot in Output 13 indicates the existence of an outlier and that it is the value for the case in row 3. This value (145cm) is well below the average height for males and its presence is also noted in the stem-and-leaf display in Output 12.

Boxplots are particularly useful for identifying outliers and extreme cases in data sets, and can be requested directly by choosing **Graphs➔Chart Builder** and selecting **Box** from the gallery (see Section 5.4 in the next Chapter).

See Section 5.4

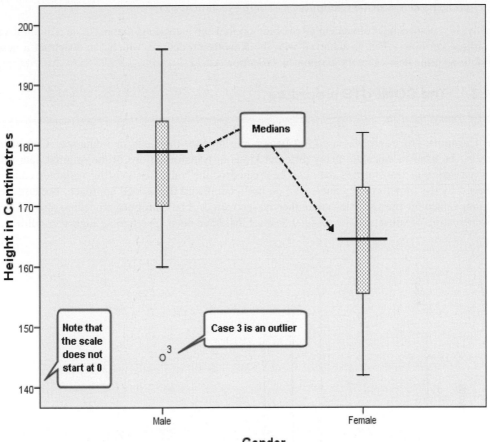

Output 13. Boxplots of *Height* categorised by *Gender*

4.4   MANIPULATION OF THE DATA SET

4.4.1   Reducing and transforming data

After a data set has been entered into SPSS, it may be necessary to modify it in certain ways. For example, an exploratory data analysis may have revealed that one or two extreme cases have exerted undue leverage upon the values of statistics such as the mean and standard deviation. One approach to this problem is to de-select the extreme cases and repeat the analysis with the remaining scores (cf. Tabachnick & Fidell, 2007). Any exclusions, however, should be mentioned in the experimental report. Cases can be dropped from the analysis by using the **Select Cases** command (Section 3.3.1).

Sometimes, in order to satisfy the distribution requirements for the use of a particular statistic, it may be necessary to **transform** the values of a variable. For example, a distribution of response latencies is often **positively skewed,** i.e. it has a long tail to the right; whereas the

116

distribution of the logarithms of the raw scores is more symmetrical. Transformations are easily implemented with the **Compute** procedure (Section 4.4.2).

Finally, it is sometimes convenient to combine or alter the categories that make up a qualitative or ordinal variable. This is achieved with the **Recode** procedure, which can construct a new variable with the new category assignments (Section 4.4.3).

4.4.2 The COMPUTE procedure

Transforming the data

The **Compute** procedure was used in Chapter 3 to number the cases in a data set. **Compute** can also be used to calculate many different kinds of transformations of the original data set. New variables of transformed data can be created or the values of existing variables can be replaced by the transformed values. We do not recommend the second approach, because the original values for the variable cannot then be recovered. The **Compute** procedure also allows transformation of subsets of the original data set that have been specified by logical conditions.

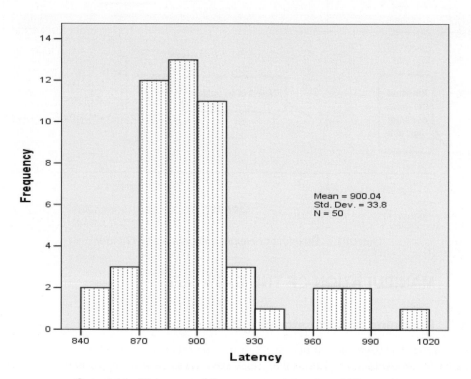

Output 14. Histogram of the response latencies of 50 people

Output 14 shows a histogram of the response latencies of fifty people. Typically, such data show a positively skewed distribution, with a long tail to the right. For the purposes of statistical testing, the investigator might want to transform the original data to make the distribution more symmetrical. Such normalisation can often be achieved by taking the logarithms, square roots, reciprocals and other functions of the original scores. These transformations, however, have different effects upon distribution shape, as the following exercise will demonstrate. We shall begin by using the **Compute** procedure to calculate the natural logarithms of the raw data.

Assuming the data set is present in the **Data Editor**,

- Choose **Transform➔Compute…** to open the **Compute Variable** dialog box (the completed version is shown in Figure 20).
- Follow the steps described in Figure 20.
- Click **OK**.

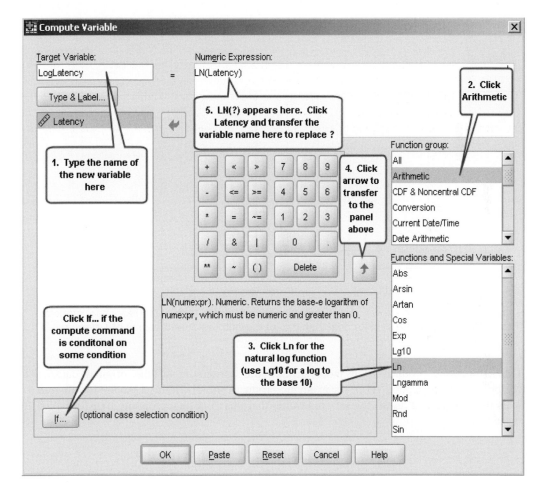

Figure 20. The completed **Compute Variable** dialog box for computing the natural logarithm of *Latency*

A new column *LogLatency*, containing the natural logs of the values of *Latencies*, will appear in **Data View**. You may wish to add a label (e.g. Log of Latency) for this new variable and to change the number of decimal places – see Section 2.3.1. A setting of two decimal places works well in this example; but with a reciprocal transformation (see below), four places of decimals would be required. Output 15 shows the histogram of the logs of the original latencies. The transformation has clearly reduced the skewness of the distribution.

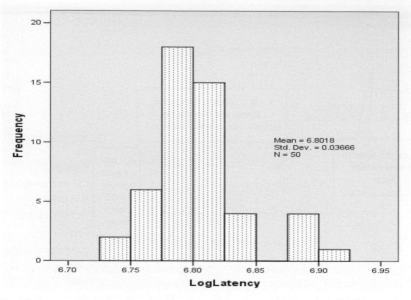

Output 15. Histogram showing the distribution of the natural logs of the response latencies. The distribution is more symmetrical than that of the untransformed values of *Latency*

Other functions produce even more striking transformations of the original data. The reciprocal transformation (1/x), for example, produces the distribution pictured in Output 16. This time, there is a tail to the left, indicating that this is an inappropriate transformation for these data.

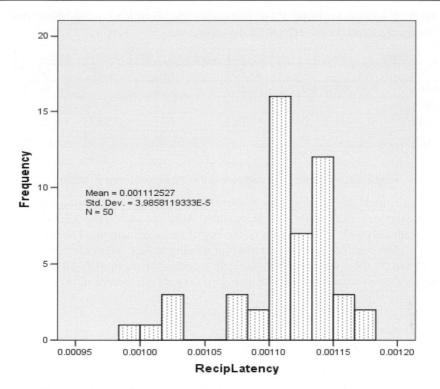

Output 16.   The distribution of a reciprocal (1/x) transformation of the response latencies. This distribution is negatively skewed, with a tail to the left

*Using **Compute** to obtain functions of several variables*

Compute can also be used to combine values of variables. Suppose you have a data set comprising the marks of schoolchildren in their French, German and Spanish examinations. You might be interested in averaging each child's score over the three examinations.

One way of doing this is to write your own numerical expression in the **Numerical Expression** box of the **Compute Variable** dialog box (e.g. name the new variable *MeanMark* and enter the expression *(French + German + Spanish)/3*.   Should any child not have taken all three examinations, however, the mean would not be calculated and a system-missing mark would appear in **Data View** instead.

Another way is to paste the **MEAN** function from the **Functions and Special Variables** list (Figure 20) into the **Numerical Expression** box and transfer the variable names *French, German* and *Spanish* into the pasted function taking care to have a comma between each name and to ensure that '?' is no longer present (e.g. **MEAN**(*French, German, Spanish*)). Should a child's mark be missing, the mean of the other two marks will be calculated. The function MEAN, therefore, calculates the mean from whatever valid values may be present. Only if a child has sat none of the three examinations, will a system-missing value of the mean be recorded.

Figure 21 is a section of **Data View** comparing the results of using these two ways, *MeanbyDiv* for the first way and *MEAN* for the second way.

ChildsN	French	German	Spanish	MeanbyDiv	MEAN
Fred	67	78	23	56.00	56.00
Mary	50	50	.	.	50.00
John	.	.	.	.	.
Peter	0	50	50	33.33	33.33
Amy	0	.	.	.	.00
Jack	23	.	.	.	23.00

Figure 21. Two ways to computing the means of three variables

It can be seen from Figure 21 that the add-then-divide way only works when there are marks on all three examinations. It fails with Mary, John, Amy and Jack. The MEAN way fails to produce a result only with John, who did not sit any of the examinations. The MEAN function also makes a clear distinction between zeros and missing values: Mary correctly receives the mean of 50 and 50 (50); whereas Peter correctly receives the mean of 0, 50 and 50 (33.33). Jack correctly receives a mean of 23 even though he sat only one examination.

Conditional computations

A medical researcher has gathered some data on the drinking and substance intake of patients. Figure 22 shows a section from **Data View**, in which *0 = No Abuse and 1 = Abuse*.

	Patient	Alcohol	Substances
1	Sarah	No Abuse	No Abuse
2	Alan	Abuse	No Abuse
3	Jim	No Abuse	Abuse
4	Joe	Abuse	Abuse

Figure 22. A section of the data set for substance abuse in patients

The researcher wants to create a third variable, *Addict*, with values as follows:

0 for patients with No Abuse on both variables
1 for patients with Abuse on *Alcohol* but No Abuse on *Substances*
2 for patients with No Abuse on *Alcohol* but Abuse on *Substances*
3 for patients with Abuse on both variables.

The problem can be solved in several ways. We could begin by letting *Addict = Alcohol + Substances + 1*. We could then instruct the **Compute** routine to proceed as follows. If either *(Alcohol = Substances = 0) or (Alcohol = 1 and Substances = 0)*, subtract *1* from *Addict*. This will solve the problem, because the remaining combinations would fail to meet either condition and no subtraction would take place.

- Choose **Transform➡Compute** to access the **Compute Variable** dialog box.
- Type *Addict* into the **Target Variable** box.
- Transfer the variable names *Alcohol* and *Substances* to the **Numeric Expression** box and create the expression *Alcohol + Substances + 1* (see Figure 23).

- Click **OK**.

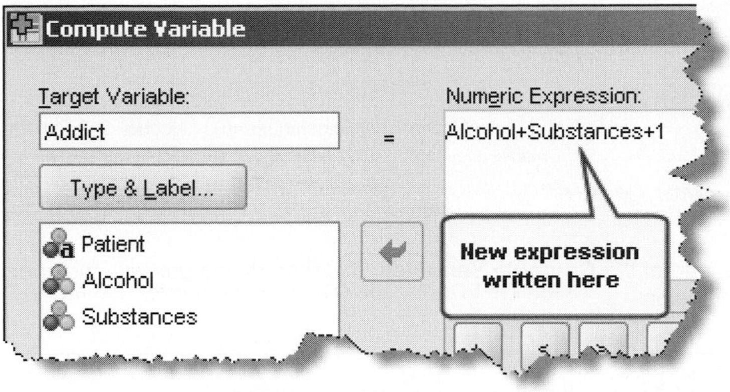

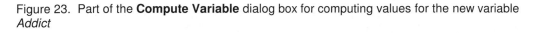

Figure 23. Part of the **Compute Variable** dialog box for computing values for the new variable
Addict

The values of *Addict* will then appear in **Data View** as shown in Figure 24.

	Patient	Alcohol	Substances	Addict
1	Sarah	No Abuse	No Abuse	1
2	Alan	Abuse	No Abuse	2
3	Jim	No Abuse	Abuse	2
4	Joe	Abuse	Abuse	3

Figure 24. **Data View** showing the newly computed variable *Addict*

These values for *Addict* are correct except for Sarah and Alan who should have a value of *0* and *1* respectively. We therefore have to modify the computation of these values of *Addict* by subtracting *1* from the total when both variables have *0*, or if *Alcohol = 1* and *Substances = 0*. This is done by constructing a conditional expression in the **Compute Variable: If Cases** dialog box.

- Return to the **Compute Variable** dialog box and change the Numeric Expression entry to *Addict – 1*.
- Click the **If...** button to open the **Compute Variable: If Cases** dialog box.
- Click the radio button labelled **Include if Case satisfies condition:**
- In the box on the right enter the expression:
         (Alcohol = 0 & Substance = 0) | (Alcohol = 1 & Substances = 0).
  The symbol **&** means **AND** and the symbol | means **OR** in this logical expression. Care must be taken with inserting brackets in the conditional expression to ensure the logical operators **AND** and **OR** operate appropriately.
- The top part of the completed dialog box will appear as in Figure 25.
- Click **Continue** to return to the **Compute Variable** dialog box.
- Click **OK** to compute the altered values of *Addict.*

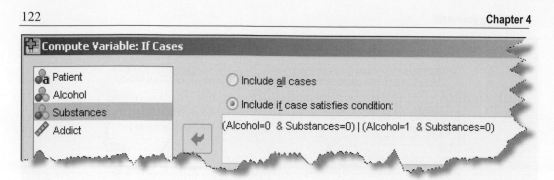

Figure 25. Top part of the **Compute Variables: If Cases** dialog box with the specially written conditional expression

The entries in **Data View** will now appear as shown in Figure 26.

	Patient	Alcohol	Substances	Addict
1	Sarah	No Abuse	No Abuse	0
2	Alan	Abuse	No Abuse	1
3	Jim	No Abuse	Abuse	2
4	Joe	Abuse	Abuse	3

Figure 26. The desired values for *Addict* after using a conditional expression in the **Compute Variable** dialog box

An alternative method would be to compute *Addict = Alcohol*10 + Substances* and then use the **Recode** procedure (next Section) to recode the resulting set of values.

4.4.3 The RECODE and VISUAL BINNING procedures

We have seen that the **Compute** procedure operates upon one or more of the variables in the data set, so that there will be as many values in the transformed variable as there were in the original variable. Sometimes, however, rather than wanting a transformation that will systematically change all the values of a variable, the user may want to assign relatively few code numbers to values that fall within specified ranges of the variable.

For example, suppose we have a set of 18 children's examination marks on a scale from 0 to 100 (Table 3). We shall recode these into three bins: 0-49 as Fail; 50-74 as Pass; 75-100 as Good. This can easily be done by using either of two other procedures on the **Transform** menu: the **Recode** procedure or the **Visual Binning** procedure.

Table 3. Children's examination marks					
Child	Mark	Child	Mark	Child	Mark
1	62	7	70	13	50
2	51	8	40	14	50
3	40	9	63	15	42
4	68	10	81	16	65
5	38	11	62	17	30
6	40	12	78	18	71

Using the **Recode** *procedure*

Enter the data into **Data View** in variables named *Case* and *Marks* and then:
- Choose **Transform➜Recode into Different Variables…** to open the **Recode into Different Variables** dialog box (Figure 27). Just as in the case of the **Compute** procedure, it is possible to change the values in the same variable to the recoded values but we recommend placing the recoded values in a new variable, perhaps *Grade*.

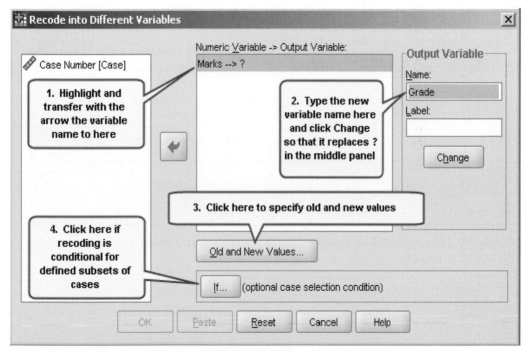

Figure 27. The **Recode into Different Variables** dialog box showing the original variable and the one to which the recoded values will be placed

- Click *Marks* and the arrow to transfer the name into the **Numeric Variable→Output Variable** box.
- Type the name of the output variable *Grade* into the **Name** box and click **Change** to insert the name into the **Numeric Variable→Output Variable** box (Figure 27).
- Click the **Old and New Values** box to open the **Recode into Different Variables: Old and New Values** dialog box.
- Follow the steps in Figures 28-29 for defining the old and new values. These will categorise all exam marks less than 50 as *Fail,* 50-74 as *Pass* and 75 and over as *Good.* The defined criteria are shown in Figure 30.
- Click **Continue** and **OK**.

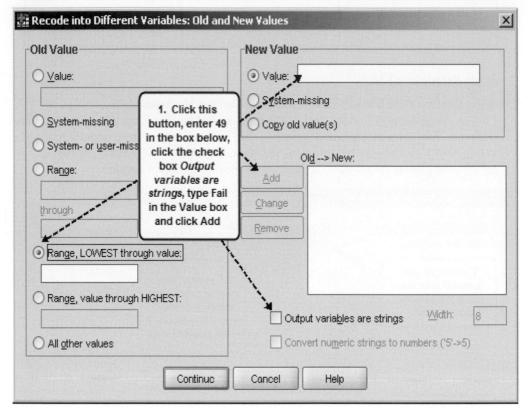

Figure 28. The **Old and New Values** dialog box with the first stage of defining ranges for Pass, Fail and Good

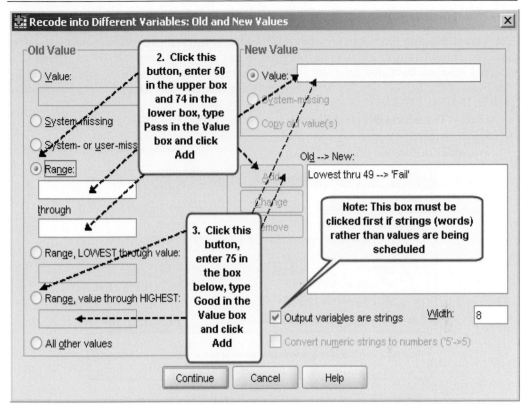

Figure 29. Continuation of defining ranges for Pass, Fail and Good

Figure 30. The appearance of the **Old -> New** panel after entering all the criteria

A new string variable *Grade* containing the recoded labels *Pass*, *Fail* and *Good* will appear in **Data View** (Figure 31).

	Case	Marks	Grade
8	8	40	Fail
9	9	63	Pass
10	10	81	Good
11	11	62	Pass
12	12	78	Good

Figure 31. Part of **Data View** showing the new string variable *Grade* with the labels Pass, Fail and Good

Using the Visual Binning

The **Visual Binning** procedure provides many different ways of categorising variables on the basis of cut-off values, equal-width intervals, equal-percentile intervals or on means and selected standard deviation intervals. We shall illustrate its use with the medical data by categorising the height data into three bins: (1) tall (greater than 180 cm); (2) intermediate (160 to 180 cm); (3) short (less than 160 cm).

- Choose **Transform➔Visual Binning** to open the **Visual Binning** dialog box.
- Select *Height in Centimetres* and click on arrowhead to transfer the variable name to the **Variables to Bin** box (Figure 32).

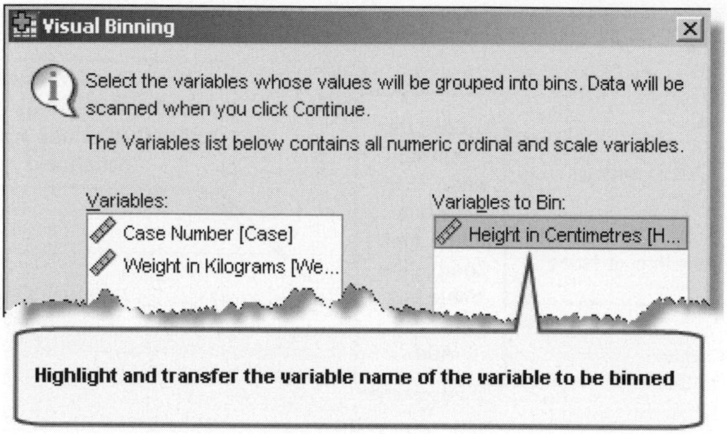

Figure 32. The upper part of the **Visual Binning** dialog box

- Click **Continue** to open the next dialog box.
- Click *Height in Centimetres* in the **Scanned Variable List** box to show the histogram of heights (Figure 33).
- Enter a variable name such as observing the usual rules for naming variables (e.g. *HeightBin*) in the **Binned Variable** cell (Figure 33).
- Enter *160* in the first **Value** cell (it overwrites HIGH) and *Short* in the first **Label** cell. Click the lower radio button **Excluded (<)** to indicate that the category *Short* is greater than 160 cm. Had we defined the category as '160 and less', then the default radio button **Included (<=)** would apply.
- Enter *180* in the second **Value** cell and *Medium* in the second **Label** cell.
- Enter *220* (any value beyond the tallest value would suffice) in the third **Value** cell and *Tall* in the third **Label** cell.
- Click **OK**.

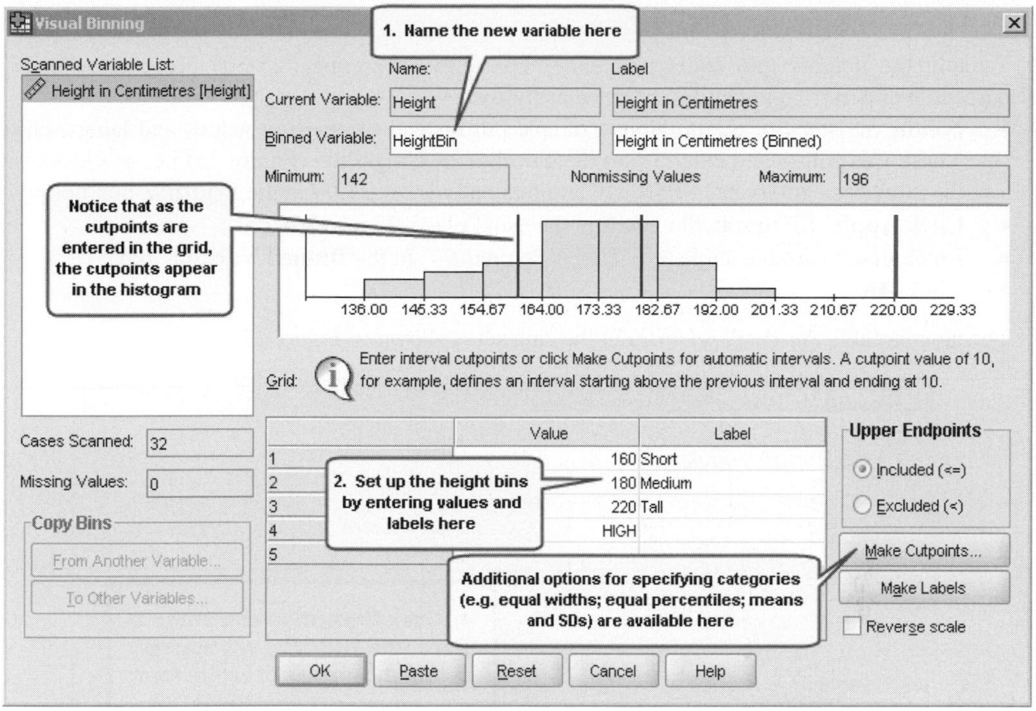

Figure 33. The histogram of *Height* is visible after clicking the variable name

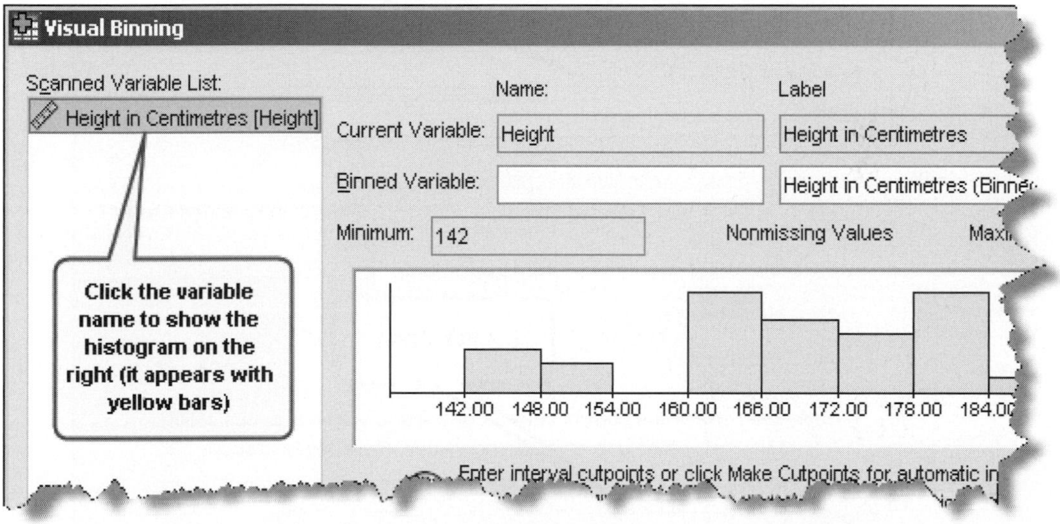

Figure 34. The completed **Visual Binning** dialog box for categorising *Height* into three bins

Notice that as each cutpoint is entered, its position is drawn into the histogram above as soon as the cursor is moved to another cell. If desired, the cursor can be positioned over one of these lines and moved left or right by clicking and dragging. The new variable *HeightBin* in the data set is shown in Figure 37.

To split the heights into equal percentiles (i.e. <25th percentile, 25-50th percentile, 50-75th percentile and >75th percentile), proceed as follows:

*   Follow the steps of the previous example but instead of entering values and labels, click **Make Cutpoints** and enter *3* into the **Number of Cutpoints** (Figure 35) i.e. one less than the number of intervals. SPSS will automatically show *25.00* in the **Width%** box below.
*   Click **Apply**, fill in suitable labels in the usual place (Figure 36).
*   Enter a new variable name (e.g. *HeightPercentiles*) in the **Binned Variable** box.
*   Click **OK**.

The new variable *HeightPercentiles* in the data set is shown in Figure 37.

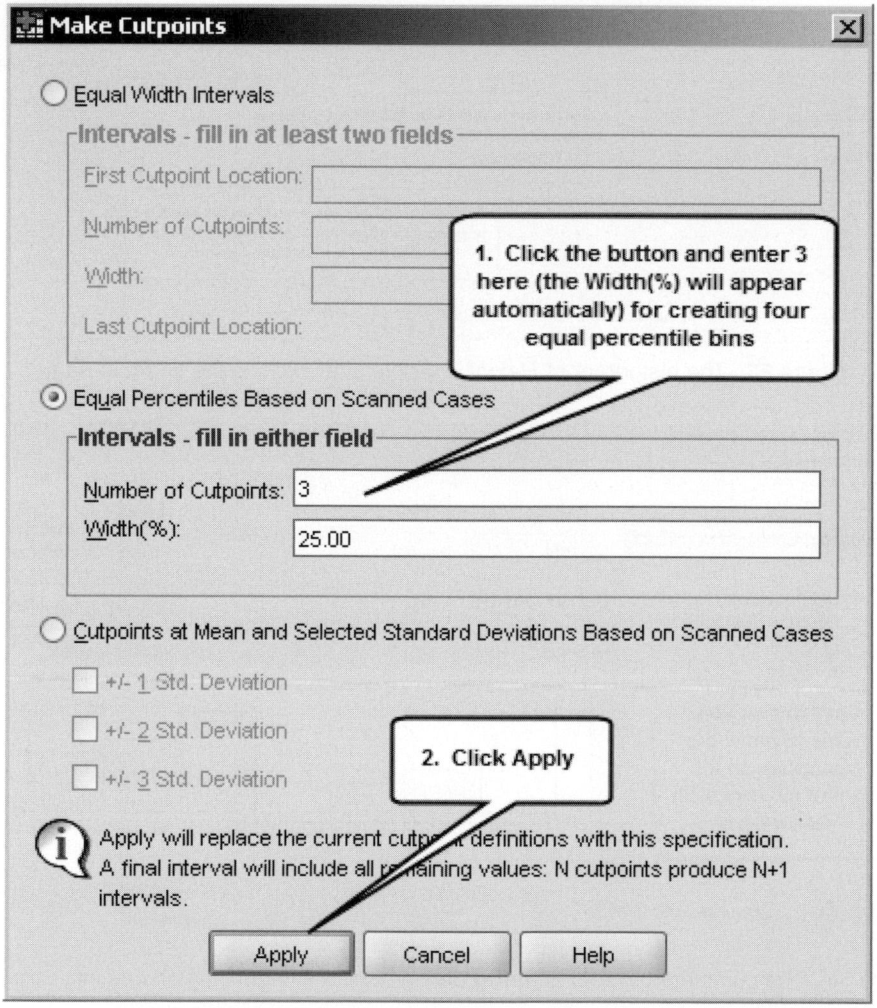

Figure 35. The completed **Make Cutpoints** dialog box for creating four equal percentile bins

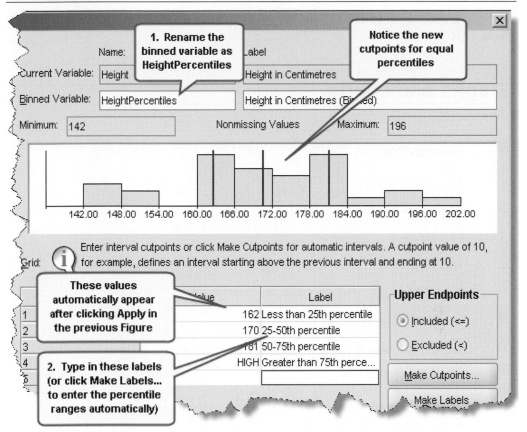

Figure 36. The **Visual Binning** dialog box with new variable name *HeightPercentiles* and labels for the percentile bins. The values were entered automatically by SPSS and are shown on the histogram above

Case	Bloodtype	Sex	Height	Weight	HeightBin	HeightPercentiles
1	Group O	Male	178	75	Medium	50th-75th percentile
2	Group O	Male	196	100	Tall	Greater than 75th percentile
3	Group A	Male	145	60	Short	Less than 25th percentile
4	Group O	Male	170	71	Medium	25th-50th percentile
5	Group B	Male	180	80	Tall	50th-75th percentile
6	Group O	Male	175	69	Medium	50th-75th percentile

Figure 37. The first six cases of the original dataset showing the new variables *HeightBin* and *HeightPercentiles* created by **Visual Binning**

Exercises

Exercise 4 *Correcting and preparing your data* and Exercise 5 *Preparing your data (continued)* are available in www.psypress.com/spss-made-simple and click on Exercises.

CHAPTER 5

Graphs and charts

5.1   INTRODUCTION

SPSS offers a wide range of graphs and charts. We shall first consider some general points about graph-drawing in SPSS. It is worth noting that the most elaborate charts do not necessarily bring out the results of an investigation in the clearest way. Three dimensional effects, for example, though they may be aesthetically attractive, can obscure the very point that you are trying to bring out.

5.1.1   Graphs and charts on SPSS

There are several different ways of producing graphics with SPSS. There is a selection of procedures on the **Graphs** menu (Figure 1) but graphs are options in analytical procedures as well. For instance, there is a **Charts** option in the **Frequencies** procedure and a **Profile Plot** option in the ANOVA procedures. These are standard charts although they can be customised to a considerable extent. The appearance of graphs can be controlled to an even greater extent by using **Chart Builder** or **Interactive** (at the foot of the **Legacy Dialogs** menu). The gallery of charts and graphs obtained by clicking on the **Chart Builder** item in the **Graphs** menu (Figure 2) is useful for selecting the type of chart or graph desired. If the gallery does not initially appear, click **Gallery** at the left of the **Chart Builder** dialog box.

Figure 1. The **Graphs** menu

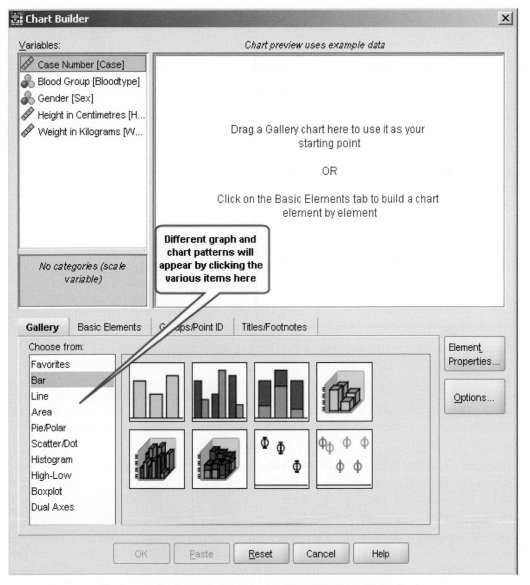

Figure 2. Options available in the **Chart Builder** dialog box

Readers who have used the graphic procedures in earlier releases of SPSS may be comforted to see that they are still available in the **Legacy Dialogs** submenu with a similar list available in the **Interactive** submenu (Figure 3). In this chapter we shall concentrate on using the **Chart Builder** as our principal means of drawing graphics.

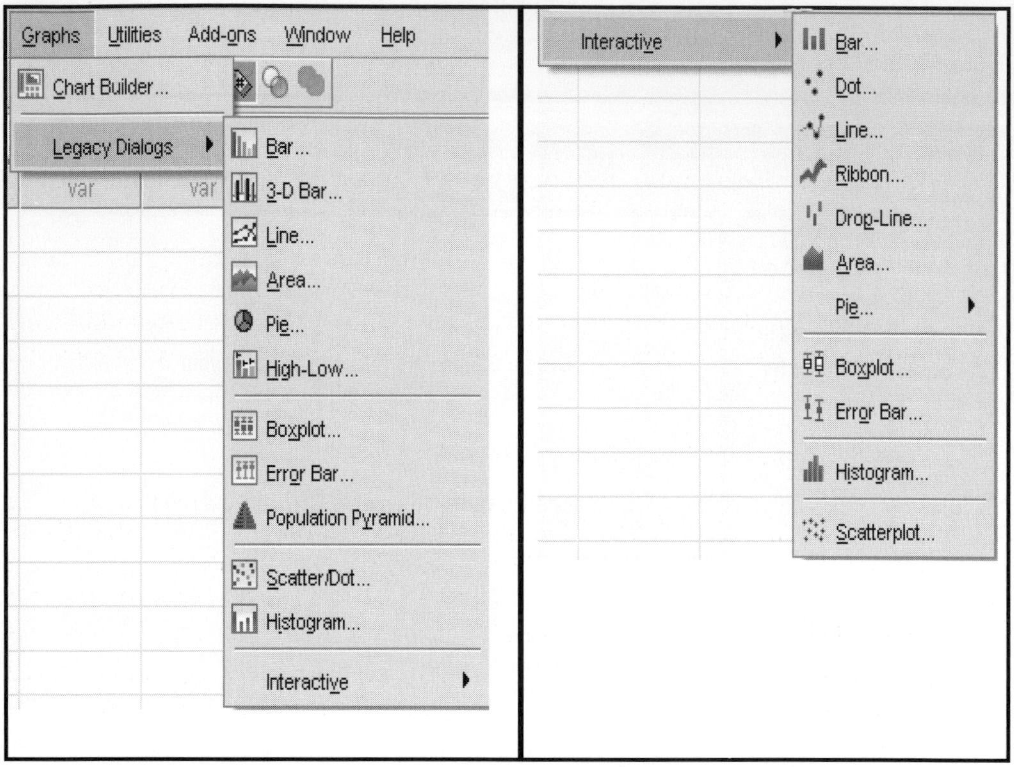

Figure 3. The list of graphical procedures in the **Legacy Dialogs** submenu (left panel) and the **Interactive** submenu (right panel)

For best results, the data set should be carefully prepared beforehand. It is easier to change variable names and labels in **Variable View** than afterwards at the editing stage of a chart.

If there are missing data, specify beforehand whether they should be included in the chart. They can be excluded from graphs by turning off the **Display groups defined by missing values** box in the **Options** dialog box. Once you are in a chart procedure, it is often easier to add a title within the **Title** option rather than at the editing stage after the chart has been produced.

When completing a dialog box for a graph, you can often leave some boxes unchecked. The acid test of whether enough information has been specified in a dialog box is whether the **OK** button is enabled: if it is not, more information is needed before the chart can be plotted.

5.1.2   Viewing a chart

A chart in **SPSS Viewer** may occasionally disappear from the screen. You can recall it by clicking its icon in the left-hand pane of SPSS Viewer. If you are working in another window, you can restore the chart by selecting it from the **Window** menu at the top of the screen.

You can make a chart narrower by clicking it and dragging the right-hand handle of the surrounding frame leftwards. If you wish to change the aspect ratio of **all** charts to make them narrower, select **Edit➔Options➔Charts** and amend the value in the **Chart Aspect Ratio** box. The default value is *1.25*, but if you change that to, say, *1,* graphs and charts will appear narrower.

Unwanted images use up memory. Bear in mind that images can always be recreated from saved data files. Save only those that you need at the moment.

Once a dialog box for a chart has been completed, the **command syntax** (see Chapter 15) can be saved to a file by clicking **Paste** from which the (unedited) graph can be generated at any time in the future. Graphs that have been edited can be stored as **chart templates** for future use. Chart templates are very useful for generating whole sets of similar graphs for analogous tables of data, such as those at different layers of a multi-way table.

5.1.3   Editing charts and saving templates

SPSS provides a special **Chart Editor** for graphic material which allows a wide range of changes to be made to a graph or chart, though proficiency takes practice. Enter the **Chart Editor** by double-clicking anywhere in the image. A single click will draw a single frame around the image. After double-clicking, the original image is shaded and a copy of it is shown in the **Chart Editor**.

The **Chart Editor** allows the user to change text, colours, type of graphic, title, axis ticks and labels, and other features. Many of these changes are made by double-clicking the item in the chart and completing dialogs.

For black-and-white printing, it is usually best to use the **Chart Editor** to remove the colours and replace them with patterns. Alternatively, the default setting for charts can be changed from cycling through colours to cycling through patterns. To do this

- Choose **Edit➔Options…** and select the **Charts** tab in the **Options** dialog box.
- Within the **Style Cycle Preference** selection panel, select **Cycle through patterns only**.
- Click **Fills…** and select whichever pattern you wish for **Simple Charts** and delete the empty pattern box in **Grouped Charts** by clicking the radio button for **Grouped Charts**, selecting the empty box pattern and clicking **Remove**. Click **Continue**.
- Click **Apply** and then **OK**.

This change will only apply for the current session if your computer is part of a networked system.

If it is likely that the same chart may be requested on subsequent occasions using different data, the user may wish to save the editing changes as a **Chart Template** so that the template can be applied to the later charts. Instructions about how to save and how to invoke a template will be given in Section 5.2.6.

5.2   BAR CHARTS

This section describes simple bar charts, clustered bar charts, panelled bar charts, 3-D charts, chart templates and how to edit bar charts.

5.2.1   Simple bar charts

A bar chart for comparing the means of groups of observers such as those of the drug experiment (see Table 1 in Section 2.1.4) is most easily obtained as follows:

- Choose **Graphs➔Chart Builder…**.
- A warning box (Figure 4) will appear asking the user to ensure that each variable has been defined in the **Measure** column of **Variable View** either as **Scale**, **Ordinal** or **Nominal**, and that each level of categorical variables has been assigned a label. **Variable View** by default assumes variables are **Scale** so it may be necessary to change categorical variables to **Nominal** either in **Variable View** or by clicking on **Define Variable Properties…** in the warning box. Click **OK** to continue.

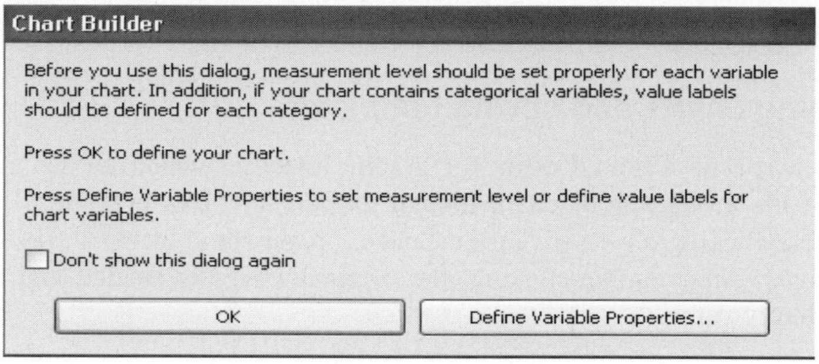

Figure 4. The warning box when **Chart Builder** is opened

- Ensure that the illustrations correspond to **Bar** by checking that **Bar** is highlighted in the **Choose from** panel (Figure 5). Click the first (top left) picture of simple bars to highlight it and then drag it to the **Chart preview** in the panel above. In addition, an **Element Properties** dialog box will also appear (Figure 6).
- Click the variable name *Score* to highlight it and then drag it to the **Y-Axis** box. Do likewise with *Experimental Condition* to the **X-Axis** box.
- To include the 95% Confidence Intervals, click the **Display error bars** box in the **Element Properties** dialog box (Figure 6) and then select the first radio button.
- To add a title, click **Titles/Footnotes** (middle of **Chart Builder** dialog box) and then click **Title 1** from the list of check-boxes which will appear in place of the gallery of graphics choices. A panel will appear in the **Element Properties** dialog box where a title such as *Means and 95% Confidence Intervals* can be typed in. Then click **Apply** followed by **Close**. Notice that **T1** would appear at the top of the preview (Figure 5) if a title is requested.
- Finally click **OK** in the **Chart Builder** dialog box to create the chart (Output 1).

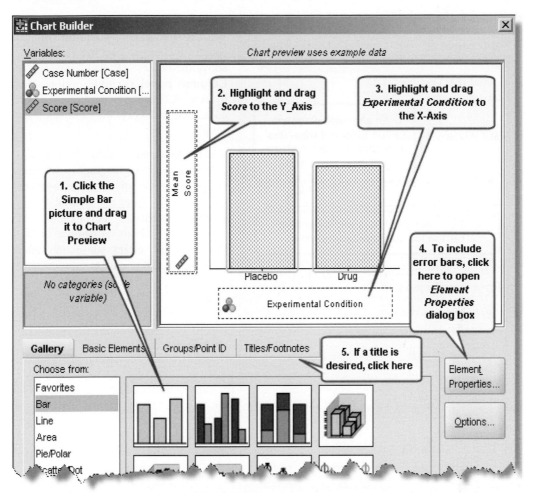

Figure 5. Part of the **Chart Builder** dialog box showing the simple bar chart preview

If the chart is to be printed in black and white, it is best to use the **Chart Editor** to change the colours of the graph to shades of grey. In fact, we have found it most effective to change the fill colour to white and mark the bars with distinguishing fill patterns. Alternatively changing the default **Chart** options to **Cycle through patterns only** as described in Section 5.1.3 renders editing unnecessary.

A simple bar chart shows only a single category variable, in this case the Experimental Condition under which the participants in the study performed. Additional category variables can be included either by using the options in **Groups/Point ID** in Figure 5 (select **Rows** panel variable or **Columns** panel variable and then transfer the appropriate variable name into the box which will appear on the right of the bar chart in the **Chart** preview) or by opting for Clustered bar charts as described in the next subsection by clicking on the second figure in the **Chart Builder** dialog box (Figure 5).

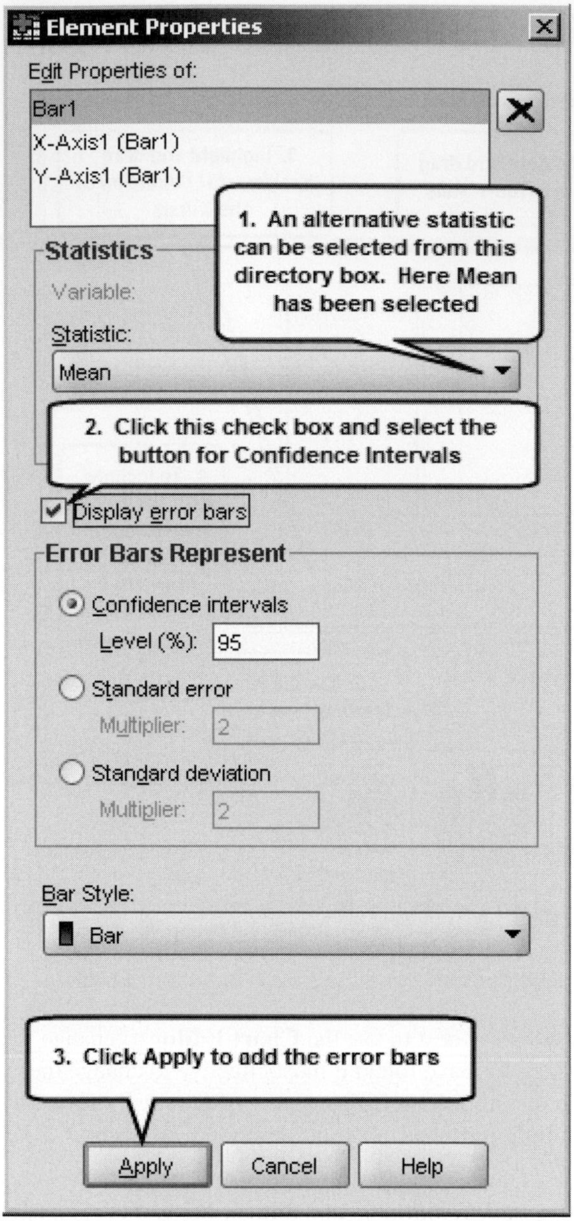

Element Properties   ✕

Edit Properties of:

Bar1   ✕
X-Axis1 (Bar1)
Y-Axis1 (Bar1)

> 1. An alternative statistic can be selected from this directory box. Here Mean has been selected

┌─Statistics─────────
Variable:

Statistic:

Mean   ▼

> 2. Click this check box and select the button for Confidence Intervals

☑ Display error bars

┌─Error Bars Represent─────────
◉ Confidence intervals
   Level (%): 95

○ Standard error
   Multiplier: 2

○ Standard deviation
   Multiplier: 2

Bar Style:

■ Bar   ▼

> 3. Click Apply to add the error bars

[Apply]   [Cancel]   [Help]

The **Rows panel variable** option enables the user to plot bar charts one-above-the-other (Rows) and the **Columns panel variable** option side-by-side (Columns) when there is an additional category variable such as sex.

When **Clustered** is used, the bars are clustered in a single graphic whereas the **panel** facility displays the levels of the second category variable in separate graphics. An example of panelled bar charts is shown in the **Panelled bar chart** subsection after the **Clustered bar charts** subsection.

Figure 6. The **Element Properties** dialog box for altering (if desired) the statistic to be used for the bars and for selecting (if desired) error bars

Means and 95% Confidence Intervals

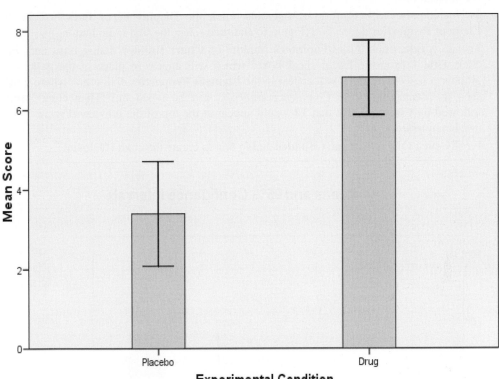

Output 1. A simple bar chart and optional 95% confidence intervals with *Experimental Condition* as the category variable

5.2.2 Clustered bar charts

A **clustered bar chart** shows two category variables in the same graphic as explained in the previous subsection. Suppose in addition to the *Experimental Condition* variable, we also knew the *Gender* of the participants. Then a clustered bar chart could be plotted with *Experimental Condition* as the first category variable subdivided according to the second category variable *Gender*. This second variable defines the **clusters**. Output 2 shows a clustered bar chart summarising the results of the drug experiment. On the horizontal axis, as before, is the independent variable *Experimental Condition*. In addition, the variable *Gender* has been used to cluster the data under the separate *Placebo* and *Drug* conditions.

To obtain such a clustered bar graph, open **Chart Builder** (see Section 5.2.1) and then:

- Ensure that the illustrations correspond to **Bar** by checking that **Bar** is highlighted in the **Choose from** panel. Click the second picture of Clustered Bar to highlight it and then drag it to the **Chart preview** in the panel above. In addition, an **Element Properties** dialog box will also appear.

- Click the variable name *Score* to highlight it and then drag it to the **Y-Axis** box. Do likewise with *Experimental Condition* to the **X-Axis** box and with *Gender* to the **Cluster: set pattern** box.
- To include the 95% Confidence Intervals, click the **Display error bars** box in the **Element Properties** dialog box (Figure 6) and then select the first radio button.
- To add a title, click **Titles/Footnotes** (middle of **Chart Builder** dialog box) and then click **Title 1** from the list of check-boxes which will appear in place of the gallery of graphics choices. A panel will appear in the **Element Properties** dialog box where a title such as *Means and 95% Confidence Intervals* can be typed in. Then click **Apply** followed by **Close**. Notice that **T1** would appear at the top of the preview (Figure 5) if a title is requested.
- Finally click **OK** in the **Chart Builder** dialog box to create the chart (Output 2).

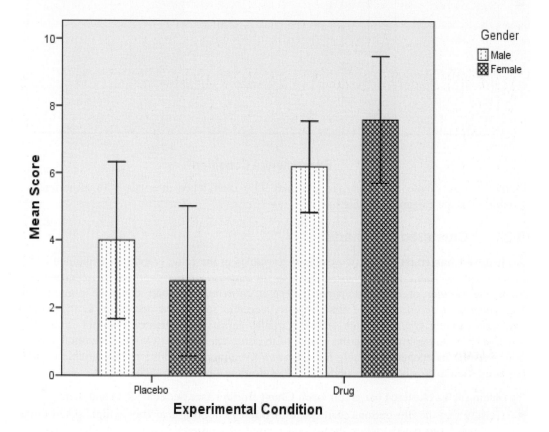

Output 2. A clustered bar chart and optional 95% confidence intervals with *Experimental Condition* as the category variable and *Gender* as the cluster variable

5.2.3   Panelled bar charts

Yet another way of including a second or third independent variable in bar charts is to panel them either by rows or by columns. For example, the data used in Chapter 8 investigating the effects upon simulated driving performance of two new anti-hay fever drugs when male and female drivers are either alert or tired could be graphically depicted as shown in Output 3. To obtain a panelled bar chart, open **Chart Builder** (see Section 5.2.1) and then:

* Ensure that the illustrations correspond to **Bar** by checking that **Bar** is highlighted in the **Choose from** panel. Click the second picture of Clustered Bar to highlight it and then drag it to the **Chart preview** in the panel above. In addition, an **Element Properties** dialog box will also appear.

* Click the variable name *Driving Performance* to highlight it and then drag it to the **Y-Axis** box. Do likewise with *Alertness* to the **X-Axis** box and with *Gender* to the **Cluster: set pattern** box.

* Click **Groups/Point ID** in the middle of the **Chart Builder** dialog box and then click the **Columns panel variable** box. This will result in another box labelled **Panel** appearing in the **Chart preview** panel. Click *Drug* to highlight it and then drag it to the **Panel** box.

* To include the 95% Confidence Intervals, click the **Display error bars** box in the **Element Properties** dialog box (Figure 6) and then select the first radio button.

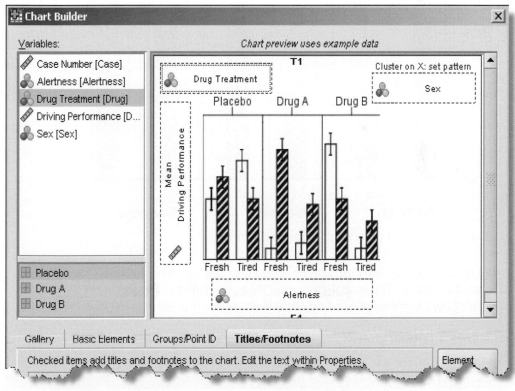

Figure 7. The **Chart preview** panel for the panelled clustered bar chart shown in Output 3 with the variable names transferred to the appropriate panels

- To add a title, click **Titles/Footnotes** (middle of **Chart Builder** dialog box) and then click **Title 1**. A panel will appear in the **Element Properties** dialog box where a title such as *Means and 95% Confidence Intervals* can be typed in. Then click **Apply** followed by **Close**. Notice that **T1** appears at the top of the preview (Figure 7).
- Finally click **OK** in the **Chart Builder** dialog box to create the chart (Output 3).

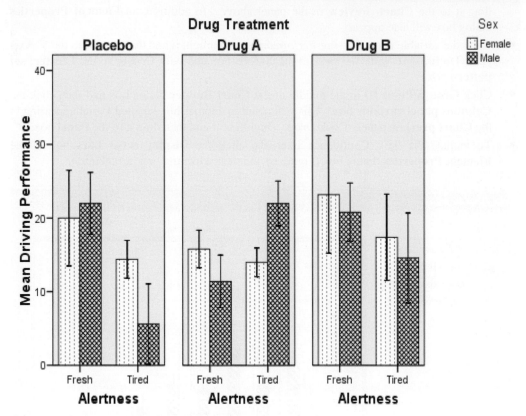

Output 3. A clustered bar chart divided into column panels

Note that simple bar charts can also be panelled so that this option could be used instead of a clustered bar chart. For example, we could have presented the data in Output 2 as simple bar charts for the *Experimental Condition* with *Males* in one row and *Females* in another row.

5.2.4   3-D charts

The **Chart Builder** can also be used to draw more exotic charts such as three-dimensional ones. As an example, a 3-D chart of *Height* against *Blood Group* and *Gender* can be drawn by selecting the image of a Simple 3-D Bar (first in second row) and filling in the variable names as shown in Figure 8. The output is shown in Output 4.

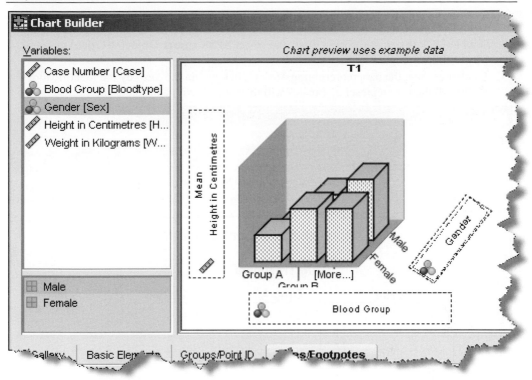

Figure 8. The upper part of the **Chart Builder** dialog box showing the selection of variables for a 3-D bar chart

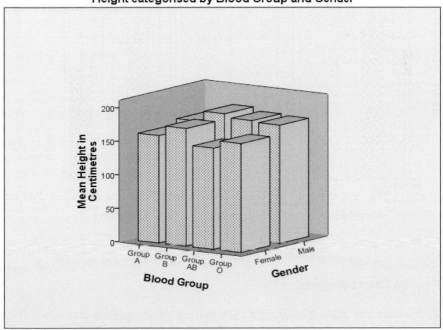

Output 4. The 3-D bar chart of *Height* categorised by *Blood Group* and *Gender*

5.2.5   Editing a bar chart

- Double-click the chart (or right click and select **SPSS Chart Object➔Open**) to open the **Chart Editor** (Figure 9).
- To change, say, the bars representing *Males*, click within the *Sex* key the identification for Male. All the bars representing males will then appear with a purple frame.

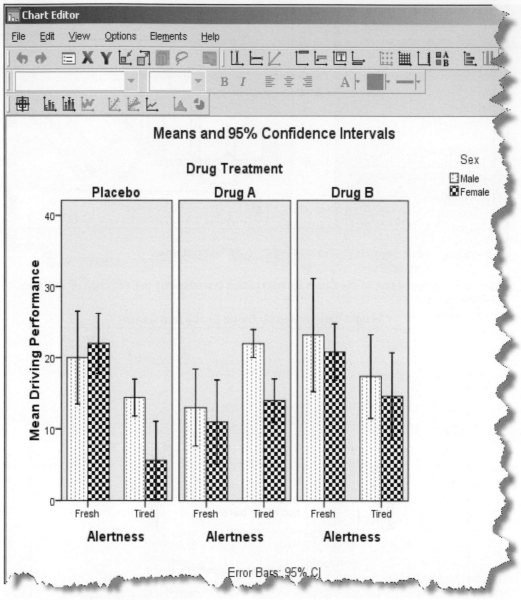

Figure 9. The **Chart Editor** window

- Double-click any of the bars or right click to open the **Properties** dialog box (Figure 10). Note that within the **Bar Options**, it is possible to change the width of the bars and the size of the gaps between clusters by moving the sliders or changing the numbers in the **%** boxes.

- To change the colour and fill of the bars, click the **Fill & Border** tab to open a dialog box for selecting fill colours, border colours and fill patterns.
- To change the fill colour, click the **Fill** box and then select a colour from the right-hand palette of colours, white and black.
- To change the fill pattern, click the **Pattern** box and select a fill.
- Click **Apply** to make these changes in the chart without leaving the editor.
- The variable bars can be rearranged by clicking the **Variables** tab, selecting the variable to be moved, pressing the right-hand mouse button, and then selecting the move to be made. For example, you can see what the chart would look like if the clustering was done by *Experimental Condition* rather than by *Gender*.
- Other changes can also be made, such as alterations to the axis labels and the bar identification key.

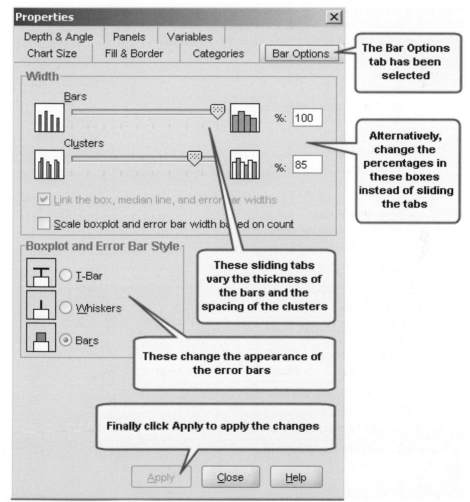

Figure 10. The **Properties** dialog box for **Bar Options** showing the various editing options for features of a graphic

5.2.6   Chart templates

If it is desired to apply these editing changes to future bar chart requests, a lot of time can be saved by saving the final format as a **Chart Template** and then invoking this template each time a similar bar chart is requested.

- Whilst still in **Chart Editor**, select **File→Save Chart Template…** to open the **Save Chart Template** dialog box (Figure 11).
- Click the **All settings** check box and type a description of the template in the panel at the foot of the dialog box e.g. *Panelled clustered bar chart with error bars*. Click **Continue**.
- The **Save Template** dialog box will appear. Select a suitable folder and file name (e.g. *Panelled clustered bar chart*) for the template and click **Save**. For networked computers it may be necessary to store the file on portable memory (e.g. a memory stick) in order to have it available on a later occasion.
- Close the **Chart Editor** to return the chart to **Output1 – SPSS Viewer**.

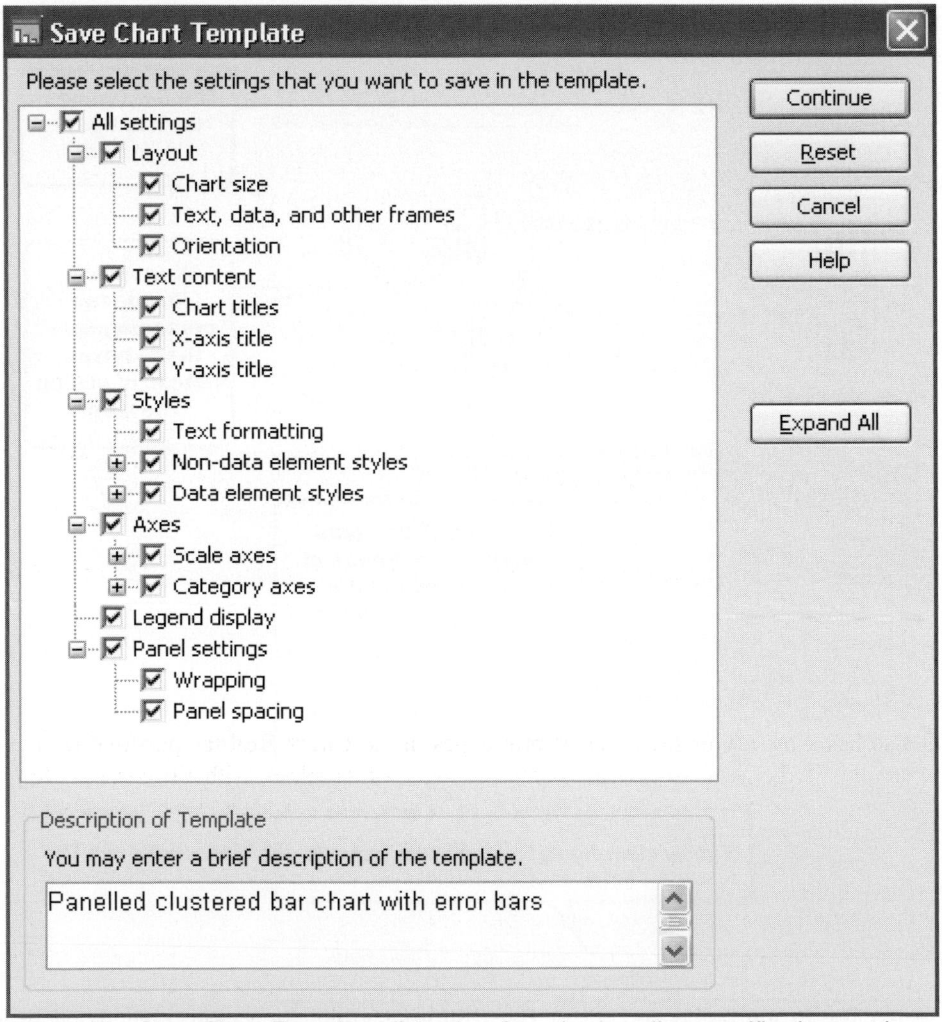

Figure 11. The **Save Chart Template** dialog box for selecting all or specific chart settings

Invoking a chart template

There are three ways of invoking a previously saved chart template. The first is to install it as the default template within the **Charts** section of the **Options** (the last item in the **Edit** drop-down menu) dialog box, the second within the **Chart Builder** dialog box, and the third within the **Chart Editor** window.

To apply our saved chart template for another panelled clustered bar chart (e.g. for a new data set), we will illustrate the second way within the **Chart Builder** dialog box. To obtain a panelled bar chart, open **Chart Builder** (see Section 5.2.1) and then:

• Click the **Options** box on the right-hand side of the **Chart Builder** dialog box to open the **Options** dialog box.
• Click the box labelled **Add…** to open the **Find Template Files** option box.
• Locate the appropriate file and click **Open** to return to the **Options** dialog box. The file name of the template file will now appear in the panel (Figure 12).
• Click **OK** to draw the panelled clustered bar chart.

The new chart will appear with the changes made to the original chart incorporated in it.

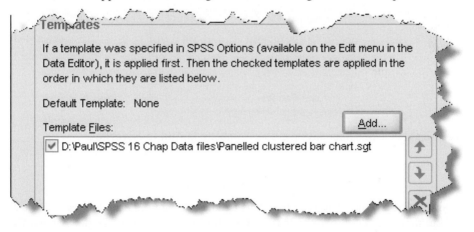

Figure 12. The **Template** section of the **Clustered Bar Chart: Options** dialog box showing the template name

Chart prototypes (SPSS calls them 'Favorites')

SPSS also has a facility of saving chart prototypes in the **Chart Builder** portfolio of images. For example, if the user wants to create a number of graphics with the same style from different data sets, then the original graphic acts as a prototype (a 'favorite') and can be invoked from the **Favorites** panel in the **Chart Builder** dialog box.

To save a prototype, proceed as follows:
• Whilst still in the **Chart Builder** dialog box after completing all the details such as including 95% confidence intervals and specifying a title, move the cursor to anywhere in the Chart preview panel and right click to open a small choice panel (Figure 13).
• Select **Add to Favorites…** and then enter a file name for the template (SPSS refers to it as prototype) such as Clustered panelled bar chart and click **OK**. The template will then

appear in a panel in the **Chart Builder** dialog box with **Favorites** highlighted in the **Choose from** directory.

Undo Apply Properties	Ctrl-Z
Redo	Ctrl-Y
Properties Window	Ctrl-T
Cut	Ctrl-X
Copy	Ctrl-C
Paste	Ctrl-V
Delete	Delete
Add Grouping Zone...	
Edit Grouping Zone...	
Delete Grouping Zone	
Transpose Axes	
Add to Favorites...	
Clear Canvas	

Figure 13. The choice panel for saving a chart template to **Add to Favorites...**

*Using a favorite in **Chart Builder** as a prototype for a graphic*

To apply our saved panelled clustered bar chart template to another data set, we will illustrate the use of our newly created **Favorite** in the **Chart Builder** dialog box. To do so, open **Chart Builder** (see Section 5.2.1) and then:

- Ensure that the illustrations correspond to **Favorites** by checking that **Favorites** is highlighted in the **Choose from** panel. Click the picture of the panelled clustered bar graphic and then drag it to the **Chart preview** in the panel above. In addition, an **Element Properties** dialog box will also appear.
- The various variable names must then be transferred but it is not necessary to specify either the title or the 95% confidence intervals.
- Click **OK** to draw the panelled clustered bar chart using the new data set.

The new chart will appear with the changes made to the original chart incorporated in it.

SPSS offers helpful tutorials on editing charts. You can access these by clicking **Help→Tutorial** and then double-clicking each of **Tutorials→Creating and Editing Charts**.

The usual buttons in the right-hand bottom corner of each page of the tutorial enable the user to see the index (magnifier), the table of

contents (house) and to navigate forward and backward through the tutorial (right and left arrows).

5.3   ERROR BAR CHARTS

An alternative to a bar graph is an **Error Bar chart**, in which the mean of the scores in a particular category is represented by a single point and the spread (confidence interval for the mean, multiples of the standard deviation or multiples of the standard error of the mean – the user can choose between these) is represented by a vertical line (T-bar or whiskers) passing through the point. Output 5 is a clustered error bar chart summarising the results of the drug experiment.

To obtain an error bar chart, open **Chart Builder** (see Section 5.2.1) and then:

- Ensure that the illustrations correspond to **Bar** by checking that **Bar** is highlighted in the **Choose from** panel. Click the fourth picture of the second row (clustered error bars shown in green and blue – see Figure 2) to highlight it and then drag it to the **Chart preview** in the panel above. In addition, an **Element Properties** dialog box will also appear.

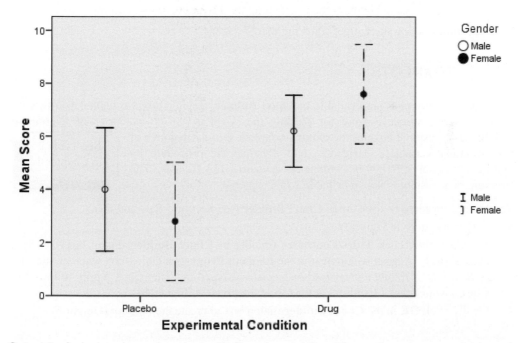

Output 5. A clustered error bar chart with *Experimental Condition* as the category variable and *Gender* as the cluster variable

- Click the variable name *Score* to highlight it and then drag it to the **Y-Axis** box. Do likewise with *Experimental Condition* to the **X-Axis** box and with *Gender* to the **Cluster: Set symbol** box.

- **95% Confidence Intervals** is the default setting appearing in the **Element Properties** dialog box. The percentage can be changed or the user can select Standard error or Standard deviation (together with the desired multiplier). If a change from the default is selected, it will be necessary to click **Apply**.

- To add a title, click **Titles/Footnotes** (middle of **Chart Builder** dialog box) and then click **Title 1**. A panel will appear in the **Element Properties** dialog box where a title such as *Means and 95% Confidence Intervals* can be typed in. Then click **Apply** followed by **Close**. Notice that **T1** would appear at the top of the preview if a title is requested.

- Finally click **OK** in the **Chart Builder** dialog box to create the chart (Output 5).

The symbols used for the means and the form of the lines used for the error bars can be changed by double-clicking anywhere within the graphic to open the **Chart Editor**. Double-clicking on the appropriate symbol or line in the *Gender* key will open the corresponding **Properties** dialog box where changes can be made.

You will notice that in Output 5, there are no lines linking the error bars. This is entirely appropriate, since the bars represent qualitatively distinct categories. In other circumstances, however, as when the categories are ordered, it may be desirable to join up the points (when there are more than two) with interpolation lines. This is easily achieved in the **Chart Editor** by clicking the means to highlight them, selecting the **Elements** drop-down menu and clicking

Interpolation line (or alternatively clicking the 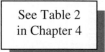 icon).

5.4   BOXPLOTS

Three types of boxplots are available in **Chart Builder**, a single boxplot (called 1-D Boxplot in the gallery), simple boxplot for plotting the boxplots across categories of a grouping variable and clustered boxplot for plotting boxplots across categories of two grouping variables. Here we shall illustrate the procedure by plotting a boxplot of *Height in Centimetres* categorised by *Gender*. The structure of a boxplot is shown in Table 2 in Chapter 4.

> See Table 2 in Chapter 4

To obtain a clustered boxplot, open **Chart Builder** (see Section 5.2.1) and then:

- Follow the steps in Figure 14.

- To add a title, click **Titles/Footnotes** (middle of **Chart Builder** dialog box) and then click **Title 1**. A panel will appear in the **Element Properties** dialog box where a title such as *Boxplots of Height categorised by Sex* can be typed in. Then click **Apply** followed by **Close**. Notice that **T1** appears at the top of the preview (Figure 14).

- Finally click **OK** in the **Chart Builder** dialog box to create the boxplot (Output 6).

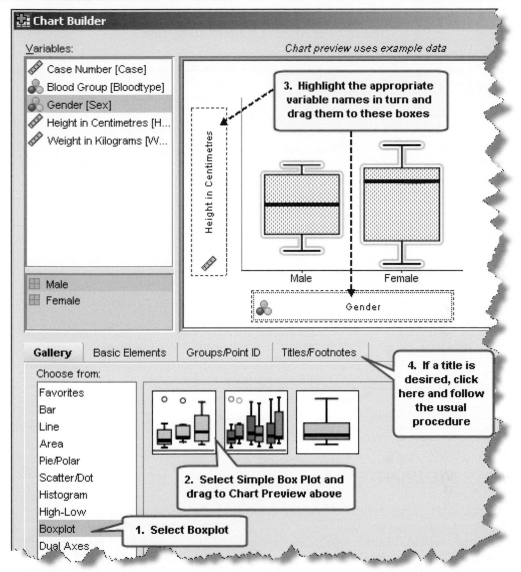

Figure 14. The completed **Chart Builder** dialog box for plotting a boxplot of *Height* for each *Sex*

Notice in the output that there is one case identified as an outlier with o. Any extreme case would have been identified with *.

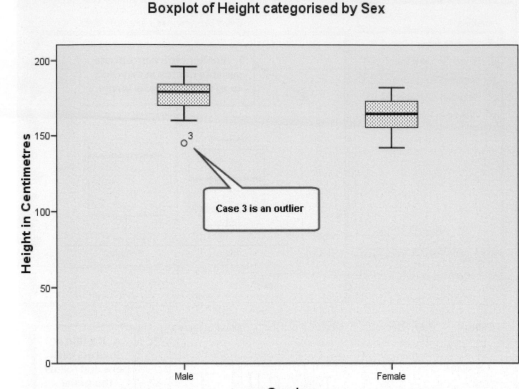

Output 6. Boxplots of *Height* categorised by *Sex*

5.5   PIE CHARTS

The **pie chart** is an alternative to a bar graph that provides a picturesque display of the frequency distribution of a qualitative variable. It is a particularly valuable kind of graph for displaying the relative frequencies of the same set of categories over time or for bringing out the varying compositions of two things. Pie charts can be panelled in a similar way to bar charts as previously described in Section 5.2.

See Section 5.2

To illustrate the production of a pie chart, we shall use the data set of blood group, gender, height and weight.

To draw a pie chart of the categories within *Blood Group*, open **Chart Builder** (see Section 5.2.1) and then:

* Ensure that the illustration corresponds to **Pie/Polar** by checking that **Pie/Polar** is highlighted in the **Choose from** panel. Click the picture and drag it to the Chart preview in the panel above. In addition, an **Element Properties** dialog box will also appear.
* Click the variable name *Blood Group* to highlight it and drag it to the **Slice by?** box. The **Angle Variable?** box will then change to **Count**.

- To change **Count** to **Percentages**, click the arrow to the right of *Count* in the **Statistic** panel within **Element Properties**, select **Percentage (?)** and then click **Apply**.
- To add a title, click **Titles/Footnotes** (middle of **Chart Builder** dialog box) and then click **Title 1**. A panel will appear in the **Element Properties** dialog box where a title such as *Blood Group Percentages* can be typed in. Then click **Apply** followed by **Close**. Notice that **T1** would appear at the top of the preview if a title is requested.
- Finally click **OK** in the **Chart Builder** dialog box to create the chart (Output 7).

Blood Group Percentages

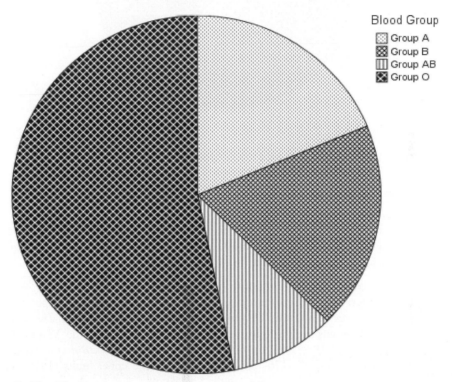

Output 7. The **Pie Chart** of the distribution of *Blood Group*

The pie chart in Output 7 can be edited (see Section 5.1.3) to change the fill patterns, to rotate the slices if it is desired to bring a particular slice to the top, to insert labels and to 'explode' a slice as shown in Output 8. If desired, the changes can be stored as a **Chart Template** and then this template can be invoked for future pie chart drawings for similar data.

See Section 5.1.3

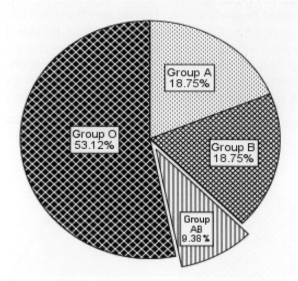

Output 8. The edited **Pie Chart** with slice labels, percentages and one slice exploded

5.6   LINE GRAPHS

Suppose that, in our analysis of the medical data, we want to produce a **line graph** of mean weight against height for both sexes. Line graphs can be drawn with just one line or more than one line in the graph; they can also be panelled as we have seen for bar and pie charts.

Along the horizontal axis, the total range of heights is divided into fixed intervals. Above the mid point of each interval is plotted for each sex the mean of the weights of people whose heights fall within the interval and adjacent points are joined by straight lines. The total range of heights of the participants is split into, say, five intervals by using the **Visual Binning** procedure (see Section 4.4.3) to create a new ordinal variable *HeightBin* consisting of the intervals <155, 156-165, 166-175, 176-185, >185. Specify the upper limits (155, 165, 175, 185, 210) in the **Value** cells and the intervals in the **Label** cells.

To plot a line graph of mean weight against height bins, open **Chart Builder** (see Section 5.2.1) and then:

- Ensure that the illustrations correspond to **Line** by checking that **Line** is highlighted in the **Choose from** panel (Figure 2). Click the second picture (Multiple Line) and drag it to the **Chart preview** in the panel above. In addition, an **Element Properties** dialog box will also appear.

- Click the variable name *Weight in kilograms* to highlight it and then drag it to the **Y-Axis** box. Do likewise with *Height in centimetres (binned)* to the **X-Axis** box and with *Gender* to the **Set pattern** box (Figure 15).

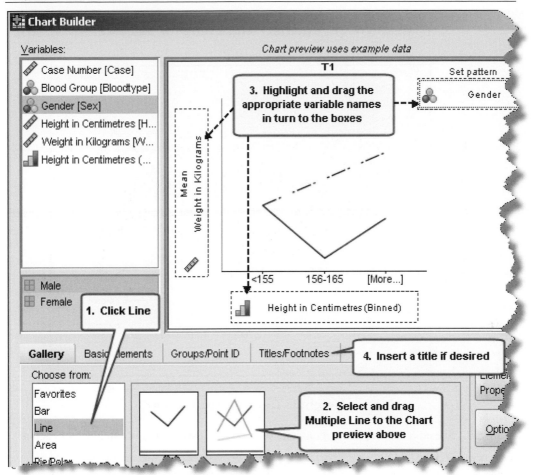

Figure 15. The upper part of the **Chart Builder** dialog box showing the transferred variable names for plotting the multiple line graph

- To add a title, click **Titles/Footnotes** (middle of **Chart Builder** dialog box) and then click **Title 1**. A panel will appear in the **Element Properties** dialog box where a title such as *Mean Weight against Height bins for each Sex* can be typed in. Then click **Apply** followed by **Close**. Notice that **T1** appears at the top of the preview (Figure 15).
- Finally click **OK** in the **Chart Builder** dialog box to create the chart (Output 9).

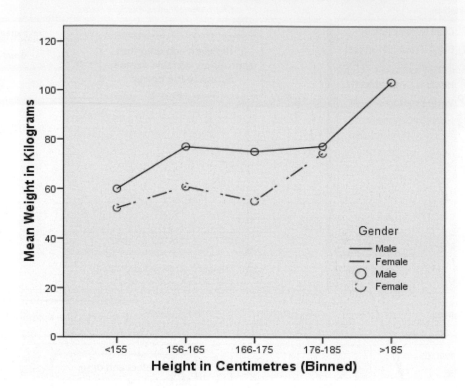

Output 9. The edited multiple line graph of mean *Weight* against *Height* category for each sex

The edited line graph is shown in Output 9. The editing operations included the following:

1. Re-setting the y-scale with a minimum of 0. This is achieved by double-clicking the graph to open the **Chart Editor**, double-clicking on the y-scale values, clicking the **Scale** tab within the **Properties** dialog box, clicking off the **Minimum** auto box, entering 0 in the **Custom** box alongside, and finally clicking **Apply**.

2. Inserting circles for the means by clicking on the **Show Line Markers** icon. Initially unfilled circles will appear: these can be made solid by clicking on them and changing **Fill** to black in the **Properties** box.

3. Moving the **Gender** legend to inside the grey panel of the graph by clicking on the legend, reducing the size of its box and dragging it to the desired position.

If preferred, the lines for males and females could have been plotted in separate line graphs side-by-side or one-above-the-other by selecting the single line graph in the **Chart Builder** dialog box, transferring the y-axis and x-axis variable names as before, clicking **Groups/Point ID**, clicking the check box for **Rows panel variable** or **Columns panel variable**, transferring *Gender* to the new box labelled **Panel** and finally clicking **OK**.

These changes can be saved as a **Chart Template** – see Section 5.2.6.

5.7   SCATTERPLOTS AND DOT PLOTS

Scatterplots

Another diagram for displaying the relationship between two variables is the **scatterplot,** in which the scales of values of the two variables (such as height and weight) are set out on the horizontal and vertical axis and each person is represented as a point whose co-ordinates are his or her particular height and weight. As with the other charts, scatterplots can also be panelled. A scatterplot should always be plotted and examined before a correlation coefficient is calculated (Chapter 11) or a regression analysis is carried out (Chapter 12).

See Chaps. 11 & 12

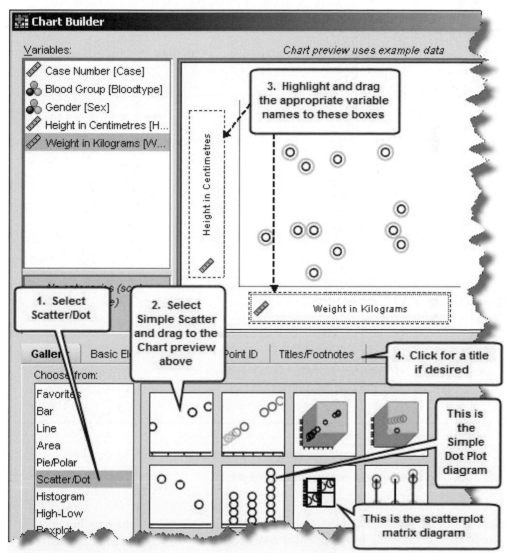

Figure 16. The **Chart Builder** dialog box with **Scatterplot/Dot** highlighted to show the various scatterplots options and with a simple scatterplot of *Height* against *Weight* prepared in the preview panel

To plot a simple scatterplot, open **Chart Builder** (see Section 5.2.1) and then:

- Ensure that the illustrations correspond to **Scatter/Dot** by checking that **Scatter/Dot** is highlighted in the **Choose from** panel (Figure 2). Click the first picture of a Simple Scatter to highlight it and then drag it to the **Chart preview** in the panel above (Figure 16). In addition, an **Element Properties** dialog box will also appear.

- Click the variable name *Height in Centimetres* to highlight it and then drag it to the **Y-Axis** box. Do likewise with *Weight in Kilograms* to the **X-Axis** box.

- To add a title, click **Titles/Footnotes** (middle of **Chart Builder** dialog box) and then click **Title 1**. A panel will appear in the **Element Properties** dialog box where a title such as *Scatterplot of Height against Weight* can be typed in. Then click **Apply** followed by **Close**. Notice that **T1** would appear at the top of the preview if a title is requested.

- Finally click **OK** in the **Chart Builder** dialog box to create the chart (Output 10).

Scatterplot of Height against Weight

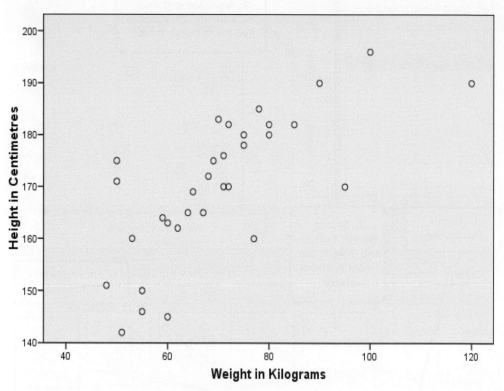

Output 10. The Scatterplot of *Height* against *Weight*

Inspection of the scatterplot shows that the line graph in Output 9, although bringing out a clear positive relationship between height and weight when average weights are considered, masks considerable individual variability. The heights of people of around 50 kg in weight range from just over 140 cm to 175 cm in height.

Dot plots

A **dot plot** plots one variable on a scale axis. The cases are represented by points that are stacked at the variable values. Thus weights for each sex could be plotted in charts side-by-side by choosing **Chart Builder** (see Section 5.2.1) and then:

- Ensure that the illustrations correspond to **Scatter/Dot** by checking that **Scatter/Dot** is highlighted in the **Choose from** panel. Click the second picture in the second row of a Simple Dot Plot to highlight it and then drag it to the **Chart preview** in the panel above (Figure 17). In addition, an **Element Properties** dialog box will also appear.

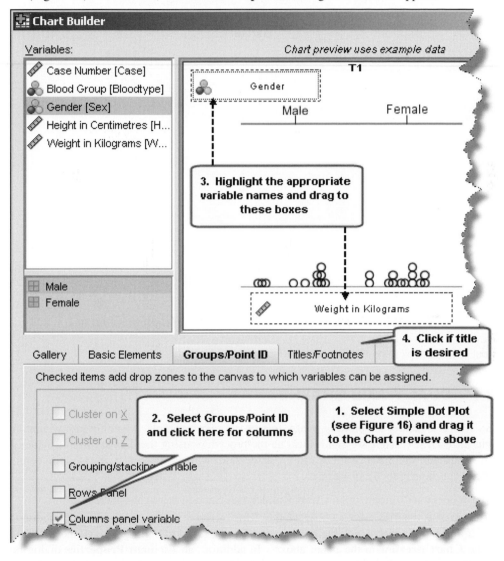

Figure 17. The upper part of the **Chart Builder** dialog box with **Groups/Point ID** highlighted to show the panel options for a simple dot plot of *Weight* for each sex prepared in the preview panel

- Follow the steps in Figure 17.
- To add a title, click **Titles/Footnotes** (middle of **Chart Builder** dialog box) and then click **Title 1**. A panel will appear in the **Element Properties** dialog box where a title such as *Dot plot of Weight for each Sex* can be typed in. Then click **Apply** followed by **Close**.
- Finally click **OK** in the **Chart Builder** dialog box to create the chart (Output 11).

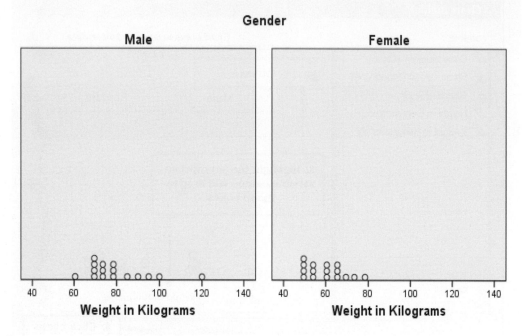

Output 11. A dot plot showing the weights of males and females

5.8   DUAL Y-AXIS GRAPHS

SPSS 16 has a facility for plotting dual y-axis charts. For example, we could plot weight and height for each sex. Here we shall illustrate the procedure using the data set from Chapter 15 to see whether competence in Latin is associated with competence in modern foreign languages such as French and German.

To plot a dual y-axis graph, open **Chart Builder** (see Section 5.2.1) and then:

- Ensure that the illustrations correspond to **Line** by checking that **Line** is highlighted in the **Choose from** panel. Click the first picture (Simple Line) to highlight it and then drag it to the **Chart preview** in the panel above. In addition, an **Element Properties** dialog box will also appear.
- Click **Basic Elements** in the middle of **Chart Builder** and then click the dual y-axis picture (the one with Y1 and Y2) to highlight it. Drag it to the **Chart preview** above (Figure 18).

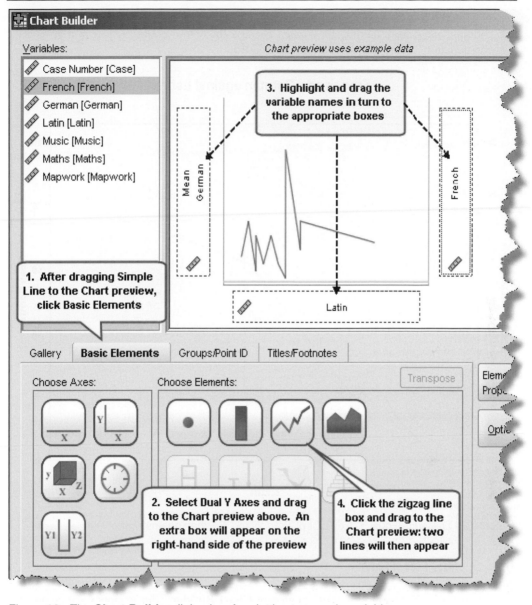

Figure 18. The **Chart Builder** dialog box for plotting two y-axis variables

- Follow the steps in Figure 18.
- To add a title, click **Titles/Footnotes** (middle of **Chart Builder** dialog box) and then click **Title 1**. A panel will appear in the **Element Properties** dialog box where a title such as *French and German against Latin* can be typed in. Then click **Apply** followed by **Close**. Notice that **T1** would appear at the top of the preview if a title is requested.

- Click **OK** to plot the graph (Output 12). The line for *German* has been edited to differentiate it from the line for *French* because the colour coding is lost in a grey-scale reproduction. Annotations have also been added.

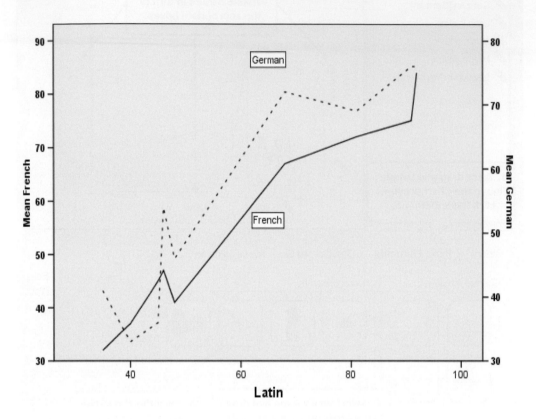

Output 12. The edited dual Y-Axis plot of *French* and *German* against *Latin*

5.9   HISTOGRAMS

Various types of histogram are easily plotted in **Chart Builder**. For example, we could plot the heights of males and females side-by-side. To plot a **Population Pyramid** (i.e. side-by-side histograms), open **Chart Builder** (see Section 5.2.1) and then:

- Follow the steps in Figure 19.
- To add a title, click **Titles/Footnotes** (middle of **Chart Builder** dialog box) and then click **Title 1**. A panel will appear in the **Element Properties** dialog box where a title such as *Histograms of height for each sex* can be typed in. Then click **Apply** followed by **Close**.
- Click **OK** to plot the histograms (Output13).

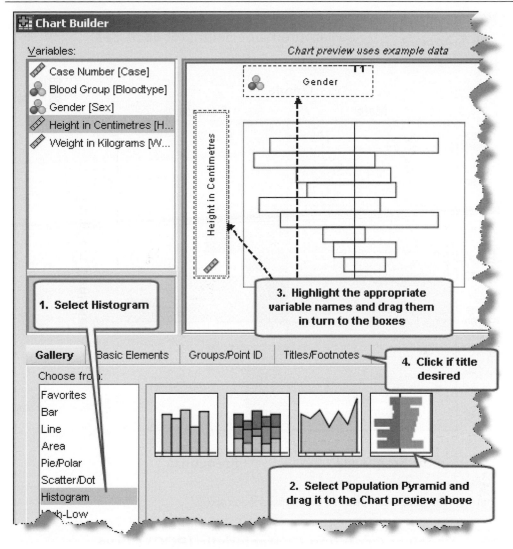

Figure 19. The upper part of the **Chart Builder** dialog box for drawing a population pyramid (side-by-side histograms) of height for each sex

Histograms of Height for each Sex

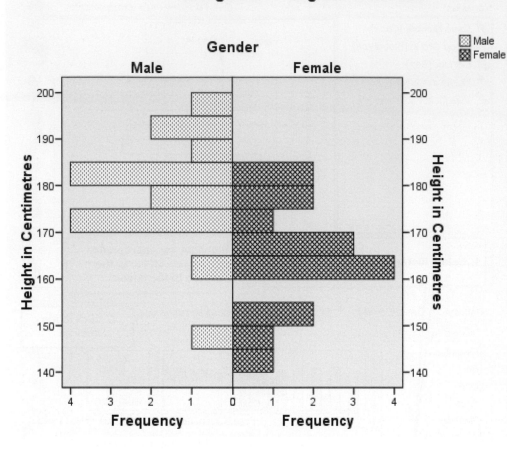

Output 13. The population pyramid of height for each sex

5.10   Receiver-Operating-Characteristic (ROC) Curve

The **ROC Curve** representation was originally developed for the detection of radio signals in the presence of noise during the Second World War. The technique has been adopted in psychophysics for detecting weak signals and in medical research for evaluating tests and drugs.

Its usefulness arises from the difficulty of determining sensory thresholds independently of how scrupulously or casually the observer is behaving. Some people will only acknowledge that they perceived (e.g. saw or heard) a signal when they are absolutely certain that they have done so whereas other people will be content to acknowledge they have done so if they felt there was the vaguest possibility that they perceived a signal. How can one determine an observer's threshold independently of their response criterion? The solution is to use an experimental paradigm in which signals are presented for some of the trials but not for all of them so that a measure of **hit rate** (saying 'yes' when there really was a signal) and of **false**

alarm rate (saying 'yes' when there was not a signal) can be determined. These rates can then be plotted on a graph of hits against false alarms. An ideal observer would be plotted in the top left-hand corner of this graph with a hit rate of 100% and a false alarm rate of 0% whereas a completely random responder with equal rates of hits and false alarms would have a point somewhere along the diagonal from the bottom left-hand corner to the top right-hand corner.

Underlying these measures are probability distributions that a given perceptual effect will be caused by noise (i.e. all other stimuli except the signal presented by the experimenter) and by the signal superimposed on the noise (i.e. the signal occurring together with the background conditions of noise). The greater the separation between the peaks of these distributions, the greater the observer's sensitivity. This separation is called d' (d-prime) whose formula will be given later. In brief, therefore, the ROC provides a means of teasing out someone's perceptual threshold independently of their response criterion (i.e. whether he/she is a scrupulous or casual responder).

Here we shall look at the hypothetical development of a test for detecting pathology of the retina (retinopathy). Ideally the test should identify those with retinopathy 100% of the time and those without retinopathy 100% of the time but in the real world there are likely to be patients with retinopathy who do not fail the test and persons without retinopathy who will fail the test. Thus the aim is to establish a cut-off point on the test scale where the clinician can be about 80% certain that the person tested has the condition (hit rate) and the false alarm rate (i.e. persons without the clinical condition failing the test) is below 20%.

Table 1. The contingency table for the type of observer and passing or failing the test			
Test Result	**Type of Observer**		
	Retinopathy	**No Retinopathy**	**Total**
Fail	A ('Hit')	B ('False Alarm')	A+B
Pass	C (False passed test)	D (True passed test)	C+D
Total	A+C	B+D	A+B+C+D

We define *sensitivity* as the probability of a failed test among patients with retinopathy and *specificity* as the probability of a passed test among those without retinopathy. If we collate frequencies in a 2 x 2 table (Table 1), then *sensitivity* = probability of a hit for retinopathy i.e. A/(A+C) and *specificity* = probability of a true passed test for persons with no retinopathy i.e. D/(B+D). Ideally we want high *sensitivity* and high *specificity* (i.e. low (1 – *specificity*)).

The SPSS ROC curve is a plot of *sensitivity* (hit rate) against *1 – specificity* (false alarm rate). High discrimination is represented by a curved line almost reaching into the top left-hand corner and zero discrimination by a diagonal line at 45° to the horizontal. As an example, suppose a new computer-based test of defective colour vision has been devised and is given to twenty patients with retinopathy and twenty persons without retinopathy. The aim is to find out whether the test can be used to discriminate these two categories of observers and if so, what cut-off point of errors should be adopted. The data are given in Table 2.

Table 2. Colour vision error scores for persons with and without retinopathy							
Retinopathy				**No Retinopathy**			
40	43	36	45	34	35	31	25
35	35	33	39	36	30	36	19
34	37	45	35	32	31	29	23
34	20	50	37	28	23	29	32
25	40	30	35	24	24	32	29

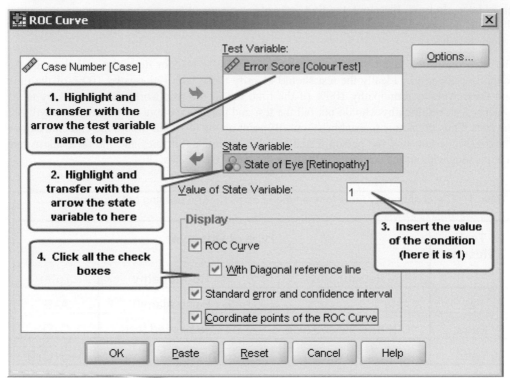

Figure 20. The completed **ROC Curve** dialog box

The data are entered into three variables in the **Data Editor**, a scale variable *Case*, a nominal variable *Retinopathy* (with variable label *State of Eye*, level 1 for Retinopathy and level 2 for No Retinopathy) and a scale variable *ColourTest* with variable label *Error Score*.

To plot the ROC Curve

• Choose **Analyze→ROC Curve...** to open the **ROC Curve** dialog box.

• Complete the dialog box as shown in Figure 20.

The first table in the output (Output 14) shows the **Case Processing Summary** – here we have 20 cases with retinopathy and 20 cases without retinopathy.

Case Processing Summary

State of Eve	Valid N (listwise)
Positive^a	20
Negative	20

Larger values of the test result variable(s) indicate stronger evidence for a positive actual state.

a. The positive actual state is Retinopathy.

Output 14. The **Case Processing Summary** table

The next output item is the **ROC Curve** (Output 15).

ROC Curve

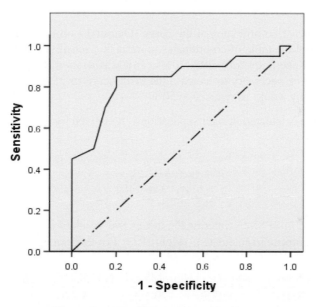

Diagonal segments are produced by ties.

Output 15. The **ROC Curve**

Output 16 is a table listing statistics relating to the area under the ROC Curve. **Area** is the probability that a randomly chosen retinopathy patient exceeds a randomly chosen person without retinopathy (here it is .838 i.e. **83.8%**) and **Asymptotic Sig.** is the probability that the test is better than guessing is less than .0005, i.e. is highly significant.

Area Under the Curve

Test Result Variable(s): Error Score

Area	Std. Error[a]	Asymptotic Sig.[b]	Asymptotic 95% Confidence Interval	
			Lower Bound	Upper Bound
.838	.067	.000	.707	.968

The test result variable(s): Error Score has at least one tie between the positive actual state group and the negative actual state group. Statistics may be biased.

a. Under the nonparametric assumption

b. Null hypothesis: true area = 0.5

Output 16. Statistics relating to the area under the **ROC Curve**

Finally there is a table of co-ordinates of the curve (Output 17 on next page). Notice that a cut-off value of 33.5 in the table of co-ordinates represents a sensitivity of 0.800 (80%) and a false alarm rate (1 − Specificity) of 0.200 (20%). If it was desired to restrict the false alarm rate to 10%, it would be necessary to increase the error score to 35.5 but then the sensitivity for detecting retinopathy would be reduced to 50%.

The statistic d′ is often calculated in such applications. It is given by the formula

$$d' = \frac{|\mu_2 - \mu_1|}{\sqrt{(\sigma_1^2 + \sigma_2^2)/2}}$$

and is easily computed in SPSS by entering the means and standard deviations into a new data file and then using **Compute** to calculate d′ (Figure 21). For this example, d′ = 1.24.

RetMean	RetSD	NormMean	NormSD	dPrime
36.400	6.809	29.100	4.778	1.241

Figure 21. The calculation of d′

The highest possible d′ (greatest sensitivity) is nearly 7 but typical values are up to 2.0: thus our value of 1.24 is typical.

Coordinates of the Curve

Test Result Variable(s): Error Score

Positive if Greater Than or Equal To[a]	Sensitivity	1 - Specificity
18.00	1.000	1.000
19.50	1.000	.950
21.50	.950	.950
23.50	.950	.850
24.50	.950	.750
26.50	.900	.700
28.50	.900	.650
29.50	.900	.500
30.50	.850	.450
31.50	.850	.350
32.50	.850	.200
33.50	.800	.200
34.50	.700	.150
35.50	.500	.100
36.50	.450	.000
38.00	.350	.000
39.50	.300	.000
41.50	.200	.000
44.00	.150	.000
47.50	.050	.000
51.00	.000	.000

The test result variable(s): Error Score has at least one tie between the positive actual state group and the negative actual state group.

a. The smallest cutoff value is the minimum observed test value minus 1, and the largest cutoff value is the maximum observed test value plus 1. All the other cutoff values are the averages of two consecutive ordered observed test values.

Output 17. The table of co-ordinates of the ROC Curve

Exercises

Exercise 6 *Charts and graphs,* and Exercise 7 *Recoding data; selecting cases; line graph* are available in www.psypress.com/spss-made-simple and click on Exercises.

CHAPTER 6

Comparing averages and frequencies: Two-sample and one-sample tests

6.1   Overview

6.2   The *t* tests

6.3   Effect size, power and the number of participants

6.4   Other tests for comparing averages

6.5   One-sample tests

6.1   OVERVIEW

In Chapter 1, five research scenarios were described (Section 1.4.1, Figure 3). In the first, the researcher has **two samples** of scores and wants to know whether the difference between their two means is significant. As an aid to choosing an appropriate test, we offered a flow chart (Figure 4 in Chapter 1), the important proviso being that the data must meet the requirements of the statistical model upon which the test is based. The first question in the flow chart concerned the number of groups or conditions. This chapter shows how to use SPSS to carry out the tests recommended by the chart when there are two samples of scores. (We shall also consider some one-sample tests.)

See Section 1.4.1

In Figure 1 in this chapter, we reproduce the flow chart for selecting a suitable test for differences between averages or (with nominal data) relative frequencies. The chart indicates whether a parametric test (e.g. a *t* test) or a nonparametric test (e.g. a chi-square test) is appropriate for the type of data in hand.

Table 1 identifies the appropriate SPSS menu items for the various two-sample tests. The left half of the table lists **parametric tests**, which make assumptions about population distributions and parameters. The right half of the table lists **non-parametric tests**, which make fewer assumptions. Each half of the table is subdivided according to whether the samples are independent or related. (Incidentally, in the context of the *t* test, SPSS uses the term **paired samples** rather than **related samples**.)

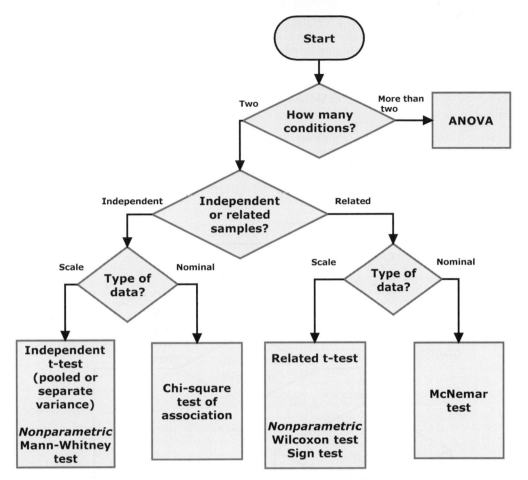

Figure 1. Flow chart showing the selection of a suitable test for differences between averages or frequencies

Table 1. Comparing the averages of two samples: The SPSS menus			
Assumptions			
Populations assumed to have normal distributions and equal variances		No specific assumptions about the population distributions	
Independent samples	Paired samples	Independent samples	Related samples
SPSS procedures			
Compare Means		**Nonparametric Tests**	
Independent-Samples T Test...	Paired-Samples T Test...	2 Independent Samples...	2 Related Samples...

In the fourth scenario in Section 1.4.1, the researcher has only a single sample of scores, on the basis of which he or she wishes either to make an inference about the mean of the population or to decide whether the distribution of the sample is sufficiently well fitted by a theoretical distribution. This chapter will describe the use of SPSS to make appropriate **one-sample tests** in such situations. Where there are two related samples of scores, the appropriate *t* test can be viewed as a one-sample test. One-sample tests, however, have many uses other than comparing means. We shall consider some of those applications as well.

In Figure 2, we reproduce the scheme we described in Chapter 1 for selecting a suitable one-sample test. This flow chart will indicate whether a parametric (e.g. a *t* test) or a nonparametric test (e.g. a chi-square test) is appropriate for the type of data in hand. Table 2 identifies the appropriate SPSS menu items for the various one-sample tests.

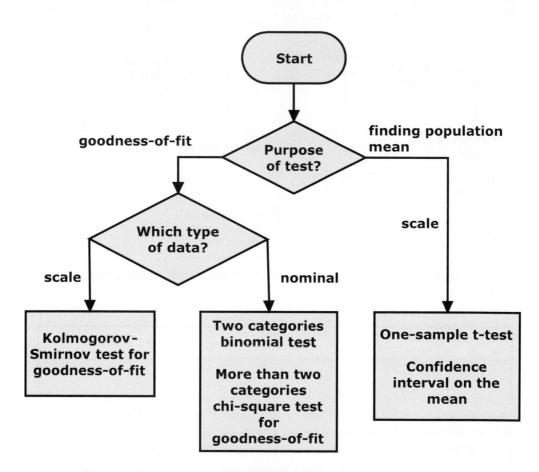

Figure 2. Flow chart showing the selection of a suitable one-sample test

Table 2. One-sample tests: Parametric and nonparametric tests in the SPSS **Analyze** and **Nonparametric Tests** procedures, respectively			
Parametric tests	**Nonparametric tests**		
SPSS procedures			
Analyze	**Nonparametric Tests**		
⬇	⬇	⬇	⬇
Compare Means (One-Sample T Test...)	Chi-Square...	Binomial...	1-Sample K-S...

⬇ indicates that the item below is part of the submenu of the item above

6.2   THE T TESTS

While we assume the reader has some familiarity with statistics, this section may serve as a review of some of the terms you will come across in the SPSS output.

6.2.1   One-sample and two-sample tests

In a one-sample test, the null hypothesis (H_0) states that, in the population, the value of the mean is some specific value, k:

$$H_0 : \mu = k$$

H_0 is tested by drawing a single sample from the population and making an inference on the basis of the statistics of the sample.

In the only two-sample test that we are going to consider, the null hypothesis states that, in the populations, the means have the same value:

$$H_0: \mu_1 = \mu_2$$

H_0 is tested by drawing a sample from each of the populations and making an inference about the truth or falsity of H_0 on the basis of the statistics of the two samples.

6.2.2   Sampling distributions

In both two-sample and one-sample tests, a key notion is that of the **sampling distribution**, that is, the distribution of a statistic when samples of the same size are repeatedly drawn from the population specified by the null hypothesis. For the one-sample test, the relevant sampling distribution is the **sampling distribution of the mean** and for the two-sample test, it is the **sampling distribution of the differences between means**.

Let X be a variable with a normal distribution and M be the mean of a sample of size n. The distribution of M (the sampling distribution of the mean) is also normal, with a mean equal to the value of the population mean μ.

Let X_1 and X_2 be scores selected at random from normal populations with means μ_1 and μ_2, respectively. Let M_1 and M_2 be the means of samples of sizes n_1 and n_2 selected from these populations. The values of the means and their difference M_1 - M_2 are also random variables. The distribution of the difference M_1 - M_2 is also normal, with a mean equal to the difference μ_1 - μ_2 between the population means. In all the examples we shall consider, the null hypothesis is that μ_1 - $\mu_2 = 0$, that is, there is no difference between the population means.

The standard error of the mean

The standard deviation of the distribution of means is known as the **standard error of the mean** σ_M, which is related to the standard deviation σ of the parent population and the size of the sample n according to

$$\sigma_M = \frac{\sigma}{\sqrt{n}} \text{ - - - (1) } \textbf{Standard error of the mean}$$

The square of the standard error of the mean $\sigma_M{}^2$ is **the sampling variance** of the mean.

The standard error of the difference between means

The standard deviation of the sample distribution of the difference between means is known as the **standard error of the difference** $\sigma_{M_1-M_2}$, which is given by

$$\sigma_{M_1-M_2} = \sqrt{\sigma_{M_1}{}^2 + \sigma_{M_2}{}^2} = \sqrt{\sigma^2\left(\frac{1}{n_1}+\frac{1}{n_2}\right)} \text{ - - - (2)}$$

Standard error of the difference between means

It is easy to understand this formula. If independent samples are drawn repeatedly from the two populations, the sample means M_1 and M_2 are independent (i.e. uncorrelated) random variables, each taking different values from sample to sample. The variance of the sum of independent random variables (or indeed, perhaps less obviously, their difference) is the sum of their variances, which in this case is the sum of the sampling variances of the means of the two samples. This is the **sampling variance of the difference**. The standard deviation of the difference, that is, the **standard error of the difference**, is the square root of the sampling variance, hence equation (2).

6.2.3   The *t* distribution, p-values, effect size & confidence intervals

If the parent populations are normally distributed, the sampling distributions of the means and the difference between means are also normal; in fact, provided the samples are sufficiently large, the sampling distributions will approach normality, even if the parent populations are not normal. Any normally distributed variable (X) can be converted to the standard normal variable z by subtracting the population mean (μ) and dividing by the population standard deviation (σ) thus:

$$z = \frac{X - \mu}{\sigma} \text{ - - - (3) } \textbf{Standard normal variable for scores}$$

The standard normal variable z has a mean of zero and a standard deviation of 1. Ninety-five per cent of values in any normal distribution lie within 1.96 standard deviations on either side of the mean, that is, within the interval $[\mu - 1.96\sigma, \mu + 1.96\sigma]$. Since the standard deviation of the standard normal distribution is 1 and its mean is zero, 95% of values of the standard normal variable z lie in the interval [-1.96, +1.96] (see Figure 3).

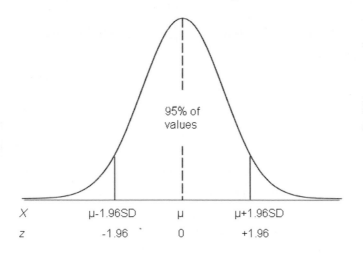

X	μ-1.96SD	μ	μ+1.96SD
z	-1.96	0	+1.96

Figure 3. Interval containing 95% of the values in the normal and standard normal distributions

If we knew the population variance σ^2, we could test the null hypothesis with the standard normal variable z, and reject H_0 if z were to fall outside the range of values between the 2.5th and 97.5th percentiles, that is, either below -1.96 or above +1.96. The statistics we should use are, for the one-sample test,

$$z = \frac{M - \mu}{\sigma_M} \text{ - - - (4)}$$

Standard normal variable for means

where M is the value of the sample mean and, for the two-sample test,

$$z = \frac{(M_1 - M_2) - (\mu_1 - \mu_2)}{\sigma_{M_1 - M_2}} \text{ - - - (5)}$$

Standard normal variable for difference between means

where M_1 and M_2 are the values of the sample means. When H_0 states that $\mu_1 = \mu_2$, $\mu_1 - \mu_2 = 0$ and the two-sample formula simplifies to

$$z = \frac{M_1 - M_2}{\sigma_{M_1 - M_2}}$$

When the population variance and standard deviation are unknown: the t distribution

Unfortunately, we rarely know the value of the population variance σ^2 and therefore cannot use the standard normal variable z as our test statistic unless the samples are very large. Instead, we use the test statistic t, which is analogous to the z statistics above, with the population variances replaced by estimates thus:

$$t = \frac{M - \mu}{s_M} \text{ where } s_M = \frac{s}{\sqrt{n}} \text{ --- (6) } \textbf{\textit{t} for a mean}$$

and

$$t = \frac{M_1 - M_2}{s_{M_1 - M_2}} \text{ where } s_{M_1 - M_2} = \sqrt{s^2 \left(\frac{1}{n_1} + \frac{1}{n_2} \right)} \text{ --- (7) } \textbf{\textit{t} for a difference between means}$$

In the estimate of the standard error of the difference $s_{M_1 - M_2}$, s^2 is an estimate of the supposedly constant population variance σ^2.

A t distribution resembles the bell-shaped standard normal distribution, but has thicker tails: large positive and negative values are more likely than large values of z. It has a single parameter, namely, the degrees of freedom (df), which is obtained from the sizes of the samples (see below). The larger the samples, the more closely the distribution of t approximates to the standard normal distribution; with very large samples, in fact, percentiles of z can be used to make the test.

In the one-sample test, the degrees of freedom of the t statistic are $n - 1$, where n is the size of the sample: this value is the degrees of freedom of the variance estimate used to calculate the estimate the standard error of the mean. A variance estimate s^2 from n scores is made as follows:

$$s^2 = \frac{\Sigma (\text{score - mean})^2}{n - 1} = \frac{SS}{df} \text{ --- (8) } \textbf{Variance estimate}$$

In the two-sample test, the degrees of freedom of the t statistic are $n_1 + n_2 - 2$, that is, the sum of the degrees of freedom of the two variance estimates used to estimate the standard error of the difference: $df_1 + df_2 = (n_1 - 1) + (n_2 - 1) = n_1 + n_2 - 2$.

The independent samples t test

Table 3 summarises the results of an experiment in which half the participants were tested on shooting accuracy after ingesting a dose of caffeine; the remaining participants took a placebo and took the same test.

	Placebo	Caffeine
Table 3. Number of hits achieved by participants under caffeine and placebo conditions		
Mean number of hits	9.25	11.90
Standard deviation	3.16	3.28
Number of cases	20	20

An experiment of this kind must be seen as a process of sampling. We have two sets of scores from two populations of possible scores: a Caffeine population; and a Placebo population. If the null hypothesis (H_0) is true and the scores achieved by the 20 participants tested under the Caffeine condition are a sample from a population with the same mean as the population of scores for the Placebo condition, the difference $M_1 - M_2$ between the means is most likely to be close to zero: only rarely would the sampling process throw up a 'large' difference, positive or negative.

Large or not, it is still necessary to verify the difference between the Caffeine and Placebo means by testing the null hypothesis that the Caffeine and Placebo score distributions have the same mean:

$$H_0: \mu_1 = \mu_2$$

Since the alternate hypothesis (H_1) is the negation of H_0, it is written as follows:

$$H_1: \mu_1 \neq \mu_2$$

If we can assume that the Caffeine and Placebo populations have the same (unknown) variance (the homogeneity of variance assumption), the null hypothesis of equality of population means can be tested with the statistic t (see (7)). When the sample sizes are equal (i.e. $n_1 = n_2$) as in the present example, s^2 is calculated simply by taking the mean of the group variance estimates s_1^2 and s_2^2:

$$s^2 = \frac{s_1^2 + s_2^2}{2} = \frac{3.16^2 + 3.28^2}{2} = 10.37$$

If $n_1 \neq n_2$, the pooled estimate of the supposedly homogeneous population variance σ^2 is given by

$$s^2 = \frac{SS_1 + SS_2}{df_1 + df_2} = \frac{SS_1 + SS_2}{n_1 + n_2 - 2} \;\text{- - -}\; (9)$$

General formula for pooling the variance estimates

where SS_1 and SS_2 are the numerators of the two variance estimates and df_1 and df_2 are their respective degrees of freedom: i.e. $df_1 = n_1 - 1$ and $df_2 = n_2 - 1$. The degrees of freedom df of the pooled estimate s^2, therefore, is $df = df_1 + df_2 = n_1 + n_2 - 2$. This is also the value of the degrees of freedom of the t statistic itself. In this example, $df = 20 + 20 - 2 = 38$. We specify the t distribution on 38 degrees of freedom with the notation $t(38)$: in general, we specify a t distribution with degrees of freedom k by the term $t(k)$.

If the significance level (α) is set at .05 (i.e., at the 5% level), the null hypothesis that, in the population, the Caffeine and Placebo means are equal is rejected if t is either greater than the 97.5th percentile or less than the 2.5th percentile. Substituting in the formula for t, we have

$$t = \frac{M_1 - M_2}{\sqrt{s\left(\frac{1}{n_1} + \frac{1}{n_2}\right)}} = \frac{2.65}{\sqrt{10.37\left(\frac{1}{20} + \frac{1}{20}\right)}} = 2.60$$

The two-tailed test

In the hypothetical population of values of t, it matters not which of the Placebo and Caffeine means the symbols M_1 and M_2 refer to. Theoretically, however, the subtraction is always in the same direction (e.g. the Caffeine mean is always be subtracted from the Placebo mean, or vice versa). If H$_0$ is true and $\mu_1 = \mu_2$, there will be as many large positive values of t as large negative values. If the significance level is set at .05, we shall reject the null hypothesis if t is either greater than the 97.5th percentile or less than the 2.5th percentile of the distribution of t on 38 degrees of freedom.

In practice, it will, of course, be more convenient simply to subtract the larger mean from the smaller one: in this example, we would subtract the Placebo mean from the Caffeine mean; had the Placebo mean been larger, we should have subtracted the Caffeine mean. Alternatively, we could simply ignore the sign of t. With either practice, however, large positive values of t will be twice as probable as they would be if we were always to subtract in the same direction and take the sign into consideration. We need to bear this in mind when calculating the p-value.

The cumulative probability and the two-sided p-value

In the present example, $t = 2.60$. The **cumulative probability** of 2.60 is the probability of a value less than or equal to 2.60 and is written as Pr[t ≤ 2.60]. The value of the cumulative probability of a specified value of t will depend upon the degrees of freedom of the distribution. For the t distribution on 38 degrees of freedom, the cumulative probability is .9934, so the probability of a value *greater* than 2.60 is $1 - .9934 = .0066$. Since large *negative* values of t are just as likely as large positive values under H$_0$, however, we must multiply the probability of obtaining a value at least as great as +2.60 by 2 in order to obtain the p-value. The p-value is therefore $2 \times .0066 = .013$. The p-value of t is automatically included in the SPSS output.

The test of the null hypothesis (H$_0$) has shown a significant difference between the Placebo and Caffeine means. We write this result briefly as follows:

$$t(38) = 2.60; p = .01.$$

The p-value should be given to two places of decimals. Should the p-value be less than .01, report it as 'p < .01'. Note that in a research report, the results of a statistical test should always be accompanied by the appropriate descriptive statistics, plus some measure of effect size (see below).

Effect size

Cohen's measure of **effect size** d (see Section 1.3.5) for the difference between the two means is

> See
> Section
> 1.3.5

$$d = \frac{\mu_1 - \mu_2}{\sigma} \; \text{- - -} \; (10) \; \textbf{Cohen's } \textbf{\textit{d}}\textbf{ statistic}$$

Assume that the sample means are the best estimates of the population means and that the population standard deviation is the square root of the pooled variance estimate s^2 in the t test formula (7): $\sqrt{10.37} = 3.22$. The effect size is thus estimated as:

$$d = \frac{11.90 - 9.25}{3.22} = 0.82$$

According to Table 3 in Chapter 1, this is a 'large' effect.

How to report the results of a statistical test

The 2001 *Publication Manual of the American Psychological Association* (APA) recommends that when reporting a statistical result, the researcher should, in general:

'…include sufficient information to allow the reader to fully understand the analysis conducted and possible alternative explanations for the results of these analyses' (p.138).

In particular, as well as the value of a statistic such as t, you should include the degrees of freedom (with other statistics such as correlation coefficients, the number of observations is given), the p-value and a statement about the statistical significance (or insignificance) of the result. The report of a statistical test should be preceded by a brief statement of the results, including relevant statistics such as the mean and standard deviation, and the effect size. Your complete report of the result of the t test would look something like this:

> The scores of the Caffeine group (M = 11.90; SD = 3.28) were significantly higher than those of the Placebo group (M = 9.25; 3.16): $t(38) = 2.60$; p = .01 (two-tailed). Cohen's $d = 0.82$, a 'large' effect.

The one-tailed test

Some would argue that, since the experiment was run in order to show that performance under the Caffeine condition is superior to that under the Placebo condition, a one-tailed test is appropriate.

Note carefully, however, that if the scientific or alternative hypothesis H_1 is that μ_2 (the Caffeine mean) is *greater than* μ_1 (the Placebo mean), the null hypothesis H_0, being the negation of H_1, is that μ_2 is *not greater* than μ_1, that is, H_0 must state that μ_2 is less than or equal to μ_1. We must write these directional hypotheses as follows:

$$H_1 : \; \mu_2 > \mu_1$$
$$H_0 : \; \mu_2 \leq \mu_1$$

When calculating the value of t, therefore, you must always subtract the Placebo mean from the Caffeine mean, *even if the former has the greater value*, with the result that t is *negative*.

Moreover, however large the absolute value of t, a negative value forces the researcher to accept the null hypothesis. This is the problem with one-tailed tests: they cannot confirm an unexpected result.

The one-tailed p-value of $t = 2.60$ is half the two-tailed value. Thus for our obtained t value of 2.60, the one-tailed p-value is half .0132 (i.e. .0066) and so t is significant beyond the .01 level.

If you are making a one-tailed test of H_0 (which we would not recommend, except in unusually compelling circumstances), you might report the result of the test as follows:

> The scores of the Caffeine group (M = 11.90; SD = 3.28) were significantly higher than those of the Placebo group (M = 9.25; 3.16): $t(38) = 2.60$; p < .01 (one-tailed). Cohen's $d = 0.82$, a large effect.

Hypothesis testing with confidence intervals

In Section 1.3.4, a confidence interval was described as a range of values built around the value of a statistic such as the mean which is constructed in such a way that it is expected to 'cover' or 'include' the value of the parameter (such as μ) with a specified probability. The 95% **confidence interval on the mean** will include μ in 95% of samples; the 99% confidence interval on the mean will include μ in 99% of samples. Naturally, the 99% confidence interval is much wider than the 95% confidence interval. Imagine you are trying to throw a hoop over an upright peg some feet away. You will achieve a higher success rate if you use a hoop with a wider diameter.

See Section 1.3.4

One can also construct a confidence interval on the difference between means $M_1 - M_2$. The 95% **confidence interval on the difference** will include the population difference $\mu_1 - \mu_2$ in 95% of samples. If the 95% confidence interval on the difference does not include $\mu_1 - \mu_2$ (zero in our example), the null hypothesis of equality of the means is rejected. The use of a confidence interval to test the null hypothesis will produce exactly the same results as the procedures described earlier in this section: if the 95% confidence interval on the difference fails to include zero, we know that t will also show significance beyond the .05 level and vice versa.

Confidence intervals are readily available on SPSS. Some journal editors like confidence intervals to be included in reports of the results of some statistical tests. Like measures of effect size, a confidence interval provides valuable information over and above that provided by the results of a significance test alone. An illustration of this will be given later in this section.

Unequal variances: The Behrens-Fisher problem

The model underlying a t test assumes that the data have been derived from normal distributions with equal variance. (This is the assumption of **homogeneity of variance**.) Computer simulations, however, have shown that even with moderate violations of these assumptions, one may still safely proceed with a t test, provided the samples are not too small, do not contain outliers (atypical scores), and are of equal (or nearly equal) size. The t test is said to be **robust** to some violation of the assumptions of the underlying statistical model.

There are limits to this robustness, however. When the sample variances are very disparate, especially in company with markedly discrepant sample sizes, error rates become unacceptably high. When the two samples have very disparate variances, so that the assumption of homogeneity of variance in the population is untenable, the statistic t^* is used, where

$$t^* = \frac{M_1 - M_2}{\sqrt{\dfrac{s_1^2}{n_1} + \dfrac{s_2^2}{n_2}}} \text{ - - - (11)} \quad \textbf{The separate-variance t statistic}$$

The statistic t^* is distributed on degrees of freedom df^*, which is smaller than df. The determination of the exact degrees of freedom of t^* is known as the **Behrens-Fisher problem**. Several formula for the degrees of freedom for t^* have been proposed, most of which are based upon one suggested many years ago by Satterthwaite (see Howell, 2007, p.214). SPSS uses one of these formulae to obtain df^* but, since the formula is complex, we shall not give it here. The greater the disparity between the two sample variance estimates, the smaller will be the value of df^* and the greater t^* will have to be for the test to show significance. There are, nevertheless, situations in which t^* may be significant when t is not. There are yet other situations, however, in which neither statistic can safely be used. When the data set is small and there are marked extreme scores or outliers, the denominator of either t or t^* can be inflated to a relatively greater extent than the numerator of t (i.e., the difference between the means). The square root operation used to estimate the standard error of the difference does not entirely negate the leverage exerted by outlying scores upon the sum of squares.

The 'pooled' and 'separate-variance' t tests

In this book, we shall use the terms **pooled** t test and **separate-variance** t test to refer to the use of the statistics t and t^*, respectively: in the former, under the assumption of homogeneity of variance, the sample variances are averaged or pooled; in the latter, they are kept separate.

6.2.4   The independent-samples *t* test

The complete data set is shown in Table 4.

Prepare the data file from this data set in Table 4 as follows:

- In **Variable View**, name the variables as *Case* for the case number, *Group* for the grouping (independent) variable, and *Hits* for the dependent variable.
- In the **Label** column, add the labels *Case Number*, *Group* and *Number of Hits*.
- In the **Values** column, define the values and their labels for the variable *Group* as follows: 1 = Placebo, 2 = Caffeine.
- In the **Measure** column, change **Scale** to **Nominal** for *Group*.
- Open **Data View** and type in the case number, the value for *Group* and number of hits for each participant.

See
Section
2.3

Case	Placebo	Case	Placebo	Case	Caffeine	Case	Caffeine
1	5	11	9	21	2	31	13
2	6	12	9	22	8	32	13
3	6	13	10	23	9	33	13
4	7	14	10	24	9	34	13
5	7	15	10	25	10	35	14
6	8	16	11	26	11	36	14
7	8	17	11	27	11	37	15
8	8	18	11	28	12	38	15
9	8	19	12	29	12	39	15
10	9	20	20	30	12	40	17

Table 4. Number of hits for the Placebo and Caffeine groups

Exploring the data

Before running the *t* test, it is important to check the data for anomalies such as extreme values or skewed distributions. Such considerations are particularly important with small data sets such as this one. Since this data set contains a grouping variable, the **Explore** procedure (Chapter 4, Section 4.3.2) is appropriate.

> See
> Section
> 4.3.2

- Choose **Analyze➔Descriptive Statistics➔Explore…** to open the **Explore** dialog box (see Chapter 4, Figure 18).
- Transfer the dependent variable *Hits* in the left-hand box to the **Dependent List:** box. Transfer the grouping variable *Group* to the **Factor List:** box.
- Click **Plots…** to open the **Explore: Plots** dialog box, deselect the **Stem-and-leaf** check box and select the **Histogram** check box. Click **Continue** to return to the **Explore** dialog box.
- Click **OK** to run the **Explore** procedure.

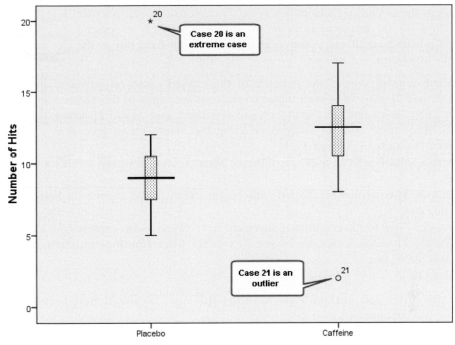

Output 1. The boxplots from the **Explore** procedure

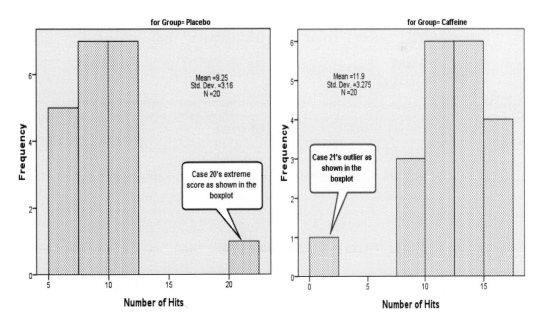

Output 2. The histograms from the **Explore** procedure

In Output 2, which shows histograms of the same distributions, the same extreme value appears as the isolated right-hand box in the *Placebo* histogram. Another score, for Case 21, appears as an outlier (o^{21} means, 'Case 21 is an outlier') in the *Caffeine* boxplot and is shown as the isolated left-hand box in the *Caffeine* histogram.

> See Table 2, Chap. 4

With such a small sample, the presence of the markedly atypical scores of Cases 20 and 21 is likely to exert undue leverage on the values of the statistics summarising the data set. We shall therefore de-select Cases 20 and 21 before running the *t* test. This is easily done using the **Select Cases** procedure described in Chapter 3, Section 3.3.1.

> See Section 3.3.1

- Choose **Data➜Select Cases…** to open the **Select Cases** dialog box (see Chapter 3, Figure 18).
- Click the **If condition is satisfied** radio button and then **If…** to open the **Select Cases: If** dialog box.
- Transfer *Case* to the conditional statement box. Type in the expression *Case* ~= 20 & *Case* ~= 21 to select all cases except 20 and 21. Click **Continue** to return to the **Select Cases** dialog box.
- Click **OK**.

Inspection of the data in **Data View** will show that cases 20 and 21 have been de-selected. Now we can continue with the *t* test.

Running the t test
- Choose **Analyze➜Compare Means➜Independent-Samples T Test …** (Figure 4) to open the **Independent-Samples T Test** dialog box (Figure 5).

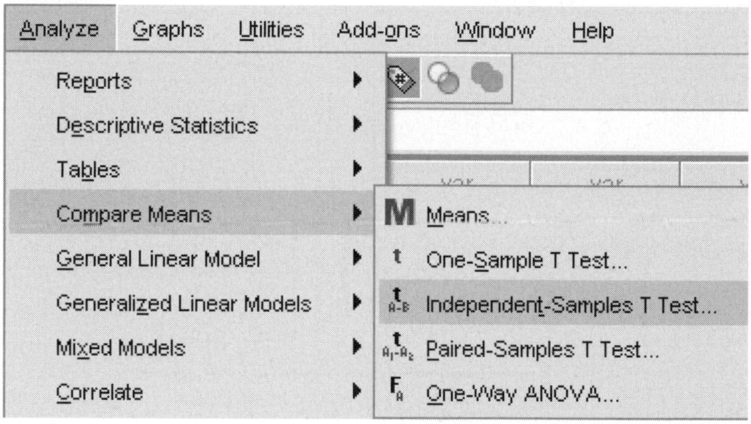

Figure 4. The **Compare Means** menu

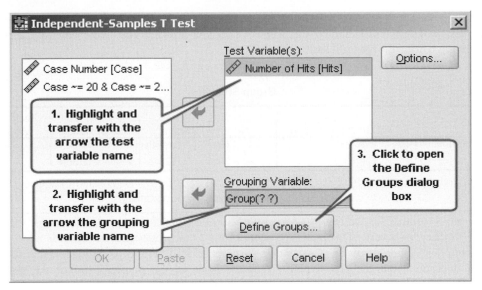

Figure 5. The **Independent-Samples T Test** dialog box

- Follow the steps in Figure 5.
- Define the values of the groups by clicking **Define Groups** to obtain the **Define Groups dialog box** (Figure 6).

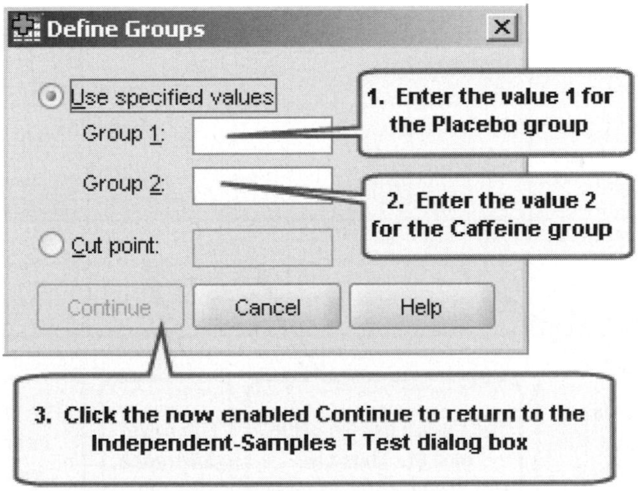

Figure 6. The **Define Groups** dialog box before defining the values of the two groups

- Type the value *1* into the **Group 1** box and the value *2* into the **Group 2** box, and click **Continue**. The values 1, 2 will then appear in brackets after *Group* in the **Grouping Variable** box:

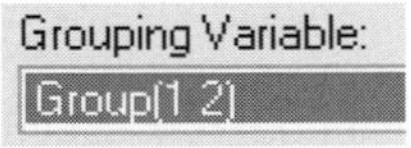

  Grouping Variable:

  Group(1 2)

- Click **OK** to run the *t* test.

Early in the output, a table of **Group Statistics** (Output 3) will appear, listing some statistics of the two samples, including the means (8.68 and 12.42). The two means are certainly different but are they significantly different?

Group Statistics

	Treatment Group	N	Mean	Std. Deviation	Std. Error Mean
Number of Hits	Placebo	19	8.68	1.945	.446
	Caffeine	19	12.42	2.364	.542

Output 3. Summary table of group statistics

Output 4 summarises the results of the *t* tests. Notice that the first two columns of the table refer to **Levene's test**. This is not the result of the *t* test proper: Levene's test is a test of the assumption of **homogeneity of variance**. Its purpose is to help us to decide whether to make our decision about the null hypothesis on the basis of the **pooled** *t* test or the **separate variance** *t* test. Notice too that, in Levene's test, the test statistic is *F*, not *t*. For the moment, we need only look at the p-value of *F*, which is .49. Since the p-value of *F* is greater than .05, the variances can be assumed to be homogeneous and the **Equal Variances** line of values for the *t* test can be used. (This is the **pooled *t* test** discussed earlier in Section 6.2.3.)

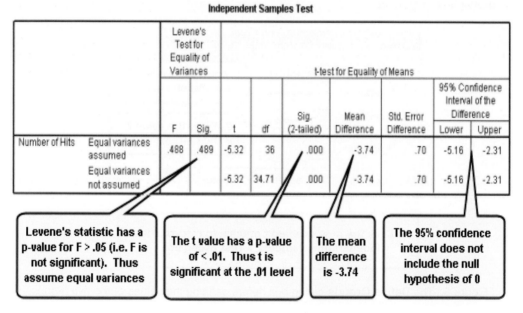

Output 4. T test output for **Independent Samples**

In summary:
- Since p > 0.05, the homogeneity of variance assumption is tenable, and the equal-variance (pooled) *t* test (**Equal variances assumed**) can be used.

- Had p been less than .05, the homogeneity of variance assumption would have been untenable and the separate variance t test (**Equal variances not assumed**) would have been used.

The reader will have observed that in this example, both the p-values and t-values for **Equal variance assumed** and **Equal variance not assumed** are identical. That would not have been the case had the variances been heterogeneous: the two t tests can lead to different decisions about the null hypothesis. In this example, the **Levene Test** is not significant (p > 0.05), so the t value calculated with the pooled variance estimate (**Equal variances assumed**) is acceptable.

Turning now to the t test itself, we see that t ($df = 36$) is 5.32 (ignore the negative sign), with a two-tailed p-value, **Sig. (2 tailed)** of <.01. (For a one-tailed test, we would halve the p-value.) The t test rejects the null hypothesis and so confirms the scientific hypothesis that the number of hits differs between participants taking a dose of caffeine or a placebo.

It will be noticed that the value of t and the p-value are different from the corresponding values we calculated using the entire data set of 40 scores. We worked with the reduced data set on the assumption that it is better to describe most of the data correctly than 100% of them badly.

Note carefully that the value in the **Sig.** column in Output 4 is the **p-value**, not the **significance level** (which is set beforehand at .05 – sometimes at .01). With a non-significant result, the p-value would be high, perhaps .6 or .7. This high value would still be reported in the **Sig.** column, even though the test has not shown significance.

The **95% Confidence Interval on the Difference** is [-5.16, -2.31], i.e. –5.16 to –2.31. Earlier, we observed that a test of significance can also be made from a confidence interval: if the interval does not include the value stated by the null hypothesis, H_0 is rejected. In this example, the confidence interval does not include zero, so H_0 is rejected. Had one of these values been positive, the interval would have included zero and the result of the t test would not have been significant.

The **effect size** (see Section 1.3.5) for a two-sample (between subjects) experiment is

$$d = \frac{\mu_1 - \mu_2}{\sigma}$$

Here we must use estimates of these values. In the numerator, we place the difference between the sample means, which Output 4 tells us is 3.74. We obtain a pooled estimate of the supposedly constant population standard deviation using

$$s = \sqrt{\frac{SS_1 + SS_2}{df_1 + df_2}} = \sqrt{\frac{(n_1 - 1) \times s_1^2 + (n_2 - 1) \times s_2^2}{n_1 + n_2 - 2}}$$

Thus

$$s = \sqrt{\frac{18 \times 1.945^2 + 18 \times 2.364^2}{36}} = 2.16$$

and so our estimate of effect strength is

$$d = \frac{3.74}{2.16} = 1.73$$

In Cohen's classification of effect size (Table 3 in Chapter 1), this is a **large** effect.

The results of the independent-samples *t* test would be reported as follows:

> The mean numbers of hits of the Placebo group (M = 8.68; SD = 1.945) were significantly different from those of the Caffeine group (M = 12.42; SD = 2.364): t(36) = 5.32; p = <.01 (two-tailed) after two cases were excluded from the analysis. Cohen's *d* = 1.73, a large effect. This confirms the hypothesis that the number of hits is affected by the ingestion of caffeine.

Demonstration of the effects of outliers and extreme scores in a small data set

Recall that the *t* test we have described was run on a data set with two outliers removed. You might wish to re-run the test on the complete data set (Table 4). You would find that the value of *t* is smaller: t(38) = 2.60; p = .01 (two-tailed), p <.01 (one-tailed). Cohen's *d* = .82. These are exactly the same values that we obtained from our calculations earlier in the chapter. The 95% confidence interval is (-4.71, -.59), which does not include zero.

The *t* value from the full data set is smaller than the value calculated from the reduced data set because the outlier and the extreme score have the effect of increasing the standard error of the difference (the denominator of *t*) from .70 to 1.02, thereby reducing the value of *t*. In small data sets such as this, the presence of outliers, even when they result in a greater difference between the means $M_1 - M_2$, can have the effect of increasing the denominator of the *t* statistic more than the numerator and so reduce the value of *t* to insignificance. (This did not happen with the full data set in the present example.) The elements of the variance (and standard deviation) are the **squares** of deviations from the mean, and large deviations thus continue to have a disproportionate influence, even after the square root operation has been carried out.

6.2.5   The related-samples *t* test

In an experiment on lateralisation of cortical functioning, a participant looks at a central spot on a computer screen and is told to press a key on recognition of a word that may appear on either side of the spot.

The experimental hypothesis is that words presented in the right visual field will be more quickly recognised than those in the left visual field, because the former are processed by the left cerebral hemisphere, which is thought to be better adapted to the processing of verbal information. For each participant, the median response time to forty words in both the right and the left visual fields is recorded, as indicated in Table 5.

Also shown in Table 5 are the differences resulting from subtracting the right field scores from the left field scores. As the researcher hoped, there is a clear tendency for the differences to be positive, that is, the right field times tend to be shorter.

Here, since each participant was tested with words in both visual hemifields, we have two related samples of scores. A **related-samples *t* test** is therefore appropriate.

The null hypothesis (H_0) we wish to test is that the 10 scores obtained under the *Left Field* and *Right Field* conditions are samples from populations with the same mean:

$$H_0: \quad \mu_1 = \mu_2$$

Table 5. Median reaction times for words presented in the left and right visual fields

Case	Left Field	Right Field	Difference (d)
1	323	304	19
2	512	493	19
3	502	491	11
4	385	365	20
5	453	426	27
6	343	320	23
7	543	523	20
8	440	442	-2
9	682	580	102
10	590	564	26

This would seem to be a situation calling for a two-sample test. There is, however, another way of conceiving the problem of testing the difference between the means of related samples for significance. The 10 difference scores in Table 5 can be regarded as a single sample from the population of such differences. Let X_1 and X_2 be the *same participant's* left hemifield and right hemifield scores, respectively. (The following move works only with *paired* data.)   Let $d = X_1 - X_2$. If H_0 is true, the mean difference in the population μ_d is zero. We can therefore re-formulate the null hypothesis as follows:

$$H_0: \mu_d = 0$$

Re-conceived in this way, the problem of testing H_0 becomes one of making a one-sample test with the statistic t, where

$$t = \frac{M_d}{s_{M_d}} = \frac{M_d}{\left(\dfrac{s_d}{\sqrt{n}}\right)} \quad \text{---} \quad (12) \ \textbf{The paired-samples } t \textbf{ statistic}$$

where M_d is the mean of $X_1 - X_2$ in the sample, s_d is the standard deviation of the differences and s_{M_d} is the estimate of the standard error of the mean (difference). Here, even though we are making a one-sample test, the denominator of t is actually an estimate of the **standard error of the difference between means** $s_{M_1-M_2}$: that is,

$$s_{M_d} = s_{M_1-M_2}$$

the numerator of t, of course, is the difference $M_1 - M_2$.

The **Descriptives...** procedure in SPSS's **Descriptive Statistics** menu will show us that $M_d = 26.50$ and $s_d = 27.814$. Substituting in the formula, we have

$$t = \frac{26.50}{\left(\dfrac{27.814}{\sqrt{10}}\right)} = 3.01$$

The two-tailed p-value of $t = 3.01$ is .02, so we have found a significant difference between the mean response latencies for the left and right visual fields: $t(9) = 3.01$; $p = .02$.

Paired-samples data file

Prepare the data file from the data set in Table 5 as follows:

- Using the techniques described in Chapter 2 (Section 2.3), open **Variable View** and name the variables *Case, LeftField* and *RightField*. Add fuller labels, such as *Case Number, Left Visual Field* and *Right Visual Field*.

See Section 2.3

- Now switch to **Data View** (which will show the variable names) and enter the data.

Notice that, since in this example the same participants perform under both the *Left Visual Field* and the *Right Visual Field* conditions, there is no grouping variable.

Exploring the data

Since each participant has performed under both conditions, we can expect some consistency in level of performance across conditions: those who are quickest to recognise words in the *Left Visual Field* should also be among the quickest to recognise words in the *Right Visual Field*; those who are slowest in *Left Visual Field* recognition should also be among the slowest in *Right Visual Field* recognition. We should therefore expect a positive correlation between reaction times under *Left Visual Field* and *Right Visual Field* conditions (see Chapter 11).

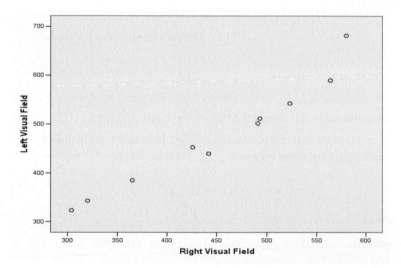

Output 5. The scatterplot of *Left Visual Field* against *Right Visual Field*

This positive correlation should be reflected in the appearance of the scatterplot (Output 5), in which the cloud of points should take the shape of a narrow ellipse sloping up from left to right.

To check for anomalies in the data before running the *t* test, plot a scatterplot as described in Section 5.7. Drag *Left Visual Field* to the **Y-Axis** dotted box and *Right Visual Field* to the **X-Axis** dotted box. The scatterplot is shown in Output 5.

See Section 5.7

No outlier appears in the scatterplot. When outliers are present, the user can either consider removing them or choosing a nonparametric method such as the **Sign test** or the **Wilcoxon matched pairs test**. The former is completely immune to the influence of outliers; the latter is much more resistant than the *t* test. Should there be no contraindications against the use of the *t* test, however, the parametric *t* test is preferable to a nonparametric test, because the latter would incur the penalty of a loss of **power** (see page 10).

Running the t test

Proceed as follows:
- Choose **Analyze➔Compare Means➔Paired-Samples T Test ...** (see Figure 4) to open the **Paired-Samples T Test** dialog box (the completed version is shown in Figure 7).
- Transfer the variable names to the **Paired Variables** box as described in Figure 7.
- Click **OK**.

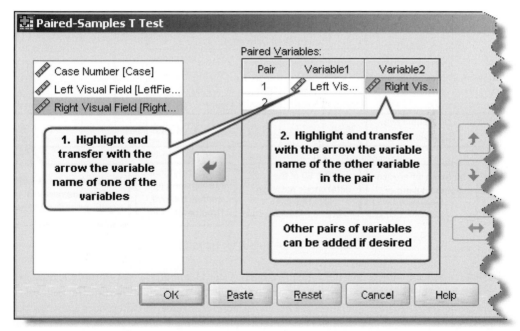

Figure 7. The **Paired-Samples T Test** dialog box for pairing *Left Visual Field* and *Right Visual Field*

Since it is possible to run *t* tests on several pairs of variables at the same time, the output specifies the pair under consideration in each sub-table. In this example, there is only one pair. The upper part of Output 6, **Paired Samples Statistics**, tabulates the statistics for each variable. The second output table (lower part of Output 6), **Paired Samples Correlations,** gives the value of the correlation coefficient, which is 0.97.

Paired Samples Statistics

		Mean	N	Std. Deviation	Std. Error Mean
Pair 1	Left Visual Field	477.30	10	112.09	35.45
	Right Visual Field	450.80	10	97.09	30.70

Paired Samples Correlations

		N	Correlation	Sig.
Pair 1	Left Visual Field & Right Visual Field	10	.97	.00

Output 6. Paired samples statistics and correlations

The final table (Output 7), **Paired Samples Test,** shows various statistics and their p-values.

Paired Samples Test

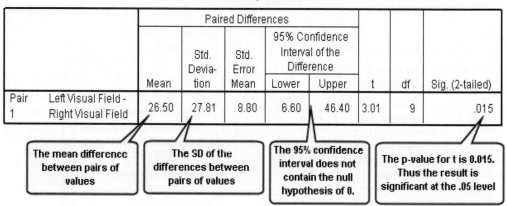

		Paired Differences							
		Mean	Std. Deviation	Std. Error Mean	95% Confidence Interval of the Difference		t	df	Sig. (2-tailed)
					Lower	Upper			
Pair 1	Left Visual Field - Right Visual Field	26.50	27.81	8.80	6.60	46.40	3.01	9	.015

The mean difference between pairs of values

The SD of the differences between pairs of values

The 95% confidence interval does not contain the null hypothesis of 0.

The p-value for t is 0.015. Thus the result is significant at the .05 level

Output 7. T test output for paired samples

Earlier, it was explained that the related-samples *t* test is actually a **one-sample** test, in which the null hypothesis states that we have a single sample from a population of **differences** *d*, with a mean of zero. All the statistics in Output 7, therefore, refer to differences between paired raw scores $X_1 - X_2$, rather than the raw scores X_1 and X_2 themselves. Notice the entry called the 'Std. Error Mean'. Its value, 8.80, was obtained as explained in Section 6.2.2:

$$s_{M_d} = \frac{s_d}{\sqrt{n}} = \frac{27.81}{\sqrt{10}} = 8.80$$

We see that the value of t (on 9 degrees of freedom) is 3.01, and that the p-value, 'Sig. (2-tailed)', is 0.015. The result of the t test is significant beyond the .05 level.

Since t is significant beyond the .05 level, we can expect that the 95% confidence interval will not include the value 0, which was specified by the null hypothesis. Indeed, the confidence interval [6.60, 46.40] does not include zero.

The **effect size**, Cohen's d, is estimated as $\dfrac{M_d}{s_d} = \dfrac{26.50}{27.81} = 0.95$

In Cohen's classification of effect size, this is a large effect.

Reporting the results of the t test

We can report the results of the test as follows.

> The mean response latency for the Left Visual Field (M = 477.30, SD = 112.09) was greater than the mean for the Right Visual Field (M = 450.80, SD = 97.09). A related-samples t test showed significance beyond the .05 level: t(9) = 3.01; p = .02 (two-tailed). The 95% confidence interval was (6.60, 46.40), which does not include the value of zero specified by the null hypothesis. Cohen's d = .95, which is a large effect.

6.3   EFFECT SIZE, POWER AND THE NUMBER OF PARTICIPANTS

6.3.1   Problems with significance testing

'Significant' versus 'substantial'

There are problems with significance testing as we have described it. A statistical test may show significance, with a p-value much smaller than .05, and yet the result may be trivial – even misleading. Suppose a manufacturer of matches claims that the mean length of their matches is 4 cm. A quality control inspector selects a sample of 900 matches and finds that the sample mean is 3.98 cm and the standard deviation is 0.15 cm (i.e. 1.5 mm). For a one-sample t test of the null hypothesis that the population mean is 4 cm, the value of t is

$$t = \frac{3.98 - 4}{\left(\dfrac{0.15}{\sqrt{900}}\right)} = 4.0$$

Locating this value of t in the distribution of t on 899 degrees of freedom, we can easily show that the p-value is 0.0000685 (2-tailed), which is significant far beyond the .01 level.

(The SPSS **CDF.T** function, available in **Compute Variable**, in the **Transform** menu, calculates the cumulative probability of a specified value of t in a distribution on any specified degrees of freedom. To obtain the two-sided p-value, we must subtract the cumulative probability from 1 and multiply by 2. All this can be done by making the appropriate specifications in the **Compute Variable** dialog box.)

The difference of .02 between the claimed mean (4 cm) and the sample mean (3.98 cm) is very small. The standard error of the mean, however, which is given by $\sigma/\sqrt{n}$, is very small indeed with such a large n. In fact, the null hypothesis can **always** be rejected, provided the sample is large enough. This is the rationale for the dictum that you **cannot prove the null hypothesis**. The eminent statistician, Sir Ronald Fisher, who pioneered significance testing, took the view that while significance implied that the null hypothesis was false, an insignificant result did not allow the researcher to accept H_0.

The 95% confidence interval on the mean is (3.970187 cm, 3.989813 cm). This tells the true story, because even the lower limit of the confidence interval is 4 cm to one decimal place. What the manufacturer is really claiming is that the mean length of the matches is 4 cm to the nearest millimetre (0.1cm), a claim which the data have shown to be substantially correct. Statistical 'significance', therefore, does not demonstrate the existence of a **substantial** difference.

Power

In Section 1.3.4, the concept of **power** in statistical testing was introduced. Here we reproduce Figure 2 in that section (Figure 8). It is clear from Figure 8 that a factor in the power of a test is the degree of overlap between the sampling distributions under the null and alternative hypotheses: the less the overlap, the greater the power. Since the standard deviation of the sampling distribution of the mean is $\sigma/\sqrt{n}$, the degree of overlap is reduced (and the power of the test increased) by increasing the sample size.

> See
> Section
> 1.3.4

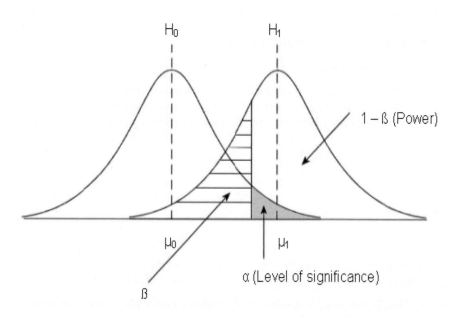

Figure 8. Relations among Type I and Type II error rates and power

Among the other factors affecting the power of a test are the type of test (parametric or nonparametric), the design of the experiment (within subjects or between subjects) and (in the latter case) the degree of discrepancy between the sizes of the samples. The reliability of the measurement is another important consideration.

Our example of the lengths of matches, which demonstrated a misleading result with a test that was too powerful, is quite unrepresentative of many areas of research, in which there is often a shortage, rather than a surplus, of data. Cohen (1962, 1988) drew attention to the low power of the tests used on the data from many of the experiments reported in the literature, a state of affairs arising from a general tendency to test too few participants. It is generally agreed that the power of a test should be at least 0.75, and in many reported studies the power is much lower than this. The issue of over-powerful tests, however, is likely to arise with modern Internet research, in which very large data sets can be gathered.

Power, however, is not the only consideration. Since P depends upon the difference between the means under the null and alternative hypotheses, we must decide upon the smallest difference that we would wish a test to show to be significant on 80% of occasions, assuming the null hypothesis to be false.

6.3.2 How many participants shall I need in my experiment?

Several authors, such as Clark-Carter (2004) have published tables giving the power that will be achieved by using different numbers of participants, given that one is hoping to reveal an effect of a minimum specified size, as measured by Cohen's statistic d and other measures of effect size. For example, suppose that you plan to carry out an experiment comparing the performance of a group of participants who have taken a supposedly performance-enhancing drug with that of a placebo group. You wish to make a t test that will reveal an effect of medium size and achieve a power of 0.8. According to Table A15.2 on p.590 of Clark-Carter's book, if you wish to achieve a power of 0.8 on a between subjects t test for an effect size of 0.5, you will need to test 60 participants in each group, that is a total of 120 participants. Clark-Carter provides a useful selection of tables giving the sample sizes necessary to achieve specified power levels in a variety of commonly used statistical tests.

6.3.3 Useful software

Some useful programs for determining the sample size necessary to achieve specified levels of power for different effect sizes are now available. One of these, G*POWER 3 (Erdfelder *et al.*, 1996; Faul *et al.*, 2007), is available on the Internet and its use is free. You can obtain information about G*POWER (and many other aspects of effect size and power analysis) by using a internet search engine such as Google. You can download G*POWER 3 into your own computer. Keppel and Wickens used G*POWER to construct a table (Keppel & Wickens, 2004: Table 8.1, p.173) showing the sample sizes necessary for a range of combinations of power, effect size and values of estimated omega-squared $\hat{\omega}^2$ (another measure of effect size). If this table is used to estimate sample size, the values obtained will be similar to those given in Clark-Carter's tables.

6.4 OTHER TESTS FOR COMPARING AVERAGES

In this section, we shall consider some equivalent tests for comparing the average performance of two groups or the average performance of the same participants under two different conditions.

6.4.1 Nonparametric tests

The *t* test is an example of a **parametric test**: that is, it is assumed that the data are samples from two normally distributed populations with the same variance. Other tests, known as **nonparametric tests**, do not make specific assumptions about population distributions and are therefore also referred to as **distribution-free tests**.

There are circumstances in which a *t* test can give misleading results. This is especially likely to occur when the data set is small and there are some highly deviant scores, or **outliers**, which can inflate the value of the denominator of *t*.

Figure 1 identifies the nonparametric equivalents of the independent and related samples *t* tests. A nonparametric alternative to the independent-samples *t* test is the **Mann-Whitney U test**. Two nonparametric equivalents of the related-samples *t* test are the **Wilcoxon test** and the **Sign test**. These are fully described in Section 6.4.2.

There has been much controversy about the use of nonparametric tests instead of *t* tests with some kinds of data. While some authors (e.g. Siegel & Castellan, 1988) strongly recommend the use of nonparametric tests, others, such as Howell (2007) emphasise the robustness of the parametric *t* tests to violations of their assumptions and the loss of power incurred by the use of the equivalent nonparametric tests. We suggest that, provided the data show no obvious contraindications, such as the presence of outliers, marked skewness or great disparity of variance (especially if the last is coupled with a large difference in sample size), a *t* test should generally be used. With some kinds of data, the presence of outliers or extreme scores is almost inevitable and there may be a good case for removing them. A good example is the recording of reaction time (RT), where a momentary lack of participant readiness can result in an atypically large RT. Here, arguably, it may be permissible to remove the outliers and repeat the analysis on the reduced data set. Otherwise, a nonparametric equivalent should be considered. Ratings are a grey area, and there has been considerable debate over whether they should be analysed with parametric or nonparametric tests. If, however, the data are measurements at the ordinal level in the first place, as with sets of ranks, or nominal data, a nonparametric test is obligatory.

Planned experiments usually produce scale or continuous data. Occasionally, however, one might have a situation in which each participant attempts a task and either a pass or a fail is recorded. If so, a two-group experiment will yield two independent samples of **nominal data**. Here the research question is still one of the significance of differences, albeit differences between relative frequencies, rather than differences between means. With independent samples, a **chi-square test of association** will answer the question of whether the success rates in the two groups are significantly different (see Chapter 11).

See
Chap.
11

Two correlated samples of dichotomous nominal data: the McNemar test

Suppose that, before they hear a debate on an issue, ten people are asked whether they are for or against the proposal. Afterwards, the same people are asked the same question again. This is a **within subjects experiment**, in which each participant is observed under two conditions: Before (an event) and After. On each occasion of testing, a person's response is coded either as 1 (For) or 0 (Against).

Since the same person produces two responses, we have a set of paired nominal data. The **McNemar test** is appropriate if one wishes to claim that the debate has resulted in a change of opinion. The McNemar test is described in Section 6.4.5.

6.4.2   Nonparametric equivalents of the *t* tests

SPSS offers a wide selection of nonparametric tests in the **Nonparametric Tests** submenu of **Analyze**. The **Mann-Whitney** test is an alternative to the independent samples *t* test; the **Sign** and **Wilcoxon** tests are nonparametric counterparts of the paired samples *t* test. Most nonparametric methods use statistics, such as the median, that are resistant to outliers and skewness. In the tests described here, H_0 states that, in the population, the two **medians** are equal.

'Asymptotic' p-values

With large samples, several of the most common nonparametric test statistics have sampling distributions approximating to known continuous distributions and the approximation is close enough to provide serviceable estimates of p-values. (The term **asymptotic** means that the approximation becomes ever closer as the sample size grows larger.) With small samples, however, the approximation can be poor.

Fortunately, with the usual reports of the approximate, **asymptotic** p-values, SPSS can also provide **exact** p-values. We recommend that, when the data are scarce, you should choose exact tests and report the **exact** p-values for nonparametric tests, rather than the **asymptotic** p-values.

6.4.3   Independent samples: Mann-Whitney test

Here we will use the original data set shown in Table 4, rather than the set after removal of the two outliers which we used for the *t* test. With the data in **Data View**,

- Choose **Analyze➔Nonparametric Tests➔2 Independent Samples ...** (Figure 9) to obtain the **Two-Independent-Samples** dialog box (Figure 10).

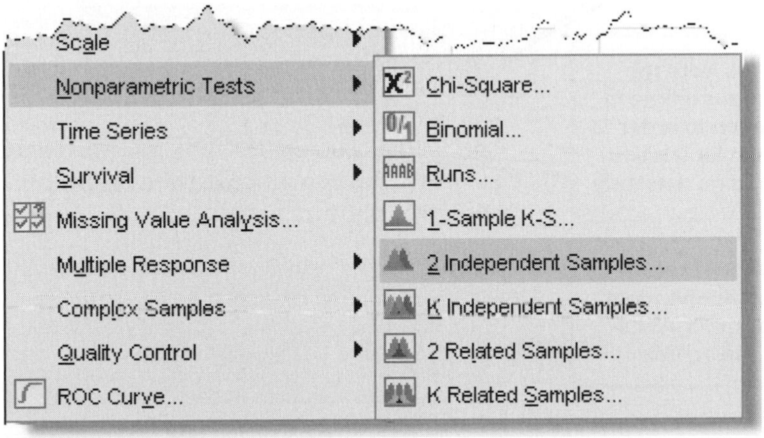

Figure 9. The **Nonparametric Tests** menu in the **Analyze** menu

- Carry out the steps shown in Figure 10.

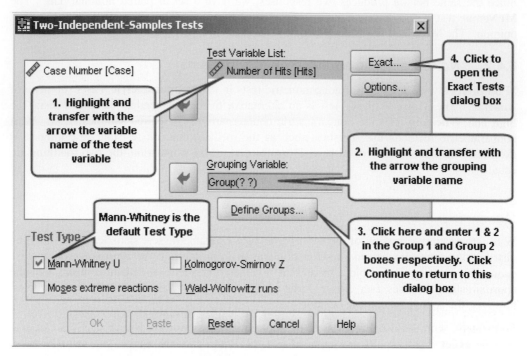

Figure 10. The **Two Independent Samples** dialog box for *Number of Hits* categorised by *Group* with the **Mann-Whitney U** test selected

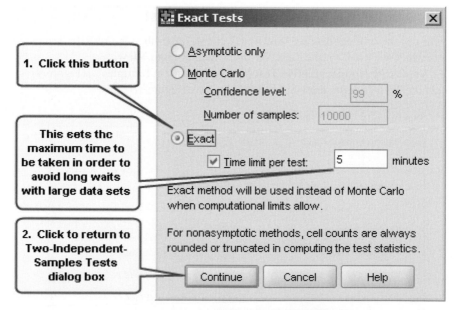

Figure 11. The **Exact Tests** dialog box

- Click the **Exact** radio button in the **Exact Tests** dialog box (Figure 11) and then **Continue** to return to the **Two-Independent-Samples Tests** dialog box.

- Click **OK** to run the test.

The first table (Output 8) in the output, **Ranks**, tabulates the mean ranks and the sums of ranks for the Placebo and Caffeine groups.

Ranks

	Treatment Group	N	Mean Rank	Sum of Ranks
Number of Hits	Placebo	20	14.50	290.00
	Caffeine	20	26.50	530.00
	Total	40		

Output 8. The table of ranks for the **Mann-Whitney test**

Test Statistics[b]

	Number of Hits
Mann-Whitney U	80.000
Wilcoxon W	290.000
Z	-3.261
Asymp. Sig. (2-tailed)	.001
Exact Sig. [2*(1-tailed Sig.)]	.001[a]
Exact Sig. (2-tailed)	.001
Exact Sig. (1-tailed)	.000
Point Probability	.000

> Take note of the exact p-values rather than the asymptotic one

a. Not corrected for ties.

b. Grouping Variable: Treatment Group

Output 9. The output for the **Mann-Whitney test**

In the process of determining the value of the test statistic U, all the scores in the data set are ranked in order of magnitude, after which the means of the ranks of the scores in each of the two groups are calculated. In Output 8, you can see that the mean rank of the scores obtained under the *Placebo* condition is less than that of the scores obtained under the *Caffeine* condition.

From Output 9, we see from the exact p-values that the **Mann-Whitney** tests shows significance on both a one-tailed or a two-tailed test. Your report of the results of the **Mann-Whitney U test** would run along the following lines.

> The mean number of hits for the Placebo group (M = 9.25, SD = 3.16) was less than the mean number of hits for the Caffeine group (M = 11.90, SD = 3.275). A Mann-Whitney U test showed this difference to be significant: U = 80.0; exact p <.01 (two-tailed).

We have already seen that with small data sets, in which there are extreme scores and outliers, parametric statistical tests such as the *t* test can produce misleading results. This is also true of nonparametric tests. Despite its greater robustness to the influence of outliers and extreme scores, the **Mann-Whitney test** is certainly not immune to the influence of disorderly data, particularly when the samples are small.

6.4.4 Related samples: Wilcoxon, Sign and McNemar tests

With the data from Table 5 in the **Data Editor**,
- Choose **Analyze→Nonparametric Tests→2 Related Samples ...** (Figure 9) to obtain the **Two-Related-Samples Tests** dialog box (Figure 12).

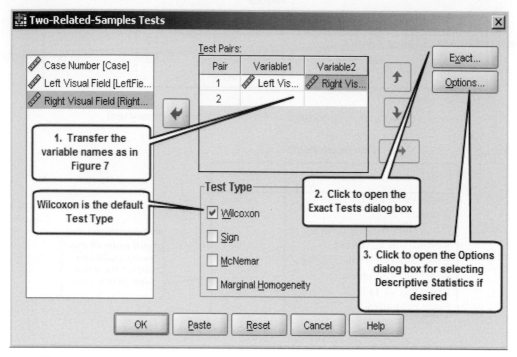

Figure 12. **Two-Related-Samples Tests** dialog box with **Wilcoxon** Test selected

- Carry out the steps described in Figure 12. The **Exact Tests** dialog box is the same as in Figure 11.

The first table in the output (Output 10) gives the means and standard deviations of the scores obtained under the *Left Visual Field* and *Right Visual Field* conditions.

Descriptive Statistics

	N	Mean	Std. Deviation	Minimum	Maximum
Left Visual Field	10	477.30	112.091	323	682
Right Visual Field	10	450.80	97.085	304	580

Output 10.   Table showing the means and standard deviations of the scores obtained under the *Left Visual Field* and *Right Visual Field* conditions

In the **Wilcoxon test**, each participant's score under the *Right Visual Field* condition is paired with the same person's score under the *Left Visual Field* condition. A set of difference scores is obtained by consistently subtracting the *Left Visual Field* score in each pair from the *Right Visual Field* score. Output 11 shows that in 9 out of 10 cases, the Left Visual Field score was greater. The differences are then ranked in order of their absolute values (that is, ignoring their signs). The test statistic W is the smaller sum of ranks of the same sign: in this case, $W = 1$.

Ranks

		N	Mean Rank	Sum of Ranks
Right Visual Field - Left Visual Field	Negative Ranks	9[a]	6.00	54.00
	Positive Ranks	1[b]	1.00	1.00
	Ties	0[c]		
	Total	10		

a. Right Visual Field < Left Visual Field

b. Right Visual Field > Left Visual Field

c. Left Visual Field = Right Visual Field

Output 11. Table of ranks for the **Wilcoxon test**. Note that W is the smaller of the two Sums of Ranks, so W = 1

Test Statistics[b]

	Right Visual Field - Left Visual Field
Z	-2.705[a]
Asymp. Sig. (2-tailed)	.007
Exact Sig. (2-tailed)	.004
Exact Sig. (1-tailed)	.002
Point Probability	.001

Take note of the Exact p-values rather than the Asymptotic one

a. Based on positive ranks.

b. Wilcoxon Signed Ranks Test

Output 12. The output for the **Wilcoxon** test

The third table (Output 12), **Test Statistics**, gives the exact two-tailed and one-tailed p-values for the statistic W (for **Wilcoxon**). Clearly the test has shown significance beyond the .01 level.

In Output 12, the statistic z is the basis of the asymptotic p-value. Since we also have available the exact p-value, however, that is the value we shall report. Your report of the results of this test would run along the following lines:

A Wilcoxon matched-pairs, signed ranks test showed that the difference between the median response time for words presented in the left visual field (M = 477.30 ms, SD = 112.09 ms) and the right visual field (M = 450.80; SD = 97.09) was significant beyond the .01 level: exact p <.01 (two-tailed). The sums of ranks were 54 and 1 for the negative and positive ranks, respectively, therefore W = 1.

6.4.5   Other nonparametric alternatives to the paired *t* test

Although the **Wilcoxon test** assumes neither normality nor homogeneity of variance, it does assume that the two samples are from populations with the same distribution shape. It is therefore also vulnerable to the influences of outliers – though not to nearly the same extent as the *t* test. The **Sign test**, which is even more robust than the Wilcoxon, can be requested by clicking its check box (report its result by quoting the p-value in the **Exact Sig. (2-tailed)** row).

The **McNemar test** is applicable to paired nominal data. Suppose that 100 people attending a debate on a contentious political issue are asked before and after hearing the debate whether they support the motion. Their responses are shown in Table 6.

Table 6. Number of people supporting a political motion		
Before	**After**	**Frequency**
Yes	Yes	27
Yes	No	13
No	Yes	38
No	No	22

You will notice that in Table 6, the cases have not been entered individually: the first row summarises the responses of the 27 people who said they were in favour of the motion both before and after hearing the debate; the fourth row summarises the responses of the 22 people who were against the motion before and after hearing the debate. The other two rows summarise the responses of those who changed their response. (The McNemar test, incidentally, uses only the data from those who *changed* their responses.)

Prepare the data file by naming two nominal variables *Before* and *After* and a scale variable *Frequency*. Name values 1 and 2 as Yes and No respectively for the nominal variables and then enter the data appropriately. At this point, SPSS must be instructed to weight the rows by their frequencies of occurrence by choosing **Data➜Weight Cases…** and, in the **Weight Cases** dialog box, transfer the variable name *Frequency* into the **Frequency Variable** box.

- To run the **McNemar** test, choose **Analyze➜Nonparametric Tests➜2 Related Samples…** to open the **Two-Related-Samples Tests** dialog box.
- Follow the steps in Figure 13.

The output (Output 13) shows that there was indeed a tendency for those of the audience who changed their position to change it in favour of the motion. We shall return to this test later (Section 6.5.2) and also in Chapter 11, when we discuss the analysis of contingency tables.

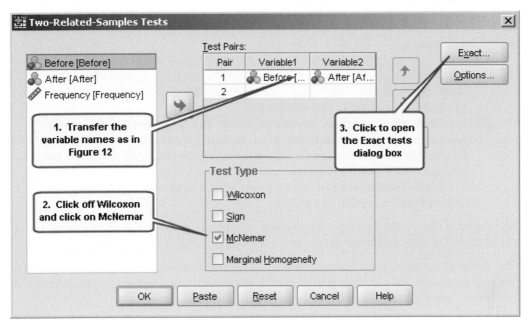

Figure 13. The **McNema**r test for paired nominal data

Before & After

	After	
Before	Yes	No
Yes	27	13
No	38	22

Test Statistics^b

	Before & After
N	100
Chi-Square^a	11.294
Asymp. Sig.	.001
Exact Sig. (2-tailed)	.001
Exact Sig. (1-tailed)	.000
Point Probability	.000

> Note the Exact p-values rather than the Asymptotic one

a. Continuity Corrected

b. McNemar Test

Output 13. The contingency table (left) and the McNemar Test results (right)

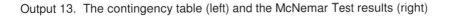

6.5   ONE-SAMPLE TESTS

In Section 1.5 of Chapter 1, two situations were identified in which a researcher might wish to make a one-sample test:

1. You may wish to compare a sample distribution with a hypothetical distribution, such as the normal distribution. On this basis, you would hope to claim that your data are (approximately) normally distributed. In technical terms, this is a question of **goodness-of-fit**.

2. You may wish to make **inferences about the parameters of a single population from the statistics of a sample**, either for the purpose of ascertaining whether the sample is from a known population or estimating the parameters of an unknown population. For example, if you have the heights of a hundred children in a certain age group, what can be said about the **typical** height of children in that age group?

Section 1.5.1 also contained a flow chart (which we reproduce here in Figure 2 in Section 6.1) for selecting the appropriate one-sample test.

The scope of goodness-of-fit tests extends far beyond ascertaining normality of distribution. With nominal data, for example, goodness-of-fit tests can be used to confirm the existence of preferences among a range of choices, or the fairness of a coin or a die.

6.5.1   Goodness-of-fit: scale or continuous data

Table 7 shows the IQs of 50 people. Have these 50 scores been drawn from a normal population? Testing for normality of distribution is one of the commonest applications of a **goodness-of-fit** test. The **Kolmogorov-Smirnov test** is appropriate for this purpose.

The **cumulative probability P** of any particular value in a distribution is the probability of obtaining a value less than or equal to that value. For example, the cumulative probability of an IQ of 100 is 0.5, because in a symmetrical distribution, the mean splits the population (and the total area under the curve) into two equal parts. For a normal distribution, the curve of P has the shape of a flattened S (Figure 14):

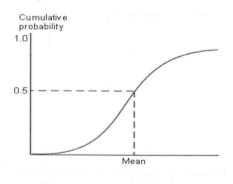

Figure 14. The cumulative probability distribution

Table 7. Fifty IQ scores sampled from a normal population with μ=100 and σ = 15									
104.6	101.1	122.5	116.5	87.7	105.9	71.7	107.4	92.4	107.3
76.4	90.5	98.6	99.3	118.5	85.7	118.5	107.1	81.8	104.3
91.4	90.7	128.7	118.7	103.7	123.0	102.7	95.3	105.0	70.7
100.3	100.0	117.1	135.1	111.0	90.8	81.8	103.1	112.1	116.8
84.4	96.4	120.6	92.1	118.3	93.7	112.3	100.9	88.7	104.5

The **Kolmogorov-Smirnov test** for goodness-of-fit compares the cumulative probabilities of values in your data set with the cumulative probabilities of the same values in a specified theoretical distribution. If the discrepancy is sufficiently great, the test indicates that your data are not well fitted by the theoretical distribution. The **Kolmogorov-Smirnov statistic** D is the greatest discrepancy in cumulative probabilities across the entire range of values. If its value exceeds a cut-off level, the null hypothesis that your sample is from the specified population is rejected. Table 7 shows some fictitious IQ data that were selected randomly by SPSS from a normal population with a mean of 100 and a standard deviation of 15, so we know the answer to our question already!

To test the distribution for goodness-of-fit to a normal distribution, use the **Kolmogorov-Smirnov test**.
- In **Variable View**, name a variable *IQ* (assign the label *Intelligence Quotient*). Enter the data in **Data View**.
- Choose **Analyze➜Nonparametric Tests➜1-Sample K-S…** (Figure 9) to obtain the dialog box for the **One-Sample Kolmogorov-Smirnov Test** dialog box (Figure 15).
- Follow the steps in Figure 15 and then click **OK**.

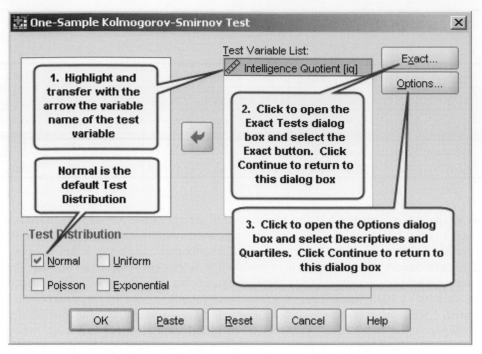

Figure 15. The **One-Sample Kolmogorov-Smirnov** dialog box

Output 14 shows the **Descriptive** statistics and **Quartiles** that we requested from **Options**.

Descriptive Statistics

			Std.			Percentiles		
	N	Mean	Deviation	Minimum	Maximum	25th	50th (Median)	75th
Intelligence Quotient	50	102.15	14.5457	70.7	135.1	91.250	102.900	113.350

Output 14. The descriptive statistics of the fifty **IQ** scores

The 'Differences' referred to in Output 15 are the differences between the cumulative probabilities for various sample values and the corresponding cumulative probabilities assuming a normal distribution. The absolute value of the largest difference (D) is 0.078. We see that the exact p-value of D (two-tailed) is .898. The null hypothesis of normality of distribution is accepted. That is exactly what you would expect, because we know that the data have indeed been drawn from a normal population.

One-Sample Kolmogorov-Smirnov Test

		Intelligence Quotient
N		50
Normal Parameters[a]	Mean	102.154
	Std. Deviation	14.5457
Most Extreme Differences	Absolute	.078
	Positive	.059
	Negative	-.078
Kolmogorov-Smirnov Z		.552
Asymp. Sig. (2-tailed)		.921
Exact Sig. (2-tailed)		.898
Point Probability		.000

Absolute value of the largest difference

Note this p-value rather than the Asymptotic value

a. Test distribution is Normal.

Output 15. Results of the **Kolmogorov-Smirnov test** of goodness-of-fit

We write the result as follows:

A one-sample Kolmogorov-Smirnov test of goodness-of-fit provided no evidence against the null hypothesis that the sample has been drawn from a normal population: D = .078; exact p = .90 (two-tailed).

6.5.2 Goodness-of-fit: nominal data

Dichotomous nominal data

Suppose a researcher wants to know whether 5-year-old children of a certain age show a preference for one of two toys (A or B). The choices of one hundred 5-year-olds are noted. Of the hundred children in the study, 60 choose toy A and 40 toy B. As another example, suppose that, in order to determine whether a coin is 'fair' (that is, heads and tails are equally likely to occur), we toss a coin 100 times, and find that the coin turns up heads on 58 tosses.

In both examples, the null hypothesis states that the probability of choosing A (or B) on each trial is 0.5. The term **Bernoulli trials** is used to denote a series of events or experiments with the following properties:
1. The outcomes of every trial can be divided into the same two dichotomous categories, one of which can be regarded as a 'success', the other as a 'failure'.
2. The outcomes of the trials are independent.
3. The probability of a 'success' is the same on all trials.

Note that (1) does not imply that there are only two outcomes, only that we can divide the outcomes into two categories. Suppose that a candidate sitting a multiple-choice examination with six alternatives per question were to choose the answer by rolling a die each time. In that case, although there are six outcomes per question, they can be classified dichotomously into Pass (with a probability of 1/6) and Fail (with a probability of 5/6).

When we have Bernoulli trials, the **Binomial test** can be used to test the null hypothesis that the probability of a success on any trial has a specified value. In the case of coin-tossing, that specified probability will usually be 0.5. The binomial test, however, can be used to test the hypothesis that the population proportion has **any** specified value.

To illustrate the binomial test, we shall use our first example of the children's choices between two toys. Of the 100 five-year-olds studied, 60 chose toy A and 40 chose toy B. Proceed as follows:

- Assign code numbers to the two choices, say 1 to toy A and 2 to toy B.
- In **Variable View**, name a variable *Toy* and assign the values 1 to Toy A and 2 to Toy B. Change **Scale** to **Nominal** in the **Measure** column.
- Name a second variable *Frequency* for the number of choices.
- Enter the data in **Data View**.
- In order to ensure that the two choices will be weighted by their frequencies of occurrence, select **Weight Cases…** in the **Data** menu to obtain the **Weight Cases** dialog box, select the **Weight Cases by** radio button, transfer *Frequency* to the **Frequency Variable** box, and click **OK**.
- Select **Analyze➔Nonparametric Tests➔Binomial …** (Figure 9) to open the **Binomial Test** dialog box (Figure 16).

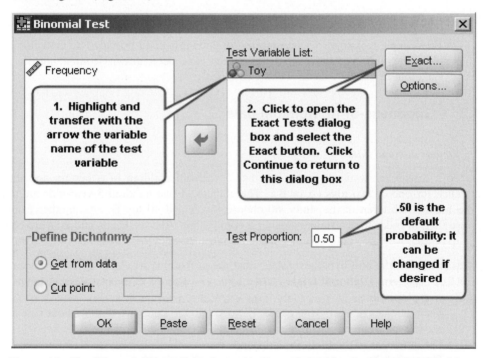

Figure 16. The **Binomial Test** dialog box with *Toy* selected for the **Test Variable List**

- Transfer *Toy* to the **Test Variable List**. Notice the small **Test Proportion** box on the right, containing the default value 0.5. This is appropriate for the present test, because if the experiment was conducted properly and the children had no preference, the probability of each choice is 0.5. In other situations, however, that would not be the case, as when a candidate is guessing the correct answers to the questions in a multiple-choice examination, in which case, if there were four choices, the **Test Proportion** would be 0.25. The **Weight Cases** procedure ensures that the two choices will be weighted by their frequencies of occurrence.

- Click **Exact…** to see the **Exact Tests** dialog box and choose **Exact**. Click **Continue** to return to the **Binomial Test** dialog box.
- Click **OK** to run the **Binomial** test.

The output is shown in Output 16.

Binomial Test

		Category	N	Observed Prop.	Test Prop.	Asymp. Sig. (2-tailed)	Exact Sig. (2-tailed)
Toy	Group 1	Toy A	60	.60	.50	.057ᵃ	.057
	Group 2	Toy B	40	.40			
	Total		100	1.00			

a. Based on Z Approximation.

> The exact p-value is > .05 so the choice of toys is not significant

Output 16. The output for the **Binomial Test**

The important item here is the rightmost entry, headed **Exact Sig (2-tailed)**. Since this p-value exceeds 0.05 (in fact, it is almost 0.06), the null hypothesis is accepted. The result of the test is written as follows:

Although more children (60%) chose toy A than toy B (40%), a binomial test failed to reject the hypothesis that there is no preference: Exact p = .06 (two-tailed).

Small numbers of trials: omitting the Weight Cases procedure

Should we have only the outcomes of a few Bernoulli trials, as when a coin is tossed twenty times, it is easier to enter the result of each toss directly, rather than aggregate the data and use the **Weight Cases** procedure. In **Variable View**, name one variable *toss* with two values (1 is a Head, 2 a Tail), enter the data in **Data View**, and complete the **Binomial Test** dialog box by transferring the variable name *Toss* to the **Test Variable List:** box.

Goodness-of-fit test with three or more categories

If, to extend the example of toy preferences, there were three or more toys to choose from, the **Chi-square goodness-of-fit test** can be used to test the null hypothesis that all three toys are equally attractive to children.

Suppose that there were three toys, A, B and C. Of 90 children tested, the numbers choosing the three toys were 20, 41 and 29, respectively. This is the distribution of **observed frequencies (O)**. If there is no preference in the population (the null hypothesis), we should expect that 30 children would choose each of the three toys. This is the distribution of **expected frequencies (E).**

	Table 8. A nominal data set showing observed and expected frequencies		
	A	**B**	**C**
O	20	41	29
E	30	30	30

The test of the null hypothesis of no preference is made with what is known as an **approximate chi-square (χ^2) test**. The test is 'approximate' because the chi-square variable is defined in the context of a normally distributed variable (see Howell, 2007). The statistic we are about to describe is only approximately distributed as χ^2. The approximate chi-square statistic is defined as follows:

$$\chi^2 = \sum \frac{(O-E)^2}{E} \qquad (\Sigma \text{ means 'sum of '}) \text{ - - - (13)} \quad \textbf{Chi-square statistic}$$

A chi-square distribution has one parameter, the **degrees of freedom**. In the context of nominal data in a one-way classification, the value of the degrees of freedom (df) is one less than the number of categories in the one-way classification. In this example, $df = 3 - 1 = 2$.

How well does this theoretical **uniform distribution** fit the observed distribution? It is clear from the formula that the greater the differences between the observed and expected frequencies, the greater will be the magnitude of the χ^2 statistic. Its value is:

$$\chi^2 = \frac{(-10)^2 + 11^2 + (-1)^2}{30} = \frac{222}{30} = 7.4$$

The **Chi-square goodness-of-fit test** is run as follows:
- In **Variable View** define the variables *Preference* and *Frequency*, the former with three levels: 1 for Toy A, 2 for Toy B, 3 for Toy C. Change **Scale** to **Nominal** for *Preference*.
- Enter the data in **Data View**.
- Use **Weight Cases…** to weight the values in *Frequency*.
- Choose **Analyze➜Nonparametric Tests➜Chi-Square…** to open the **Chi-Square Test** dialog box (Figure 17).
- Follow the steps in Figure 17.
- Click **OK**.

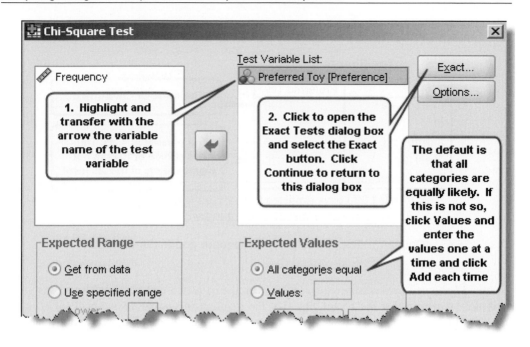

Figure 17. The **Chi-Square Test** dialog box with *Preferred Toy* transferred to the **Test Variable List** box

The first table (Output 17) in the output shows the observed and expected frequencies.

Preferred Toy

	Observed N	Expected N	Residual
Toy A	20	30.0	-10.0
Toy B	41	30.0	11.0
Toy C	29	30.0	-1.0
Total	90		

Output 17. The observed and expected frequencies

Any transcription errors will immediately be apparent here. Notice that the expected frequencies are 30 for each choice, because if there is no preference, the three choices are equally likely, and we should have approximately equal numbers of children choosing A, B and C.

The next table (Output 18) presents the results of the Chi-square goodness-of-fit test.

Test Statistics

	Preferred Toy
Chi-Square a	7.400
df	2
Asymp. Sig.	.025
Exact Sig.	.026
Point Probability	.003

The value of Chi-square

The p-value is < .05. Thus the choice of toys is not equally likely at the .05 level

a. 0 cells (.0%) have expected frequencies less than 5. The minimum expected cell frequency is 30.0.

Output 18. The output for the **Chi-square goodness-of-fit test**

Output 17 showed marked discrepancies between the expected and observed frequencies, and it is not surprising that the **Exact Sig.** (i.e. the p-value) in Output 18 is small (.026). The report of the results of this test would run along the following lines. (The bracketed value with the chi-square symbol is the degrees of freedom, which is the number of categories minus one.)

> Inspection of the frequency distribution shows that twice as many children (41) chose Toy B as chose Toy A (20). Approximately the expected number (29) preferred Toy C. A chi-square test of the null hypothesis that the three toys were equally attractive to the children showed significance beyond the .05 level: $\chi^2(2) = 7.4$; exact $p = .03$.

The interpretation of the results of this test requires care. The experimenter may have had theoretical reason to expect that Toy B would be preferred to the other toys. All the chi-square test has shown, however, is that the hypothesis of no preference is untenable. We have not demonstrated that any one toy was preferred significantly more (or less) than either of the others. Had the purpose of the investigation been to show that Toy B was preferable to the other two, a better analytic strategy would have been to dichotomise a child's choice as either B or NotB. This can be done by dichotomising the data into B and NotB: 49 for B and 41 for NotB. A binomial test would test the null hypothesis that the number of children choosing B exceeded the expected value. In the **Binomial Test** dialog box, the **Test Proportion** would be set at $1/3 = .33$. The binomial test shows significance beyond the .05 level: p = .01. This result does support the scientific hypothesis that Toy B is preferred to either of the other two toys.

The McNemar test again

In Table 9, we reproduce the data in Table 6.

Table 9. Number of people supporting a political motion		
Before	**After**	**Frequency**
Yes	Yes	27
Yes	No	13
No	Yes	38
No	No	22

We run the **McNemar** test by choosing **Analyze➡Nonparametric Tests➡2 Related Samples ...** as described more fully in Section 6.4.5.

It can be seen from Table 10, that of the 100 people studied, 51 appear to have changed their minds. The rationale of the McNemar test is that, under the null hypothesis that hearing the debate has no effect, we can expect half of those who changed their minds to change in one direction; the other half should change in the other direction. We can therefore prepare the following table:

Table 10. Number of participants changing their minds		
	No➔Yes	**Yes➔No**
Observed	38	13
Expected	25.5	25.5

The original McNemar test is an approximate chi-square goodness-of-fit test. It has been argued that the approximation is poor when there are only two categories and that the **Yates correction for continuity** should be used to remedy this. Essentially, the Yates correction subtracts .5 from the absolute (sign ignored) value of each O – E difference before squaring it thus:

$$\chi^2 = \sum \frac{\left(|O-E|-.5\right)^2}{E} \text{ --- (14) } \textbf{Chi-square statistic with Yates correction}$$

Applying this formula to the data in Table 10, we have

$$\chi^2 = \frac{\left(|38-25.5|-.5\right)^2 + \left(|12-25.5|-.5\right)^2}{25.5} = \frac{144+169}{25.5} = 12.27$$

There has been much discussion about whether the Yates correction is really necessary. Fortunately, we now have access to exact tests. Note that if the responses of those 51 participants who changed their opinions are viewed as 51 Bernoulli trials, the Binomial test can be used to test the null hypothesis that p = .5. There is now no need to use an approximate test.

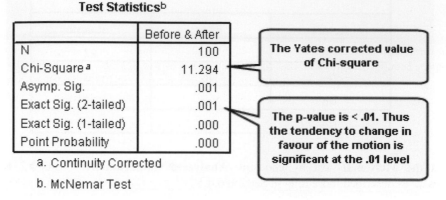

Test Statistics[b]

	Before & After
N	100
Chi-Square[a]	11.294
Asymp. Sig.	.001
Exact Sig. (2-tailed)	.001
Exact Sig. (1-tailed)	.000
Point Probability	.000

> The Yates corrected value of Chi-square

> The p-value is < .01. Thus the tendency to change in favour of the motion is significant at the .01 level

a. Continuity Corrected

b. McNemar Test

Output 19. Results of the **McNemar** test

The results of the McNemar test are shown in Output 19. The Yates-corrected value of chi-square is 11.29, in agreement with our calculated value. Since the case for a one-tailed test does not appear to us to be very strong, we suggest you should use the **Exact Sig. (2-tailed)** p-value, which is less than .01. We can report this result as follows:

> A McNemar test for the significance of changes showed a significant tendency for those who changed their responses to do so in favour of the motion: $\chi^2(1) = 11.29$; Exact p <.01.

6.5.3   Inferences about the mean of a single population

The mean and standard deviation of the 50 IQ scores in Table 7 (Section 6.5.1) are 102.15 and 14.6 respectively. (You can confirm this with **Descriptives...** in **Descriptive Statistics** submenu in the **Analyze** menu.) What can we infer about the population mean?

On the sample mean, a **95% confidence interval** can be constructed, that is, a range of values centred on the sample mean which will include the population mean in 95% of samples. Once we have found this range of values, we can say, with '95% confidence', that the population mean μ lies within this range.

If a variable is normally distributed, the sampling distribution of the mean of n scores is also normally distributed. 95% of values of M lie within the range from $\mu - 1.96\sigma_M$ to $\mu + 1.96\sigma_M$: that is,

$$\Pr[(\mu - 1.96\sigma_M) \le M \le (\mu + 1.96\sigma_M)] = 0.95$$

By manipulating this inequality, it is easy to show that the probability that μ will be included in an interval centred on M is also 0.95: that is,

$$\Pr[(M - 1.96\sigma_M) \le \mu \le (M + 1.96\sigma_M)] = 0.95$$

Since we rarely know the population standard deviation σ^2, we must estimate the value of σ_M from sample statistics and replace the values ± 1.96, which are the 2.5^{th} and 97.5^{th} percentiles of the standard normal distribution with the 2.5^{th} and 97.5^{th} percentiles of the appropriate t distribution

$$\Pr[(M - t_{.975}s_M) \leq \mu \leq (M + t_{.975}s_M)] = 0.95$$

where $t_{.975}$ is the 97.5^{th} percentile of the t distribution on $n - 1$ degrees of freedom and n is the size of the sample.

In this case, since $n = 50$, $df = 49$. A simple operation with SPSS's **Compute Variable...** command (Section 6.2), tells us that the critical value of t is 2.0096. (To obtain this critical value, we can use SPSS's **inverse distribution function** thus: IDF.T[.975, 49].) Since $M = 102.154$, $s_M = 14.5546/\sqrt{50} = 2.05833$ and $t = 2.0096$, the 95% confidence interval on the mean is

$$[(102.154 - 2.0096 \times 2.05833), (102.154 + 2.0096 \times 2.05833)] = [98.02, \ 106.29]$$

Note that, when interpreting this confidence interval, it is incorrect to infer that the probability that μ lies between 98.02 and 106.29 is 0.95. A confidence interval is not a sample space. The die, as it were, has already been rolled: either the interval [98.02, 106.29] includes μ or it does not. The '95% confidence' that we should feel arises from the fact that this interval was generated by a process which, over many repeated samples, could be expected to cover μ on 95% of occasions.

To find this confidence interval with SPSS, proceed as follows.
- Choose **Analyze➔Descriptive Statistics➔Explore...** to obtain the **Explore** dialog box.
- Transfer the variable name Intelligence Quotient (*IQ)* to the **Dependent List** box.
- If you click **Statistics...** (not the **Statistics** radio button), you will obtain the **Explore: Statistics** subdialog box, in which it can be seen that the **Descriptives** check box has been selected, and a **Confidence Interval for Mean** with *95* in the % box has already been specified by default. (The user may wish to specify a higher confidence level, such as 99%.)
- Click **Continue** to return to the **Explore** dialog box.
- Click **OK**.

An edited version of the output is shown in Output 20. The output gives the sample **Mean** as *102.154* and the **95% Confidence Interval for Mean** as extending from *98.020* to *106.288*, which agrees with the calculation above.

Descriptives

			Statistic	Std. Error
Intelligence Quotient	Mean		102.154	2.0571
	95% Confidence Interval for Mean	Lower Bound	98.020	
		Upper Bound	106.288	

Output 20. The mean and the **95% Confidence Interval for Mean**

Not surprisingly, the actual population mean (100) lies within this range since, as we have seen, the data were actually generated by commanding SPSS to select 50 scores from a normal population with a mean of 100 and a standard deviation of 15. Note, incidentally, that, because of sampling error, the sample mean is not *exactly* 100: in fact, we should be very surprised indeed to find that it was.

6.5.4   Using a confidence interval to test a hypothesis about the mean of a single population

A hypothesis about the mean of a single population can be tested by constructing a confidence interval on the sample mean. If the hypothetical mean value lies outside the confidence interval, the null hypothesis can be rejected beyond the .05 level (for the 95% confidence interval) and the .01 level (for the 99% confidence interval). In the present case, the null hypothesis that the population mean IQ is 100 must be accepted, which (since we know the true parent population) is the correct decision.

6.5.5   Using a one-sample *t* test to test a hypothesis about the mean of a single population

We have claimed that the fifty IQ scores are a random sample from a normal population with a mean of 100 and a standard deviation of 15. We have seen that one way of testing this hypothesis is to construct a 95% confidence interval on the mean and reject the hypothesis if the sample mean falls outside this interval.

Another approach is to make a **one-sample *t* test** of the null hypothesis that the mean is 100.

To do so:

- Choose **Analyze➔Compare Means➔One-Sample T Test…** to open the **One-Sample T Test** dialog box (Figure 18).
- Follow the steps in Figure 18.
- Click **OK**.

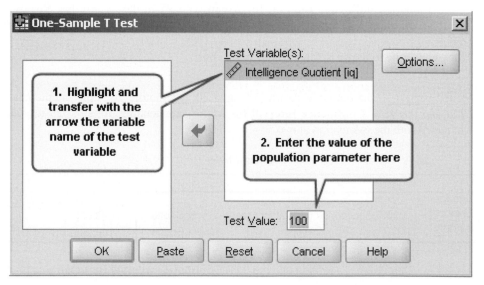

Figure 18. The **One-Sample T Test** dialog box with *IQ* transferred to the **Test Variable(s)** box and *100* entered for the **Test Value**

The first table in the output (Output 21), **One-Sample Statistics**, tabulates some descriptive statistics.

One-Sample Statistics

	N	Mean	Std. Deviation	Std. Error Mean
Intelligence Quotient	50	102.15	14.55	2.06

Output 21. The descriptive statistics table

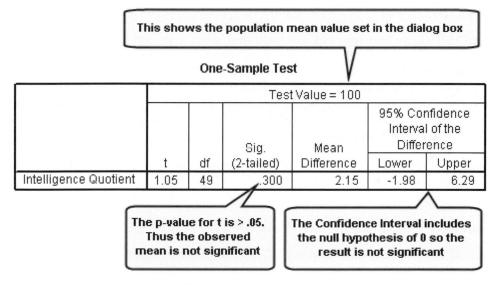

Output 22. The output for the one-sample *t* test

The second table (Output 22) includes the *t* **test** results and the **95% Confidence Interval**. It can be seen from the table that the null hypothesis must be accepted.

The **effect size** (see Section 1.3.5) here is

$$d = \frac{M - \mu_0}{s} = \frac{102.15 - 100}{14.55} = 0.15$$

In Cohen's Table, this is less than the lowest value for a **Small** effect.

This result of the one-sample *t* test is written as follows:

> The mean intelligence quotient (M = 102.15, SD = 14.55) was greater than the population value of 100. A one-sample *t* test showed that this value was not significant: $t(49) = 1.05$; p = .30 (two-tailed). The 95% confidence interval on the mean is (-1.98, 6.29), which includes the population mean difference of 0 specified by the null hypothesis. Cohen's $d = 0.15$, which is a small effect.

The related t test as a special case of the one-sample t test

Earlier we said that a related-samples *t* test was a special case of a one-sample *t* test. From a set of paired data, we can obtain a single column of differences by consistently subtracting, say the scores on the right from those on the left. The null hypothesis states that, in the population, the mean of these **difference scores** is zero. If we enter the differences as the **Test Variable** in the **One-Sample T Test** dialog box, enter 0 in the **Test Value** box and run the test, we shall obtain exactly the same result as we would have done if we had run a related-samples *t* test on the two columns in the original data set.

Recommended reading

In this chapter, we have reviewed some statistical ideas, terms and concepts that we thought you might require in order to understand the SPSS output for the various tests that we described. We realise, however, that, should you be unfamiliar with statistics, you may have found Section 2 rather indigestible. Howell (2007) provides a lucid coverage of most of the terms and formulae used in this chapter: in Chapter 6 of his book, he describes the use of the chi-square test in the analysis of nominal data; in Chapter 7, he explains the *t* tests; in Chapter 8, he discusses power and effect size.

Howell, D. C. (2007). *Statistical methods for psychology (6th ed.)*. Belmont, CA: Thomson/Wadsworth.

Exercises

Exercise 8 *Comparing the averages of two independent samples of data,* Exercise 9 *Comparing the averages of two related samples of data* and Exercise 10 *One-sample tests* are available in www.psypress.com/spss-made-simple and click on Exercises.

CHAPTER 7

The one-way ANOVA

7.1   INTRODUCTION

In Chapter 6, we discussed the use of the t test and other techniques for comparing mean levels of performance under *two* different conditions. In this chapter, we shall also be describing techniques for comparing means, but in the context of more complex experiments with *three or more* conditions or groups.

7.1.1   An experiment with five treatment conditions

If two groups of participants perform a task under different conditions, an independent samples t test can be used to test the null hypothesis (H_0) of equality of the two population means:

$$H_0 : \mu_1 = \mu_2$$

If the test shows significance, we can reject H_0 and conclude that there is a difference between the two population means.

The analysis of variance (ANOVA for short) is another technique (actually a set of techniques) for comparing means; in fact, the ANOVA is applicable to data from the same simple experiments (with only two groups or conditions) to which one would normally apply a t test. The ANOVA, however, was designed for the analysis of data from more complex experiments, with three or more groups or conditions.

217

Suppose that in an investigation of the effects of four supposedly performance-enhancing drugs upon skilled performance, five groups of participants are tested:

1.   A control group, who have received a Placebo.
2.   A group who have received Drug A.
3.   A group who have received Drug B.
4.   A group who have received Drug C.
5.   A group who have received Drug D.

Does any of these drugs affect level of performance? Our scientific hypothesis is that at least one of them does. The null hypothesis, however, (and the one directly tested in ANOVA) is the *negation* of this assertion: H_0 states, in effect, that *none* of the drugs affects performance: in the population (if not in the sample), the mean performance score is the same under all five conditions:

$$H_0: \mu_1 = \mu_2 = \mu_3 = \mu_4 = \mu_5$$

The **ANOVA** provides a direct test of this null hypothesis.

The results of the experiment are summarised in Table 1, which shows the group means of the scores and their standard deviations.

Table 1. Summary of the results of a one-factor, between subjects experiment					
	Placebo	**Drug A**	**Drug B**	**Drug C**	**Drug D**	
Mean	8.00	7.90	12.00	14.40	13.00	GM* 11.06
SD	1.83	2.13	2.49	4.50	3.74	
					* Grand Mean

There are obviously marked differences among the five group means in Table 1. Another way of saying this is to observe that the treatment means show considerable variability, or variance. This variance among the treatment means is termed **between groups variance**. Drugs B, C and D do seem to have boosted performance: the means for those conditions are substantially greater than the Placebo mean; Drug A, on the other hand, seems to have been ineffective. The question is, could the null hypothesis actually be true and the differences we see in the table have come about merely through sampling error? We need a formal statistical test to confirm what appear to be markedly higher levels of performance in some of the drug groups.

7.1.2   Some basic terms in ANOVA

The ANOVA is based upon a statistical **model**, or interpretation, of how the data were generated and culminates in an appropriate test, *provided that the assumptions of the model apply to the data*. It is therefore important to be clear about the nomenclature of ANOVA designs, so that SPSS will run the correct tests. In this book, only a few of the most common kinds of ANOVA will be described. There are many others, which can be found in standard statistics textbooks such as Winer, Brown & Michels (1991) and Keppel & Wickens (2004).

Factors, levels and measures

In ANOVA, a **factor** is a set of related conditions or categories. The conditions or categories making up a factor are known the **levels** of the factor, even though, as in the qualitative factors of gender or blood group, there is no sense in which one category can be said to be 'higher' or 'lower' than another. In ANOVA, the term **factor** has a meaning similar to the term **independent variable** elsewhere in the methodology literature. In the ANOVA, the **dependent variable** *(DV)* is known as a **measure**. In our current example, the measure is the score that the participant achieved on the skilled task.

Between subjects and within subjects factors

In Chapter 1 (Section 1.4.3), we observed that **between subjects** experiments, in which different groups of participants (subjects) are tested under the different conditions, result in independent samples of scores; whereas **within subjects** experiments, in which each participant is tested under all conditions, result in related samples of scores. This distinction, as we saw in Chapter 6, is very important for the selection of an appropriate statistical test, because different statistical models are appropriate for the two kinds of experiment.

The distinction is also of great importance in the analysis of variance because, as with the *t* tests, different statistical models (and therefore different tests) apply when the levels of factors vary between and within subjects. In ANOVA designs, a factor is said to be **between subjects** if each participant is either tested under only one condition or has been selected from one of a set of mutually exclusive natural categories. In our drugs experiment, *Drug Condition* (whose levels are Placebo, Drug A, Drug B, Drug C, Drug D) is a between subjects factor. Between subjects factors must be distinguished from **within subjects** factors, in which the participant is tested at all levels (i.e. under all the conditions making up the factor). In ANOVA designs, an experiment with a within subjects factor is also said to have **repeated measures** on that factor: the measure or *DV* is taken at all levels of the factor.

Our drug experiment is a **one-factor between subjects** experiment. The **completely randomised** or **one-way ANOVA** is applicable here.

7.2   HOW THE ONE-WAY ANOVA WORKS

Table 2 shows, in addition to the group means and standard deviations, the raw scores from which the means and standard deviations were computed.

We have already drawn attention to the **between groups variance**, the variability among the five treatment means. Within any of the five treatment groups, however, there is also dispersion of the scores about their group mean. This **within groups variance** reflects, among other things, individual differences. When several people attempt exactly the same task under exactly the same conditions, their performance is likely to vary considerably, provided the task is at the right level of difficulty and there is no floor or ceiling effect. There is also random **experimental error**, that is, random variation arising from such things as sudden background noises, changes in the tone or clarity of the experimenter's tone of voice and so on. Together, individual differences and random experimental error contribute to **error variance**, that is, variability among the scores that is not attributable to variation among the experimental conditions. Error variance has been likened to the background crackle one used to experience with pre-digital radios and is thus sometimes referred to as data **noise**.

Table 2.	The results of a one-factor, between subjects experiment, including the raw data, the group means, the grand mean, and the standard deviations					
	Placebo	**Drug A**	**Drug B**	**Drug C**	**Drug D**	
	10	8	12	13	11	
	9	10	14	12	20	
	7	7	9	17	15	
	9	7	7	12	6	
	11	7	15	10	11	
	5	12	12	24	12	
	7	7	14	13	15	
	6	4	14	11	16	
	8	9	11	20	12	
	8	8	12	12	12	
Mean	8.00	7.90	12.00	14.40	13.00	GM* 11.06
SD	1.83	2.13	2.49	4.50	3.74	

* Grand Mean

In the one-way ANOVA, it is assumed that the within groups or error variance σ_e^2 is homogeneous across treatment groups. This is the same assumption of **homogeneity of variance** that underlies the pooled-variance version of the independent-samples t test. The group sample variances, of course, will vary because of sampling error. If, however, they are all estimates of the supposedly constant variance σ_e^2, they can be pooled (as in the t test) to give a combined estimate of within groups variance. Note that, since the variance estimates are each based on the deviations of the individual scores in a group from their group mean, the pooled variance estimate is unaffected by the values of the group means. The converse, however, is not true: the values of the group means and therefore the between groups variance also do reflect, in part, within groups or error variance.

A second determinant of the between groups variance is the magnitude of any real differences there may be among the population means for the five treatment groups. If a sample of ten scores is taken from each of two populations centred on different mean values, we can expect the sample means to have different values; and the greater the difference between the populations means, the greater the difference between the sample means is likely to be. Real differences between population means inflates differences between sample means beyond what would be expected from sampling error.

The one-way ANOVA works by comparing the variability *between* the treatment means (the **between groups** variance) with the typical spread of scores *within* groups around their group means (the **within groups** variance), which is measured by the standard deviations and variances of scores within their treatment groups.

In the ANOVA, a variance estimate is known as a **mean square** (MS). The between groups variance estimate is the **between groups mean square** $MS_{between}$. The within groups variance estimate is the **within groups mean square** MS_{within}. The larger the value of $MS_{between}$ compared with that of MS_{within} , the stronger the evidence against the null hypothesis. ANOVA compares these two variance estimates by means of a statistic known as an **F ratio**, where

$$F = \frac{MS_{between}}{MS_{within}} \quad ---(1) \ \textbf{An } \textit{F} \textbf{ ratio}$$

The denominator of the F statistic is known as the **error term**. (The correct error term, however, depends upon which particular ANOVA model applies to the data in hand.) If the null hypothesis is true, both mean squares reflect merely within groups error variance and the value of F should be around 1. If the null hypothesis is false, the numerator of F will be inflated by real differences among the population means and F may be very large. If so, there is evidence against the null hypothesis (Figure 1).

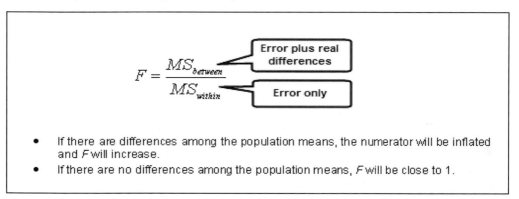

Figure 1. What *F* is measuring

Expected value of F

Imagine the drug experiment were to be repeated an unthinkably large number of times, with a fresh total number of 50 participants each time the experiment is repeated. The result would be millions of data sets, upon each of which an ANOVA could be run and an F value calculated. Through sampling error, the value of F will vary considerably. The population or distribution of F is fixed by the degrees of freedom of the numerator and denominator mean squares. The mean value of a statistic such as F is known as the **expected value** or **expectation** of F. The expectation of F is written as $\mathbf{E(F)}$.

It might be thought that, because the expected value of the between groups mean square under the null hypothesis of no treatement effect is σ_e^2 and the expected value of the within groups mean square is also σ_e^2, the expected value of F should be exactly 1. In fact, this is not the case: it can be shown that

$$E(F) = \frac{df_{error}}{df_{error} - 2} \quad \text{- - - (2)}$$

The expected value of F under the null hypothesis

It is clear from (2), however, that the value of E(F) approaches unity as the sample size becomes large.

7.2.1   The between and within groups mean squares

In ANOVA, the numerator of a variance estimate is known as a **sum of squares (SS)**. The denominator is known as the **degrees of freedom (df)**. (The meaning of degrees of freedom has already been explained in Chapter 6, Section 6.2.3.) In ANOVA, the variance estimate itself is known as a **mean square (MS)**, so that $MS = SS/df$. The familiar formula for the variance estimate s^2 from a sample of n scores may therefore be re-written as follows:

$$s^2 = \frac{\sum_{all\ scores} (score - mean)^2}{n - 1} = \frac{SS}{df} = MS \quad \text{- - - (3)}$$

ANOVA notation for a variance estimate

The partition of the total sum of squares

There is a relationship which affords insight not only into the workings of the one-way ANOVA, but also some of the statistics used in various follow-up analyses.

The total sum of squares SS_{total} is the sum of the squares of the deviations of all the scores from the experiment from the grand mean:

$$SS_{total} = \sum_{all\ scores} (X - M)^2 \quad \text{- - - (4)} \ \textbf{Total sum of squares}$$

We can think of SS_{total} as measuring the total variability of the scores in the entire data set of 50 scores. It can be shown that the total sum of squares is the sum of the between and within sums of squares, a relationship known as the **partition of the total sum of squares**:

$$\begin{matrix} SS_{total} & = & SS_{between} & + & SS_{within} \\ \begin{bmatrix} total \\ variability \end{bmatrix} & & \begin{bmatrix} between\ groups \\ variability \end{bmatrix} & & \begin{bmatrix} within\ groups \\ variability \end{bmatrix} \end{matrix} \quad \text{- - - (5)}$$

Partition of the total sum of squares

The partition of the total sum of squares divides the total variability among the scores into between groups and within groups components.

The partition also provides a framework for the comparison of the one-way ANOVA with other kinds of ANOVA. The one-way ANOVA can be represented schematically as shown in Figure 2. In other kinds of ANOVA, the total sum of squares is partitioned differently, sometimes in a complex way.

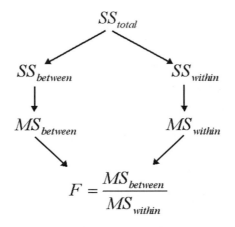

Figure 2. Schematic picture of the one-way ANOVA

Degrees of freedom of the between subjects and within subjects mean squares

Since there are 50 scores, the degrees of freedom of the total sum of squares is 49 (i.e. 50 – 1) because, of the 50 deviations from the grand mean, only 49 are free to vary independently. Although there are also fifty terms in the between groups sum of squares, there are only five *different* values of the treatment mean and the values of four of the deviations from the grand mean fully determine the value of the remaining deviation. The degrees of freedom of the between groups sum of squares is therefore 5 – 1 = 4. Turning now to the within group sum of squares, there are 10 scores in each group, but only 9 of their deviations about their group mean are free to vary independently. Over the entire data set, therefore, deviations about the group means have 5×9 = 45 degrees of freedom.

Partition of the total degrees of freedom

It is worth noting that the total degrees of freedom can also be partitioned in the manner of the total sum of squares:

$$df_{total} = df_{between} + df_{within} \quad - - - (6)$$

Partition of the total degrees of freedom

In ANOVA, much of what is true of the sums of squares is true also of the degrees of freedom. A knowledge of the degrees of freedom of the various sources of variance, therefore, is of great assistance when one is interpreting the SPSS output for more complex ANOVA designs.

Calculating the sums of squares

You may wish to confirm, from the scores in Table 2, that the values of the three sums of squares are as follows and that the sum of $SS_{between}$ and SS_{within} is SS_{total}:

$$SS_{total} = \sum (X - M)^2$$
$$= (10 - 11.06)^2 + (9 - 11.06)^2 + ... + (12 - 11.06)^2$$
$$= 786.820$$

$$SS_{between} = \sum (M_j - M)^2$$
$$= 10(8.00 - 11.06)^2 + 10(7.90 - 11.06)^2 + ... + 10(13.00 - 11.06)^2$$
$$= 351.520$$

$$SS_{within} = \sum (X - M_j)^2$$
$$= (10 - 8.00)^2 + ... + (12 - 13.00)^2$$
$$= 435.30$$

(These operations are carried out very easily by using SPSS's **Compute** command.)

Finding the Mean Squares and F

It is now a simple matter to calculate the between groups and within groups mean squares and the value of F: just divide the sums of squares by their respective degrees of freedom; then divide the between groups mean square by the within groups mean square to obtain the value of F:

$$MS_{between} = \frac{SS_{between}}{df_{between}} = \frac{351.520}{4} = 87.880$$

$$MS_{within} = \frac{SS_{within}}{df_{within}} = \frac{435.30}{45} = 9.673*$$

$$F = \frac{MS_{between}}{MS_{within}} = \frac{87.880}{9.673} = 9.09$$

*When (as in the present example) there are equal numbers of scores in all groups (the 'equal-n case'), we can obtain the within subjects means square simply by taking the mean of the within-group variances across the five groups.

7.2.2   Testing F for significance

The value of F that we have calculated from the data (9.09) is several times the expected value of F under the null hypothesis, which is about 1. But is this value of F large enough for us to be able to reject H_0?

Suppose that the null hypothesis is true and that our drug experiment were to be repeated many times. Through sampling error, we can expect very large values of F (much greater than 9.09) to occur occasionally. The distribution of F is known as its **sampling distribution**. To make a test of significance, we must locate our obtained value within the sampling distribution of F so that we can determine the probability, under the null hypothesis, of obtaining a value at least as extreme as the one we obtained.

Parameters of the F distribution

To specify a particular F distribution, we must assign values to its **parameters**.

The F distribution has two parameters:
1. The degrees of freedom of the between groups mean square $df_{between}$;
2. The degrees of freedom of the within groups mean square df_{within} .

An F distribution is positively skewed, with a long tail to the right (Figure 3). In our own example, in order to make a test of the null hypothesis that, in the population, all five means have the same value, we must refer specifically to the F distribution with 4 and 45 degrees of freedom: $F(4, 45)$.

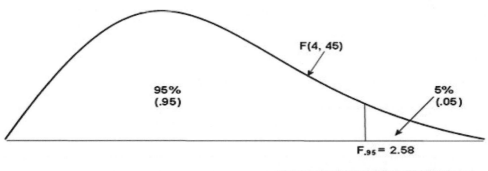

95th percentile of F distribution

Figure 3. Distribution of F with 4 and 45 degrees of freedom. The critical value of F (2.58) is the 95th percentile of this distribution

The critical region and critical value of F

Since a variance, which is the sum of squared deviations, cannot have a negative value, the value of F cannot be less than zero. On the other hand, F has no upper limit. Since only large values of F cast doubt upon the null hypothesis, we shall be looking only at the *upper* tail of the distribution of F.

It can be seen from Figure 3 that, under the null hypothesis, only 5% of values in the distribution of $F(4, 45)$ have values as great as 2.58. Our obtained value of F, 9.09, greatly exceeds this critical value; in fact, fewer than 1% of values of F are as large as this.

The p-value of 9.09 (made available by editing the SPSS output) is 0.000018, which is very small indeed. The null hypothesis of equality of the treatment means is therefore rejected. The result of the F test is written as follows:

A one-way ANOVA rejected the null hypothesis of equality, in the population, of the five treatment means: $F(4, 45) = 9.09$; $p < .01$.

Note that, in accordance with APA recommendations, the p-value is reported to two decimal places only: where the p-value is very small (as in the present example), the inequality sign ($<$) is used and the probability expressed to two places of decimals. It is now common practice to give the p-value with the report of *any* statistical test to two places of decimals, even when the result is statistically insignificant ('p = 0.56', or 'p = 0.95'). When the p-value is very small, avoid the expression '0.00': write '<0.01' .

When reporting the result of any statistical test, make sure that the reader has ready access to the descriptive statistics: the fact that F is significant tells the reader nothing whatsoever about either the directions or the magnitudes of differences among the group means. Either give the values of the relevant means in the same paragraph or have a table of means nearby to which the reader can be referred.

The ANOVA summary table

It is useful for the researcher to have what is known as a **summary table**, which includes, not only the value of F, but also the between groups and within groups sums of squares and mean squares, with their degrees of freedom. Nowadays, the ANOVA summary table is not usually included in research papers: the results of an ANOVA are reported in the body of the text in the manner described above. Nevertheless, the full summary table, which is included in the SPSS output, is a valuable source of information about the results of the analysis.

Table 3 shows the ANOVA summary table for our present example.

Table 3. The **ANOVA Summary Table**					
	Sum of squares	**df**	**Mean square**	**F**	**p-value***
Between groups	351.520	4	87.880	9.085	< 0.01
Within groups	435.30	45	9.673		
Total	786.820	49			

*SPSS calls this 'Sig.', an abbreviation for 'Significance probability', a term synonymous with 'p-value'.

Note carefully that the total sum of squares is the sum of the squared deviations of all the scores from the grand mean. In accordance with the partition of the total sum of squares, either the between groups or the within groups sum of squares could be obtained by subtracting the value of the other from the total sum of squares. The same is true of the degrees of freedom.

7.2.3   The special case of two groups: equivalence of *F* and *t*

Since the one-way ANOVA is a technique which enables us to test the null hypothesis of equality of treatment means, it is natural to consider its application to data from an experiment with only two groups, as when we are comparing the performance of a group who performed under an active or experimental condition with that of a comparison or control group. In Chapter 6, we saw that the null hypothesis of equality in the population of the two group means could be tested by using an independent-samples *t*-test. Would the ANOVA lead to the same decision about the null hypothesis as the independent samples *t*-test? In fact, it would.

In Chapter 6, we compared the mean level of performance of a group of 20 participants who had ingested a dose of caffeine (the Caffeine group) with that of another group of 20 participants who had ingested a neutral saline solution (the Placebo group). The Caffeine group (Mean 11.90, SD 3.28) outperformed the Placebo group (Mean 9.25, SD 3.16). The independent-samples *t*-test confirmed that there was a significant difference between the mean levels for performance of the Drug and Placebo groups: t(38) = 2.604; p = 0.013. (Here we have given the p-value to three places of decimals for the purposes of comparison later.)

If a one-way ANOVA is run on the same data set, the summary table appears as in Table 4.

Table 4. Summary table of the ANOVA of the data from the two-group Caffeine experiment

	Sum of squares	df	Mean square	F	p-value*
Between groups	70.225	1	70.225	6.781	0.013
Within groups	393.550	38	10.357		
Total	463.775	39			

*SPSS calls this 'Sig.', an abbreviation for 'Significance probability', a term synonymous with 'p-value'.

The p-value from the ANOVA is exactly the same as the p-value from the *t* test: the two tests lead to exactly the same decision about the null hypothesis. Notice also that $F = 6.781$: this is the same value as t^2 (2.6042^2). The *t* distribution has a mean of zero and an infinite range of values in the positive and negative directions. The distribution of t^2, however, has a minimum value of zero and an infinite range in the positive direction only. It can be shown the square of the distribution of *t* on 38 degrees of freedom is distributed as F (1, 38). In general,

$$t^2(df) = F(1, df) \text{ - - - (7) } \textbf{ Relation between } t \textbf{ and } F$$

Note also that the p-value of *F* is equal to the *two-tailed* p-value of *t*: thus, although the critical region of *F* lies in the upper tail of the distribution only, a sufficiently large difference between the means in *either* direction will result in a large positive value of *F*.

7.2.4   The fixed effects model for the one-way ANOVA

The one-way ANOVA (and indeed any kind of ANOVA) is based upon an interpretation of the data, usually in the form of an equation, known as a **model**.

An observed score X can be expressed as the sum of three components:

$$ X \quad = \quad M \quad + \quad \left(M_j - M \right) \quad + \quad \left(X - M_j \right) $$

$$ \begin{bmatrix} estimate \\ of \\ grand \\ mean \end{bmatrix} \quad \begin{bmatrix} estimate \\ of \\ treatment \\ effect \end{bmatrix} \quad \begin{bmatrix} estimate \\ of \\ random \\ error \end{bmatrix} \quad - - - (8) $$

Breakdown of an individual score

All the terms on the right-hand side of (8) are *statistics* calculated from the data set. They are, however, estimates of their corresponding population parameters as follows:

$$ \begin{pmatrix} Statistic & Parameter & Explanation \\ \\ M & \mu & population\ grand\ mean \\ \left(M_j - M \right) & \left(\mu_j - \mu \right) = \alpha_j & effect\ of\ treatment\ j \\ \left(X - M_j \right) & \left(X - \mu_j \right) = e & random\ error \end{pmatrix} $$

The model for the fixed effects, one-way ANOVA is, therefore,

$$ X = \mu + \alpha_j + e \quad - - - (9) \text{ \textbf{The fixed effects model}} $$

In words, a score has a fixed part, consisting of the grand population mean plus the deviation of the population group mean from the population grand mean, plus a random error component, which is the deviation of the score from the population group mean.

This, we should note, is the **fixed effects** model: the effects α_j have been systematically selected and are not a random sample from a pool of possible effects. In ANOVA (and elsewhere), the distinction between fixed and random effects has important implications, both for the making of statistical tests and for their power.

The random error component e is assumed to be normally distributed with a mean of zero. The error components of any score is assumed to be independent of the error component in any other score and to have uniform variance across groups. This supposedly uniform variance is denoted by σ_e^2. This is the **homogeneity of variance** assumption.

7.3   THE ONE-WAY ANOVA IN THE COMPARE MEANS MENU

There are several ways of running a one-way ANOVA on SPSS. The easiest method is to select an option in the **Compare Means** menu (Figure 4).

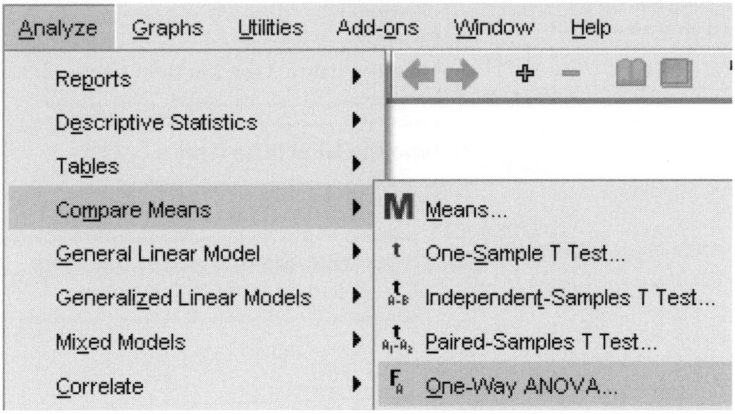

Figure 4. One route to the **One-Way ANOVA**

For the experienced user, however, the **General Linear Model (GLM)** offers a wider range of statistics; although the preliminary dialog and the output are more complex than in **Compare Means**. The preliminary work in **Variable View** and the entry of the data in **Data View** are the same for either approach.

7.3.1   Entering the data

As with the independent samples *t* test, you will need to define two variables:

1. A grouping variable with a simple name such as *Group*, which identifies the condition under which a score was achieved. (The grouping variable should also be given a more meaningful variable label such as *Drug Condition*, which will appear in the output.)
2. A variable with a name such as *Score*, which contains all the scores in the data set. This is the measure, or dependent variable.

The grouping variable will consist of five values (one for the placebo condition and one for each of the four drugs). We shall arbitrarily assign numerical values thus: 1 = Placebo; 2 = Drug A; 3 = Drug B; 4 = Drug C; 5 = Drug D.

Proceed as follows:

- Open **Variable View** first and amend the settings so that when you enter **Data View**, your variables are already labelled and the scores appear without unnecessary decimals. When you are working in **Data View**, you will have the option of displaying the value labels of your grouping variable, either by checking **Value Labels** in the **View** menu or clicking on the easily-identifiable label icon (it looks like a suitcase label) at the top of the window.
- In the **Values** column, assign clear value labels to the code numbers you choose for grouping variables (Figure 5). When you are typing data into **Data View**, having the value labels available can help you to avoid transcription errors.

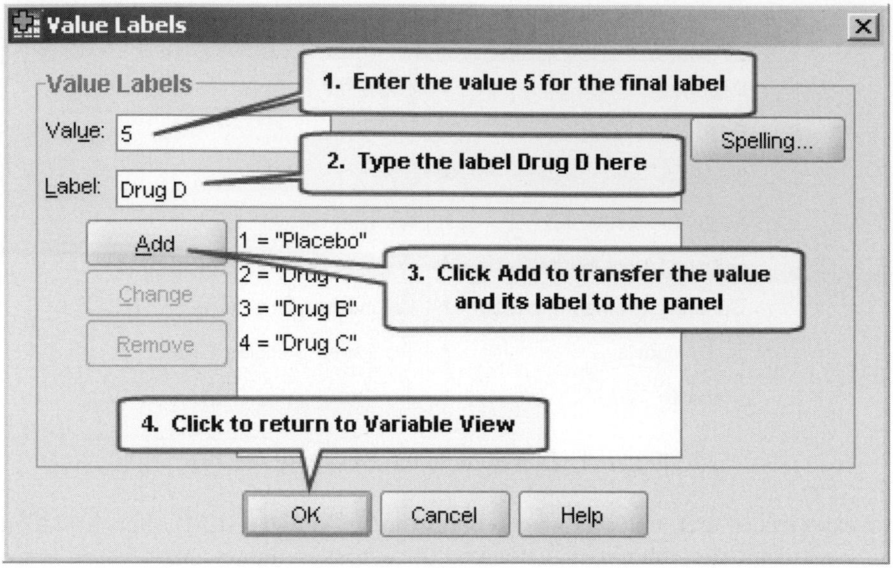

Figure 5. Assigning value labels to the code numbers making up the grouping variable

- In the **Measure** column of **Variable View**, specify the level of measurement of your grouping variable, which is at the nominal level of measurement (Figure 6). (The numerical values that we have assigned were arbitrary and are merely labels for the five different treatment conditions.)

	Name	Type	Width	Decimals	Label	Values	Missing	Columns	Align	Measure
1	Group	Numeric	8	0	Drug Condition	{1, Placebo}...	None	8	Right	Nominal
2	Score	Numeric	8	0		None	None	8	Right	Scale

Figure 6. The completed **Variable View** window, specifying the nominal level of measurement for the grouping variable *Group*.

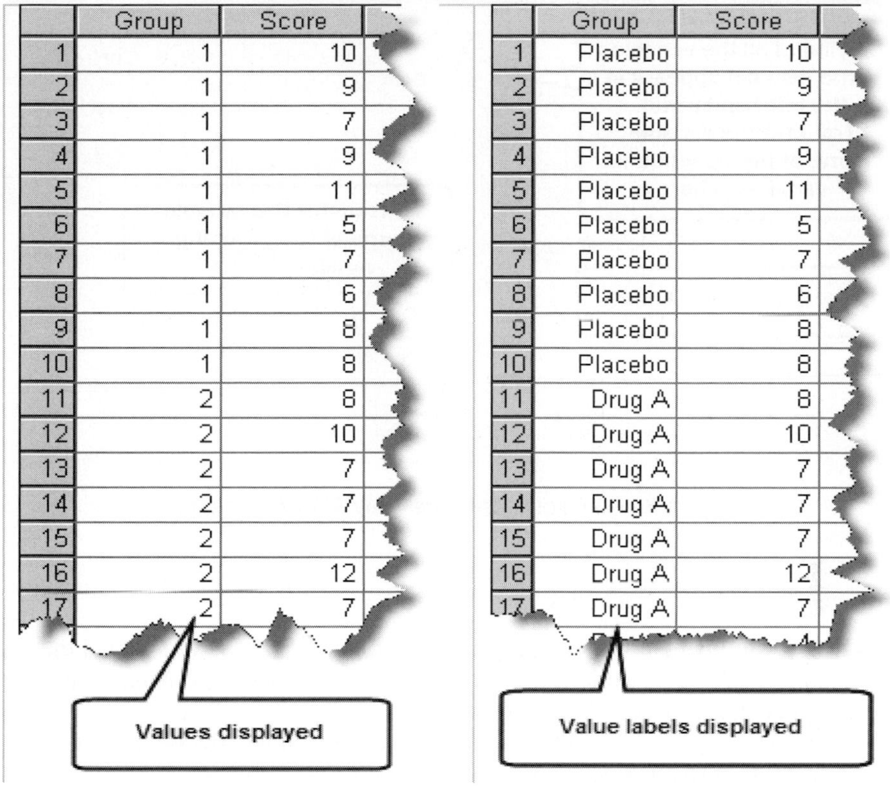

	Group	Score	
1	1	10	
2	1	9	
3	1	7	
4	1	9	
5	1	11	
6	1	5	
7	1	7	
8	1	6	
9	1	8	
10	1	8	
11	2	8	
12	2	10	
13	2	7	
14	2	7	
15	2	7	
16	2	12	
17	2	7	

Values displayed

	Group	Score	
1	Placebo	10	
2	Placebo	9	
3	Placebo	7	
4	Placebo	9	
5	Placebo	11	
6	Placebo	5	
7	Placebo	7	
8	Placebo	6	
9	Placebo	8	
10	Placebo	8	
11	Drug A	8	
12	Drug A	10	
13	Drug A	7	
14	Drug A	7	
15	Drug A	7	
16	Drug A	12	
17	Drug A	7	

Value labels displayed

Figure 7. Two displays of the same part of **Data View** after the data have been entered: on the left, in the *Group* column, the values are shown; on the right, in the same column, the value labels are shown

Having prepared the ground in this way while in **Variable View**, you will find that when you enter **Data View**, the names of your variables appear at the heads of the first two columns. When you type in the values of the grouping variable, you can view their labels by checking the value labels option in the **View** menu or by clicking the ⬚ icon. Figure 7 shows the same part of **Data View** after the data have been entered, with and without value labels.

7.3.2   Running the one-way ANOVA in Compare Means

Click **Compare Means** to open the **One-Way ANOVA** dialog box (Figure 8). The basic ANOVA can be requested very easily as shown. Click **OK** to run the ANOVA.

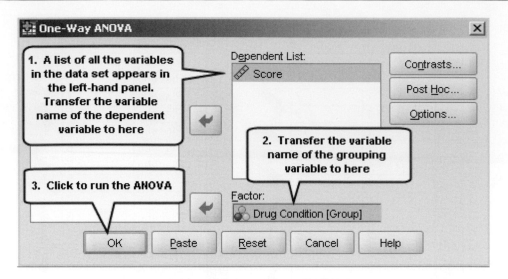

Figure 8. Completing the **One-Way ANOVA** dialog box

SPSS output for the one-way ANOVA

In the **ANOVA summary table** (Output 1), the values of F, the SS, the MS and the df are the same as those we calculated earlier. Confirm also that the values in the **Mean Square** column are the **Between Groups** and **Within Groups** sums of squares divided by their respective degrees of freedom. The value of F has been obtained by dividing the **Between Groups** mean square by the **Within Groups** mean square.

In the df column, note that, as we showed earlier, the between groups sum of squares has 4 degrees of freedom and the within groups sum of squares has 45 degrees of freedom.

Notice that in Output 1, the p-value is given as .000. The exact p-value can be obtained by double-clicking on the ANOVA table in the output, choosing **Cell Properties** and resetting the number of decimal places to a higher value. We stress that a p-value should never be reported as it appears in Output 1: write 'p < 0.01'.

ANOVA

Score

	Sum of Squares	df	Mean Square	F	Sig.
Between Groups	351.52	4	87.88	9.08	.000
Within Groups	435.30	45	9.67		
Total	786.82	49			

Notice that the Total Sum of Squares is the sum of the Between Groups and Within Groups values

The associated p-value for F is <.01 (i.e. significant at the .01 level). Write it as 'p<.01'

Output 1. The **One-way ANOVA** summary table

7.4   MEASURES OF EFFECT SIZE IN ONE-WAY ANOVA

Several measures of effect size have been proposed and there is an extensive (indeed confusing) literature on the topic. The first measure to be proposed was a statistic known as η^2 (**eta squared**), where eta is known as the **correlation ratio**. Some authors define eta squared in terms of population parameters; others, however, define the measure in terms of the statistics of their own data. Here we shall take the second approach and treat eta squared as a purely descriptive measure of the strength of the treatment effect.

Eta squared is defined as the between groups sum of squares divided by the total sum of squares:

$$\eta^2 = \frac{SS_{between}}{SS_{total}} \quad \text{- - - (10) \textbf{Eta squared}}$$

Using the values in the ANOVA summary table (Output 1), we have

$$\eta^2 = \frac{SS_{between}}{SS_{total}} = \frac{351.520}{786.820} = 0.447$$

It is clear from the partition of the total sum of squares (5) that, for a given value of the total sum of squares, the larger the value of the between groups sum of squares, the smaller must be the within sum of squares and vice versa. The greater the value of the between groups sum of squares in relation to that of the within groups sum of squares, the greater the proportion of the total sum of squares that is accounted for by differences among the group means. A small value of eta squared, on the other hand, indicates a predominance of error variance, as we should expect if the null hypothesis is true and, in the population, there are no differences among the treatment or group means.

The term **correlation ratio** is not particularly transparent. Eta, however, is indeed a correlation; moreover, as we have seen, it is also a ratio. If each of the fifty scores in our data set is paired with its group mean (so that each of the ten scores in each group is paired with the same sample mean), the correlation between the scores and the group means has the value of eta. This value, moreover, like those of the statistics from the one-way ANOVA itself, is unaffected by the ordering of the scores from the different groups. Eta can be regarded as a **function-free correlation** expressing the total regression (linear and curvilinear) of the scores upon the treatments, which are represented as arbitrary code numbers. For reasons that will be fully explained in Chapter 12, eta squared is also known as R^2 and is referred to as such in the SPSS output. Eta is, in fact, a **multiple correlation coefficient** and, as such, cannot have a negative value.

Effect size in the population

Despite its cogent rationale and intuitive appeal, eta squared as we have defined it is a purely descriptive statistic. It can be shown that, as a measure of effect size, eta squared overstates the effect size in the population, that is, as an estimate of effect size in the population, it is **positively biased**.

To obtain some idea of the meaning of effect strength in the population (as opposed to the sample), we can think of the between groups and within groups sums of squares as the variance of the population group means and the variance of the scores within their groups, respectively. In words, therefore, we can express (10) in words as follows:

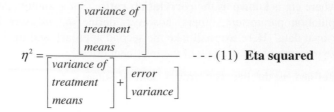

$$\eta^2 = \frac{\begin{bmatrix} variance\ of \\ treatment \\ means \end{bmatrix}}{\begin{bmatrix} variance\ of \\ treatment \\ means \end{bmatrix} + \begin{bmatrix} error \\ variance \end{bmatrix}} \quad \text{- - - (11) \textbf{Eta squared}}$$

If we take the variances referred to in (11) as population parameters, rather than statistics of the sample, we have a measure of effect size in the population, which we shall term **omega squared** ω^2 :

$$\omega^2 = \frac{\sigma_\mu^2}{\sigma_\mu^2 + \sigma_e^2} = \frac{\sigma_\mu^2}{\sigma_{total}^2} \quad \text{- - - (12) \textbf{Omega squared}}$$

where σ_μ^2 is the variance of the treatment means in the population, (that is $\sigma_\mu^2 = \frac{\sum (\mu_j - \mu)^2}{k}$)

and σ_{total}^2 is the long run mean value of $(X - \mu)^2$, the squared deviation of the individual score X from the grand mean μ. By 'long run mean value', we mean that if the experiment were to be run an unthinkable number of times (with exactly the same number of fresh participants each time) and we were to calculate the value of $(X - \mu)^2$ each time and take the mean of this huge number of values, we should have σ_{total}^2 .

As an estimate of omega squared, the statistic eta squared is positively biased: in the long run, it overstates the strength of the treatment effect. In this respect, a better estimate of omega squared is $\hat{\omega}^2$, which can be calculated from the following formula:

$$\hat{\omega}^2 = \frac{(k-1)(F-1)}{(k-1)(F-1) + kn} \quad \text{- - - (13) \textbf{Estimated omega squared}}$$

where k is the number of treatment groups, and n is the number of participants in each group. Substituting the values given in Output 1 into (12), we have

$$\hat{\omega}^2 = \frac{(5-1)(9.085-1)}{(5-1)(9.085-1) + 50} = 0.39$$

Notice that the value of estimated omega squared ($\hat{\omega}^2$) is less than that of eta squared, because it is correcting the positive bias.

Adjusted R^2

SPSS does not include an estimate of omega squared in its output for the one-way ANOVA. It does, however, give a statistic it terms **adjusted R^2**, that is, adjusted eta squared. Adjusted R^2 (or adjusted eta squared) is a modification of eta squared which incorporates a correction for positive bias. In the special case of the one-way ANOVA, the values of adjusted R^2 and the estimate of omega squared are quite similar. (In the ANOVA of more complex experiments, however, where there are several different effects to be investigated, adjusted R^2 will not fit the bill as a measure of effect size for any particular source.)

Cohen's f statistic

We have already encounted **Cohen's d**, a measure of effect size applicable to the results of two-group experiments:

$$d = \frac{\mu_1 - \mu_2}{\sigma} \quad \text{- - - (14)} \quad \textbf{Cohen's } d$$

In practice, the population means in (14) are estimated with the sample means and the two sample variances are pooled to give an estimate of the supposedly constant population variance.

As a summary measure of effect size, however, Cohen's d is inapplicable to data from experiments with three or more treatment conditions. For that purpose, Cohen developed another measure of effect size which he termed f. Cohen's f is defined as the standard deviation of the treatment means in the population, divided by the within groups error variance:

$$f = \frac{\sigma_\mu}{\sigma_e} = \frac{\sqrt{\dfrac{\sum (\mu_j - \mu)^2}{k}}}{\sigma_e} \quad \text{- - - (15)} \quad \textbf{Cohen's } f$$

As with d, the parameters in (15) must be estimated from the statistics of the sample.

The **G*Power** package, which we shall discuss below, refers to Cohen's f statistic in its classification of effect size.

Relation between Cohen's f and omega squared

The two statistics omega squared and f are closely related:

$$\omega^2 = \frac{f^2}{1 + f^2}$$

$$\text{- - - (16)} \quad \textbf{Relation between Cohen's } f \textbf{ and omega squared}$$

$$f^2 = \frac{\omega^2}{1 - \omega^2}$$

In terms of Cohen's f statistic, our obtained omega squared value of 0.39 becomes

$$f = \sqrt{\frac{0.14}{0.14 - 0.39}} = 0.80$$

Interpreting measures of effect size

To interpret an obtained value of a measure of effect size such as estimated omega squared, we can turn to a table similar to Table 3 in Chapter 1. Table 5 gives ranges of values that are regarded as 'Small', 'Medium' and 'Large' effects.

Table 5. A scheme for assessing values of omega squared		
Size of Effect	**Omega squared**	**Cohen's** f
Small	$0.01 \le \omega^2 < 0.06$	$0.10 \le f < 0.25$
Medium	$0.06 \le \omega^2 < 0.14$	$0.25 \le f < 0.40$
Large	$\omega^2 \ge 0.14$	$f \ge 0.40$

It is perhaps worth noting that, while Cohen's measure d does not generalise beyond the two-group case, eta squared and f are applicable in a situation where there are only two treatment or group means. Where there are only two groups (with equal n), eta squared and Cohen's d are related as follows:

$$\eta^2 = \frac{d^2}{d^2 + 4} \quad \text{- - - (17)}$$

In the two-group situation, where both d and f are defined, $f = \dfrac{d}{2}$.

7.5   THE ONE-WAY ANOVA IN THE GLM MENU

In addition to all the techniques in the **One-Way ANOVA** procedure, the **General Linear Model** (GLM) menu offers measures of effect size, as well as other important procedures, such as **Analysis of covariance (ANCOVA)**. In this subsection, we shall describe how to run the one-way ANOVA in GLM.

7.5.1   Some key terms

First, however, it will be necessary to explain some of the terms that will appear in the GLM dialog box.

Factors with fixed and random effects

The experimenter does not usually select experimental conditions at random: their inclusion is driven either by theory or by the need to resolve some practical issue. A factor consisting of a set of theoretically-determined conditions is said to have **fixed effects**. Most factors in experimental research are fixed effects factors.

There are occasions, however, on which the conditions making up a factor can be viewed as a random sample from a large (perhaps infinitely large) pool of possible conditions. In research on reading skills, for example, an investigator studying the effects of sentence length upon passage readability may select or prepare some passages which vary systematically in sentence length. With such a procedure, however, reading performance may reflect passage properties other than sentence length; moreover, these additional properties cannot be expected to remain the same from passage to passage. The effects of using different passages must be included as a factor in the analysis, even though the experimenter is not primarily interested in this nuisance variable. Since, arguably, additional passage characteristics are a random selection from a pool of possible conditions, the passage factor is said to have **random effects**. Factors with random effects arise more commonly in applied, correlational research and their presence has important implications for the analysis.

Covariates

Often the researcher has available information about participants other than that directly relevant to the research project. A **covariate** is a variable which, because it can be expected to correlate (i.e. 'co-vary') with the DV, is likely to add to the variability (or 'noisiness') of the data and inflate the error term, with a consequent loss of power in the statistical test. An obvious example of a covariate is IQ, which can be expected to correlate substantially with any measure of cognitive or skilled performance.

The **analysis of covariance** (**ANCOVA**) is a technique whereby the effects of a covariate upon the DV are removed from the data, thus reducing their 'noisiness' and increasing the power of the F test. The manner in which this is achieved is described in statistical texts such as Winer, Brown & Michels (1991) and Keppel & Wickens (2004).

Univariate versus multivariate ANOVA

In all the experiments we have considered so far, there has been a single DV. In the current example, the DV is the score a participant achieves on a task. The one-way ANOVA and the *t test* are **univariate tests**, because they were designed for the analysis of data from experiments with a single DV. If, however, we had also recorded the time the participant took to complete the task, there would have been two DVs. **Multivariate tests** are techniques designed for the analysis of data from experiments with two or more DVs. An example of a multivariate technique is **Multivariate Analysis of Variance** (**MANOVA**), which is a generalisation beyond the univariate ANOVA to the analysis of data from experiments with several DVs. This technique is described and illustrated in Chapter 10 (Section 10.4).

7.5.2   Using the GLM menu for one-way ANOVA

The **General Linear Model** (GLM) menu is shown in Figure 9. The **Univariate** option is clearly appropriate for our example, since there is only one dependent variable.

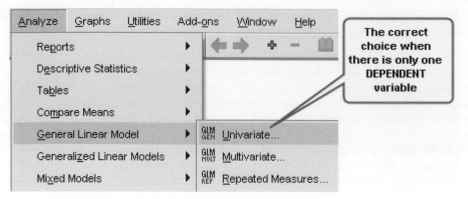

Figure 9. The **General Linear Model** menu

In this section, we shall use **GLM** to run the basic one-way ANOVA only, so that we can compare the output with the **Compare Means** One-Way ANOVA summary table.

Proceed as follows:

- Choose **Analyze➜General Linear Model➜Univariate...** to open the **Univariate** dialog box (the completed box is shown in Figure 10).

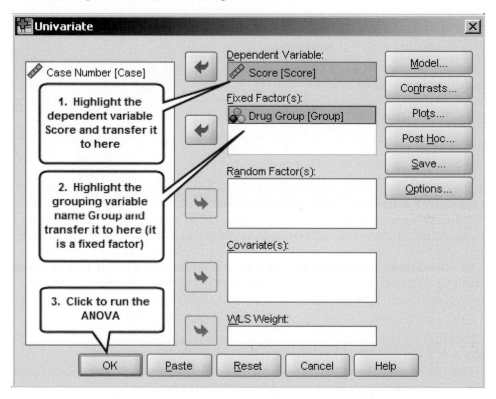

Figure 10. Completing the GLM **Univariate** dialog box

- As before, the left panel of the dialog box will contain a list of all the variables in the data set. Transfer the variable names as shown in Figure 10. In our example, the *Drug Group* factor has fixed effects, since its levels were selected systematically.
- Click **OK** to run the basic one-way ANOVA.

The **GLM ANOVA** summary table is shown in Output 2, with the table from the **Compare Means One-Way ANOVA** procedure below it for comparison.

Univariate Analysis of Variance

Tests of Between-Subjects Effects

Dependent Variable: Score

Source	Type III Sum of Squares	df	Mean Square	F	Sig.
Corrected Model	351.52[a]	4	87.88	9.08	.000
Intercept	6116.18	1	6116.18	632.27	.000
Group	351.52	4	87.88	9.08	.000
Error	435.30	45	9.67		
Total	6903.00	50			
Corrected Total	786.82	49			

a. R Squared = .447 (Adjusted R Squared = .398)

Oneway

The sums of squares in the grey area have the same values in both tables. The corrected total sum of squares in the GLM table is the same as the total in the ANOVA table.

The values of *F* are the same

ANOVA

Score

	Sum of Squares	df	Mean Square	F	Sig.
Between Groups	351.52	4	87.88	9.08	.000
Within Groups	435.30	45	9.67		
Total	786.82	49			

Output 2. Comparison of the **Univariate ANOVA** summary table from the **GLM** menu (upper panel) with the **One-Way ANOVA** summary table from the **Compare Means** menu (lower panel).

The GLM table contains some additional terms: **Corrected Model**, **Intercept**, **Corrected Total** and **Type III Sum of Squares**. These are terms from another statistical technique called **regression**, which is discussed in Chapter 12. As we shall see in Chapter 12, it is quite possible to recast the one-way ANOVA (or, indeed, *any* ANOVA) as a problem in regression and make exactly the same test of the null hypothesis. If that is done (as in the GLM procedure), the mean squares, their degrees of freedom, the value of *F* and the p-value will all be exactly the same as those produced by the ANOVA procedure. In the GLM summary table, the rows labelled as **Corrected Model**, **Group**, **Error** and **Corrected Total** contain exactly the same information that we shall find in the **Between Groups**, **Within Groups** and **Total** rows of the One-Way ANOVA table below. The values of F are also exactly the same in both tables.

Output 2 also contains another item that is missing from the table we obtained from the **One-Way** procedure in **Compare Means** (Output 1). Underneath the table is the information that **R Squared** (that is, η^2) = .447 and that **Adjusted R Squared** = .398.

7.5.3   Additional items with GLM Univariate

The basic ANOVA output includes little other than the ANOVA summary table. We shall require several other statistics, which can be selected from the GLM **Univariate** dialog box (Figure 10). For clarity, we shall consider these measures separately here; but they would normally be requested with the basic ANOVA. Among the items we shall select are the **descriptive statistics** (including the means and standard deviations for the five conditions in the experiment), **homogeneity tests** (testing the assumption of homogeneity of variance among the levels of the DV), **estimates of effect size** and a **profile plot** (a line graph of the treatment means). These are obtained by making the appropriate responses in the **Univariate** dialog box.

Requesting various statistics

The first three recommended options are obtained by clicking **Options…** in the **Univariate** dialog box (Figure 10) to open the **Options** dialog box (Figure 11).

When the box labelled **Estimates of effect size** is checked in **Options**, the ANOVA summary table will include **partial eta squared (η_p^2)** which, in the context of the one-way ANOVA, is identical with eta squared (R^2 in Output 2). You may wish to confirm that when the **Estimates of effect size** box is checked, the output will give the value of partial eta squared as 0.447. As we have seen, however, eta squared is positively biased as a measure of effect size in the population and many reviewers (and journal editors) would expect the value of a statistic such as omega squared to be reported.

It is now usual to include a measure of effect size with reports of statistical tests. We suggest that your complete report of the results of the ANOVA might run along the following lines:

> The mean skill score for the placebo was M = 8.00 (SD = 1.83) and for the four drugs respectively, the means were: M = 7.90 (SD = 2.13); M = 12.00 (SD = 2.49); M = 14.40 (SD = 4.50); M = 13.00 (SD = 3.742). The one-way ANOVA showed F to be significant beyond the .01 level: $F(4, 45) = 9.08$; p <.01. Estimated omega squared = 0.39.

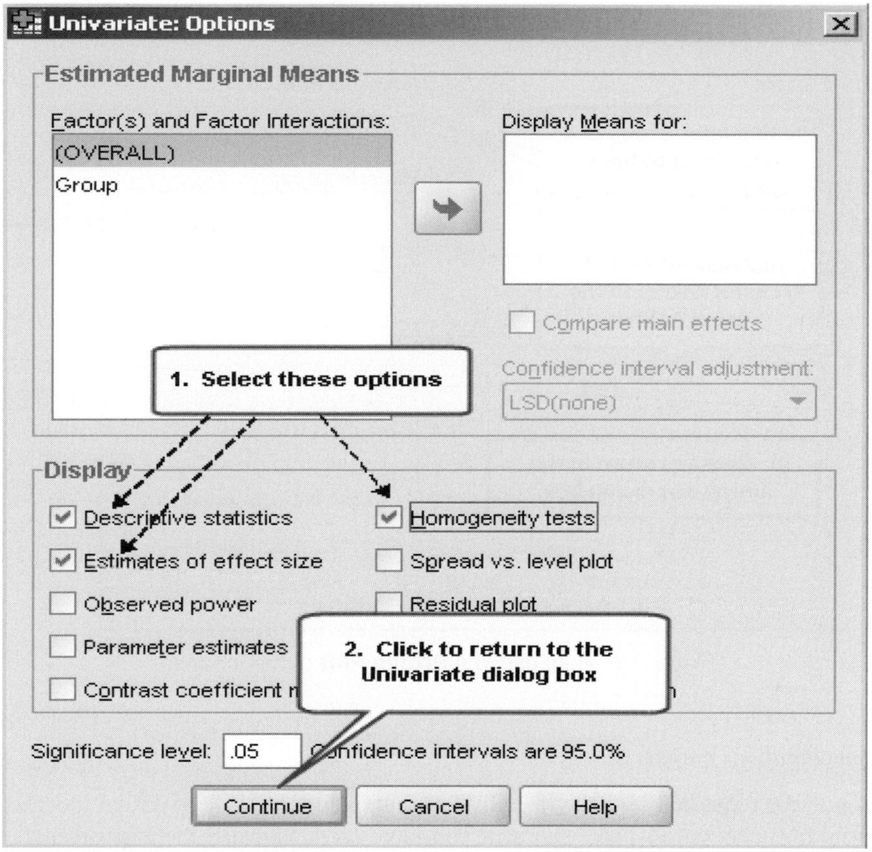

Figure 11. The **Options** dialog box with **Descriptive statistics**, **Estimates of effect size** and **Homogeneity tests** selected

Requesting profile plots of the five treatment means

Click **Plots...** (Figure 10) to open the **Profile Plots** dialog box (Figure 12) and follow the procedure shown in Figure 12.

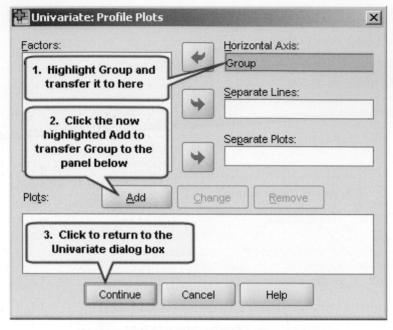

Figure 12. Requesting a **Profile Plot** of the means

Design specifications output

In addition to the requested statistics, the GLM output includes a table of design specifications. These should be checked to make sure that you have communicated the experimental design correctly to SPSS. Output 3 shows the specifications of the independent variable *Drug Condition.*

Between-Subjects Factors

		Value Label	N
Drug Condition	1	Placebo	10
	2	Drug A	10
	3	Drug B	10
	4	Drug C	10
	5	Drug D	10

Output 3. Design specifications: the values and value labels of the grouping variable

Check this table to make sure that SPSS agrees that the factor has five levels, that 10 participants are tested at each level and that the code numbers are correctly paired with the five conditions. Incorrect specifications in **Variable View** can emerge at this point. Transcription errors in **Data View** could result in incorrect entries in the *N* column.

Descriptive statistics output

Output 4 tabulates the requested **Descriptive statistics**.

Descriptive Statistics

Dependent Variable:Score

Drug ...	Mean	Std. Deviation	N
Placebo	8.00	1.826	10
Drug A	7.90	2.132	10
Drug B	12.00	2.494	10
Drug C	14.40	4.502	10
Drug D	13.00	3.742	10
Total	11.06	4.007	50

Output 4. The **Descriptive Statistics** output: means and standard deviations for the five groups.

The Levene test output

Output 5 shows the result of Levene's test for homogeneity of variance.

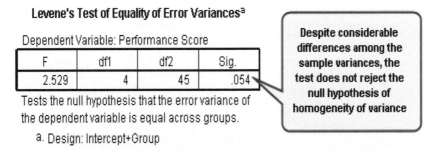

Levene's Test of Equality of Error Variances[a]

Dependent Variable: Performance Score

F	df1	df2	Sig.
2.529	4	45	.054

Tests the null hypothesis that the error variance of the dependent variable is equal across groups.

a. Design: Intercept+Group

> Despite considerable differences among the sample variances, the test does not reject the null hypothesis of homogeneity of variance

Output 5. **Levene's Test** for homogeneity of variance

The non-significance of the **Levene F Statistic** for the test of equality of error variances (homogeneity of variances) indicates that the assumption of homogeneity of variance is tenable; however, considerable differences among the variances are apparent from inspection. The one-way ANOVA is to some extent robust to violations of assumptions of normality of distribution and homogeneity of variance, especially when, as in the present example, there are equal numbers of observations in the different groups. When there are marked differences in sample size from group to group, however, this robustness tends to break down and the true Type I error rate may increase to an unacceptable level. We shall return to this matter later in Section 8.

The profile plot of means output

The requested profile plot of the means is shown in Output 6. Observe that the zero point of the vertical scale does not appear on the axis. This is something that still happens in default profile plots on SPSS. Always be suspicious of such a graph, because it can give the appearance of a strong effect when actually there is very little happening. The difficulty can easily be remedied by double-clicking on the graph to bring it into the **Chart Editor**, double-clicking on the vertical axis and specifying zero as the minimum point on the vertical scale (Output 7).

In this case, the profile flattens out a little; but the effect of including the zero point can sometimes be quite dramatic: with some data sets, an exciting-looking range of peaks suddenly becomes a monotonous level plain. In this case, however, it is clear that even when the zero point is shown on the vertical axis, something is really happening in this data set.

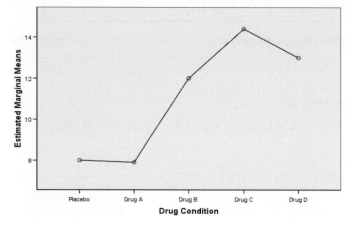

Output 6. The plot of the means as originally shown in SPSS output

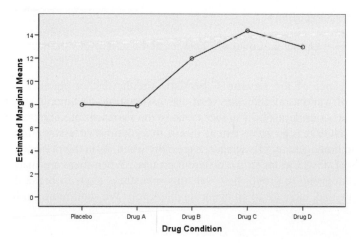

Output 7. The plot of the means with the ordinate scale now including zero

It is important to be clear that the profile plot in Output 7 is not to be seen as depicting a functional relationship between the five conditions in the experiment and the mean scores: the five conditions making up the single factor in the experimental design are *qualitative* categories, which have *no intrinsic order*. The results of the ANOVA would be exactly the same were we to rearrange the data so that the scores obtained under Drug C followed those for the Placebo condition; in fact, *any* ordering of the data from the five conditions in the **Data Editor** would produce exactly the same result from the ANOVA. What we learn from the profile plot in Output 7 is that there are marked differences among the five group means and we can expect this to be reflected in the value of *F*. The more mountainous the profile of means, the more reason we have to doubt the null hypothesis of equality.

7.6   MAKING COMPARISONS AMONG THE TREATMENT MEANS

We have found evidence against the null hypothesis (H_0: all five means in the population have the same value) but what can we conclude from this? If H_0 states that all the means are equal, the alternative hypothesis is simply that they are not all equal. The falsity of H_0, however, does not imply that the difference between any and every pair of group means is significant. If the ANOVA *F* test is significant, there should be at least one difference *somewhere* among the means; but we cannot claim that the mean for any particular group is significantly different from the mean of any other group. Further analysis is necessary to confirm whatever differences there may be among the individual treatment means. We shall consider some techniques for making comparisons among means in Section 7.6.

Planned and unplanned comparisons

Before running an experiment such as the one in our current example, the experimenter may have some very specific questions in mind. It might be expected, for example, (perhaps on theoretical grounds) that the mean score of every group who have ingested one of the drugs will be greater than the mean score of the Placebo group. This expectation would be tested by comparing each drug group with the Placebo group. Perhaps, on the other hand, the experimenter has theoretical reasons to suspect that Drugs A and B should enhance performance, but Drugs C and D should not. That hypothesis would be tested by comparing the Placebo mean with the average score for groups A and B combined and with the average score for groups B and C combined. These are examples of **planned comparisons**.

Often, however, the experimenter, perhaps because the field has been little explored, has only a sketchy idea of how the results will turn out. There may be good reason to expect that *some* of the drugs will enhance performance; but it may not be possible, *a priori*, to be more specific. Unplanned, *a posteriori* or **post hoc**, comparisons are part of the 'data-snooping' that inevitably follows the gathering of a data set.

*The **per comparison** and **familywise** Type I error rates*

We have seen that when we use the *t* test to compare two means, the significance level α is the probability of a Type I error, that is, the rejection of the null hypothesis when it is actually true. When, however, we intend to make several comparisons among a group of means, we must distinguish between the individual comparison and the whole set, or **family**, of comparisons that we intend to make. It can be shown that if we make a set of comparisons, the probability, under the null hypothesis, of at least one of them being significant, may be considerably greater than α. We must, therefore, distinguish between the Type I error rate *per comparison* (*α*) and the Type I error rate *familywise* (α_{family}). If we intend to make c comparisons, the *familywise* Type I error rate can be shown to be approximately $c\alpha$

$$\alpha_{family} \approx c\alpha \quad \text{- - -} (18) \quad \textbf{The familywise Type I error rate}$$

The import of (18) is that when the researcher is making many comparisons among the treatment means of data from complex experiments, the probability of at least one test showing significance can be very high: with a large array of treatment means, the probability of obtaining at least one significant difference might be 0.8, 0.9 or even greater! It is therefore essential to control the *familywise* Type I error rate by making data-snooping tests more conservative. Several procedures for doing this have been proposed.

The **Bonferroni** method

Equation (18) is the basis of the *Bonferroni method* of controlling the *familywise* Type I error rate. If c is the number of comparisons in the family, the p-value for each test is multiplied by c. This procedure obviously makes the test of a comparison more conservative. For example, suppose that, having decided to make 4 comparisons, we were to make an ordinary t test of one comparison and find that the p-value is 0.04. In the Bonferroni procedure, we must now multiply this p-value by 4, obtaining 0.16, a value well above the desired *familywise* error rate of 0.05. We must, therefore, accept the null hypothesis (or, at any rate, not conclude that we have evidence to reject it).

It is common practice, following the running of an experiment with several different conditions, to make unplanned or **post hoc** multiple pairwise comparisons among the treatment means: that is, the difference between every possible pair of means is tested for significance. Here, the Bonferroni method can result in extremely conservative tests, because in this situation c (the size of the comparison family) is arguably the number of different pairs that can be drawn from the array of k treatment means; otherwise we risk capitalising upon chance and making false claims of differences among the population means.

The great problem with the Bonferroni correction is that when the array of means is large, the criterion for significance becomes so exacting that the method finds too few significant differences. In other words, the Bonferroni tests are conservative to the point that they may have very little power to reject the null hypothesis. The **Tukey** tests and the **Newman-Keuls** test are less conservative, the Tukey test itself (or a variant known as Tukey-b) being generally preferred for *post hoc* tests of pairwise differences following the one-way ANOVA. For more complex comparisons, such as the comparison of one mean with the mean of several others, the **Scheffé test** is highly regarded; but it is thought to be over-conservative when used for pairwise comparisons.

The situation may arise in which the researcher wishes to compare performance under each of several active conditions with that of a baseline control group. The **Dunnett test**, described in Howell (2007; p.374), is regarded as the most powerful test available for this purpose.

These tests (and many others) are available within SPSS.

7.6.1   Unplanned or post hoc multiple comparisons with SPSS

Click **Post Hoc...** (Figure 10) to open the **Post Hoc** dialog box (Figure 13). Follow the directions in Figure 13 in order to run the **Bonferroni**, **Tukey** and **Dunnett** tests.

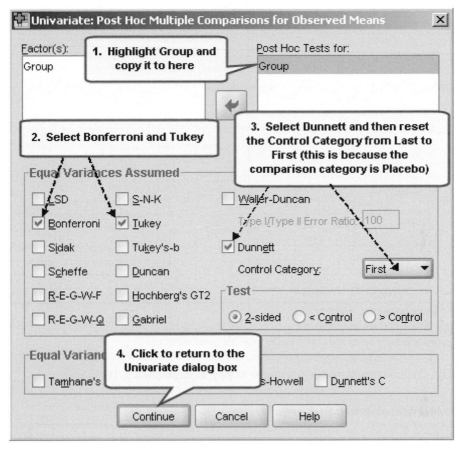

Figure 13. Selecting **Post Hoc** tests

Output 8 is only part of an extensive table of the results of multiple pairwise comparisons with the **Tukey**, **Bonferroni** and **Dunnett** tests. The most conservative test of the three, the Bonferroni, has the widest confidence intervals and the largest p-values; the least conservative test, the Dunnett test, has the smallest p-values and the narrowest confidence intervals.

Output 9 shows a second part of the output for the **Tukey** test. The output shows that there are two subgroups of tests. Within each subgroup there are no significant pairwise differences; on the other hand, any member of either subgroup is significantly different from any member of the other subgroup. For example, there are no differences among Drugs B, C and D; but each of those is significantly different from both the Placebo and Drug A. In a word, of the four drugs tested, the only one not to produce an improvement over the Placebo was Drug A.

Multiple Comparisons

Dependent Variable: Score

	(I) Drug Condition	(J) Drug Condition	Mean Difference (I-J)	Std. Error	Sig.	95% Confidence Interval Lower Bound	95% Confidence Interval Upper Bound
Tukey HSD	Placebo	Drug A	.10	1.391	1.000	-3.85	4.05
		Drug B	-4.00*	1.391	.046	-7.95	-.05
		Drug C	-6.40*	1.391	.000	-10.35	-2.45
		Drug D	-5.00*	1.391	.007	-8.95	-1.05
Bonferroni	Placebo	Drug A	.10	1.391	1.000	-4.01	4.21
		Drug B	-4.00	1.391	.061	-8.11	.11
		Drug C	-6.40*	1.391	.000	-10.51	-2.29
		Drug D	-5.00*	1.391	.008	-9.11	-.89
	Drug A	Placebo	-.10	1.391	1.000	-4.21	4.01
		Drug C	-1.40	1.391	1.000	-5.51	2.71
Dunnett t (2-sided)a	Drug A	Placebo	-.10	1.391	1.000	-3.62	3.42
	Drug B	Placebo	4.00*	1.391	.021	.48	7.52
	Drug C	Placebo	6.40*	1.391	.000	2.88	9.92
	Drug D	Placebo	5.00*	1.391	.003	1.48	8.52

Based on observed means.

*. The mean difference is significant at the .05 level.

a. Dunnett t-tests treat one group as a control, and compare all other groups against it.

Output 8. Comparison of the outputs for the **Tukey**, **Bonferroni** and **Dunnett** tests

Homogeneous Subsets

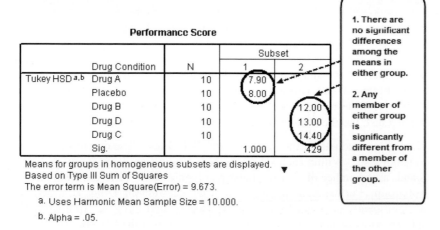

Performance Score

	Drug Condition	N	Subset 1	Subset 2
Tukey HSD a,b	Drug A	10	7.90	
	Placebo	10	8.00	
	Drug B	10		12.00
	Drug D	10		13.00
	Drug C	10		14.40
	Sig.		1.000	.429

Means for groups in homogeneous subsets are displayed.
Based on Type III Sum of Squares
The error term is Mean Square(Error) = 9.673.

a. Uses Harmonic Mean Sample Size = 10.000.

b. Alpha = .05.

1. There are no significant differences among the means in either group.

2. Any member of either group is significantly different from a member of the other group.

Output 9. The two subgroups of treatment means identified by the **Tukey** multiple comparisons test

7.6.2   Linear contrasts

We have data from a one-factor between subject experiment with five treatment groups, the mean levels of performance of which are M_1, M_2, M_3, M_4 and M_5.

A comparison between two of an array of k treatment means (or combinations of the means) can be expressed as a **linear contrast**, that is, a linear sum of the five treatment means, with the constraint that the coefficients (weights) add up to zero. We have 5 treatment means and we want to compare M_1 with M_2. The difference $M_1 - M_2$ can be expressed as the linear contrast ψ_1, where

$$\psi_1 = (1)M_1 + (-1)M_2 + (0)M_3 + (0)M_4 + (0)M_5 \ \text{- - - (19)} \ \textbf{Linear contrast}$$

Since we are interested in comparing only two of the five means, the inclusion of all five means in (19) may seem highly artificial; but we need to develop a notation for a whole *set* of contrasts that might be made among a given set of treatment means. We must have the same number of terms in all contrasts, even if we have to have coefficients of zero for the irrelevant terms. In a situation such as our current example, in which there are five treatment means, one of which is a control or comparison, the researcher may wish to compare the control mean with each of the others. Such pairwise contrasts are known as **simple contrasts**. As in (19), the formulation of each of a set of simple contrasts must include all the treatments means, the irrelevant means having coefficients of zero:

$$M_2 - M_1 = (-1)M_1 + (+1)M_2 + (0)M_3 + (0)M_4 + (0)M_5$$
$$M_3 - M_1 = (-1)M_1 + (0)M_2 + (+1)M_3 + (0)M_4 + (0)M_5$$
$$M_4 - M_1 = (-1)M_1 + (0)M_2 + (0)M_3 + (+1)M_4 + (0)M_5$$
$$M_5 - M_1 = (-1)M_1 + (0)M_2 + (0)M_3 + (0)M_4 + (+1)M_5$$

This set of four simple contrasts can be represented more compactly by the four rows of coefficients alone:

$$\begin{pmatrix} -1 & +1 & 0 & 0 & 0 \\ -1 & 0 & +1 & 0 & 0 \\ -1 & 0 & 0 & +1 & 0 \\ -1 & 0 & 0 & 0 & +1 \end{pmatrix}$$

The same notation extends easily to more complex contrasts involving three or more treatment means. If we wish to compare M_3 with the mean of M_1 and M_2, the difference $M_3 - \dfrac{(M_1 + M_2)}{2}$ can be expressed as the linear contrast ψ_2, where

$$\psi_2 = (-0.5)M_1 + (-0.5)M_2 + (1)M_3 + (0)M_4 + (0)M_5 \ \text{- - - (20)}$$

It is worth bearing in mind that although in (20) three means have coefficients, the contrast involves only *two* means: M_3 and a composite derived from means M_1 and M_2. This has the important implication that *a contrast sum of squares must always have one degree of freedom*, however complex the contrast and however many means may be involved. We shall return to this point when we discuss the testing of contrasts for significance.

In general, for a set of k treatment means M_j, any contrast Ψ can be represented as

$$\psi = \sum_j^k c_j M_j \quad \text{---(21)} \quad \textbf{General equation for a linear contrast}$$

where c_j is the coefficient of the treatment mean M_j and $\sum c_j = 0$.

Sums of squares for contrasts

Associated with a particular contrast ψ is a sum of squares SS_ψ, the formula for which is

$$SS_\psi = \frac{n\psi^2}{\sum c_j^2} = \frac{n\left[\sum_j c_j M_j\right]^2}{\sum c_j^2} \quad \text{---(22)} \quad \textbf{Contrast sum of squares}$$

This sum of squares can be thought of as the variability of the scores that can be attributed to the difference between the two means (or composite means) that are being compared. The term $\sum_j c_j^2$ in the denominator acts as a scaling factor, ensuring that the sum of squares attributable to a particular contrast can be compared in magnitude with the ANOVA between groups mean square $SS_{between}$.

Table 6 shows the application of formula (22) to the first contrast that we considered (19).

Table 6. Steps in calculating a contrast sum of squares					
	Placebo	**Drug A**	**Drug B**	**Drug C**	**Drug D**
Mean	8.00	7.90	12.00	14.40	13.00
c_j	1	−1	0	0	0	$\sum_j c_j^2 = 2$
$c_j M_j$	8.00	-7.90	0	0	0	$\sum_j c_j M_j = 0.10$

It can be seen from Table 6 that

$$\psi_1 = (1)M_1 + (-1)M_2 + (0)M_3 + (0)M_4 + (0)M_5 = 8.00 - 7.90 = 0.10$$

$$SS_1 = \frac{n\psi_1^2}{\sum c_j^2} = \frac{10(0.10^2)}{2} = 0.5$$

As we pointed out earlier, this sum of squares has one degree of freedom because we are comparing two means. In fact, for *any* linear contrast, the sum of squares has one degree of freedom because, however complex the comparison, only two means are being compared and the specification of a value for one deviation fully determines the value of the other.

Testing a contrast for significance

A contrast is a comparison between two means. In this special two-group case, therefore, we can either make an independent samples *t* test to test the difference for significance or we can run a one-way ANOVA – the two procedures will produce the same decision about the null hypothesis. The value of *F* will be the square of the value of *t*; but the p-values will be the same for both statistics.

Since any contrast is a comparison between two means, a contrast sum of squares always has one degree of freedom. This means that, in this special case, the mean square has the same value as the sum of squares, so that

$$F_{contrast} = \frac{MS_{contrast}}{MS_{within}} = \frac{SS_{contrast}}{MS_{within}} \quad \text{- - - (23) F ratio for a contrast}$$

where the degrees of freedom of $F_{contrast}$ are 1 and df_{within} .

We can therefore make the test of the contrast in Table 6 with the statistic $F_1(1,45)$, where

$$F_1(1,45) = \frac{MS_1}{MS_{within}} = \frac{SS_1}{SS_{within}} = \frac{0.05}{9.673} = 0.005$$

Alternatively, we can make the test with $t(45)$, where *t* is the square root of *F*:

$$t(45) = \sqrt{F(1,45)} = \sqrt{0.005} = 0.07$$

The p-value of either statistic is 0.943.

Since SPSS gives the result of the *t* test rather than the *F* test, we should perhaps look a little more closely at the *t* test. In the equal-*n* case, the usual formula for the independent-samples *t* statistic becomes:

$$t = \frac{M_1 - M_2}{\sqrt{MS_{within}\left(\frac{1}{n} + \frac{1}{n}\right)}} = \frac{M_1 - M_2}{\sqrt{2MS_{within}/n}} \quad \text{- - - (24) Independent-samples t statistic}$$

When we are making a test of a contrast, the numerator of (24) becomes the value of the contrast, i.e., $\sum_j c_j M_j$. The denominator changes too, the constant 2 being replaced with $\sum_j c_j^2$. The t statistic for testing the contrast is therefore

$$t = \frac{\sum_j c_j M_j}{\sqrt{\sum_j c_j^2 MS_{within}/n}} \quad \text{- - - (25) The t statistic for a contrast}$$

Substituting the values we calculated in Table 6 into (25) and putting $MS_{within} = 9.673$, we have

$$t = \frac{0.10}{\sqrt{2 \times 9.673 / 10}} = 0.07$$

which is the value we obtained above simply by taking the square root of F.

Helmert contrasts

Suppose, as in our present example, we have an array of five treatment means. We construct a set of contrasts as follows:
   1. We compare the first mean with the average of the other four means.
   2. We drop the first mean and compare the second mean with the average of means three four and five.
   3. We drop the second mean and compare the third with the average of means four and five.
   4. Finally, we compare the fourth mean with the fifth.

This set of Helmert contrasts can be represented by four rows of coefficients as follows:

$$\begin{pmatrix} +1 & -1/4 & -1/4 & -1/4 & -1/4 \\ 0 & +1 & -1/3 & -1/3 & -1/3 \\ 0 & 0 & +1 & -1/2 & -1/2 \\ 0 & 0 & 0 & +1 & -1 \end{pmatrix}$$

We can remove the fractions by multiplying each of the coefficients in the first row by 4, those of the second by 3, and those of the third by two thus:

$$\begin{pmatrix} +4 & -1 & -1 & -1 & -1 \\ 0 & +3 & -1 & -1 & -1 \\ 0 & 0 & +2 & -1 & -1 \\ 0 & 0 & 0 & +1 & -1 \end{pmatrix}$$

While multiplying the coefficients by four multiplies the value of the contrast by the same factor, the value of $\sum c^2$ in the denominator of (21) also increases, so that the value of the contrast sum of squares is unaltered.

Orthogonal contrasts

A set of Helmert contrasts has the property that each contrast is independent of the others, in the sense that its value is neither constrained by nor constrains those of any of the others. The first contrast does not affect the value of the second, because the first mean is not involved in the second contrast. Similarly, the values of neither of the first two contrasts affect the value of the third, because the latter involves neither of the first two means. Finally, the fourth contrast is independent of the first three because the first three means have now been dropped. Taken together, these Helmert contrasts make up a set of **orthogonal contrasts**.

In either version of the set of Helmert contrasts, the sum of the products of the corresponding coefficients in any two rows is zero. For contrasts 1 and 2, for instance, $\sum c_1 c_2 = 0$. This is the criterion for the orthogonality (independence) of a set of contrasts. You might wish to confirm, for example, that the sum of products of the corresponding coefficients in the first two rows of either matrix is zero; moreover, you can easily check that the sum of products is zero for *any* two rows.

In our current example, with five treatment means, we were able to construct a set of four orthogonal contrasts. In general, with k treatment means, sets of only $(k - 1)$ orthogonal contrasts are possible; though it may be possible to construct more than one orthogonal set. The limit to the size of any one set of orthogonal contrasts is, of course, the degrees of freedom of the between groups sum of squares.

An advantage of orthogonal contrasts is that it is possible to assign to each contrast a sum of squares that is attributable to that contrast alone and to none of the others in the set. Moreover, when the sums of squares of the $(k - 1)$ orthogonal contrasts are added together, we shall obtain the between groups treatment sum of squares.

If we apply formula (22) to the set of four Helmert contrasts and calculate the sum of squares for each contrast, you may wish to confirm that four contrast sums of squares add up to 351.52, the between groups sum of squares given in the ANOVA summary table.

$$
\begin{pmatrix}
& M_1 & M_2 & M_3 & M_4 & M_5 & & & \\
Contrast & 8.00 & 7.90 & 12.00 & 14.40 & 13.00 & \sum c_j^2 & \sum c_j M_j & SS_{contrast} \\
1 & +4 & -1 & -1 & -1 & -1 & 20 & -15.3 & 117.04 \\
2 & 0 & +3 & -1 & -1 & -1 & 12 & -15.7 & 205.41 \\
3 & 0 & 0 & +2 & -1 & -1 & 6 & -3.4 & 19.27 \\
4 & 0 & 0 & 0 & +1 & -1 & 2 & 1.40 & 9.80 \\
& & & & & & & & 351.52
\end{pmatrix}
$$

> The sum of the contrast sums of squares is equal to $SS_{between}$ in the ANOVA summary table.

What we have shown is that the partition of the total ANOVA sum of squares can be extended in the following way:

$$ SS_{between} = SS_1 + SS_2 + SS_3 + SS_4 \quad \text{- - - (26)} \quad \textbf{Partition of the between groups SS} $$

where the sums of squares on the right-hand side of (26) are those associated with each of the four contrasts in the orthogonal set.

Testing contrasts in the One-Way ANOVA procedure

The GLM menu offers several entire sets of contrasts, each set serving a different purpose. To make a test of a few specified contrasts, however, we shall turn to the **One-Way ANOVA** procedure in the **Compare Means** menu. In the **One-Way ANOVA** dialog box (Figure 8), click on the **Contrasts ...** button at the top right of the dialog box and proceed as shown in Figure 14.

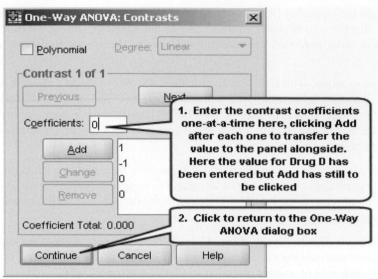

Figure 14. Specifying a specific contrast in the **One-Way ANOVA: Contrasts** dialog box.

Output 10 shows the result of the t test of the contrast ψ_1. In the upper panel, the coefficients of the contrast ψ_1 are listed. The t-value (0.07) agrees with the result of our previous calculation.

Contrast Coefficients

Contrast	Drug Condition				
	Placebo	Drug A	Drug B	Drug C	Drug D
1	1	-1	0	0	0

Contrast Tests

		Contrast	Value of Contrast	Std. Error	t	df	Sig. (2-tailed)
Score	Assume equal variances	1	.10	1.391	.072	45	.943
	Does not assume equal	1	.10	.888	.113	17.584	.912

Output 10. Result of the test of the contrast ψ_1

Running contrasts in the GLM procedure

Table 7 shows the different types of contrasts that can be requested from the GLM dialog box.

Table 7. The types of contrast sets available on GLM	
Type	**Description**
Simple	A pre-specified reference or control mean is compared with each of the other means.
Helmert	Starting from the leftmost mean in the array, each mean is compared with the mean of the remaining means.
Difference (Reverse Helmert)	Starting from the leftmost mean in the array, each mean is compared with the mean of the means that preceded it.
Repeated	First with second, second with third, third with fourth, …
Deviation	Each mean is compared with the grand mean.

We shall illustrate the procedure by requesting a set of simple contrasts. Click **Contrasts…** (Figure 10) to open the **Contrasts** dialog box (Figure 15) and follow the directions in Figure 15.

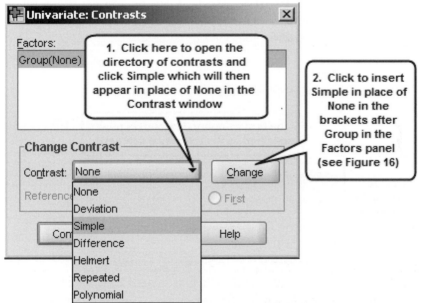

Figure 15. Requesting simple contrasts

The **Contrasts** dialog box will now appear as in Figure 16. To specify the *Placebo* category as the **Reference Category**, you will need to click the appropriate radio button at the foot of the dialog box and click **Change** to complete the specification (Figure 16, lower slot).

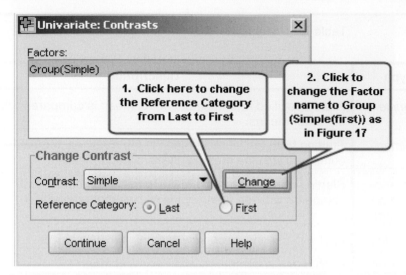

Figure 16. Completing the specifications of simple contrasts with *Placebo* as the reference category.

In Figure 17, it is clear from the entry in the upper panel not only that **Simple** contrasts have been specified, but also that the reference category is now the Placebo group, with which all the other means (that is the means of the four drug groups) will each be compared.

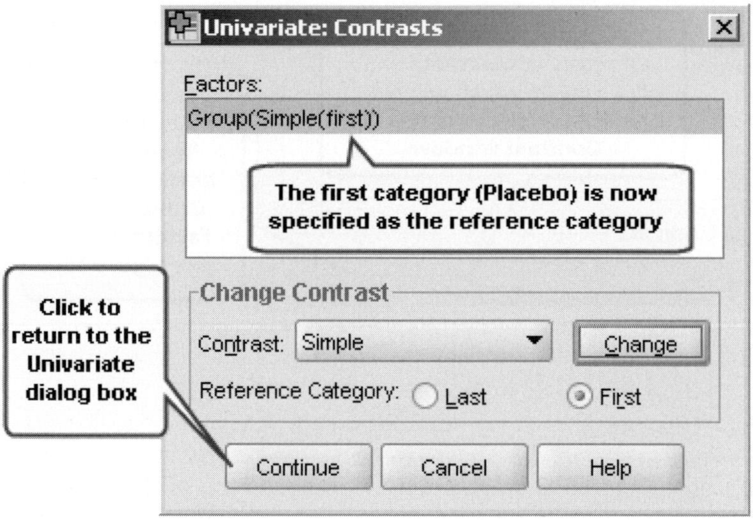

Figure 17. The **Univariate: Contrasts** dialog has now been completed, with the first (Placebo) condition as the reference category

Output 11 shows part of the table of results of the set of simple contrasts. No *t*-values are given; but if the 95% confidence interval fails to include zero, the contrast is significant. The first test reported in Output 11 is the one we made by specifying the same contrast in the **One-**

Way ANOVA procedure. To obtain the value of t, we need only divide the 'Contrast Estimate' by the 'Std. Error':

$$t(35) = \frac{-0.10}{1.391} = -0.07 \quad \text{(as before)}$$

Custom Hypothesis Tests

Contrast Results (K Matrix)

Drug Condition Simple Contrast[a]			Dependent Variable Performance Score
Level 2 vs. Level 1	Contrast Estimate		-.100
	Hypothesized Value		0
	Difference (Estimate - Hypothesized)		-.100
	Std. Error	Not significant since p-value > .05	1.391
	Sig.		.943
	95% Confidence Interval for Difference	Lower Bound	-2.901
		Upper Bound	2.701
Level 3 vs. Level 1	Contrast Estimate		4.000
	Hypothesized Value		0
	Difference (Estimate - Hypothesized)		4.000
	Std. Error	Significant since p-value < .05	1.391
	Sig.		.006
	95% Confidence Interval for Difference	Lower Bound	1.199
		Upper Bound	6.801
Level 4 vs. Level 1	Contrast Estimate		6.400

Output 11. Part of the **Simple Contrasts** output with *Placebo* as the reference category

7.7   TREND ANALYSIS

In the data sets that we have been considering so far, the sets of categories or conditions making up the treatment factor differ qualitatively, so that, as far as the results of the analysis are concerned, the order in which the levels of the factor are defined in the **Labels** column in **Variable View** and the consequent order of entry of the data in **Data View** are entirely arbitrary. In our example, suppose that the levels of the Drug factor had been defined in the order: Drug C, Placebo, Drug D, Drug B, Drug D. The outcome of the one-way ANOVA would have been exactly the same as it was before. Moreover, as we shall explain in Chapter 12, the various measures of effect strength such as eta squared and estimated omega squared would have exactly the same values as they did when the conditions appeared in their original order in the Data Editor. (It's more convenient to begin or end the SPSS data set with the Placebo scores, but that variable could have been placed anywhere in the data set without affecting the results.)

Now suppose that the levels making up a treatment factor are equally-spaced points on a single quantitative dimension, so that the treatment factor is a continuous independent variable, rather than merely a set of unordered categories. Suppose, for example, that in our drug experiment, the factor or independent variable had consisted not of a set of active conditions with *different* drugs, but of different dosages of *the same* drug. Our five treatment conditions now make a set of *ordered* categories. The purpose of such an investigation is no longer simply to establish whether differences exist among the group treatment means, but to investigate the precise nature of the functional relationship between the factor (independent variable) and the measure (dependent variable).

It might be well to review the possible types of functional relationships that might obtain between the independent variable (the Drug dosage factor) and Performance (the measure or dependent variable). (The reader who is familiar with the term **polynomial** may wish to skip the next section.)

Polynomials

A **polynomial** is a sum of terms, each of which is a product of a constant and a power of the same variable: e.g. $y = 6 + 2x$, $y = 2 + x + 3x^2$, $y = -4 + 3x^2 - 4x^3$ and $y = 3 - x - x^2 - 2x^3 - x^4$ are all polynomials. The general definition of a polynomial is as follows:

$$y = a_0 + a_1 x + a_2 x^2 + ... + a_n x^n \quad ---(27) \text{ \bf General equation of a polynomial}$$

where $a_0, a_1, ..., a_n$ are constants, and $a_1, a_2, ..., a_n$ are **coefficients** of the single variable x, which is raised to increasing powers. up to a maximum of n.

The highest power n of x is known as the **order** or **degree** of the polynomial. The graph of the equation of a polynomial of the first degree (Figure 18, leftmost panel), such as $y = x - 3$, is a straight line: that is, a first order polynomial is a **linear function**.

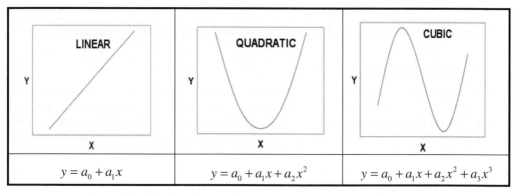

Figure 18. The first three polynomials and their general equations

A straight line obviously does not change direction at all. By choosing the right values for the constants a_0 and a_1, however, a straight line can be made to fit any *two* points in the plane of the graph that are separated along the x-axis.

A polynomial of the second degree, such as $y = 7 + x - 6x^2$ (Figure 18, middle panel), is known as a **quadratic function**. The graph of a quadratic function is a curve which changes direction only once. Although a quadratic curve changes direction only once, values for the three constants can always be found so that the curve will fit any three points that are separated along the x-axis. The graph of a polynomial of the third degree, such as $y = -14 + x - 8x^2 + 20x^3$ (Figure 18, rightmost panel), is termed a **cubic function**. The graph of a cubic function changes direction twice. Although the graph of a cubic function changes direction only twice, values of the four constants can always be found so that the curve fits any four points separated along the x-axis. In general, a polynomial of degree n changes direction $(n - 1)$ times and can be made to fit any $(n + 1)$ points separated along the x-axis.

The graphs in Figure 18 depict polynomial relationships in their pure forms. In a real data set, however, more than one kind of relationship, or **trend** may be evident: for example, the graph of a data set may be of linear shape in the middle of the range of values, but have a curve at one end, suggesting the presence of both linear and quadratic trends. In **trend analysis**, it is possible to attribute portions of the total variability of the scores to specific polynomial relationships in the data and to test these components of trend for significance.

In a trend analysis, a special set of orthogonal contrasts, known as **orthogonal polynomial coefficients** is constructed. In any row, the coefficients are values of a polynomial of one particular order: the first row is a first order (linear) polynomial; the second row is a second order (quadratic) polynomial and so on. Since each row of coefficients is a contrast, the coefficients sum to zero; moroever, as with all orthogonal sets, the products of the corresponding coefficients in any two rows also sum to zero. The sum of squares associated with each contrast (row) captures one particular type of functional trend in the data; moreover, because we have an orthogonal set, each contrast sum of squares measures that kind of trend and no other. The sum of squares for the first row captures the linear component of trend, the SS for the second row the quadratic component, that for the third row the cubic and so on. As in the ANOVA of data from an experiment with a qualitative treatment factor, it is possible to partition the between groups sum of squares into the sums of squares associated with the different contrasts and test each contrast for significance; in trend analysis, however, each test confirms the presence of a specific polynomial relationship in the data.

A drug experiment with a quantitative independent variable

The purpose of the drug experiment was essentially to compare the performance of participants who had ingested different drugs with a comparison, Placebo group. For our second example, the purpose of the investigation changes. This time, the investigator wishes to determine the effects upon performance of varying the dosage of a single drug – possibly the one that seemed to have the strongest effect in the first experiment. Suppose that, in a drug experiment of similar design to our running example, the groups vary, in equal steps of 2 units, in the size of the dosage of a single drug that they have ingested: zero (the Placebo), 2mg, 4mg, 6mg and 8mg. The profile plot appears as in Output 12. It is important to be clear about the differences between this second experiment and the previous one. In the first experiment, the Drug factor was a set of qualitative (and therefore unordered) categories, so that the order in which the 'levels' were defined in Variable View (and their corresponding ordering in Data View) was entirely arbitrary. The results of the analysis would be the same regardless of the order. In this new experiment, the five conditions are equally spaced points on a quantitative dimension: dosage. Here, the ordering of the data is crucial, because the purpose of the exercise is to investigate (and confirm) any possible functional relationships between the scores and the dosage level that might emerge. Does performance increase continuously as the dosage increases? Or does it increase at first, but fall off with higher dosages?

Inspection of the profile plot suggests that the means show a basically linear trend in the middle of the range; the changes in direction at the extremes of the dosage scale, however, may indicate the presence of an additional (perhaps cubic) component.

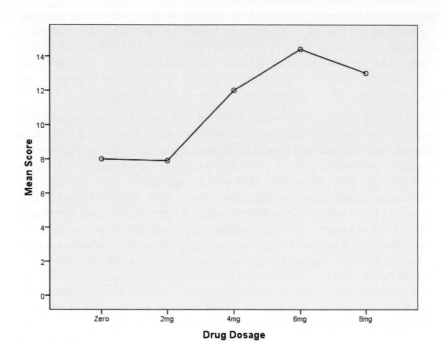

Output 12. Profile plot of the group means from an experiment with a quantitative treatment factor

Almost any standard statistics textbook will contain a table of sets of orthogonal polynomial coefficients for a wide range of values of k, where k is the number of levels in the quantitative treatment factor. (We should note that the use of such tables assumes that the levels of the factor are equally spaced on the scale of the continuous independent variable.) When, as in the present example, there are five conditions, the set of orthogonal polynomial coefficients contains only four rows:

$$\begin{pmatrix} -2 & -1 & 0 & 1 & 2 \\ 2 & -1 & -2 & -1 & 2 \\ -1 & 2 & 0 & -2 & 1 \\ 1 & -4 & 6 & -4 & 1 \end{pmatrix}$$

The top row of coefficients captures the linear trend, the second row captures the quadratic trend and so on. Each contrast is tested in the manner described in Section 7.6.

7.7.1   Trend analysis with SPSS

SPSS offers powerful facilities for the running of trend analyses. It is, of course, possible to run a trend analysis with GLM. As with the basic one-way ANOVA, however, it may, in the first instance, be more illuminating to access a trend analysis through the **One-Way ANOVA** procedure in the **Compare Means** menu.

In the **One-Way ANOVA** dialog box, trend analysis is accessed by clicking the **Contrasts** button (Figure 19).

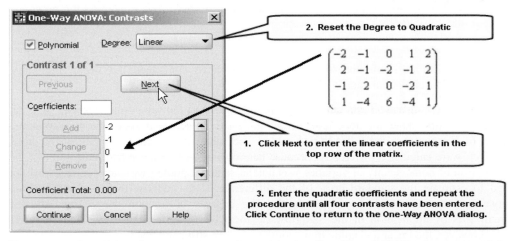

Figure 19. Accessing a trend analysis

When requesting a trend analysis in the **One-Way ANOVA: Contrasts dialog box** (Figure 20), check the **Polynomial** box and (after the first row of coefficients has been entered) adjust the **Degree** setting to the polynomial of the next order of magnitude. When all four sets of coefficients have been entered, click **Continue** to return to the **One-Way ANOVA** dialog.

Figure 20.   Specifying the components of trend in the **One-Way ANOVA: Contrasts** dialog box.

Output of a trend analysis

The first item in the output (not shown) is the full ANOVA summary table. Since this data set is exactly the same as the one we used for the basic one-way ANOVA, the table is identical with Output 1. We shall need to recall, however, that the between groups sum of squares is 351.520.

The output also contains a table of **Contrast Coefficients** (not shown). Check the entries in the table to make sure that you specified the contrasts correctly. The results of the trend analysis itself are contained in two tables, the first of which is the full ANOVA table, in which the between groups sum of squares (with value 351.520 as above) is broken down into the sums of squares accounted for by each of the four orthogonal polynomial contrasts (Output 13).

ANOVA

Performance

			Sum of Squares	df	Mean Square	F	Sig.
Between Groups	(Combined)		351.520	4	87.880	9.085	.000
	Linear Term	Contrast	272.250	1	272.250	28.144	.000
		Deviation	79.270	3	26.423	2.732	.055
	Quadratic Term	Contrast	13.207	1	13.207	1.365	.249
		Deviation	66.063	2	33.031	3.415	.042
	Cubic Term	Contrast	64.000	1	64.000	6.616	.013
		Deviation	2.063	1	2.063	.213	.646
	4th-order Term	Contrast	2.063	1	2.063	.213	.646
	Within Groups		435.300	45	9.673		
	Total		786.820	49			

The between groups sum of squares is the sum of the four contrast sums of squares

The linear and cubic components of trend have been confirmed by the statistical tests.

Output 13. The full ANOVA table, showing that statistical tests have confirmed the presence of linear and cubic trends.

It is clear from the table that the statistical tests have confirmed the linear and cubic components of trend in the data.

There is also a **Contrast Tests** table, which reports t tests of the same four contrasts (Output 14). The values of t in the upper part of this table are the square roots of the corresponding values of F reported in the full ANOVA table. The values of t in the lower part of the table, however, were calculated differently, because heterogeneity of variance had indicated that the assumption of homogeneity of variance was untenable and a pooled variance estimate was not used to estimate the standard error of the difference. Consequently, the usual relationship between t squared and F no longer holds. The degrees of freedom have been adjusted downwards by application of the Satterthwaite formula. Even on these more conservative tests, however, the linear and cubic trend components are still confirmed.

Contrast Tests

		Contrast	Value of Contrast	Std. Error	t	df	Sig. (2-tailed)
Performance	Assume equal variances	1	16.50	3.110	5.305	45	.000
		2	-4.30	3.680	-1.168	45	.249
		3	-8.00	3.110	-2.572	45	.013
		4	3.80	8.229	.462	45	.646
	Does not assume equal variances	1	16.50	3.068	5.378	21.299	.000
		2	-4.30	3.450	-1.246	29.217	.223
		3	-8.00	3.414	-2.343	17.205	.031
		4	3.80	7.989	.476	22.802	.639

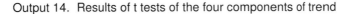

The degrees of freedom have been reduced because of heterogeneity of variance

The linear and cubic components are confirmed even by conservative tests

Output 14. Results of t tests of the four components of trend

The results of this trend analysis might be reported as follows.

A trend analysis confirmed the linear appearance of the profile plot: for the linear component, t(21.30) = 5.38; p < 0.01; for the cubic component, t(17.21) = 3.34; p = 0.03.

Note, once again, the manner in which small p-values are reported: avoid expressions such as '.000' and give the probability to two places of decimals, using the inequality sign < for probabilities that are less than 0.01.

Trend analysis with GLM

We have recommended that you make your first acquaintance with trend analysis through the **One-way ANOVA** procedure in the **Compare Means** menu. We did so because the exercise should help to clarify the link between contrasts and trend analysis. On the other hand, this approach requires the user to look up tables to produce a set of orthogonal polynomial coefficients. On GLM, the whole process is streamlined, so that the user is not required to enter the coefficients as required in the **One-Way ANOVA** approach. We think, however, that working through the procedures we have described will make the output of trend analysis with GLM easier to understand.

7.8   POWER AND EFFECT SIZE IN THE ONE-WAY ANOVA

When planning research, it is now standard practice to calculate the numbers of observations that will enable tests of sufficient power to be made. (The power of a statistical test is the probability that the test will show significance if the null hypothesis is false.) One determinant of the power of a test is the size of the effect that is being studied: a given test has greater power to obtain significance when there is a large effect than when there is a small one. In order to plan a test with a specified power, a decision must be made about the minimum size that effects must reach before they are sufficiently substantial to be worth reporting.

There are several determinants of the power of a statistical test. The factor most under the control of the researcher, however, is usually the size of the sample: the more data you have, the greater the power of your statistical tests.

Statistical textbooks show that the sample sizes necessary to achieve an acceptable level of power (at least 0.75) for small, medium and large effects vary considerably: to be sufficiently powerful to reject the null hypothesis when there is a small effect, a sample must be several times as large as one necessary for a large effect. The higher the level of power you require, the greater the differential in sample size (Keppel & Wickens, 2004; p169, Figure 8.1).

How many participants shall I need?   Using G*Power

We have seen that when the null hypothesis is true, the expected value of F is $df_{error}/(df_{error}-2)$. This is the mean of the **central F distribution**. If the null hypothesis is false, the distribution of F is centred on a value above $df_{error}/(df_{error}-2)$ and is said to be distributed as **noncentral F**. The noncentral F distribution has three parameters: $df_{between}$, df_{within}, and the **noncentrality parameter (lambda λ)**. Lambda is related to Cohen's f statistic as follows:

$$lambda = f^2 \times N \quad \text{- - - (28)} \textbf{ The noncentrality parameter}$$

where N is the total sample size.

Cohen suggested the value 0.25 as a tentative benchmark for an effect of 'medium' size. Let us suppose that a researcher plans to run an experimenter similar to the first drug experiment in this chapter and is considering having 10 participants in each of the five groups, making a total of 50 participants in all. To determine the power of the ANOVA F test, we need to know the critical value for F and locate that value in the noncentral F distribution corresponding to a lambda of $0.25^2 \times 50 = 3.08$. The cumulative probability of F (that is, the probability of a value less than or equal to F) is β, the **Type II error rate**. $(1 - \beta)$ is the power of the test.

The user who is planning an experiment could make decisions about sample size in trial-and-error fashion, by trying various numbers and determining the power of the test each time. It is much more convenient, however, to work back from the desired power level and the minimum effect size that you would want to report to the size of the sample that would be required to meet those criteria.

There are several ways of determining the power of a test given the sample size and of solving the obverse problem of finding the sample size necessary to achieve a test at a specified minimum level of power. The traditional method was to look up tables of key percentiles of the noncentral F distribution, which are available in any standard work on ANOVA. Nowadays, however, the user of a statistical package such as SPSS can also obtain a computed value of the cumulative probability and subtract its value from 1 to obtain the power of the test.

The easiest way to answer questions about power and sample size, however, is to use one of the several dedicated statistical packages that are available. **G*Power 3** (Erdfelder, Faul & Buchner, 1996; Faul, Erdfelder, Lang & Buchner, 2007) is freely on the Internet. The answers

G*Power gives to questions about power and sample size agree with those that you would obtain if you were to consult standard tables or use a statistical computing package.

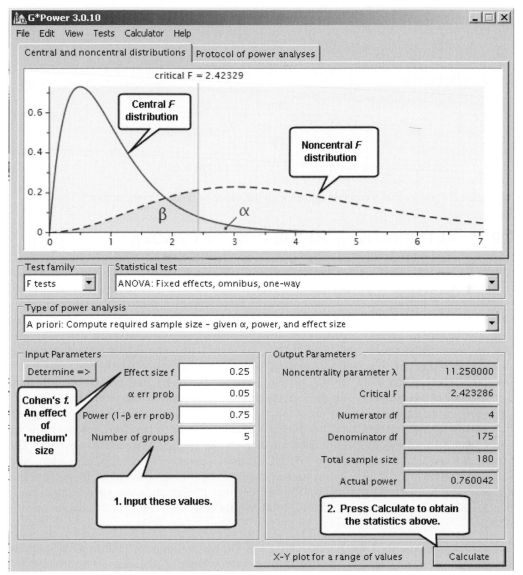

Figure 21. The **G*Power** window for the ANOVA F test

Suppose that we are planning to run an experiment of the same design as our first drug experiment. There will be five treatment groups. The desired power to detect an effect of 'medium' size is 0.75, and the significance level will be set at 0.05. Figure 21 shows the G*Power 3 window for the ANOVA F test. (We have added an explanatory label or two.) The values required for the input are shown in the left-hand panel. In addition to the alpha-rate, the minimum power and the number of groups, we must enter a value for Cohen's f. The input value 0.25 is an effect of 'medium' size. The output, which is shown in the panel on the right, includes the total number of participants that will be required to achieve the required level of power: 180. We shall need 36 participants in each group.

We can compare the value for power in the G*Power output with one we obtain when we insert the other values from the G*Power output into the cumulative distribution function of the noncentral F distribution, which is available in SPSS's **Compute Variable** command, in the **Transform** menu:

$$Power = 1 - NCDF \left(\begin{bmatrix} \text{critical} \\ \text{value} \\ \text{of F} \end{bmatrix} df_{between}, \text{df}_{within}, lambda \right)$$

$$= 1 - NCDF \left(2.423, \ 4, 55, \ 11.25 \right) = 0.76$$

The value for power that we obtain agrees with the value in the G*Power output.

7.9   ALTERNATIVES TO THE ONE-WAY ANOVA

Monte Carlo studies have shown that the one-way ANOVA is, to some extent, robust to small to moderate violations of the assumptions of the model, such as homogeneity of variance and normality of distribution. The general import of these studies is that, if the sample sizes are similar in the various groups, and the distributions of the populations are, if not normal, at least similar from group to group, variances can differ by a factor of four without the Type I or Type II error rates rising unacceptably (see Howell, 2007; p 316). The risk of error, however, is much increased in data sets with very unequal sample sizes in the groups. Occasionally, a data set, even when 'cleaned up' to the greatest possible extent by the removal of obviously aberrant extreme scores, may still show contraindications against the use of the usual one-way ANOVA. Nonparametric equivalents of the one-way ANOVA are available. Since, however, these involve an initial process of converting a scalar data set to ranks (a process which we might term 'ordinalisation'), we do not think they should be used as a matter of course. The choice of a nonparameteric test over the ANOVA pays a penalty of loss of power. Moreover, some nonparametric tests are by no means immune to the baleful influence of outliers and extreme scores. There are many who would say that if your data are good enough for a nonparametric method such as the **Kruskal-Wallis** test, they are good enough for the ANOVA.

The techniques described by Welch (1951) and Brown & Forsythe (1974) were specially designed for use with data sets showing marked heterogeneity of variance. They are reported to keep the error rates within acceptable limits. Both are available within SPSS and we feel that these should be one's first port of call when there are strong contraindications against the usual ANOVA procedure.

There is one kind of data, however, that has been the focus of dispute more than almost any other. Many would dispute the claim that ratings are measures on an independent scale with units. From a psychological point of view, the use of anchor points seems to impart ratings with an independence of scale that a set of ranks would lack. Many journal editors, however, when presented with the ANOVA of data in the form of ratings, are uneasy about the unquestionable fact that with ratings, means and variances tend to be associated; indeed the variance is artificially constrained by the nature of the measure being used. They would prefer the researcher to use a nonparametric equivalent of ANOVA, such as the **Kruskal-Wallis** test (see the next section). When the data are at the ordinal or nominal level of measurement in the first place (an unlikely occurrence), the researcher has, of course, no choice but to use a nonparametric technique.

7.9.1   The Kruskal-Wallis k-sample test

This non-parametric equivalent of ANOVA was designed for use with scalar data from a one-factor, between subjects experiment. In such a test, the data are first converted to ranks and the distribution of the ranks among the various groups determines the value of the test statistic.

Proceed as follows:

*   **Choose➜Analyze➜Nonparametric Tests➜K Independent Samples…** (Figure 22) to open the **Tests for Several Independent Samples** dialog box (the completed version is shown in Figure 23).

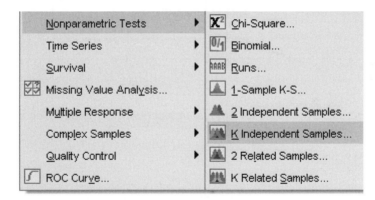

Figure 22. Part of the **Analyze** menu showing **Nonparametric Tests** and its submenu with **K Independent Samples** selected

*   Transfer the variable names and define the range of the grouping variable as shown in Figure 23.
*   Since the **Exact** tests can take some time, we shall content ourselves with the **asymptotic** p-value.
*   Click **OK**.

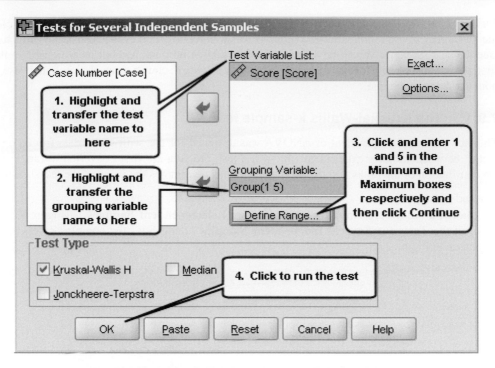

Figure 23. The **Tests for Several Independent Samples** dialog box

The test results are shown in Output 15.

Kruskal-Wallis Test

Ranks

	Drug Condition	N	Mean Rank
Score	Placebo	10	12.95
	Drug A	10	13.10
	Drug B	10	31.50
	Drug C	10	36.60
	Drug D	10	33.35
	Total	50	

Test Statistics[a,b]

	Performance Score
Chi-Square	25.376
df	4
Asymp. Sig.	.000

With a p-value < .01, the result is significant at the .01 level

a. Kruskal Wallis Test

b. Grouping Variable: Drug Condition

Output 15. The **Kruskal-Wallis One-Way ANOVA** output

The first subtable, **Ranks**, tabulates the mean rank for each group. The second subtable, **Test Statistics**, lists the value of Chi-Square, its *df* and its p-value (**Asymp. Sig.**). Since the p-value is much smaller than 0.01, the Kruskal-Wallis test agrees with the parametric test that the five groups do not perform equally well. We can report this result as follows:

> The mean rank under the Placebo condition is 12.95 and for Drugs A to D the mean ranks are respectively 13.10, 31.50, 36.60 and 33.35. The Kruskal-Wallis chi-square test is significant beyond the .01 level: $\chi^2 (4) = 25.38$; $p < .01$.

7.9.2   Dichotomous nominal data: the chi-square test

Suppose that participants in an experiment are divided randomly into three equally-sized groups: two experimental groups (Group A and Group B) and a Control group (Group C). Each participant is tested with a criterion problem, a 1 being recorded if they pass, and a 0 if they fail.

This experiment would result in a nominal data set. With such data, a **chi-square test** for association can be used to test the null hypothesis that, in the population, there is no tendency for the criterion problem to be solved more often in one condition than in the other (see Chapter 11).

7.10   A FINAL WORD

The one-way ANOVA provides a direct test of the null hypothesis that, in the population, all treatment or group means have the same value. When the value of *F* is sufficient large to cast doubt upon the null hypothesis, further questions arise, the answers to which require further testing. The ANOVA itself is therefore merely the first step in the process of statistical analysis.

A significant value of *F*, while implying that, in the population, there is a difference *somewhere* among the treatment means, does not locate the difference and it would be illegitimate to infer, on the basis of a significant *F*, that any two means (or combinations of means) are significantly different. On the other hand, the process of data-snooping, that is, the making of follow-up statistical tests, runs a heightened risk of a **Type I error**. A key notion here is the *familywise* Type I error rate. This is the probability, under the null hypothesis, of obtaining *at least one* significant result when several tests are made subsequently. The familywise Type I error rate may be very much higher than the *per comparison* Type I error rate, which is usually 0.05. It is essential to distinguish the Type I error rate per comparison with the Type I error rate familywise. Several ways of achieving control over the familywise Type I error rate were discussed.

Since statistical significance and a small p-value do not necessarily mean that a substantial effect has been found, it is now expected that the report of the results of a statistical test should include a measure of effect size, such as eta squared or (preferably) omega squared. The researcher should also ensure that sufficient numbers of participants are tested to allow statistical tests of sufficient power to be made.

When there are strong contraindications against the use of the normal one-way ANOVA, as when the sample variances and samples sizes vary markedly, the researcher must consider more robust methods, some of which are available as alternatives to the ANOVA in the same

SPSS program. These robust variants of ANOVA should be the first alternatives to be considered. There are also available nonparametric counterparts of the one-way ANOVA which, since they involve an initial process of converting scores on the original scale to ranks, incur an automatic loss in power. The most arguable case for their use is with data in the form of ratings.

When the conditions making up the treatment factor vary along a continuous dimension, as when different groups of participants perform a skilled tasks after ingestion of varying doses of the same drug, the technique of trend analysis can be used to investigate and confirm the polynomial components of the functional relationship between the independent and dependent variables. In trend analysis, the components of trend are captured in contrasts whose coefficients are values of polynomials of specified order. These contrasts are tested for significance in the usual way.

Recommended reading

There are available many textbooks on analysis of variance. Two excellent examples are:

Howell, D. C. (2007). *Statistical methods for psychology (6th ed.)*. Belmont, CA: Thomson/Wadsworth.

Keppel, G., & Wickens, T. D. (2004). *Design and Analysis: A researcher's handbook (4th ed.)*. Upper Saddle River, New Jersey: Pearson/Prentice Hall.

Both books also present ANOVA in the context of the **general linear model** (GLM).

Exercise

Exercise 11 *One-factor between subjects ANOVA* is available in www.psypress.com/spss-made-simple and click on Exercises.

CHAPTER 8

Between subjects factorial experiments

8.1   INTRODUCTION

Experiments with two or more factors are known as **factorial** experiments. In the simplest case, there is a different sample of participants for each possible combination of conditions. This arrangement is known as a **between subjects** (or **completely randomised**) **factorial** experiment. In this chapter, we shall discuss between subjects factorial experiments with two and three factors. For the analysis of data from such experiments, the **two-way** and **three-way** **ANOVA** are appropriate techniques.

8.1.1   An experiment with two treatment factors

Suppose that a researcher has been commissioned to investigate the effects upon simulated driving performance of two new anti-hay fever drugs, A and B. It is suspected that at least one of the drugs may have different effects upon fresh and tired drivers, and the firm developing the drugs needs to ensure that neither drug has an adverse effect upon driving performance.

The researcher decides to carry out a two-factor factorial experiment, in which the factors are:
1.   Drug Treatment, with levels Placebo, Drug A and Drug B;
2.   Alertness, with levels Fresh and Tired.

All participants are asked to take a flavoured drink containing either (in the Drug A and Drug B conditions) a small quantity of the drug or (in the control or Placebo condition) no drug. Half the participants are tested immediately on rising; the others are tested after doing without sleep for twenty-four hours. A different sample of ten participants is tested under each of the six treatment combinations: (Fresh, Placebo); (Fresh, Drug A); (Fresh, Drug B); (Tired, Placebo); (Tired, Drug A); (Tired, Drug B).

In this experiment, each level of either factor is to be found in combination with every level of the other. The two factors are said to **cross**. There are experimental designs in which the factors do not cross (not all combinations of conditions or groups are present), but such designs will not be considered in this book. The two-factor between subjects factorial experiment can be represented as a table in which each row or column represents a particular level of one of the treatment factors, and a **cell** of the table (i.e. a single rectangle in the grid) represents one particular treatment combination (Table 1). In Table 1, the cell on the bottom right represents the combination (Tired, Drug B). The ten participants in Group 6 were tested under that particular treatment combination.

Table 1. A completely randomised, two-factor factorial experiment on the effects of two factors upon simulated driving performance

	Levels of the Drug Treatment factor		
Levels of the Alertness factor	Placebo	Drug A	Drug B
Fresh	Group 1	Group 2	Group 3
Tired	Group 4	Group 5	Group 6

The mean scores of the participants are shown in Table 2. The row and column means are known as **marginal means**. They are the means of all the scores at each level of either factor, ignoring the other factor in the classification. Inspection of the column means shows that the mean score of all those who ingested Drug B, irrespective of whether they were fresh or tired, is 19.0, a higher level of performance than that of the Placebo or Drug A groups. Inspection of the row means shows that the mean score of the Fresh participants, ignoring the drug group to which they had been assigned, is greater than that of the Tired participants.

Table 2. Mean scores achieved by the participants in the drugs experiment

	Placebo	Drug A	Drug B	*Mean*
Fresh	21.0	12.0	22.0	18.3
Tired	10.0	18.0	16.0	14.7
Mean	15.5	15.0	19.0	16.5

To say that the mean for the fresh participants is greater than that for the tired participants does not, of course, imply that this superiority is necessarily true of the scores at any particular level of the Drug factor. In fact, when we move from consideration of the marginal means to the cells within the body of the table, we see that with the scores achieved under the Drug A condition, the opposite is the case: the Tired participants outperformed the Fresh participants!

The most interesting features of the data from factorial experiments often emerge from consideration of the cell means in the body of the table, rather than the marginal means. This is because the cell means show how the factors in a factorial experiment interplay or **interact**, often in complex ways. The interaction of the factors is a source of variance over and above any main effect and the possibility of such an interaction is often the principal purpose of a factorial experiment.

8.1.2   Main effects and interactions

The introduction of a second factor into the experimental design extends the range of questions that can be investigated. In this two-way factorial experiment, there are two kinds of effects, both of which can be tested with an appropriate F statistic:

1.   **Main effects**;
2.   The **interaction**.

Main effects may be evident from inspection of the marginal means. Should at least one of the differences among the column means for the three levels of the *Drug* factor be sufficiently great as to indicate a difference in the population and should this pattern be confirmed by statistical testing, the *Drug* factor is said to have a **main effect**. Similarly, a large difference between the two row means would indicate that the *Alertness* factor also has a main effect. Since Table 2 shows that there are indeed marked differences among both row and column marginal means, it looks as if both factors have main effects. Not surprisingly the fresh participants, on average, outperformed the tired participants. In the participants as a whole, Drug A did not produce a higher overall level of performance in comparison with the mean score of those participants who received a placebo. Drug B, on the other hand, did produce a higher overall level of performance.

Simple main effects

The effect of one treatment factor (such as *Alertness*) at one particular level of another factor (e.g. on the Drug A participants only) is known as a **simple main effect**. From inspection of Table 2, it would appear that the *Alertness* factor has different simple main effects at different levels of the *Drug* factor: its effect is diminished with Drug B and actually reversed with Drug A.

Interactions

When the simple main effects of one treatment factor are not homogeneous at all levels of another, the two factors are said to **interact**. An interaction between two factors, such as *Drug* and *Alertness*, is indicated by a multiplication sign thus: *Drug* × *Alertness*. (In computer output, multiplication is indicated by an asterisk: *Drug*Alertness*.) The results of the drug experiment, therefore, suggest the presence of a *Drug* × *Alertness* interaction.

8.1.3   Profile plots

The interaction pattern that we have just described can be pictured graphically, as plots of the cell means for the Fresh and the Tired participants against Drug Treatment (see Figure 1). Such graphs are called **profile plots**. In the present example, the Fresh participants' performance profile is V-shaped, plunging under the Drug A condition. The Tired participants' profile, on the other hand, rises to higher levels under both the Drug A and Drug B conditions. The presence of an interaction is indicated by **profile heterogeneity** from level to level of one of the factors, that is, by *non-parallel* profiles. This is certainly the case in the present example with the profiles of the Fresh and Tired participants across the three *Drug Treatment* conditions.

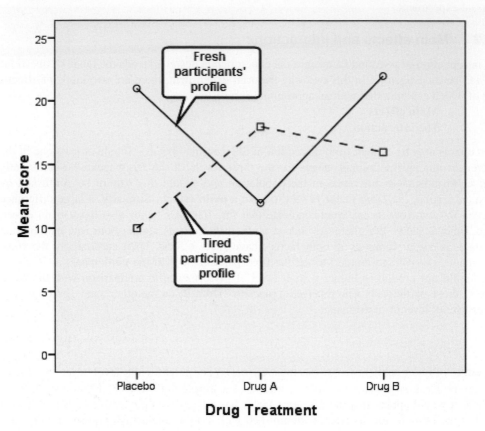

Figure 1. A pattern of cell means suggestive of an interaction

It is important to be clear that an interaction effect is a source of variance over and above the effect of either factor considered alone or, indeed, the main effects of both factors combined. Main effects and interactions are independent: it is quite possible to obtain significant main effects without any significant interaction between the factors; it is also possible to have significant interactions without any significant main effects. As well as showing an interaction pattern, however, the appearance of the profiles in Figure 1 is affected partly by the presence of main effects. Had there been an even greater difference in overall performance level between the Fresh and Tired participants, for example, the Fresh and Tired profiles might have become completely separated at all three levels of the *Drug* factor. It is the *convergence or divergence* of the profiles, rather than their separation or slope, that indicates the presence of an interaction. There is no need for the profiles to cross one another. When the profiles are parallel, there is no interaction – even if they both slope sharply upwards or downwards or are widely separated on the vertical axis of the graph. Either of those tendencies indicates a main effect, not an interaction.

8.2   HOW THE TWO-WAY ANOVA WORKS

Recall that in the one-way ANOVA, the total sum of squares can be taken to represent the total variability of the scores and that this total variability can be divided or partitioned into a between groups and a within groups component thus:

$$SS_{total} = SS_{between} + SS_{within} \quad \text{- - - (1)}$$

Partition of the total sum of squares in the one-way ANOVA

In (1), the element of SS_{total} is $(X - M)$, the deviation of the individual score from the grand mean, so that $SS_{total} = \sum_{all\ scores} (X - M)^2$. In the one-way ANOVA, the element of $SS_{between}$ is $(M_j - M)$, the deviation of the mean score for group j from the grand mean; the element of SS_{within} is $(X - M_j)$, the deviation of the individual score from the mean score for group j.

In the two-way ANOVA, a similar partition holds. As in the one-way ANOVA, the total sum of squares can be partitioned into between groups and within groups component sums of squares. As before, the element of the total sum of squares is the deviation of the individual score from the grand mean. This time, however, the element of $SS_{between}$ is the between groups deviation $(M_{jk} - M)$, the deviation of the *cell mean* for row j and column k (M_{jk}) from the grand mean. This between groups deviation can itself be divided into main effects components and the interaction component, so that the between groups sum of squares does not appear explicitly in the final partition. The main effect components are the deviations $(M_j - M)$ and $(M_k - M)$, of the *marginal means* for row j and column k from the grand mean. The interaction effect for cell ij is what remains of the between groups deviation when the main effects have been subtracted:

$$(M_{jk} - M) - (M_j - M) - (M_k - M) = (M_{jk} - M_j - M_k + M) \quad \text{- - - (2)}$$

Interaction component of the between groups deviation

In the two-way ANOVA, the element of SS_{within} is $(X - M_{jk})$, the deviation of a score in group jk from the cell mean M_{jk}.

It can be shown that in the two-factor case, the partition of the total sum of squares becomes:

$$SS_{total} = SS_{Alertness} + SS_{Drug} + SS_{Alertness \times Drug} + SS_{within} \quad \text{- - - (3)}$$

Partition of the total sum of squares in the two-way ANOVA

where the between groups sum of squares does not appear, because it has been further partitioned into the two main effect sums of squares and the sum of squares for the interaction.

We should note that, as in the one-way ANOVA, the total degrees of freedom (total number of scores – 1) can be partitioned in a similar way:

$$df_{total} = df_{Alertness} + df_{drug} + df_{Alertness \times Drug} + df_{within} \quad \text{- - - (4)}$$

Partition of the total degrees of freedom in the two-way ANOVA

The two main effects sum of squares and the interaction sum of squares are divided by their respective degrees of freedom to obtain mean squares, that is, variance estimates for the main effects and the interaction. As in the one-way ANOVA, the within groups sum of squares can be divided by its degrees of freedom to obtain an estimate of the error (within cell) variance. Finally, the two main effects and the interaction are tested with *three* F statistics, each of which has the same within groups mean square as its error term or denominator:

$$F_{Alertness} = \frac{MS_{Alertness}}{MS_{within}}$$

$$F_{Drug} = \frac{MS_{Drug}}{MS_{within}} \quad \text{- - - (5)}$$

$$F_{Alertness \times Drug} = \frac{MS_{Alertness \times Drug}}{MS_{within}}$$

The three F tests in the two-way ANOVA

Figure 2 summarises the two-way ANOVA.

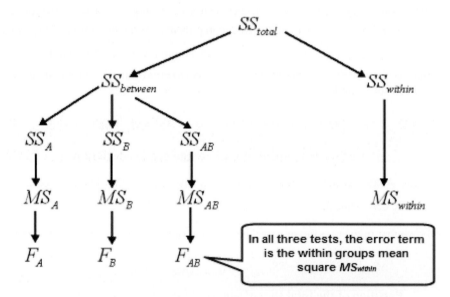

Figure 2. Diagram summarising the two-way ANOVA. (In the subscripts, the specific labels *Alertness* and *Drug* have been replaced by the generalised factor labels A and B, respectively.)

Degrees of freedom

In the one-way ANOVA of data from an experiment with k treatment groups, the degrees of freedom df of the between groups mean square is the number of treatment groups minus one: $df = k - 1$. In a similar way, in a two-way ANOVA, the degrees of freedom of each of the source mean squares for main effects is the number of levels making up the source, minus one: thus for the *Alertness* factor (Fresh, Tired), $df = (2 - 1) = 1$; for the *Drug* factor (Placebo, Drug A, Drug B), $df = (3 - 1) = 2$.

Turning now to the degrees of freedom of the interaction, the rule is as follows: the degrees of freedom of an interaction mean square is the product of the degrees of freedom of the factors involved. Since $df_{Alertness} = 1$ and $df_{Drug} = 2$, $df_{Interaction} = 1 \times 2 = 2$. In general, if Factor A and Factor B have a and b levels, respectively, the degrees of freedom of their interaction $df_{Interaction} = (a-1)(b-1)$.

In the two-way ANOVA, the within groups mean square is the average of the variance estimates for every *combination* of treatment conditions and is essentially the mean of the cell variances. In the present example, there are 6 cells, each cell representing a different combination of the factors of *Alertness* and *Drug*. Each of the six cells yields a variance estimate which, since it is based upon ten observations, has 9 degrees of freedom. The pooled within cells variance estimate, therefore, has $6 \times 9 = 54$ degrees of freedom.

In the two-way ANOVA, the within cell pooled variance estimate MS_{within} is the error term in all three F tests. Table 3 shows the ANOVA summary table for the data summarised in Table 2. Notice that there are three F statistics: one for each of the two factors considered separately; the third for the interaction. Consistent with our inspection of Table 2, the two-way ANOVA has shown that all three tests show significance beyond the .05 level; and the *Alertness* factor and the interaction are significant beyond the .01 level.

Table 3. The two-way ANOVA summary table						
Source	**df**	**SS**	**MS**	**F**	**p**	**Partial eta squared**
Main effects						
Alertness (A)	1	201.67	201.67	8.71	<.01	.14
Drug (D)	2	190.00	95.00	4.10	.02	.13
Interaction						
Interaction (A×D)	2	763.33	381.67	16.49	<.01	.38
Error						
Within groups (Error)	54	1250.00	23.15			
Total	59	2405.0				

The two-way ANOVA has confirmed the most interesting feature of the data, namely, the presence of an interaction between the *Drug* and *Alertness* factors: while the *Drug* improved the performance of the tired participants, it impeded the performance of the fresh participants. It is this ability to confirm the existence of an interaction that accounts for the fact that the factorial ANOVA is one of the most widely used statistical techniques in some fields of research, such as experimental psychology; indeed, the main effects of factors considered separately are often of little interest in themselves. It is not surprising, for example, to learn that fresh participants outperform tired participants; but it is of considerable interest to learn that while a drug improves the performance of tired participants, this effect is reversed with fresh participants.

The entries under the headings 'Partial eta squared' (an option in SPSS) are included in Table 3 at this point for the sake of completeness. Partial eta squared is a measure of effect size. We shall return to the measurement of effect size in a later section.

8.2.1   Reporting the results of the two-way ANOVA

The results of the three F tests shown in Table 3 should be reported by specifying the name of the factor, followed by the value of the F ratio (with the df of the numerator and denominator separated by a comma in brackets), the p-value and a measure of effect size as follows:

For the Alertness factor: $F(1, 54) = 8.71$; $p < 0.01$; partial eta squared $= 0.14$.
For the Drug factor: $F(2, 54) = 4.10$; $p = 0.02$; partial eta squared $= 0.13$.
For the interaction: $F(2, 54) = 16.49$; $p < 0.01$; partial eta squared $= 0.38$.

A reader, however, should never be confronted with the result of a statistical test (or, worse, a list of results like this) without also being given instant access to the descriptive statistics, either in the body of the text or in a table or figure nearby. A measure of effect size should also be included. The following report embodies these requirements; though a table would have made it less cluttered. The main thing is, the descriptives must be there as well as the test results. Note that p-values are given to two places of decimals only; with probabilities less than 0.01, the inequality sign $<$ is used thus: $p < 0.01$. Probabilities *greater* than 0.05 should also be given (to two places of decimals). Insignificant results are also of interest and their p-values should also be given.

The mean Driving Performance scores for the Fresh (M = 18.33, SD = 6.35) and Tired (M = 14.67, SD = 5.97) conditions of the Alertness factor differed significantly beyond the 0.01 level: $F(1, 54) = 8.71$; $p < 0.01$. Partial eta squared $= 0.14$, a 'large' effect. The means and standard deviations of the three condition making up the Drug factor were: Placebo (M = 15.5, SD = 7.47); Drug A (M = 15.0, SD = 5.38); Drug B (M = 19.00, SD = 5.65). The Drug factor had a significant main effect: $F(2, 54) = 4.10$; $p = 0.02$. Partial eta squared $= 0.13$, a 'large' effect. There was also a significant Alertness × Drug interaction, as might be expected from perusal of Figure 1: $F(2, 54) = 16.49$; $p < 0.01$. Partial eta squared $= 0.38$, a 'large' effect.

The precise manner in which the quantities in Table 2 are calculated is lucidly described in many excellent textbooks, such as Howell (2007) and Keppel & Wickens (2004).

8.2.2   The fixed effects model for the two-way ANOVA

In Chapter 7, we saw that the score model for the one-way ANOVA is as follows:

$$X = \begin{bmatrix} grand \\ mean \end{bmatrix} + \begin{bmatrix} treatment \\ effect \end{bmatrix} + \begin{bmatrix} random \\ error \end{bmatrix} \quad - - - (6)$$

Model for the one-way ANOVA

The random error component is assumed to be normally distributed with mean 0 and variance σ_e^2. By the assumption of **homogeneity of variance**, the random error variance is constant across groups.

The fixed effects model for the two-way ANOVA is a simple extension of the one-way model:

$$X = \begin{bmatrix} grand \\ mean \end{bmatrix} + \begin{bmatrix} main \\ effect\ of \\ Factor\ A \end{bmatrix} + \begin{bmatrix} main \\ effect\ of \\ Factor\ B \end{bmatrix} + \begin{bmatrix} interaction \\ effect \end{bmatrix} + \begin{bmatrix} random \\ error \end{bmatrix} \quad - - - (7)$$

Model for the two-way ANOVA

The random error component e is assumed to be normally distributed with a mean of zero and its distribution for any score is assumed to be independent of its distribution for any other score. Its variance σ_e^2 is assumed to be constant across all cells of the two-way table. This, in the context of the two-way ANOVA, is the assumption of **homogeneity of variance**.

As in the model for the one-way ANOVA, all the terms on the right-hand side of (7) involve population parameters, rather than the statistics of any one data set. The effect estimates and their corresponding parameters are shown below in (8).

Statistic	Parameter	Explanation	
M	μ	Population grand mean	
$M_j - M$	$(\mu_j - \mu) = \alpha_j$	Main effect of Factor A, treatment j	
$M_k - M$	$(\mu_k - \mu) = \beta_j$	Main effect of Factor B, treatment k	$- - - (8)$
$M_{jk} - M_j - M_k + M$	$(\alpha\beta)_{jk} = \mu_{jk} - \alpha_j - \beta_k + \mu$	Interaction at cell jk	
$X - M_i$	$X - \mu_i = e$	Random error	

Effects and their estimates in the two-way ANOVA model

8.3   FURTHER ANALYSIS

In Chapter 7, we observed that the ANOVA itself is just the first stage in the analysis of a set of data from a complex experiment: inevitably, further analysis will be required to clarify the result of the initial ANOVA F test. This is true, a fortiori, of factorial ANOVA. In the first place, the researcher will wish to establish the strength of the effects the experiment has demonstrated. It will also be necessary to pinpoint and confirm differences among the individual treatment or group means. Should a significant interaction be obtained, it may be necessary to 'unpack' it by making comparisons among the individual cell means.

8.3.1   Measuring effect size in the two-way ANOVA

In Chapter 7, we introduced the measure of effect size known as **eta-squared** η^2, which is the proportion of variance in the dependent variable accounted for by differences in the levels of the independent variable. In the case of the one-way ANOVA, η^2 is defined as follows:

See Section 7.4

$$\eta^2 = \frac{SS_{\text{treatment}}}{SS_{\text{total}}} = \frac{SS_{\text{between}}}{SS_{\text{total}}} \quad \text{--- (9)}$$

Eta squared in the one-way ANOVA

Factorial experiments: complete eta squared

Let Factor A and Factor B be the factors in a two-way ANOVA. We have seen that in the two-way ANOVA, there are three between groups sources of variance: two main effect sources; and the interaction. For Factor A, the measure of effect size known as **complete** η^2 is defined as follows:

$$\eta^2 = \frac{SS_A}{SS_{total}} = \frac{SS_A}{SS_A + SS_B + SS_{A\times B} + SS_{within}} \quad \text{--- (10)}$$

Complete eta squared

Applying (10) to the information in Table 3, we find that, for the *Alertness* factor,

$$\eta^2 = \frac{SS_{Alertness}}{SS_{Total}}$$

$$= \frac{SS_{Alertness}}{SS_{Alertness} + SS_{Drug} + SS_{Alertness \ x \ Drug} + SS_{Within}}$$

$$= \frac{201.67}{2405.00} = 0.08$$

Partial eta squared

There are two major problems with complete eta squared. One is that its value is affected by the variance arising from the presence of the other factors in the experiment, which would make it difficult to compare the effect size of the same factor in two experiments with different numbers of factors. Some authors therefore advocate an alternative form of η^2, called **partial** η^2 or η_p^2 in which the variance of the sums of squares for a particular effect is expressed as a proportion, not of the *total* sum of squares, but of the sum of squares of *that effect alone* plus the error sum of squares:

$$\eta_p^2 = \frac{SS_A}{SS_A + SS_{within}} \quad \text{- - - (11)} \quad \textbf{Partial eta squared}$$

Applying Formula (11) to the information in Table 3, we find that, for the *Alertness* factor, partial eta squared is

$$\eta_p^2 = \frac{201.667}{201.667 + 1250} = 0.139$$

which is the value given in Table 3. The value of partial eta squared is, of course, appreciably larger than that of complete eta squared for the same effect.

SPSS includes partial eta squared as an option (**Estimates of effect size**) in the **Options...** dialog box. The choice between the **complete** η^2 and **partial** η^2 statistics depends upon the design of the experiment and purpose of the investigation (see Keppel & Wickens, 2004; p.235). As we shall see, however, better measures of effect size are available.

Omega squared

The other major problem with eta squared (and this applies to both the complete and partial versions) is that it is a purely descriptive measure and overstates the strength of the effect in the population. The omega squared statistics correct this positive bias and allow for shrinkage with resampling.

The omega squared statistics corresponding to eta squared and partial eta squared are, respectively, complete omega squared (ω^2) and partial omega squared (ω_p^2) – see Keppel & Wickens, 2004; pp. 232 – 233. Here (Table 4) we reproduce the table from Chapter 7 comparing Cohen's measure of effect size (f) with omega squared.

Table 4. A scheme for assessing values of omega squared		
Size of Effect	**Omega squared**	**Cohen's f**
Small	$0.01 \leq \omega^2 < 0.06$	$0.10 \leq f < 0.25$
Medium	$0.06 \leq \omega^2 < 0.14$	$0.25 \leq f < 0.40$
Large	$\omega^2 \geq 0.14$	$f \geq 0.40$

The formula for partial omega squared is as follows:

$$\hat{\omega}^2_{source} = \frac{df_{source}(F_{source}-1)}{df_{source}(F_{source}-1)+abn} \quad \text{- - - (12)} \quad \textbf{Partial omega squared}$$

where a, b and n are the number of levels of Factor A, the number of levels of Factor B and the number of observations per cell, respectively.

Returning to Table 3, we see that, for the *Alertness* factor, partial eta squared is given as 0.14. Applying Formula (12), we find that the estimate of partial omega squared for the same source is

$$partial \ \hat{\omega}^2_{source} = \frac{df_{Alertness}(F_{Alertness}-1)}{df_{Alertness}(F_{Alertness}-1)+(2\times3\times10)}$$

$$= \frac{1\times7.712}{1\times7.712+60} = 0.114$$

As we should expect, this value is somewhat less than the value of partial eta squared for the same source, because the estimate of omega squared incorporates a correction for positive bias.

The formula for the estimate of complete omega squared is

$$\hat{\omega}^2_{source} = \frac{df_{source}(F_{source}-1)}{\sum\limits_{\substack{all \\ treatment \\ sources}} df_{source}(F_{source}-1)+abn} \quad \text{- - - (13)} \quad \textbf{Complete omega squared}$$

Applying Formula (13) to the information in Table 3, we see that, for the *Alertness* factor, the value of the estimate of complete omega squared is

$$complete \ \hat{\omega}^2_{Alertness} = \frac{df_{Alertness}(F_{Alertness}-1)}{\sum\limits_{all \ treatment \ sources} df_{source}(F_{source}-1)+abn}$$

$$= \frac{1(7.712)}{1(7.712)+2(3.10)+2(15.49)+60} = 0.07$$

Since the estimate of complete omega squared has the full denominator and incorporates the correction for bias, we can expect it to be the smallest of the four estimates that we have calculated.

8.3.2 How many participants shall I need for my two-factor experiment?

Suppose that we plan to run a two-factor between subjects factorial experiment of the same design as the one in our current example. How many people would we need to test in order to achieve, say, a power of 0.75 for an effect of medium size, that is, Cohen's $f = 0.25$ (see Section 7.8)?

See Section 7.8

When deciding upon the numbers of participants necessary to achieve a specified level of power for, say, an effect of 'medium' size ($f = 0.25$) the user should bear in mind that in factorial experiments, the tests of the various effects do not always have the same power to reject the null hypothesis: e.g. if both factors have three or more levels, the test for an interaction will have less power than a test for a main effect. You may have sufficient participants to achieve a power of at least 0.75 for your tests of main effects; but your test for an interaction may have lower power. Since the interaction is often the main focus in a factorial experiment, the researcher should give this effect source special attention.

As with the earlier versions, G*Power 3 will answer questions about the power of an experimental design with specified numbers of participants and about the numbers of participants that will be needed to achieve tests at a minimum specified level of power. Returning to our original question, we shall need to enter the following items: the effect size (0.25); the alpha-level (0.05); the desired power level (0.75); the numerator degrees of freedom (in the present example, $df_{Interaction} = 2$); and the total number of groups (6). In the output, we shall learn that a total sample size of 141 will be required. In practical terms, this means we shall actually require 24 participants in each group, i.e. 144 participants in all.

8.3.3 Making multiple comparisons among the treatment means

A data set from a complex experiment with two or more treatment factors is likely to show some interesting patterns: the more complex the experiment, in fact, the more likely you are to find something interesting in the results. Unfortunately, this 'discovery' might be the result of sampling error! You will therefore want to follow up the original ANOVA with additional analysis and make several (perhaps many) additional tests of significance. The problem with that procedure, however, is that the more significance tests you make, the more significant results you will obtain – even if the null hypothesis is true!

By making many tests of significance without taking certain precautions, the researcher is 'capitalising upon chance'. In order to avoid such capitalisation, the researcher must make conservative tests in order to control the **per family** Type I error rate, that is, the probability, under the null hypothesis, that at least one test will show significance. There has been much dispute about which of several possible strategies one should follow and none has emerged as a clear winner. Here, we outline just one approach.

8.3.4 The analysis of interactions

When the two-way ANOVA has produced a significant interaction between the two factors, it is often necessary to 'unpack' the interaction to determine which differences among the individual treatment or group means are significant.

In Figure 3, we have re-plotted the means from the drug experiment, so that the profiles are now the three different *Drug* conditions and on the horizontal axis are the levels of the *Alertness* factor. We have done so because ultimately we shall want to make comparisons among the means for the three drug conditions and the new arrangement will help.

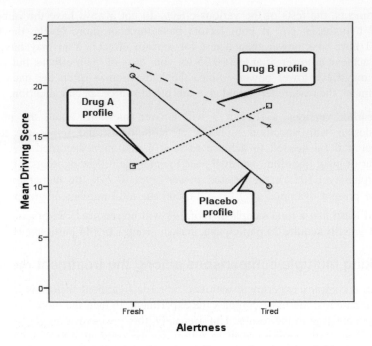

Figure 3. Profile plot of levels of *Drug* against levels of *Alertness*

From the graph it seems that, in the Fresh participants, performance is considerably better under the Placebo and Drug B conditions than it was under Drug A; whereas in the Tired participants, performance with both drugs seems superior to performance under the Placebo condition. Are these differences significant: that is, would these patterns survive a replication of the experiment?

One approach to the problem of making conservative multiple comparisons among the individual means is to inform SPSS that this is really a one-factor experiment with six groups and request a **Tukey** test. The problem with that approach is that, even with an array of six means, the number of possible pairwise comparisons is quite large (fifteen) and this is reflected in a large critical value for the **studentized range statistic** (q). In the next subsection, we shall describe another strategy, which provides a justification for defining a smaller comparison 'family', thus enabling the user to make tests of greater power.

Testing for simple main effects

We have seen that in a factorial experiment, a **simple main effect** is the effect of a factor at one particular level of another. It would appear from Figure 3, for example, that there is a simple main effect of the *Drug* factor at each of the two levels of the *Alertness* factor. If we could demonstrate that these effects are robust, we should have justification for defining the comparison families on the basis of three means, rather than six, and so run more powerful Tukey pairwise multiple comparisons tests.

To test for a simple main effect of the *Drug* factor with the Fresh participants only, one could select the data for the fresh participants only and run a one-way ANOVA, compensating for what would otherwise be a loss of power by using the error term (and its associated degrees of freedom) for the whole design. This, however, cannot be done simply by completing dialogs in the windowed ANOVA procedure. An easier approach is to automate this follow-up analysis by using SPSS control language, or **syntax**. We shall describe the use of SPSS syntax to run tests for simple main effects later in this chapter.

8.4   THE TWO-WAY ANOVA WITH SPSS

Table 5 shows the raw data from the two-factor factorial *Drug × Alertness* experiment.

Table 5. Results of the Drug Treatment × Alertness factorial experiment			
Levels of the Alertness factor:	**Levels of the Drug Treatment factor:**		
	Placebo	**A**	**B**
Fresh	24 25 13 22 16	18 8 9 14 16	27 14 19 29 27
	23 18 19 24 26	15 6 9 8 17	23 19 17 20 25
Tired	13 12 14 16 17	21 24 22 23 20	21 11 14 22 19
	13 4 3 2 6	13 11 17 13 16	9 14 11 21 18

8.4.1   Preparing the data for the factorial ANOVA

Since there are two factors, two **grouping variables** will be required to specify the treatment combination under which each score was achieved. If the grouping variables are *Alertness* and *Drug*, and performance in the driving simulator is *DrivingPerf*, the data file will consist of a column for case numbers, two for the grouping variables, and a fourth for *DrivingPerf*.

Proceed as follows:
- In **Variable View**, use the **Name** column to create the variables, as described in Chapter 2, Section 2.3.
  > See Section 2.3
- In the **Decimals** column, change the values to 0 to display whole numbers.
- In the **Label** column, enter informative variable labels, such as *Case Number, Alertness, Drug Treatment,* and *Driving Performance.*
- In the **Values** column, add values and labels for the grouping variables, such as 1 and 2 (with labels Fresh and Tired, respectively) for the variable *Alertness* and 1, 2, and 3 (with labels Placebo, Drug A, and Drug B, respectively) for the variable *Drug.*
- In the **Measure** column, ensure that *Case Number* and *Score* are Scale variables, *Drug Treatment* and *Alertness* are Nominal variables.
- Enter **Data View**. To display the labels for the values entered for the grouping variables, check the View menu to make sure that **Value Labels** is ticked.

Part of the completed data set is shown in Figure 4. Note that the values for the grouping variables *Alertness* and *Drug* have been replaced by their corresponding labels. For example, in case 28, the value 1 has been replaced by Fresh and 2 has been replaced by Drug B. Likewise, in case 31, the value 2 has been replaced by Tired and 1 by Placebo.

Case	Alertness	Drug	DrivingPerf
27	Fresh	Drug B	19
28	Fresh	Drug B	17
29	Fresh	Drug B	20
30	Fresh	Drug B	25
31	Tired	Placebo	13
32	Tired	Placebo	12
33	Tired	Placebo	14
34	Tired	Placebo	16

Figure 4. Part of **Data View** showing some of the data from Table 5

8.4.2   Exploring the data: boxplots

Before running the ANOVA, it is important to explore the data to check for any problems with the distributions.   To obtain the boxplots under each of the six treatment combinations, proceed as follows:

- Choose **Graphs➜Chart Builder…** and select **Boxplot** from the gallery.
- Drag the **Clustered Boxplot** image to the **Chart preview** and fill in the variable names with *Driving Performance* in the **Y-Axis** box, *Drug* in the **X-Axis** box and *Alertness* in the **Cluster: set pattern** box.
- Complete the details as in Section 5.4 to obtain the boxplot (Output1).

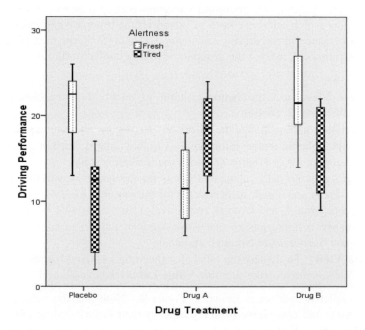

Output 1. Boxplots clustered for *Alertness* at each level of *Drug Treatment*

These boxplots show no extreme cases, each of which would have been flagged with an asterisk. (See Chapter 4, Table 2, for details of the structure of a boxplot.) None of the distributions is markedly skewed. There is therefore no need to remove any cases or apply a transformation to make the distribution more symmetrical. We can safely proceed with the ANOVA.

See Table 2 in Chap. 4

8.4.3   Choosing a factorial ANOVA

In SPSS, a factorial ANOVA is run by choosing from the **General Linear Model (GLM)** menu (see Figure 9 in Chapter 7).

For a between subjects factorial ANOVA, we must choose the **Univariate** option, bearing in mind that, although there are two independent variables (factors), namely, *Drug Treatment* and *Alertness*, there is only one dependent variable, *Driving Performance*. See Figure 10 in Chapter 7 for details.

WLS Weight

The **WLS Weight** box in Chapter 7, Figure 10, is used for identifying a variable containing weights for weighted least-squares analysis. We do not consider this type of analysis in this book.

Factors with Fixed and Random effects

The box labelled **Random Factor(s)** is used only if the levels of a factor must be viewed as a random sample from a large pool of possible levels, as opposed to exhausting the possibilities, as in *Sex*, or having been chosen systematically, in accordance with a hypothesis or an experimental design, as in the drug experiment, in which case the factor is said to have **fixed effects** (Section 7.5.1). *Alertness* and *Drug* are both fixed effects factors. Random factors are rare in experimental research.

Analysis of covariance

We have seen (Chapter 7) that there are techniques known as **Analysis of Covariance (ANCOVA)** that essentially remove the effects of covariates upon the scores and re-run the ANOVA on a 'purified' data set. The advantage of ANCOVA is often a reduction of 'data noise' and a resulting increase in the power of the ANOVA tests. To run an ANCOVA, transfer the name(s) of the covariate(s) into the covariate box.

Profile plots

To obtain a profile plot of the means, click **Plots...** in the **Univariate** dialog box (Chapter 7, Figure 10) to open the **Univariate: Profile Plots** dialog box and follow the steps in Figure 5.

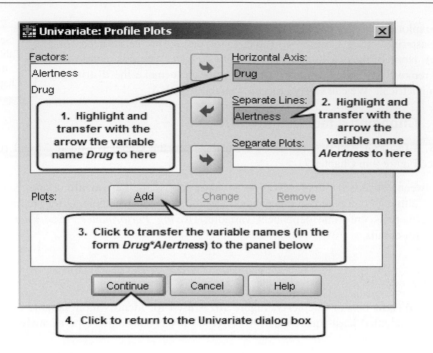

Figure 5. The **Profile Plots** dialog box for plotting *Drug*Alertness* i.e. plotting *Drug* along the horizontal axis with the separate lines representing the levels of *Alertness*

Note that by completing the dialog as we have in Figure 5, we have requested the profile plot shown in Figure 2. Had we wished to obtain the plot in Figure 3, we should have transferred *Alertness* to the slot labelled **Horizontal Axis** and *Drug* to the **Separate Lines** slot.

8.4.4   Output for a factorial ANOVA

The results are shown in Output Listings 2-5. The table in Output 2, **Between-Subjects Factors**, summarises the factor names and level labels, together with the number of cases at each level.

Between-Subjects Factors

		Value Label	N
Alertness	1	Fresh	30
	2	Tired	30
Drug Treatment	1	Placebo	20
	2	Drug A	20
	3	Drug B	20

Output 2. The table of **Between-Subjects Factors**

Output 3 is the table of descriptive statistics requested from **Options…** .

Descriptive Statistics

Dependent Variable: Driving Performance

Alertness	Drug Treatment	Mean	Std. Deviation	N
Fresh	Placebo	21.00	4.29	10
	Drug A	12.00	4.42	10
	Drug B	22.00	4.94	10
	Total	18.33	6.35	30
Tired	Placebo	10.00	5.66	10
	Drug A	18.00	4.64	10
	Drug B	16.00	4.78	10
	Total	14.67	5.97	30
Total	Placebo	15.50	7.47	20
	Drug A	15.00	5.38	20
	Drug B	19.00	5.65	20
	Total	16.50	6.38	60

Output 3. The table of **Descriptive Statistics**

The table in Output 4, **Tests of Between-Subjects Effects**, is the ANOVA summary table, which tabulates the sources of variation, their **Sums of Squares**, degrees of freedom (**df**), mean squares, *F* ratios and p-values (**Sig.**). Note that, in the between subjects factorial ANOVA, each *F* ratio is the Mean Square for the source divided by the Error Mean Square (23.15). The final column **Partial Eta Squared** is the estimate of effect size (explained in Section 8.3).

This table was edited in **SPSS Viewer** to reduce the display of values from three decimal places to two decimal places. This was done by double-clicking the whole table so that it showed a hashed border, highlighting the five columns of numbers so that they appeared in inverse video, clicking the right-hand mouse button to show a menu, selecting the item **Cell Properties...**, selecting in the **Format** box the item *#.#*, changing the number of decimals shown in the **Decimals** box to 2, and finally clicking **OK**.

The terms **Corrected Model** and **Intercept** refer to the regression method used to carry out the ANOVA and can be ignored. The three rows **Alertness, Drug** and **Alertness*Drug** are of most interest, since these report tests for the two main effects and the interaction. Note the **Sig.** (i.e. p-value, or tail probability) for each *F* ratio. There are significant main effects for both the *Alertness* and *Drug* factors: the former is significant beyond the 0.01 level, the latter beyond the 0.05 level, but not beyond the 0.01 level. In addition to main effects of both treatment factors, there is a significant interaction. The p-value is given as .000, which means that it is less than 0.0005. Write 'p < .01', not 'p = .000'. Clearly, the *Drug* factor has different effects upon Fresh and Tired participants. To ascertain the nature of these effects, however, we shall need to examine the pattern of the treatment means more closely.

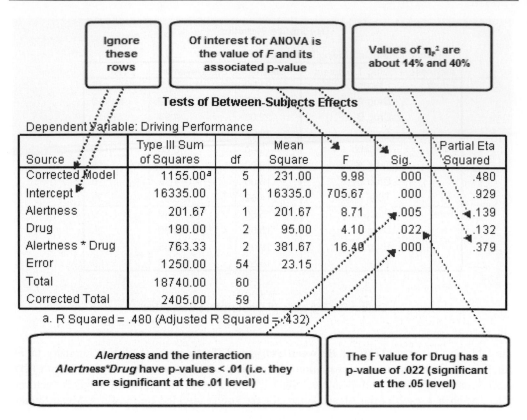

Output 4. The **ANOVA** summary table

Optional post hoc tests following significant main effects

The optional **Tukey** Post Hoc test results for the factor Drug Treatment are shown in Output 5. It can be seen that the means for Drug A and Drug B differ significantly from one another, but neither differs significantly from the Placebo mean.

The optional profile plot has already been shown in Figure 1. It has been edited in **SPSS Viewer** to replace the colours with different textures of lines and markers that are clear in black and white.

Since the ANOVA summary table has confirmed the interaction pattern that was strikingly evident in Figure 1 and in Figure 2, further analysis is necessary in order to pinpoint the crucial differences among the cell means. We have suggested that a first step in this follow-up analysis might be to test for the presence of simple main effects. In Figure 3, for example, interest now centres upon comparisons among the individual cell means for the three drug groups at each level of the *Alertness* factor. If we could demonstrate that there are significant simple main effects of the *Drug* factor at either or both levels of *Alertness*, we would be justified in reducing the size of each comparison 'family' to three means, rather than six and proceeding with a post hoc test such as the **Tukey** on that basis.

Multiple Comparisons

Dependent Variable: Driving Performance

Tukey HSD

(I) Drug Treatment	(J) Drug Treatment	Mean Difference (I-J)	Std. Error	Sig.
Placebo	Drug A	.50	1.52	.942
	Drug B	-3.50	1.52	.064
Drug A	Placebo	-.50	1.52	.942
	Drug B	-4.00*	1.52	.029
Drug B	Placebo	3.50	1.52	.064
	Drug A	4.00*	1.52	.029

Based on observed means.

*. The mean difference is significant at the .05 level.

> The only difference with a p-value < .05 is *Drug A* and *Drug B*.
> Note these rows are highlighted with *

Output 5. **Multiple Comparisons** with the **Tukey Post Hoc** test for the *Drug Treatment* factor

Should it be more meaningful to view the data as in Figure 1, with the three levels of the *Drug* factor on the horizontal axis of the graph and different profiles for the Fresh and Tired participants, we should need to test for simple main effects of *Alertness* at each of the three levels of the *Drug* factor. In that case, the demonstration of a significant simple main effect at any one level would itself imply that the individual means are significantly different, since there are only two of them: there would be no need for any further statistical testing.

In the next subsection, we shall describe how to use SPSS syntax to test for simple main effects. Here we note that, if we follow our usual procedure with dialog boxes, we can test for a simple main effect of *Alertness* in the data from the Placebo participants by choosing **Data➜Select Cases** and running a one-way ANOVA. We shall find that $F(1, 18) = 23.99$; $p < .01$. This confirms the simple main effect of *Alertness* at the Placebo level of the *Drug* factor and hence that the difference between the means for the (Placebo, Fresh) and (Placebo, Tired) conditions is significant. The procedure is more complicated if we test for simple main effects of the *Drug* factor at each level of *Alertness*: a significant result would have to be followed by a conservative multiple-comparisons method such as the Tukey test to pinpoint the robust differences among the three individual treatment means at each level of *Alertness*.

8.5   TESTING FOR SIMPLE MAIN EFFECTS WITH SYNTAX

So far throughout this book, the statistics provided by SPSS have been accessed by opening windows and completing dialog boxes. Although this is the easy way to learn SPSS, there is another approach which, though it requires practice, has considerable advantages.

It is also possible to run SPSS procedures and analyses by writing instructions in a control language known as **SPSS syntax**. (In fact, until a few years ago, that was the only way of using SPSS or any of the other major statistical packages.) It is useful to learn how to use SPSS syntax if only because some SPSS routines are available through syntax only. Moreover, the syntax for a particular analysis (even one set up initially from dialog boxes – see below) can be saved as a syntax file and re-used later, with enormous savings in time.

The commands are written in a special window known as the **Syntax Editor**, either by typing them in from the keyboard or by pasting them in from syntax files. The Syntax Editor window can be opened by making a selection from the File drop-down menu as shown in Figure 6.

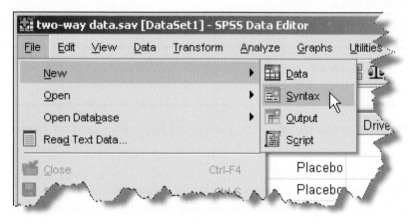

Figure 6. Accessing the syntax window

The window of the **SPSS Syntax Editor** is shown in Figure 7.

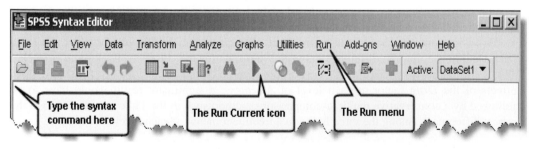

Figure 7. The **Syntax Editor**

All the commands in the syntax window can be executed by selecting the **Run** menu and clicking **All**. Should you wish to run only one of the commands, highlight that command and click the (**Run current**) icon ▶ at the top of the syntax window (see Figure 7).

If an analysis has been set up from dialog boxes, pressing **Paste** (instead of **OK**) in the final dialog box will paste the hitherto hidden syntax into the **syntax window** from which it can be saved to a file in the usual way. Once an SPSS data file is active, the syntax file can be opened and the procedure can be run immediately: there is no need to complete any dialog boxes. In no time at all, the user will become practised in the use of syntax and familiar with the general form of syntax commands. We believe that the most efficient way of learning SPSS syntax is by working from the dialog boxes in this way, rather than ploughing through the available texts on the topic, which tend to be rather compendious and are better left until one has already acquired a working knowledge of the language.

8.5.1   Using the MANOVA command to run the univariate ANOVA

In the ANOVA, there is just one dependent variable or measure, no matter how many independent variables or factors there may be. The ANOVA, that is, is a **univariate** statistical technique – even though there may be several factors in the design. In **multivariate statistics**, there are two or more dependent variables. The **multivariate analysis of variance** (**MANOVA**) is a generalisation of the ANOVA to data sets in which there are two or more dependent variables or measures. We shall have more to say about MANOVA in later chapters. For present purposes, it is only necessary to bear in mind that, for some purposes, the ANOVA can be viewed as a special case of MANOVA and that, in SPSS syntax, the MANOVA command can be used to run ANOVA. We shall do this because there are some ANOVA procedures which can be run by including them in a MANOVA command.

Running a two-way ANOVA on the MANOVA command

Like a paragraph of English, every SPSS command ends in a full stop or period. In fact, the procedure will not run otherwise. An SPSS command must also begin with a command **keyword**, which SPSS must recognise or, once again, the procedure will not run. Within each command, are **subcommands**, each being preceded by a forward 'slash' / sign. This, too, is essential. A subcommand will not run on its own: it must appear within a recognised command.

Figure 8 shows a syntax command which will run a two-way ANOVA on the same drug and alertness data that we have already analysed.

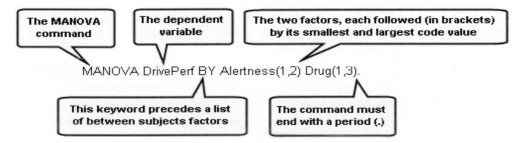

Figure 8. Syntax for running ANOVA with the MANOVA command

Note the following points. The first word of the syntax must be the command keyword MANOVA and the command must end with a full stop or period. In the middle of the command is the keyword BY, on the left of which is the measure or dependent variable and on the right is the list of between subjects factors. The numbers in brackets after each factor name are the lowest and highest code numbers assigned to the groups or conditions.

The ANOVA summary table

The ANOVA summary table is shown in Output 6. The values of the sums of squares, the mean squares, the degrees of freedom and F are exactly as they were in Output 4. The term UNIQUE indicates that the ANOVA has been run by using the MANOVA command. This is a special application of MANOVA: the MANOVA output normally looks different from this.

> This term indicates that MANOVA has run a univariate ANOVA.

```
Tests of Significance for DrivePerf using UNIQUE sums of squares
Source of Variation            SS      DF       MS        F  Sig of F

WITHIN CELLS               1250.00     54     23.15
Alertness                   201.67      1    201.67     8.71    .005
Drug                        190.00      2     95.00     4.10    .022
Alertness BY Drug           763.33      2    381.67    16.49    .000

(Model)                    1155.00      5    231.00     9.98    .000
(Total)                    2405.00     59     40.76

R-Squared =         .480
Adjusted R-Squared =  .432
```

> These are terms in regression (Chapter 12). A regression method was used to run the ANOVA.

Output 6. The **ANOVA** summary table obtained from running the **MANOVA** command

Including simple effects within the MANOVA subcommand

There is more than one way of writing the syntax for simple main effects. The easiest way is shown in Figure 9. In SPSS syntax, a subcommand always begins with a forward slash /. The commands for all the simple main effects of one factor at the different levels of another can be included in the same /DESIGN subcommand.

Note carefully the subcommand /ERROR. If this subcommand is not included, MANOVA will use a composite error term which includes an extra RESIDUAL component. The inclusion of the /ERROR subcommand is not the only way of avoiding this problem: as we shall see, it is possible to absorb the residual component of the error term into effect sums of squares by amending the /DESIGN subcommand.

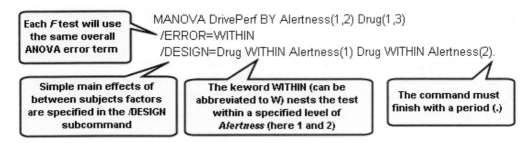

Figure 9. Syntax for simple main effects the *Drug* factor at each level of *Alertness*

Output for the simple main effects analysis

Part of the analysis is shown in Output 7.

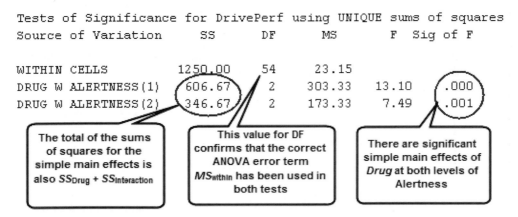

Output 7. Results of tests for simple main effects of the *Drug* factor at each level of *Alertness*

The analysis has confirmed the presence of simple effects of the *Drug* factor at both levels of *Alertness*: both p-values are very small. The correct error term has been used, as requested in the /ERROR subcommand. (Compare with values of SS and DF in the full two-way ANOVA summary table in Output 6.)

The comparison of the values in Output 7 with the ANOVA summary table in Output 6 also confirms another interesting identity. Earlier, we observed that the appearance of profile plots (such as those in Figure 1 p. 274) reflects the presence of the main effect of the factor whose simple main effects we are testing, as well as the interaction. In Output 7, you can see that

$$SS_{Drug\ at\ Alertness(1)} + SS_{Drug\ at\ Alertness(2)} - 606.666... + 346.666...$$

$$= 953.33$$

This is the total of the sums of squares for the Drug factor and the interaction in the ANOVA summary table (Output 6):

$$SS_{Drug} + SS_{Alertness\ BY\ Drug} = 190.00 + 763.33$$

$$= 953.33$$

The above comparison illustrates the general point that, in a factorial experiment A × B, design, the sums of squares of the simple main effects of A at B_1, A at B_2, and so on, across all levels of B, add up to the sum of squares for the main effect of A plus the sum of squares for the interaction:

$$\sum_k SS_{A\ at\ B_k} = SS_{A\ at\ B_1} + SS_{A\ at\ B_2} + ... + SS_{A\ at\ B_k}$$

$$= SS_A + SS_{AB} \qquad \text{--- (14)}$$

Simple main effects reflect main effect plus interaction

Effectively, the simple main effects terms in Output 7 have replaced the main effect and interaction terms in the full ANOVA shown in Output 6.

An alternative syntax for testing simple main effects

The manner in which the ANOVA run by the MANOVA procedure has repartitioned the total sum of squares becomes explicit when another wording of the MANOVA syntax command is used to test for the same simple main effects.

We have seen that the full ANOVA can be run from the MANOVA command with a single line of syntax, namely,

MANOVA DrivePerf BY Alertness(1,2) Drug(1,3).

The same result can also be achieved by adding a /DESIGN subcommand as in Figure 10.

MANOVA DrivePerf BY Alertness(1,2) Drug(1,3)
/DESIGN=Alertness Drug Drug BY Alertness.

The /DESIGN subcommand partitions the between groups sums of squares into main effect and interaction components

Figure 10. Ordering a full ANOVA by specifying the components in the DESIGN subcommand

The same simple effects analysis discussed above can also be implemented by rewriting the DESIGN subcommand to repartition the between groups sum of squares into a main effect of Alertness, plus simple effects of the Drug factor at each level of Alertness (see Figure 11).

MANOVA DrivePerf BY Alertness(1,2) Drug(1,3)
    /DESIGN=Alertness Drug WITHIN Alertness(1) Drug WITHIN Alertness(2).

> These simple effects replace the *Drug* and *Drug* BY *Alertness* components in the /DESIGN subcommand for the full ANOVA

Figure 11. Specifying tests for simple main effects without also specifying the error term

Output 8 shows the result of the analysis.

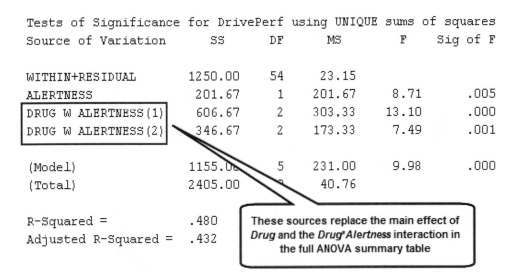

Source of Variation	SS	DF	MS	F	Sig of F
WITHIN+RESIDUAL	1250.00	54	23.15		
ALERTNESS	201.67	1	201.67	8.71	.005
DRUG W ALERTNESS(1)	606.67	2	303.33	13.10	.000
DRUG W ALERTNESS(2)	346.67	2	173.33	7.49	.001
(Model)	1155.00	5	231.00	9.98	.000
(Total)	2405.00		40.76		

Tests of Significance for DrivePerf using UNIQUE sums of squares

R-Squared =   .480
Adjusted R-Squared =   .432

> These sources replace the main effect of *Drug* and the *Drug*Alertness* interaction in the full ANOVA summary table

Output 8. Tests for simple effects in the context of a model repartitioning the main effect of the *Drug* factor and the *Drug* by *Alertness* interaction.

Several features of Output 8 are worthy of note. The source labelled WITHIN + RESIDUAL is actually the WITHIN error term in the full ANOVA, as you can see from the degrees of freedom (54) and the agreement between the sum of squares value (1250) and that given as WITHIN CELLS in Output 7. The sums of squares for ALERTNESS and (Total) have exactly the same values as those given in the full ANOVA summary table (Output 6). Once again, the sums of squares for the simple effects of the *Drug* factor at the different levels of *Alertness* sum to the total of the *Drug* and *Drug* × *Alertness* sums of squares in the full ANOVA.

Multiple comparisons following tests of simple main effects

Figure 12 is an alternative set of profile plots of the two-way table of means for the Drug and Alertness experiment, with the profiles for the three different drug conditions being plotted against the two levels of the *Alertness* factor on the horizontal axis. From the graph, it would appear that, with the Fresh participants, Drug A lowered the performance level in comparison with the Drug B and Placebo conditions, which produced similar levels of performance.

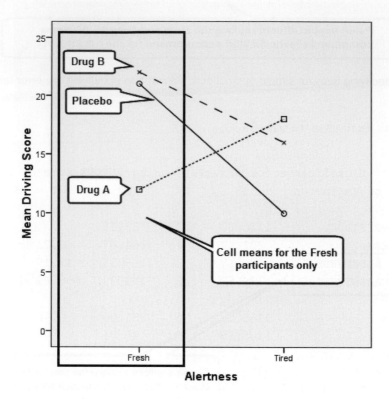

Figure 12. Profile plots showing the effect of the *Drug* factor upon the Fresh participants

Now that we have established that there is a significant simple main effect of the *Drug* factor with the Fresh participants, we can proceed with *post hoc* pairwise comparisons on the basis that the comparison 'family' is the number of possible pairs in the three cell means for the Fresh participants. From Figure 12, we can expect that the mean for Drug A will turn out to be significantly less than the means for the Placebo and Drug B groups; whereas it seems likely that there is no significant difference between Drug B and the Placebo.

To select Fresh participants only, choose **Data→Select Cases...** and click the **If condition satisfied** radio button to open the **Select Cases: If** dialog box (Figure 13). Follow the instructions in Figure 13 and then click **OK** in the **Select Cases** dialog box.

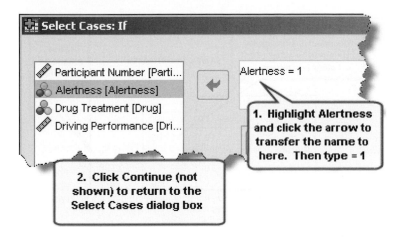

Figure 13. Selecting the data from the Fresh participants only

Back in the **Univariate** dialog box, click the **Post Hoc** button and choose the **Tukey** test, specifying the factor as *Drug* (Figure 14).

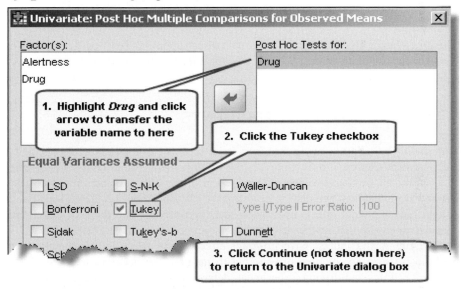

Figure 14. Choosing **Tukey** post hoc tests for the *Drug* factor

Output for the Tukey test

Output 9 shows that the **Tukey** test has identified two subgroups:

1. The mean for Drug A;
2. The means for the Placebo and Drug B groups.

Should you require further details for your report, the SPSS output includes another table showing the p-values and confidence intervals for these tests.

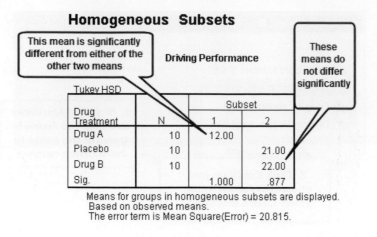

Output 9. Summary of the results of the **Tukey** test

The **Tukey** test has clearly confirmed that, in the data from the Fresh participants only, the mean for the Drug A group is significantly lower than the means for either the Drug B group or the Placebo group, which do not differ significantly from one another.

Since the *Drug* factor also has a significant main effect upon the Tired participants, a similar Tukey test can be run on those data as well to confirm the pattern of differences that appears in Figure 1.

8.6   MORE COMPLEX EXPERIMENTS

SPSS can readily be used to analyse data from more complex factorial experiments, with three or more treatment factors. In Section 8.2, we described the two-way ANOVA, which we illustrated with data from an imaginary investigation of the effects of two new anti-hay fever drugs, A and B, upon simulated driving performance. It was suspected that at least one of the drugs might have different effects upon fresh and tired drivers, and the firm developing the drugs needed to ensure that neither had an adverse effect upon driving performance. It was found that Drug A did indeed have different effects upon fresh and tired participants: it improved the performance of tired drivers; but it impaired the performance of fresh drivers. The two-factor drugs-and-driving experiment demonstrated the presence of an interaction between the two treatment factors of *Alertness* (Fresh, Tired) and *Drug* (Placebo, Drug A, Drug B).

Our hypothetical researcher was aware that much of the previous research on the hay fever drugs had used male participants. Recent pilot work, however, had suggested that the striking interaction between *Alertness* and *Drug* might not occur in female drivers. It was therefore decided to include females in a new investigation and run a **three-factor between subjects factorial experiment**, in which the factors were:
  1.   Drug Treatment, with levels Placebo, Drug A and Drug B.
  2.   Alertness, with levels Fresh and Tired.
  3.   Sex, with levels Female and Male.

An experiment with three factors allows the investigation of more complex hypotheses than does a two factor experiment: in particular, the addition of the third factor brings the possibility of a complex interplay among all three factors which is known as a **three-way interaction**.

8.6.1   Three-way interactions

In a factorial experiment with three factors, the interaction between two factors at one particular level of the third factor is known as a **simple interaction**. For example the interaction between the *Drug* and *Alertness* factors with the female participants only is a simple interaction, as is the interaction between the same two factors with the male participants.

Three-way interactions

A **three-way interaction** is said to occur when the simple interaction between two factors is not the same at all levels of a third factor. This is exactly what is implied by the investigator's hypothesis: we can expect a three-way interaction among the factors of *Alertness*, *Drug* and *Sex* because we have reason to suspect that the simple interaction between *Drug* and *Alertness* is not homogeneous in the two sexes.

The results of the three-factor experiment are summarised in Figure 15.

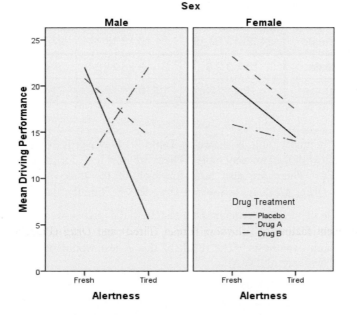

Figure 15. The two-way graphs for the female and male participants, illustrating a three-way interaction among the factors of *Alertness*, *Drug* and *Sex*. The simple two-way interaction between *Drug* and *Alertness* is clearly heterogeneous across the sexes.

It is quite clear from the graph that the two-way interaction between the *Alertness* and *Drug* factors is different in the female and the male participants: while the simple interaction is strikingly evident in the males, it is not apparent in the data from the females. Here we have what appears to be a three-way interaction among the factors *Alertness*, *Drug* and *Sex*. We can hope that the three-way ANOVA will confirm this complex interaction.

In the males, Drug A had a dampening effect on the performance of the fresh participants; whereas the same drug improved the performance of the tired participants. In the female participants, there is little sign of an interaction; though the Drug A profile is shallower than those of the Drug B or Placebo groups. There is here no evidence that either drug boosted the performance of tired female drivers.

8.6.2   The three-way ANOVA

The results of the experiment are shown in Table 6.

Table 6. Results of a three-way factorial experiment				
Levels of the Alertness factor:	Levels of the Sex factor:	Levels of the Drug Treatment factor:		
		Placebo	A	B
Fresh	Male	23 18 19 24 26	11 16 11 8 11	23 19 17 20 25
	Female	24 25 13 22 16	14 18 15 18 14	27 14 19 29 27
Tired	Male	13 4 3 2 6	21 19 25 21 24	9 14 11 21 18
	Female	13 12 14 16 17	13 16 14 15 12	21 11 14 22 19

The three-way ANOVA summary table is shown in Table 7. It is worth examining Table 7 carefully and comparing it with the two-way table. There are now tests for three main effects: *Drug*, *Alertness* and *Sex*. There are also tests for each of the three possible two-way interactions: *Alertness* × *Drug*, *Alertness* × *Sex* and *Drug* × *Sex*. Finally, there is a test for a three-way interaction.

The most interesting result in Table 7 is the significance of the three-way interaction, which is consistent with the research hypothesis. The result of this F test would be reported in the manner described for the two-way ANOVA:

$$F(2, 48) = 11.15; p < .01$$

A measure of effect size (preferably omega squared, rather than partial eta squared) would also be included.

Table 7. Three-way ANOVA table for the data in Table 6.					
Source	df	SS	MS	F	p
Main effects					
Alertness (A)	1	264.60	264.60	17.49	<.01
Drug (D)	2	150.53	75.27	4.97	.01
Sex (S)	1	29.40	29.40	1.94	.17
Two-way interactions					
A × D	2	617.20	308.60	20.39	<.01
A × S	1	.60	.60	.04	.84
D × S	2	78.40	39.20	2.59	.09
Three-way interaction					
A × D × S	2	337.60	168.80	11.15	<.01
Error term					
Within groups (Error)	48	726.40	15.13		
Total	59	2204.73			

In this context, it is worth observing that a list of ANOVA test results means very little without a clear demonstration of the patterns of differences responsible. The mere fact that the three-way interaction is significant does not necessarily mean that the cell means show the patterns of those in Figure 15. Rather than presenting the reader of your report with a long list of results of the seven F tests, you should 'talk the reader through' the patterns of means in a graph such as Figure 15 or a table, explaining the relevant significant (and insignificant) results with reference to the descriptive statistics.

8.6.3 How the three-way ANOVA works

The rationale of the three-way ANOVA is a simple extension of the two-way ANOVA.

In the three-way ANOVA, the between groups sums of squares is partitioned into 3 main effects sums of squares, 3 two-way interaction sums of squares and the three-way interaction sum of squares. In our current example, the partition is:

$$SS_{between} = SS_{Alertness} + SS_{Drug} + SS_{Sex} + SS_{A\times D} + SS_{A\times S} + SS_{D\times S} + SS_{A\times D\times S} \quad \text{- - - (15)}$$

Partition of the total sum of squares in the three-way ANOVA

As with the one-way and two-way ANOVA, the mean squares are obtained by dividing the sums of squares by their degrees of freedom. The general form of the F statistic for any between subjects factorial design is as follows:

$$F_{df\ source,\ df\ within} = \frac{MS_{source}}{MS_{within}} \quad ---(16)$$

General form of the F statistic in the between subjects factorial ANOVA

Degrees of freedom of the mean squares

It is important, with complex experimental designs especially, to be clear about the degrees of freedom of the various sources in the ANOVA. This knowledge is very helpful when you are interpreting the SPSS output, or when you want to use a package such as G*Power to determine the number of participants that will be needed in a study you plan to run.

The degrees of freedom are obtained in a manner analogous with the one-way and two-way ANOVA. For main effects, *df* is the number of conditions or groups minus 1.

$$df_A = (a-1); \ df_B = (b-1); \ df_C = (c-1)$$

In our current example,

$$df_{Drug} = (3-1) = 2; \ df_{Alertness} = (2-1) = 1; \ df_{Sex} = (2-1) = 1$$

For two-way interactions, the *df* is the product of the degrees of freedom of the sources considered separately.

$$df_{A\times B} = (a-1)(b-1); \ df_{A\times C} = (a-1)(c-1); \ df_{B\times C} = (b-1)(c-1)$$

In our current example,

$$df_{Alertness \times Drug} = (2-1)(3-1) = 2;$$
$$df_{Alertness \times Sex} = (2-1)(2-1) = 1;$$
$$df_{Drug \times Sex} = (3-1)(2-1) = 2$$

The degrees of freedom of the three-way interaction is the product of the degrees of freedom of the three component sources.

$$df_{A\times B\times C} = (a-1)(b-1)(c-1) \quad ---(17)$$

Degrees of freedom of the three-way interaction

In our current example, if A, B and C are the *Alertness*, *Drug* and *Sex* factors, respectively, $a = 2$, $b = 3$, $c = 2$ and

$$df_{A\times B\times C} = (2-1)(3-1)(2-1) = 2$$

The error term for the three-way ANOVA

As in the two-way ANOVA, all the *F* tests in the three-way ANOVA have the same denominator, namely, MS_{within}. As in the one-way and two-way ANOVA, the within groups mean square is the average of the variance estimates calculated from each sample of participants.

In general, if the three factors A, B and C have a, b & c levels, respectively, n is the number of participants in each combination of conditions and N is the total number of observations, there will be $a \times b \times c = abc$ combinations of treatments, that is, cells in the design. In our example, $abc = 2 \times 3 \times 2 = 12$. If n is the sample size (in our fictitious example, $n = 5$), the total number of observations is $N = abcn$. In our example, $N = 2 \times 3 \times 2 \times 5 = 60$.

As in the one-way and two-way ANOVAs, the error term in the three-way ANOVA is a pooled estimate of the supposedly uniform population variance σ_e^2. In general, since there are abc cells in the design, there will be abc variance estimates, each with $(n-1)$ degrees of freedom. The degrees of freedom of the within groups mean square MS_{within} is therefore given by

$$df_{within} = abc(n-1) = N - abc \quad \text{- - - (18)}$$

Degrees of freedom of the within groups mean square

In our current example,

$$df_{within} = 60 - 12 = 48$$

which is the value given in Table 7.

8.6.4   Measures of effect size in the three-way ANOVA

Since the various measures of effect size are defined and calculated as simple generalisations from the two-way ANOVA, we shall only consider partial omega squared here.

$$\hat{\omega}_{source}^2 = \frac{df_{source}\left(F_{source} - 1\right)}{df_{source}\left(F_{source} - 1\right) + abcn} \quad \text{- - - (19)}$$

Partial omega squared for the three-way ANOVA

Note the difference in the denominator of (19): into the rightmost term, we must introduce the multiplier c, the number of levels making up the third factor.

8.6.5   How many participants shall I need?

Proceed with G*Power 3 in a manner similar to the two-factor ANOVA, supplying the degrees of freedom for the various sources and the error term as described in Section 8.3.2.

8.6.6   The three-way ANOVA with SPSS

For the three-way ANOVA, the data set in **Data View** will now include three grouping variables (*Alertness*, *Sex*, and *Drug*), as well as a column for the dependent variable *DrivingPerf*. Figure 16 shows a section of **Data View**, showing the third grouping variable *Sex*, representing the third factor in the experimental design.

	Case	Alertness	Drug	DrivingPerf	Sex
1	1	Fresh	Placebo	23	Male
2	2	Fresh	Placebo	18	Male
3	3	Fresh	Placebo	19	Male
4	4	Fresh	Placebo	24	Male
5	5	Fresh	Placebo	26	Male
6	6	Fresh	Placebo	24	Female
7	7	Fresh	Placebo	25	Female
8	8	Fresh	Placebo	13	Female

Figure 16. Part of **Data View** showing some of the data in Table 6

To run the three-factor ANOVA, proceed as follows:

- Open the **General Linear Model - Univariate** dialog box and complete it as in Chapter 7, Figure 10, with *Driving Performance* in the **Dependent Variable** box and the three grouping factors *Alertness*, *Drug* and *Sex* in the **Fixed Factors** box.
- Select the optional **Descriptive statistics** and **Estimates of effect size** check boxes from **Options...** and the **Tukey Post Hoc** test for *Drug* from **Post Hoc...**, clicking **Continue** each time to return to the **Univariate** dialog box.
- To obtain the profile plots of the means that we have shown in Figure 15, click **Plots...** to open the **Univariate: Profile Plots** dialog box. Select *Alertness* for the **Horizontal Axis** box, *Drug* for the **Separate Lines** box and *Sex* for the **Separate Plots** box. Click **Add** to add the plot to the **Plots** list and then **Continue** to return to the **Univariate** dialog box. (Note that, should you want to have the *Drug* factor on the horizontal axis of the graphs and show the profiles of the two *Alertness* conditions, you would transfer *Drug* to the Horizontal Axis box, *Alertness* to the **Separate Lines** box and *Sex* to the **Separate Plots** box as before.)
- Click **OK**.

Output for the three-way ANOVA

The first table in the output describes the factors in the experiment and lists the number of cases for each level of every factor (Output 10). Check this information carefully to ensure that there have been no transcription errors and that the design specifications have been correctly communicated to SPSS.

Between-Subjects Factors

		Value Label	N
Alertness	1	Fresh	30
	2	Tired	30
Drug Treatment	1	Placebo	20
	2	Drug A	20
	3	Drug B	20
Sex	1	Male	30
	2	Female	30

Output 10. The table of **Between-Subjects Factors**

The next table in the output (not reproduced here) shows the descriptive statistics you should always request in the **Options…** dialog box.

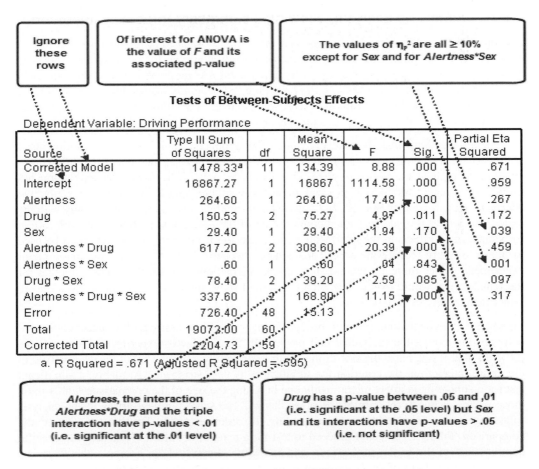

Ignore these rows

Of interest for ANOVA is the value of *F* and its associated p-value

The values of η_p^2 are all $\geq 10\%$ except for *Sex* and for *Alertness*Sex*

Tests of Between-Subjects Effects

Dependent Variable: Driving Performance

Source	Type III Sum of Squares	df	Mean Square	F	Sig.	Partial Eta Squared
Corrected Model	1478.33[a]	11	134.39	8.88	.000	.671
Intercept	16867.27	1	16867	1114.58	.000	.959
Alertness	264.60	1	264.60	17.48	.000	.267
Drug	150.53	2	75.27	4.97	.011	.172
Sex	29.40	1	29.40	1.94	.170	.039
Alertness * Drug	617.20	2	308.60	20.39	.000	.459
Alertness * Sex	.60	1	.60	.04	.843	.001
Drug * Sex	78.40	2	39.20	2.59	.085	.097
Alertness * Drug * Sex	337.60	2	168.80	11.15	.000	.317
Error	726.40	48	15.13			
Total	19073.00	60				
Corrected Total	2204.73	59				

a. R Squared = .671 (Adjusted R Squared = .595)

Alertness, the interaction *Alertness*Drug* and the triple interaction have p-values < .01 (i.e. significant at the .01 level)

Drug has a p-value between .05 and ,01 (i.e. significant at the .05 level) but *Sex* and its interactions have p-values > .05 (i.e. not significant)

Output 11. The three-way factorial **ANOVA** summary table

The ANOVA summary table (Output 11) shows that of the three main effects, *Alertness* and *Drug* are significant; but *Sex* is insignificant. Of the three two-way interactions, *Alertness* × *Drug* is significant, but neither *Alertness* × *Sex* nor *Drug* × *Sex* is significant. There is a significant three-way interaction, in line with the experimental hypothesis.

The full SPSS ANOVA summary table is a useful source of information for the researcher who is analysing data with a view to publishing a research paper. Such a table, on the other hand, would rarely appear in the body of the text of a paper; moreover, little would be achieved by including, in the body of the text, a comprehensive list of all the test results in the ANOVA summary table. Instead, the reader should be guided through only those results that are relevant to the principal research hypotheses, each result being explained with reference to the appropriate descriptive statistics.

Whether a table or a graph is the more suitable vehicle for the descriptive statistics is a matter of opinion and different reviewers and journal editors have different views. With a complex experiment such as the present one, we think it makes life easier for the reader to be referred to a graph such as Figure 15, rather than a complex table; but others would certainly disagree.

8.6.7 Follow-up analysis following a significant three-way interaction

Having obtained a three-way interaction, you will certainly want to follow this up with further analysis. In an experiment of this degree of complexity, however, the perils of data-snooping are even greater than they are in a two-factor experiment. As far as we can see from our study of the literature, there seems to be, in this situation, no generally acceptable way of avoiding inflation of the **Type I error rate** to at least some extent. The following suggestions, though defensible, would certainly not be accepted by all.

In general, we think that the risk of capitalising upon chance is reduced by following a multistage decision process, in which tests at any stage would only be made following a significant result at the previous stage. For example, only if the three-way interaction has proved significant, would one proceed to test for simple interactions between *Drug* and *Alertness* at each level of *Sex*. Should you obtain a significant simple interaction only with the males, this would provide additional confirmation of the research hypothesis. As with testing for simple main effects in the two-factor experiment, the Bonferroni correction could be used to make a more conservative test for simple two-way interactions in the three-factor experiment. Since there are two possible simple interactions, one for the males, the other for the females, you would require that each test should show significance beyond the 0.25 level, rather than merely at the 0.05 level.

Should a simple interaction prove to be significant, you will naturally wish to make unplanned comparisons among the individual cell means. In the two-factor experiment, there was the difficulty that if one bases the size of the comparison family upon the set of means involved in the entire interaction, the criterion for significance is very stringent. Arguably, a significant test for a simple main effect might justify one in basing the size of the comparison family upon those means at one level only of the other factor. The same problem arises in the analysis following a significant three-way interaction. In order to justify limiting the size of the comparison 'family', you could proceed to test for a main effect of the *Drug* factor at specific combinations of the factors of *Alertness* and *Sex*. Should you find, for example, that there is a significant main effect of the *Drug* factor in those participants who were both Fresh and Male, you could then proceed to run a Tukey test on the three cell means involved, basing the size of the comparison family upon those means alone, rather than upon all those involved in the interaction. A test for a main effect of one factor at a specific combination of two other factors is known as a **simple, simple main effect**. A significant simple, simple main effect might justify reducing the size of the comparison family when making unplanned multiple comparison among the cell means. Once again, the test for a significant simple, simple main effect should be protected by the Bonferroni procedure: in the present example, the test would have to show significance beyond the 0.025 level, rather than the 0.05 level.

If, on the other hand, the tests for simple, simple main effects should fail to show significance, the obtaining of a significant three-way interaction might be justification for proceeding with a more stringent Tukey test with the size of the comparison family being based upon all the means involved in the interaction.

In the next section, we shall describe the use of SPSS syntax to test for simple interactions and simple, simple main effects.

8.6.8 Using SPSS syntax to test for simple interactions and simple, simple main effects

Tests for simple effects of various kinds are accessed by the use of the DESIGN subcommand within the MANOVA command. Here we shall consider the syntax for simple interactions and simple, simple main effects separately. In practice, of course, both types of subcommand could be subsumed under the same MANOVA command.

The full ANOVA can be run with a one-line MANOVA command very similar to the one we used for the two-factor ANOVA (Figure 17):

Figure 17. The MANOVA command for the three-way ANOVA

The ANOVA summary table is shown in Output 12. The values given, of course, agree exactly with the corresponding values in the GLM output (Output 11).

```
Tests of Significance for DrivingPerf using UNIQUE sums of squares
Source of Variation           SS          DF        MS          F   Sig of F

WITHIN CELLS               726.40         48      15.13
Alertness                  264.60          1     264.60      17.48    .000
Drug                       150.53          2      75.27       4.97    .011
Sex                         29.40          1      29.40       1.94    .170
Alertness BY Drug          617.20          2     308.60      20.39    .000
Alertness BY Sex              .60          1        .60        .04    .843
Drug BY Sex                 78.40          2      39.20       2.59    .085
Alertness BY Drug BY       337.60          2     168.80      11.15    .000
  Sex


(Model)                   1478.33         11     134.39       8.88    .000
(Total)                   2204.73         59      37.37


R-Squared =                  .671
Adjusted R-Squared =         .595
```

Output 12. Results of the three-way ANOVA from the MANOVA procedure.

Testing for simple interactions

Figure 18 shows the syntax for tests of simple interactions at each level of the *Sex* factor. The keyword BY specifies an interaction.

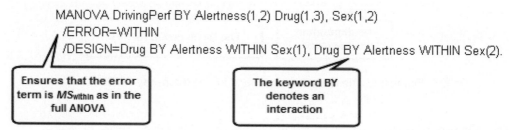

Figure 18. Tests for the simple *Drug* by Alertness interaction at each level of *Sex*

The results of the tests for simple interactions are shown in Output 13.

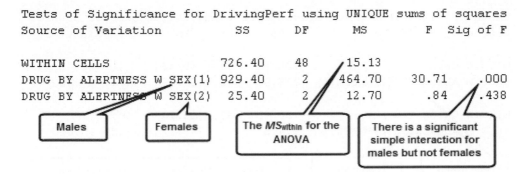

Output 13. Tests for a simple interaction between *Drug* and *Alertness* at each level of *Sex*

There is a significant simple *Drug* × *Alertness* interaction in the Males, but not in the Females. This result is consistent with the experimenter's hypothesis that the interaction may not occur in Female drivers.

Notice that if we add the sums of squares for the two simple interactions, we obtain the sum of the sums of squares for the Drug × Alertness interaction and the Drug × Alertness × Sex interaction from the full ANOVA summary table. Simple effects confound the target interaction with certain lower-order effects: simple main effects confound the two-way interaction with the main effect; simple interactions confound the three-way interaction with the two-way interaction.

Testing for a simple, simple main effect of the Drug factor at each level of Sex

Figure 19 shows the syntax for testing for simple, simple main effects. A specific combination of *Alertness* and *Sex* is specified by a second use of the keyword WITHIN.

```
MANOVA DrivingPerf BY Alertness(1,2) Drug(1,3) Sex(1,2)
    /ERROR=WITHIN
    /DESIGN=Drug WITHIN Alertness(1) WITHIN Sex(1)
    /DESIGN=Drug WITHIN Alertness(2) WITHIN Sex(1).
```

> **The use of the keyword WITHIN twice nests the simple effect of the *Drug* factor within one combination of the *Alertness* and *Sex* factors**

Figure 19. Testing for simple, simple main effects of the *Drug* factor at different combinations of *Alertness* and *Sex*

The results of the tests for simple, simple main effects are shown in Output 14.

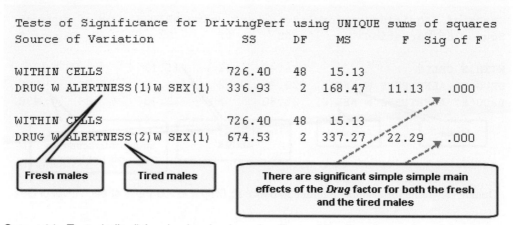

```
Tests of Significance for DrivingPerf using UNIQUE sums of squares
Source of Variation                  SS     DF    MS       F   Sig of F

WITHIN CELLS                       726.40   48   15.13
DRUG W ALERTNESS(1)W SEX(1)        336.93    2  168.47   11.13    .000

WITHIN CELLS                       726.40   48   15.13
DRUG W ALERTNESS(2)W SEX(1)        674.53    2  337.27   22.29    .000
```

Fresh males   **Tired males**

There are significant simple simple main
effects of the *Drug* factor for both the fresh
and the tired males

Output 14. Tests (edited) for simple, simple main effects of the *Drug* factor at each level of *Alertness* in the Male participants only.

Since both tests show significance beyond the 0.01 level, there is, some would argue, justification for making unplanned multiple comparisons among the three cell means at either level of *Alertness*.

8.6.9   Unplanned multiple comparisons following a significant three-way interaction

We have seen that the appearance of the cell means in Figure 3 has been confirmed by the finding that there is a significant simple interaction between the factors of *Drug* and *Alertness* among the male participants. We have also found that there is a significant simple, simple main effect of the *Drug* factor in the data from the Fresh Males. We now want to unpack the interaction more completely by making unplanned multiple comparisons among the Placebo, Drug A and Drug B cell means from the data on the Fresh Males only. The first step is to filter out all the data except the scores obtained by the Fresh Male participants. Figure 20 shows the appropriate **Select Cases: If** command.

Figure 20. Selecting only those performance scores that were produced by the Fresh Males in the study.

Figure 21 shows the appearance of part of **Data View** with the filter in operation. It will be seen that only the data from the Fresh Males have been selected for the **Tukey** analysis.

	Case	Alertness	Drug	Sex	DrivingPerf	filter_$
8	8	Fresh	Placebo	Male	19	Selected
9	9	Fresh	Placebo	Male	24	Selected
10	10	Fresh	Placebo	Male	26	Selected
11	11	Fresh	Drug A	Female	14	Not Selected
12	12	Fresh	Drug A	Female	18	Not Selected
13	13	Fresh	Drug A	Female	15	Not Selected
14	14	Fresh	Drug A	Female	18	Not Selected
15	15	Fresh	Drug A	Female	14	Not Selected
16	16	Fresh	Drug A	Male	11	Selected
17	17	Fresh	Drug A	Male	16	Selected

Figure 21. The appearance of **Data View** after the user has selected the data from the Fresh Males only

The **Tukey** test can now be run from the by clicking **Post Hoc** to access a wide choice of **Post Hoc** tests (Figure 22).

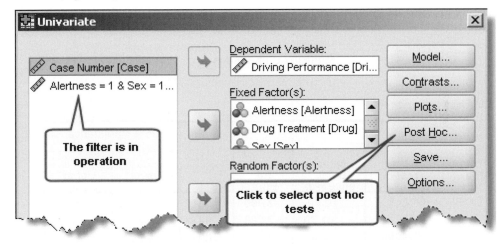

Figure 22. Accessing **Post Hoc** tests from the **Univariate** dialog box

In the **Univariate: Post Hoc Multiple Comparisons for Observed Means** dialog, move the variable name *Drug* to the right-hand panel and check the **Tukey** box (see Figure 14). The results of the Tukey test are shown in Output 15.

Homogeneous Subsets

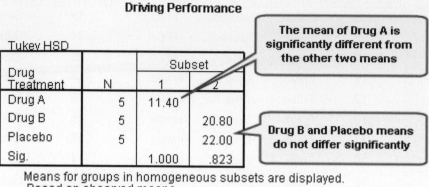

Driving Performance

Tukey HSD

Drug Treatment	N	Subset 1	Subset 2
Drug A	5	11.40	
Drug B	5		20.80
Placebo	5		22.00
Sig.		1.000	.823

Means for groups in homogeneous subsets are displayed.
Based on observed means.
The error term is Mean Square(Error) = 10.000.

Callout: The mean of Drug A is significantly different from the other two means

Callout: Drug B and Placebo means do not differ significantly

Output 15. Results of **Tukey** post hoc tests following a significant simple, simple main effect of *Drug* in the Fresh Male participants

The **Tukey** tests have confirmed that the mean for Drug A is significantly less than the means for the Drug B and Placebo groups, which do not differ significantly. Should it be felt necessary to report the p-values for the individual tests, this more detailed information is given in another table, shown here in Output 16.

Multiple Comparisons

Driving Performance
Tukey HSD

(I) Drug Treat-ment	(J) Drug Treat-ment	Mean Differ-ence (I-J)	Std. Error	Sig.	95% Confidence Interval Lower Bound	95% Confidence Interval Upper Bound
Placebo	Drug A	10.60*	2.000	.001	5.26	15.94
	Drug B	1.20	2.000	.823	-4.14	6.54
Drug A	Placebo	-10.60*	2.000	.001	-15.94	-5.26
	Drug B	-9.40*	2.000	.001	-14.74	-4.06
Drug B	Placebo	-1.20	2.000	.823	-6.54	4.14
	Drug A	9.40*	2.000	.001	4.06	14.74

Based on observed means.
The error term is Mean Square(Error) = 10.000.

*. The mean difference is significant at the 0.05 level.

Output 16. Details of the **Tukey** multiple comparison tests, including confidence intervals and p-values

8.7   A FINAL WORD

In this chapter, we have tried to provide information that will be helpful to the reader who wishes to interpret the results of factorial experiments and to confirm that the findings have not merely arisen through sampling error.

We strongly recommend that you should try to avoid factorial designs with more than three factors. While we agree that many variables may affect scores in a situation, it is usually possible to arrange that theoretically unimportant potential sources of variance, such as positional and sequential contingencies, can be made to balance by careful experimental design and need not emerge explicitly as factors in the analysis.

There are several good reasons for avoiding complex factorial designs with four or more factors. Four-way interactions are always exceedingly difficult to interpret. Moreover, although the follow-up methods we have described can, in principle, be extended to the analysis of more complex experiments, there remains the potential problem of over-analysis and hence capitalising upon chance. The more factors, the greater the risk that the anlysis will turn up one unexpected and striking effect or another. If a comparison is of such vital theoretical importance, there is much to be said for designing a new, simpler experiment to confirm that it has nor arisen merely through sampling error.

Some would certainly disapprove of the use of simple effects analysis to reduce the size of the comparison 'family' when one is unpacking a significant interaction; and the testing of simple, simple main effects for the purpose of reducing the size of the comparison family when unpacking a significant three-way interaction is even more questionable. Others, however, would agree that if such analyses are untaken only after an interaction (or simple interaction) has proved to be significant, the risk of capitalising upon chance has at least been reduced. In our view, an experiment of complex factorial design is perhaps most appropriate when the hypotheses driving the research are still somewhat tentative. At a later stage, when the focal hypothesis has crystallised, the researcher should test it with an experiment of simple design.

Recommended Reading

In this chapter, we could do no more than touch upon the analysis of data from complex factorial experiments. Howell (2007; Chapter 13) gives a lucid treatment of the analysis of interactions.

Howell, D. C. (2007). *Statistical methods for psychology (6th ed.).* Belmont, CA: Thomson/Wadsworth.

Exercise

Exercise 12 *Between subjects factorial ANOVA (two-way ANOVA)* is available in www.psypress.com/spss-made-simple and click on Exercises.

CHAPTER 9

Within subjects experiments

9.1   Introduction

9.2   A one-factor within subjects ANOVA with SPSS

9.3   Nonparametric equivalents of the within subjects ANOVA

9.4   The two-factor within subjects ANOVA

9.5   A final word

9.1   INTRODUCTION

9.1.1   Rationale of a within subjects experiment

A potential problem with between subjects experiments (Chapters 7 & 8) is that if there are large individual differences in performance, searching for a meaningful pattern in the data can be like trying to listen to an old-fashioned radio against a loud background crackle of interference. For example, in a Drug experiment such as the one described in Chapter 7, some of the scores obtained by participants in the Placebo condition may well be higher than those of participants tested under any of the drug conditions. There are some people who can bring a natural dexterity and flair to almost any test of skill; others, on the other hand, are clumsy and inept. Since, in a between subjects experiment, a different sample of participants performs under each condition, variation in natural aptitude is likely to introduce considerable **noise** into the data and inflate the error terms of the F statistics.

Another drawback with the between subjects experiment is that it is wasteful of participants: if the experimental procedure is a short one, a participant may spend more time travelling to and from the place of testing than actually performing the experimental task. We shall now consider another experimental strategy which allows the researcher to make fuller use of the participant's time and trouble.

A researcher wishes to investigate the effects upon shooting accuracy of the shape of the target. Each participant is asked to shoot twenty times at each of four differently-shaped targets. Since each participant is tested under all the conditions making up the factor of target shape, this experiment is said to be of **within subjects** design, or to have **repeated measures** on target shape. Table 1 compares the design of this one-factor, within subjects experiment with that of a one-factor between subjects experiment similar to the drug experiment in Chapter 7.

Table 1. Between subjects and within subjects experiments in which there is one treatment factor with four levels			

(a) A one-factor between subjects experiment			
	Levels of the Drug factor		
	Control	**Drug A**	**Drug B**	**Drug C**
Participants	Group 1	Group 2	Group 3	Group 4

(b) A one-factor within subjects experiment			
	Levels of the Shape factor		
	Circle	**Square**	**Triangle**	**Diamond**
Participants	The same participants perform with all four shapes. The order of presentation of the four conditions is varied, or **counterbalanced**, so that each condition occurs with equal frequency in each of the four ordinal positions across all the participants in the study.		

The variance in the scores from the Shape experiment will certainly reflect individual differences every bit as marked as they are likely to be in the Drug experiment. There is, however, an important difference between the two experiments. In being tested under every condition, each participant is effectively serving as his or her own control. That person's average performance over all conditions will provide a baseline against which performance under the different conditions can be evaluated.

While the within subjects experiment has obvious advantages over the between subjects experiment, it should also be said that this data-gathering strategy raises problems that are not encountered with the between subjects experiment. All these difficulties stem ultimately from the fact that within subjects experiments yield correlated data. The manner in which the data are correlated has important implications, both for the making of the statistical tests in the ANOVA itself and for such considerations as the measure of power and effect size.

9.1.2 How the within subjects ANOVA works

In Figure 1, we reproduce from Chapter 7 a diagram of the one-way between subjects ANOVA. In Chapter 7, we saw that the total sum of squares (representing the total variability of the scores) could be partitioned into between groups and within groups components, $SS_{between}$ and SS_{within}, which formed the basis of two variance estimates, $MS_{between}$ and MS_{within}, respectively. The null hypothesis of equality, in the population, of the treatment means was tested with the statistic F, where $F = \dfrac{MS_{between}}{MS_{within}}$.

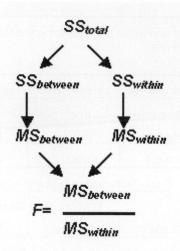

Figure 1. Summary of the one-way (between groups) ANOVA

In the one-factor within subjects ANOVA, the total sum of squares is partitioned somewhat differently. In the first place, since the participants are not grouped, there is no between groups sum of squares. The fact that each participant (subject) is tested under all conditions, however, allows a mean score for each subject to be calculated. The deviation of this mean score from the grand mean is the basis of the **between subjects** sum of squares $SS_{between \ subjects}$.

This between subjects sum of squares is not to be confused with the between *groups* sum of squares in the one-way ANOVA.

The total sum of squares can be partitioned into between subjects and within subjects components. The within subjects component can itself be subdivided into two sub-components:

1. The **treatments** sum of squares;
2. The **residual** sum of squares, which is what remains of the total sum of squares when the between subjects and treatment sums of squares have been removed.

As in the one-way ANOVA, the treatment sum of squares is the sum of the squares of the deviations of the individual scores X achieved under condition j from the mean score achieved under that condition:

$$SS_{treatments} = \sum \left(X - M_j \right)^2 \quad \text{--- (1)}$$

The treatments sum of squares

Since each participant is tested at all levels of the treatment factor, we could regard *Subjects* as a second factor which crosses with *Treatments*: we could think of the within subjects experiment as a two-factor experiment with one observation per cell. In fact, in some textbooks, the one-factor within subjects experiment is described as being of 'Subjects ×
Treatments' design. That designation makes explicit the possibility of an interaction between the *Subjects* 'factor' and the true treatments factor. The residual component of the total sum of

squares is, in fact, the sum of squares for the interaction between *Subjects* and the treatment factor, this sum of squares having $(n-1)(k-1)$ degrees of freedom, where n is the number of participants (subjects) in the experiment and k is the number of different treatment conditions making up the single treatment factor in the design. The residual sum of squares is the basis of the error term in the F test:

$$MS_{residual} = MS_{Subjects \times Treatments} = \frac{SS_{residual}}{df_{residual}} = \frac{SS_{residual}}{(n-1)(k-1)} \quad ---(2)$$

The error term in the one-factor within subjects experiment

In the one-factor within subjects ANOVA, the partition of the total sum of squares is as follows:

$$SS_{total} = SS_{between\ subjects} + SS_{Treatments} + SS_{residual:\ Subjects \times Treatments} \quad ---(3)$$

Partition of the total sum of squares in the within subjects ANOVA

Figure 2 summarises the one-factor within subjects ANOVA:

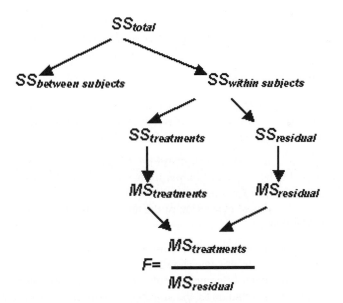

Figure 2. Summary of the one-factor within subjects ANOVA

In Table 2, are sketches of the ANOVA summary tables for a between groups ANOVA and a within subjects ANOVA. Both experiments have yielded the same number of scores (40). One advantage of the within subjects strategy is apparent from inspection of the ANOVA tables for the two experiments.

Table 2. The ANOVA summary tables for the one-factor between subjects (the one-way ANOVA) and within subjects experiments

Between groups one-way ANOVA					Within subjects ANOVA				
Source	df	SS	MS	F	Source	df	SS	MS	F
Drug	3			$\dfrac{MS_{Drug}}{MS_{within}}$	Shape	3			$\dfrac{MS_{Shape}}{MS_{Residual}}$
Within	36				Subjects	9			
					Residual	27			
Total	39				Total	39			

We do not need any entries in Table 2 for the values of the sums of squares in order to understand what is going on: the degrees of freedom tell the whole story. From the degrees of freedom in the between groups ANOVA table on the left, we can see that there were 10 participants in each group, making a total of 40 participants in the experiment; whereas, from the within groups ANOVA summary table on the right, we can see that there were only 10 participants but, since each was tested under all four conditions, 40 scores were generated, as in the Drug experiment. The total degrees of freedom therefore has the same value in both experiments, namely, $40 - 1 = 39$. In both experiments, the total sum of squares is $\sum (X - M)^2$, the sum of the squares of the deviations of scores X from the grand mean M.

In the within subjects Shape experiment, the degrees of freedom of the Subjects and Residual sources add up to 36, which is the degrees of freedom of the within groups sums of squares in the Drug experiment. The residual sum of squares itself has only 27 degrees of freedom.

If Subjects is a 'factor', it is one with **random effects**: that is, the participants in the experiment are assumed to be a random sample from a large pool of possible participants. This is why the residual (Subjects × Treatments) mean square is suitable as the error term for the F test. (Howell, 2007, gives a lucid discussion of the theory of the F tests in ANOVA, including the within subjects ANOVA.)

Since the degrees of freedom of the residual sum of squares is less than the df of MS_{within}, the critical value for F is larger. In practice, however, the partialling out of a major part of the variance arising from individual differences results in an increase in power, so that the power efficiency (that is, power in relation to the number of participants) of the within subjects experiment is greater than that of the between subjects experiment.

In summary, therefore, the within subjects experiment has two advantages over the between subjects experiment:
1. It cuts down data noise, resulting in a test of greater power in relation to the number of participants in the experiment.
2. It makes more efficient use of time and resources, requiring fewer participants and making more use of those participants.

The within subjects experiment, however, also has disadvantages, which in some circumstances can outweigh considerations of convenience and the maximisation of the signal-to-noise ratio. One of these problems is discussed in Section 9.1.4.

> See Section 9.1.4

9.1.3 A within subjects experiment on the effect of target shape on shooting accuracy

Table 3 shows the results of an experiment on the effects of target shape on shooting accuracy. (In this experiment, there were three target shapes.) The order of presentation of the three targets was counterbalanced across participants in an attempt to neutralise any order effects.

	Table 3. Results of a one-factor within subjects experiment		
Participant (Subject)	**Circle**	**Target** **Square**	**Triangle**
1	10	12	14
2	18	10	16
3	20	15	16
4	12	10	12
5	19	20	21
6	25	22	20
7	18	16	17
8	22	18	18
9	17	14	12
10	23	20	18

The ANOVA summary table is shown in Table 4.

Table 4. The ANOVA summary table.					
Source	**df**	**SS**	**MS**	**F**	**p**
Shape	2	39.267	19.633	4.86	.02
Subjects	9	370.170	40.608		
Residual (Shape × Subjects)	18	72.730	4.04		
Total	29	482.167			

We can report the result of the *F* test as follows:

The factor of Target Shape had a significant main effect: $F(2, 18) = 4.86$; p = .02.

This result, of course, would be accompanied by the descriptive statistics (preferably in a table or graph) and some measure of effect size such as partial omega squared (see Section 9.1.7).

9.1.4 Order effects: counterbalancing

A potential problem with repeated measures is that a participant's performance on one task may well be affected by the experience of having performed another task, particularly when the two tasks are attempted in close succession. Such an effect upon performance is an example of a **carry-over** (or **order**) **effect**. Sometimes, of course, carry-over effects are of focal interest, as in memory research, where the researcher might wish to demonstrate the proactive interference of learning one list of words with the recall of the words in another list learned subsequently. More usually, however, carry-over effects in within subjects experiments are potential **confounds**, whose influence can be difficult to disentangle from that of the treatment factor itself.

If participants are tested on a succession of tasks, their performance on the later tasks may improve through a **practice effect**. Practice effects, however, are only one type of carry-over effect. Not all carry-over effects are positive: proactive and retroactive interference in memory are negative carry-over effects. In within subjects experiments, carry-over effects are potential **extraneous variables**, whose effects may be confounded with those of the treatment factor.

The possibility of carry-over effects confounding the effects of the treatment factor is reduced by the procedure known as **counterbalancing**, in which the order of the conditions making up a within subjects factor is varied from participant to participant, in the hope that carry-over effects will balance out across conditions. Counterbalancing is not always effective, however, because order effects can be quite asymmetrical. There are also situations in which a within subjects strategy would be quite inappropriate: the drug experiment in Chapter 7 is a good example.

9.1.5 Assumptions underlying the within subjects ANOVA: homogeneity of covariance

We shall not describe the model underlying the within subjects ANOVA explicitly here. Recall, however, that in the model for the one-way ANOVA, certain assumptions are made about the random error component of each score, such as normality of distribution and homogeneity of variance.

Another important assumption in the one-way ANOVA is the independence of the error components of different scores. The within subjects ANOVA, however, is based upon a model of a situation in which the same participant is tested under all experimental conditions. Here, the assumption of independence of the error components is untenable. The within subjects model, therefore, makes an additional assumption about the scores, namely, that they have the property of **homogeneity of covariance**, or **sphericity**.

The covariance

Since the same participants shoot at all three targets, we can expect strong statistical **associations** or **correlations** between the scores that the participants achieved under any two of the conditions: high scores with one target are likely to be paired with high scores on the other; and low scores on one target are likely to be accompanied by low scores on the other. (We shall consider the topic of correlation more closely in Chapter 11.)

Figure 3 is the scatterplot of *Square Target* against *Triangular Target*. This plot shows evidence of a positive association or correlation between the scores the participants achieved under these two conditions. (For the meaning of **positive correlation**, see Chapter 11.)

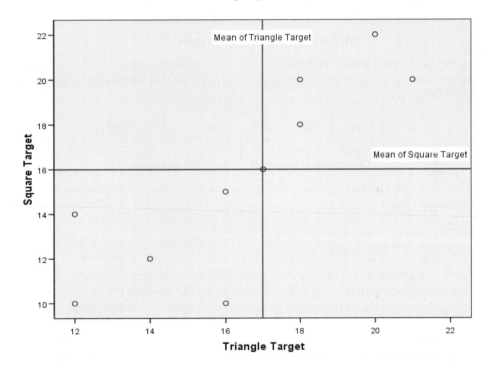

Figure 3. Scatterplot of *Square target* against *Triangle target* scores showing a high positive correlation between them

The **covariance**, like the correlation coefficient, is a measure of the strength of the association between two variables. In fact, the correlation coefficient is simply the covariance between two variables that have been transformed to standard scores, so that their means are zero and the variances and their standard deviations are 1. The formula for the covariance is analogous with the formula for the variance: the difference is that the sum of squares in the numerator of the variances is replaced with the sum of the products of corresponding deviations from the means of X and Y:

Variance of X   Variance of Y

$$s_X^{\,2} = \frac{\Sigma\left(X - M_X\right)^2}{n-1} \qquad\qquad s_Y^{\,2} = \frac{\Sigma\left(Y - M_Y\right)^2}{n-1}$$

Covariance

$$COV_{XY} = \frac{\Sigma\left(X - M_X\right)\left(Y - M_Y\right)}{n-1}$$

The variance and the covariance - - - (4)

In the formulae for the variance and covariance, it is often more convenient to write the sum of squares and sum of products (the numerators of the variance and covariance, respectively) as SS and SP, respectively:

$$S_X^{\,2} = \frac{SS_X}{n-1} \quad S_Y^{\,2} = \frac{SS_Y}{n-1} \quad COV_{XY} = \frac{SP}{n-1} \text{ - - - (5)}$$

Variance & covariance in SS/SP notation

The covariance of a variable with itself is simply its variance: the sum of products SP becomes a sum of squares SS.

The variance-covariance matrix

In Table 5, the entries in which have been calculated from the data in Table 3, is shown the **variance-covariance matrix**. The values in bold along the diagonal (21.60; 18.23; 9.38) are the variances (each is the covariance of a variable with itself); the off-diagonal elements are covariances.

Table 5. Variance-covariance matrix for the scores in Table 3.			
	Circle	**Square**	**Triangle**
Circle	**21.60**	15.91	10.38
Square	15.91	**18.23**	10.80
Triangle	10.38	10.80	**9.38**

Notice the symmetry of the variance-covariance matrix: the covariance of X with Y is identical with the covariance of Y with X, so the entries in the cells below the diagonal of bold entries (the **principal diagonal**) duplicate those in the cells above the diagonal.

As we have said, the values in the variance-covariance matrix must show a uniformity or consistency known as **homogeneity of covariance** or **sphericity**: that is, there should be comparable levels of association among the scores at different levels of the treatments factor. If this assumption is violated, the **Type I error rate** (i.e. the probability of rejecting H_0 when it is true) may be inflated. Tests for homogeneity of covariance are made on the variance-covariance matrix. SPSS uses the **Mauchly Sphericity Test**. Should the data fail the sphericity test (i.e. p-value < 0.05), the ANOVA F test must be modified to make it more *conservative* (less likely to reject the null hypothesis). SPSS offers three such conservative tests, varying in their degree of conservativeness: the **Greenhouse-Geisser**, the **Huynh-Feldt**, and the **Lower-bound**. All three tests reduce the degrees of freedom of the numerator and the denominator of the F ratio (by multiplying them by a factor termed **epsilon**), thus increasing the value of F required for significance.

9.1.6   Effect size in within subjects ANOVA

As with the between subjects ANOVA, SPSS provides, as a measure of the size of the effect of an independent variable, the statistic known as **partial eta-squared $\eta_p{}^2$**, where

$$\eta_p{}^2 = \frac{SS_{treatment}}{SS_{treatment} + SS_{error}} \quad \text{- - - (6)} \quad \textbf{Partial eta squared}$$

Eta squared, however, is not the best measure of effect size available and we suggest that **omega squared** should be reported instead.

For the one-factor within subjects experiment, an estimate of **partial omega squared** is given by

$$\hat{\omega}^2_{treatments} = \frac{(k-1)(F-1)}{(k-1)(F-1) + kn} \quad \text{- - - (7)}$$

**Estimate of partial omega squared for
the one-factor within subjects experiment**

In the current example,

$$\hat{\omega}^2_{treatments} = \frac{(3-1)(4.86-1)}{(3-1)(4.86-1) + 3 \times 10} = 0.20$$

Below, in Table 6, we reproduce Table 5 from Chapter 7, which gives guidelines for the interpretation of values of omega squared and Cohen's f.

We should note that, although the eta squared measures can readily be extended to within subjects designs with two or more factors, the estimation of omega squared is deeply problematic. (See, for example, Keppel & Wickens, 2004; p 427.) For a detailed discussion of these issues, see Dodd & Schultz (1973).

Table 6. A scheme for assessing values of omega squared		
Size of Effect	**Omega squared**	**Cohen's _f_**
Small	$0.01 \leq \omega^2 < 0.06$	$0.10 \leq f < 0.25$
Medium	$0.06 \leq \omega^2 < 0.14$	$0.25 \leq f < 0.40$
Large	$\omega^2 \geq 0.14$	$f \geq 0.40$

9.1.7 Power and effect size: how many participants shall I need?

The correlated nature of the data from within subjects experiments has implications for the determination of power and effect size. We have already seen that the correlations among the scores that participants achieve at different levels of the within subjects treatment factor must show a degree of uniformity or sphericity if the F statistics in the ANOVA are to have the distributions that would normally be fixed by the numerator and denominator degrees of freedom. The multiplier epsilon determines the extent to which the nominal degrees of freedom must be adjusted downwards to locate the obtained value of F in the correct sampling distribution.

To determine the power of the F test in a within subjects experiment, we also need to be able to locate the critical value for F in the noncentral F distribution, where its cumulative probability is beta, the Type II error rate, and (1 – the cumulative probability) is the power of the test. In Chapter 7, we saw that for the kind to data to which the one-way ANOVA is applicable, the noncentrality parameter lambda is simply the square of Cohen's f statistic multiplied by N, the total sample size. In the one-factor within subjects experiment, which will yield correlated data, matters are by no means as simple. The noncentrality parameter is affected by several factors, including the average correlation among the scores at the different levels of the treatment factor. It is also affected by epsilon, the multiplier for the degrees of freedom that is obtained from the variance-covariance matrix. The import of all this is that, in order to determine, a priori, the power of a within subjects experiment that you are planning to run, you will require information that may not readily be available unless you have already run some pilot studies of the measures you intend to use in your experiment.

The **G*Power 3** package available freely on the Internet (Erdfelder, Faul & Buchner, 1996; Faul, Erdfelder, Lang & Buchner, 2007) can answer questions about power and effect size in within subjects experiments. Suppose that you are planning to run a within subjects experiment with three treatment conditions. You want to make a test with a power of at least 0.75 to reject the null hypothesis for an effect of 'medium' size (Cohen's f = 0.25). You will set the alpha-level at 0.05. How many participants will you need? In G*Power, in the **ANOVA: repeated measures: within factors** menu, you would choose **A priori: Compute required sample size – given α, power and effect size**.

In the **Input Parameters** panel on the left, you will be asked to enter values for the Number of groups and the Repetitions. In this case, the number of groups is 1, because there is a single sample of participants. The number of repetitions is three, the number of levels in the within subjects treatment factor. There are no problems there; but in addition, you will be required to supply the average correlation among the three levels of the treatment factor and the value of epsilon. You might, of course, decide on some plausible level for the correlation, such as 0.6, and set epsilon at 1, which would be justified should the data from such an experiment be 'spherical', that is, have the property of homogeneity of covariance. Without additional information, however, you cannot know this; nor can one know how closely the scores in the three different conditions are correlated. (The higher the inter-correlation, the greater is the power of the test for a given number of participants.) Some pilot work with the planned measures, of course, could supply the necessary information.

9.2 A ONE-FACTOR WITHIN SUBJECTS ANOVA WITH SPSS

The one-factor within subjects ANOVA is accessed through **Repeated Measures...** in the **General Linear Model** menu. As always, however, we strongly recommend that you begin your analysis by getting to know your data first, before embarking on any formal statistical tests.

9.2.1 Entering the data

Since the participants have not been divided into groups, no grouping variable is required for entry of these data into the **SPSS Data Editor**. In **Variable View**, using the procedures described in Section 2.3, define the variables *Case*, *Circle*, *Square* and *Triangle*. Using the **Label** column, expand the variable names to *Case Number*, *Circle Target*, *Square Target* and *Triangle Target*. Set

See
Section
2.3

the number of decimal places displayed to zero. In **Data View**, enter the data from Table 3 into the first four (pre-labelled) columns.

9.2.2 Exploring the data: Boxplots for within subjects factors

*   To draw boxplots of the data at the various levels of a within subjects factor, select **Analyze➜Descriptive Statistics➜Explore...** to open the **Explore** dialog box (Figure 4).
*   Follow the steps shown in Figure 4.
*   In the **Explore: Plots** dialog box (Figure 5), click on the **Dependents together** button and click off the **Stem-and-leaf** check box. Click **Continue** and then **OK**.

The boxplots (Output 1) reveal no extreme cases (which would have been flagged by * - see Table 2 in Section 4.3.2 for details of the structure of a boxplot). None of the distributions is markedly skewed. There is therefore no need to remove any cases or apply any transformation to symmetrise the distribution. We can carry on with the ANOVA.

See Table 2 in
Section 4.3.2

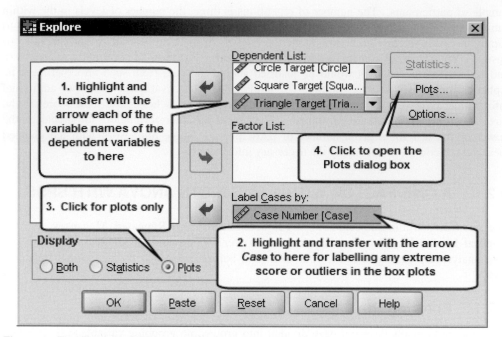

Figure 4. The **Explore** dialog box with the dependent variable names transferred to the **Dependent List** panel and the **Plots** button checked

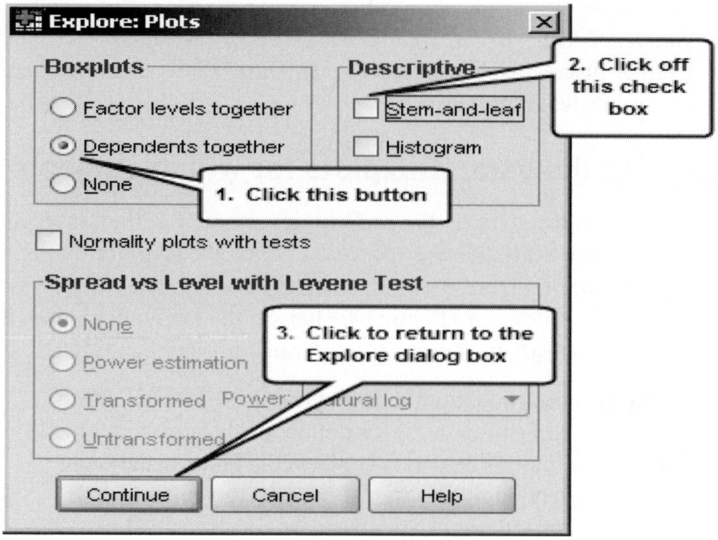

Figure 5. The **Explore: Plots** dialog box with **Dependents together** selected and **Stem-and-leaf** deselected

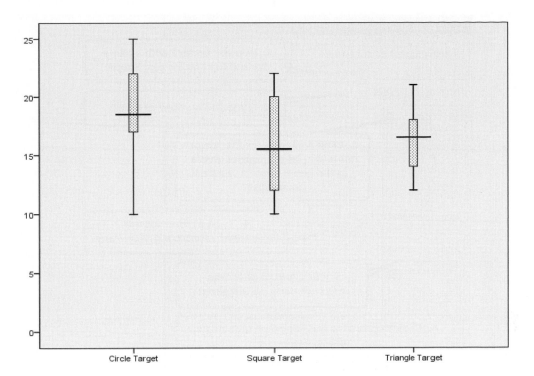

Output 1. Boxplots of the data for the three shapes

9.2.3   Running the within subjects ANOVA

The within subjects ANOVA is selected as follows:

• Select **Analyze➔General Linear Model➔Repeated Measures...** (Figure 6) to open the **Repeated Measures Define Factors** dialog box (Figure 7).

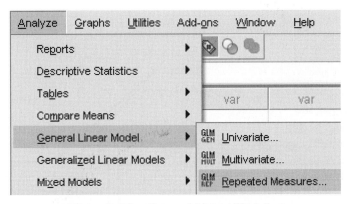

Figure 6. The **General Linear Model** menu

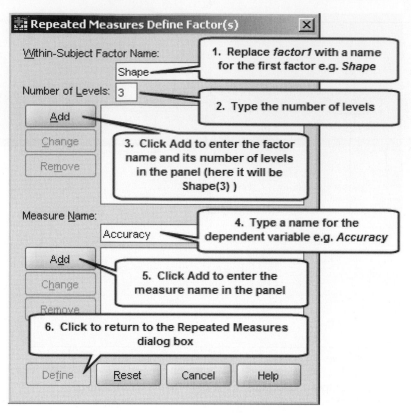

Figure 7. The **Repeated Measures Define Factor(s)** dialog box

- Follow the steps described in Figure 7 to obtain the situation in Figure 8.
- Click **Define** to return to the **Repeated Measures ANOVA** dialog box (the upper half of which is shown in Figure 8).

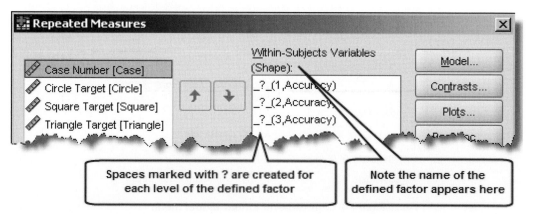

Figure 8. The upper half of the **Repeated Measures** dialog box after defining the **Within-Subjects Variables** factor as *Shape* with three levels and naming the measure as *Accuracy*

- Highlight the variables *Circle, Square* and *Triangle* (Figure 9) by clicking-and-dragging the cursor down over them and clicking the arrow to transfer all three into the **Within Subjects Variables [Shape]** box. The question marks will be replaced by the variable names as shown in Figure 9.

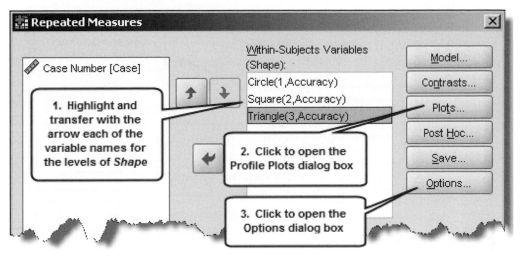

Figure 9. The completed **Repeated Measures** dialog box

- There are some useful options with a repeated measures ANOVA. For example, you can obtain a profile plot of the levels of the within subjects factor by clicking **Plots...** and following the steps shown in Figure 10. Click **Continue** to return to the original dialog box.

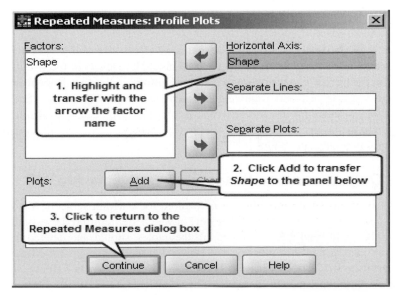

Figure 10. The **Profile Plots** dialog box for a plot at each level of a factor

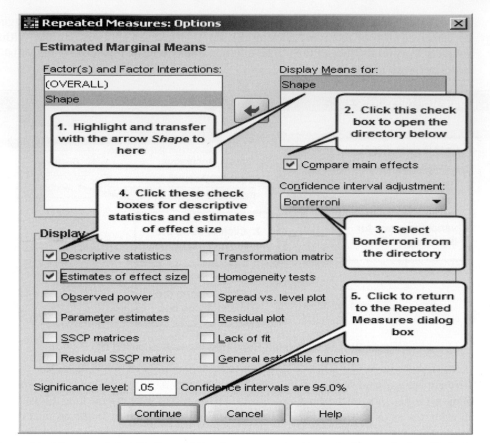

Figure 11. The completed **Options** dialog box requesting **Descriptive statistics**, **Estimates of effect size** and **Bonferroni** comparisons

- A table of **Descriptive statistics**, **Estimates of effect size** and a table of **Bonferroni adjusted pairwise comparisons** among the levels of the within subjects factor are requested by clicking **Options...** in the **Repeated Measures** dialog box and following the steps shown in Figure 11. See Section 9.2.5 regarding the choice of the Bonferroni test. Click **Continue** to return to the original dialog box.

See Section 9.2.5

- Click **OK** to run the procedure.

9.2.4   Output for a one-factor within subjects ANOVA

The output is extensive, but not all of it is required for a within subjects ANOVA. Output 2 shows the left-hand pane of the **SPSS Viewer**, in which are itemised the various subtables that appear in the right-hand pane. Three of the tables should be deleted immediately by highlighting each in turn and pressing the **Delete** key on the keyboard: **Multivariate Tests**; **Tests of Within-Subjects Contrasts**; **Tests of Between-Subjects Effects** (in this example, there are no between subjects factors). The **Multivariate Tests** in **Estimated Marginal Means** can also be deleted.

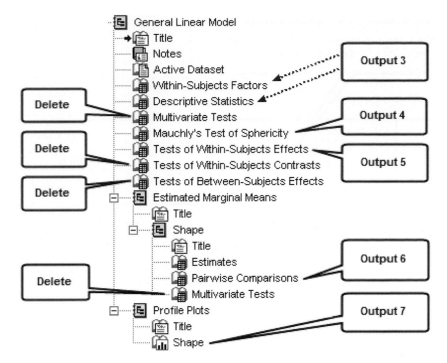

Output 2. The left-hand pane of the **SPSS Viewer** for the Repeated Measures (within subjects) analysis

Output 3 shows the **Title**, the **Within-Subjects Factors** list for the measure *Accuracy* and the specially requested **Descriptive Statistics** table.

Within-Subjects Factors

Measure: Accuracy

Shape	Dependent Variable
1	Circle
2	Square
3	Triangle

Descriptive Statistics

	Mean	Std. Deviation	N
Circle Target	18.40	4.648	10
Square Target	15.70	4.270	10
Triangle Target	16.40	3.062	10

Output 3. The **Within-Subjects Factors** list and **Descriptive Statistics** table

Output 4 reports the result of the **Mauchly's Test of Sphericity**, a test for homogeneity of covariance (see Section 9.1). There are two possible results. If the p-value (**Sig.**) is greater than .05, the null hypothesis of homogeneity of covariance (sphericity) is accepted. If the p-value is less than .05, the null hypothesis of homogeneity of covariance is rejected. The result of Mauchly's Test indicates how we should read the final ANOVA summary table.

The chi-square value is 0.76 and its associated
p-value (Sig.) is 0.68 (i.e. not significant)

Mauchly's Test of Sphericity[b]

Measure: Accuracy

Within Subjects Effect	Mauchly's W	Approx. Chi-Square	df	Sig.	Epsilon[a]		
					Greenhouse-Geisser	Huynh-Feldt	Lower-bound
Shape	.909	.760	2	.684	.917	1.000	.500

Tests the null hypothesis that the error covariance matrix of the orthonormalized transformed dependent variables is proportional to an identity matrix.

a. May be used to adjust the degrees of freedom for the averaged tests of significance. Corrected tests are displayed in the Tests of Within-Subjects Effects table.

b.
Design: Intercept
Within Subjects Design: Shape

Output 4. **Mauchly's Test of Sphericity** and values of epsilon for conservative **ANOVA** F tests

The ANOVA summary table (Output 5) shows the results of four F tests of the null hypothesis that, in the population, shooting accuracy for all three shapes is the same.

The results of the tests are given in separated rows, labelled **Sphericity Assumed**, **Greenhouse-Geisser**, **Huynh-Feldt** and **Lower-Bound**. In the lower part of the table, the same row labels are used for the error terms of the four F statistics reported in the top half of the table. Each F ratio was obtained by dividing the treatment mean square in its row by the error mean square in the row of the same name in the lower half of the table. If Mauchly's Test does not show significance, we can read, in the ANOVA summary table, only the rows labelled **Sphericity Assumed**. If Mauchly's Test does show significance, we suggest that, in the ANOVA summary table, you read the rows labelled **Greenhouse-Geisser**.

The conservative test only makes a difference when:
1. There is heterogeneity of covariance (i.e. Mauchly's Test is significant).
2. The F with unadjusted degrees of freedom (i.e. the values shown in the **Sphericity Assumed** rows) is barely significant beyond the 0.05 level.

Should F have a low tail probability (say p<0.01), the null hypothesis can be safely rejected without making a conservative test. In the present case, Mauchly's Test gives a p-value of 0.68, so there is no evidence of heterogeneity of covariance. The usual ANOVA F test can therefore be used.

Tests of Within-Subjects Effects

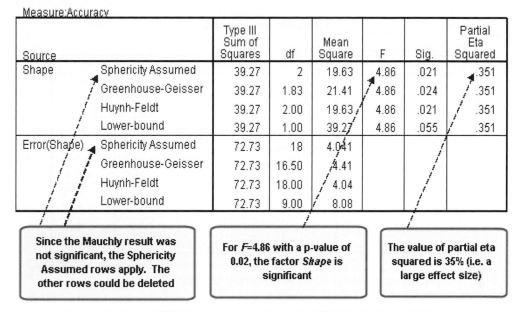

Measure:Accuracy

Source		Type III Sum of Squares	df	Mean Square	F	Sig.	Partial Eta Squared
Shape	Sphericity Assumed	39.27	2	19.63	4.86	.021	.351
	Greenhouse-Geisser	39.27	1.83	21.41	4.86	.024	.351
	Huynh-Feldt	39.27	2.00	19.63	4.86	.021	.351
	Lower-bound	39.27	1.00	39.27	4.86	.055	.351
Error(Shape)	Sphericity Assumed	72.73	18	4.04			
	Greenhouse-Geisser	72.73	16.50	4.41			
	Huynh-Feldt	72.73	18.00	4.04			
	Lower-bound	72.73	9.00	8.08			

Since the Mauchly result was not significant, the Sphericity Assumed rows apply. The other rows could be deleted

For *F*=4.86 with a p-value of 0.02, the factor *Shape* is significant

The value of partial eta squared is 35% (i.e. a large effect size)

Output 5. The **ANOVA** summary table for the **Within-Subjects Effects**

The main result in Output 5 is the value of **F** and its associated p-value (**Sig.**) for the within subjects factor *Shape*. This table has been edited to reduce the number of decimal places to two in some of the columns and to narrow some of the columns.

In the case of the factor *Shape*, note that the p-value for *F* in the **Sphericity Assumed** row is *0.021*: that is, the obtained value of *F* is significant beyond the five per cent (.05) level, but not beyond the 0.01 level. We can therefore conclude that the shape used does affect shooting accuracy. We can write this result as:

> The mean scores for the three shapes of target differed significantly at the 5% level: $F(2, 18) = 4.86$; p = .02 Partial eta squared = .35, which is a large effect.

Since this within subjects experiment has only a single treatment factor, a preferable measure of effect size is an estimate of omega squared, rather than partial eta squared. As you would expect, the value of the estimate of omega squared is less than that of eta squared:

$$\hat{\omega}^2 = \frac{(k-1)(F-1)}{(k-1)(F-1)+kn} = \frac{2(3.86)}{2(3.86)+30} = 0.20$$

The value of 18 for the error *df* can be seen in the row labelled **Error (Shape) Sphericity Assumed**. In the present case, there was no need to make a conservative *F* test because Mauchly's Test was not significant. It is apparent from the **Sig.** column that *in this particular example* the conservative tests make no difference to the result of the ANOVA *F* test.

The next table (Output 6) shows the pairwise comparisons adjusted according to the **Bonferroni** method.

Pairwise Comparisons

Measure: Accuracy

(I) Shape	(J) Shape	Mean Differ- ence (I-J)	Std. Error	Sig.[a]	95% Confidence Interval for Difference[a]	
					Lower Bound	Upper Bound
1	2	2.70*	.90	.044	.075	5.325
	3	2.00	1.01	.238	-.966	4.966
2	1	-2.70*	.90	.044	-5.325	-.075
	3	-.70	.78	1.000	-2.974	1.574
3	1	-2.00	1.01	.238	-4.966	.966
	2	.70	.78	1.000	-1.574	2.974

Based on estimated marginal means

*. The mean difference is significant at the .05 level.

a. Adjustment for multiple comparisons: Bonferroni.

> Only one comparison has a p-value (Sig.) < .05

Output 6. The Bonferroni adjusted **Pairwise Comparisons** among the levels of the within subjects factor *Shape* for the measure *Accuracy*

The requested profile plot is shown in Output 7, which is an edited version of the default plot, adjusted to include zero on the vertical scale. The default plot, with only a small section of the scale on the vertical axis, makes the differences among the means look enormous.

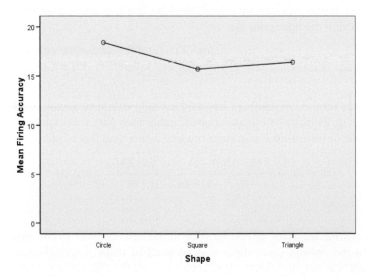

Output 7. The plot of the mean shooting accuracy for the three shapes

9.2.5   Unplanned multiple comparisons

There is some doubt as to whether, following significant main effects of within subjects factors, the **Tukey test** affords sufficient protection against inflation of the *per family* type I error rate. It is thought that the **Bonferroni** correction affords better protection.

9.3   NONPARAMETRIC EQUIVALENTS OF THE WITHIN SUBJECTS ANOVA

As with the one-factor completely randomised experiment, nonparametric methods are available for the analysis of ordinal and nominal data. Once again, we suggest that if your measurements are on a continuous scale, the first possibility to consider is the running of the within subjects ANOVA on cleaned-up data, rather than 'nonparametrisation' by conversion to ranks, which is what happens when you choose a nonparametric test. The decision to opt for a nonparametric test incurs the immediate penalty of a loss of power. In the next example, however, the raw data are ranks in the first place and the researcher has no option but to use a nonparametric test.

9.3.1   The Friedman test for ordinal data

Suppose that six people rank five objects in order of 'pleasingness'. Their decisions might appear as in Table 7.

If we assume that the highest rank is given to the most pleasing object, it would appear, from inspection of Table 7, that Object 3 is more pleasing to most of the raters than is Object 1. Since, however, the numbers in Table 7 are not independent measurements but ranks, the one-factor within subjects ANOVA cannot be used here. The Friedman test is suitable for such ordinal data. In **Variable View**, name the variables *Object1, Object2, ... Object5* (with no spaces before the digits). In **Data View**, enter the data in the usual way.

Table 7. Six people's ranks of five objects in order of 'pleasingness'					
	Object 1	Object 2	Object 3	Object 4	Object 5
Person 1	2	1	5	4	3
Person 2	1	2	5	4	3
Person 3	1	3	4	2	5
Person 4	2	1	3	5	4
Person 5	2	1	5	4	3
Person 6	1	2	5	3	4

To run the Friedman test:
* Choose **Analyze➔Nonparametric Tests➔K Related Samples…** to obtain the **Tests for Several Related Samples** dialog box (Figure 12).

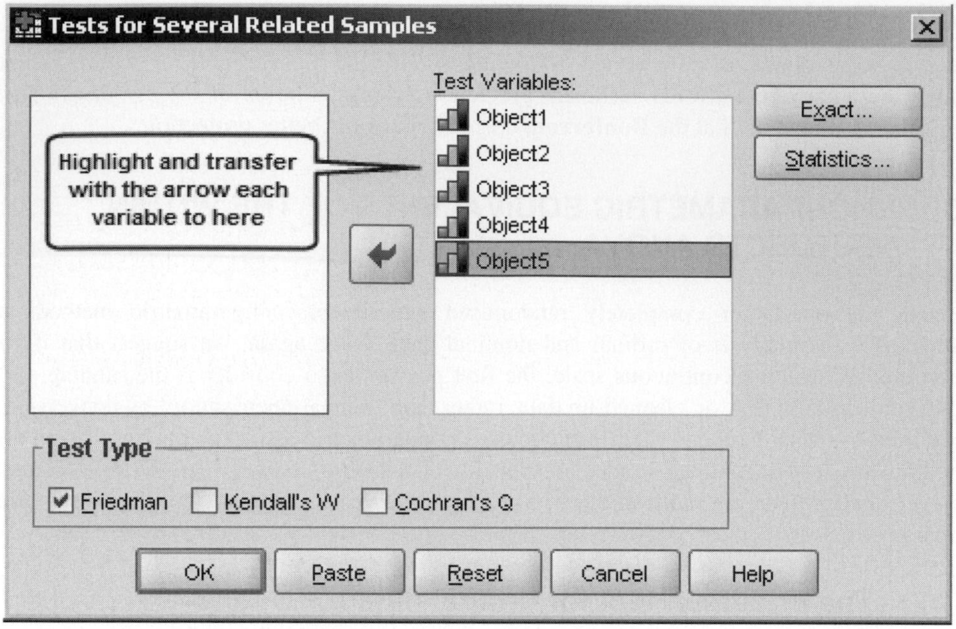

Figure 12. The **Tests for Several Related Samples** dialog box with the **Friedman** Test selected

- In the panel on the left, will appear a list of the variables. This list should include the items *Object1*, *Object2*, ..., *Object5*, which will contain the numbers shown in Table 7. Simply transfer these names to the **Test Variables:** box in the usual way. Make sure the **Friedman** check box has been ticked.
- Click the **Exact...** button to see the **Exact Tests** dialog box and activate the **Exact** radio button. Click **Continue** and then **OK**.

The **Friedman Test** results are shown in Output 8.

Friedman Test

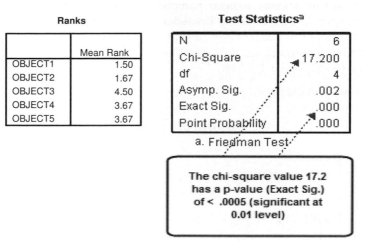

Ranks

	Mean Rank
OBJECT1	1.50
OBJECT2	1.67
OBJECT3	4.50
OBJECT4	3.67
OBJECT5	3.67

Test Statistics[a]

N	6
Chi-Square	17.200
df	4
Asymp. Sig.	.002
Exact Sig.	.000
Point Probability	.000

a. Friedman Test

The chi-square value 17.2 has a p-value (Exact Sig.) of < .0005 (significant at 0.01 level)

Output 8. **Friedman** test results

Clearly the rankings differ significantly across the objects since the p-value is less than 0.01. We can write this result as:

$$\chi^2 \ (4) = 17.2; \ p < 0.01.$$

9.3.2   Cochran's Q test for nominal data

Suppose that six children are asked to imagine they were in five different situations and had to choose between Course of Action *A* (coded *0*) and *B* (coded *1*). The results might appear as in Table 8. From inspection of Table 8, it would seem that Course of Action B (i.e. cells containing *1*) is chosen more often in some scenarios than in others. A suitable confirmatory test is **Cochran's Q** test, which was designed for use with related samples of dichotomous nominal data.

Table 8. Courses of action chosen by six children in five scenarios					
	Scene 1	Scene 2	Scene 3	Scene 4	Scene 5
Child 1	0	0	1	1	1
Child 2	0	1	0	1	1
Child 3	1	1	1	1	1
Child 4	0	0	0	1	0
Child 5	0	0	0	0	0
Child 6	0	0	0	1	1

To run Cochran's Q test:

- Bring the **Tests for Several Related Samples** dialog box to the screen (see previous section and Figure 12), click off the **Friedman** check box and click the **Cochran** check box.
- Click the **Exact...** button to see the **Exact Tests** dialog box and activate the **Exact** radio button. Click **Continue** and then **OK**.

The results are shown in Output 9.

Cochran Test

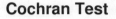

Frequencies

	Value	
	0	1
SCENE1	5	1
SCENE2	4	2
SCENE3	4	2
SCENE4	1	5
SCENE5	2	4

Test Statistics

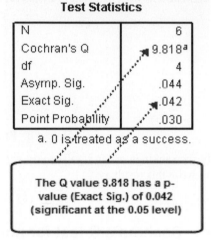

N	6
Cochran's Q	9.818[a]
df	4
Asymp. Sig.	.044
Exact Sig.	.042
Point Probability	.030

a. 0 is treated as a success.

The Q value 9.818 has a p-value (Exact Sig.) of 0.042 (significant at the 0.05 level)

Output 9. **Cochran** test results

It is clear that the same course of action is not taken in all five scenarios:

$$\text{Cochran Q} = 9.82; \text{ df} = 4; \text{ p} = .04.$$

Note that, as always, we must be cautious in our statement of the implications of statistical significance. We can reject the null hypothesis that there is, in the population, no difference among the five scenarios, confirming the variation among the scenarios apparent in Table 8. We cannot, however, conclude from this that the difference between any two particular scenarios is also significant. Further pairwise post hoc comparisons could be made by using the **Sign Test**, controlling the **Type I error rate** with the **Bonferroni** procedure previously described.

9.4   THE TWO-FACTOR WITHIN SUBJECTS ANOVA

An experiment is designed to investigate the effects of the shape and solidity of patterns shown on a screen upon the ease with which they are detected. The dependent variable (DV) is the Number of Errors made in responding to the pattern, and the two factors Shape (Circle, Square, or Triangle) and Solidity (Outline or Solid) are the independent variables (IVs). The same sample of participants is used for all the possible treatment combinations: that is, there are two within subjects (repeated measures) factors in the experiment. The results are shown in Table 9.

Table 9. Results of a two-factor within subjects experiment						
SHAPE:-	**Circle**		**Square**		**Triangle**	
SOLIDITY:-	**Solid**	**Outline**	**Solid**	**Outline**	**Solid**	**Outline**
Participant						
1	4	2	2	8	7	5
2	3	6	2	6	8	9
3	2	10	2	5	5	3
4	1	8	5	5	2	9
5	4	6	4	5	5	10
6	3	6	4	6	9	12
7	7	12	2	6	4	8
8	6	10	9	5	0	10
9	4	5	7	6	8	12
10	2	12	12	8	10	12

The ANOVA summary table for the data of Table 9 is shown in Table 10 below.

Table 10. Summary table for the ANOVA of the data in Table 9					
Source	**Degrees of freedom**	**Sum of squares**	**Mean square**	**F**	**p**
Subjects	9				
Shape	2	46.03	23.02	2.98	.08
Error (Shape)	18	138.97	7.72		
Solidity	1	117.60	117.60	54.56	<.01
Error (Solidity)	9	19.40	2.16		
Shape × Solidity	2	23.70	11.85	1.41	.27
Error (Shape × Solidity)	18	151.30	8.41		

There are three treatment sources of variance in this ANOVA: the two main effect sources Shape and Solidity; and the Shape × Solidity interaction. Each of these sources has its own error term. The error term is always the interaction between the source (i.e. Shape, Solidity or Shape × Solidity) and Subjects. So the error term for Shape is the Shape × Subjects interaction, with $2 \times 9 = 18$ degrees of freedom; the error term for Solidity is the Solidity × Subjects interaction, with $1 \times 9 = 9$ degrees of freedom; the error term for Shape × Solidity is Shape × Solidity × Subjects, with $2 \times 1 \times 9 = 18$ degrees of freedom.

A full explanation of this rule for finding the correct error term lies beyond the scope of this book. Basically, the Subjects source can be regarded as a factor with random effects, so that the various combinations of Subjects and treatments do not cancel out across the experiment as a whole. The interaction, therefore, adds to the expected value of the treatments sum of squares. (For more on this, see a statistical textbook such as Howell, 2007 or Keppel & Wickens, 2004.)

9.4.1 Preparing the data set

The first four rows of data in **Data View** appear as in Figure 13.

Case	CircleSolid	CircleOutline	SquareSolid	SquareOutline	TriangleSolid	TriangleOutline
1	4	2	2	8	7	5
2	3	6	2	6	8	9
3	2	10	2	5	5	3
4	1	8	5	5	2	9

Figure 13. Part of **Data View** for the two-factor within subjects ANOVA

Extra care is needed when entering data from experiments with two or more within subjects factors. It is essential to ensure that SPSS understands which data were obtained under which combination of factors. In the present example, there are six data for each participant, each datum being a score achieved under a different combination of the two factors. We can name the data variables as *CircleSolid*, *CircleOutline*, *SquareSolid*, *SquareOutline*, *TriangleSolid* and *TriangleOutline*, representing all possible combinations of the shape and solidity factors. Such systematic, left-to-right naming not only helps to avoid transcription errors at the data entry stage, but also prevents incorrect responses when you are in the **Repeated-Measures Define Variable(s)** dialog box and are naming the within subjects factors.

Note that the left-to-right ordering of the variable names is exactly the order in which they appeared in the original table of results (Table 9).

9.4.2 Running the two-factor within subjects ANOVA

- Select **Analyze➔General Linear Model➔Repeated Measures...** and complete the various dialog boxes by analogy with the one-factor example, defining a second within subjects (repeated measures) factor and the dependent measure as *Errors*.
- The completed **Repeated Measures Define Factor(s)** dialog box, with the two within subjects factor names *Shape* and *Solidity*, is shown in Figure 14, together with a measure name *Errors*. (This is the name of the dependent variable in the study.)

- After **Define** has been clicked, the **Repeated Measures** dialog box appears with the six variables listed in alphabetical order on the left. (The top half is reproduced in Figure 15).

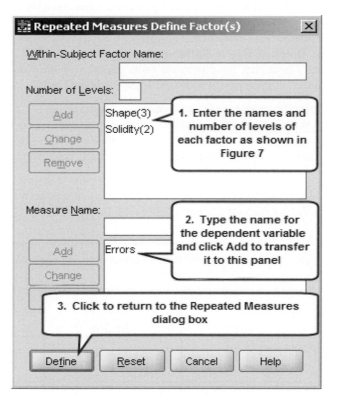

Figure 14. The **Repeated Measures Define Factor(s)** dialog box with two factors and their numbers of levels defined as well as a name for the dependent variable

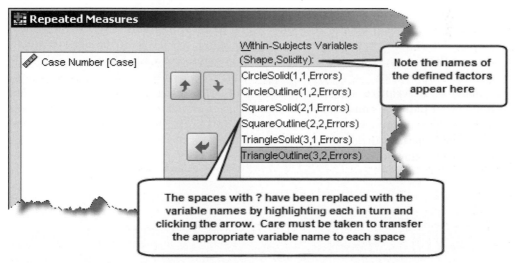

Figure 15. The top half of the **Repeated Measures** dialog box for two factors *Shape* and *Solidity* after transferring the variable names

On the right (Figure 15), in the box labelled **Within-Subjects Variables [Shape, Solidity]**, appears a list of the various combinations of the code numbers representing the levels of each of the two treatment factors. It will be noticed that, as one reads down the list, the first number in each pair changes more slowly than the second. When there is more than one within subjects factor, it is inadvisable immediately to transfer the variable names in a block from the left-hand box to the **Within-Subjects Variables** box by a click-and-drag operation, as in the one-factor situation. Check that the downward order of the variable names in the left-hand panel matches the order of the names in **Variable View** (or **Data View**).

Should your experiment be more complex, with more levels in the factors, it is safer to transfer the variables to the **Within-Subjects Variables** slots one at a time, noting the numbers in the square brackets and referring to the names of the newly defined within subjects factors (in this case *Shape* and *Solidity*) inside the square brackets in the caption above the **Within-Subjects Variables** box.

A table such as Table 11 clarifies the numbering of the levels of within subjects factors. Thus the variable *CircleSolid* is [Shape 1, Solidity 1] i.e. [1,1], *CircleOutline* is [1,2] and so on.

Table 11. Numbering of levels in within subjects variables						
Shape Factor	**Shape 1** (Circle)		**Shape 2** (Square)		**Shape 3** (Triangle)	
Solidity Factor	Solidity 1 (Solid)	Solidity 2 (Outline)	Solidity 1 (Solid)	Solidity 2 (Outline)	Solidity 1 (Solid)	Solidity 2 (Outline)
Variable name	*Circle Solid*	*Circle Outline*	*Square Solid*	*Square Outline*	*Triangle Solid*	*Triangle Outline*

- There are some useful options associated with a repeated measures ANOVA. Request a profile plot of the levels of one of the factors across the levels of the other factor by clicking **Plots…** and following the steps shown in Figure 16. Click **Continue** to return to the original dialog box.
- A table of **descriptive statistics**, **estimates of effect sizes** and a table of post hoc **Bonferroni pairwise comparisons** among the levels of within subjects factors with more than two levels (here only *Shape*) are requested by clicking the **Options…** button in the **Repeated Measures** dialog box and following the steps shown earlier in Figure 11. Click **Continue** to return to the original dialog box and then **OK**.

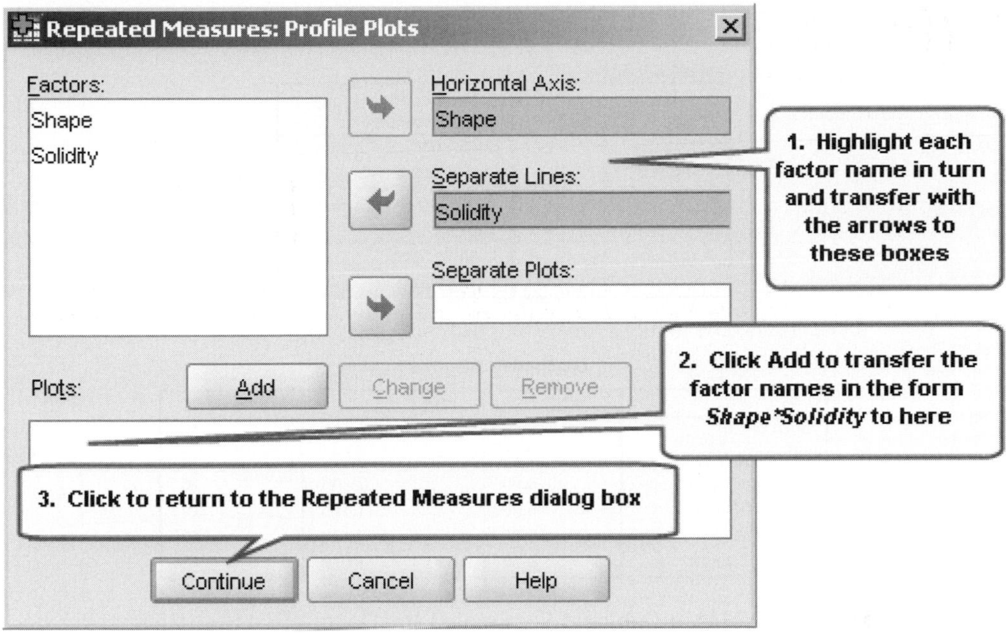

Figure 16. Part of the **Profile Plots** dialog box for requesting a profile plot *Shape*Solidity*

9.4.3 Output for a two-factor within subjects ANOVA

As in the case of the one-factor within subjects ANOVA, the output is extensive, and not all of it is required. You can make life easier by pruning some items and removing others altogether. Three of the subtables in the left-hand pane of the **SPSS Viewer** can be immediately deleted by highlighting each in turn and then pressing the **Delete** key on the keyboard: **Multivariate Tests**; **Tests of Within-Subjects Contrasts**; **Tests of Between-Subjects Effects** (in this example, there are no between subjects factors).

> See
> Output 2
> in Section
> 9.2.4

Output 10 shows the **Title**, **Within-Subjects Factors** list and the specially requested **Descriptive Statistics** table.

Within-Subjects Factors

Measure: Errors

Shape	Solidity	Dependent Variable
1	1	CircleSolid
	2	CircleOutline
2	1	SquareSolid
	2	SquareOutline
3	1	TriangleSolid
	2	TriangleOutline

Descriptive Statistics

	Mean	Std. Deviation	N
Solid Circle	3.60	1.838	10
Outline Circle	7.70	3.268	10
Solid Square	4.90	3.446	10
Outline Square	6.00	1.155	10
Solid Triangle	5.80	3.190	10
Outline Triangle	9.00	3.018	10

Output 10. The **Within-Subjects Factors** list and **Descriptive Statistics** table

The next table (Output 11) reports the result of the **Mauchly's Test of Sphericity** for homogeneity of covariance (see Section 9.3).

The table is more extensive than that in Output 4, because there are two factors. Notice that the test is not applied when a factor has only two levels, as in the case of *Solidity*. The test is not significant (i.e. there is no evidence of heterogeneity of covariance) for either *Shape* or the interaction of *Shape* and *Solidity*, so the significance levels in the rows labelled **Sphericity Assumed** can be accepted. You should now remove from the ANOVA table the rows giving the results of the various conservative *F* tests.

The edited ANOVA summary table (minus the rows with the conservative tests and the words Sphericity Assumed) for the within subjects factors *Shape* and *Solidity*, and their interaction is shown in Output 12. Notice that, in contrast with a two-factor between subjects ANOVA, there are three error terms, one for each main effect and one for the interaction.

The chi-square values and their associated p-values (Sig.) show that none is significant. Note the test does not apply to factors with only two levels (e.g. *Solidity*)

Mauchly's Test of Sphericity[b]

Measure: Errors

Within Subjects Effect	Mauchly's W	Approx. Chi-Square	df	Sig.	Epsilon[a]		
					Greenhouse-Geisser	Huynh-Feldt	Lower-bound
Shape	.67	3.25	2	.197	.750	.866	.500
Solidity	1.00	.00	0	.	1.000	1.000	1.000
Shape * Solidity	.90	.82	2	.663	.911	1.000	.500

Tests the null hypothesis that the error covariance matrix of the orthonormalized transformed dependent variables is proportional to an identity matrix.

  a. May be used to adjust the degrees of freedom for the averaged tests of significance. Corrected tests are displayed in the Tests of Within-Subjects Effects table.

  b.
     Design: Intercept
     Within Subjects Design: Shape+Solidity+Shape*Solidity

Output 11. **Mauchly's Test of Sphericity** and more conservative statistics for *Shape* and for the interaction of *Shape* and *Solidity*

Tests of Within-Subjects Effects

Measure:Errors

Source	Type III Sum of Squares	df	Mean Square	F	Sig.	Partial Eta Squared
Shape	46.03	2	23.02	2.98	.076	.249
Error(Shape)	138.97	18	7.72			
Solidity	117.60	1	117.60	54.56	.000	.858
Error(Solidity)	19.40	9	2.16			
Shape * Solidity	23.70	2	11.85	1.41	.270	.135
Error(Shape*Solidity)	151.30	18	8.41			

The factor *Shape* has F = 2.98 with a p-value (Sig.) > .05 (i.e. not significant)	The factor *Solidity* has F = 54.56 with a p-value < .0005 (i.e. significant at .01 level)	The interaction *Shape*Solidity* has F = 1.41 with a p-value > .05 (i.e. not significant)	The values of partial eta squared vary from 13.5% to 86%

Output 12. The edited **ANOVA** summary table for the **Within-Subjects Effects**

Output 12 shows that the factor *Shape* has no significant main effect, since the p-value for *F* in the column headed **Sig.** is greater than 0.05. We can write this result as follows:

> There was no significant effect of the Shape factor: F(2, 18) = 2.98; p = .08.

The factor *Solidity* is significant, since its p-value is less than 0.01 (the output value 0.000 means that the p-value is less than .0005). We can write this result as:

> The Solidity factor had a main effect that was significant beyond the 1%
> level: F(1, 9) = 54.6; p <.01. Partial eta squared = .86. This is a large effect.

As we said earlier, it would be desirable to be able to use the partial omega squared measure instead of eta squared; however, as Keppel & Wickens observe (2004; p427), we almost never have sufficient information about the sources of random error to be able to supply the necessary estimates for the equations. It is, perhaps, better to report the values of partial eta squared (biased though they are) than no measures of effect size at all.

Finally, there was no significant *Shape*Solidity* interaction: F(2, 18) = 1.41; p = .27.

Since the factor *Shape* is not significant, the **Bonferroni pairwise comparisons** table should be ignored.

The edited profile plot is shown in Output 13. An interaction is indicated when the profiles cross one another, diverge or converge. Obviously the slight difference between the profiles here is insufficient for a statistically significant interaction.

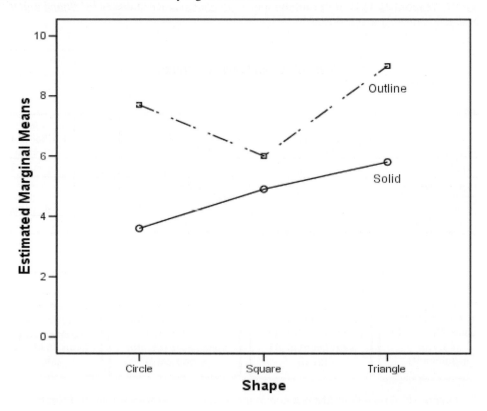

Output 13. The profile plots of the two levels of *Solidity* across the three shapes

In conclusion, Output 12 shows that only the *Solidity* factor has a significant effect: the other factor, *Shape* and its interaction with *Solidity*, are not significant.

9.4.4   Unpacking a significant interaction with multiple comparisons

In the example we have just considered, the question of unplanned multiple comparisons among the means for combinations of the two treatment factors did not arise, because the interaction was insignificant. In fact, since the only significant source of variance was Solidity, which had only two levels, no further analysis was necessary, since a significant main effect implies that the difference between the two means is significant.

Table 12 shows an alternative set of results from the Shape and Solidity experiment.

Table 12. An alternative set of results from the Shape and Solidity experiment						
SHAPE:-	**Circle**		**Square**		**Triangle**	
SOLIDITY:-	**Solid**	**Outline**	**Solid**	**Outline**	**Solid**	**Outline**
Participant						
1	8	2	3	8	5	7
2	7	6	3	6	6	11
3	6	10	3	5	3	5
4	5	8	6	5	2	11
5	8	6	5	5	3	12
6	7	6	5	6	7	14
7	11	12	3	6	2	10
8	10	10	10	5	0	12
9	8	5	8	6	6	14
10	6	12	13	8	8	14

The profile plots of the two different conditions of *Solidity* against the *Shape* factor are shown in Output 14. The ANOVA of this set of results (we shall not show the summary table here) confirms the presence of a marked interaction between the factors *Solidity* and *Shape*.

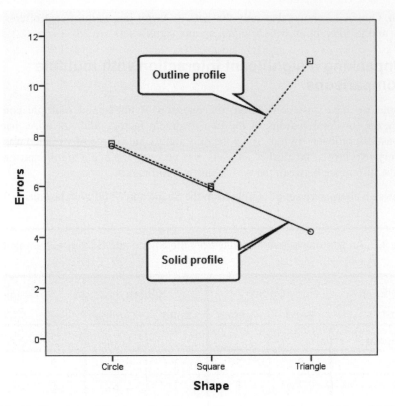

Output 14. Profile plots of the two *Solidity* conditions suggesting a striking simple main effect of *Solidity* when the target is a triangle

The appearance of the profiles in Output 14 suggest that if we test for simple main effects of *Solidity* at each of the three levels of the *Shape* factor, we can expect to confirm the existence of an effect with the triangle only. The SPSS syntax for testing for simple main effects of *Solidity* at the Circle, Triangle and Square levels of *Shape* is shown in Figure 17.

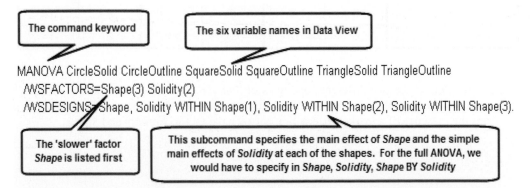

Figure 17. Syntax for testing simple main effects of *Solidity* at the Circle, Triangle and Square levels of *Shape*. Note that for within subjects factors, the subcommand /WSDESIGNS replaces /DESIGNS

The results of the tests for simple main effects are shown in Output 15. They are entirely consistent with the pattern that is so evident in the graph in Output 14: there is a significant simple main effect of *Solidity* at the Triangle level of *Shape*, but not at the Square or Circle levels.

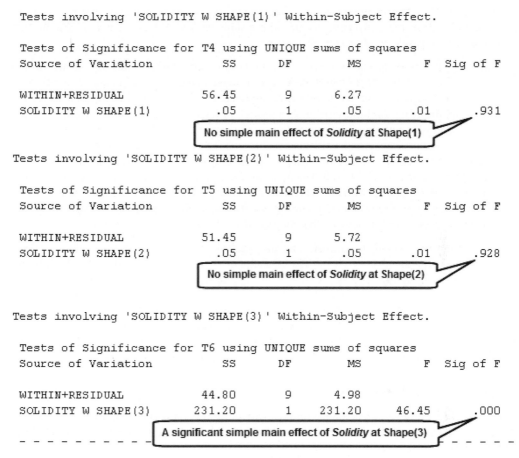

```
Tests involving 'SOLIDITY W SHAPE(1)' Within-Subject Effect.


Tests of Significance for T4 using UNIQUE sums of squares
Source of Variation          SS        DF        MS          F   Sig of F

WITHIN+RESIDUAL            56.45        9       6.27
SOLIDITY W SHAPE(1)          .05        1        .05        .01      .931
```
No simple main effect of *Solidity* at Shape(1)

```
Tests involving 'SOLIDITY W SHAPE(2)' Within-Subject Effect.


Tests of Significance for T5 using UNIQUE sums of squares
Source of Variation          SS        DF        MS          F   Sig of F

WITHIN+RESIDUAL            51.45        9       5.72
SOLIDITY W SHAPE(2)          .05        1        .05        .01      .928
```
No simple main effect of *Solidity* at Shape(2)

```
Tests involving 'SOLIDITY W SHAPE(3)' Within-Subject Effect.


Tests of Significance for T6 using UNIQUE sums of squares
Source of Variation          SS        DF        MS          F   Sig of F

WITHIN+RESIDUAL            44.80        9       4.98
SOLIDITY W SHAPE(3)       231.20        1     231.20      46.45      .000
```
A significant simple main effect of *Solidity* at Shape(3)

Output 15. The results of tests (edited) for simple main effects of the *Solidity* factor at the three levels of *Shape*

Simple main effects analysis has implications for unplanned comparisons among the cell means following a significant interaction. (In the present example, since *Solidity* has only two levels, no further analysis is required.) The confirmation of a simple main effect of one factor at one particular level of another might be regarded as a justification for calculating the size of the comparison family from the cell means at that level only. The **Bonferroni** correction might be made on that basis.

9.5   A FINAL WORD

In this chapter, we have considered the analysis of variance of data from within subject experiments, in which the participant performs at all levels of the treatment factors. Despite the practical efficiency of this research strategy and the increase in power that results from using participants as their own controls, the within subjects ANOVA encounters problems that do not arise with between subjects experiments.

Within subjects experiments produce correlated data; and therein lies the heart of the difficulty. The within subjects ANOVA model must make the additional assumption of homogeneity of variance. Violation of this requirement can have serious consequences for the ANOVA, arising from the failure of the F statistics to have the distributions specified by the degrees of freedom, with consequent inflation of the error rates. There are available tests for homogeneity of covariance and adjustments that can be made to the F tests as a result of violation of this assumption. Heterogeneity of covariance, however, has ramifications that extend far beyond the ANOVA iself which, as we have pointed out, is usually merely the first stage in the analysis of a set of data. The measurement of effect size, power and the making of specific contrasts are all problematic; even if the data meet the requirement of sphericity, the researcher is pressed for information that may be difficult or impossible to obtain.

There is, however, another approach to the analysis of the data from within subjects experiments. Rather than viewing the participant's performance under the k different conditions making up a treatment factor as values of one dependent variable measured under different conditions, the same data could be viewed as measures on k different dependent variables. The **Multivariate Analysis of Variance** (or **MANOVA** for short) is a generalisation of ANOVA, which is applicable to correlated experimental data and yet does not require homogeneity of covariance. In the final section of the next chapter, we shall take a closer look at the MANOVA and its application to within subjects experiments.

Recommended reading

There are available several readable textbooks with clear yet comprehensive accounts of within subjects ANOVA. The treatments of ANOVA in the following books are particularly accessible.

Field, A. (2005). *Discovering statistics using SPSS (2nd ed.)*. London: Sage.

Howell, D. C. (2007). *Statistical methods for psychology (6th ed.)*. Belmont, CA: Thomson/Wadsworth.

Keppel, G., & Wickens, T. D. (2004). *Design and analysis: A researcher's handbook (4th ed.)*. Upper Saddle River, NJ: Pearson Prentice Hall.

Tabachnick, B.G., & Fidell, L.S. (2007). *Using multivariate Statistics (5th ed.)*. Boston: Allyn & Bacon (Pearson International Edition).

Two useful additional references

Dodd, D. H., & Schultz, R. F. (1973). Computational procedures for estimating magnitude of effect for some analysis of variance designs. *Psychological Bulletin, 79*, 391-395.

Faul, F., Erdfelder, E., Lang, A-G., and Buchner, A. (2007). G*Power 3: A flexible statistical power analysis program for the social, behavioral and biomedical sciences. *Behavior Research Methods*, *39*, 175 – 191.

Exercises

Exercise 13 *One-factor within subjects (repeated measures) ANOVA* and Exercise 14 *Two-factor within subjects ANOVA* are available in www.psypress.com/spss-made-simple and click on Exercises.

CHAPTER 10

Mixed factorial experiments

10.1   INTRODUCTION

In the experimental designs we have considered so far, the factors have been of one type: in the completely randomised factorial experiment, the factors are all between subjects; in the within subjects factorial experiment all factors are within subjects. In this chapter, we shall consider designs in which there are both between subjects and within subjects factors.

10.1.1   Mixed factorial or split-plot designs

A researcher designs an experiment to explore the hypothesis that engineering students, because of their training in two-dimensional representation of three-dimensional structures, have a more strongly developed sense of shape discrimination than do psychology students, whose training places a greater emphasis upon verbal and numerical skills. This, he reasons, should enable the engineers to make more accurate drawings of projections in the fronto-parallel plane of the gable-ends of buildings photographed from varying angles. The investigator creates a set of solid building-like structures with triangular, square and rectangular 'gable-ends' and the participant is required to judge which of a set of comparison shapes presented on a screen is the correct projection, in the fronto-parallel plane, of the 'gable-end' of the object. A scoring system is devised which assigns the highest marks for selections that are closest to the correct projection of the gable end of the real structure. The dependent variable (or measure) is the participant's score. The results of the experiment are shown in Table 1.

It can be seen from Table 1 that there were two factors in this experiment:
1.   Student Category, with levels Psychology and Engineering.
2.   Shape, with levels Triangle, Square and Rectangle.

Since each participant was tested with all three shapes, Shape is a within subjects factor; Student Category is, of course, a between subjects factor. It is very common for factorial designs to have within subjects (repeated measures) factors on *some* (but not *all*) of their treatment factors. Since such experiments have a mixture of between subjects and within subjects factors, they are often said to be of **mixed** design. A common alternative term for this kind of design is **split-plot**, which reflects the agronomic purposes for which this type of experiment was originally designed.

Table 1. Results of a two-factor mixed factorial experiment with one within subjects factor and one between subjects factor

Group	Case	Shape		
		Triangle	Square	Rectangle
Psychology	1	2	12	7
	2	8	10	9
	3	4	15	3
	4	6	9	7
	5	9	13	8
	6	7	14	8
Engineering	7	13	3	35
	8	21	4	30
	9	26	10	35
	10	22	8	30
	11	20	9	28
	12	19	8	27

In this chapter, we shall follow a common convention for labelling different kinds of mixed factorial designs, in which the between subjects factors are represented by letters without brackets and the within subjects factors are bracketed. The present experiment, for example, is of type A × (B), where Factor A is Professional Group, Factor B is Shape and the brackets around B indicate that there are repeated measures on *Shape*. Later in the chapter, we shall consider more complex mixed factorial experiments with three factors:

1. Design A × (B × C) has one between subjects factor and two within subjects factors;
2. Design A × B × (C) has two between subjects factors and one within subjects factor.

In the same notation, the completely randomised two-factor factorial experiment is of type A × B and the two-factor within subjects experiment is S × A × B. (Subjects crosses with the treatment factors.) We shall label the one-factor between subjects experiment as type A.

In Figure 1, three experimental designs with two factors, A and B, are shown for comparison. The two-factor mixed factorial experiment of which our current experiment is an example, is shown in Figure 1c. This design is clearly a hybrid of the completely randomised and within subjects designs. Nested within each group in a one-factor between subjects (type A) design is a one-factor within subjects S × B experiment.

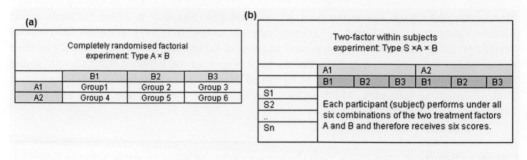

Figure 1. Three two-factor factorial designs

10.1.2　Rationale of the mixed ANOVA

The ANOVA of the data in Table 1 is a hybrid of the ANOVA for the between subjects and within subjects experiments. If we were to ignore the Shape factor and calculate the mean performance of each participant across the three shapes, we should have data suitable for a one-way ANOVA, the results of which are shown in Table 2.

Table 2. The ANOVA summary table for the one-way ANOVA of the mean scores of participants in the two groups

ANOVA

Mean

	Sum of Squares	df	Mean Square	F	Sig.
Between Groups	359.343	1	359.343	98.952	.000
Within Groups	36.315	10	3.631		
Total	395.657	11			

Turning now to the right-hand side of Table 1, we see that we have, within each professional group, the results of a Subjects × Treatments (one-factor within subjects) experiment, with Shape as the single factor. In the experiment as a whole, however, the Group and Shape factor cross, so that we can include the Group × Shape interaction as another within subjects source of variance in the analysis of variance.

In Chapter 9, we saw that in the two-factor within subjects S × A × B experiment, the Subjects 'factor' crosses with the two treatment factors, so that the correct error term for the F-test of the interaction is the three way interaction A × B × S. In the present case, however, it is clear that the Subjects 'factor' does not cross with the Group factor, so that there can be no A × B × S interaction; there is, however, a B × S (Shape × Subjects) interaction nested within levels of the group factor A. These nested interactions are pooled to give the error term for the F tests for the within subjects sources.

The ANOVA summary table is shown in Table 3. There are both between subjects and within subjects sources. We have already seen that the between groups sources are Group and the Within Groups error term. Among the within subjects sources are Shape and the interaction between the Group and Shape factors. There is also a second error term, Error(Shape), for the F tests for the within subjects treatment sources.

The term Error (Shape) is simply a pooled estimate constructed from the Shape × Subjects interactions in the two groups. You can see this from the degrees of freedom. Since there are six participants (subjects) within each group, the degrees of freedom of the error term for either one-factor within subjects experiment is $(6 - 1)(3 - 1) = 10$. Pooling across both groups doubles this value, producing the tabled df value of 20.

The composite error term Error (Shape) is appropriate not only for the test for a main effect of Shape, but also for a test for the Group × Shape interaction. Essentially, this is because since Subjects is a 'factor' with random effects, the expected value of the composite Subjects × Shape interaction mean square includes a Group × Shape component. (For a full explanation of why this is so, see a statistics textbook such as Howell, 2007 or Keppel & Wickens, 2004.)

Table 3. ANOVA summary table for the data in Table 1					
Source	**df**	**SS**	**MS**	**F**	**p**
Between subjects					
Group	1	1078.03	1078.83	98.95	<.01
Error: Within Groups	10	108.94	10.89		
Within subjects					
Shape	2	533.56	266.78	32.62	<.01
Shape × Group	2	1308.22	654.11	79.99	<.01
Error (Shape): Pooled Shape × Subjects	20	163.56	8.18		

10.2   THE TWO-FACTOR MIXED FACTORIAL ANOVA WITH SPSS

In Chapter 9, we saw that the within subjects ANOVA is available in **Repeated Measures** in the **General Linear Model** menu. The mixed ANOVA is also run with the **Repeated Measures** procedure.

See Chap. 9

10.2.1   Preparing the SPSS data set

In Table 1, we represented the experimental design with the levels of the within subjects factor arrayed horizontally and those of the between subjects factor stacked vertically, with Engineering under Psychology. We did so because this arrangement corresponds to the way in which the results will be arranged in **Data View**.

As always, the first column of **Data View** will contain the case numbers. The second column will contain a single grouping variable *Category* representing the Psychologists (1) and the Engineers (2). The third, fourth and fifth columns will contain the results at the three levels of the *Shape* factor (Triangle, Square, and Rectangle).

Using the techniques described in Chapter 2, Section 2.3, enter **Variable View** and name five variables: *Case*, *Category* (the grouping variable), *Triangle*, *Square*, and *Rectangle*. Use the **Label** column to assign more meaningful variable names (Case Number, Category of Student) and the **Values** column to assign labels to the numerical values of the grouping variable *Category* (such as 1 = 'Psychology Student', 2 = 'Engineering Student'). Ensure that the **Decimals** column is set at 0 for each variable.

See Section 2.3

Click the **Data View** tab and enter the data into **Data View** (Figure 2). If values rather than labels appear in the variable Category, enter the **View** menu and click **Value Labels**.

Case	Category	Triangle	Square	Rectangle
1	Psychology Student	2	12	7
2	Psychology Student	8	10	9
3	Psychology Student	4	15	3
4	Psychology Student	6	9	7
5	Psychology Student	9	13	8
6	Psychology Student	7	14	8
7	Engineering Student	13	3	35
8	Engineering Student	21	4	30
9	Engineering Student	26	10	35
10	Engineering Student	22	8	30
11	Engineering Student	20	9	28
12	Engineering Student	19	8	27

Figure 2. The data from Table 1 in **Data View**

10.2.2   Exploring the results: Boxplots

As usual, the first step is to explore the data set. The boxplot was described in Section 4.3.2. Here, however, the **clustered boxplot** (which clusters the levels of the within subjects factor within levels of the between subjects factor) is appropriate.

To obtain a clustered boxplot, proceed as follows:

- Click **Analyze➜Descriptive Statistics➜Explore...** to open the **Explore** dialog box.
- Complete the details as in Section 9.2.2, but with the addition of the variable name *Category of Student* transferred to the **Factor List** panel.
- Click **OK**.

The edited boxplot is shown in Output 1.

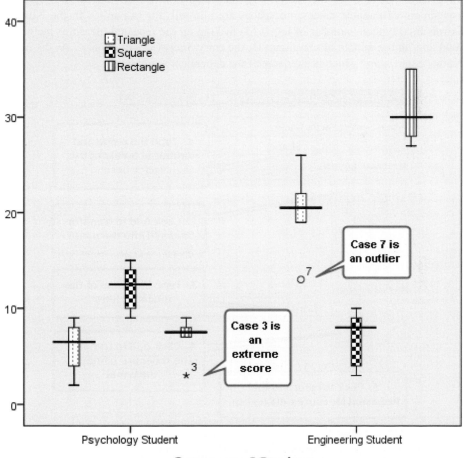

Output 1. Edited boxplots of the three shapes for each student category

Notice the extreme score (case 3) for the number of rectangles identified by a Psychology student and the outlier (case 7) for the number of triangles identified by an Engineering student. In a real research situation, it might have been worth eliminating the two deviant scores and comparing the analyses with and without the outliers, but here we shall work with the entire data set. Extreme scores may simply be clerical errors or the results of misunderstandings; but they may simply be normal scores in the tail of the distribution.

10.2.3 Running the ANOVA

- Select **Analyze➔General Linear Model➔Repeated Measures…** to open the **Repeated Measures Define Factor(s)** dialog box. (The completed version is shown in Figure 3.)
- In the **Within-Subject Factor Name** box, delete *factor1* and type a generic name (such as *Shape*) for the repeated measures factor. This variable name must not be that of any of the three levels making up the factor. It must also conform to the rules governing the assignment of variable names: no spaces are allowed, for example. In the **Number of Levels** box, type the number of levels (3) making up the repeated measures factor. Click **Add** and, in the middle box in Figure 3, the entry *Shape*(3) will appear. As the **Measure Name**, enter *Score*, which is the name of the dependent variable.

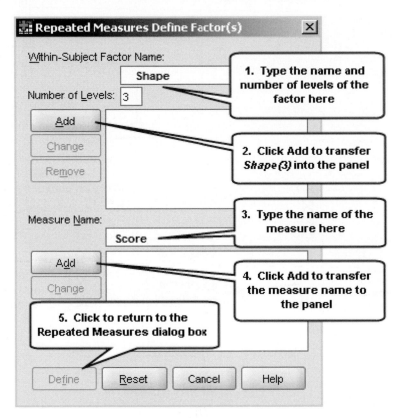

Figure 3. The **Repeated Measures Define Factor(s)** for three levels of *Shape*

- Click **Define** to open the **Repeated Measures ANOVA** dialog box.

- Transfer the variable names *Rectangle*, *Square*, *Triangle* to the **Within-Subjects Variables** box as shown in Figure 4.
- The new element is the presence of the between subjects factor *Category of Student*. Transfer this factor to the **Between-Subjects Factor(s)** box as shown in Figure 4.
- You should also request a number of useful additional options. A profile plot of the levels of the within subjects factor *Shape* for each level of the between subjects variable *Category* is requested by clicking **Plots…** and following the steps shown in Figure 16 in Chapter 9. Click **Continue** to return to the **Repeated Measures** dialog box.
- A table of **descriptive statistics**, **estimates of effect size** and a table of **Bonferroni adjusted pairwise comparisons** among the levels of the within subjects factor *Shape* are requested by clicking **Options…** and following the steps shown in Figure 11 in Chapter 9. Click **Continue** to return to the **Repeated Measures** dialog box.

  See Section 9.4.2

- Had there been more than two levels in the between subjects variable *Category*, a Tukey post-hoc test could have been requested by clicking **Post Hoc…**, transferring the variable name *Category* to the **Post Hoc Tests for** box, and clicking the **Tukey** check box. Click **Continue** to return to the original dialog box.
- Click **OK** to run the ANOVA.

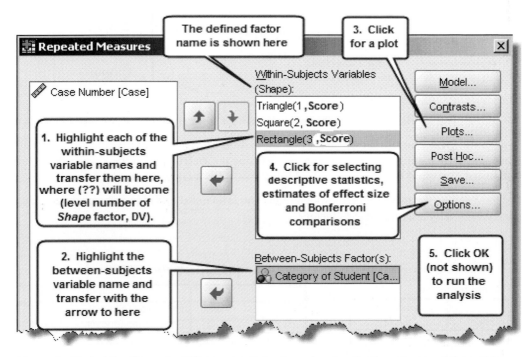

Figure 4. Part of the **Repeated Measures** dialog box showing the three levels of the within subjects factor *Shape* and the between subjects factor *Category*

10.2.4   Output for the two-factor mixed ANOVA

Output 2 shows the left-hand pane of the **SPSS Viewer**, in which the various items appearing in the right-hand pane are listed.

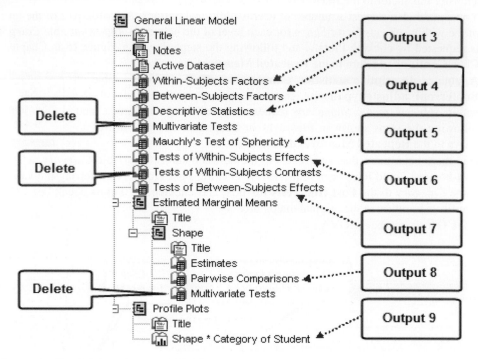

Output 2. The left-hand pane of **SPSS Viewer** listing the output items for the mixed ANOVA

Two items, **Multivariate Tests** and **Tests of Within-Subjects Contrasts**, can be deleted immediately by highlighting each in turn and pressing the **Delete** key on the keyboard. In the **Estimated Marginal Means** section, the **Multivariate Tests** table can also be deleted.

Output 3 shows the two SPSS tables identifying the levels of the Within-Subjects factors and the levels of the Between-Subjects factors.

Within-Subjects Factors

Measure: Score

Shape	Dependent Variable
1	Triangle
2	Square
3	Rectangle

Between-Subjects Factors

		Value Label	N
Category of Student	1	Psychology Student	6
	2	Engineering Student	6

Output 3. The **Within-Subjects Factors** list of levels and the **Between-Subjects Factors** list of levels

Output 4 shows the table of descriptive statistics requested in **Options**. Inspection of the means shows different profiles across the factor *Shape* for the two student categories.

Descriptive Statistics

	Category of Student	Mean	Std. Deviation	N
Triangle	Psychology Student	6.00	2.61	6
	Engineering Student	20.17	4.26	6
	Total	13.08	8.13	12
Square	Psychology Student	12.17	2.32	6
	Engineering Student	7.00	2.83	6
	Total	9.58	3.65	12
Rectangle	Psychology Student	7.00	2.10	6
	Engineering Student	30.83	3.43	6
	Total	18.92	12.74	12

Output 4. The optional table of **Descriptive Statistics**

The next table, in Output 5, reports the result of the **Mauchly's Test of Sphericity** for homogeneity of covariance. (Section 9.2.4 describes the correct procedure when the Mauchly statistic is significant.)

See Section 9.2.4

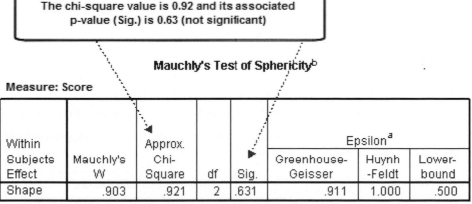

The chi-square value is 0.92 and its associated p-value (Sig.) is 0.63 (not significant)

Mauchly's Test of Sphericity[b]

Measure: Score

Within Subjects Effect	Mauchly's W	Approx. Chi-Square	df	Sig.	Epsilon[a]		
					Greenhouse-Geisser	Huynh-Feldt	Lower-bound
Shape	.903	.921	2	.631	.911	1.000	.500

Tests the null hypothesis that the error covariance matrix of the orthonormalized transformed dependent variables is proportional to an identity matrix.

    a. May be used to adjust the degrees of freedom for the averaged tests of significance. Corrected tests are displayed in the Tests of Within-Subjects Effects table.

    b.
      Design: Intercept+Category
      Within Subjects Design: Shape

Output 5. **Mauchly's Test of Sphericity** and values of **Epsilon** for more conservative tests

In the present case, the **Mauchly** statistic has a p-value of 0.63, so there is no evidence of heterogeneity of covariance. The usual (**Sphericity Assumed**) F test can therefore be used. You should simplify the ANOVA table in Output 6 accordingly by removing the information about the conservative F tests.

Tests for within subjects and interaction effects

Tests of Within-Subjects Effects

Measure: Score

Source	Type III Sum of Squares	df	Mean Square	F	Sig.	Partial Eta Squared
Shape	533.56	2	266.78	32.62	.000	.765
Shape * Category	1308.22	2	654.11	79.99	.000	.889
Error(Shape)	163.56	20	8.18			

> Both the *F* values for the factor *Shape* and the interaction *Shape*Category* have associated p-values (Sig.) < .01 (significant at the .01 level)

> The values of $h_p{}^2$ are 77% (medium) and 89% (large) respectively

Output 6. The edited ANOVA summary table for the within-subjects factor *Shape* and its interaction with the between-subjects factor *Category*

Note that in Output 6, the factor *Shape* is significant beyond the 1 per cent level: the p-value (**Sig.**) 0.000 is computerese for 'less than 0.0005'. Write p < .01, not .000. This result would be reported as:

> The mean scores for the three shapes differed significantly beyond the .01 level: F(2, 20) = 32.62; p < 0.01. Partial eta squared = .765, a 'large' effect.

The *Category* × *Shape* interaction is also significant beyond the 1% level: the p-value is less than 0.0005. This result would be reported as:

> There was a significant interaction between *Category* and *Shape*: F(2, 20) = 79.99; p < 0.01. Partial eta squared = .889, a large effect.

Test for between subjects effects

Output 7 shows the ANOVA summary table for the between subjects factor *Category*.

Tests of Between-Subjects Effects

Measure: Score

Transformed Variable: Average

Source	Type III Sum of Squares	df	Mean Square	F	Sig.	Partial Eta Squared
Intercept	6916.69	1	6916.69	634.9	.000	.984
Category	1078.03	1	1078.03	98.95	.000	.908
Error	108.94	10	10.89			

Ignore the *Intercept* row. The *F* value for the factor *Category* is 98.95 with an associated p-value < .01 (significant at the .01 level)

The value of h_{p^2} is 91% (large effect)

Output 7. The ANOVA summary table for the between-subjects factor *Category*

Ignore the terms **Intercept** and **Type III**: these refer to the regression method that was used to perform the analysis. With a p-value (**Sig.**) of less than 0.0005, there is clearly a significant difference in performance between the two groups of students. This result would be reported as:

> The mean scores for the categories of student differed significantly at the 1% level: F(1,10) = 98.95; p < 0.01. Partial eta squared = .91, a 'large' effect.

The ANOVA strongly confirms the patterns discernible in Table 2: the *Shape* and *Category* factors both have significant main effects; the interaction between the factors is also significant. You will notice that although the value given for *F* is exactly the same as in the one-way ANOVA of the mean scores of the participants over all three shapes, the mean squares for the *Category* and *Error* sources are three times the values in the one-way table. For each of the six means for each group, there were three times that number of raw scores, increasing the multiplier of the sum of the squares of the deviations by a factor of three.

Bonferroni Pairwise Comparisons for the within subjects factor

Output 8 shows the pairwise comparisons requested in **Options**.

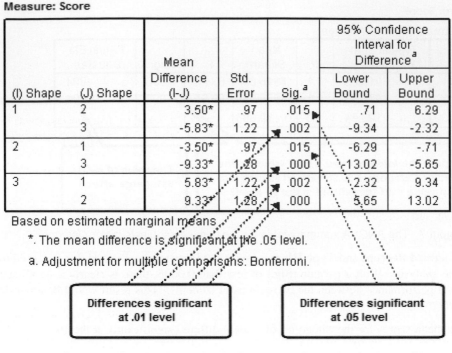

Pairwise Comparisons

Measure: Score

(I) Shape	(J) Shape	Mean Difference (I-J)	Std. Error	Sig.[a]	95% Confidence Interval for Difference[a]	
					Lower Bound	Upper Bound
1	2	3.50*	.97	.015	.71	6.29
	3	-5.83*	1.22	.002	-9.34	-2.32
2	1	-3.50*	.97	.015	-6.29	-.71
	3	-9.33*	1.28	.000	-13.02	-5.65
3	1	5.83*	1.22	.002	2.32	9.34
	2	9.33*	1.28	.000	5.65	13.02

Based on estimated marginal means

*. The mean difference is significant at the .05 level.

a. Adjustment for multiple comparisons: Bonferroni.

Differences significant at .01 level

Differences significant at .05 level

Output 8. The **Bonferroni pairwise comparisons** for the factor *Shape*

Profile plot

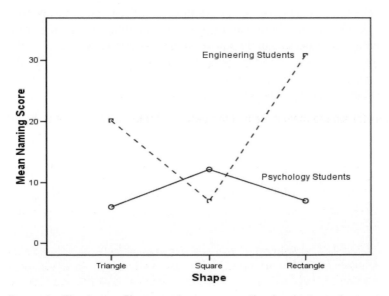

Output 9. The factor *Shape* performance profiles for each student category

The requested profile plot is shown (edited) in Output 9. The plot confirms the pattern of the boxplots in Output 1. With squares, the Psychology students improved, while the Engineering students' scores tended to slump in that condition.

10.2.5   Simple effects analysis with syntax

Given that the *Group* × *Shape* interaction has proved significant, the researcher might wish to 'unpack' it by making tests for the simple effects of *Group* at each of the three levels of the *Shape* factor.

The syntax for testing for simple main effects of a factor in a mixed design at specific levels of a factor of the opposite type (i.e. a between factor at one level of a within factor and vice versa) is tricky, because the /DESIGN subcommand permits the explicit mention of between subjects factors only; while the /WSDESIGN subcommand allows the naming of within subjects factors only. In other words, for an experiment of mixed factorial A × (B) design, a phrase such as A WITHIN B(1) will not be permitted in either the /DESIGN or the /WSDESIGN subcommand.

The trick here is, when (in the two-factor mixed factorial A × (B) experiment) we want to specify the simple main effect of the between subjects factor A at each level of B, we use the keyword MWITHIN to refer to the effects of A; moreover, this reference is in the /WSDESIGN subcommand which, hitherto, we have used exclusively for within subjects sources (Figure 5).

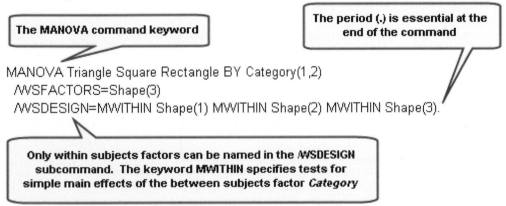

Figure 5. Syntax for simple main effects of the between factor at each level of the within factor

In this particular example, where there is only one between subjects factor, there will be an automatic link between that factor and the MWITHIN statements. In more complex mixed designs, where there are two or more between subjects factors, we shall need to write an additional /DESIGN subcommand to make the link between the specific effect that we want and the MWITHIN phrase.

The results of the tests for simple main effects of the *Group* factor at the three levels of the *Shape* factor are shown in Ouput 10 (edited). The desired simple main effects are labelled as if they were *interactions*: that is, the keyword BY which, hitherto has always indicated an interaction, appears before MWITHIN. The simple main effect of *Group* at the first level of

Shape is labelled as 'Category BY MWITHIN SHAPE(1); the simple main effect of *Group* at the second level of *Shape* is 'Category BY MWITHIN SHAPE(2)'. These are NOT interactions: they are simple effects. The sources labelled 'MWITHIN SHAPE(1)' and 'MWITHIN SHAPE(2)' test the null hypothesis that the average score across the groups is zero within each level of *Shape*. Unless we are dealing with difference scores, this test is not usually of interest.

We can see from Output 10, that formal testing has confirmed the existence of simple main effects of *Group* at all three levels of *Shape*. Since there were only two groups, we can infer that the difference between the two group means is significant at all three levels of the *Shape* factor.

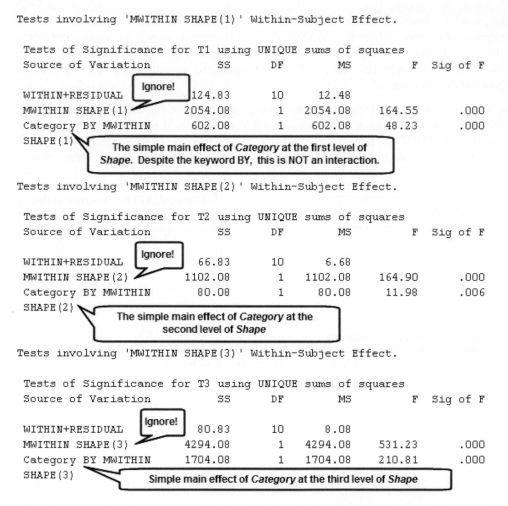

Output 10. Results of the tests for simple main effects of *Category* at each level of *Shape*

The syntax for testing for simple main effects of *Shape* at each level of the *Group* factor is shown in Figure 6.

```
MANOVA Triangle Square Rectangle BY Category(1,2)
    /WSFACTORS=Shape(3)
    /DESIGN=MWITHIN Category(1) MWITHIN Category(2).
```

> This time the subcommand /DESIGN is being used to test for simple effects of the within subjects factor *Shape*

Figure 6. Syntax for testing for simple main effects of the within subjects factor (*Shape*) at each level of the between groups factor.

Note once again that, although we are testing for simple main effects of the *within subjects* factor, we use the /DESIGN subcommand, not /WSDESIGN. This is because only the /DESIGN subcommand allows you to name a between subjects factor. Since there are only two factors, the link between MWITHIN and the within subjects factor is automatic.

The results of the simple effects analysis are shown in Output 11. The arrangement of this output is somewhat different from the output for the simple main effects of *Group* at each level of *Shape*: the output is divided explicitly into between subjects and within subjects effects. The same points about the output, however, apply here too. In the between subjects output, the sources MWITHIN GROUP(1) and MWITHIN GROUP(2) test the hypothesis that, within each group, the mean score averaged across the three shapes is zero. The results we are looking for are in the within subjects section. Once again, the labels of the simple effects contain the keyword BY as if they were interactions.

```
Tests of Between-Subjects Effects.
```
> These are not generally of interest. Ignore!

```
Tests of Significance for T1 using UNIQUE sums of squares
Source of Variation          SS        DF        MS           F  Sig of F

WITHIN+RESIDUAL            108.94      10       10.89
MWITHIN CATEGORY(1)       1266.72       1     1266.72      116.27     .000
MWITHIN CATEGORY(2)       6728.00       1     6728.00      617.56     .000
```

```
Tests involving 'SHAPE' Within-Subject Effect.
```
> Tests for simple main effects of *Shape* at each level of *Group*.

```
AVERAGED Tests of Significance for MEAS.1 using UNIQUE sums of squares
Source of Variation          SS        DF        MS           F  Sig of F

WITHIN+RESIDUAL            163.56      20        8.18
MWITHIN CATEGORY(1)       131.44       2       65.72        8.04     .003
BY SHAPE
MWITHIN CATEGORY(2)      1710.33       2      855.17      104.57     .000
BY SHAPE
```

> Despite the keyword BY, these are simple *main effects*.

Output 11. Tests for simple main effects of the within subjects factor *Shape* at each level of the between groups factor

Output 11 (edited) shows that there are significant simple main effects of *Shape* at both levels of *Group*. Should you wish to make multiple comparisons among the cell means, this might be seen as justification for defining the comparison family in relation to the three means at each level of the *Group* factor, rather than the six means in the entire experiment.

Figure 7 presents the syntax for testing for simple main effects of either factor in the A × (B) design in more abstract notation, representing the scores obtained under the conditions of the within subjects factor B as B1 and B2. In the current example, B1, B2, B3 and A are *Triangle*, *Square*, *Rectangle* and *Category*, respectively.

In Figure 7, the /DESIGN and /WSDESIGN subcommands are presented as alternatives, the choice between them depending upon which set of simple main effects are required; but both subcommands can be run on a single MANOVA command. Have a separate subcommand for each set of simple main effects: the two sets of simple effects are alternative partitions of the same interaction and main effect terms in the model.

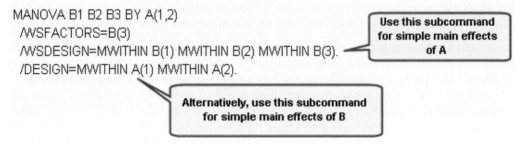

Figure 7. Using the MWITHIN keyword to test for simple main effects in the A × (B) mixed design

Including comments with SPSS syntax

As an *aide-memoire*, it can be useful to include in syntax files reminders of the purpose of various subcommands and phrases. If added in the proper format, such comments are ignored by the computer and the syntax will run in the usual way. The rules for comments are as follows.

- If a comment requires several lines, write it before or after a command.
- If a comment occurs in the middle of a command, it must not spill over into a second line.
- All comments begin with an asterisk * and end with a period or full stop.
- When a comment occurs before or after a command, the asterisk and full stop are all that is necessary.
- A comment in the middle of a line of syntax must begin with the /* and end with */.
- When a comment comes in the middle of a command, but at the end of a line, the right-hand sequence of characters */ after the period is unnecessary.

The format for comments in various positions is illustrated in Figure 8.

> A comment occupying more than one line must come before or after a command

> This period is essential after a long comment

*Mixed A by (B) design. Test for simple effects of B at A1 and A2. Here the keyword MWITHIN must be used to avoid naming both between and within subjects factors in the same subcommand, which is not permitted.
MANOVA B1 B2 B3 /* Listing the levels of the within subejcts factor. */ BY A(1,2)
   /WSFACTORS=B(3) /* Defines the within subjects factor.

> The characters */ are unnecessary at the end of a line

   /DESIGN=MWITHIN A(1), MWITHIN A(2).
*The /DESIGN subcommand will run tests of simple main effects of the within subjects factor at each level of the between subjects factor.

Figure 8. Illustration of the formatting for comments inserted in syntax

10.3   THE THREE-FACTOR MIXED ANOVA

The procedures described in Section 10.2 can readily be extended to the analysis of data from mixed factorial experiments with three treatment factors.

Table 4. The 'mixed' or 'split-plot' experimental designs, as elaborations of the simple, two-group between subjects experiment

(a) Type A design	**Women**	**Men**					
	Group 1	Group 2					

(b) Type A × (B) design	Gender	Task 1	Task 2	Task 3	Task
	Women	Group 1			
	Men	Group 2			

(c) Type A × (B×C) design	Gender	Task 1		Task 2		Task 3		Task
		L	**R**	**L**	**R**	**L**	**R**	Hand
	Women	Group 1						
	Men	Group 2						

(d) Type A × B × (C) Design	Gender	Hand	Task 1	Task 2	Task 3	Task
	F	**R**	Group 1			
		L	Group 2			
	M	**R**	Group 3			
		L	Group 4			

There are two possible mixed three-factor factorial experiments:

1. Two within subjects factors and one between subjects factor: $A \times (B \times C)$
2. One within subjects factor and two between subjects factors: $A \times B \times (C)$.

In Table 4, are shown the most common mixed ANOVA designs, all of which can be seen as elaborations of between subjects experiments, the simplest of which we shall term the 'Type A' design. In Table 4, the within subject factors are bracketed.

10.3.1 Two within subjects factors and one between subjects factor: the A × (B × C) mixed factorial design

Suppose that to the experiment described in Section 10.2, we were to add an additional within subjects factor, such as *Solidity* (of the shape), with two levels, Solid or Outline. The participants (either Psychology or Engineering students) now have to try to recognise both Solid and Outline Triangles, Squares, and Rectangles. Since there are six combinations of the *Shape* and *Solidity* factors, we shall need to have six variables in **Data View** to contain all the scores. Prepare the named columns systematically in **Variable View** by taking the first level of one factor (say, *Shape*) and combining it in turn with each of the levels of the second factor (*Solidity*), and then doing the same with the second and third levels of the first factor. The top part of **Data View** might appear as in Figure 9. As we read from left to right across the variable labels for the various combinations of *Shape* and *Solidity*, we see that, whereas the third column is still a triangle (we are still at the first level of the *Shape* factor), the level of the *Solidity* factor has changed to Outline. In this sense, the levels of the *Shape* factor can be said to 'change more slowly' as we scan the variable names from left to right.

Case	Category	Triangle Solid	Triangle Outline	Square Solid	Square Outline	Rectangle Solid	Rectangle Outline
1	Psychology Student	13	15	12	23	12	14

Figure 9. The variable names for a three-factor mixed factorial experiment with two within subjects factors

When you are working in the **Repeated Measures** dialog box, take care when transferring variable names from the list in the panel on the left to the **Within-Subjects Variables** panel on the right. If, in **Data View**, you have arranged the variables systematically as we have described, you will be able to transfer the variables *en bloc* to the Within-Subjects Variables panel, where each will occupy the correct slot. The contents of the slots in the panel are determined by the order in which the factors were defined and the numbers of levels that were given for each factor. In this case, the contents of the brackets should read as follows: (1, 1), (1, 2), (2, 1), (2, 2), (3, 1), (3, 2). Should the order of the variables in the left-hand panel fail to correspond with the numbering in the right-hand panel, something has gone wrong. You may, for instance, have defined the factors in the wrong order. Had you defined the factors in the order Solidity(2), Shape(3), the numbering in the slots would have been wrong for some of the variables: the third slot would still contain the variable *SquareSolid*, but the programme would treat this variable as the scores for the solid triangle; and the slot that should contain data for the solid triangle would be treated as an outline square.

The upper part of the completed dialog box is shown in Figure 10.

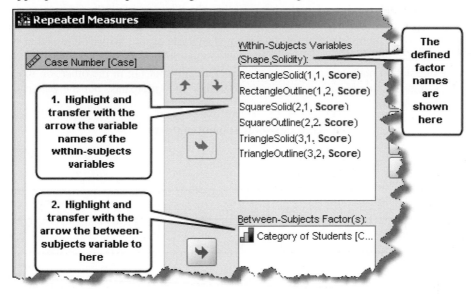

Figure 10. The upper part of the **Repeated Measures** dialog box for a three-factor mixed factorial experiment, with two within subjects factors and one between subjects factor

The output includes Output 12, which shows the tests for the main effects of the within subjects factors and their various interactions with each other and with the between subjects factor. Output 13 shows the test for the between subjects factor.

Tests of Within-Subjects Effects

Measure:**Score**

Source	Type III Sum of Squares	df	Mean Square	F	Sig.	Partial Eta Squared
Shape	166.17	2	83.08	7.11	.017	.640
Shape * Category	109.06	2	54.53	4.67	.045	.539
Error(Shape)	93.44	8	11.68			
Solidity	25.00	1	25.00	11.25	.028	.738
Solidity * Category	28.44	1	28.44	12.80	.023	.762
Error(Solidity)	8.89	4	2.22			
Shape * Solidity	15.17	2	7.58	2.74	.124	.407
Shape * Solidity * Category	193.39	2	96.69	34.98	.000	.897
Error(Shape*Solidity)	22.11	8	2.76			

Output 12. The edited **Within-Subjects Effects** table showing the **F ratio** and **Partial Eta Squared** for the within subjects factors *Shape* and *Solidity* and their various double and triple interactions with each other and with the between subjects factor *Category*

In the ANOVA, having equal sample sizes ensures the sums of squares for the various effects can vary independently. Nevertheless, a significant higher order effect is often of more interest than a lower order effect and supersedes the former as the focus of attention and further analysis. In Output 12, for example, we see that the *Shape* × *Solidity* interaction is not significant. The finding that there is a significant three-way *Shape* × *Solidity* × *Category* interaction, however, shows that a more fine-grained analysis of the two-way interaction within the data from each group of participants is indicated. One obvious possibility is that the *Shape* × *Solidity* interaction may occur in one participant category but not in the other; on the other hand, there may be simple interactions in both groups of participants, but the patterns they show may be different.

Tests of Between-Subjects Effects

Measure:Score
Transformed Variable:Average

Source	Type III Sum of Squares	df	Mean Square	F	Sig.	Partial Eta Squared
Category	18.78	1	18.78	.538	.504	.119
Error	139.56	4	34.89			

Output 13. The edited **Between-Subjects Effects** table showing the **F ratio** and **Partial Eta Squared** for the between subjects factor *Category*

The profile plots of *Shape* against *Solidity* for the two student groups suggest heterogeneity of the simple interactions: the simple interaction appears to be more striking in the Engineers than it is in the Psychologists; but in the psychologists, although the profiles do not cross, they are still far from being parallel (Output 14). The patterns shown by the two sets of profiles are quite consistent with the finding that the three-way interaction is significant.

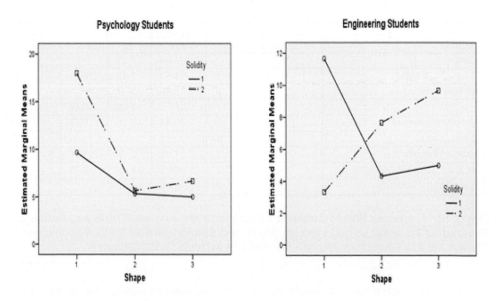

Output 14. Profile plots of *Solidity* against *Shape* for the two groups of participants

10.3.2   Using syntax to test for simple effects

Since the three-way interaction has proved to be significant, the researcher might wish to 'unpack' it by making further tests. Should at least one of the simple interactions turn out be significant, one might consider further analysis of simple, simple main effects of *Solidity* at different levels of the *Category* factor (i.e. in the psychologists and the engineers considered separately).

As we observed in our discussion of the syntax for simple effects in the two-factor A × (B) mixed factorial experiment, in order to avoid naming both a between subjects factor and a within subjects factor in the same subcommand (whether that is /DESIGN or /WSDESIGN), we shall need to use the keyword MWITHIN. If the experimental design is of the type A × (B × C), for instance, a statement such as B BY C at A(1), for instance, is unacceptable in either subcommand, because it involves both within subjects and between subjects factors. Once again, the MWITHIN keyword is included in the subcommand we would normally use for effects of the other type: that is, if we want simple effects of within subjects factors (or their simple interactions), the MWITHIN keyword is included in the /DESIGN command, not the /WSDESIGN subcommand, as might be expected. The same is true of simple effects and (in designs with more than one between subjects factor) interactions among between subjects sources: in such cases, the MWITHIN keyword occurs in the /WSDESIGN, not the /DESIGN, subcommand.

For a mixed factorial design of type A × (B × C), that is, one in which factor A is between subjects and B and C are within subjects as in the current example, the following syntax will run the full ANOVA:

```
MANOVA B1C1 B1C2 B2C1 B2C2 B3C1 B3C2 BY A(1,2)
    /WSFACTORS=B(3) C(2).
```

In terms of the variable names in the current example, the syntax will appear as follows:

```
MANOVA RectangleSolid RectangleOutline SquareSolid SquareOutline
TriangleSolid TriangleOutline BY Category(1,2)
    /WSFACTORS=Shape(3) Solidity(2).
```

We shall be testing the simple interactions between *Shape* and *Solidity* at each level of the *Category* factor. As a check on the output, we shall want to satisfy ourselves that the sum of the sums of squares for the simple interactions is equal to the sum of squares for the three-way interaction plus the sums of squares for the two-way interaction between *Shape* and *Solidity*.

We expect this because, in general,

$$\sum_{j} SS_{BC\,at\,A_j} = SS_{BC} + SS_{ABC} \quad \text{- - - (1)}$$

Alternative partitioning of interaction terms

We shall not show the MANOVA output for the full ANOVA again, since the values given are identical with those shown in Outputs 12 and 13. We note from Output 12 that

$$SS_{Shape \times Solidity} + SS_{Shape \times Solidity \times Category} = 15.17 + 193.39 = 208.56$$

We shall make use of this value when we examine the output for the tests for simple interactions.

The syntax for testing for simple interactions between two within subjects factors at specified levels of a between subjects factor is as follows:

```
MANOVA B1C1 B1C2 B2C1 B2C2 B3C1 B3C2 BY A(1,2)
    /WSFACTORS=B(3) C(2)
    /WSDESIGN=B BY C
    /DESIGN=MWITHIN A(1) MWITHIN A(2).
```

Notice that, since there are three factors in the current experiment, we shall need both /DESIGN and /WSDESIGN subcommands to link the simple interactions to the MWITHIN statements. In terms of the variable names in the current example, the syntax for testing for simple interactions between *Shape* and *Solidity* at each level of the *Category* factor is as follows:

```
MANOVA RectangleSolid RectangleOutline SquareSolid SquareOutline
TriangleSolid TriangleOutline BY Category(1,2)
    /WSFACTORS=Shape(3) Solidity(2)
    /WSDESIGN=Shape BY Solidity
    /DESIGN= MWITHIN Category(1) MWITHIN Category(2).
```

The results of the tests for simple interactions are shown in Output 15, which forms the final part of an extensive list of test results, the rest of which has been omitted.

```
Tests involving 'SHAPE BY SOLIDITY' Within-Subject Effect.

  AVERAGED Tests of Significance for MEAS.1 using UNIQUE sums of squares
  Source of Variation             SS       DF       MS          F   Sig of F

  WITHIN+RESIDUAL               22.11       8      2.76
  MWITHIN CATEGORY(1)           55.11       2     27.56       9.97      .007
  BY SHAPE BY SOLIDITY

  MWITHIN CATEGORY(2)          153.44       2     76.72      27.76      .000
  BY SHAPE BY SOLIDITY
```

Output 15. Tests for simple interactions *Shape* and *Solidity* at both levels of the *Category* factor

Notice that, once again, the second occurrence of the keyword BY in connexion with the keyword MWITHIN suggests a three-factor interaction; but these are simple two-factor interactions of *Shape* with *Solidity* at each level of the *Category* factor.

When we add together the sums of squares for the sources labelled as MWITHIN CATEGORY(1) BY SHAPE BY SOLIDITY and MWITHIN CATEGORY(2) BY SHAPE BY SOLIDITY, we obtain the value 208.56, which, as we have seen (1), is the sum of the sums of squares for the *Shape × Solidity* interaction and the *Shape × Solidity × Category* interaction. This is further confirmation that our interpretation of the output is correct.

Our formal tests have confirmed the existence of simple interactions between *Shape* and *Solidity* in both groups of participants. Arguably, therefore, we can proceed to test for simple, simple main effects of solidity in order to cast further light on the profile patterns in Output 14. The syntax for these tests is as follows:

```
MANOVA
B1C1 B1C2 B2C1 B2C2 B3C1 B3C2  BY A(1,2)
   /WSFACTORS = B(3), C(2)
   /WSDESIGN C W B(1), C W B(2)  C W B(3)
   /DESIGN MWITHIN A(1), MWITHIN A(2).
```

In terms of the variable names of the current example, the syntax reads as follows:

```
MANOVA RectangleSolid RectangleOutline SquareSolid
SquareOutline TriangleSolid TriangleOutline BY Category)(1,2)
   /WSFACTORS=Shape(3) Solidity(2)
   /WSDESIGN=Solidity WITHIN Shape(1) Solidity
      WITHIN Shape(2) Solidity WITHIN Shape(3)
   /DESIGN=MWITHIN Category(1) MWITHIN Category(2).
```

Since the MWITHIN keywords in the /DESIGN subcommand nest the three simple main effects within each level of the between subjects factor *Category*, the analysis will run tests of six simple, simple main effects: Solidity at Shape(1), Shape(2) and Shape(3) at Category(1); and Solidity at Shape(1), Shape(2) and Shape(3) at Category(2).

Output 16 shows the results of the six tests for simple simple main effects of *Solidity* at the six combinations of the *Shape* and *Solidity* factors.

Source of Variation	SS	DF	MS	F	Sig of F
WITHIN+RESIDUAL	13.67	4	3.42		
MWITHIN CATEGORY(1) BY SOLIDITY W SHAPE(1)	104.17	1	104.17	30.49	.005
MWITHIN CATEGORY(2) BY SOLIDITY W SHAPE(1)	104.17	1	104.17	30.49	.005
WITHIN+RESIDUAL	15.67	4	3.92		
MWITHIN CATEGORY(1) BY SOLIDITY W SHAPE(2)	.17	1	.17	.04	.847
MWITHIN CATEGORY(2) BY SOLIDITY W SHAPE(2)	16.67	1	16.67	4.26	.108
WITHIN+RESIDUAL	1.67	4	.42		
MWITHIN CATEGORY(1) BY SOLIDITY W SHAPE(3)	4.17	1	4.17	10.00	.034
MWITHIN CATEGORY(2) BY SOLIDITY W SHAPE(3)	32.67	1	32.67	78.40	.001

Callouts: C at B(1)A(1), C at B(1)A(2), C at B(2)A(1), C at B(2)A(2), C at B(3)A(1), C at B(3)A(2)

Output 16. Tests for simple, simple main effects of *Solidity* at each of the six combinations of *Shape* and *Category*

Since the factor of *Solidity* has only two levels, a significant simple, simple main effect implies that the difference between the means for the Solid and Outline conditions is also significant. Had we tested for simple, simple main effects of *Shape* at each of the four combinations of the *Solidity* and *Category* factors, further testing of pairwise comparisons would have been required. Once again, the presence of a significant simple, simple main effect might be seen as justification for defining the size of the comparison family on the basis of three means only.

10.3.3   One within subjects factor and two between subjects factors: the A × B × (C) mixed factorial design

Suppose the experiment described in Section 10.3.1 were to have an additional between subjects factor, such as *Sex* (Male, Female) but just one within subjects factor *Shape*. Our mixed factorial design is now of type A × B × (C). The participants (either Psychology or Engineering Students, and either Male or Female) have to try to recognise different shapes of targets (Triangles, Squares and Rectangles). In **Variable View**, it will now be necessary to add a second grouping variable *Sex* (Figure 11).

Case	Category	Sex	Triangle	Square	Rectangle
1	Psychology Student	Male	2	12	7

Figure 11. The variable names for a three-factor mixed factorial experiment with one within subjects and two between subjects factors

The completed **Repeated Measures ANOVA** dialog box would then appear as in Figure 12.

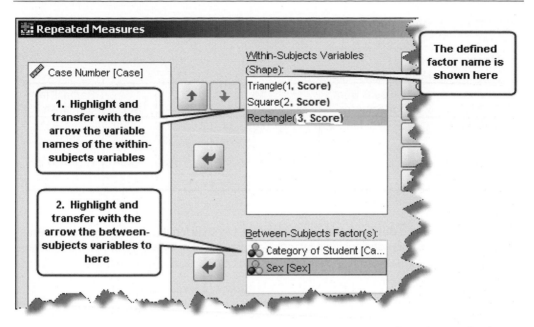

Figure 12. The upper part of the **Repeated Measures** dialog box for a three-factor mixed factorial experiment with one within subjects factor and two between subjects factors

The output includes the following tables. Output 17 shows the tests of the within subjects factor *Shape* and its various interactions with the two between subjects factors and Output 18 shows the tests of the between subjects factors *Category* and *Sex*. The results in Output 17 show that the factor *Shape* and the interaction of *Shape* and *Category* are significant at the 1% level but the interaction of *Shape* and *Sex* and the triple interaction are not significant. The results in Output 18 show that the factor *Category* is significant at the 1% level but neither the factor *Sex* nor the interaction between *Sex* and *Category* is significant.

The profile plot in Output 19 shows a crossing-over of the lines for the significant interaction of *Shape* and *Category*.

Tests of Within-Subjects Effects

Measure: Score

Source	Type III Sum of Squares	df	Mean Square	F	Sig.	Partial Eta Squared
Shape	519.62	2	259.81	29.39	.000	.786
Shape * Category	1277.74	2	638.87	72.27	.000	.900
Shape * Sex	14.92	2	7.46	.84	.448	.095
Shape * Category * Sex	7.86	2	3.93	.44	.649	.053
Error(Shape)	141.44	16	8.84			

Output 17. The edited **Within-Subjects Effects** table showing the **F ratio** and **Partial Eta Squared** for the within subjects factor *Shape* and its interactions with the two between subjects factors *Category* and *Sex*

Tests of Between-Subjects Effects

Measure: Score
Transformed Variable: Average

Source	Type III Sum of Squares	df	Mean Square	F	Sig.	Partial Eta Squared
Category	1093.34	1	1093.34	107.69	.000	.931
Sex	22.75	1	22.75	2.24	.173	.219
Category * Sex	6.28	1	6.28	.62	.454	.072
Error	81.22	8	10.15			

Output 18. The edited **Between-Subjects Effects** table showing the **F ratio** and **Partial Eta Squared** for the two between subjects factors *Category* and *Sex* together with their interaction

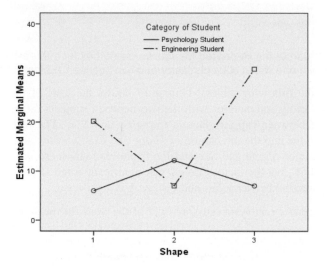

Output 19. The profile plot showing the significant interaction of *Shape* and *Category*

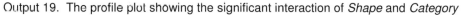

Testing for simple main effects and interactions in the A ×B ×(C) mixed factorial experiment

In the event of a significant two-factor interaction, the researcher might well proceed to test for simple main effects. Since the procedure presents no new issues, we shall not describe the syntax for the tests for simple main effects here.

Since, in the current example, the three-factor interaction is statistically insignificant, we would not go on to test for simple interactions. Had the interaction proved to be significant, however, we would certainly have considered testing the simple interactions for significance.

In general notation, the syntax for testing for a simple interaction between factors A and B at each of the three levels of factor C is as follows:

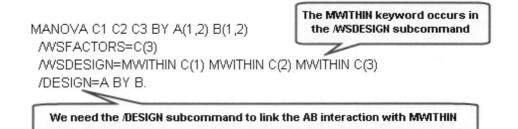

MANOVA C1 C2 C3 BY A(1,2) B(1,2)
/WSFACTORS=C(3)
/WSDESIGN=MWITHIN C(1) MWITHIN C(2) MWITHIN C(3)
/DESIGN=A BY B.

> The MWITHIN keyword occurs in the /WSDESIGN subcommand

> We need the /DESIGN subcommand to link the AB interaction with MWITHIN

Should a test for a simple interaction show significance, you might wish to proceed to make tests of simple, simple main effects. The syntax reads as follows:

MANOVA C1 C2 C3 BY A(1,2) B(1,2)
/WSFACTORS=C(3)
/WSDESIGN=MWITHIN C(1) MWITHIN C(2) MWITHIN C(3)
/DESIGN=A WITHIN B(1) A WITHIN B(2) A WITHIN B(3).

Here, we are asking for tests of simple, simple main effects of factor A at combinations of factors B and C: B(1)C(1), B(2)C(1), B(3)C(1) and so on. In the output (not shown here), these simple, simple main effects will look like interactions, because their labels contain the keyword BY with MWITHIN.

10.4 THE MULTIVARIATE ANALYSIS OF VARIANCE (MANOVA)

In the analysis of variance (ANOVA), there is just ONE dependent variable. There may, as we have seen, be several factors (that is, independent variables) and, as a consequence, **Data View** will contain several variables. Such a data set, however, is still regarded as **univariate**, because it contains only one variable, namely the DV, that is of central interest and is measured during the investigation. This is still essentially true if the researcher has further data on the participants in the form of measurements on a **covariate**, that is, a variable which correlates (or covaries) with the DV and may inflate the error term in the F tests. We shall have two measured variables; but interest still focuses on the DV and the purpose of the technique known as **analysis of covariance (ANCOVA)** is to 'purify' the data by removing the effects of the covariate, thereby reducing their 'noisiness' and permitting a more powerful ANOVA F test.

A researcher, however, will often wish to study the effects of experimental or group factors upon more than one DV. For example, in an experiment on the influence of drugs upon skilled performance, there might be measures of speed and errors, as well as the participant's performance score. Such an experiment will result in a **multivariate** data set, that is, one in which two or more of the variables are measured during the course of the investigation with a view to investigating how they are affected by the factors in the experimental design. Such additional DVs are quite different from covariates, in that, far from being merely potential causes of noise in the data (which must therefore be cleansed of their contamination), they are of central interest in their own right.

A researcher with a multivariate data set of this kind might be tempted to run a univariate ANOVA on each of the measures in the study. This, indeed, has been (and still is) a very common approach to the analysis of multivariate data. A major problem, however, is that the DVs are highly likely to be correlated. As a result, the outcomes of the various univariate ANOVAs are not independent. This can have serious consequences for the interpretation of the p-values from the F tests: the type I error rate, for example, may increase to an unacceptably high level.

The **multivariate analysis of variance (MANOVA)** is a set of techniques designed specially for the purpose of analysing simultaneously the results of experiments with several DVs.

10.4.1 What the MANOVA does

The MANOVA is an extension or generalisation of the univariate ANOVA to multivariate data sets. We have seen that the one-way ANOVA tests the null hypothesis that any differences there may be among the group means on a single DV have arisen merely through sampling error. In MANOVA, the object of the exercise is to decide whether inter-group differences on a *linear combination of the DVs* could have arisen through sampling error.

The linear functions that emerge from the MANOVA are known as **discriminant functions**. They have the general form:

$$D = b_0 + b_1 DV_1 + b_2 DV_2 + ... + b_p DV_p \quad \text{- - - (2)}$$

A discriminant function

where it is assumed that there are p dependent variables in the experiment. Each of the participants in the experiment will receive, in addition to scores on the DVs, an additional score on the discriminant function D. The values of the constants $b_0, b_1, ... b_p$ are chosen so that the distributions of D among the groups are spread out on the range of variation of D to the greatest possible extent: that is, the variability of D between groups is maximised. In this sense, the function D can be said to 'discriminate' among the groups.

If there are more than two groups, more than one discriminant function will be extracted. If there are k groups, there will be $k - 1$ discriminant functions. During the MANOVA, the extraction of the first discriminant function D_1 is followed by the extraction of the second discriminant function D_2, which is so constructed that it is independent of (the technical expression is **orthogonal to**) D_1. The process continues until all $k - 1$ discriminant functions have been extracted. Each participant will now have, in addition to a score on each DV, $k - 1$ extra scores, one on each of the discriminant functions.

MANOVA, then, finds orthogonal linear combinations of the DVs known as **discriminant functions** which maximise inter-group differences on their mean values, which are known as **group centroids**. The one-way MANOVA, in fact, is mathematically identical with the technique known as **discriminant analysis**: the meaning of the term 'discriminant' is exactly the same in both cases. The differences lie in the context and emphasis of the research. The MANOVA is used to analyse the results of experiments with several dependent variables to investigate and confirm differences among treatment groups; whereas discriminant analysis is used, usually with correlational (rather than experimental) data, to predict group membership from various measures. The researcher, for instance, might use discriminant analysis to predict diagnostic categories from scores on a battery of clinical scales. The output from discriminant analysis (see Chapter 14) reflects the difference in orientation. Although it contains many of the core statistics in the MANOVA output (with identical values), there are additional statistics of particular interest to the researcher who is trying to predict group membership.

While discriminant functions can each be analysed with a univariate, one-way ANOVA to compare the group centroids or means, additional techniques are available enabling the researcher to ascertain the relative contribution of each discriminant function to the between groups variance and of the DVs to the variance accounted for by each discriminant function. It is also possible, from the discriminant functions, to predict group membership, a process known as **classification**.

For these various purposes, SPSS computes a variety of statistics. One of the most important of these statistics is **Wilks's Lambda (Λ)**, which enables the researcher to ascertain not only the significance of differences among the group centroids or means of the discriminant functions, but also the contributions of each of the functions to the total variance (Tabachnick and Fidell, 2007).

10.4.2   How the MANOVA works

The presence of several DVs makes the mathematics of the MANOVA more complicated than that of the ANOVA. In the one-way ANOVA, the total variability, as measured by the total sum of squares, is partitioned into between groups and within groups components and (after adjustments for their different degrees of freedom), the two variance estimates are compared by means of an F ratio to test the null hypothesis of equality, in the population, of the group means. Something basically similar happens in the MANOVA as well; but the analogues of point (or scalar) quantities such as the between and within sums of squares are rectangular arrays of numbers, known as **matrices**. Conceptually, though, the parallels are very close.

We have already encountered the **variance-covariance** matrix in Chapter 9, where we discussed the within subjects ANOVA. The values running along the principal diagonal of the variance-covariance matrix (the cells running from the top left to the bottom right of the matrix) are variances and the off-diagonal values are covariances between pairs of the repeated measures. The safe use of the within subjects ANOVA requires that the variance-covariance matrix must have the property of **sphericity**, that is, the values of the covariances must be (within sampling error) uniform. One of the great advantages of the MANOVA over the within subjects ANOVA is that sphericity is not required. This is especially relevant when the MANOVA is used as an alternative to the ANOVA to analysis data from within subjects experiments (see below).

In the MANOVA, the point values embodying the total variability, the between groups variability and the within groups variability that are used in the ANOVA, namely, SS_{total}, $SS_{between}$ and SS_{within}, respectively, are replaced by values calculated from variance-covariance matrices. We have seen that the building block from which a covariance is calculated is the **cross-product** $(X - M_X)(Y - M_Y)$. The numerator of the covariance is the sum of cross-products SP. If we take deviations of the scores on the DVs from their respective grand means, ignoring the group means, we have a variance-covariance matrix which is the analogue of the total sum of squares in the ANOVA. If we take the deviations of the group means from the grand means, we have a matrix corresponding to the between groups sum of squares in

ANOVA. If we take the deviations of the scores from their group means, we have a matrix corresponding to the within groups sum of squares in the ANOVA. We shall term the total, between groups and within groups matrices T, B and W, respectively. Rather than merely measuring variance or variability, however, as in the ANOVA, these matrices also measure covariance, or shared variability.

Matrices with the same numbers of rows and columns can be added, producing a matrix of the same **dimensions** (i.e. the same numbers of rows and columns), whose elements are the sums of the corresponding elements in the component matrices. For example,

$$\underbrace{\begin{pmatrix} 2 & 1 & 3 & 1 \\ 5 & 0 & 1 & 2 \end{pmatrix}}_{M_1} + \underbrace{\begin{pmatrix} 2 & 1 & 3 & 1 \\ 5 & 0 & 1 & 2 \end{pmatrix}}_{M_2} = \underbrace{\begin{pmatrix} 4 & 2 & 6 & 2 \\ 10 & 0 & 2 & 4 \end{pmatrix}}_{M_3 = M_1 + M_2}$$

So, in MANOVA, we have a partition of the total variance-covariance matrix into between groups and within groups components thus:

$$T = B + W \ \text{- - - (3)}$$

Partition of the total variance-covariance

where B and W are the between groups and within groups variance-covariance matrices, respectively. From such a matrix, however, a point analogue of the variance can be calculated, namely, the **determinant** of the variance-covariance matrix. The determinant can be thought of as measuring variance plus covariance. A determinant is denoted by the use of two vertical lines: $|\ \ |$: the determinants of the between groups and within groups matrices are $|B|$ and $|W|$, respectively.

In the one-way ANOVA, the F statistic is used to test the null hypothesis of equality of the group means. In MANOVA, several statistics have been proposed for testing the null hypothesis of equality of the group centroids. These statistics include **Wilks's lambda**, **Pillai's criterion**, **Hotelling's trace** and **Roy's principal root**. Wilks's lambda divides the determinant of the within groups matrix by the sum of the determinants of the within groups and between groups matrices:

$$\Lambda = \frac{|W|}{|W| + |B|} \ \text{- - - (4)} \ \textbf{Wilks's lambda}$$

We can think of Wilks's lambda as expressing the error variance as a proportion of the total variance. From Wilks's lambda, an approximate F statistic can be calculated. (An approximate chi-square statistic can also be used.) The degrees of freedom of F are given by complex formulae with which we shall not concern ourselves here (see Tabachnick & Fidell, 2007, p259).

Recall that in univariate one-way ANOVA, a measure of effect size is eta squared (η^2), where

$$\eta^2 = \frac{SS_{between}}{SS_{total}} \ \text{- - - (5)} \ \textbf{Eta squared}$$

For simplicity, Wilks' lambda can be thought of as the proportion of the total variance that is *within* groups, rather than *between* groups, as in eta squared. In the context of one-way ANOVA (where there is just one DV), in fact, lambda is simply 1 minus eta squared:

$$\Lambda = 1 - \eta^2 \text{ - - - (6)}$$

Wilks' lambda and eta squared

This comparison extends to the situation where, rather than one DV, we have a discriminant function of several DVs. The value of Λ, like that of η^2, can range in value from 0 to 1. Since, however, lambda is measuring *within* groups rather than *between* groups variability, a value of Λ close to zero indicates a *large* separation among the means; whereas a value close to unity indicates a *small* separation.

How discriminant functions are constructed: eigenvectors and eigenvalues

We have seen that a discriminant function D is of the form shown earlier in equation (2):

$$D = b_0 + b_1 DV_1 + b_2 DV_2 + ... + b_p DV_p$$

where p is the number of dependent variables. A **vector** is a row or column of values, as opposed to a **scalar**, which is a single value. In a matrix, any row or column is a vector. From some matrices, it is possible to calculate a special vector known as an **eigenvector**. In the MANOVA, the values in an eigenvector are the coefficients of a discriminant function: there is an eigenvector for each discriminant function extracted by the MANOVA. Associated with each eigenvector and discriminant function is an **eigenvalue** (λ) (or **characteristic root**). The eigenvalue measures the proportion of the variance accounted for by that function. An eigenvalue has a maximum value of 1, which would mean that its discriminant function accounts for 100% of the variance.

Eigenvectors and eigenvalues are ubiquitous in multivariate statistics: 'Most of the multivariate procedures rely on eigenvalues and their corresponding eigenvectors (also called characteristic roots and vectors) in one way or another because they consolidate the variance in a matrix (the *eigenvalue*) while providing the linear combination of variables (the *eigenvector*) to do it' (Tabachnick & Fidell, 2007; p931).

We have already looked at Wilks's lambda in the context of the comparison between within groups and between groups variance-covariance matrices. Lambda can also be expressed in terms of eigenvalues:

$$\Lambda = \prod_i^d \frac{1}{(1 + \lambda_i)} \text{ - - - (7)}$$

Wilks's lambda expressed in terms of eigenvalues

where d is the number of discriminant functions extracted by the MANOVA. The symbol Π (pi) stands for 'product': the d terms $1/(1 + \lambda_i)$ are multiplied together. The greater the eigenvalues, the smaller the value of Wilks's lambda, bearing in mind that lambda is the *error* variance-covariance expressed as a proportion: the *smaller* the value of lambda, the greater the power of the discriminant function to discriminate among the groups.

The other principal statistics that appear in the SPSS MANOVA output, namely, the **Pillai-Bartlett trace**, **Hotellings T^2 (Hotelling-Lawley trace)** and **Roy's largest root**, are all functions of the eigenvalues λ. The simplest of these measures, Roy's largest root, is simply the largest value of λ. Since the first eigenvector (and discriminant function) to be extracted has the largest eigenvalue, Roy's statistic is the ratio of the between groups to the within groups variance for the first discriminant function.

10.4.3   Assumptions of MANOVA

In univariate ANOVA, the data should be normally distributed. In MANOVA, the distributions of the DVs should be **multivariate normal**: if there are k DVs, then for any set of fixed values of k – 1 of them, the distribution of the remaining variable is also normal. The assumption of multivariate normality is the counterpart, in multivariate statistics, of the assumption of normality of distribution in univariate ANOVA.

In univariate ANOVA, the data should meet the requirement of homogeneity of variance. In MANOVA, the counterpart of this assumption is **homogeneity of variance-covariance matrices**: that is, it is assumed that the variance-covariance matrices in the different groups have all been sampled from the same population and so can be combined to give a pooled estimate of error, just as in the ANOVA, the cell variances are combined in the within groups mean square. The assumption of homogeneity of variance-covariance matrices (which is tested by Box's test) is quite a separate property from **sphericity**, that is, the homogeneity of the covariances among the repeated measures in the within subjects ANOVA, which is tested with the Mauchly test. The great advantage of MANOVA is that homogeneity of covariance is not a requirement and for this reason, some prefer to use MANOVA for the analysis of data from within subjects experiments.

To some extent, MANOVA is robust to some violation of the assumptions of multivariate normality and homogeneity of variance-covariance matrices. As in the case of between subjects ANOVA, when sample sizes are large and equal among groups, all is likely to be well. In the ANOVA, the greatest threat to the accuracy of the p-values of the F tests is a combination of unequal sample sizes and heterogeneity of variance. In the MANOVA, the parallel is a combination of unequal sample sizes and disparities among the variance-covariance matrices in different groups: if the larger samples have larger variances and covariances, the p-values are likely to be too large; whereas if the smaller samples have larger variances and covariances, the p-values are likely to be too small (Tabachnick & Fidell, 2007; p252). This consideration has implications for the choice between the various test statistics that are available.

The presence of strong associations among the variables is known as **multicollinearity**. In the extreme case of a perfect correlation between two of the DVs, the variance-covariance matrix is **singular**, that is, the determinant does not exist and the key statistics cannot be calculated. If the data show multicollinearity, one or more of the dependent variables must be removed before the MANOVA can run successfully.

10.4.4   Relation of MANOVA to within subjects ANOVA

The reader will recall that in Section 10.2.4, the output for the within subjects ANOVA included a table of **Multivariate tests** (see Output 2) which at that stage was ignored. Here we can note that if we consider the levels of the within subjects factor in an ANOVA as a set of DVs, then we shall have a set of data suitable for analysis with MANOVA.

10.4.5   Application of MANOVA to the shape recognition example

In Section 10.1.1, we described the analysis of data from an experiment of design A × (B) using the mixed or split-plot ANOVA. Included in the SPSS output is a table of **Multivariate Tests** which we omitted from that section, but which is shown in Output 20 below.

Multivariate Tests[b]

Effect		Value	F	Hypothesis df	Error df	Sig.
Shape	Pillai's Trace	.841	23.884[a]	2.000	9.000	.000
	Wilks' Lambda	.159	23.884[a]	2.000	9.000	.000
	Hotelling's Trace	5.308	23.884[a]	2.000	9.000	.000
	Roy's Largest Root	5.308	23.884[a]	2.000	9.000	.000
Shape * Category	Pillai's Trace	.941	71.159[a]	2.000	9.000	.000
	Wilks' Lambda	.059	71.159[a]	2.000	9.000	.000
	Hotelling's Trace	15.813	71.159[a]	2.000	9.000	.000
	Roy's Largest Root	15.813	71.159[a]	2.000	9.000	.000

a. Exact statistic

b. Design: Intercept + Category
Within Subjects Design: Shape

Output 20. Table of results of multivariate tests for the data in Table 1

The results in Output 20 were obtained by running the MANOVA on the same data that we used for the mixed ANOVA. It is clear that, on all four criteria, there is both a significant main effect of *Shape* and a significant *Shape*Category* interaction. These results are consistent with those of the mixed ANOVA, which also gave significant results for *Shape* and for the interaction. We should note, however, that the ANOVA and the MANOVA do not always agree when applied to the same data. The purpose of this section is to show how the results in Output 20 were obtained.

Suppose we were to re-analyse the data set in Table 1 with the MANOVA, treating the three levels of the *Shape* factor as three DVs (*Triangles*; *Squares*; *Rectangles*), rather than different levels of a within subjects factor. The IV, as before, is the group factor *Category*. Thus we now have an experiment with one IV and three DVs. The reader, however, will see that there is a problem. In redefining the data set as having one between subjects factor and three measures or dependent variables, we effectively 'lose' a factor! How, then, can we use the MANOVA to test for the presence of an interaction between the factors of *Shape* and *Group*?

Figure 13 shows **Data View** with the grouping variable and the participants' scores with the Triangle, the Square and the Rectangle. There are also, however, two extra variables: SquareMinusTriangle and RectangleMinusSquare. These variables, whose names are self-explanatory, were added to the original data set very quickly by using the **Compute Variable** command in the **Transform** menu (Figure 14):

	Case	Category	Triangle	Square	Rectangle	SquareMinus Triangle	RectangleMinus Square
1	1	1	2	12	7	10	-5
2	2	1	8	10	9	2	-1
3	3	1	4	15	3	11	-12
4	4	1	6	9	7	3	-2
5	5	1	9	13	8	4	-5
6	6	1	7	14	8	7	-6
7	7	2	13	3	35	-10	32
8	8	2	21	4	30	-17	26
9	9	2	26	10	35	-16	25
10	10	2	22	8	30	-14	22
11	11	2	20	9	28	-11	19
12	12	2	19	8	27	-11	19

Figure 13. **Data View**, showing the addition to the data set of two difference variables

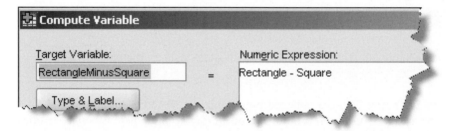

Figure 14. Compute Rectangle – Square with the **Compute Variable** command

An interaction between the *Group* and *Shape* factors would be captured in an inter-group difference between either or both these new difference variables. Should a comparison, using the MANOVA, of these two new variables show a significant difference between the two groups, we can conclude that an interaction is indeed present.

We shall begin by running a MANOVA on the three columns containing the participants' raw scores under the Triangle, Square and Rectangle conditions.

- Select **Analyze→General Linear Model→Multivariate...** to open the **Multivariate** dialog box (Figure 15).
- Transfer the DVs to the **Dependent Variables** box.
- Click **Options** and select **Descriptive statistics**, **Estimates of effect size**, and **Homogeneity tests** for checking the assumption of homogeneity of the variance-covariance matrix (Figure 16). Click **Continue** to return to the **MANOVA** dialog box.
- Click **OK** to run the MANOVA.

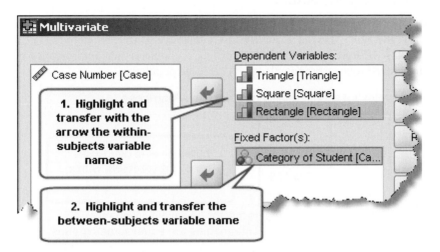

Figure 15. The **Multivariate** dialog box with the DVs transferred to the **Dependent Variables** box and the IV to the **Fixed Factor(s)** box

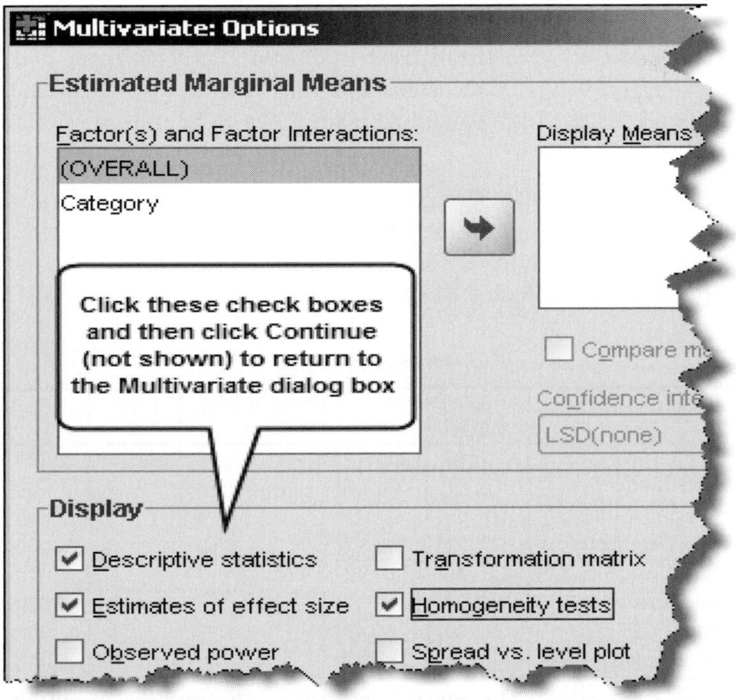

Figure 16. The **Multivariate: Options** dialog box with **Descriptive statistics**, **Estimates of effect size** and **Homogeneity tests** selected

10.4.6 The MANOVA output

After tables of the **Between Subjects Factors** and **Descriptive Statistics** (not reproduced here), there is the **Box's Test of Equality of Covariance Matrices** (Output 21). With a p-value of 0.628, we have no evidence against the hypothesis that the variance-covariance matrices in the two groups were sampled from the same population.

Box's Test of Equality of Covariance Matrices[a]

Box's M	6.539
F	.727
df1	6
df2	724.528
Sig.	.628

With a p-value (Sig.) > .05, there is no problem with a lack of homogeneity

Tests the null hypothesis that the observed covariance matrices of the dependent variables are equal across groups.

a. Design: Intercept+Category

Output 21. The **Box's Test of Equality of Covariance Matrices** table

The results of the MANOVA are summarised in Output 22. The upper part of the table (labelled Intercept) reports tests of the null hypothesis that the overall mean score on the discriminant function is zero. Since we did not expect that to be true anyway, we can ignore the upper four rows in the table.

The lower part of the table (labelled Category) table is the multivariate equivalent of the one-way ANOVA that was carried out on the participants' average scores over the three shape conditions. The two group centroids are significantly different. This result is consistent with the result of the one-way ANOVA on the average scores.

Multivariate Tests[b]

Effect		Value	F	Hypothesis df	Error df	Sig.	Partial Eta Squared
Intercept	Pillai's Trace	.99	271.18[a]	3	8	.000	.990
	Wilks' Lambda	.01	271.18[a]	3	8	.000	.990
	Hotelling's Trace	101.69	271.18[a]	3	8	.000	.990
	Roy's Largest Root	101.69	271.18[a]	3	8	.000	.990
Category	Pillai's Trace	.96	63.47[a]	3	8	.000	.960
	Wilks' Lambda	.04	63.47[a]	3	8	.000	.960
	Hotelling's Trace	23.80	63.47[a]	3	8	.000	.960
	Roy's Largest Root	23.80	63.47[a]	3	8	.000	.960

a. Exact statistic

b. Design: Intercept+Category

The p-value (Sig.) for the factor *Category* associated with all the multivariate statistics is <.01 (significant at the .01 level)

Output 22. The **Multivariate Tests** table

Just as in the case of ANOVA, this table shows a highly significant difference for *Group*. The effect size (.96) is larger than the ANOVA value (.91). The next table (not reproduced here) is **Levene's Test of Equality of Error Variances** which tests the null hypothesis that the error variance of the dependent variable is equal across groups.

The final edited table (Output 23) lists the univariate tests on each of the DVs for the IV in the row labelled *Group* (the three groups).

Tests of Between-Subjects Effects

Source	Dependent Variable	Type III Sum of Squares	df	Mean Square	F	Sig.	Partial Eta Squared
Category	Triangle	602.08	1	602.08	48.23	.000	.828
	Square	80.08	1	80.08	11.98	.006	.545
	Rectangle	1704.08	1	1704.08	210.81	.000	.955
Error	Triangle	124.83	10	12.48			
	Square	66.83	10	6.68			
	Rectangle	80.83	10	8.08			
Total	Triangle	2781.00	12				
	Square	1249.00	12				
	Rectangle	6079.00	12				

The relative magnitudes of *F* show that the two categories of students differ most greatly in recognising rectangles followed by triangles and finally squares

Output 23. The univariate tests for each DV

In Output 23, the values of partial eta squared show that for recognising squares, the between-groups difference is less than the differentials for the other shapes. This finding is in agreement with the outcomes of the ANOVA Bonferroni comparisons (see Output 8).

Testing for the presence of an interaction

If we return to the **Multivariate** dialog box, remove the three *Shape* variables from the right-hand box, replace them with the two difference variables and re-run the analysis, we shall obtain the multivariate test results shown in Output 24.

Multivariate Tests[b]

Effect		Value	F	Hypothesis df	Error df	Sig.
Intercept	Pillai's Trace	.841	23.884[a]	2.000	9.000	.000
	Wilks' Lambda	.159	23.884[a]	2.000	9.000	.000
	Hotelling's Trace	5.308	23.884[a]	2.000	9.000	.000
	Roy's Largest Root	5.308	23.884[a]	2.000	9.000	.000
Category	Pillai's Trace	.941	71.159[a]	2.000	9.000	.000
	Wilks' Lambda	.059	71.159[a]	2.000	9.000	.000
	Hotelling's Trace	15.813	71.159[a]	2.000	9.000	.000
	Roy's Largest Root	15.813	71.159[a]	2.000	9.000	.000

a. Exact statistic

b. Design: Intercept + Category

Output 24. Results of the MANOVA of the difference variables *SquareMinusTriangle* and *RectangleMinusSquare*

Although the upper and lower part of the table are labelled 'Intercept' and 'Category', respectively, we have the results of the tests for a main effect of the *Shape* factor and the *Shape* × *Category* interaction (compare with Output 20). The use of difference variables rather than raw scores has captured both the main effect of *Shape* and the interaction.

There are several ways of proceeding when a MANOVA main effect or an interaction is significant but details of these lie beyond the scope of this book. SPSS provides a step-by-step tutorial - click the **Help** button in the **MANOVA** dialog box and then click **Show me** at the foot of the resulting text box. Books such as Tabachnick & Fidell (2007) and Field (2005) suggest further procedures such as Roy-Bargmann Stepdown Analysis and Discriminant Analysis.

10.5   A FINAL WORD

In this chapter, we have described the analysis of data from experiments of mixed factorial (or split-plot) design, in which some (but not all) factors have repeated measures. Experiments of this type are very widespread in research.

On the positive side, the presence of within subjects factors has both convenience and improved power for the statistical tests. On the negative side, the very considerable difficulties with within subjects designs that we discussed in Chapter 9, together with their implications for the determination of power and effect size and their consequences for error rates, all apply to the designs we have described in this chapter. The main problem is that having repeated measures on some factors produces correlated data; and the patterns of those correlations can have consequences for the statistical tests. Should the variance-covariance matrices lack the property of homogeneity of covariance or sphericity, the F tests will produce too many significant results. Conservative tests are available to attempt to control the **Type I error rate**; but there has been considerable discussion about how effective they really are.

An alternative approach to the analysis of data from experiments of mixed factorial design is the multivariate analysis of variance (MANOVA). The MANOVA does not require sphericity; although the variance-covariance matrices in the various groups should be homogeneous.

We have taken only a very brief look at MANOVA using a simple example. MANOVA designs can have many more factors and DVs as well as covariates, and can include contrast analyses. To learn more about these techniques, you should consult textbooks such as those already cited before embarking on a MANOVA.

Recommended reading

There are many readable textbooks on ANOVA, which provide extensive coverage of within subjects ANOVA. These include:

Howell, D. C. (2007). *Statistical methods for psychology (6th ed.).* Belmont, CA: Thomson/Wadsworth.
Keppel, G., & Wickens, T. D. (2004). *Design and analysis: A researcher's handbook (4th ed.).* Upper Saddle River, New Jersey: Pearson Prentice Hall.

There are now several excellent textbooks on multivariate statistics, including MANOVA. These include:

Field, A. (2005). *Discovering Statistics Using SPSS (2nd ed.).* London: Sage.

Tabachnick, B. G., & Fidell, L. S. (2007). *Using multivariate statistics (5th ed.).* Boston: Allyn & Bacon (Pearson International Edition).

Todman, J., & Dugard, P. (2006). *Approaching multivariate statistics: An introduction for psychology.* Hove: Psychology Press.

Exercises

Exercise 15 *Mixed ANOVA: two-factor experiment* and Exercise 16 *Mixed ANOVA: three-factor experiment* are available in www.psypress.com/spss-made-simple and click on Exercises.

CHAPTER 11

Measuring statistical association

11.1   INTRODUCTION

So far, this book has been concerned with comparing the averages of different samples with respect to one variable: for example, a drug group might be compared with a placebo group; right-handed people might be compared with left-handed people; the trained might be compared with the untrained; males might be compared with females. In this chapter, we shall be concerned with the presence and strength of the statistical association between two variables.

11.1.1   A correlational study

Suppose that a researcher believes that exposure to screen violence promotes actual violence in children. Ethical and practical considerations rule out an experiment in which the independent variable of amount of exposure to screen violence is manipulated to determine its effects upon the incidence of violent behaviour. The investigator, therefore, decides upon a correlational strategy. Twenty-seven children are measured on two variables:
  1. Their exposure to screen violence (*Exposure*).
  2. Their actual violence (*Actual*).

The researcher measures these variables in the expectation that they will show a positive association: there should be a tendency for those with high *Exposure* also to score highly on *Actual* violence; those low on *Exposure* should also be low on *Actual* violence; and those with average *Exposure* should fall within the normal range on *Actual* violence. This strategy will not yield the strong evidence for causation that a true experiment would yield; however, an association would at least be consistent with the researcher's view that exposure to screen violence encourages actual violence in children.

Correlational research like this results in a **bivariate** data set, which can be depicted in a **scatterplot**. The scatterplot of the children's actual violence against their exposure to screen violence is shown in Figure 1. In the scatterplot, each person is represented as a point, the coordinates of which are the person's scores on the *Exposure* and *Actual* scales, which are marked out on the vertical and horizontal axes, respectively.

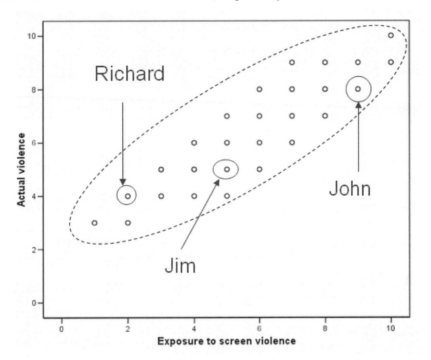

Figure 1. Scatterplot of *Actual Violence* against *Exposure to Screen Violence*

It is evident from the scatterplot that there is indeed an association between *Exposure* and *Actual* violence: John was highest on *Exposure* and he was also the most violent of the three children identified in the figure; Richard, with least *Exposure*, was also the least violent; Jim had intermediate scores on both variables. On the other hand, the association is imperfect: four children, including Jim, scored 5 on *Exposure*; but their *Actual* violence scores ranged from 4 to 7.

11.1.2 Linear relationships

One variable is said to be a **linear function** of another if the graph of the first upon the second is a straight line. Temperature in degrees Fahrenheit is a linear function of temperature in degrees Celsius, as shown in Figure 2.

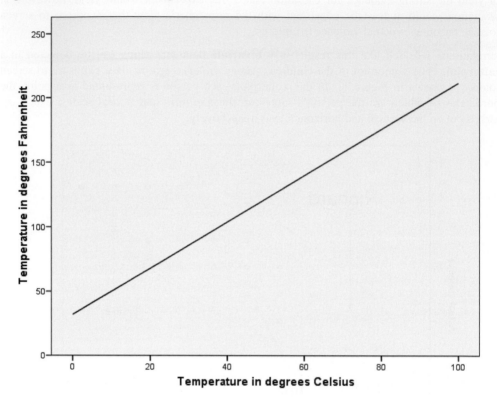

Figure 2. A linear (straight line) relationship

Errors of measurement

In many empirical disciplines, including medicine, biology and psychology, measurements have associated with them a considerable random, or **error** component. This means that, even if two variables do have a linear relationship, the points in their scatterplot will never lie on a straight line, as in Figure 2. Provided, however, that the scatterplot has an elliptical shape as in Figure 1, the relationship between the variables is *basically* linear in nature, subject to random errors of measurement.

If the slope of the longer axis of the ellipse is positive, the variables are said to be **positively correlated**; if it is negative, they are **negatively correlated**. The thinner the ellipse, the stronger the degree of linear relationship; the fatter the ellipse, the weaker the relationship.

If two variables are dissociated or independent, their scatterplot will be a circular cloud of points. Suppose two coins are each tossed 100 times and the number of heads recorded for each. The experiment is repeated, so that there are 1000 pairs of scores. We should not expect any association between the values for the first and second coins. The scatterplot will appear as in Figure 3.

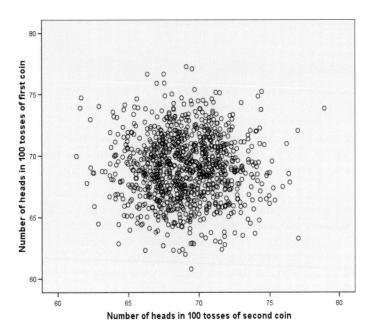

Figure 3. Scatterplot showing absence of association between two variables

11.2 THE PEARSON CORRELATION

The Pearson correlation is a measure of a supposed linear relationship between two variables. There are several different formulae for the Pearson correlation, two of the most common of which are as follows:

$$r_{XY} = \frac{\Sigma(X - M_X)(Y - M_Y)}{\sqrt{\Sigma(X - M_X)^2 \, \Sigma(Y - M_Y)^2}} = \frac{SP}{\sqrt{SS_X \, SS_Y}} \quad \text{- - - (1)} \quad \textbf{The Pearson correlation}$$

In the SS/SP version of the formula, SS stands for 'Sum of Squares' (i.e. the sum of the squared deviations from the mean) and SP stands for 'Sum of Products' (i.e. the sum of the products of the deviations from M_X and M_Y over all the participants in the study).

The range of values of the Pearson correlation

By definition, the value of r can vary only within the range from -1 to $+1$, inclusive.

$$-1 \le r \le +1 \quad \text{- - - (2)} \quad \textbf{Range of possible values of } r$$

This property confers upon the Pearson correlation a great advantage over another measure of association known as the **covariance**, which was described in Chapter 9. Unlike the covariance, the correlation coefficient is 'unit-free', in that it can be used to compare the degrees of association between pairs of variables measured in different units. A correlation between the heights and weights of fifty people measured in centimetres and grams respectively has the same value as the correlation between their heights and weights measured in inches and pounds.

The sign of a correlation

The sign of a correlation may reflect the natures of the variables being measured: one would not expect height to correlate negatively with weight. Often, however, the sign of a correlation is merely a matter of definition and scaling and therefore arbitrary. There exist measures of Decisiveness and Indecisiveness, which show a strong association. The strong negative correlation between the two measures, however, merely reflects the fact that the numerical scales progress in opposite directions. The two scales are, to a large extent, measuring the same dimension.

The important thing about a correlation is often its *absolute* value, i.e., its value with the sign ignored. Figure 4 shows two scatterplots: the first is the scatterplot of *Actual* violence upon *Exposure* to violence; the second is a scatterplot with the direction of the *Exposure* scale reversed (by multiplying the original *Exposure* scores by -1). In either case, the absolute value of the Pearson correlation is 0.90. A negative correlation of $-.0.90$ represents the same (strong) degree of linear association as a positive correlation of $+ 0.90$.

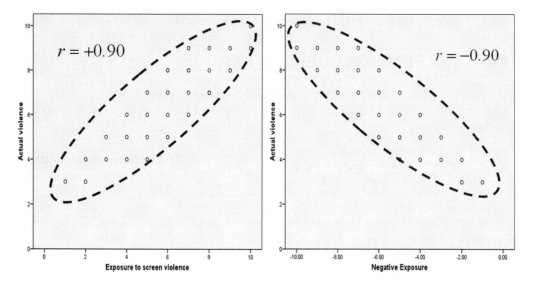

Figure 4. Scatterplots of data sets showing the same degree of association, but with correlations of opposite sign

A perfect linear association, with all the points in the scatterplot lying along the same straight line, would be reflected either in a correlation of $+1$ or a correlation of -1: either value would represent a perfect linear relationship.

Testing an obtained value of r for significance

The test for the significance of a correlation coefficient presupposes that the data have the property of **bivariate normality**, that is, at any particular value of either variable, the other variable has a normal distribution. If that requirement is met, the test of the null hypothesis that, in the bivariate normal population, the correlation is zero is made with the statistic *t*, where

$$t = \frac{r\sqrt{(n-2)}}{\sqrt{(1-r^2)}} \quad \text{with } (n-2) \text{ degrees of freedom.} \quad \text{- - - (3)} \quad \textbf{Testing } r \textbf{ for significance}$$

A word of warning

It is quite possible, from inspection of a scatterplot, to do two useful things:
1. See whether there is indeed a linear relationship between the variables, in which case the Pearson correlation would be a meaningful statistic to use;
2. Guess fairly accurately what the value of the Pearson correlation would be if calculated.

In other words, from inspection of the scatterplot alone, one can discern the most important features of the true relationship (if any) between two variables. So if we reason from the scatterplot to the statistics, we shall never go seriously wrong.

The converse, however, is not true: *given only the value of a Pearson correlation, one can say nothing whatsoever about the relationship between two variables*. Many years ago, in a famous paper, the statistician Anscombe (1973) presented some bivariate data sets which illustrate how misleading the value of the Pearson correlation can be. In one set, for instance, the correlation was high, yet the scatterplot showed no association whatsoever; in another, the correlation was zero, but the scatterplot showed a perfect, but nonlinear, association. The moral of this cautionary tale is clear: when studying the association between two variables, always construct a scatterplot, and interpret (or disregard) the Pearson correlation accordingly.

In the same paper, Anscombe gave us a useful rule for deciding whether there really is a robust linear relationship between two variables: should the shape of the scatterplot be unaltered by the removal of a few observations at random, the plot is an accurate depiction of the true relationship between the variables.

To sum up, the Pearson correlation is a measure of a *supposed* linear relationship between two variables; but the supposition of linearity must always be confirmed by inspection of the scatterplot.

11.2.1 Effect size

Unlike *t*, *F* or chi-square, the value of a correlation is, in itself, a measure of 'effect' size, bearing in mind that correlation does not imply causation. However, for the purposes of comparison with other measures of effect size, the **square** of the correlation r^2, which is known as the **coefficient of determination**, is often used instead. The reason for this will be explained in Chapter 12, where we shall see that the square of the Pearson correlation is the proportion of the variance of the scores on the target or criterion variable that is accounted for by regression upon another variable.

The Pearson correlation between the *Actual* and *Exposure* scores is .89. The value of the coefficient of determination (CD) is therefore $0.89^2 = 0.80$. This means that 80% of the variance of *Actual* scores is accounted for by regression.

It may be helpful to think of the coefficient of determination as the proportion of the variance of either variable that is shared with the other variable. This sharing of variance can be depicted by two overlapping circles, where the overlapping area represents the proportion of the variance of either variable that is shared with the other (Figure 5).

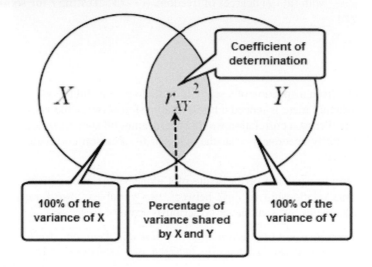

Figure 5. The coefficient of determination as the percentage of the variance of either variable that is shared with the other

In the coefficient of determination (r^2), we have a measure of effect size which is comparable to those we have met in the context of *t* tests and ANOVA. The ANOVA eta squared η^2 and adjusted R^2 statistics are actually coefficients of determination: they represent the proportion of the variance of the scores on the dependent variable that can be predicted from grouping variables representing the treatment categories, that is, as the proportion of shared variance. Effect size, therefore, might be classified as follows:

Effect size (r^2)	Size of Effect
<0.01 (<1%)	Small
0.01 to 0.10 (1-10%)	Medium
>0.10 (>10%)	Large

11.3   CORRELATION WITH SPSS

Table 1 shows the raw data that were pictured in the scatterplot in Figure 1.

	Exposure	Violence			Exposure	Violence
1	1	3	15	5	7
2	2	3	16	6	7
3	2	4	17	7	7
4	3	4	18	8	7
5	4	4	19	6	8
6	5	4	20	7	8
7	3	5	21	8	8
8	4	5	22	9	8
9	5	5	23	7	9
10	6	5	24	8	9
11	4	6	25	9	9
12	5	6	26	10	9
13	6	6	27	10	10
14	7	6			

Table 1. The raw data from the violence study

Preparing the SPSS data set

As usual, begin in **Variable View**. Name the variables *Actual* and *Exposure* and assign full variable labels, such as *Actual Violence* and *Exposure to Screen Violence*. Set the **Decimals** specification to zero in order to avoid unnecessary clutter in **Data View**. Switch to **Data View** and enter the data. Save the data set.

11.3.1 Obtaining a scatterplot

The procedure for plotting a scatterplot using **Chart Builder** is described in Section 5.7. Here we want a scatterplot of *Actual* against *Exposure*.

The default scatterplot will not show the zero point on the vertical scale. This can be done either by editing the obtained scatterplot or, beforehand, in the **Chart Builder**, by altering the specifications in the **Element Properties** dialog box. Follow the steps in Figure 6 to plot the scatterplot starting at zero on the **Y-Axis**.

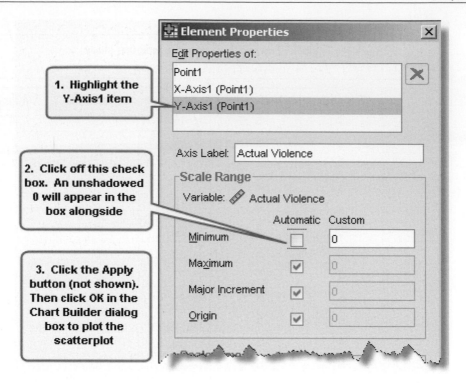

Figure 6. Editing the **Element Properties** dialog box to obtain a scatterplot showing the entire Y-Axis scale starting at zero

11.3.2   Obtaining the Pearson correlation

*   Choose **Analyze➔Correlate➔Bivariate…** (Figure 7) to open the **Bivariate Correlation** dialog box (Figure 8).
*   Complete the dialog as in Figure 8.

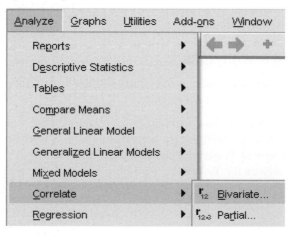

Figure 7. The **Correlate** menu with **Bivariate** highlighted

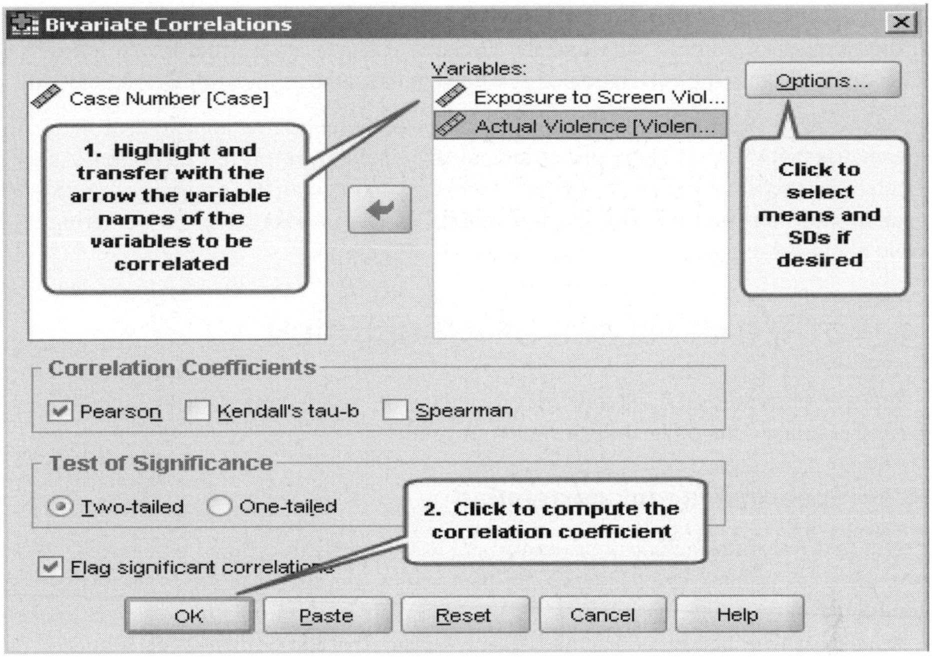

Figure 8. The **Bivariate Correlations** dialog for computing the Pearson correlation coefficient

11.3.3 Output for the Pearson correlation

Output 1 tabulates the Pearson correlation, with its p-value. The value for r is 0.892, which is significant beyond the 0.01 level. This is written as:

$$r(27) = 0.892; p < .01. \quad r^2 = 0.80$$

Since 80% of the variance is shared, the association is obviously a strong one.

Correlations

		Exposure to Screen Violence	Actual Violence
Exposure to Screen Violence	Pearson Correlation	1	.892**
	Sig. (2-tailed)		.000
	N	27	27
Actual Violence	Pearson Correlation	.892**	1
	Sig. (2-tailed)	.000	
	N	27	27

**. Correlation is significant at the 0.01 level (2-tailed).

> r = 0.892 and is significant at .01 level

> There are 27 pairs of values

> Since the correlation of Exposure with Actual is the same as the correlation of Actual with Exposure, the second row is a repeat of the first row

Output 1. The Pearson **Correlations** table

Notice that in Output 1, the information we need in the upper right cell of the table (the value of r, the number of pairs of data and the p-value) is duplicated in the lower left cell of the table. This is because the correlation of A with B is the same as the correlation of B with A.

Were we to have more than two variables, the results would have appeared in the form of a square matrix with entries above the principal diagonal (from top left to bottom right) being duplicated in the cells below it. When there are more than two variables, SPSS can be commanded to construct this **correlation matrix** (or **R-matrix**) simply by entering as many variable names as required into the **Variables** box (Figure 8).

11.4   OTHER MEASURES OF ASSOCIATION

The Pearson correlation is suitable only for data on continuous or scale variables. With ordinal or nominal data, other statistics must be used.

11.4.1   Spearman's rank correlation

The term **ordinal data** includes both ranks and assignments to ordered categories. When the same objects are ranked independently by two judges, the question arises as to the extent to which the two sets of ranks agree. This is a question about the strength of association between two variables which, although quantitative, are measured at the ordinal level. Suppose that the ranks assigned to ten paintings by two judges are as in Table 2.

Table 2. Ranks assigned by two judges to each of ten paintings										
Painting	A	B	C	D	E	F	G	H	I	J
First Judge	1	2	3	4	5	6	7	8	9	10
Second Judge	1	3	2	4	6	5	8	7	10	9

It is obvious that the judges generally agree closely in their rankings: at most, their assignments differ by a single rank. One way of measuring the level of agreement between the two judges is by calculating the Pearson correlation between the two sets of ranks. This correlation is known as the **Spearman rank correlation** r_S or as **Spearman's rho** ρ. Like eta squared, Spearman's rho is a *statistic*, not a parameter, and is thus an exception to the general rule about reserving Greek and Roman letters for parameters and statistics, respectively. While the defining formula for the Spearman rank correlation looks very different from that for the Pearson correlation, the two formulae are actually equivalent, provided that no ties are allowed.

The use of the Spearman rank correlation is not confined to ordinal data. Suppose the scatterplot of the bivariate distribution of two continuous variables shows that they are in a **monotonic** (increasing or decreasing together) but non-linear relationship, rendering the Pearson correlation an unsuitable measure of degree of association. The scores on both variables can be converted to ranks and the Spearman rank correlation calculated instead.

11.4.2   Kendall's tau statistics

The **Kendall's tau** (τ) statistics offer an alternative to the Spearman rank correlation as measures of agreement between rankings, or assignments to ordered categories. The basic idea is that one set of ranks can be converted into another by a succession of reversals of pairs of ranks in one set: the fewer the reversals needed to achieve the conversion (in relation to the total number of possible reversals), the larger the value of tau. The numerator of Kendall's tau is the difference between the number of pairs of objects whose ranks are concordant (i.e. they go in the same direction) and the number of discordant pairs. If the former predominate, the sign of tau is positive; if the latter predominate, tau is negative.

There are three different versions of Kendall's tau: **tau-a**, **tau-b** and **tau-c**. All three measures have the same numerator, the difference between the numbers of concordant and discordant pairs. In their denominators, however, they differ in the way they handle tied observations.

The denominator of the correlation **tau-a** is simply the total number of pairs. The problem with tau-a is that when there are ties, its range quickly becomes restricted, to the point where it becomes difficult to interpret.

The correlation **tau-b** has terms in the denominator that consider, in either variable, pairs that are tied on one variable but not on the other. (When there are no ties, the values of tau-a and tau-b are identical.)

The correlation **tau-c** was designed for situations where one wishes to measure agreement between assignments to unequal-sized sets of ordered categories. Provided the data meet certain requirements, the appropriate tau correlation can vary throughout the complete range from -1 to $+1$.

Note that the calculation of Kendall's statistics with ordinal data, in the form of assignments of target objects to ordered categories, is best handled by the **Crosstabs** procedure (see next section); indeed, **tau-c** (which is appropriate when the two variables have different numbers of categories) can only be obtained in **Crosstabs**.

11.4.3   Rank correlations with SPSS

In **Variable View**, name two variables, *Judge1* and *Judge2*. Click the **Data View** tab to switch to **Data View** and, from Table 2, enter the ranks assigned by the first judge into the *Judge1* column and those assigned by the second judge into the *Judge2* column.

- Choose **Analyze➜Correlate➜Bivariate...** to obtain the **Bivariate Correlations** dialog box (the completed version of which is shown in Figure 9). By default, the **Pearson** check box will be marked. Click off the **Pearson** check box and click the **Kendall's tau-b** and the **Spearman** check boxes.
- Transfer the variable names *Judge1* and *Judge2* to the **Variables:** box.
- Click **OK** to obtain the correlations shown in Output 2.

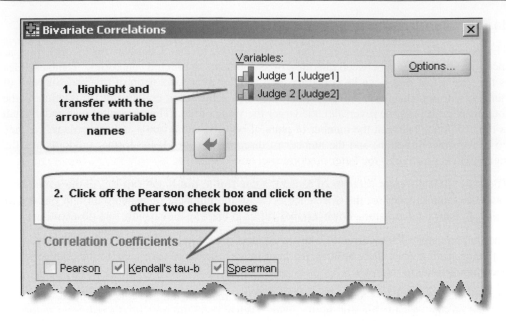

Figure 9. The completed **Bivariate Correlations** dialog for **Kendall's tau-b** and Spearman's rho

Correlations

			Judge 1	Judge 2
Kendall's tau_b	Judge 1	Correlation Coefficient	1.000	.822**
		Sig. (2-tailed)	.	.001
		N	10	10
	Judge 2	Correlation Coefficient	.822**	1.000
		Sig. (2-tailed)	.001	.
		N	10	10
Spearman's rho	Judge 1	Correlation Coefficient	1.000	.952**
		Sig. (2-tailed)	.	.000
		N	10	10
	Judge 2	Correlation Coefficient	.952**	1.000
		Sig. (2-tailed)	.000	.
		N	10	10

> Tau-b correlation is .822 with an associated p-value < .01

> Spearman's correlation is .952 with an associated p-value < .01

**. Correlation is significant at the 0.01 level (2-tailed).

Output 2. **Kendall** and **Spearman**'s rank correlations

Output 2 shows that the **Kendall correlation** is 0.82 and the **Spearman correlation** is 0.95. These values differ, but there is nothing untoward in this. The two statistics are based on quite different theoretical foundations and often take noticeably different values when calculated from the same data set. Incidentally, the Pearson option would have given the same value as the Spearman (0.95), because the procedure first transforms the raw data to ranks. The results of the Spearman test would be written as follows:

$$rho\ (10) = 0.95;\ p = < .01.$$

$$rho^2\ = 0.91,\ \text{a large effect.}$$

11.5 TESTING FOR ASSOCIATION IN NOMINAL DATA

A **nominal** data set consists of assignments of individuals to the categories making up qualitative attributes or variables, such as gender, blood group or nationality.

In Chapter 6, we discussed the use of the approximate **chi-square statistic** χ^2 to test the **goodness-of-fit** of a theoretical distribution of expected frequencies E to the distribution of the observed frequencies O over a set of categories.

If the attribute has k categories, the value of chi-square for the goodness-of-fit test is given by

$$\chi^2 = \sum_{\substack{all \\ categories}} \frac{(O-E)^2}{E} \text{ with } df = k - 1 \text{ - - - (4) \textbf{Chi-square goodness-of-fit test}}$$

The value of df is needed to specify the sampling distribution of χ^2 so that the null hypothesis (that the theoretical distribution gives a good account of the data) can be tested.

We have also seen that when people's membership of two sets of mutually exclusive and exhaustive categories (such as sex or blood group) is recorded, it is possible to construct a **crosstabulation**, or **contingency table** (see Chapter 4, Section 4.3.1). In the analysis of **categorical data** (that is nominal assignments or assignments to ordered categories), the crosstabulation is the equivalent of the scatterplot. Like the scatterplot, the contingency table provides an excellent means of inspecting a bivariate distribution in order to ascertain the presence of an association between the variables concerned.

See
Section
4.3.1

11.5.1 The chi-square test for association

A researcher has reason to believe that there should be a higher incidence of a potentially harmful antibody in patients whose tissue is of a certain 'critical' type. In a study of 79 patients, the incidence of the antibody in patients of four different tissue types, including the 'critical' category, are recorded. The results are presented in Table 3.

Table 3. Contingency table with a pattern of observed frequencies suggesting an association between *Tissue Type* and *Presence* of an antibody

Tissue type	Presence		Total
	No	Yes	
Critical	6	21	27
A	5	7	12
B	11	7	18
C	14	8	22
Total	36	43	79

Confirming the pattern: testing for the presence of an association

The pattern of the frequencies appears to confirm the research hypothesis: there is a noticeably higher incidence of the antibody in the Critical group.

The researcher's hypothesis is that there is an association between the variables of *Group* (the type of tissue) and the *Presence* (Yes or No) of the antibody. The null hypothesis H_0 is the negation of this: there is no association between the two attributes. While it would appear from Table 3 that the null hypothesis is false, a formal statistical test is required.

The null hypothesis that there is no association between the *Group* and *Presence* variables can be tested with the **chi-square test for association**. For each cell of the contingency table, the expected frequency E is calculated on the assumption that the attributes of *Group* and *Presence* are independent, and the values of E are compared with the corresponding observed frequencies O by means of the statistic χ^2, where

$$\chi^2 = \sum_{all\ cells} \frac{(O-E)^2}{E} \quad \text{- - - (5) \textbf{Chi-square association test}}$$

In general, if the attributes A and B consist of a and b categories, respectively, the value of the degrees of freedom of this chi-square statistic is given by

$$df = (a-1)(b-1) \quad \text{- - - (6) \textbf{Degrees of freedom}}$$

In the present example, $df = (4 - 1)(2 - 1) = 3$. In a 4×2 table with fixed marginal totals, the assignment of frequencies to only 3 cells completely determines the values of the frequencies in the remaining 5 cells.

The expected frequencies are calculated using estimates of probability derived from the marginal totals and the total frequency N in the following way. If R and C are the marginal totals of the row and the column that locate the cell in the contingency table, the expected frequency E_{RC} is given by

$$E_{RC} = \frac{R \times C}{N} \quad \text{- - - (7)} \quad \textbf{Expected frequency}$$

For example, for the top left cell in the contingency table, E = (27×36)/79 = 12.30. The expected frequencies in all 8 cells of the table are shown in Output 3.

Tissue Type * Presence Crosstabulation

| | | | Presence | | |
			No	Yes	Total
Tissue Type	Critical	Count	6	21	27
		Expected Count	12.3	14.7	27.0
	Type C	Count	5	7	12
		Expected Count	5.5	6.5	12.0
	Type B	Count	11	7	18
		Expected Count	8.2	9.8	18.0
	Type A	Count	14	8	22
		Expected Count	10.0	12.0	22.0
Total		Count	36	43	79
		Expected Count	36.0	43.0	79.0

Output 3. The observed and expected frequencies of observations in the cells of the contingency table in Table 3.

The value of chi-square is

$$\chi^2 = \sum_{cells} \frac{(O-E)^2}{E} = \frac{(6-12.3)^2}{12.3} + \frac{(21-14.7)^2}{14.7} + ... + \frac{(14-10.0)^2}{10.0} + \frac{(8-12.0)^2}{12.0} = 10.66$$

The p-value of the chi-square value 10.66 on df = 3 is < .05. The null hypothesis is therefore rejected and we report this result as follows:

$$\chi^2(3) = 10.66; \; p < .05$$

Formula 7 is a straightforward application of the multiplication rule for independent events in elementary probability. Events are independent if the probability of their joint occurrence is the product of their separate probabilities: for example, if a coin is tossed and a die is rolled, the joint probability of a head and a six is $1/2 \times 1/6 = 1/12$.

If, in a two-way contingency table, the row and columns represent attributes A and B, respectively, and R and C are the marginal totals of the row and column intersecting in a cell of the table, the probabilities of those particular levels of A and B are R/N and C/N, respectively. According to the null hypothesis, the occurrence of this level of A with that level of B are independent events, so the probability of their joint occurrence $p = (R/N)(C/N)$. We can regard the total frequency N as the number of times an experiment of chance is replicated, so the expected cell frequency E is $p \times N = (R/N)(C/N)N = RC/N$.

Likelihood ratio (or Maximum Likelihood) chi-square

So far, both in testing for goodness-of-fit and association, we have used the traditional **Pearson chi-square** statistic. Both types of tests, however, can also be made with another chi-square statistic known variously as the **likelihood ratio**, **maximum likelihood** or **log-likelihood** chi-square. Like the Pearson chi-square, the likelihood ratio chi-square is distributed approximately as a true chi-square variable on the same degrees of freedom; although for small samples, the Pearson chi-square is perhaps the better approximation (Agresti, 1990).

For a test of goodness-of-fit with a single qualitative variable comprising g categories, the formula for the likelihood-ratio chi-square is

$$\chi^2_{g-1} = 2 \sum_{all\ groups} O\ ln\left(\frac{O}{E}\right) \quad \text{---}\ (8)\ \textbf{LR goodness-of-fit chi-square}$$

where the function *ln* is the natural log (to the base *e*) of the ratio of the observed to the expected frequency. For a test of association, the formula is

$$\chi^2_{(r-1)(c-1)} = 2 \sum_{all\ cells} O\ ln\left(\frac{O}{E}\right) \quad \text{---}\ (9)\ \textbf{LR association chi-square}$$

where r and c are the numbers of rows and columns, respectively. The likelihood ratio chi-square is distributed approximately as chi-square on $(r-1)(c-1)$ degrees of freedom.

For the data in Table 3, the value of the likelihood ratio chi-square is

$$\chi^2_{3\times1} = 2\sum O\ ln\left(\frac{0}{E}\right)$$

$$= 2\left[6\ ln\left(\frac{6}{12.3}\right) + 21\ ln\left(\frac{21}{14.7}\right) + \dots + 36\ ln\left(\frac{14}{10}\right) + 43\ ln\left(\frac{8}{12.0}\right)\right]$$

$$= 11.09$$

which is close to 10.66, the value of the value of the Pearson chi-square.

The likelihood ratio chi-square is ubiquitous in log-linear analysis (Chapter 13) because, unlike the Pearson chi-square, the values of chi-square associated with the various components in a model add up to the total chi-square value: the likelihood chi-square, that is, has the **additive property**.

11.5.2   Measures of strength of association for nominal data

The rejection of the null hypothesis establishes the presence of an association between the two attributes. The chi-square statistic itself, however, is not a satisfactory measure of association strength, because its magnitude is affected by the total frequency of observations in the contingency table. From the chi-square statistic itself, however, several statistics designed to measure strength of association have been devised.

An ideal measure of association should mimic the correlation coefficient by having a maximum absolute value of 1 for a perfect association, and a value of 0 for dissociation or independence. The choice of the appropriate statistic depends on whether the contingency table is 2×2 (each variable has two categories) or larger.

Several measures of strength of association for nominal data have been proposed. For two-way 2×2 contingency tables, the **phi coefficient** φ is applicable. The phi coefficient is defined as follows:

$$\varphi = \sqrt{\frac{\chi^2}{N}} \quad \text{- - - (10)} \; \textbf{Phi coefficient}$$

For two-way contingency tables involving variables with more than two categories, another statistic, known as **Cramér's V**, is preferred. Cramér's measure, unlike the phi coefficient, can still, as in the 2×2 case, achieve its maximum value of unity.

Other measures of association, such as **Goodman & Kruskal's lambda**, measure the proportional reduction in error achieved when membership of a category on one attribute is used to predict category membership on the other.

More information on the various measures of association can be found by clicking the SPSS **Help** box in the **Crosstabs: Statistics** dialog box.

Two by two contingency tables: the odds and odds ratio

Table 4 is a contingency table in which both attributes (Presence of the antibody and tissue Group) are dichotomous, i.e., they consist of only two categories. (Table 4 was constructed from Table 3 by 'collapsing' across the three non-critical tissue types to produce a single category named 'Other'.)

Table 4. A 2 × 2 contingency table			
Tissue type	**Presence**		**Total**
	No	**Yes**	
Critical	6	21	27
Other	30	22	52
Total	36	43	79

The **odds** is a measure of likelihood which, like probability, arises in the context of an experiment of chance, that is, a procedure with an uncertain outcome, such as tossing a coin or rolling a die. The odds in favour of an outcome is the number of ways in which the outcome could occur divided by the number of ways in which it could fail to occur.

$$odds = \frac{number\ of\ ways\ in\ which\ an\ outcome\ can\ occur}{number\ of\ ways\ in\ which\ it\ can\ fail\ to\ occur} \quad \text{- - - (11)}$$

When a die is rolled, for example, the odds in favour of a six are 1 to 5 or, to express this as a fraction, 1/5.

We can compare the incidence of an outcome in two groups of participants simply by dividing the odds in favour of the outcome in one category by the odds for the other category, the resulting statistic being known as the **odds ratio** *OR*:

$$OR = \frac{odds\ in\ favour\ in\ first\ group}{odds\ in\ favour\ in\ second\ group} \quad \text{- - - (12)}$$

In Table 4, we see that for the Critical category, the value of the odds in favour of the presence of the antibody is 21/6 = 3.5 and for the category Other, the odds = 22/30 = 0.7333. The odds ratio is calculated simply by dividing the odds for the Critical group by the odds for the Other group: *OR* = 3.5/0.7333 = 4.77. The odds ratio tells us that when we move from the category Other to the Critical category, the odds in favour of the occurrence of the antibody increase nearly fivefold.

The odds ratio is useful for exploring any contingency table where at least two of the attributes are dichotomous. We shall make use of this statistic later, when we consider multi-way frequency tables in Chapter 13.

11.5.3   Analysis of contingency tables with SPSS

In the usual research situation, the data on the participants would be entered on an individual basis. **Data View** would then contain as many rows of data as there were participants in the study. From these raw data, SPSS would produce the contingency table shown in Table 3. Here, for convenience, rather than having 79 rows of data in **Data View**, we shall enter the frequencies of individuals in the four combinations of the two qualitative variables *Group* and *Presence*. Normally, of course, these frequencies would not be available and we would rely upon SPSS to calculate them for us.

When the data have already been grouped in this way, the SPSS data set for a contingency table must include two grouping variables to identify the various cell counts, one representing the rows (*Group*), and the other the columns (*Presence*) of the contingency table in Table 3. In this example, since the data are counts, not individual records of presence or absence, a third variable (*Count*) is needed for the cell frequencies.

- In **Variable View**, name the variables *Group*, *Presence*, and *Count*.
- In the **Values** column, define the numerical values and their labels for the two grouping variables. For the *Group* variable, assign the code numbers 1, 2, 3 and 4 to tissue types A, B, C and Critical, respectively. For the *Presence* variable, assign the numbers 1 and 2 to No and Yes, respectively.
- When you have finished working in Variable View, Click the **Data View** tab to switch to **Data View** and enter the data into the three columns, as shown in Figure 10.

	Group	Presence	Count
1	Type A	No	14
2	Type A	Yes	8
3	Type B	No	11
4	Type B	Yes	7
5	Type C	No	5
6	Type C	Yes	7
7	Critical	No	6
8	Critical	Yes	21

Figure 10. **Data View** showing the two grouping variables and the counts of presence or absence of the antibody

When you have grouped data as in this example, the next step is essential. Since the data in the *Count* column represent cell frequencies of a variable (not values), SPSS must be informed of this by means of the **Weight Cases** procedure in the **Data** menu. The procedure for weighting cases is illustrated in Figure 11.

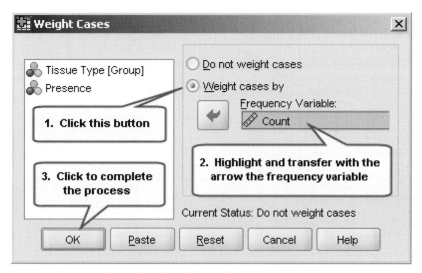

Figure 11. The **Weight Cases** procedure

Had the data been recorded case by case in the data file (i.e. not collated), there would have been no need to use the **Weight Cases** procedure because the **Crosstabs** procedure would have counted up the cases automatically.

Find the **Crosstabs** procedure in the **Descriptives** menu as shown in Figure 12.

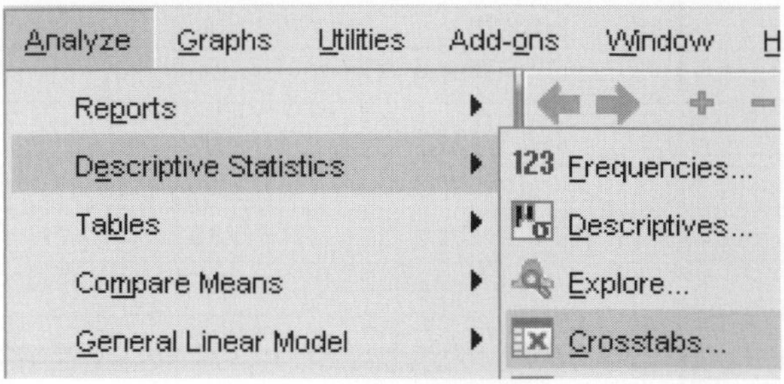

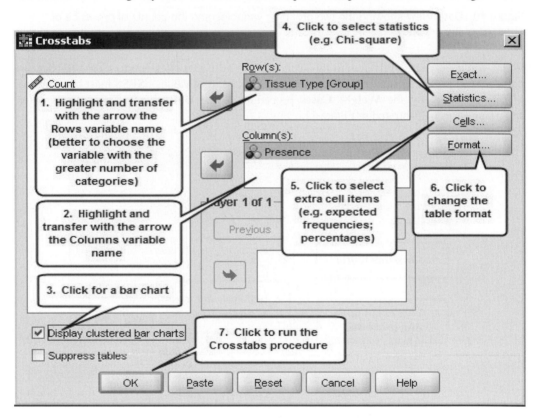

Figure 12. Finding **Crosstabs** in the **Analyze** menu

To obtain the contingency table and make the chi-square test, proceed as shown in Figure 13.

Figure 13. The **Crosstabs** dialog box for *Tissue Type* in the rows and *Presence* in the columns

Complete the **Statistics…**, **Cells…**, and **Format…** dialog boxes as shown in Figures 14 - 16. The **Format…** dialog controls the order in which rows for the values of the grouping variable appear in the contingency table. The default setting is **Ascending**, meaning that the top row of entries in the table will be the data for the value 1 and the bottom row will be the data for the value 4 (the Critical group). By changing the setting to **Descending**, this order will be reversed: the row with the value 4 (the Critical group) will now appear at the top and the row with the value 1 will appear at the bottom.

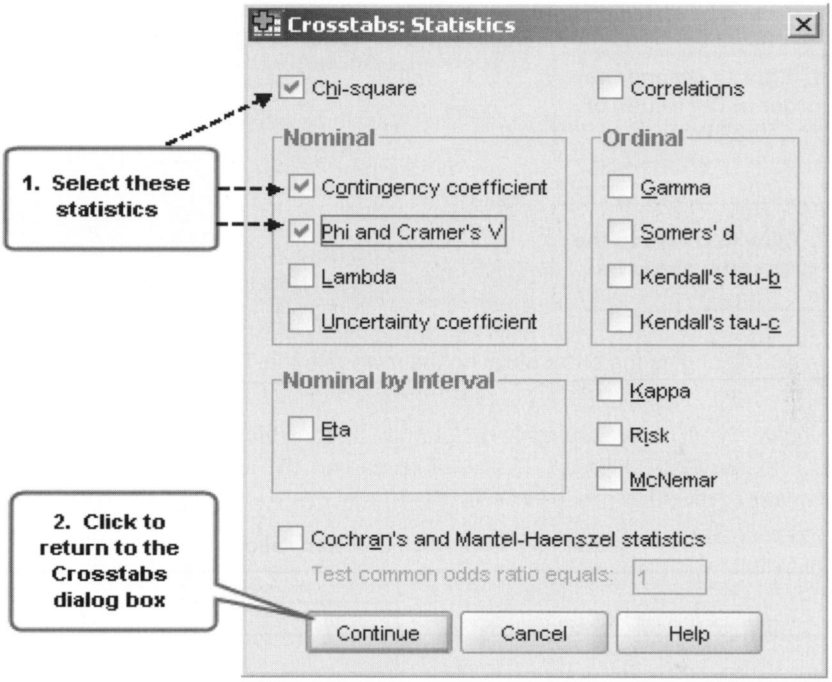

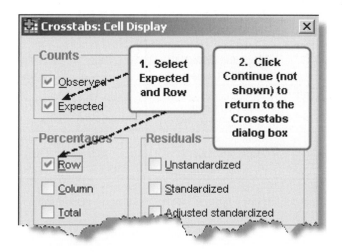

Figure 14. Appropriate choices of statistics in the **Statistics** dialog box

Figure 15. The **Cell Display** dialog box with **Expected** and **Row** ticked

The option of **Expected** cell frequencies in **Counts** enables the user to check that the prescribed minimum requirements for the valid use of chi-square have been fulfilled. Although there has been much debate about these, some leading authorities have proscribed the use of chi-square when:

1. In 2×2 tables, any of the expected frequencies is less than 5;
2. In larger tables, any of the expected frequencies is less than 1 or more than 20% are less than 5.

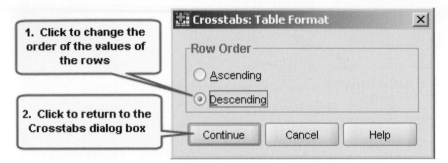

Figure 16. Changing the order of listing the rows with the **Table Format** dialog box

Output 4 shows the contingency table in Output 3, to which have been added the row percentages. In the Critical group, 77.8% of cases had the antibody; whereas the highest percentage in any of the other groups was 58.3%.

Tissue Type * Presence Crosstabulation

			Presence		Total
			No	Yes	
Tissue Type	Critical	Count	6	21	27
		Expected Count	12.3	14.7	27.0
		% within Tissue Type	22.2%	77.8%	100.0%
	Type C	Count	5	7	12
		Expected Count	5.5	6.5	12.0
		% within Tissue Type	41.7%	58.3%	100.0%
	Type B	Count	11	7	18
		Expected Count	8.2	9.8	18.0
		% within Tissue Type	61.1%	38.9%	100.0%
	Type A	Count	14	8	22
		Expected Count	10.0	12.0	22.0
		% within Tissue Type	63.6%	36.4%	100.0%
Total		Count	36	43	79
		Expected Count	36.0	43.0	79.0
		% within Tissue Type	45.6%	54.4%	100.0%

Output 4. The contingency table, to which have been added the row percentages

Output 5 shows the (edited) clustered bar chart, in which the colours in the original chart have been replaced by black and white patterns. The chart provides a striking demonstration of the predominance of the antibody in the Critical tissue group.

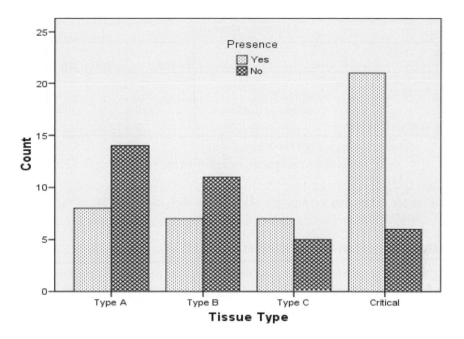

Output 5. Clustered bar chart showing the relatively high incidence of the antibody in the Critical tissue group.

Chi-Square Tests

	Value	df	Asymp. Sig. (2-sided)
Pearson Chi-Square	10.655[a]	3	.014
Likelihood Ratio	11.093	3	.011
Linear-by-Linear Association	9.850	1	.002
N of Valid Cases	79		

> Chi-square has a p-value .014 (significant at .05 level)

a. 0 cells (.0%) have expected count less than 5. The minimum expected count is 5.47.

> As shown in Output 4, none of the expected counts was <5

Output 6. Result of the chi-square test

Output 6 shows the results of the chi-square test. The chi-square value 10.66 is significant beyond the 0.05 level:

$$\chi^2 (3) = 10.66; \quad p < .05$$

Note the remark under the table in Output 6 about expected cell frequencies, which assures the user that the data are sufficiently plentiful to permit the usual chi-square test.

Output 7 gives the values of the tests of strength of association. In this particular example, where one of the attributes is a dichotomy, the values of phi and Cramer's V are the same. That would not necessarily be so in more complex tables.

Symmetric Measures

		Value	Approx. Sig.
Nominal by Nominal	Phi	.367	.014
	Cramer's V	.367	.014
	Contingency Coefficient	.345	.014
N of Valid Cases		79	

a. Not assuming the null hypothesis.

b. Using the asymptotic standard error assuming the null hypothesis.

Output 7. Statistics measuring the strength of the association between *Tissue Type* and *Presence* of the antibody

11.5.4   Getting help with the output

Should any item in the SPSS output be unfamiliar, you can find an explanation by double-clicking on the item to highlight it and right-clicking with the mouse (Figure 17).

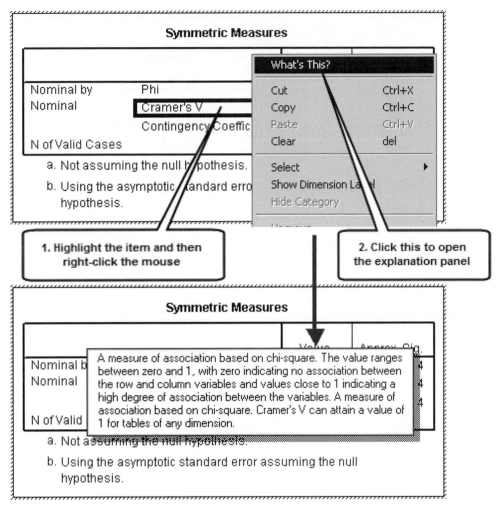

Figure 17. Getting help with unfamiliar terms in the output

11.5.5   Some cautions and caveats

Low expected frequencies

A word of warning about the misuse of chi-square should be given here. In the first place, it is important to bear in mind that, as we pointed out in Chapter 6, the 'chi-square' statistic is only **approximately** distributed as chi-square: the higher the expected frequencies, the better the approximation, hence the rule about minimum expected frequencies. When the expected frequencies fall below the recommended levels, the traditional chi-square test can produce misleading p-values. SPSS, however, provides **exact p-values**, which should be requested when the data are scarce.

Here is an example of what can go wrong if the expected frequencies fall below the acceptable limits. Returning to our example of the presence of the antibody in patients of a certain tissue type, suppose that the study has involved only 19 patients. The contingency table (Output 8) shows the same pattern as before: there is a clear predominance of the antibody in the Critical tissue group.

Tissue Type * Presence Crosstabulation

Count

		Presence		Total
		No	Yes	
Tissue Type	Critical	2	7	9
	Type C	1	0	1
	Type B	3	0	3
	Type A	4	2	6
Total		10	9	19

Output 8. A contingency table summarising a small data set

When completing the **Crosstabs** dialog, the researcher, realising that the data are less plentiful than one would wish, clicks the **Exact ...** button at the side of the dialog box (see Figure 13), enters the **Exact Tests** dialog box, and activates the **Exact** radio button (Figure 18).

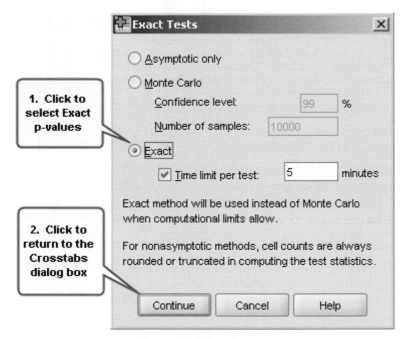

Figure 18. Choosing an exact test

The results of both the approximate (Asymptotic) chi-square test and the exact test are shown in Output 9. The exact tests do not agree with the asymptotic tests: on the exact tests, the result is significant beyond the .05 level.

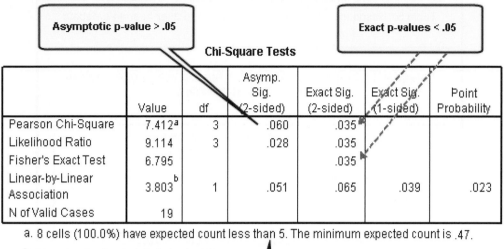

Output 9. Results of the exact tests

Non-independent observations

The use of the chi-square statistic requires that **each individual studied contributes to the count in only one cell in the crosstabulation**. Returning to a situation we described in Chapter 6, suppose that 100 people were asked whether they supported a motion before and after hearing a debate. The people were identified, so that it could be seen whether or not members of the audience had changed their opinions and, if so, in which direction. From this information, Table 5 was constructed.

We saw that the correct procedure here was to analyse only the responses of those who *changed* their opinion and run a goodness-of-fit test of the null hypothesis that there was no systematic tendency for those who changed their views as a result of hearing the debate to do so in one particular direction. The **McNemar** test uses the Yates-corrected chi-square approximation; but the **binomial test** with p set at .5 would serve equally well. Since 38 participants changed from No to Yes, whereas only 13 changed from Yes to No, we were not surprised when the McNemar test showed significance.

Table 5. Responses of an audience before and after hearing a debate

Agreed with motion after debate? * Agreed with motion before debate? Crosstabulation

Count

		Agreed with motion before debate?		Total
		Yes	No	
Agreed with motion after debate?	Yes	27	38	65
	No	13	22	35
Total		40	60	100

Now suppose that the researcher had merely asked people to respond before and after hearing the debate, but didn't bother to identify the people on either occasion or even, after the debate, to ask them whether they had changed their views and, if so, in which direction. That would have produced the data in Table 6.

Table 6. Table showing the frequencies of positive and negative responses of an audience before and after hearing a debate. A chi-square test is inadmissible here

Before or after the debate * Response to proposed legislation Crosstabulation

Count

		Response to proposed legislation		Total
		Yes	No	
Before or after the debate	Before	40	60	100
	After	65	35	100
Total		105	95	200

He then decides that, since he wants to see whether there was an association between the time at which an opinion was sought (Before, After) and the response to the proposed legislation (Yes, No), he will run a chi-square. The result is positive and the researcher concludes that hearing the debate influenced the opinions of the audience.

The display in Table 6 breaks the important rule that, in contingency tables, each person must contribute to the tally in one cell only. In Table 6, each person makes two contributions and, as a result, although 100 people participated in the investigation, there are 200 responses!

When the assumptions underlying a statistical test are so seriously violated, no reliance can be placed upon the p-value.

The information that we need, it is worth noting, cannot be recovered from Table 6: in a contingency table, the cell totals cannot be deduced from the marginal totals alone.

There are several other potential problems with the making of chi-square tests that the user should be aware of. A lucid account of the rationale and assumptions of the chi-square test is given by Howell (2007).

11.6 DO DOCTORS AGREE? COHEN'S KAPPA

Suppose that two psychiatrists assign each of 50 patients to one of a set of five diagnostic categories, A, B, C, D and E. Their assignments are shown in Table 7.

Table 7. Assignments of patients to categories A to E					
Doctor1	Doctor2	Count	Doctor1	Doctor2	Count
A	A	4	C	D	1
A	B	1	C	E	1
A	C	1	D	A	1
A	D	1	D	B	1
A	E	1	D	C	2
B	A	1	D	D	8
B	B	4	D	E	2
B	C	0	E	A	1
B	D	4	E	B	0
B	E	2	E	C	1
C	A	2	E	D	3
C	B	0	E	E	2
C	C	6			

When these assignments are cast into a contingency table, the data appear as in Table 8.

The marked diagonal cells in Table 8 contain the numbers of patients who were assigned to the same diagnostic category by the two doctors. Intuitively, it might seem reasonable to divide the sum of the judgements on the marked diagonal by the total number of judgements and argue that the percentage of agreement is 24/50 = 48%. As with the analysis of any contingency table, however, we must take into consideration the different numbers of patients with different kinds of problem, as indicated by the varying row and column frequencies. Such discrepancies may merely reflect a tendency to make more use of some diagnostic categories than others, rather than reliable diagnosis. Accordingly, we need to obtain the **expected frequencies (E)** for the cells along the marked diagonal, given the values of the marginal row and column totals. We obtain the value of E for each cell by multiplying the marginal totals in the row and column and dividing by the total frequency (50). For example, 4 patients were assigned to diagnostic category B by both doctors. Since the row and column totals for the assignments by the first and second doctor are 6 and 11, respectively, E = 66/50 = 1.32.

Table 8. Contingency table showing the diagnoses of 50 patients by two doctors

(The observed frequencies are given in the rows labelled O; the expected frequencies are given in the rows labelled E.)

Second Doctor * First Doctor Crosstabulation

			First Doctor					Total
			A	B	C	D	E	
Second Doctor	A	O	4	1	2	1	1	9
		E	1.4	2.0	1.8	2.5	1.3	9.0
	B	O	1	4	0	1	0	6
		E	1.0	1.3	1.2	1.7	.8	6.0
	C	O	1	0	6	2	1	10
		E	1.6	2.2	2.0	2.8	1.4	10.0
	D	O	1	4	1	8	3	17
		E	2.7	3.7	3.4	4.8	2.4	17.0
	E	O	1	2	1	2	2	8
		E	1.3	1.8	1.6	2.2	1.1	8.0
Total		O	8	11	10	14	7	50
		E	8.0	11.0	10.0	14.0	7.0	50.0

Cohen (1960) offered the statistic **kappa (κ)** as a measure of agreement between the doctors. Kappa is defined as

$$\kappa = \frac{\sum_{diagonal} O - \sum_{diagonal} E}{N - \sum_{diagonal} E} \quad \text{--- (13) } \textbf{Kappa coefficient}$$

where O and E are, respectively, the observed and expected frequencies *for the diagonal cells only in Table 8* and N is the *total* number of patients. (For the *entire* contingency table, the totals for O and E would have the same value.) Substituting in the formula, we have

$$\sum_{diagonal} O = 4 + 4 + 6 + 8 + 2 = 24$$

$$\sum_{diagonal} E = 1.44 + 1.32 + 2.00 + 4.76 + 1.12 = 10.64$$

$$\kappa = \frac{24 - 10.64}{50 - 10.64} = 0.34$$

The value 0.34 is even lower than the 48% agreement we arrived at using the intuitive measure.

Cohen's kappa statistic is available in SPSS.

- In **Variable View**, set up the variables *Doctor1* and *Doctor2* as string variables and *Count* as a numeric variable. Enter all the data for each combination of doctors (Table 7).

- Follow the path **Data➔Weight Cases...** to weight the cases by *Count*.
- Choose **Analyze➔Descriptive Statistics➔Crosstabs...** to open the **Crosstabs** dialog box.
- Highlight and transfer the grouping variable names to the **Row(s)** and **Column(s)** boxes respectively
- Click the **Statistics...** button and select the **Kappa** check box (see earlier Figure 14). Click **Continue** to return to the **Crosstabs** dialog box and then click **OK**.

The output starts with a **Case Processing Summary** table and then the **Doctor1*Doctor2 Crosstabulation** table. The value of κ is shown in the next table (Output 10).

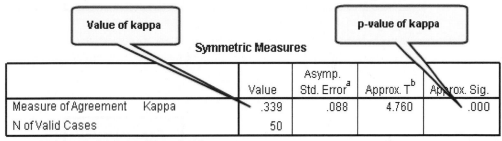

Symmetric Measures

	Value	Asymp. Std. Error[a]	Approx. T[b]	Approx. Sig.
Measure of Agreement Kappa	.339	.088	4.760	.000
N of Valid Cases	50			

a. Not assuming the null hypothesis.

b. Using the asymptotic standard error assuming the null hypothesis.

Output 10. The kappa statistics

The value of kappa is given as .34, as calculated previously. The output also contains a test of the significance of kappa which is of little importance, because a value such as .34, while significant beyond the .01 level, is much too low for a reliability: a minimum value of .75 would be expected with a reliable diagnostic system.

The result should be reported as follows:

> Cohen's kappa statistic was used as a measure of diagnostic agreement between the two doctors: κ = .34; p < .01.

11.7   PARTIAL CORRELATION

Correlation does not imply causation

In experimental (as opposed to correlational) research, provided there are adequate controls, the independent variable (IV) can be shown to have a causal effect upon the dependent variable (DV). In correlational research, however, in which variables are measured as they occur in participants, it can be difficult or impossible to demonstrate unequivocally that one variable in any sense 'causes' another. In some situations, in fact, even when two variables are substantially correlated, *neither* variable causes the other: both are at least partly determined by a third variable. Although the correlation between the two variables may be both statistically significant and substantial, it is a 'spurious' correlation, in the sense that it suggests the presence of a direct causal link between the two variables when actually there is none.

Suppose, for example, we have a bivariate data set showing a strong positive correlation (r = +0.89) between the amount of screen violence that children witness and an independent measure of the extent to which they are actually violent. Let us call these variables *Exposure* and *Actual*. The supposition that *Exposure* increases *Actual* violence was what motivated the researcher to measure these variables in the first place: that is, the researcher wishes to sustain the following model of causation:

Model 1

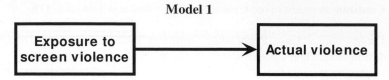

The existence of a positive correlation, however, is equally compatible with the view that the amount of screen violence a child watches is a reflection of his or her own violent tendencies:

Model 2

There is, however, still another possibility. Neither *Exposure* nor *Actual* causes the other: they are both determined by a third variable, parental aggression (*Parental*):

Model 3

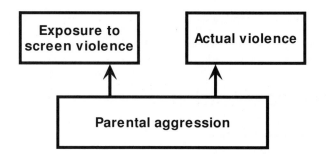

It is often impossible to determine unequivocally which of these three causal models is the correct interpretation of a correlation coefficient, unless additional data are available or theoretical considerations compel the acceptance of one particular model.

Partial correlation

A **partial correlation** is what remains of the correlation between two variables when their correlations with a third variable have been taken into consideration. If r_{AB} and r_{AC} are, respectively, the correlations of variables A and B with a third variable C, the partial correlation between A and B with C 'partialled out' ($r_{AB.C}$) is given by the following formula:

$$r_{AB.C} = \frac{r_{AB} - r_{AC} r_{BC}}{\sqrt{\left(1 - r_{AC}^2\right)\left(1 - r_{BC}^2\right)}} \quad \text{--- (14)} \quad \textbf{Partial correlation}$$

If the two variables correlate substantially with the third variable, the partial correlation between them may be much smaller than the original correlation; indeed, it may be statistically insignificant. In that case, it may be reasonable to interpret the original correlation as having been driven by the third variable, as in the third causal model shown above. Let us suppose that, in our current example, we have data on the *Parental* variable.

To run a partial correlation within SPSS, proceed as follows:

- Select **Analyze➔Correlate➔Partial...** to enter the **Partial Correlations** dialog box.
- Complete the dialog box as shown in Figure 19.
- By clicking the **Options** button and checking the **Zero-order correlations** box in the **Options** dialog, you can obtain the original Pearson correlation between *Exposure* and *Actual* violence for comparison.

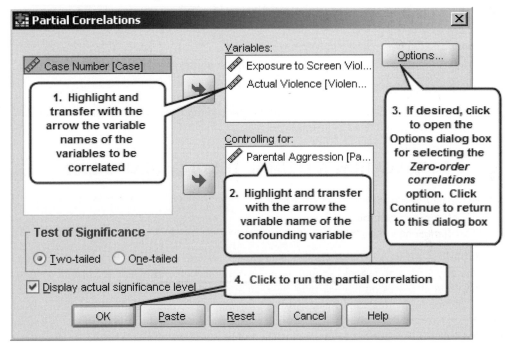

Figure 19. The **Partial Correlations** dialog box

The upper part of the edited output (Output 11) gives the Pearson correlations among the three variables. The second row gives the partial correlation between *Actual Violence* and *Exposure to Screen Violence*, after the potential confounding variable of *Parental Aggression* has been controlled or **partialled out**. The original value of .89 has been reduced to .33: rather little of the original correlation remains when the correlations of *Exposure to Screen Violence* and

Actual Violence with the *Parental Aggression* variable have been taken into consideration. It would appear that the original correlation was driven largely by the *Parental* variable.

Correlations

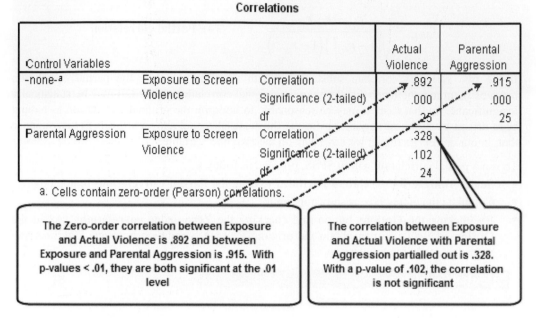

Control Variables			Actual Violence	Parental Aggression
-none-[a]	Exposure to Screen Violence	Correlation	.892	.915
		Significance (2-tailed)	.000	.000
		df	25	25
Parental Aggression	Exposure to Screen Violence	Correlation	.328	
		Significance (2-tailed)	.102	
		df	24	

a. Cells contain zero-order (Pearson) correlations.

> The Zero-order correlation between Exposure and Actual Violence is .892 and between Exposure and Parental Aggression is .915. With p-values < .01, they are both significant at the .01 level

> The correlation between Exposure and Actual Violence with Parental Aggression partialled out is .328. With a p-value of .102, the correlation is not significant

Output 11. Edited table of correlations showing the partial correlation in the second row

Report this result as follows:

> The partial correlation between *Actual* violence and *Exposure* with *Parental Aggression* partialled out is insignificant: $r_{partial}(27) = .33$; $p = .10$.

11.8   CORRELATION IN MENTAL TESTING: RELIABILITY

A psychological test must have two attributes:
1. It must be **reliable**;
2. It must be **valid**.

A **reliable** test gives *consistent* results: a person, if tested with the instrument on different occasions by different testers, should score at similar percentile levels. Implicit in this definition is that scores on the test must have an appropriate distribution, so that the variance reflects natural individual differences in the property concerned. Ceiling and floor effects, whereby everyone either achieves perfection or fails, vitiate reliability. A **valid** test is one that measures what it is supposed to measure. The brevity of that definition belies the complexity of the problems involved in the establishment of the validity of a test: in his Dictionary of Psychology, Reber (1985) gives more than twenty definitions of validity. In this section, however, we shall be concerned with reliability only. Reliability is a necessary – but not a sufficient – condition for validity (in any of its conceptions). An unreliable measuring instrument would be like an elastic tape measure or a rubber ruler: even when used to measure a property of the same object, it would never give the same result twice. In particular, we shall be concerned with how the reliability of a composite test consisting of a set of items increases with the number of items.

There are several approaches to the measurement of reliability, all of which utilise the Pearson correlation. Three of these are:
  1. Test-retest;
  2. Parallel forms;
  3. Split-half.

In the first two methods, each participant is tested twice, either (as in 1) with the same test or (as in 2) with parallel (or equivalent) forms of the same test. A Pearson correlation is then used to measure the association between the participants' scores on the two occasions of testing and thus determine the reliability of the test. It is generally accepted that the reliability of a test should be at least 0.80 for the test to be useful. In the **split-half** approach, the component items must be divisible into two equal-sized equivalent subgroups, perhaps the odd-numbered and even-numbered items. Each participant receives two subtotal scores: one for the even items, the other for the odd. The split-half reliability is the Pearson correlation between the odd totals and the even totals. In the split-half approach, the participant is tested only once. Split-half reliability can be viewed as a special case of the general problem of establishing the reliability of the total score on any composite test yielding an aggregate total in relation to that of its component items.

In psychometric theory, a score X on a test is regarded as the sum of two components:
  1. A **true** component t, which is that part of x that truly expresses the property;
  2. An **error** component e.

Thus

$$X = t + e \quad \text{- - - (15)} \quad \textbf{Components of a score}$$

On the basis of some reasonable assumptions, such as the independence of the true and error components, it can be shown that

$$\sigma_{total}^2 = \sigma_{true}^2 + \sigma_{error}^2 \quad \text{- - - (16)} \quad \textbf{Partition of the total variance of the scores}$$

In words, the total variance of a score is the sum of the variances of the true component and random error, remembering that different participants will be in possession of the property to varying degrees.

Earlier in this chapter, we observed that the square of the Pearson correlation could be interpreted as the proportion of the variance of a variable that was shared with another variable. In the special context of reliability, however, the *unsquared* reliability coefficient itself can be interpreted as the ratio of the variances of the true and the total scores:

$$reliability = \frac{\sigma_{true}^2}{\sigma_{total}^2} \quad \text{- - - (17)} \quad \textbf{Reliability as a ratio of variances}$$

The notion of a reliability as a ratio of true to total variance extends to composite scores that are aggregates of scores on individual items.

Reliability and number of items: coefficient alpha

Psychometric theory shows that the reliability of a test increases with the number of items it contains, according to the following formula:

$$alpha = \frac{i}{i-1}\left(\frac{\sigma_Y^2 - \sum\limits_{items}\sigma_{item}^2}{\sigma_Y^2}\right) \text{ --- (18) } \textbf{Coefficient alpha}$$

where i is the number of items in the test and σ_Y^2 is the variance of the complete test.

Formula (18) brings out the intimate connection between variance and reliability. The relationship between number of items and reliability obtains because the items in a test constitute a sample from a domain of possible items and, other things being equal, the statistics of large samples are less subject to variability than those of small samples.

There are several equivalent versions of the formula for **coefficient alpha**, one of which is the **Spearman-Brown formula**, which expresses the reliability of a test in terms of the mean of the correlations between every possible pair of items:

$$reliability = \frac{i\bar{r}}{1+(i-1)\bar{r}} \text{ --- (19) } \textbf{Spearman-Brown formula}$$

where i is the number of items in the test and $\bar{r}$ is the mean of the correlations between all pairs of items. It is clear from (19) that even if the average inter-item correlation is low, the total score on a test with many items can achieve a very high level of reliability.

Suppose that a test contains four items, all of which are intended to measure the same property. Table 9 shows the scores of 6 people on the test. (These data have been borrowed from Winer, 1962, p127.)

Table 9. The scores of six participants on a four-item test					
Participant	Item 1	Item 2	Item 3	Item 4	Sum
1	2	4	3	3	12
2	5	7	5	6	23
3	1	3	1	2	7
4	7	9	9	8	33
5	2	4	6	1	13
6	6	8	8	4	26

From the **Spearman-Brown** formula, we can expect the reliability of the sum of the four test items to be greater than that of any of the individual items. Table 10 shows the intercorrelations among the four items. The mean inter-item correlation is 0.84.

Table 10. Intercorrelations among the four items in the test

Inter-Item Correlation Matrix

	Item 1	Item 2	Item 3	Item 4
Item 1	1.000	1.000	.865	.865
Item 2	1.000	1.000	.865	.865
Item 3	.865	.865	1.000	.586
Item 4	.865	.865	.586	1.000

Applying the Spearman-Brown formula, we find that the estimate of the reliability for the aggregrate test score is

$$reliability = \frac{i\bar{r}}{1+(i-1)\bar{r}} = \frac{4(0.84)}{1+3(0.84)} = 0.95$$

There were only four items in this test; but the reliability of a test with many items can be expected to be very high indeed – even if the mean inter-item correlation is low.

Measuring agreement among judges: the intraclass correlation

So far, we have been considering the question of the consistency of a test when used repeatedly on the same individuals. A related problem is the measurement of the level of agreement among *different* measuring instruments when used on the same set of objects or people. A particular instance is the measurement of the extent to which judges agree when, for example, rating the performance of musicians or skaters on a 10-point scale. Table 11 shows the marks assigned by four judges to six performers.

Table 11. Marks assigned by four judges to six performers

Performer	Judge1	Judge2	Judge3	Judge4	MeanRating
1	2	4	3	3	3.00
2	5	7	5	6	5.75
3	1	3	1	2	1.75
4	7	9	9	8	8.25
5	2	4	6	1	3.25
6	6	8	8	4	6.50

The four marks given to each performer can be regarded as belonging to a category or **class**: they all refer to the same person and should tend to be more similar to one another than they are to the marks assigned to the other performers. The total variance of the ratings σ_{total}^2 is made up of two components:

1. The variance of the true extent to which people possess the property, which we shall term σ_{people}^{2};

2. The error variance $\sigma_{within\ people}^{2}$, which depends partly upon differences among the judges. The larger the first component of the total variance in relation to the second, the closer the agreement among the judges.

In summary, we can break down the total variance of the ratings as follows:

$$\sigma_{total}^{2} = \sigma_{between\ people}^{2} + \sigma_{within\ people}^{2} \quad \text{- - - (20) \textbf{Partition of the total sum of squares}}$$

Conceptually, the **intraclass correlation (ICC)** is defined as follows:

$$ICC = \frac{\sigma_{between\ people}^{2}}{\sigma_{between\ people}^{2} + \sigma_{within\ people}^{2}} \quad \text{- - - (21) \textbf{Intraclass correlation}}$$

Comparison of (21) with (17) shows that the *ICC* is actually the ratio of the variance of the hypothetical true scores to the total variance and is therefore a reliability. This is why (21) is termed a 'correlation'. In fact, measuring agreement among the judges and assessing the reliability of an aggregate score are actually one and the same problem. In our second example, the judges are the equivalent of separate test items measuring one and the same property in the person being tested. The *ICC* is, at the same time, both a measure of agreement among judges and a measure of the reliability of their average ratings of the performers. In fact, the *ICC* is yet another form of coefficient alpha.

Reliability analysis with SPSS

We shall illustrate SPSS's computation of reliability using the scores of six people on four items (Table 9).

- Select **Analyze➔Scale➔Reliability Analysis...** (Figure 20) to open the **Reliability Analysis** dialog box (Figure 21).

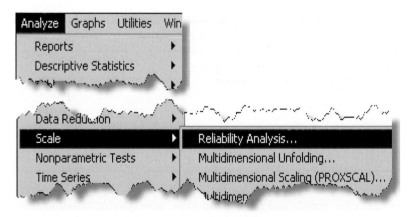

Figure 20. The menu for **Reliability Analysis**

- Complete the **Reliability Analysis** dialog boxes as shown in Figures 21 and 22.

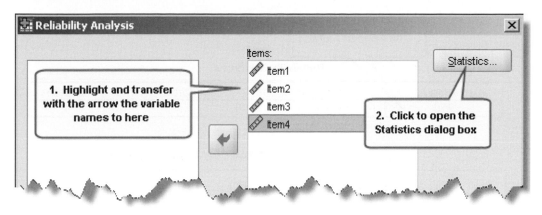

Figure 21. The completed **Reliability Analysis** dialog box

In choosing the default **Two-Way Mixed** model from the **Statistics** menu, we have assumed that four judges are the only ones of interest, whereas the performers are a random sample from a large pool of potential performers.

It can be seen in Output 12 that both **Cronbach's Alpha** and the **Intraclass Correlation Coefficient** (*ICC*) for **Average Measures** is 0.95, as calculated previously from the Spearman-Brown formula. As we should expect, the value of *ICC* for individual items (.825) is lower than it is for the whole test (.950).

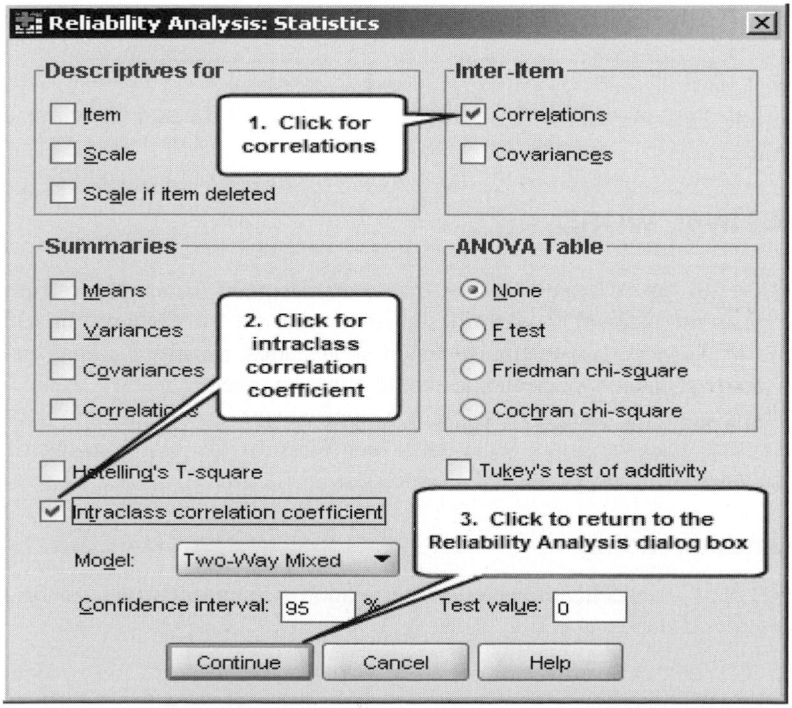

Figure 22. The completed **Statistics** dialog box for **Reliability Analysis**

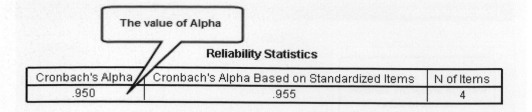

Reliability Statistics

Cronbach's Alpha	Cronbach's Alpha Based on Standardized Items	N of Items
.950	.955	4

Intraclass Correlation Coefficient

	Intraclass Correlation[a]	F Test with True Value 0			
		Value	df1	df2	Sig
Single Measures	.825[b]	19.865	5.0	15	.000
Average Measures	.950[c]	19.865	5.0	15	.000

Two-way mixed effects model where people effects are random and measures effects are fixed.

 a. Type C intraclass correlation coefficients using a consistency definition-the between-measure variance is excluded from the denominator variance.

 b. The estimator is the same, whether the interaction effect is present or not.

 c. This estimate is computed assuming the interaction effect is absent, because it is not estimable otherwise.

The value of *ICC* and its significance (p < .01)

Output 12. The values of Alpha and ICC and its significance for the aggregate and single items

11.9   A FINAL WORD

In this chapter, we turned from statistics that were designed to compare means (or other averages such as the median) to those designed to measure association. In particular, we discussed two of the most used (and misused) of all statistics, namely, the Pearson correlation and the chi-square statistic. A correlation should never be taken at its face value without first examining the scatterplot; and the user of the approximate chi-square test for association should make sure that the contingency table conforms to the requirements of minimum expected frequencies and independence of responses.

Recommended reading

Howell (2007) has an excellent chapter on correlation (Chapters 9) and on the analysis of contingency tables (Chapter 6).

Howell, D. C. (2007). *Statistical methods for psychology (6th ed.)*. Belmont, CA: Thomson/Wadsworth.

Exercises

Exercise 17 *The Pearson correlation*, Exercise 18 *Other measures of association* and Exercise 19 *The analysis of nominal data* are available in www.psypress.com/spss-made-simple and click on Exercises.

CHAPTER 12

Regression

12.1   INTRODUCTION

The associative coin has two sides.   On the one hand, a single number, a correlation coefficient, can be calculated which expresses the *strength* of the association between two variables.   On the other, however, there is a set of techniques, known as **regression**, which utilise the presence of an association between two variables to predict the values of one variable (the **dependent**, **target** or **criterion** variable) from those of another (the **independent variable**, or **regressor**).   In **simple** regression, there is just one regressor or IV; in **complex** regression there are two or more IVs.   It is with this predictive aspect of association that the present chapter is concerned.

12.1.1   Simple, two-variable regression

Returning to the study of the association between Actual Violence and Exposure to Screen Violence (Chapter 11), our starting point in this chapter is the same elliptical scatterplot that served as our point of departure in the earlier chapter.   The cautions and caveats about the use and abuse of the Pearson correlation all apply, with equal force, to regression as well.   In particular, the scatterplot must either be elliptical in shape (indicating a basically linear relationship between the criterion or DV and the regressor or IV) or circular (indicating the complete absence of any association).

Figure 1 shows the **regression line** drawn through the points in the scatterplot.   The equation of this line is

$$Y' = 2.09 + 0.74X$$

436

where Y' is the point on the line above X. (It is important to distinguish carefully between the observed values Y and the corresponding points on the line Y' for the same values of X.)

The general form of this **linear regression equation** is

$$Y' = b_0 + b_1 X \ \text{- - -} \ (1)$$

The linear regression line

where b_0 is the **intercept** of the line and b_1 is its **slope**. The intercept is the distance from the origin to the point at which the line cuts the y-axis. At this point, $X = 0$: that is, $Y' = b_0$ (Figure 1). In SPSS output, the intercept b_0 is referred as the **constant**.

The slope of the regression line b_1 is known as the **regression coefficient**. The regression coefficient measures the estimated average change in the criterion variable Y that results from increasing the value of X, the regressor or IV, by one unit. In our example, $b_1 = 0.74$, so an increase of one unit in Exposure (Exposure to screen violence) results in an estimated average increase of 0.74 units in the Actual Violence score.

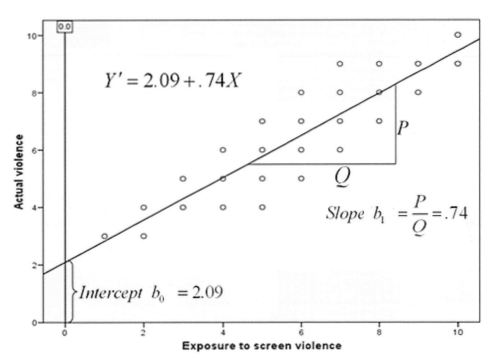

Figure 1. The regression line of Actual Violence upon Exposure to Screen Violence

Suppose that all the points in the scatterplot were to be removed and we knew only that the mean score on Actual Violence is 6.37. We are told that John has an Exposure score of 9. Without further information, our best guess of John's Actual Violence score would be the mean Actual Violence score M_Y, that is, 6.37. In the absence of further information, we should be obliged to make this guess whatever the value of John's Exposure score. We could do much better, however, if we knew the equation of the regression line and were to take as our guess of John's Actual Violence score the point on the line above $X = 9$. From (1), we see that John's predicted Actual Violence score (the point on the regression line above Exposure = 9) is

$$Y' = 2.091 + 0.7359 \times 9 = 8.714$$

This value is much closer to John's real score Y on Actual Violence, which was 8 (Figure 2).

12.1.2   Residuals

Although we can predict the participants' real scores on Actual Violence more accurately when we use the regression line, we shall still make errors. The error or **residual** (e) is the participant's real score on Actual Violence minus the prediction from regression:

$$e = Y - Y' \; \text{---} \; (2) \quad \textbf{The residual score}$$

In John's case, since $Y = 8$ and $Y' = 8.714$, $e = 8 - 8.714 = -0.714$. John's residual score is shown in Figure 2.

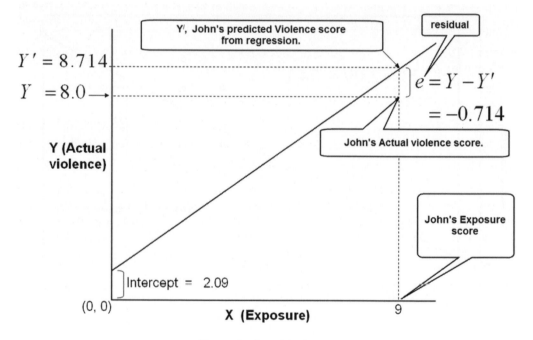

Figure 2. A residual score

In regression, the study of the residuals is of great importance, because they form the basis for measures of the accuracy of the estimates and of the extent to which the **regression model** (see below) gives a good account of the data in question. (See Tabachnick & Fidell, 2007, for advice on **regression diagnostics**, which are based largely upon residuals and their transformations.)

12.1.3 The least squares criterion

The regression line shown in Figure 1 is the line that 'fits' the data best according to what is known as the **least squares criterion**, whereby the values of b_0 and b_1 must be such that that the sum of squares of the residuals Σe^2 is a minimum. There is a unique mathematical solution to this problem. The values of b_0 and b_1 that meet the criterion are given by the following formulae:

$$b_1 = \frac{SP}{SS_X}$$

--- (3) **Slope and intercept of the regression line**

$$b_0 = M_Y - b_1 M_X$$

where SS and SP are, respectively, the sum of squares and cross-products, as in the formula for the Pearson correlation (Chapter 11):

$$SS_X = \Sigma(X - M_X)^2 \qquad SP = \Sigma(X - M_X)(Y - M_Y)$$

The technique we have been describing is known as **ordinary least squares (OLS)** regression. There are other kinds of regression (such as logistic regression) which do not work in this way. It is not our intention here to present a comprehensive account of regression, simple or complex. There are, however, certain features that are common to all types of regression and therefore particularly deserving of attention.

12.1.4 Partition of the sum of squares in regression

The element of the variance of the scores Y on the target or criterion variable (DV) is the deviation $(Y - M_Y)$: $SS_Y = \Sigma(Y - M_Y)^2$. Associated with the regression line is the regression sum of squares $SS_{regression}$, the formula for which is $SS_{regression} = \Sigma(Y' - M_Y)^2$. With error-prone measured variables, even if they are in a basically linear relationship, the regression sum of squares cannot account for all the variance in the target variable. The residuals e in the current data set are pictured in Figure 3. From the residuals, can be calculated the **residual sum of squares**, $SS_{residual}$, the formula for which is $SS_{residual} = \Sigma(Y - Y')^2 = \Sigma e^2$.

It can be shown that the total sum of squares of the target variable can be partitioned into regression and residual components according to

$$SS_Y = SS_{regression} + SS_{residual} \quad \text{--- (4)}$$

Partition of the total sum of squares in simple regression

In a manner reminiscent of the partition of the total sum of squares in the one-way ANOVA, the sum of squares of the criterion or DV has similarly been partitioned into two components. As in the ANOVA, the sums of squares can also be regarded as measures of variability uncorrected by their respective degrees of freedom.

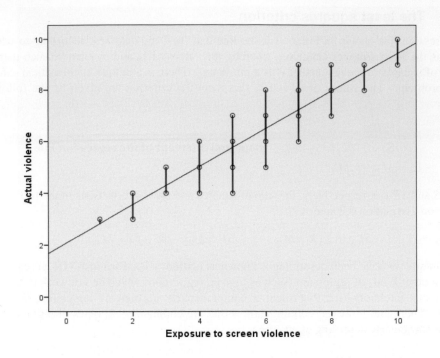

Figure 3. The residuals, which form the basis of the residual sum of squares

Degrees of freedom of the regression sums of squares

The degrees of freedom of SS_Y can be partitioned in a manner similar to the sum of squares:

$$df_Y = df_{regression} + df_{residual}$$
$$(n-1) \qquad\qquad 1 \qquad\qquad (n-2) \qquad \text{- - - (5)}$$

Partition of the degrees of freedom of the DV

If we assume that there are n (X, Y) pairs in the data set, the degrees of freedom of SS_Y are ($n - 1$), because the specification of ($n - 1$) deviations from M_Y fixes the remaining deviation.

Turning now to the regression sum of squares $SS_{regression} = \sum (Y' - M_Y)^2$, although there are n values of Y', these are all completed fixed by the value of the regression coefficient b_1. The regression sum of squares, therefore, has only ONE degree of freedom.

The element of the residual degrees of freedom is $Y - Y' = Y - M_Y - b_1 (X - M_X)$, from which it is clear that TWO parameters are being estimated, M_Y and b_1. As a result, another degree of freedom is lost and so the residual sum of squares has ($n - 2$) degrees of freedom.

12.1.5   Effect size in regression

It can be shown that, in regression, the proportion of the variance of the target variable accounted for by regression is given by the square of the Pearson correlation r^2, a statistic known as the **coefficient of determination (CD)**:

$$CD = r^2 = \frac{SS_{regression}}{SS_Y} \quad - - - (6)$$

The coefficient of determination

The Pearson correlation between the *Actual* and *Exposure* scores is 0.89. The value of the coefficient of determination is therefore $0.89^2 = 0.80$. This means that 80% of the variance of *Actual* scores is accounted for by regression of *Actual* violence upon *Exposure* to violent programmes.

We have already encountered the coefficient of determination in Chapter 11. There, we suggested that it is helpful to think of the *CD* as the proportion of the total variance of either variable that is shared with the other. Here, however, in the regression context, we see that the *CD* is the proportion of the variance of the criterion or target variable that is accounted for by the linear regression of the criterion variable on the regressor or IV.

In the coefficient of determination, we have a useful measure of effect size applicable to regression. Here we reproduce the table from Chapter 11, which offers a rough guide to the classification of effect size in regression.

Effect size (r^2)	Size of Effect
<0.01 (<1%)	Small
0.01 to 0.10 (1-10%)	Medium
>0.10 (>10%)	Large

Picturing effect size in simple regression

In Chapter 11, it was observed that the CD can be represented diagrammatically as the proportion of overlap between two circles, the total area of each circle representing 100% of the variance of one of the variables (Figure 4). In the context of regression, as opposed to correlation, we think of the degree of overlap as the proportion of the DV that is accounted for by regression upon the IV.

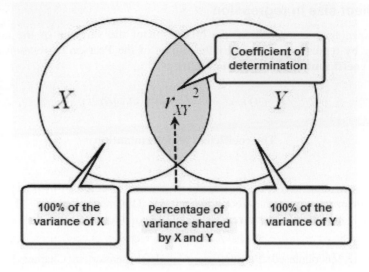

Figure 4. Diagrammatic representation of the coefficient of determination (CD)

12.1.6   Shrinkage

So far, all the statistics we have described refer to a single sample of scores. The purpose of the regression exercise, however, is ultimately to generalise beyond our data to the bivariate population or joint distribution of *Actual* violence and *Exposure*, which can be visualised as a scatterplot with an infinite number of points. The statistics of our sample, including the coefficient of determination, will tend to overstate the predictive power of regression in the population, with the consequence that predictive power will be lost if the regression equation we have just arrived at is re-applied to a fresh data set. This loss in predictive power with re-sampling is known as **shrinkage**. The CD, as calculated from a set of data, is positively biased as an estimate of the corresponding parameter (population value). In practice, where we are attempting to generalise beyond our own data to the population, we need to use the degrees of freedom of the relevant statistics to adjust the value of r^2 downwards to remove its positive bias. This is the reason for the 'adjustment' referred to in the SPSS output for various regression-related routines; in fact, **adjusted R^2** is referred to by some authors as '**shrunken R^2**'.

12.1.7   Regression models

The violence study was motivated by the desire to show that *Actual* violence is a linear function of *Exposure* to violence: that is, an observed score Y is made up according to the following equation:

$$Y = \beta_0 + \beta_1 + e \text{ - - - (7) A linear regression model}$$

where β_0 and β_1 are the parameters corresponding to the intercept b_0 and slope b_1, respectively, of the sample regression line that we have been discussing and e is a random error component corresponding to the residual score.

In regression theory and tests for significance of estimates of the parameters of the regression equation, important assumptions are made about the random component e, including normality of distribution and independence of e across different values of X. The purpose of regression diagnostics (referred to earlier) is to ascertain whether these assumptions have been met.

12.1.8 Beta-weights

The **beta weight** β_1 is the slope of the regression line when the criterion or DV Y and the regressor or IV X have both been standardised to produce the standardised variables z_Y and z_X, respectively, where

$$z_Y = \frac{Y - M_Y}{s_Y} \text{ and } z_X = \frac{X - M_X}{s_X} \quad \text{- - - (8)}$$

Standardised variables

It follows immediately from (3) that since the mean and standard deviation of a set of standardised scores are 0 and 1, respectively, the intercept in the regression equation of z_Y upon z_X is zero and the regression equation of z_Y upon z_X is

$$z_Y{}' = \beta_1 z_X \quad \text{- - - (9)}$$

Standardised form of the simple regression equation

where $z_Y{}'$, a point on the regression line, is the estimate of the observed standard score z_Y for a particular value of z_X.

The slope β_1 of the standardised form of the regression equation is the average change in the DV Y, measured in standard deviation units, produced by an increase of one standard deviation in the regressor or independent variable X. The beta-weight therefore has the advantage of providing a unit-free measure of the slope of the regression line.

Regression and correlation

The slope of the regression line of Y upon X is related to the Pearson correlation r as follows:

$$b_1 = r_{XY} \frac{s_Y}{s_X} \quad \text{- - - (10)}$$

**Relation between the regression coefficient
and the Pearson correlation**

Since the standard deviations of z_Y and z_X are both unity, the slope of the standardised regression line is simply the Pearson correlation r and we can write:

$$z_Y{}' = \beta_1 z_X = r_{XY} z_X \quad \text{- - - (11)}$$

**Identity of beta with r in
the standardised simple regression equation**

Effects of linear transformations on the correlation and regression coefficients

A *linear* transformation of either X or Y leaves the *absolute* value of the correlation unaltered; however, if the slope of the transformation is negative, the sign of the correlation changes. For example, if the correlation between X and Y, is $+0.6$, the correlation between X and $100Y$ is still $+0.6$. The correlation between X and $-100Y$, however, is -0.6.

It is clear from (10) that the regression coefficient must always have the same sign as the correlation. The effect upon the regression coefficient of a linear transformation of either X or Y with a negative slope is to reverse the sign of both the correlation and the regression coefficient b_1. We shall make use of these two facts about linear transformations later, when we consider the **multiple correlation coefficient**.

12.1.9   Significance testing in simple regression

In Chapter 11, we saw that, provided the data have a bivariate normal distribution, the null hypothesis of independence (which states that in the population, the correlation is zero) can be tested with the statistic t with $n-2$ degrees of freedom, where

$$ t = \frac{r\sqrt{(n-2)}}{\sqrt{(1-r^2)}} \quad \text{- - - (12)} \ \textbf{\textit{t} test for significance of correlation} $$

In this chapter, we have seen that the Pearson correlation r is closely related to the regression coefficient b_1, so that the value of one fully determines that of the other:

$$ r = b_1 \left(\frac{s_Y}{s_X} \right) $$

A test of the significance of the sample correlation r, therefore, is also a test of the significance of the regression coefficient b_1. The testing of a regression coefficient for significance can be thought of in two equivalent ways:

1.   The making of a point estimate of the population value and dividing that by an estimate of the standard error of the regression coefficient to produce a t statistic.
2.   The testing of an estimate of the variance accounted for by regression (the coefficient of determination). This is achieved by an analysis of variance, in which the test statistic is F which, in the present context (where the regression sum of squares has one degree of freedom), is the square of t.

In the t-test approach, the test statistic is

$$ t_{n-2} = \frac{b_1}{s_{b_1}} \quad \text{- - - (13)} $$

t test for the significance of the regression coefficient

where the standard error estimate in the denominator is given by

$$ s_{b_1} = \sqrt{\frac{SS_{residual} \, /(n-2)}{SS_X}} \quad \text{- - - (14)} $$

The standard error of b

In the ANOVA approach, the test statistic is

$$F(1, df_{residual}) = \frac{MS_{regression}}{MS_{residual}} = \frac{SS_{regression} / 1}{SS_{residual} / (n-2)} = \frac{SS_{regression}(n-2)}{SS_{residual}} \quad \text{- - -} \quad (15)$$

F test for the significance of b

Since $SS_{regression} = r^2 SS_Y$ and $SS_{residual} = (1-r^2)SS_Y$, we see that

$$F(1, df_{residual}) = \frac{r^2 SS_Y (n-2)}{(1-r^2)SS_Y} = \frac{r^2(n-2)}{(1-r^2)} \quad \text{- - -} \quad (16)$$

The F statistic as a function of the correlation

Notice that (16) is t^2 (see formula 12). In words, the value of t fully determines that of F, and vice versa, because $F = t^2$. The two tests are exact equivalents.

12.2 SIMPLE REGRESSION WITH SPSS

As always, we recommend that you should get to know your data before making any formal statistical tests. In regression, as well as correlation, the graphical approach is the best way of doing this. In this example, we shall want to see the scatterplot and regression line first.

12.2.1 Drawing scatterplots with regression lines

Our starting point is the scatterplot of *Actual* violence upon *Exposure* (Figure 1). To add a regression line to this scatterplot, double-click on the plot to enter the **Chart Editor**, then click on the icon marked by the white cursor in Figure 5 labelled **Add Fit Line at Total**.

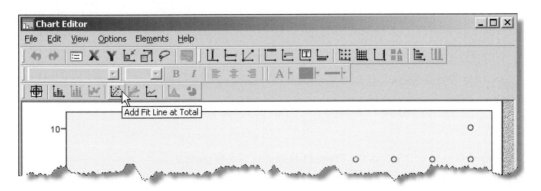

Figure 5. Choosing **Fit Line at Total** to draw the regression line

Clicking on **Fit Line at Total** will access the **Properties** dialog box, in which the **Linear** radio button is checked as the default setting. Close the **Properties** dialog box to see the complete regression line (Figure 6).

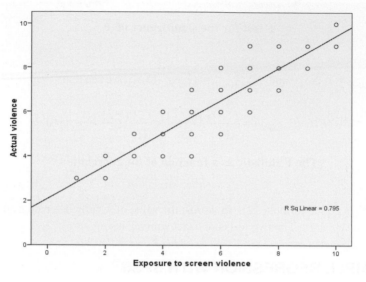

Figure 6. The regression line

In Figure 6, the vertical axis has been displaced slightly to the left, with the result that the intercept appears to be nearer the origin that the correct value of 2.09 (the intercept or regression constant). To rectify this, enter the **Chart Editor** again and click the icon labelled **Add a reference line to the X axis** (Figure 7).

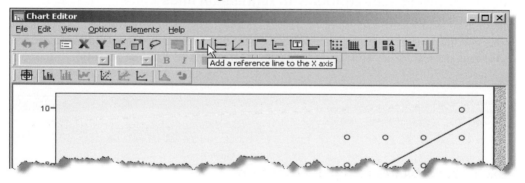

Figure 7. Adding a vertical reference line to the X axis

Clicking this icon will access the **Properties** dialog box (Figure 8).

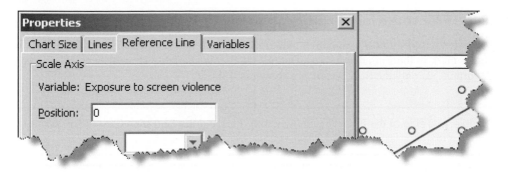

Figure 8. The **Properties** dialog box for drawing a vertical reference line on the X axis

Set the **Position** to zero and click the **Apply** button at the foot of the dialog box. The graph will now appear as in Figure 9. The regression line intercepts the vertical reference line 2.09 units above zero on the vertical axis. The value 2.09, as we know, is the correct value of the intercept.

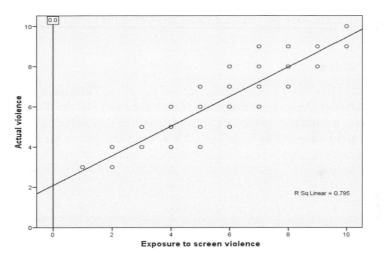

Figure 9. Scatterplot with regression line and vertical reference line above the zero point on the X axis

12.2.2   A problem in simple regression

In some North American universities, there is concern with the efficacy of the methods used to select students for entry. How closely are scores on the entrance tests and final exam results associated? If there is an association, how accurately can we predict university performance from students' marks on the entrance tests?

Given that we have each student's final exam mark and entrance test mark, a Pearson correlation can be used to measure the degree of statistical association between these two variables. Simple regression can be used to predict final exam performance from marks on the entrance test.

12.2.3 Procedure for simple regression

In Table 1, the score *Fin* is a student's mark in the Final University Exam, and *Ent* is the same student's mark in the Entrance Exam. The full data set is available at www.psypress.com/spss-made-simple, so only the first 2 cases are shown in Table 1.

Table 1. Table of the Final University Exam (Fin) and the Entrance Exam (Ent) scores

Case	Fin	Ent	Case	Fin	Ent	Case	Fin	Ent	Case	Fin	Ent
1	38	44	10	81	53	19	105	43	28	142	56
2	49	40	11	86	47	20	106	55	29	145	60
3	6		12	91		21	107	48		50	

The table contains the marks of 34 students: Student 1 (whose data are in the first row of the first two columns from the left) got 44 in the Entrance Exam and 38 in the Final University Exam. Student 34, on the other hand, (whose data are shown in the seventh row of the last two columns on the right), got 49 in the Entrance Exam and 195 in the Final University Exam.

Preparing the SPSS data set

Using the techniques described in Chapter 2, Section 2.3, enter **Variable View** and name the variables *Case*, *FinalExam* and *EntranceExam*. In the **Label** column, add more informative variable labels such as *Case Number*, *Final University Exam* and *Entrance Exam*. In **Data View**, enter the data in the pre-labelled columns.

See Section 2.3

Exploring the data

Usually the user would explore the data to check for incorrect enries and examine the scatterplot to detect any outliers. Here, in the interests of brevity, we shall proceed directly with the regression analysis and rely upon the regression procedure itself to find any problem cases.

Running simple regression

- Choose **Analyze➔Regression** (see Figure 10) and click **Linear...** to open the **Linear Regression** dialog box (the completed dialog is shown in Figure 11).
- Transfer the variable names as shown in Figure 11, taking care to select the appropriate variable names for the dependent variable (target) and the independent variable (regressor).
- Request additional descriptive statistics and a residuals analysis by clicking the **Statistics...** button to open the **Linear Regression: Statistics** dialog box (Figure 12) and activating the **Descriptives** checkbox. Analysis of the residuals gives a measure of how good the prediction is and whether there are any cases that are so discrepant as to be considered outliers and perhaps dropped from the analysis. Click the **Casewise**

diagnostics checkbox to include a listing of any exceptionally large residuals in the output. Click **Continue** to return to the **Linear Regression** dialog box.

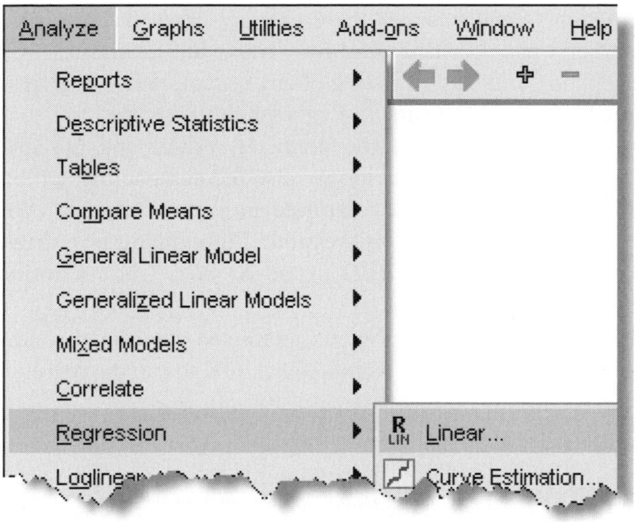

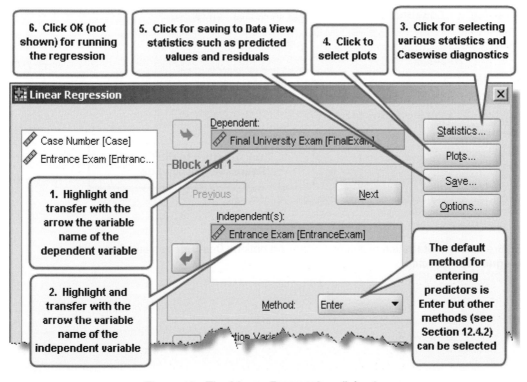

Figure 10. Finding the **Linear Regression** procedure

Figure 11. The **Linear Regression** dialog box

- Request additional descriptive statistics and a residuals analysis by clicking the **Statistics...** button to open the **Linear Regression: Statistics** dialog box (Figure 12) and activating the **Descriptives** checkbox. Analysis of the residuals gives a measure of how good the prediction is and whether there are any cases that are so discrepant as to be considered outliers and perhaps dropped from the analysis. Click the **Casewise diagnostics** checkbox to include a listing of any exceptionally large residuals in the output. Click **Continue** to return to the **Linear Regression** dialog box.
- Since systematic patterns between the predicted values and the residuals can indicate violations of the assumption of linearity, we also recommend that a plot of the standardised residuals (*ZRESID*) against the standardised predicted values (*ZPRED*) be requested. Click **Plots...** to open the **Linear Regression: Plots** dialog box (Figure 13) and transfer *ZRESID* to the **Y:** box and *ZPRED* to the **X:** box. Click **Continue** to return to the **Linear Regression** dialog box.
- Back in the **Linear Regression** dialog box, predicted values and residuals can be saved to **Data View** by clicking the **Save...** button. Click **OK** to run the regression.

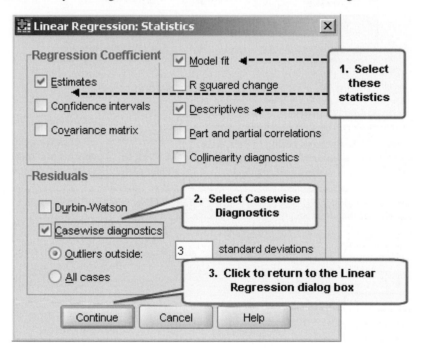

Figure 12. The **Statistics** dialog box with extra options **Descriptives** and **Casewise diagnostics** selected

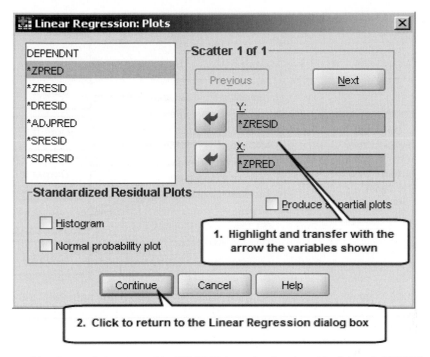

Figure 13. The **Plots** dialog box with *ZRESID* (standardised residuals) and *ZPRED* (standardised predicted scores) selected for the axes of the plot

12.2.4   Output for simple regression

The various tables and charts in the output are listed in the left-hand pane of **SPSS Viewer**, as shown in Output 1. After the requested descriptive statistics and correlations (plus several other tables), the first table to scrutinise is **Casewise Diagnostics**. The information it contains may indicate that the regression analysis should be terminated and re-run after outliers have been removed from the data set. The table can be selected directly by moving the cursor to **Casewise Diagnostics** in the left-hand pane and clicking the left-hand mouse button.

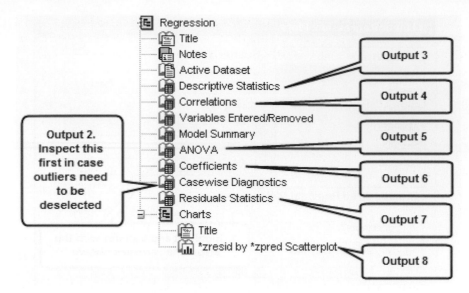

Output 1. The left-hand pane listing the tables and charts in the right-hand pane

Indication of residual outliers

The table of cases (**Casewise Diagnostics**) in Output 2 shows only one outlier with an absolute standardised residual greater than 3. This is Case 34, with a score of *195* for *Final University Exam*. From past experience, this is a suspiciously high mark and is almost certainly a typo; moreover, the candidate concerned got only 49 in the entrance exam, which is not an outstanding mark. The next section describes how to eliminate this outlier and re-run the regression analysis.

Casewise Diagnostics [a]

Case Number	Std. Residual	Final University Exam	Predicted Value	Residual
34	3.12	195	110.95	84.05

a. Dependent Variable: Final University Exam

Output 2. A list of cases with residuals greater than ± 3 standard deviations

Elimination of outliers

A more reliable regression analysis can be obtained by eliminating suspicious outliers. Use the **Select Cases** procedure described in Section 3.3.1.

See Section 3.3.1

- Choose **Data➜Select Cases…** to open the **Select Cases** dialog box.
- Click the **If condition is satisfied** radio button and define the condition as *Case ~=34* (the symbol ~= means 'not equal to').
- Click **Continue** and then **OK** to deselect this case.

If there are several suspicious outliers (obvious typographical errors, perhaps), it might be simpler to deselect them all by using a cut-off value for one of the variables (e.g. defining the condition with an inequality operator, as in the specification: *FinalExam* > 190). Sometimes, in order to see what value to use in the inequality, it is convenient to arrange scores in order of value by entering the **Data** menu and choosing **Sort Cases...** .

Output for simple regression after elimination of the outliers

When the regression analysis is re-run after deleting the original output, there will be no table of **Casewise Diagnostics**, since no cases will now have outlying residuals. We can therefore begin with the various tables and plots in the output. In Output 3, are the tables of descriptive statistics and the correlation coefficient for the 33 cases remaining in the data set.

Descriptive Statistics

	Mean	Std. Deviation	N
Final University Exam	102.82	32.633	33
Entrance Exam	47.27	7.539	33

Correlations

		Final University Exam	Entrance Exam
Pearson Correlation	Final University Exam	1.00	.73
	Entrance Exam	.73	1.00
Sig. (1-tailed)	Final University Exam	.	.00
	Entrance Exam	.00	.
N	Final University Exam	33	33
	Entrance Exam	33	33

Output 3. The **Descriptive Statistics** and **Correlations** tables for the data set without the outlier

Output 4 gives the value of **Multiple R**, where *R* is the **multiple correlation coefficient**. We shall explain the meaning of *R* when we discuss multiple regression.

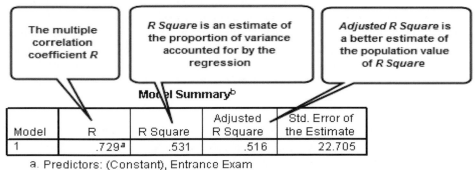

Model	R	R Square	Adjusted R Square	Std. Error of the Estimate
1	.729a	.531	.516	22.705

a. Predictors: (Constant), Entrance Exam

b. Dependent Variable: Final University Exam

Output 4. The values of the multiple correlation coefficient *R* and other statistics

For the moment, note that when, as in the present example, there is only one regressor, *R* is simply the *absolute value* of the Pearson correlation between the criterion or DV and the regressor (IV).

The other statistics listed in Output 4 are **R Square** (a positively biased estimate of the proportion of the variance of the dependent variable accounted for by regression), **Adjusted R Square** (which corrects this bias and therefore has a lower value), and the **Standard Error of the Estimate** (the standard deviation of the residuals). The **effect size**, as estimated by **adjusted R^2** is 0.516 (52%). This, following Cohen's classification, is a 'large' effect.

Output 5 shows the regression ANOVA, which tests for a linear relationship between the variables. The *F* statistic is the ratio of the mean square for regression to the residual mean square. In this example, the value of *F* in the ANOVA Table is significant beyond the .01 level. *It should be noted, however, that only an examination of their scatterplot can confirm that the relationship between two variables is genuinely linear.*

The value of *F* and its associated p-value (significant at the .01 level)

ANOVA^b

Model		Sum of Squares	df	Mean Square	F	Sig.
1	Regression	18096.33	1	18096.3	35.10	.000^a
	Residual	15980.58	31	515.50		
	Total	34076.91	32			

a. Predictors: (Constant), Entrance Exam

b. Dependent Variable: Final University Exam

Output 5. The **ANOVA** for the regression

Output 6 presents the kernel of the regression analysis, the regression equation. The values of the **regression coefficient** and **constant** are given in column **B** of the table. Two further features of Output 6 are worthy of note. In the column headed 'Standardized Coefficients', there is no entry in the row labelled 'Constant'. This is because, as we have seen, the intercept of the regression equation disappears when the scores are standardised. In the same column, the regression coefficient is given as 0.73, which is the value of the Pearson correlation *r* because, as we have seen, the slope of the regression line of one standardised variable upon another is the Pearson correlation.

Coefficientsᵃ

Model		Unstandardized Coefficients		Standardized Coefficients	t	Sig.
		B	Std. Error	Beta		
1	(Constant)	-46.30	25.48		-1.82	.079
	Entrance Exam	3.15	.53	.73	5.92	.000

a. Dependent Variable: Final University Exam

> The regression equation includes this constant and coefficient

> *Beta* is the regression coefficient whan all the variables are expressed in standardised form

> This tests the null hypothesis that there is no linear relationship between the variables (i.e. H₀ states that the regression coefficient is 0)

Output 6. The regression equation and associated statistics

From the values for the intercept and slope given in Output 6, the regression equation is

$$\left(Final\ University\ Exam\right)' = -46.30 + 3.15 \times \left(Entrance\ Exam\right)$$

where *(Final University Exam)'* is the predicted value of the actual *Final University Exam* mark. Thus a person scoring 60 in the *Entrance Exam* would have a predicted *Final* mark of

$$-46.30 + 3.15 \times 60 = 142.7 \quad \text{(i.e. 143).}$$

Notice that in Table 1, the person who scored 60 on the *Entrance Exam* actually scored 145 on the *Final University Exam*. So $Y' = 143$ and $Y = 145$. The residual $e = (Y - Y')$ is

$$145 - 143 = +2.$$

Other statistics are also listed in Output 6. The **Std. Error** is the standard error of the regression coefficient, B. **Beta** is the beta coefficient, which is the estimated average change in the dependent variable (expressed in standard deviation units) that would be produced by a positive increment of one standard deviation in the independent variable. The t statistic tests the regression coefficient for significance, and **Sig.** is the p-value of t. (Here .00 means <0.01, i.e. t is significant beyond the 0.01 level for the variable *Entrance Exam*. Write this p-value as '<.01', not as '.00'.)

Output 7 is a table of the statistics of the residuals. The row labelled **Predicted Value** summarises the unstandardised predicted values. The row labelled **Residual** summarises the unstandardised residuals. The row labelled **Std. Predicted Value** (identified as *ZPRED* in the **Plots** dialog box in Figure 13) summarises the standardised predicted values (i.e. *Predicted Value* transformed to a scale with mean 0 and SD 1). You can see that the calculated value for the SD (.98) is approximately 1. The row labelled **Std. Residual** (identified as *ZRESID* in the **Plots** dialog box in Figure 13) summarises the standardised residuals (with mean 0 and SD 1).

Residuals Statistics [a]

	Minimum	Maximum	Mean	Std. Deviation	N
Predicted Value	60.95	152.43	102.82	23.780	33
Residual	-54.49	30.97	.00	22.35	33
Std. Predicted Value	-1.76	2.09	.00	1.00	33
Std. Residual	-2.40	1.36	.00	.98	33

a. Dependent Variable: Final University Exam

Output 7. Table of statistics relating to the residuals

Output 8 is the scatterplot of the standardised residuals (*ZRESID*) against the standardised predicted values (*ZPRED*). The plot shows an essentially shapeless pattern, thereby confirming that the assumptions of linearity and homogeneity of variance are tenable. A crescent-shape or a 'funnel' would have indicated that a linear regression model was not a convincing interpretation of the data.

Other diagnostic plots could have been selected from within the **Standardized Residual Plots** box in Figure 13: for example, we could obtained a histogram of the standardised residuals (see Output 8) and a cumulative normal probability plot (in which, ideally, the points should lie along or adjacent to the diagonal).

Dependent Variable: Final University Exam

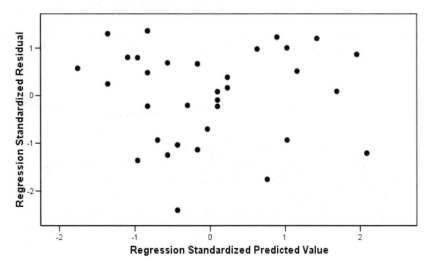

Output 8. Scatterplot of standardised residuals against standardised predicted scores

12.3   MULTIPLE REGRESSION

In **multiple regression**, the values of one variable (the target, criterion or dependent variable Y) are estimated from those of two or more (in the general case, p) independent variables or regressors (X_1, X_2, ..., Xp). This is achieved by the construction of a **multiple linear regression equation** of the general form:

$$Y' = b_0 + b_1 X_1 + b_2 X_2 + ... + b_p X_p \ \text{- - -} \ (17)$$

Multiple linear regression equation

where the parameters b_1, b_2, ..., b_p are the **partial regression coefficients** and the intercept b_0 is the **regression constant**. This equation is known as the **multiple linear regression equation of Y upon X_1, X_2, ... X_p.**

In simple regression, where there is only one IV or regressor, the graph of the regression equation is a straight line. In multiple regression, where there are two or more IVs, the graph is a plane or an abstract generalisation of a plane known in mathematics as a **hyperplane**.

Associated with each IV or regressor is a **partial regression coefficient**, which is the average change in the criterion variable that would be produced by a positive increase of one unit in the IV, with the effects of the other IVs upon either variable being held constant. Consider the partial regression coefficient b_1. Suppose we were to fix the values of all variables except regressor X_1, regress the criterion Y upon X_1 and calculate the regression coefficient. If we were to do this for every possible combination of fixed values for the other regressors and average the regression coefficients, we should have the partial regression coefficient b_1.

12.3.1   The multiple correlation coefficient *R*

One simple measure of the efficacy of regression for the prediction of Y is the Pearson correlation between the true values of the target variable Y and the estimates Y' obtained by substituting the corresponding values of X_1, X_2, ..., Xp into the regression equation. The correlation between Y and Y' is known as the **multiple correlation coefficient R**. Notice that the upper case is used for the multiple correlation coefficient, to distinguish it from the correlation between the target variable and any one independent variable considered separately.

Range of the multiple correlation coefficient

Returning for a moment to simple regression, where there is only one IV, recall that, while a linear transformation of one of the variables in a correlation leaves the absolute value of the correlation unaltered, a negative slope changes the sign of the correlation. Even in simple regression, the multiple correlation coefficient is defined, because R is simply the correlation between the predictions from regression, Y', that is, a linear function of the IV (X), and Y, the true values of the scores on the DV. The linear function, as we also saw, must always have the same sign as the correlation. The value of R can never be negative, because if the Pearson correlation is negative, the negative sign of the regression coefficient ensures that the correlation between Y and Y' is positive in that case also.

In multiple regression, the situation is obviously more complicated, because there are several IVs. It can be shown, nevertheless, that there too, the correlation between Y and Y' can never be negative. Basically, the reasoning is the same: if the partial correlation between an IV and the DV is negative, the Pearson correlation between the two is also negative and the negative sign of the regression coefficient converts the correlation between Y and Y' to a positive value.

The multiple correlation R, therefore, can only take values in the range from zero to +1, inclusive. (In practice, with measured variables, neither of these theoretical limits is ever achieved.)

As in simple regression, a measure of **effect size** in multple regression is provided by the **coefficient of determination R^2** which, by analogy with bivariate regression, is the proportion of variance in the dependent variable that can be accounted for by regression upon the independent variables or regressors. The positive bias in R^2 is partially corrected in the statistic known as **adjusted R^2**.

12.3.2   Significance testing in multiple regression

Statistical testing is more complex in multiple regression than it is in simple regression. As in simple regression, an overall F test can be made of the null hypothesis of complete independence. In multiple correlation, however, the significance of F does not imply that any one of the partial regression coefficients is significant. Another problem is that when there are two or more correlated IVs, it is impossible to attribute variance in the DV unequivocally to any particular IV, without additional collateral evidence or a well-conceived and empirically supported causal model.

If we assume that there are p independent variables, the (very unlikely) null hypothesis that all the regression coefficients are zero is, by analogy with (15), tested with the statistic

$$F(p, df_{residual}) = \frac{MS_{regression}}{MS_{residual}} = \frac{SS_{regression} / p}{SS_{residual} /(n-1-p)} = \frac{R^2(n-1-p)}{(1-R^2)p} \;\text{- - -}\; (18)$$

F ratio for testing the null hypothesis
that all regression coefficients are zero

where p, the number of regressors in the multiple regression, replaces 1 in (16).

Associated with the independent variable X_k is the regression coefficient b_k. The null hypothesis that, in the population, this regression coefficient is zero is tested with the statistic

$$t_k = \frac{b_k}{s_{b_k}} \quad \text{where } s_{b_k} = \sqrt{\frac{SS_{residual} /(n-1-p)}{\sum X_k^2 (1-R^2)}} \;\text{- - -}\; (19)$$

t test for significance of a partial regression coefficient

where the s_{b_k} is the estimated standard error of the partial regression coefficient b_k. Here, R is the multiple correlation coefficient between the DV and the estimates from regression Y' when all p IVs or regressors are in the regression equation.

Provided various assumptions are met, this statistic is distributed as t on $(n - 1 - p)$ degrees of freedom. Formula (19) is an obvious generalisation of (15) from the case with one IV to the case with p IVs.

12.3.3   Partial and semipartial correlation

Partial correlation

We made the acquaintance of partial correlation in Chapter 11. The **partial correlation** between two variables is what remains of the association between them when their associations with a third variable have been taken into account. Consider the multiple regression of Y (the DV) upon X_1 and X_2 (the IVs). Let e_Y and e_1 be the residuals of Y and X_1 when both variables are regressed upon independent variable X_2. The correlation between the residuals e_Y and e_1 is the partial correlation between Y and X_1. In Chapter 11, we saw that this correlation is readily obtained from the values of the correlations among the three variables.

In this chapter, we shall denote the partial correlation between Y and X_1 by using subscript notation thus $r_{Y1.2}$. In the subscript, the IV or regressor on the right of the point has been removed or 'partialled out' of the variables on the left of the point: X_2 has been removed from both Y and X_1.

We gave a formula for the partial correlation in Chapter 11. Amending the notation to apply to the present (regression) situation, the partial correlation $r_{Y1.2}$ is given by

$$r_{Y1.2} = \frac{r_{Y1} - r_{Y2}.r_{12}}{\sqrt{(1 - r_{Y2}^2)(1 - r_{12}^2)}} \quad \text{- - - (20) \textbf{Partial correlation}}$$

The partial correlation is tested for significance with

$$t = \frac{r\sqrt{(n-3)}}{\sqrt{(1 - r^2)}} \quad \text{- - - (21) \emph{t} \textbf{test for significance of partial correlation}}$$

on $(n - 3)$ degrees of freedom. A degree of freedom has been lost from the residual variance because an additional regression coefficient has been estimated.

Semipartial (or part) correlation

Since in multiple regression we are trying to account for the variance of the DV in terms of regression upon two or more IVs, interest centres upon the proportion of the *total* variance of the DV that is accounted for, rather than the residual variance. To determine this proportion, we need to know the correlation between Y and the residual variance of X_1 after the influence of X_2 has been removed from X_1 only. The **semipartial** (or **part**) **correlation** between Y and the residuals of X_1 after the influence of X_2 has been removed is written as $r_{Y(1.2)}$. In the subscript of r, $Y(1.2)$, the dot between the numbers 1 and 2 inside the brackets indicates that X_2 has been partialled out from X_1, but from Y.

The semipartial correlation $r_{Y(1.2)}$ is given by

$$r_{Y(1.2)} = \frac{r_{Y1} - r_{Y2}.r_{12}}{\sqrt{(1 - r_{12}^2)}} \quad \text{- - - (22) \textbf{Semipartial correlation}}$$

The formulae for the partial and semipartial correlations are very similar. The only difference is the additional factor in the denominator of the partial correlation, which ensures that its value is always at least as great as that of the semipartial correlation. Generally, the value of the partial correlation will be greater: it is highly unlikely that either Y or X_1 will show a correlation of exactly zero with X_2, in which case the partial and semipartial correlations would have the same value. The semipartial correlation can be tested for significance in the same way as the partial correlation. If, however, the semipartial correlation is significant, then the partial correlation must also be significant.

Variance interpretation of partial and semipartial correlations

Figure 14 depicts the relationships among the three variables when Y is regressed upon two independent variables X_1 and X_2.

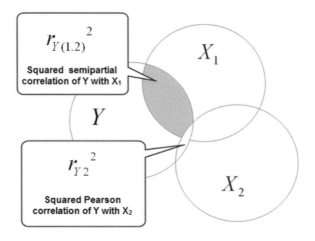

Figure 14. Variance interpretation of the semipartial correlation

Figure 14 shows that the square of the *semipartial* correlation $r^2_{Y(1.2)}$ (the grey area) is the additional proportion of the *total* variance of Y that is accounted for when the independent variable X_1 is added to the regression equation of Y upon X_2. The square of the *partial* correlation $r_{Y1.2}{}^2$, on the other hand, is the proportion of the *unexplained* variance of Y (the residuals when Y is regressed upon X_2) that is accounted for when X_1 is added to the regression equation. In the figure, the partial correlation is the grey area divided, not by 100% (the area of the whole circle), but by the area of the circle from which the white area of overlap has been subtracted. (The denominator of the partial correlation is thus smaller, making its value greater than that of the semipartial correlation.)

The foregoing notation for the semipartial correlation generalises to any number of independent variables. Suppose there are, not two but four independent variables X_1, X_2, X_3, X_4 and that we regress X_1 upon the other independent variables X_2, X_3, X_4. The semipartial correlation of Y with X_1 is the correlation between Y and the residuals of X_1 when X_2, X_3 and X_4 have been removed by multiple regression. This semipartial correlation is written as $r_{Y(1.234)}$, the subscripts 234 to the right of the point and the brackets signifying that the effects of X_2, X_3, X_4 have been removed from X_1 but not from Y.

Semipartial correlation and multiple correlation

If we regress Y upon two independent variables X_1 and X_2, the Pearson correlation between Y and the estimates from regression Y' is the multiple correlation coefficient, which we shall write as $R_{Y.12}$. In this expression, the subscript '$Y.12$' indicates that Y is being correlated with a function of X_1, X_2 (the linear regression function). As we have seen, the square of the multiple correlation $R_{Y.12}{}^2$ is the proportion of the total variance of the dependent variable Y that is accounted for by regression upon the independent variables X_1 and X_2 and is known as the **coefficient of determination**.

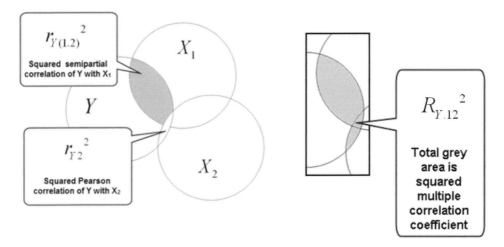

Figure 15. Relation between total proportion of variance accounted for by regression (R^2) and the squared semipartial correlation

In Figure 15, the total grey area in the right part of the figure is the coefficient of determination, that is, the total proportion of the variance of Y that is accounted for by multiple regression upon the two independent variables. The left-hand part of Figure 15 shows that the coefficient of determination can be partitioned into two components:

1. The square of the Pearson correlation between Y and X_2;
2. The squared semipartial correlation between Y and the residuals of X_1 after regression of X_1 upon X_2. We can therefore write

$$R^2_{Y.12} = r_{Y2}{}^2 + r_{Y(1.2)}{}^2 \quad \text{--- (23) \ \textbf{Partition of} } R^2_{Y.12}$$

We can also partition the coefficient of determination $R_{Y.12}{}^2$ as if the initial regression has been Y upon X_1 as follows:

$$R^2_{Y.12} = r_{Y1}{}^2 + r^2_{Y(2.1)} \quad \text{--- (24) \ \textbf{Alternative partition of} } R^2_{Y.12}$$

where $r^2_{2.1}$ is the squared semipartial correlation between Y and the residuals of X_2 after regression upon X_1.

Obtaining semipartial correlations from multiple correlations: ΔR^2

We now consider a more complex example, in which there are four independent variables X_1, X_2, X_3, X_4. In this case, the multiple correlation coefficient is $R_{Y.1234}$ to indicate that the dependent variable Y is being correlated with a linear function of X_1, X_2, X_3, X_4.

We can partition the squared multiple correlation $R^2_{Y.1234}$ as follows:

$$R^2_{Y.1234} = r^2_{Y4} + r^2_{Y(3.4)} + r^2_{Y(2.34)} + r^2_{Y(1.234)} \text{ --- (25)} \textbf{ Partition of } R^2_{Y.1234}$$

The first three terms on the right of equation (25), however, are a partition of the squared multiple correlation when Y is regressed upon the three independent variables X_2, X_3, X_4:

$$r^2_{Y4} + r^2_{Y(3.4)} + r^2_{Y(2.34)} = R^2_{Y.234} \text{ --- (26)} \textbf{ Partition of } R^2_{Y.234}$$

We may therefore express the squared semipartial correlation of Y with X_1 as the difference between the two squared multiple correlation coefficients thus

$$r^2_{Y(1.234)} = R^2_{Y.1234} - R^2_{Y.234} \text{ --- (27)} \textbf{ Delta } R^2$$

From (27), we see that the squared semipartial correlation is the increase in R^2 that results from adding that particular independent variable to the regression equation. For this reason, the squared semipartial correlation is referred to by some authors as ΔR^2 (**delta R^2**).

Uncorrelated independent variables

If, in the example of four independent variables, those variables were to be uncorrelated, we could represent the situation as in Figure 16. In Figure 16, none of the independent variables overlaps with any of the others, reflecting the total lack of correlation among them. In this case, the coefficient of determination (the total proportion of the variance of the dependent variable that is accounted for by regression) is given by

$$R_{Y.1234}{}^2 = r_{Y1}{}^2 + r_{Y2}{}^2 + r_{Y3}{}^2 + r_{Y4}{}^2 \text{ --- (28)}$$

Partition of $R^2_{Y.1234}$ when the IVs are uncorrelated

The partition in (28) permits an unequivocal attribution of a portion of the variance of Y accounted for by regression to a particular independent variable.

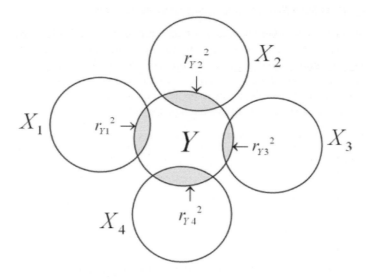

Figure 16. Regression with uncorrelated independent variables

Variance interpretation of the test of the partial regression coefficient

The situation depicted in Figure 16 is, in practice, never encountered when the independent variables X are measured in the units of study, because such measurements are always subject to error. More typically, the IVs are correlated, as in Figure 15. There, the squared semipartial correlation between Y and either dependent variable is less than the square of the simple Pearson correlation between Y and that independent variable alone. The squared semipartial correlation effectively places an independent variable 'at the end of the queue', as far as the attribution of variance in Y to each IV is concerned.

It can be shown that the test for the significance of a regression coefficient b_k, that is,

$$t_k = \frac{b_k}{s_{b_k}}$$

is equivalent to the test of the significance of the squared semipartial correlation, or ΔR_k^2 :

$$F(1,\ n-1-p) = \frac{\Delta R_k^2}{SS_{residual}\ /(n-1-p)} = \frac{R_{Y.all}^2 - R_{Y.all\ except\ X_k}^2}{\left(1 - R_{Y.12...k}^2\right)/(n-1-p)} \ \text{- - -}\ (29)$$

F ratio for significance of squared semipartial correlation

where ΔR_k^2 is the squared semipartial correlation been Y and X_k when all the other $p-1$ independent variables or regressors have been entered into the regression equation first.

'Importance' of the independent variable considered separately

The sharing of variance among the independent variables in multiple regression makes it impossible to assign variance in *Y* unequivocally to any of the independent variables. There is, therefore, a large literature on the question of which of the variables in a multiple regression is the 'most important' in explaining the variance of the dependent variable. The paper and textbook by Darlington (1968, 1990) provide a lucid discussion of the problems with the various measures of 'importance' that have been proposed.

We have already seen that the unstandardised regression coefficient is unsuitable as a measure of 'importance'. It might be thought that the simple Pearson correlation between an independent variable and the criterion would be an appropriate measure; but there are situations in which the largest squared semipartial correlation ΔR^2 does not belong to the variable showing the highest Pearson correlation with the criterion.

Suppressors

Some independent variables in a regression analysis are 'important', not in the sense that they predict the dependent variable, but because when their effects are removed from other independent variables with which they correlate substantially, those other variables predict the criterion with greater accuracy, even though the suppressor variable may itself show a negligible correlation with the criterion.

12.4   MULTIPLE REGRESSION WITH SPSS

One potential problem with multiple regression is that if we have measured several variables, some of which are highly correlated, the multiple regression package the researcher is using may not work at all. This is known as the problem of **multicollinearity**. A key notion here is that of the **tolerance** of a regressor, that is, one minus the square of the multiple correlation between the regressor and estimates of its values from its regression upon all the other regressors. If the tolerance is too low, the multiple regression will fail to run.

Even if multiple regression is feasible, there remains the problem of ascertaining which of the many variables in a study are crucial. In a situation where everything correlates with everything else, it is impossible to attribute variance in the target, criterion or dependent variable unequivocally to any one regressor or independent variable. Should the researcher be armed with a well-developed causal model of the focal health variables, this can drive both the selection of regressors and establish their relative importance. Often, however, especially in the early stages of research in an area, the researcher has no such model; indeed, the motivation for the research may be little more than the suspicion that certain variables might be important.

In Table 2, three extra variables, the subject's *Age*, the score obtained on a relevant academic *Project*, and *IQ* have been added to the original variables in Table 1. The outlier that was detected in the preliminary regression analysis, however, has been removed. Only a few cases are shown in Table 1. The full data set is available at www.psypress.com/spss-made-simple.

In the following discussion, we shall be concerned with two main questions:

1. Does the addition of more independent variables improve the accuracy of predictions of the value of *Final University Exam*?
2. Of these new variables, are some more useful than others for prediction of the dependent variable?

We shall see that the answer to the first question is 'Yes, up to a point'. It can be shown, in fact, that (providing the tolerance is sufficient) adding more regressors will result in a value for *R* which is at least as high as the previous value. On the other hand, this does not mean that more regressors should necessarily be added as a matter of course because, in some circumstances, that can result in highly unstable estimates. More is not necessarily better.

Table 2. An extension of Table 1, with data on three additional independent variables

Case	Fin	Ent	Age	Pro	IQ	Case	Fin	Ent	Age	Pro	IQ
1	38	44	21.9	50	110	18	103	48	22.3	53	134
2	49	40	22.6	75	120	19	105	43	21.8	72	140
3	61	43	21.8	54	119	20	106	55	21.4	69	127

The second question, concerning the relative importance of the various regressors, is particularly problematic, and none of the available approaches to it is entirely satisfactory (see, for example, the references to Darlington's work above and Howell, 2007, for a review).

In this section, we shall consider two general approaches to multiple regression. In **simultaneous** multiple regression, all the relevant regressors are entered in the equation directly, so that the tests for each regression coefficient effectively put it 'at the end of the queue' and test ΔR^2 in the presence of all the other variables. In **stepwise** multiple regression, the more controversial of the two techniques, the independent variables are added to (or taken away from) the equation one at a time, the order of entry (or removal) being determined by preset statistical criteria. Many would say, however, that no statistical model alone can justify such 'queue-jumping': a substantive causal model is also essential.

In this section, we shall begin with an example of the use of simultaneous regression. After that, for the sake of completeness (and with considerable reservations), we shall turn to stepwise regression. In fact, despite the theoretical problems with stepwise regression, we have found that the method often yields sensible results that are very similar to those from a simultaneous regression on the same data.

Constructing the SPSS data set

Restore the original data set (minus the outlier) to **Data View**. In **Variable View**, name the three new variables (e.g. *Age*, *Project* and *IQ*). Use the **Label** column to assign a variable label such as *Project Mark*. Now enter the scores in **Data View**. The first three cases are shown in Figure 17.

Case	FinalExam	EntranceExam	Age	Project	IQ
1	38	44	21.9	50	110
2	49	40	22.6	75	120
3	61	43	21.8	54	119

Figure 17. The first three cases in **Data View**

12.4.1 Simultaneous multiple regression

- In the **Linear Regression** dialog box, transfer the variable name *Final University Exam* into the **Dependent Variable:** and *Entrance Exam*, *Age*, *Project Mark* and *IQ* into the **Independent Variables:** box.
- Select the other optional items as in Section 12.2.3, then click **OK**.

Output for simultaneous multiple regression

The first table in the output is a table of the requested descriptive statistics for each variable (Output 9).

Descriptive Statistics

	Mean	Std. Deviation	N
University Exam	102.82	32.63	33
Entrance Exam	47.27	7.54	33
Age	22.518	3.046	33
Project Mark	67.94	9.14	33
IQ	129.03	9.66	33

Output 9. The Descriptive Statistics table

The next item is an edited table of correlations (Output 10) showing that the target variable *Final University Exam* correlates significantly with three of the regresssors but not with the fourth (*Age*).

Correlations

		University Exam
Pearson Correlation	University Exam	1.00
	Entrance Exam	.73
	Age	-.03
	Project Mark	.40
	IQ	.65
Sig. (1-tailed)	University Exam	.
	Entrance Exam	.00
	Age	.43
	Project Mark	.01
	IQ	.00

Output 10. Edited table of Correlations

Output 11 lists the variables entered in the model.

Variables Entered/Removed[b]

Model	Variables Entered	Variables Removed	Method
1	IQ, Age, Project Mark, Entrance Exam [a]	.	Enter

a. All requested variables entered.

b. Dependent Variable: Final University Exam

Output 11. List of variables entered, the dependent variable and the method of analysis

Output 12 shows that the multiple correlation coefficient R is 0.87 and the **Adjusted R Square** is 0.73. The effect size represented by adjusted R^2 is 73% i.e. a **large** effect.

Model Summary [b]

Model	R	R Square	Adjusted R Square	Std. Error of the Estimate
1	.87[a]	.76	.73	16.92

a. Predictors: (Constant), IQ, Age, Project Mark, Entrance Exam

b. Dependent Variable: Final University Exam

Output 12. Value of *R* and other statistics

Recall that when one regressor (*Entrance Exam*) was used to predict *Final University Exam*, the value of *R* was 0.73 and **Adjusted R Square** (the estimate of the proportion of variance accounted for by regression) was 0.52 (52%). With *R* now at 0.87 and **Adjusted R Square** up from 52% to 73%, we see that the answer to the question of whether adding more independent variables improves the predictive power of the regression equation is definitely 'Yes'. There remains, however, the question of which of the new variables is responsible for the improvement.

Not surprisingly, the ANOVA (Output 13) shows that the regression is significant beyond the 0.01 level.

ANOVA[b]

Model		Sum of Squares	df	Mean Square	F	Sig.
1	Regression	26059.63	4	6514.91	22.75	.000[a]
	Residual	8017.28	28	286.33		
	Total	34076.91	32			

a. Predictors: (Constant), IQ, Age, Project Mark, Entrance Exam

b. Dependent Variable: Final University Exam

Output 13. The **ANOVA** for regression

Output 14 tables the values of the regression coefficients. From column **B**, we see that the multiple regression equation of *Final University Exam* upon *Entrance Exam*, *Age*, *Project Mark* and *IQ* is:

$$Final' = -272.13 + 2.49 \times Entrance + 1.24 \times Age + 0.50 \times Project + 1.51 \times IQ$$

where *Final'* is the predicted *Final University Exam* mark.

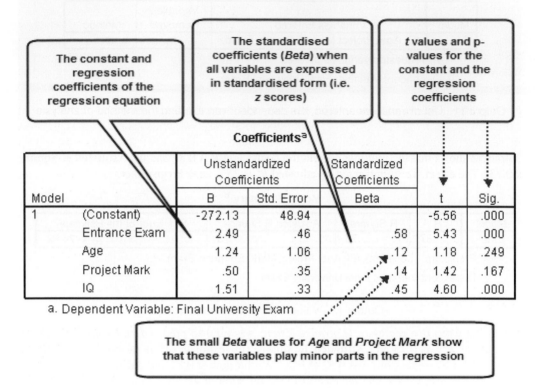

Model		Unstandardized Coefficients		Standardized Coefficients	t	Sig.
		B	Std. Error	Beta		
1	(Constant)	-272.13	48.94		-5.56	.000
	Entrance Exam	2.49	.46	.58	5.43	.000
	Age	1.24	1.06	.12	1.18	.249
	Project Mark	.50	.35	.14	1.42	.167
	IQ	1.51	.33	.45	4.60	.000

a. Dependent Variable: Final University Exam

The small *Beta* values for *Age* and *Project Mark* show that these variables play minor parts in the regression

Output 14. The regression equation and associated statistics

A person with *Age 21.6* and scoring *60* on the *Entrance Exam*, *84* on the *Project* and having an *IQ* of *132* would have an estimated score of

$$-272.13 + 2.49 \times (60) + 1.24 \times (21.6) + 0.50 \times (84) + 1.51 \times (132) = 145.37$$

Notice that case 29, who meets these specifications, actually scored 145 in the *Final University Exam*. However, not all cases have estimates so close to the actual values: for case 6, the estimate is 113.34, but the actual value is 73.

But what about the second question? Do all the new variables contribute substantially to the predictive power of the regression equation, or is one or more a passenger in the equation? We can learn little about the relative importance of the variables from the sizes of their regression coefficients B, because *the values of the partial regression coefficients reflect the original units in which the variables were measured.* For this reason, although the coefficient for *Age* is larger than that for *Project*, we cannot thereby conclude that *Age* is the more important predictor.

The **beta coefficients** (in the column headed **Beta**) tell us rather more, because each gives the estimate of the average number of standard deviations change in the criterion that will be produced by a change of one standard deviation in the regressor concerned. On this count, *Entrance Exam* still makes by far the greatest contribution, because a change of one standard deviation on that variable produces a change of 0.58 standard deviations on *Final University Exam*. Next is *IQ* with a change of 0.45, but *Project Mark* produces a change in *Final University Exam* of only 0.14 standard deviations and *Age* a change of 0.12 SDs. This ordering of the standardised beta coefficients is supported by consideration of the correlations between the criterion and each of the three regressors (Output 10). If ***R* square change** (ΔR^2) had been selected in Figure 12, the output would have shown that the regressor with the largest beta coefficient also has the largest value of R square change.

The remaining items of output (the table of **Residual Statistics** and the scatterplot of standardised predicted values against standardised residuals) are not shown here. There were no residual outliers. Residuals are the basis of **regression diagnostics**, that is, set of procedures for identifying rogue scores that can distort the values of multiple regression statistics. The raw residuals *e* are themselves valuable measures of **distance**. But distances exert more **leverage** on the regression statistics if they are far from the mean of the IV concerned than if they are near. Leverage is captured by the statistic known as h_i, where *h* stands for 'hat'. To have influence, however, a score must have both distance and leverage. The statistic known as **Cook's D** is a respected measure of influence, which is sensitive to both distance and leverage. (See Howell, 2007, pages 515-520, for a helpful introduction to regression diagnostics.)

12.4.2 Stepwise multiple regression

If, in the **Linear Regression** dialog box, the choice of **Method** is changed to **Stepwise**, rather than **Enter**, a stepwise regression will be run, whereby predictors are added to (or subtracted from) the equation one at a time. In **Forward selection**, predictors are added one a time, provided they meet an entry criterion: we could decide, for example, that a variable makes a robust contribution if the increase in the variance it explains is significant beyond the 0.05 level. In **Backward deletion**, the predictors are all present initially and are removed one at a time if they do not meet a retention criterion: we could decide, for example, that a variable will be removed if the resulting reduction in the value of R^2 has an associated p-value of greater than 0.10. The SPSS **Stepwise regression** routine is a combination of these two processes: a variable, having been added at an early stage, may subsequently be removed. Selected portions of the results of a **Stepwise regression** analysis are shown in Outputs 15-19.

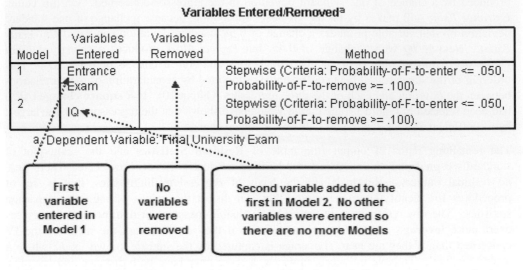

Output 15. List of variables entered (only two achieved entry in the stepwise regression)

The value of *R* for Model 2 is smaller than the value (0.87) given for simultaneous regression of *Final University Exam* upon *Entrance Exam*, *Project Mark*, *Age* and *IQ* but only slightly so. This shows the lack of predictive value of the two excluded variables (*Age* and *Project Mark*). The values of adjusted R^2 for Model 1 and Model 2 are large (52% & 71%, respectively) so the **effect sizes** are large.

Model Summary[c]

Note the increase in the value of *R* (and *R²*) after the addition of a second variable

Model	R	R Square	Adjusted R Square	Std. Error of the Estimate
1	.73[a]	.53	.52	22.70
2	.85[b]	.73	.71	17.62

a. Predictors: (Constant), Entrance Exam

b. Predictors: (Constant), Entrance Exam, IQ

c. Dependent Variable: Final University Exam

Output 16. Value of ***R*** and associated statistics for each Model

The ANOVA (Output 17) for each regression Model is significant.

ANOVA[c]

Model		Sum of Squares	df	Mean Square	F	Sig.
1	Regression	18096.33	1	18096.33	35.10	.000[a]
	Residual	15980.58	31	515.50		
	Total	34076.91	32			
2	Regression	24757.87	2	12378.93	39.85	.000[b]
	Residual	9319.04	30	310.63		
	Total	34076.91	32			

a. Predictors: (Constant), Entrance Exam

b. Predictors: (Constant), Entrance Exam, IQ

c. Dependent Variable: Final University Exam

Output 17. The **ANOVA** for each regression Model

The decision of the SPSS stepwise procedure is that, since the increment in R with the inclusion of either of the remaining variables (*Project Mark* and *Age*) does not reach the necessary statistical criterion, these variables are excluded from the final equation (Output 18).

From column **B** in Output 18, we see that the multiple regression equation of *Final University Exam* upon *Entrance Exam* and *IQ* is

$$(Final\ University\ Exam)' = -219.07 + 2.51 \times (Entrance\ Exam) + 1.58 \times IQ$$

where *(Final University Exam)'* is the predicted value of the *Final University Exam* mark.

Thus the estimated score of a person with *Age 21.6* scoring *60* on the *Entrance Exam* and having an *IQ* of *132* is

$$-219.07 + 2.51 \times (60) + 1.58 \times (132) = 140.09$$

Notice that case 29, who meets these specifications, scored 145 in the *Final University Exam*. In this case the 'simultaneous' regression equation provides a better estimate than the stepwise regression equation; but there are other cases in which the opposite is true.

	The constants and regression coefficients for each Model's regression equation	The standardised coefficents (*Beta*) when all the variables are expressed in *z* scores	*t* values and p-values for the constants and coefficients

Coefficients[a]

Model		Unstandardized Coefficients		Standardized Coefficients		
		B	Std. Error	Beta	t	Sig.
1	(Constant)	-46.30	25.48		-1.82	.079
	Entrance Exam	3.15	.53	.73	5.92	.000
2	(Constant)	-219.07	42.22		-5.19	.000
	Entrance Exam	2.51	.44	.58	5.75	.000
	IQ	1.58	.34	.47	4.63	.000

a. Dependent Variable: Final University Exam

Output 18. The regression coefficients tables for the single variable (Model 1) and the two variables (Model 2) remaining in the stepwise regression analysis

Output 19 lists the statistics for the excluded variables. Note the low values of *t* and their correspondingly high (i.e. > 0.05) p-values.

Excluded Variables [c]

Model		Beta In	t	Sig.	Partial Correlation	Collinearity Statistics Tolerance
1	Age	.18[a]	1.42	.167	.25	.93
	Project Mark	.21[a]	1.69	.102	.29	.92
	IQ	.47[a]	4.63	.000	.65	.90
2	Age	.15[b]	1.56	.129	.28	.92
	Project Mark	.17[b]	1.77	.088	.31	.91

a. Predictors in the Model: (Constant), Entrance Exam

b. Predictors in the Model: (Constant), Entrance Exam, IQ

c. Dependent Variable: Final University Exam

Output 19. The variables excluded from the stepwise regression analysis

In the table in Output 19, **Beta In** is the standardised regression coefficient that would result if the variable were entered into the equation at the next step. The *t* test is the usual test of significance of the regression coefficient. Partial correlation is the correlation that remains between two variables after removing the correlation that is due to their mutual association with the other variables. As we have seen, **multicollinearity** is the undesirable situation where the correlations among the regressors are high. Multicollinearity can be detected by the

Tolerance statistic, which is the proportion of a variable's variance not accounted for by other independent variables in the equation. A variable with very low tolerance contributes little information to a model, and can cause computational problems.

In conclusion, the **stepwise regression** confirms the conclusion from the beta coefficients in the simultaneous regression that only the variables *Entrance Exam* and *IQ* are useful for predicting *Final University Exam* marks. The other two variables can be dropped from the analysis.

12.5 REGRESSION AND ANALYSIS OF VARIANCE

In this section, we shall show that the similarities between the regression output and that of ANOVA are by no means coincidental; in fact, as we shall see in this section, the ANOVA itself can be viewed as a special case of multiple regression.

The link between the ANOVA and regression may seem far from self-evident. In the one-way ANOVA, for example, there is no continuous IV: we have a set of qualitatively different categories among which there is no inherent order. The results of the one-way ANOVA are, as we have seen, quite unaffected by the order in which the scores achieved in the various groups are entered in the Score column in Data View. In this section, however, we shall show that the one-way ANOVA can be viewed as the multiple regression of the scores (the DV) upon a set of artificial coding variables (known as **dummy variables**) and the resulting regression statistics are exactly equivalent to the usual ANOVA F test and to tests of differences among the treatment means.

12.5.1 The point-biserial correlation

In Chapter 6, we used an independent samples *t* test to compare the mean performance score of 20 participants who had ingested caffeine with the mean performance of a comparison or placebo group. It was found that the Caffeine group ($M = 11.90$; $SD = 3.28$) outperformed the Placebo group ($M = 9.25$; $SD = 3.16$). The *t* test showed the difference to be significant: $t(38) = 2.60$; $p = 0.01$.

To run a *t* test on the caffeine data, group membership is indicated by a **grouping variable**, that is, a set of code numbers, each number serving as a label for one group or condition. For the purposes of the *t* test, it doesn't matter what the code numbers are, as long as they are different. If, however, we let the value 0 denote the Placebo group and 1 denote the Caffeine group, we shall be using what is known as **dummy coding**. In some applications of regression, the choice of numbers for grouping variables is very important and different codes are appropriate for different purposes. Dummy coding, as we shall see, highlights the equivalence of the regression and ANOVA statistics.

When we introduced the Pearson correlation *r* in Chapter 11, we emphasised that *r* was a measure of linear association suitable for continuous or scale data. There is, however, a special application of the Pearson correlation which breaks this rule. A **point-biserial** correlation is the Pearson correlation between a continuous variable and a dichotomous grouping variable. In the caffeine example, we would calculate the correlation between the column of scores in Data View and the grouping variable consisting of the code numbers for the different groups.

When, from the caffeine data set, we calculate the point-biserial correlation between the scores and the grouping variable, we obtain $r(40) = 0.389$. In Chapter 11, we said that, provided a bivariate data set consisting of n pairs of scores was bivariate-normal, we could test the significance of r with the statistic t, where

$$t = \frac{r\sqrt{n-2}}{\sqrt{1-r^2}} \text{ - - - (30) } \textbf{\textit{t} test for significance of correlation}$$

on $(n-2)$ degrees of freedom.

When we apply this formula to the correlation between the dummy-coded grouping variable and the scores in the caffeine data (adding a few more decimal places when entering the value of r), we find that

$$t = \frac{.38913\sqrt{38}}{\sqrt{1-.38913^2}} = 2.604$$

which is exactly the value for t that we obtained when using the independent t test to compare the means of the Caffeine and Placebo groups.

This is, of course, no coincidence. There is, as we shall see, an intimate link between using techniques such as t and F to compare group means and the regression of scores upon grouping variables. The point-biserial correlation forms an important conceptual bridge between the statistics of comparison and those of association.

12.5.2   Regression and the one-way ANOVA for two groups

In Chapter 7, we saw that if the one-way ANOVA were to be applied to the data from the two-group Caffeine experiment, the ANOVA F-test would result in exactly the same decision about the null hypothesis of equality of the population means as would the independent-samples t test. In general, F and t are related according to

$$F_{1,2(n-1)} = t_{2(n-1)}^2 \text{ - - - (31)}$$

Relation between F and t in the two-group case

where n is the size of a sample (equal-n case).

In this particular example,

$$F_{1,38} = 6.781 = 2.604^2 = t_{38}^2$$

In Table 3, is shown the summary table for the one-way ANOVA for comparison with the output table for regression of the scores in the Caffeine experiment upon the dummy variable.

You will notice immediately that the regression sum of squares $SS_{\text{regression}}$ has exactly the same value as the one-way ANOVA between groups sum of squares SS_{between}. Moreover, the regression residual sum of squares SS_{residual} has the same value as the within groups sum of squares SS_{within} in the one-way ANOVA.

We have also seen that, in regression, the coefficient of determination (CD or r^2) is the proportion of the variance of the criterion or DV that is accounted for by regression. When we square the point-biserial correlation between the scores in the Caffeine experiment and the grouping variable, we obtain the coefficient of determination (r^2):

$$r^2 = 0.38913^2 = 0.1514$$

When the CD is multiplied by the total regression sum of squares SS_{total}, we obtain

$$r^2 (SS_{total}) = .1514 \times 463.775 = 70.22$$

which is not only the value of the regression sum of squares, but also the value of $SS_{between}$ in the one-way ANOVA.

Table 3. Comparison between the one-way ANOVA summary table (upper panel) with the ANOVA table in the output for the regression of the scores in the Caffeine experiment upon the grouping variable (lower panel)

ANOVA

Performance Score

	Sum of Squares	df	Mean Square	F	Sig.
Between Groups	70.225	1	70.225	6.781	.013
Within Groups	393.550	38	10.357		
Total	463.775	39			

ANOVA[b]

Model		Sum of Squares	df	Mean Square	F	Sig.
1	Regression	70.225	1	70.225	6.781	.013[a]
	Residual	393.550	38	10.357		
	Total	463.775	39			

a. Predictors: (Constant), Treatment Group

b. Dependent Variable: Performance Score

In this special case of two groups, therefore, we can interpret the between groups sum of squares in the one-way ANOVA as a regression sum of squares. We can also interpret the square of the point-biserial correlation as the proportion of the one-way ANOVA total sum of squares that is accounted for by the difference between the means of the two groups.

We have been considering the two-group case; but we know that the equivalence of F and t breaks down with three or more groups. The equivalence of regression and ANOVA generalises, however, to any number of groups.

12.5.3 Regression and dummy coding: the two-group case

In the previous section, we remarked upon the identity of the regression with the ANOVA statistics and showed that this is true in the special two-group case. In this session, we shall explain why the two sets of statistics are identical.

Equivalence of the t test and regression with a dummy variable

Figure 18 shows the scatterplot of performance scores against the values of the dummy variable X. The ordinary least squares regression line of the scores Y upon the dummy variable X will pass through the group means. (This is because the sum of the squared deviations about the mean is a minimum: that is, its value is less than the sum of the squared deviations about any other value.)

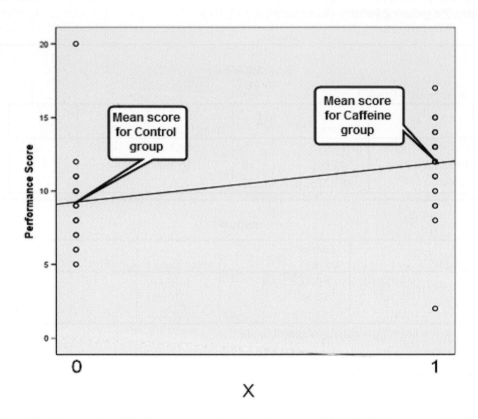

Figure 18. Scatterplot of Performance against the dummy variable X with the regression line passing through the group means

Let Y_0' and Y_1' be the points on the regression line when X has the values 0 and 1, respectively. Applying the regression equation $Y' = b_0 + b_1 X$, we find that

$$Y_0' = M_{Placebo} = b_0 \qquad Y_1' = M_{Caffeine} = M_{Placebo} + b_1 \qquad b_1 = M_{Caffeine} - M_{Placebo}$$

In words, with dummy coding, the intercept of the regression line is the mean score of the control group and the slope of the line is the difference between the mean scores under the two conditions. As a consequence, a test of the null hypothesis that the regression coefficient is zero is also a test of the null hypothesis that, in the population, the difference between the Caffeine and Placebo means is zero. This is why the regression on a dummy variable and the two-group ANOVA are equivalent: the regression predicts the group means exactly.

The lower part of Table 4 shows that the intercept (constant) is 9.25, the value of the Placebo mean. The slope of the line is 2.65, which is $11.90 - 9.25$, the difference between the means for the Caffeine and Placebo groups. Finally, $t(38) = 2.604$; $p = 0.013$. This is exactly the result we obtained from the independent samples t test.

Table 4. The intercept and regression coefficient from regression on the dummy variable. Notice that the value of F in the upper part of the table is the square of the value of t in the lower part

ANOVA[b]

Model		Sum of Squares	df	Mean Square	F	Sig.
1	Regression	70.225	1	70.225	6.781	.013[a]
	Residual	393.550	38	10.357		
	Total	463.775	39			

a. Predictors: (Constant), Treatment Group

b. Dependent Variable: Performance Score

Coefficients[a]

Model		Unstandardized Coefficients		Standardized Coefficients		
		B	Std. Error	Beta	t	Sig.
1	(Constant)	9.250	.720		12.854	.000
	Treatment Group	2.650	1.018	.389	2.604	.013

a. Dependent Variable: Performance Score

12.5.4   Regression and the one-way ANOVA

In a one-factor experiment with k treatment groups, the between groups (or treatment) sum of squares has $k - 1$ degrees of freedom, because there are only $k - 1$ deviations about the grand mean. We can carry group membership in $k - 1$ dummy variables. If we regress the scores on the $k - 1$ dummy variables, the multiple regression equation will predict the group means exactly, because the regression follows the least squares criterion, whereby the sum of squared deviations about the mean is a minimum. The multiple regression sum of squares will have $k-1$

degrees of freedom – one degree for each dummy variable. In the one-way ANOVA of Chapter 7, there were 5 treatment groups. If, therefore, we regress the scores upon 4 dummy variables, we shall predict the treatment means exactly and the regression sum of squares will be equal to the between groups mean square from the one-way ANOVA.

The four dummy variables are shown in Table 5. Every member of each of the five treatment groups will be assigned the same row of values of the four dummy variables.

Table 5. Four dummy variables specifying membership of the five treatment groups in the drug experiment

Group	X_1	X_2	X_3	X_4
Placebo	0	0	0	0
Drug A	1	0	0	0
Drug B	0	1	0	0
Drug C	0	0	1	0
Drug D	0	0	0	1

In Table 6, a section of **Data View** is shown, with the scores in the *Placebo* and **Drug A** groups alongside the assigned values of the four dummy variables.

Table 6. A fragment of **Data View**, showing the scores of some of the participants in the *Placebo* and *Drug A* groups, together with their assigned values of the four dummy variables

	Group	Score	X1	X2	X3	X4
7	Placebo	7	0	0	0	0
8	Placebo	6	0	0	0	0
9	Placebo	8	0	0	0	0
10	Placebo	8	0	0	0	0
11	Drug A	8	1	0	0	0
12	Drug A	10	1	0	0	0
13	Drug A	7	1	0	0	0

While completing the regression dialog, Click the **Save** button and, in the **Predicted Values** panel, check the **Unstandardised** check box. This choice will have the effect of placing the predicted values from regression into a new column in **Data View**, which will be assigned the heading PRE_1.

In Data View

Figure 19 is a fragment of **Data View**, showing (in the column labelled PRE_1) the predicted values that the multiple regression has assigned to the Placebo and Drug A groups.

	Group	Score	X1	X2	X3	X4	PRE_1
7	Placebo	7	0	0	0	0	8.00000
8	Placebo	6	0	0	0	0	8.00000
9	Placebo	8	0	0	0	0	8.00000
10	Placebo	8	0	0	0	0	8.00000
11	Drug A	8	1	0	0	0	7.90000
12	Drug A	10	1	0	0	0	7.90000
13	Drug A	7	1	0	0	0	7.90000
	Drug A	7	1	0	0	0	7.90000

Figure 19. Predicted values from the multiple regression for the *Placebo* and *Drug A* groups

As expected, the multiple regression of the scores upon the four dummy variables has predicted the values of the means of the *Placebo* and *Drug A* groups exactly.

The regression output

As in the case of two groups, the results of the one-way ANOVA and the regression are identical. (See Output 20.)

ANOVA[b]

Model		Sum of Squares	df	Mean Square	F	Sig.
1	Regression	351.52	4	87.88	9.08	.000[a]
	Residual	435.30	45	9.67		
	Total	786.82	49			

a. Predictors: (Constant), X4, X3, X1, X2

b. Dependent Variable: Score

Same value as the one-way ANOVA value

B for Constant is the Placebo mean

Coefficients[a]

Model		Unstandardized Coefficients		Standardized Coefficients	t	Sig.
		B	Std. Error	Beta		
1	(Constant)	8.000	.984		8.13	.000
	X1	-.100	1.391	-.010	-.07	.943
	X2	4.000	1.391	.403	2.88	.006
	X3	6.400	1.391	.645	4.60	.000
	X4	5.000	1.391	.504	3.59	.001

a. Dependent Variable: Score

The B values for X1-X4 are the differences between the respective means and the Placebo mean

Output 20. Output from regression of the scores in the 5-group drug experiment in Chapter 7 upon four dummy variables.

The Constant (intercept) is the mean for the *Placebo* group. The regression coefficients are the differences between the group means and the *Placebo* mean. The regression sum of squares is equal to $MS_{between}$ in the one-way ANOVA; so also are the results of the F tests in the two analyses.

Eta squared revisited

In Chapter 7, we discussed the measure of effect size known as **eta squared** (η^2), where η, the **correlation ratio**, is the proportion of the variance of the scores that is attributable to differences among the group means. The positive square root of this measure, eta, is the correlation between the scores the participants achieved in the experiment and their group means. Since the value of eta, like those of the statistics from the one-way ANOVA itself, is unaffected by the ordering of the scores from the different groups, it is applicable to a situation in which there is no continuous independent variable.

In Chapter 7, in the context of the analysis of trend, it was observed that if the members of a set of k treatment means are assigned arbitrarily to the counting numbers from 1 to k, the graph of a polynomial of degree $k - 1$ will fit the values perfectly. This will be true regardless of which mean value is paired with which number; although, of course, the coefficients of the polynomial will be different with different pairings. The values of the polynomial coefficients do not matter: the point is that the fit of the curve to the values of the means will be perfect, whatever the order of the means. If the IV is continuous and there are k treatment means, $k - 1$ sets of contrast coefficients can be constructed, each of which captures one particularly type of polynomial trend. Regression of the scores upon the $k - 1$ polynomials will predict the group means perfectly and the between groups sum of squares can be partitioned among the various different components of trend.

In the usual one-way ANOVA, however, there is no continuous IV: a factor is usually a set of qualitatively different categories among which there is no intrinsic order. We have seen, nevertheless, that by assigning the means of the five treatment groups in the ANOVA from Chapter 7 to different combinations of the values of 4 dummy variables, the multiple regression of the scores upon the dummy variables predicts the values of the five treatment means exactly; moreover, the regression statistics capture and test differences among the group means.

In fact, if we assign any sequence of four numbers to the participants in the Placebo group, another sequence to those in the Drug A group and so on, and run a multiple regression of the participants' scores on the four new coding variables, it will be found that, once again, the regression equation predicts the values of the group means exactly. For example, the Placebo group could be assigned the sequence: 1, 2, 3, 4; the Drug A group could be assigned the sequence 4, 1, 2, 3; the Drug B group could be assigned the sequence 3, 4, 1, 2; the Drug C group could be assigned the sequence 2, 3, 4, 1 and the Drug D group could be assigned the sequence 1, 3, 4, 2 (to avoid repetition of the first sequence of numbers). Run the regression and check that the values in the new column PRE_2 are indeed those of the five treatment means.

The **eta squared** ($\eta2$) statistic is the square of the multiple correlation between the scores and their predicted values from multiple regression upon the 4 dummy (or other grouping) variables. For each individual in a group, the predicted score will be the same, namely, the group mean. A multiple correlation is the Pearson correlation between the observed scores Y and the corresponding predicted values from regression Y'. Eta is, in fact, a multiple correlation coefficient. Since η is a multiple correlation, its value cannot be negative.

Since the value of η is independent of the ordering of the scores in the different groups, this statistic can be regarded as a **function-free correlation** expressing the total regression (linear and curvilinear) of the scores upon the numbers that have been assigned to the treatment groups.

12.6   MULTILEVEL REGRESSION MODELS

Underlying all the methods described so far in this chapter has been a very important assumption, namely, that the observations are independent. Suppose, however, that we are interested in the factors that lead to school success and that we have data on the exam results of a large number of children, together with their scores on a reading test, as well as information about their school's gender policy and other variables.

If we are interested in the effect of the children's reading levels on their exam success at school, it might seem natural to regress their school exam scores on their reading scores in the manner described earlier in this chapter. We could easily enter the data into SPSS and apply the methods of least squares regression to estimate the regression coefficient and test it for significance. The difficulty with this approach is that the assumption of independence of observations is manifestly false: it is well known that schools vary considerably in the stringency of their selection processes, their policy with regard to the issue of segregation of boys and girls and so on. For a variety of reasons, therefore, observations from one school will tend to be more similar to one another than they are to observations from another school.

Data of this kind are not a simple random sample from a pool of possible observations, as required by ordinary least squares regression models: on the contrary, they are clustered in a hierarchical fashion: students are nested within schools; schools are nested within districts and so on. It is likely that the data of children within a particular school will be more similar than the data of children from different schools. The same applies to districts. Research in many areas of study (e.g. education and health psychology) typically yield data that are hierarchically clustered in this way.

If the hierarchical dependencies in such a data set are ignored, the consequences can be serious. OLS regression will produce underestimates of the standard errors of the test statistics and the researcher may be led to conclude that there is strong evidence for non-existent effects. Rasbash et al. (2004) provide some striking examples of the consequences of inappropriate use of OLS regression with clustered data and the different conclusions the researcher would come to using multilevel modelling.

There is now available some excellent software for multilevel or hierarchical modelling, including the SPSS MIXED procedure. Jon Rasbash and his associates (Rasbash et al., 2004) have developed MLwiN, a dedicated package which provides excellent graphical feedback and an interactive learning environment for the user, backed up by an excellent manual and other documentation.

12.7   A FINAL WORD

Multiple regression is a highly complex topic and we can only touch upon it in a book of this kind. The following is a small selection from the wide choice of excellent books available.

Recommended reading

Ordinary least squares regression

Many years ago Jacob Cohen co-authored a book on multiple regression which, perhaps more than any other, made this difficult topic accessible to those other than professional statisticians.

The book has continued to be updated and the latest edition has kept fully abreast with recent developments. It is strongly recommended to anyone wishing to make progress in multiple regression.

Cohen, J., Cohen, P., West, S. G., & Aiken, L. S. (2003). *Applied multiple regression/correlation analysis for the behavioral sciences (3rd ed.)*. Mahwah, NJ: Lawrence Erlbaum Associates.

Todman and Dugard have written a readable practical guide to multivariate analysis, including multiple regression:

Todman, J., & Dugard, P. (2006). *Approaching multivariate analysis: An introduction for psychology*. London: Psychology Press.

A more comprehensive, in-depth treatment of multiple regression will be found in

Tabachnick, B. G., & Fidell, L. S. (2007). *Using multivariate statistics (5th ed.)* Boston: Allyn & Bacon (Pearson International Edition).

The article and book by Darlington are well worth reading:

Darlington, R. B. (1968). Multiple regression in psychological research and practice. *Psychological Bulletin,* 69, 161 – 182.

Darlington, R. B. (1990). *Regression and linear models*. New York: McGraw-Hill.

Multilevel modelling

The topic of multilevel modelling is introduced in Tabachnick & Fidell (2007), Chapter 15. The manual by Jon Rasbash and his associates would be an excellent follow-up:

Rasbash, J., Steele, F., Browne, W., & Prosser, B. (2004). *A User's Guide to MLwiN Version 2.0*. London: Centre for Multilevel Modelling, University of London.

Exercises

Exercise 20 *Simple, two-variable regression* and Exercise 21 *Multiple regression* are available in www.psypress.com/spss-made-simple and click on Exercises.

CHAPTER 13

Analyses of multiway frequency tables & multiple response sets

13.1   Introduction

13.2   Some basics of loglinear modelling

13.3   Modelling a two-way contingency table

13.4   Modelling a three-way frequency table

13.5   Multiple response sets

13.6   A final word

13.1   INTRODUCTION

A contingency table is a crosstabulation showing the frequencies of observations in different combinations of the categories making up two qualitative or categorical variables. The construction of a contingency table is the first step in the investigation of a possible association between categorical variables in a set of nominal data. The contingency table is the equivalent, for nominal data, of the scatterplot used to investigate associations in continuous bivariate (or multivariate) data sets. In Chapter 11, we described the use of approximate chi-square tests to test for the presence of an association between two categorical variables: 1. *Tissue type*; 2. *Presence of an antibody*.

In this chapter, we shall consider the investigation of associations among the variables in multivariate nominal data sets with three or more attributes. The traditional Pearson chi-square test was designed for use with two-way frequency tables. The situation often arises, however, in which the researcher has nominal data on three or more attributes and wants to test for associations among the attributes. For many years, the standard approach to this problem was to combine or 'collapse' the frequencies across the categories of some of the variables, thus creating a two-way table, upon which the usual chi-square test could then be made. This is a dangerous practice. Todman & Dugard (2007), for example, show how an apparent association between sex and mathematical ability (seemingly revealed by collapsing across a third variable and testing in the usual way) actually arises from the association of both gender and mathematical aptitude with the third variable, namely, the relative lengths of the index and third fingers. (Later in this chapter, we shall see that there are circumstances in which multiway frequency tables can safely be collapsed across the categories of some variables, but this move must be justified by preliminary analysis.)   It is also possible to generalise the traditional chi-square test to multi-way tables without collapsing across any of the attributes. Such an approach, however, as we shall see, rarely answers the researcher's specific questions.

Recent years have seen great advances in the analysis of multi-way contingency tables, and these new methods, collectively known as **loglinear analysis**, are now available in computing packages such as SPSS. Loglinear analysis allows the user to do much more than merely reject the hypothesis of independence of all the variables in the classification, which (when there are three or more attributes) is often very unlikely to be true anyway. The great advantage of loglinear analysis is that it makes possible the formulation of a model of the data which shows the unique contribution of each attribute and of its interactions with the other attributes.

Multiple response sets

This chapter will be devoted largely to the loglinear analysis of multiway frequency tables to which an individual contributes only one unit to the tally of frequencies of one combination of attributes. There are, however, data sets, such as responses to questionnaires, in which the individual may have made responses in two or more categories. For example, when asked which means of transport he or she uses to get to work, a respondent may be allowed to tick two or more items from the selection of possible means.

The final sections of the chapter illustrate how SPSS can be used to identify distinct response patterns for different categories of a variable. For instance, do males and females show different patterns in their use of transport?   The testing of such patterns for statistical robustness is problematic; but some tests are available for determining whether differences in frequencies are statistically significant.

13.2   SOME BASICS OF LOGLINEAR MODELLING

There is general agreement that there is little or no advantage in using loglinear analysis to analyse a two-way contingency table: the Pearson and likelihood ratio chi-square tests which we described in Chapter 11 (together with follow-up measures of strength of association) are sufficient for this purpose. In the simple context of the two-way table, however, the essential features of loglinear modelling emerge particularly clearly; moreover, the comparison with the traditional chi-square analysis of the same data is also instructive. In this section, therefore, we shall apply loglinear analysis to the same data that we analysed in Chapter 11, namely, the incidence of an antibody in four different tissue groups. The data are reproduced in Table 1 below.

Table 1. Contingency table with a pattern of observed frequencies suggesting an association between *Tissue Type* and *Presence* of an antibody

Tissue type	Presence		Total
	Yes	No	
A	8	14	22
B	7	11	18
C	7	5	12
Critical	21	6	27
Total	43	36	79

13.2.1 Loglinear models and ANOVA models

The full loglinear model of a two-way contingency table is very similar in appearance to the fixed-effects model for the two-factor, between subjects ANOVA. In the ANOVA model, each score X is expressed as the sum of several components:

1. The **grand mean** μ;
2. A **main effect** of factor A which, in the population, is the deviation of a marginal group mean on the A classification from the grand mean;
3. A **main effect** of factor B, which is the deviation of a marginal mean on the B classification from the grand mean;
4. The **interaction** AB, which is what remains of the deviation of a cell mean from the grand mean when the two main effects have been subtracted;
5. A random **error** component.

The **two-way ANOVA model** states that:

$$X = \begin{bmatrix} grand \\ mean \end{bmatrix} + \begin{bmatrix} main\ effect \\ of\ factor\ A \end{bmatrix} + \begin{bmatrix} main\ effect \\ of\ factor\ B \end{bmatrix} + \begin{bmatrix} AB \\ interaction \end{bmatrix} + \begin{bmatrix} random \\ error \end{bmatrix} ---(1)$$

The main effect of factor A is estimated with $M_j - M$, the deviation of the mean on the A classification from the grand mean. The main effect of factor B is estimated with $M_k - M$, the deviation of the mean on the B classification from the grand mean. The interaction component AB is what is left of the deviation of the cell mean from the grand mean when the main effects have been removed: $M_{jk} - M_j - M_k + M$.

With the exception of the grand mean, the components of the fixed effects ANOVA model are deviation scores, which have the property that they sum to zero at any level of either factor.

A loglinear model of a two-way contingency table

The full loglinear model for the cell frequencies in a two-way contingency table is similar in form to the ANOVA model:

$$ln\,E = \text{constant} + \begin{bmatrix} \text{main effect} \\ \text{of A} \end{bmatrix} + \begin{bmatrix} \text{main effect} \\ \text{of B} \end{bmatrix} + \begin{bmatrix} \text{interaction} \\ \text{AB} \end{bmatrix} \;\text{- - - (2)}\;\textbf{Loglinear model}$$

In equation 2, $ln\,E$ is the natural logarithm of the cell frequency. (Should you be rusty on logarithms and unsure about the difference between common [base *10*] and natural [base *e*] logs, you might look at the Appendix about logarithms.)

Notice that, rather than modelling the individual score *X* as in the two-way ANOVA, we are modelling the cell frequency in the contingency table. There is no separate random error term in the ANOVA model. Moreover, rather than modelling the cell frequency itself, we are modelling the natural logarithm of the cell frequency. The reason for this is basically that, as we said in Chapter 11, value of the expected frequencies are derived from *products* of the marginal frequencies in the contingency table. Equation 2 is linear in form because the log of a product is the *sum* of the logs of the factors involved. In fact, there is a multiplicative equivalent of the model in equation 2, in which the expected frequencies themselves (rather than their logs) are modelled as a *product* of main effect and interaction terms. This multiplicative model is obtained from (2) by taking antilogs of both sides of the equation.

These differences aside, there are important similarities between the ANOVA and loglinear models. The 'constant' in the loglinear model is the equivalent of the grand mean in the ANOVA model: it is the mean of the logs of the cell frequencies. The main effects are the deviations of the logs of the marginal frequencies from the grand mean. The interaction effect (there is one for each cell in the table) is what remains of the deviation of the log of the cell mean from the grand mean when the main effects have been removed. Once again, the main effects sum to zero over all the levels of either factor; and the interaction effects sum to zero at any level of either factor.

Although the ANOVA is predicated upon a score model, the ANOVA is not an exercise in modelling as such: the various components of the model (main effects and interactions) are tested for significance and the results interpreted accordingly. Throughout the testing process, the same model remains intact with all its original components, regardless of the outcomes of the tests.

In contrast, loglinear analysis is a process of **model-building**, the aim of the exercise being to find the model which, while having as few components as possible, accounts for the cell frequencies adequately. In the tissue type example, for instance, the hypothesis that the two attributes are independent implies that the cell frequencies can be modelled adequately by omitting the interaction term and retaining only the main effect components of the model.

13.2.2 Model-building and the hierarchical principle

Having identified important similarities with the ANOVA model, we must now draw your attention to a very important difference. In the ANOVA, we are dealing with the means of samples of scores. The values of means are independent of the numbers of observations from which they are calculated. In ANOVA, therefore, the values of the various effects are unaffected by the sizes of the samples. In loglinear analysis, however, we are modelling cell frequencies as a function of other frequencies. As a consequence, the values of the marginal frequencies do affect estimates of the main effects and the interaction.

In loglinear analysis, therefore, model-building should generally follow what is known as the **hierarchical principle**: that is, if an interaction term is included in the model, the main effects of all the factors involved in the interaction must also be included; and if the interaction involves three or more factors, the model must include all the lower-order interactions involving those factors. For example, if the model includes the three-way interaction term ABC, it must also include the main effects A, B and C, plus the two-way interactions AB, AC and BC. In most (though not all) SPSS loglinear procedures, it is necessary to specify the highest-order interaction term only: the procedure will automatically **generate** the lower-order effects. Hence a model which includes the effects A, B, C, D, BC, BD, CD and BCD is said to be of **generating class** A, BCD: the term BCD implies the presence in the model of the main effects B, C and D, and also of the two-way interactions BC, BD and CD.

Saturated models

A loglinear model that contains all the possible effect terms is known as a **saturated model**. A saturated model will always predict the observed cell frequencies exactly. In our current example, since the interaction has been defined as the residual difference between the (logs of the) cell frequencies and the grand mean when the main effects have been removed, the sum of the main effects plus the interaction is the (log of the) cell frequency.

Each effect term in a loglinear model has an associated number of degrees of freedom and parameters that must be estimated. In our 4×2 contingency table, the Group variables has $(4 - 1) = 3$ degrees of freedom, the Presence variable has $(2 - 1) = 1$ degree of freedom and the Group $\times$ Presence interaction has $(4 - 1)(2 - 1) = 3$ degrees of freedom. That makes 7 degrees of freedom in total, making 7 parameters that would be estimated with the saturated model. If we add the grand mean, we have as many parameters as there are cells in the contingency table, leaving no room for any deviation from the observed cell frequencies.

Unsaturated models

The purpose of a loglinear analysis is often to see whether the cell frequencies can be adequately approximated by a model that contains *fewer* than the full set of possible treatment effects, subject to the hierarchical constraint. A model that contains fewer than the total number of possible terms is known as an **unsaturated model**.

When there is no association between two variables, the expected frequencies can be accounted for adequately in terms of the marginal frequencies in the table and the model will contain no interaction terms. This model is known as the **total independence** or **main-effects-only** model:

$$ln\, E = \text{constant} + \begin{bmatrix} \text{main effect} \\ \text{of A} \end{bmatrix} + \begin{bmatrix} \text{main effect} \\ \text{of B} \end{bmatrix} \quad \text{- - - (3)} \;\; \textbf{Loglinear main-effects model}$$

Note the absence of the interaction term from this unsaturated model.

The role of the chi-square test in loglinear model-building

When we make a traditional chi-square test for an association in a contingency table, the null hypothesis states that the attributes are independent. On that assumption, expected frequencies are calculated from the marginal frequencies in the table and the chi-square test statistic expresses the extent to which the observed cell frequencies O deviate from the corresponding expected frequencies E. The greater the values $(O - E)$ tend to be, the greater the value of chi-square and the stronger the evidence against the null hypothesis of independence. In Chapter 11, we described two versions of the chi-square statistic: the Pearson version and the likelihood ratio version. It is the likelihood ratio chi-square that is used in loglinear analysis.

In Chapter 11, we observed that the traditional chi-square test is used for two purposes. When we have data on a single variable, we can use the chi-square statistic to measure the extent to which our data are approximated by a theoretical distribution and test the null hypothesis that the data have been sampled from this theoretical population. This is a **goodness-of-fit** test. Where we have data on two attributes in the form of a contingency table, we can use chi-square to test for an **association** between the two attributes. In a test of goodness-of-fit, a *small* value of chi-square indicates a *good* fit. In a test for association, a *large* value of chi-square indicates the presence of an association.

In loglinear modelling, the (likelihood ratio) chi-square statistic is used as a measure of goodness-of-fit of the model to the data. A small value for chi-square indicates a good fit; a large value indicates a poor fit. There are several approaches to loglinear modelling. In the **backward hierarchical** approach, we begin with the saturated model, which we know in advance will predict the cell frequencies perfectly. Next, we remove the most complex interaction term from the model. The expected frequencies and LR chi-square are now recalculated on the basis of the simpler model. The effect of this simplification of the model will be to increase the value of chi-square from zero, because there are now fewer parameters in the model than there are cells in the table and the degrees of freedom of the chi-square statistic will increase from zero to the degrees of freedom of the effect that has been removed. This increment in chi-square can be tested to see whether the removal of the interaction significantly worsens the goodness-of-fit of the model to the data. If the goodness-of-fit is not significantly worse, that is, the value of chi-square has not been significantly increased, we remove the term from the model. We continue the process of removing terms, recalculating the expected frequencies and re-testing with chi-square. The process ends when the removal of a term from the model results in a significant increase in chi-square, indicating that the term should be retained in the model. (If the term is an interaction, we must also, in accordance with the hierarchical principle, retain any lower order interactions and the main effects of all the factors involved.)

In the context of loglinear modelling, the likelihood ratio chi-square measure of goodness-of-fit is often known as G^2 (or as the **Goodman statistic**, in honour of his pioneer work in this area). A great advantage of the Goodman statistic over the traditional Pearson chi-square is that it has the **additive property**: that is, its total value can be apportioned among the different terms being tested, enabling us to see whether the removal of any term from the model makes a significant difference to the model's goodness-of-fit. By 'total value' here, we mean the value of chi-square that we should obtain if we tried to fit the data with a model containing only a constant and no effect terms at all.

The significance of any particular interaction effect is tested with G^2_{effect} , where

$$G^2_{effect} = G^2_{effect\ present} - G^2_{effect\ absent} \quad \text{- - - (4)}$$

Partition of LR chi-squares (Goodman statistics)

which is distributed approximately on chi-square with degrees of freedom equal to that of the effect itself.

13.2.3   The main-effects-only loglinear model and the traditional chi-square test for association

The **main-effects-only** model is the equivalent, in loglinear analysis, of the null hypothesis of no association between two variables that is tested by the traditional chi-square test. In the loglinear analysis of a two-way contingency table, the value of the Goodman statistic will be exactly that of the likelihood ratio chi-square, obtained from the formula:

$$\chi^2_{(r-1)(c-1)} = 2 \sum_{all\ cells} O\ ln\left(\frac{O}{E}\right) \quad \text{- - - (5)} \quad \textbf{Likelihood ratio chi-square}$$

where r and c are the numbers of rows and columns, respectively. The likelihood ratio chi-square is distributed approximately as chi-square on $(r - 1)(c - 1)$ degrees of freedom. For the data in Table 1, the value of the likelihood ratio chi-square is

$$\chi^2_{3 \times 1} = 2 \sum O\ ln\left(\frac{0}{E}\right)$$
$$= 2\left[6\ ln\left(\frac{6}{12.3}\right) + 21\ ln\left(\frac{21}{14.7}\right) + ... + 36\ ln\left(\frac{14}{10}\right) + 43\ ln\left(\frac{8}{12.0}\right)\right]$$
$$= 11.09$$

We shall see that this is exactly the value of G^2 when the interaction term has been removed from the loglinear model and the main effects model is tested for goodness-of-fit.

Note carefully that when we apply the main-effects-only model to the data and run a test of significance, we are not testing the *main effects* for significance: we are testing the increase in the value of chi-square resulting from the *removal* of the interaction term from the model. We are, in fact, testing the *interaction term* for significance.

13.2.4   Analysis of the residuals

As in regression analysis, it is good practice to assess the goodness-of-fit of a loglinear model by examining the distribution of the **residuals** (the differences between the observed and expected frequencies). There are different kinds of residuals, designed for different purposes. The **raw** residuals are obtained by subtracting the expected frequencies generated by the model from the observed frequencies. Other residuals have been rescaled, so that they have a mean of zero and a standard deviation of 1. **Adjusted residuals** and **deviance residuals** are more useful than raw residuals for identifying outliers and the cells where the estimates of the expected frequencies are particularly poor.

Quantile-quantile and detrended Q-Q plots

Other kinds of graph, which are included in the SPSS output if requested, examine the distribution of the residuals. A **quantile-quantile Q-Q plot** is a plot of the quantiles (quantiles are points taken at regular intervals from the cumulative distribution function of a random variable – the 100-quantiles are called percentiles) of the standardised scores of the obtained distribution against the values of the standard normal distribution that have the same quantile values. The same range of values of the standard normal variable is stepped out on both axes. If the points tend to lie (approximately) along the straight line running diagonally from bottom left to top right, the obtained distribution is normal; non-normal distributions have points that deviate systematically from the line in an obviously non-linear fashion.

In a **detrended Q-Q plot**, the deviations of the scores from the line in the Q-Q plot (i.e. their deviations from expectation) are plotted against their standard scores. If the distribution is normal, all values will lie reasonably close to the horizontal baseline through zero on the vertical axis. The important point is that the points should show no obvious pattern: should, for instance, those points on the left tend to lie above the horizontal baseline and those to the right below (or vice versa), non-normality of distribution is indicated.

13.3   MODELLING A TWO-WAY CONTINGENCY TABLE

We shall now run a loglinear analysis of the *Tissue Type × Presence* contingency table in Table 1. Since we have already explored this table thoroughly in Chapter 11, we can dispense with the preliminaries here and proceed with the loglinear analysis proper.

Follow the usual procedure to enter the data into the **Data Editor**, which will appear as in Figure 1.

	Group	Presence	Count
1	Type A	No	14
2	Type A	Yes	8
3	Type B	No	11
4	Type B	Yes	7
5	Type C	No	5
6	Type C	Yes	7
7	Critical	No	6
8	Critical	Yes	21

Figure 1. **Data View** showing the two grouping variables and the counts of presence or absence of the antibody

(To view the value labels rather than the numerical values themselves, check **Value Labels** in the **View** menu or click the label icon at the tops of either of the **Data Editor** windows.)

13.3.1   SPSS procedures for loglinear analysis

Figure 2 shows the menu for loglinear analysis.

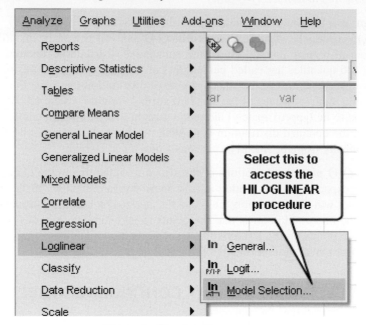

Figure 2. The **Loglinear** menu

Any of the three choices on the **Loglinear** menu will fit a loglinear model to the data. **Model Selection**, however, accesses the HILOGLINEAR program; whereas the **General** and **Logit** choices access the GENLOG program. Here we shall concentrate on the **Model Selection** choice.

There are important differences between the HILOGLINEAR and GENLOG programs. All three choices from the **Loglinear** menu will produce parameter estimates and tests of significance of these estimates. **Model Selection**, however, will run a backward elimination analysis and report direct tests of significance of the various components of the model. In our view, this is the easiest way of testing the components of the loglinear model. Tests of the significance of model components can also be made in GENLOG; but in order to make such tests, the user must take extra steps. We shall therefore take the **Model Selection** approach first.

* Select **Data➔Weight Cases…** to open the **Weight Cases** dialog box and transfer the variable *Count* to the **Frequency Variable** box. Click **OK**. (This move is not necessary for a loglinear analysis; however, loglinear analysis should be run in conjunction with the Crosstabs procedure, which does require that the cases be weighted according to frequency.)
* Select **Analyze➔Loglinear➔Model Selection…** to enter the **Model Selection Loglinear Analysis** dialog box (Figure 3).

- Transfer the variable names *Group* and *Presence* to the **Factor(s)** panel on the right. Each factor name in the **Factor(s)** box will be followed by the expression (? ?), which is a request for the minimum and maximum values of the code numbers that have been selected for the categories.
- Follow the steps described in Figure 3 to specify the minimum and maximum values of each factor.
- Click **OK** to run the procedure.

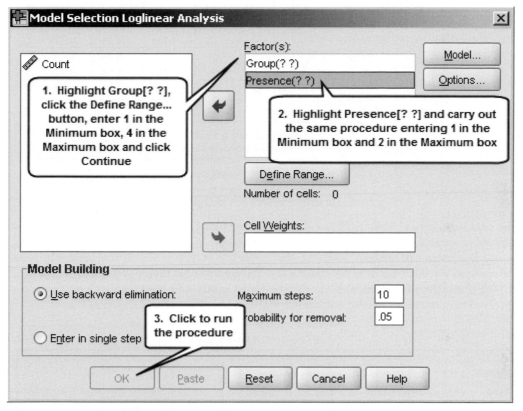

Figure 3. The **Model Selection Loglinear Analysis** dialog box (HILOGLINEAR) showing how to define the range of the factor values

Table of contents of the Output window

The output of many SPSS procedures is extensive. SPSS has therefore provided a useful navigational aid. In the SPSS Output window, there is a vertical grey pillar, to the left of which is a table of contents of the output. Clicking on any item in the table will bring it into view in the pane on the right of the pillar (Figure 4).

An early item in the output (not shown here) is a table headed **Convergence Information**. In this table, check that the generating class is given as Group*Presence, which means that SPSS has applied a saturated model to the data.

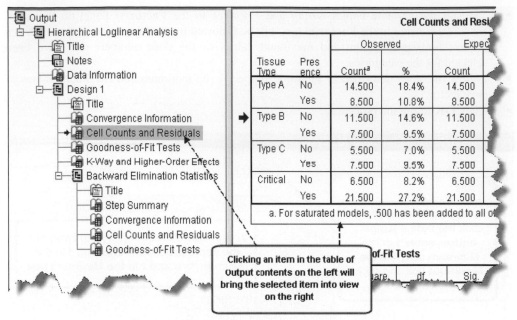

Figure 4. Table of contents of the Output window

The next item (partly shown in Figure 4) is a table of **Cell Counts and Residuals**. From this table, it is immediately apparent that the saturated model is a perfect fit: all the residuals are zero. For technical reasons, however, the frequency in every cell in the table has been incremented by 0.5. Later in the **Backward Elimination Statistics** section of the output, however, another table, also with the caption **Cell Counts and Residuals**, appears with the observed frequencies as they were in the original data set. This table is shown in Output 1.

Cell Counts and Residuals							
Tissue Type	Presence	Observed		Expected		Residuals	Std. Residuals
		Count	%	Count	%		
Type A	No	14.000	17.7%	14.000	17.7%	.000	.000
	Yes	8.000	10.1%	8.000	10.1%	.000	.000
Type B	No	11.000			13.9%	.000	.000
	Yes	7.000			8.9%		
Type C	No	5.000			6.3%		
	Yes	7.000			8.9%		
Critical	No	6.000	7.6%	6.000	7.6%	.000	.000
	Yes	21.000	26.6%	21.000	26.6%	.000	.000

In every cell, the expected frequency predicted from the saturated model is equal to the observed frequency.

Since the saturated model predicts the frequencies exactly, the residuals are all zero.

Output 1. Table of **Cell Counts and Residuals**, showing that the saturated model predicts the cell frequencies perfectly

The table headed **Goodness-of-fit Tests** (Output 2) shows that the chi-square statistic has no degrees of freedom and hence a value of zero: this is entirely consistent with information in the table of cell counts and residuals.

Goodness-of-Fit Tests

	Chi-Square	df	Sig.
Likelihood Ratio	.000	0	.
Pearson	.000	0	.

Output 2. The **Goodness-of-Fit Tests**. The saturated model leaves chi-square with no degrees of freedom

Note carefully that the test reported in Output 2 is not a test of the significance of any of the components of the model: the chi-square statistic measures any residual difference that might remain (in this case there is none) between the predictions of the model and the actual cell frequencies.

The tests of significance for individual components of the model are reported in the table of **Backward Elimination Statistics**, which is shown in Output 3. In this table, it can be seen that when the interaction term is removed from the model, the value of the **LR chi-square** (i.e. G^2) increases from zero to 11.093 on 3 degrees of freedom. Since this value is significant beyond the 0.05 level, the interaction term must be retained in the model. Note that the value 11.093 is *exactly the value we obtained when we applied the likelihood ratio chi-square formula to the same contingency table.*

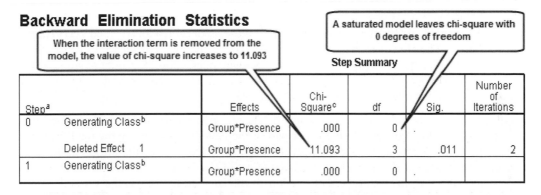

Backward Elimination Statistics

> When the interaction term is removed from the model, the value of chi-square increases to 11.093

> A saturated model leaves chi-square with 0 degrees of freedom

Step Summary

Step[a]		Effects	Chi-Square[c]	df	Sig.	Number of Iterations
0	Generating Class[b]	Group*Presence	.000	0	.	
	Deleted Effect 1	Group*Presence	11.093	3	.011	2
1	Generating Class[b]	Group*Presence	.000	0	.	

a. At each step, the effect with the largest significance level for the Likelihood Ratio Change is deleted, provided the significance level is larger than .050
b. Statistics are displayed for the best model at each step after step 0
c. For 'Deleted Effect', this is the change in the Chi-Square after the effect is deleted from the model

Output 3. Table of backward elimination statistics

The process of backward elimination ceases after the first step because, by the hierarchical principle, the retention of an interaction necessitates also the retention of its component factors.

Output 4 is part of a table with the caption **K-Way and Higher Order Effects**. (In the original table, the Pearson chi-square values were also given. They present a very similar picture to the LR chi-square statistics.) Here the term **Order** refers to the number of factors involved in the effects concerned: a first-order effect (K=1) is a main effect; a second-order effect (K = 2) is a two-way interaction, and so on.

| | | | K-Way and Higher-Order Effects | | |
| | | | Likelihood Ratio | | Pearson |
	K	df	Chi-Square	Sig.	Chi-Square
K-way and Higher Order Effects[a]	1	7	18.048	.012	20.342
	2	3	11.093	.011	10.655
K-way Effects[b]	1	4	6.955	.138	9.686
	2	3	11.093	.011	10.655

$df_{Group} + df_{Presence}$

$df_{Group} + df_{Presence} + df_{Group \times Presence}$

a. Tests that k-way and higher order effects are zero.

b. Tests that k-way effects are zero.

Output 4. Table showing the chi-square values associated with the effects at different levels. The upper part of the table gives the chi-square value associated with effects at a level as high as or higher than a specified level; the lower part gives the total chi-square associated with the effects at each level alone

In the upper part of Output 4, the chi-square value opposite each level of effect is the chi-square attributable to all effects at that level, *plus* those associated with any (and every) higher-order effect. The chi-square value for K = 1 (18.048) is the total chi-square value of the two main effects, plus the chi-square value for the two-way interaction. Since there are no effects of order higher than K = 2, the chi-square for K = 2 is, in this example, the chi-square associated with the interaction alone, namely, 11.093.

The meaning of the terms in Output 4 may be clearer upon consideration of the values in the degrees of freedom column. In the upper part of the table, the entries are the total degrees of freedom of all effects at each level, *plus* the degrees of freedom of the effects at all higher levels. Thus at level K = 1, we have the main effect of *Group* (df = 3), plus the main effect of *Presence* (df = 1), *plus* the degrees of freedom of the interaction (3), making seven degrees of freedom in all. At level K = 2, there is only one effect, namely, the interaction (*df* = 3).

In the lower half of the table, the *df* value for K = 1 is now 4 (not 7), because here we are being given the total degrees of freedom of the effects at one level only. The total degrees of freedom for the two main effects is 4 (1 for *Presence* plus 3 for *Group*), which is the value opposite K = 1.

The topmost entry for the LR chi-square (or G^2) is 18.048. This is the total value of chi-square: it is the increment in G^2 that would result from applying a model that contained no effects at all, that is, one containing the constant only. You will see that when we add the two values in the lower part of the table (those associated with the main effects and the interaction), we obtain 18.048, which is exactly the value of the total G^2 in the upper part of the table. (This is also approximately true of the corresponding Pearson chi-square values.)

Notice also that the value of G^2 given for the interaction alone (11.093) is what remains of the total G^2 when the portion attributable to the main effects only (6.955) has been subtracted.

Finally, we note from the entry for K − 1 in the lower part of Output 4 that the tests for main effects do not show significance. The only significant component in the model, therefore, is the interaction.

13.3.2   Fitting an unsaturated model

A saturated model, which contains all possible effect terms, must (as explained earlier) always predict the cell frequencies exactly, as in the present example.

We have also seen, however, that in order to account adequately for the pattern of frequencies in Table 1, we must include the interaction term in the model; otherwise, the value of chi-square increases significantly. We know, therefore, that an unsaturated model containing only main effect terms will fit the data poorly. It is, however, instructive to apply an ill-fitting main-effects-only model to the data of our current example, so that we can obtain some of the graphs from SPSS's regression diagnostics. The goodness-of-fit of a model is readily apparent from the appearance of such diagnostic graphs. We shall begin at the point where we have completed the dialog shown in Figure 3. In that exercise, we were then able to proceed with the backward elimination simply by clicking **OK**.

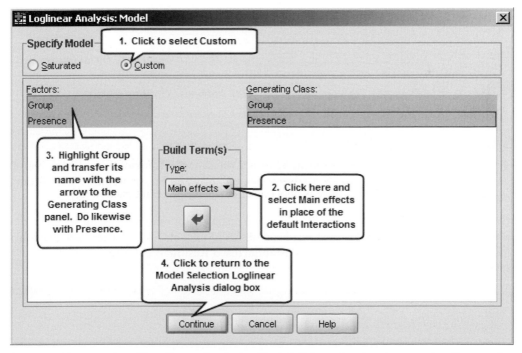

Figure 5. The completed **Loglinear Analysis: Model** dialog, showing that a main-effects-only model has been specified

- This time, click the **Model** button in the top right-hand corner of the dialog box, to obtain the **Loglinear Analysis: Model** dialog box (Figure 5). Follow the steps shown in Figure 5 to specify a main-effects-only model. In the central pillar in the dialog box is the **Build Term(s)** caption, with the **Type** button underneath. The default setting is *Interactions*. Change this setting to *Main effects* and return to **Model Selection Loglinear Analysis**.

- In the **Model Selection Loglinear Analysis** dialog box, click the **Options** button to open the **Loglinear Analysis: Options** dialog box (Figure 6). Select a **Residuals** plot and click **Continue** to return to **Model Selection Loglinear Analysis**.

- Finally click **OK** to run the procedure.

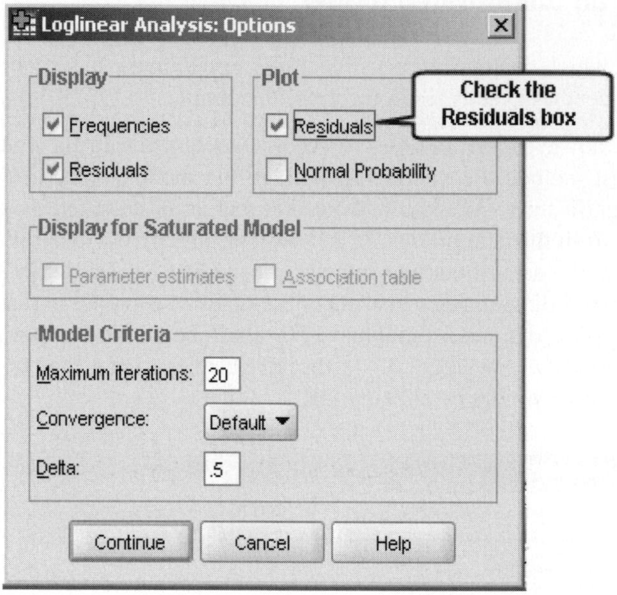

Figure 6. The completed **Loglinear Analysis: Options** dialog

Output for an unsaturated model

The first table in the output (not shown here) is **Convergence Information**. Check that the generating class is given as *Group*, *Presence*, not *Group*Presence*, as when we were fitting a saturated model.

Output 5 shows the plots of observed counts and residuals for our current data set. The fit is now clearly far from perfect: the expected and observed frequencies no longer match and there are non-zero entries in the **Residuals** and **Standardised Residuals** columns.

Cell Counts and Residuals							
Tissue Type	Presence	Observed		Expected		Residuals	Std. Residuals
		Count	%	Count	%		
Type A	No	14.000	17.7%	10.025	12.7%	3.975	1.255
	Yes	8.000	10.1%	11.975	15.2%	-3.975	-1.149
Type B	No	11.000	13.9%	8.203	10.4%	2.797	.977
	Yes	7.000	8.9%	9.797	12.4%	-2.797	-.894
Type C	No	5.000	6.3%	5.468	6.9%	-.468	-.200
	Yes	7.000	8.9%	6.532	8.3%	.468	.183
Critical	No	6.000	7.6%	12.304	15.6%	-6.304	-1.797
	Yes	21.000	26.6%	14.696	18.6%	6.304	1.644

Output 5. **Cell Counts and Residuals** table when the main-effects-only model is applied

Output 6 summarises the **Goodness-of-fit Tests**. The significant increase in G^2 shows that the main-effects-only (independence) model is not a good fit for these data.

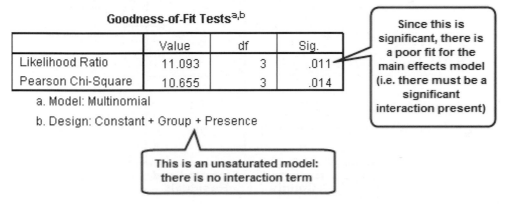

Goodness-of-Fit Tests[a,b]	Value	df	Sig.
Likelihood Ratio	11.093	3	.011
Pearson Chi-Square	10.655	3	.014

a. Model: Multinomial
b. Design: Constant + Group + Presence

Since this is significant, there is a poor fit for the main effects model (i.e. there must be a significant interaction present)

This is an unsaturated model: there is no interaction term

Output 6. Summary of the **Goodness-of-Fit Tests**

The values of the **Likelihood Ratio** and **Pearson Chi-Square** are exactly the same as those we obtained by the backward elimination analysis in the previous section. They are also the values we obtain when we make the traditional chi-square test of association between *Presence* and *Group*. The significance test for the goodness-of-fit of a main-effects-only loglinear model is the exact equivalent of the traditional likelihood-ratio chi-square test for association, in which the null hypothesis is that the two variables are independent.

It may be worth repeating our earlier point that the test reported in Output 6 is a test of the component *omitted* from the model, not of those remaining in the model. The test of G^2 when the main-effects-only model is applied is a test of the *interaction* component of the full model.

The residual plots

If a loglinear model is a good fit and the observed cell counts are plotted against the expected counts from the loglinear model, the points on the graph should lie close to a straight line. Another characteristic of a good fit is that both the adjusted and deviance residuals should have approximately normal distributions. Thirdly, a plot of either kind of residual against the expected values should result in an amorphous cloud of points, and there should be no outstandingly large values.

Output 7 shows what the residual plots would look like if the main-effects-only model were a good fit for the data, as it would be with a data set showing no association between *Group* and *Presence*. Only the cells either above or below the diagonal of blank cells are relevant: the other three cells simply reproduce the same plots with the axes reversed.

Hiloglinear Model

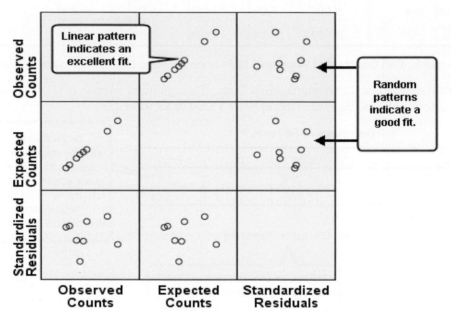

Cases weighted by Count

Output 7. Plots of **Observed Counts, Expected Counts** and **Standardized Residuals** when a model fits the data well

The strongly linear pattern in the plot of observed counts against expected counts indicates an excellent fit, as do the shapeless plots of observed counts against standardised residuals.

Output 8 shows the plots of counts and residuals for the data in our current example (the data in Table 1). The plots clearly do not meet the criteria for a good fit: the plot of observed counts against expected counts is far from linear; and the plots of the observed and expected counts against the standardised residuals show patterns that are far from random.

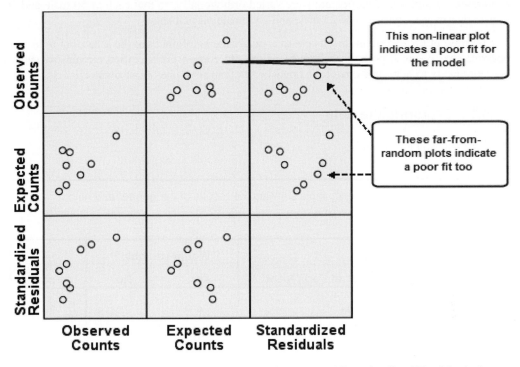

Output 8. Plots of **Observed Counts, Expected Counts** and **Standardized Residuals** for the data in Table 1 showing that the main-effects model fits the data poorly

13.3.3 Summary

The purpose of the foregoing sections has been to introduce the fundamentals of loglinear modelling in the simplest possible context and to familiarise the reader with the general procedure and the main features of the output. As we said in Section 13.1, if you actually have a two-way contingency table you want to analyse, you should use one of the chi-square tests described in Chapter 11: there would be no advantage in running a loglinear analysis (although that would produce the same result). In the next section, however, the essential features we have discussed in this section will be put to good use in the analysis of a three-way frequency table, where the loglinear analysis has great advantages over the traditional chi-square approach. Faced with a more complex table, loglinear modelling can not only confirm the existence of associations among the data, but also pinpoint the precise nature of those associations.

13.4 MODELLING A THREE-WAY FREQUENCY TABLE

We shall illustrate the application of loglinear modelling of a three-way frequency table with some entirely fictitious data from an imaginary experiment on gender and helpfulness. Suppose that male and female interviewers asked 50 male and 50 female participants whether, in a hypothetical situation, they would offer to help someone in difficulties. The factors of sex of interviewer and sex of participant were varied orthogonally, so that each of 50 male and 50 female interviewers interviewed 25 male and 25 female participants.

The purpose of the investigation was not to compare the helpfulness of the sexes, but to test the opposite-sex dyadic hypothesis, which holds that, in certain pre-specified circumstances, we are more likely to help someone of the opposite sex than someone of our own.

13.4.1   Exploring the data

The data are shown in Table 2.

Table 2. Three-way contingency table showing the results of the gender and helpfulness experiment

		Would you help?		
Sex of Interviewer	Sex of Participant	Yes	No	Total
Male	Male	4	21	25
	Female	16	9	25
Female	Male	11	14	25
	Female	11	14	25
	Total	42	68	100

The measures known as the **odds** and the **odds ratio** were introduced in Chapter 11. There, we used them to explore the pattern of the frequencies in a two-way contingency table. These measures can also be used to explore more complex frequency tables, provided at least two of the factors are dichotomies.

What is the effect of the sex of the interviewer on whether male participants will help or not? When the interviewer is male (first data row in the table), the odds in favour of males helping are 4/21 = 0.190. When the interviewer is female (third data row in the table), the odds in favour of males helping are 11/14 = 0.786. Male participants, then, are more likely to help when the interviewer is female. The *OR* is 0.786/0.190 = 4.13: that is, male participants are four times as likely to help when the interviewer is a female.

When we turn to the female participants, we find that, when we compare their helpfulness with male and female interviewers, the odds ratio is 2.26. Again, the participants are more likely to help someone of the opposite sex than one of their own. A superficial exploration of the data, therefore, seems to confirm the opposite-sex dyadic hypothesis.

Suppose for a moment that instead of recording whether someone was prepared to help or not, we had taken some continuous measure of helpfulness on an independent scale with units. We should then have had an experiment of between subjects, two-factor design and could consider running an ANOVA on the data. The opposite-sex dyadic hypothesis implies what, in the context of ANOVA, would be a two-way interaction between *Sex of Participant* and *Sex of Interviewer*. In the present context of loglinear modelling, however, the same hypothesis implies a *three-way* interaction between the factors of *Sex of Participant*, *Sex of Interviewer* and whether *Help* was given. Here, the *Help × Sex of Participant* interaction has replaced the continuous measure of helpfulness. In Chapter 9, we saw that a three-way interaction is said to occur when the interaction between two of the variables is not homogeneous across the levels of the third factor. In the present example, the opposite-sex dyadic hypothesis implies that the interaction between *Gender* and *Help* will be different with male and female interviewers: with male interviewers, females will be more helpful than they would be with female interviewers; with female interviewers, the reverse pattern should be obtained.

We have used the odds ratio to explore the three-way frequency table. The clustered bar charts offered as options in SPSS's crosstabulation procedure can also be illuminating.

Output 9 shows rather different patterns for the Male and Female interviewers. A pattern consistent with the opposite-sex dyadic hypothesis is clearly evident when the interviewer is male. With a female interviewer, however, the incidence of help is rather less than 50% in both male and female participants; nevertheless, comparisons between the heights of the bars in the graphs on the right and on the left show that once again, the males were more helpful when the interviewer was female, and vice versa for the females, again a pattern consistent with the hypothesis.

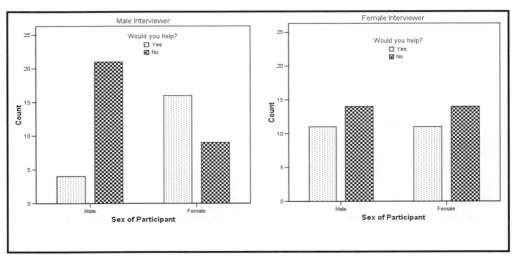

Output 9. Bar charts of the helpfulness of male and female participants with male and female interviewers showing an interaction pattern

13.4.2   Loglinear analysis of the data on gender and helpfulness

An important consideration before embarking upon a loglinear analysis of a multiway frequency table is whether the data are sufficiently numerous to meet the requirements of loglinear modelling. According to Tabachnick and Fidell (2007; p862), there should be at least five times as many cases as there are cells in the multi-way table. Those authors also recommend that, in every two-way association among the variables, all expected frequencies must be greater than 1 and no more than 20% should be less than 5. Since, in our data set, there are 100 cases and 8 cells in the multiway table, the first criterion is satisfied. We can test the data on the second criterion by using **Crosstabs** to create three two-way tables (*Interviewer × Help*, *Participant × Help* and *Participant × Interviewer*) and calculate the expected frequencies for each table.

Proceed as follows:

- In **Variable View**, create three grouping variables: *Participant (Sex of Participant), Interviewer (Sex of Interviewer), Help (Would you help?)* and a fourth variable, *Count*, for the frequencies. Use the **Values** column to assign values to the code numbers, such as, for the *Help* variable, 1 = Yes, 2 = No. The complete SPSS data set is shown in Figure 7.

	Interviewer	Participant	Help	Count
1	Male	Male	Yes	4
2	Male	Male	No	21
3	Female	Male	Yes	11
4	Female	Male	No	14
5	Male	Female	Yes	16
6	Male	Female	No	9
7	Female	Female	Yes	11
8	Female	Female	No	14

Figure 7. **Data View** showing the Gender and Helping data set

- We now need to weight the cases with the frequencies in *Count*. (This step would not be required if the data consisted of records of individual cases.) Choose **Data➔Weight Cases...** to open the **Weight Cases** dialog box and transfer the variable *Count* to the **Frequency Variable** box. Click **OK**.

- The next stage is to confirm, with **Crosstabs**, that the expected frequencies are sufficiently large. (The procedure is described in Section 11.5.3.) The output tables (which we have omitted) show that no cell has an expected frequency of less than 1 and over 80% of cells have expected frequencies of 5 or more. We have, therefore, sufficient data for a loglinear analysis.

  See Section 11.5.3

- Select **Analyze➔Loglinear➔Model Selection...** to open the **Model Selection Loglinear Analysis** dialog box (the completed version is shown in Figure 8).

- Follow the steps in Figure 8. You will notice that, since each variable contains two categories, to which we have consistently assigned the values 1 and 2, we need only complete the **Define Range** dialog once; had the variables had different numbers of categories or different values been used from variable to variable, it would have been necessary to enter the ranges separately for each grouping variable.

- The default model is **backward elimination**. Makes sure its radio button is on.

- Click **OK**.

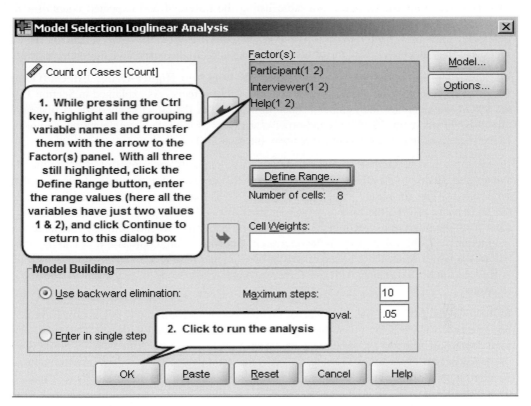

Figure 8. The completed **Model Selection Loglinear Analysis** dialog box for three factors

The output for the loglinear analysis

The first table in the output (Output 10) lists the number of cases and the names of the variables (factors) in the analysis. Check that the information is consistent with the design of the experiment as we have described it: in this example, there should be three factors, each having two levels. In Output 10, the factors, *Help*, *Interviewer* and *Participant*, are listed under the heading 'Categories'.

Data Information

		N
Cases	Valid	8
	Out of Range a	0
	Missing	0
	Weighted Valid	100
Categories	Help	2
	Interviewer	2
	Participant	2

a. Cases rejected because of out of range factor values.

Output 10. Information about the number of cases and the category names (factors)

The next item (not shown here) is a table listing the observed and expected counts for the combinations of the three factors. At this stage, SPSS is fitting a **saturated model**, with generating class *Sex of Interviewer × Sex of Participant × Help* to the cell frequencies. In this section of the output, therefore the observed and expected frequencies have the same values.

The third item in the output, with the caption **K-Way and Higher-Order Effects** (Output 11), lists the results of the statistical tests for the various effects. As explained in Section 13.3, the term **Order** denotes the number of factors involved in the effect concerned: a first-order effect (K=1) is a main effect; a second-order effect (K = 2) is a two-way interaction, and so on. In the present example, there is one three-way interaction (K = 3).

In the upper part of Output 11, the chi-square value opposite each level of effect is the chi-square attributable to all effects at that level, *plus* that associated with any (and every) higher-order effect. The chi-square value for K = 1 (15.382) is the *total* of the chi-squared values for the three main effects, the three two-way interactions and the three-way interaction. This is clear from the degrees of freedom: 3 (main effects) + 3 (two-way interactions) + 1 (three-way interaction) = 7, the value given in the degrees of freedom column opposite K = 1 in the upper half of the table. Since there are no effects of order higher than K = 3, the chi-square for K = 3 is the chi-square associated with the three-way interaction alone (6.659), on one degree of freedom.

In the lower half of the table, the value of the degrees of freedom for K = 1 is now 3 (not 7), because now we are being given the degrees of freedom associated with *one* level only. The total degrees of freedom for the three main effects alone is 3, which is the value opposite K = 1 in the lower part of the table. The chi-square value (and degrees of freedom) are the same for K = 3 in both the upper and lower parts of the table, because in either case, there is just one three-way interaction. From the entries for K = 3 in either half of the table, we see that, as we should expect from the hypothesis, there is indeed a significant three-way interaction (*Sex of Interviewer × Sex of Participant × Help*) : Chi-Square = 6.659 on one degree of freedom; p = 0.01.

K-Way and Higher-Order Effects

	K	df	Likelihood Ratio Chi-Square	Sig.	Pe: Chi-Squar
K-way and Higher Order Effects[a]	1	7	15.382	.031	14.24...
	2	4	12.811	.012	11.98...
	3	1	6.659	.010	6.52
K-way Effects[b]	1	3	2.571	.463	2...
	2	3	6.152	.104	5...
	3	1	6.659	.010	6.5...

$df_P + df_I + df_H + df_{P \times I} + df_{P \times H} + df_{I \times H} + df_{P \times I \times H}$

$df_{P \times I \times H}$

a. Tests that k-way and higher order effects
b. Tests that k-way effects are zero.

Only the three-way interaction is significant

Output 11. Part of the **Tests of Effects** table. The subscripts P, I and H represent Participant, Interviewer and Help respectively

From the lower part of Output 11, which gives the results of tests of the individual components of the model, we also learn that no other effect makes a significant contribution to the total chi-square value, as can be seen from the p-values in the rows for K = 1 and K = 2. Loglinear analysis, therefore, has given us something that the traditional chi-square test cannot offer: a direct test for a three-way interaction.

The fourth part of the SPSS output, the **Backward Elimination Statistics** (Output 12) shows that the saturated model containing the three-way interaction is the best one for the data, because removal of the interaction term would result in a significant increase in Chi-square. At Step 1, the saturated model is therefore adopted as the final model.

Backward Elimination Statistics

> Since deletion of the three-way interaction term results in a significant increase in chi-square, this term must be retained in the final model

Step Summary

Step[a]		Effects	Chi-Square[c]	df	Sig.	Number of Iterations
0	Generating Class[b]	Participant*Interviewer*Help	.000	0	.	
	Deleted Effect 1	Participant*Interviewer*Help	6.659	1	.010	2
1	Generating Class[b]	Participant*Interviewer*Help	.000	0	.	

a. At each step, the effect with the largest significance level for the Likelihood Ratio Change is deleted, provided the significance level is larger than .050

b. Statistics are displayed for the best model at each step after step 0

c. For 'Deleted Effect', this is the change in the Chi-Square after the effect is deleted from the model

Output 12. The final model for the gender and professed helpfulness data

The loglinear analysis has confirmed the opposite-sex dyadic hypothesis, which implies that the best-fitting loglinear model contains the three-way interaction term.

13.4.3   The main-effects-only model and the traditional chi-square test

The formula for the likelihood ratio chi-square statistic (and indeed the Pearson formula also) can readily be adapted for use with multiway contingency tables. We can represent a three-way frequency table as a set of two-way tables, one at each level of the third attribute, where r and c are the number of rows and columns in each table and each table is said to be at a different **layer** of the third attribute, which has l layers. Let R, C and L be the marginal totals associated with a particular combination of the categories of the three attributes. By extension of the reasoning for the two-way contingency table, the expected cell frequency E under the null hypothesis of total independence among the three attributes is given by

$$E = \frac{R}{N} \times \frac{C}{N} \times \frac{L}{N} \times N = \frac{RCL}{N^2} \ \text{- - - (6)}$$

Expected cell frequency for total independence model

For the three-way frequency table, the likelihood ratio chi-square statistic is

$$\chi^2_{(r-1)(c-1)(l-1)} = 2 \sum_{all\ cells} O\ ln\left(\frac{O}{E}\right) \text{ - - - (7) } \textbf{LR Chi-square}$$

which is distributed approximately as chi square on $(r-1)(c-1)(l-1)$ degrees of freedom.

Table 3 shows the observed frequencies O, together with the expected frequencies E for each of the eight cells in the frequency table of the results of the helping experiment. Also given are the marginal total frequencies for the three variables: *Sex of Participant*; *Sex of Interviewer*; *Help*.

Table 3. Observed and expected frequencies for the data in Table 2. (In (a), the observed frequencies are shown in brackets.)

(a) Table of observed and expected frequencies

Sex of Interviewer	Sex of Participant	Would you help?	
		Yes	No
Male	Male	4 (10.5)	21 (14.5)
	Female	16 (10.5)	9 (14.5)
Female	Male	11 (10.5)	14 (14.5)
	Female	11 (10.5)	14 (14.5)

(b) Marginal row frequencies

Sex of Interviewer		Sex of Participant		Was Help Given?	
Male	Female	Male	Female	Yes	No
50	50	50	50	42	58

For the cell in Table 3(a) with entries in bold font (Male Interviewer, Male Participant, No Help Given) and the values of the marginal totals in Table 3(b), we see from the formula for the expected frequencies that the expected frequency for that cell is $(50\times50\times58)/100^2 = 14.5$. The expected frequencies for the other cells are found in a similar way. Applying the likelihood ratio chi-square formula, we have

$$\chi^2(1) = 2 \sum_{all\ cells} O\ ln\left(\frac{O}{E}\right)$$

$$= 2\left[4 \times ln\left(\frac{4}{10.5}\right) + 21 \times ln\left(\frac{21}{14.5}\right) + ... + 14 \times ln\left(\frac{14}{14.5}\right)\right]$$

$$= 12.81$$

This value is significant beyond the 0.05 level: $\chi^2(1) = 12.81; p = 0.012$.

If you follow the procedure described in Section 13.3.2 and apply a main-effects-only model to the three-way frequency table, you will find that the value for chi-square given in the output is exactly the value that we have just obtained by applying the likelihood-ratio formula. Output 13 shows the result of the goodness-of-fit test of the main-effects-only model. The value of chi-square is exactly the same as the one we have just calculated from the extension of the usual likelihood ratio formula.

Goodness-of-Fit Tests

	Chi-Square	df	Sig.
Likelihood Ratio	12.811	4	.012
Pearson	11.987	4	.017

Output 13. The result of the goodness-of-fit test of the main-effects-only model

The main-effects-only model is the exact equivalent, in loglinear analysis, of the traditional chi-square test for an association. The problem with the traditional chi-square test is that it can merely reject the total independence (main-effects-only) model. This is fine if there are only two attributes, because in that situation only one association is possible. With multi-way frequency tables, however, it can tell us only that there are at least some dependencies among the variables: it cannot tell us which of several possible effects is responsible for the pattern of frequencies in the frequency table. Could these cell frequencies have arisen from one or more of the possible two-way interactions? Does the three-way interaction account for a significant portion of the chi-square value? Only modern methods such as loglinear analysis can provide the answers to such questions.

13.4.4 Collapsing a multi-way table: the requirement of conditional independence

We might reasonably ask another question of our data: are female participants more inclined to help than male participants? The traditional approach to this question was to create a two-way table by 'collapsing' across the levels of the *Interviewer* variable. By adding the data for the male interviewers to that of the female interviewers, we can produce a two-way table in which only the variables of *Sex of Participant* and *Help* remain. We have already said, however, that there are dangers in 'collapsing' a table in this way. In Output 14, the variable *Sex of Interviewer* has disappeared and, in both the table and the clustered bar chart, we see a pattern of cell frequencies suggesting that there may be a tendency for female participants to be more helpful. Moreover, this impression is seemingly confirmed by formal statistical testing: **Fisher's Exact** two-tailed probability = 0.03. On the other hand, we have previously seen that the loglinear analysis does not confirm *any* of the two-way interactions: the only statistically robust effect to emerge from the loglinear analysis is a three-way interaction.

Our variables are *Help*, *Participant* and *Interviewer*. In collapsing the three-way table across the *Interviewer* variable to obtain a two-way *Help × Participant* table, we have ignored the fact (confirmed by the three-way interaction that emerged from the loglinear analysis) that the *Interviewer* variable is correlated with the interaction between the other two variables and therefore confounds the simple comparison of males and females on helpfulness.

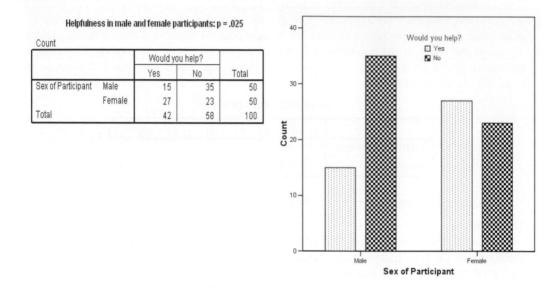

Output 14. Collapsed table, showing levels of helpfulness in male and female participants

An important concept in loglinear modelling is that of **conditional independence**. Two variables A and B are said to be conditionally independent at one level of a third variable C if, at that level of C, they show no association. Only if A & B are conditionally independent at *every* level of C, is it permissible to collapse the frequency table across C to investigate the association between A and B with a traditional chi-square test. In our example, *Help*, *Participant* and *Interviewer* are A, B and C, respectively. If we follow the Select Cases procedure and test for an association between *Help* and *Participant* in the male inverviewers, we find a striking tendency for the females to be more helpful: $\chi^2(1) = 12.647$; $p < 0.01$. (If, however, we make a similar test with the female interviewers, $\chi^2(1) = 0$; $p = 1$.) Clearly the requirement of conditional independence of A and B (Help and Participant) at all levels of C (male and female interviewers) has not been met and it is unsafe to collapse the three-way table by combining the data for the male and female interviewers.

A better case can be made for collapsing the data across the *Participant* variable and studying the association between *Interviewer* and *Help*. It will be found that if tests for association between *Interviewer* and *Help* are made on the data from the male and female participants separately, the chi-square test fails to show significance in either case. When the three-way table is collapsed across *Participants* (i.e. the data for male and female participants are combined so that we have a two-way *Interviewer × Help* table), the chi-square test fails to provide evidence for an association. That conclusion is consistent with the results of the loglinear analysis.

13.4.5 An alternative data set for the gender and helpfulness experiment

The presence of a three-way interaction, together with the absence of any other significant effects, made the interpretation of the output of the gender and helping experiment very simple. Often, however, several steps will be needed to locate the significant effects. Let us suppose that the data from the gender and helping experiment had been as in Table 4.

Table 4. Three-way contingency table showing a more complex outcome of the gender and helping experiment.

		Would you help?		
Sex of Interviewer	Sex of Participant	Yes	No	Total
Male	Male	4	10	14
	Female	10	20	30
Female	Male	47	10	57
	Female	58	17	75
	Total	119	57	176

Notice that in Table 4, the row marginal totals show some variation: there were differences both in the numbers of male and female interviewers and in the numbers of male and female participants.

In the table of **Convergence Information** (Output 15), we learn that the generating class is *Interviewer*Help, Participant*. Remembering the hierarchical principle by which the retention of an interaction term in the model requires the retention of all lower order effect involving the factors in the interaction, we write the final model as follows:

$$\ln(E) = \text{constant} + \begin{bmatrix} \text{main effect} \\ \text{of} \\ \text{Interviewer} \end{bmatrix} + \begin{bmatrix} \text{main effect} \\ \text{of} \\ \text{Help} \end{bmatrix} + \begin{bmatrix} \text{Interviewer} \times \text{Help} \\ \text{interaction} \end{bmatrix} + \begin{bmatrix} \text{main effect} \\ \text{of} \\ \text{Participant} \end{bmatrix} \text{ -- (8)}$$

Final loglinear model

This unsaturated model fits the data quite well: the table of **Cell Counts and Residuals** (not shown) shows no residual value larger than 0.713. The **Goodness-of-Fit Tests** (Output 16) show that G^2 is small and insignificant, confirming the appearance of the table of observed and expected frequencies.

Convergence Information[a]

Generating Class	Interviewer*Help, Participant	
Number of Iterations		.000
Max. Difference between Observed and Fitted Marginals		.000
Convergence Criterion		.250

a. Statistics for the final model after Backward Elimination.

Output 15. The **Convergence Information** table in the **Backward Elimination Statistics** section of the output

Goodness-of-Fit Tests

	Chi-Square	df	Sig.
Likelihood Ratio	2.435	3	.487
Pearson	2.393	3	.495

Output 16. **Goodness-of-Fit Tests** for the unsaturated model

Output 17 shows the table of **K-Way and Higher-Order Effects**. The total **Likelihood Ratio Chi-Square** (G^2) is 110.282; but, unlike the equivalent table from the analysis of the previous data set, most of this value is accounted for by main effects and two-way interactions. There is no evidence for a three-way interaction in these data. There is, therefore, here no evidence to support the opposite-sex dyadic hypothesis.

K-Way and Higher-Order Effects

	K	df	Likelihood Ratio		Pearson		Number of Iterations
			Chi-Square	Sig.	Chi-Square	Sig.	
K-way and Higher Order Effects[a]	1	7	110.282	.000	123.000	.000	0
	2	4	35.310	.000	37.077	.000	2
	3	1	.431	.512	.425	.514	4
K-way Effects[b]	1	3	74.972	.000	85.923	.000	0
	2	3	34.879	.000	36.651	.000	0
	3	1	.431	.512	.425	.514	0

a. Tests that k-way and higher order effects are zero.

b. Tests that k-way effects are zero.

Output 17. The **K-Way and Higher-Order Effects** table

Output 18 shows the **Backward Elimination Statistics**. At Step 0, a saturated model is applied first, after which the three-way interaction is tested by fitting a model with the three-way component absent. Since there is no significant increase in G^2, the three-way interaction term is dropped from the model.

At Step 1, each of the three two-way interactions is tested by removing it from the model. Only for the *Interviewer* × *Help* interaction is the increase in G^2 significant. At Step 2, therefore, the other two two-way interactions are removed from the model. At Step 3, it is found that if either *Interviewer* × *Help* or *Participant* is removed from the model, G^2 is significantly increased. At Step 4, therefore, both terms are retained and the final model is of generating class *Interviewer × Help, Participant*.

Backward Elimination Statistics

Step[a]			Effects	Chi-Square[c]	df	Sig.	Number of Iterations
0	Generating Class[b]		P*I*H	.000	0	.	
	Deleted Effect	1	P*I*H	.431	1	.512	4
1	Generating Class[b]		P*I, P*H, I*H	.431	1	.512	
	Deleted Effect	1	P*I	1.029	1	.310	2
		2	P*H	.198	1	.656	2
		3	I*H	32.098	1	.000	2
2	Generating Class[b]		P*I, I*H	.629	2	.730	
	Deleted Effect	1	P*I	1.806	1	.179	2
		2	I*H	32.875	1	.000	2
3	Generating Class[b]		I*H, P	2.435	3	.487	
	Deleted Effect	1	I*H	32.875	1	.000	2
		2	P	6.610	1	.010	2
4	Generating Class[b]		I*H, P	2.435	3	.487	

Step Summary

Abbreviations for Participant, Interviewer and Help, respectively

a. At each step, the effect with the largest significance level for the Likelihood Ratio Change is deleted, provided the Significance level is larger than .050.

b. Statistics are displayed for the best model at each step after Step 0.

c. For 'Deleted Effect', this is the change in the Chi-square after the effect is deleted from the model

Output 18. The **Backward Elimination Statistics** table

While the loglinear analysis of this second data set does not confirm the opposite-sex dyadic hypothesis, it should serve as an illustration of how this technique can pinpoint the key associations among the variables in a multi-way frequency table.

From inspection alone, it is much more difficult to discern any clear-cut pattern in the data of Table 4 than it is in Table 3. The import of the loglinear analysis is that the only robust effects are an *Interviewer × Help* interaction and a main effect of *Sex of Participant*. Since the interaction has received confirmation from the loglinear analysis, there is justification for creating a two-way table by collapsing across the factor of *Sex of Participant*.

The significant main effect of the *Participant* factor arises simply because there were more male participants in the study. While that fact is of no scientific interest, this factor must be retained in the model to achieve an adequate goodness-of-fit to the cell frequencies.

The cross-tabulation of the *Interviewer × Help* interaction is shown in Output 19. There is an obvious tendency for the participants to be helpful when the interviewer is female:

$$\text{LR } \chi_1^2 = 32.875; \ p < 0.01. \ OR = 8.33.$$

This odds ratio $(105/27)/(14/30)$ is very large indeed.

Sex of Interviewer * Was help given? Crosstabulation				
Count				
		Was help given?		
		Yes	No	Total
Sex of Interviewer	Female	105	27	132
	Male	14	30	44
	Total	119	57	176

Output 19. Crosstabulation showing that participants were more likely to help a female interviewer

13.4.6   Reporting the results of a loglinear analysis

Reports of loglinear analyses in the literature have yet to follow a standard format. For example, once a model has been fitted, it would be possible to write out the equation of the loglinear model and report the estimates of each of the terms in the equation. Many journal editors, however, would take the view that such a mathematical presentation is unnecessary and would serve only to obscure the findings of the research.

One of the many excellent features of the book by Tabachnick & Fidell (2007) is their inclusion of sample write-ups of the results of the multivariate procedures they describe, including a report of a loglinear analysis on pages 906-908. In their report they (quite rightly, in our view) do not include any formal equations. They do, however, include the following:
1.   Details of the data that were used in the analysis, including information about the incidence of cells with low expected frequencies and the presence of outliers. It is essential to establish that there are no contraindications against the use of loglinear analysis. Make sure that you have sufficient data.
2.   The maximum likelihood chi square and p-value for the final model.
3.   A table showing the results of the significance tests of the various effects on an individual basis. The entries in the table are chi-square tests of partial association, each on one degree of freedom.
4.   A larger table showing the parameter estimates and the ratios of the estimates to their standard errors. This table, however, is very extensive, so the researcher submitting an article might omit it from the first draft (or include it as an appendix): the table can always be included in the body of the text in a revision of the article should the editor require this.

13.5   MULTIPLE RESPONSE SETS

A researcher wishes to determine the most typical combination of modes of travel used by commuters in a particular area in order to compare the profiles of male and female commuters. Hundreds of commuters fill in a questionnaire about how they get to work. Do they walk, cycle, drive, take the train or bus and, if they use more than one mode of transport, which ones?   Many commuters, of course, use more than one form of transport to get to work. For example, Respondent A uses her car for the entire journey; Respondent B drives his car to a station and take a train; Respondent C walks to a bus stop, takes the bus to the railway station, takes the train to a railway station near work and finally takes a taxi to complete her journey.

This research is not just about the simple frequencies with which the different forms of transport are used. Which *combinations* of transport mode are the most common? Which are the least common? Do the sexes differ in their combinations of transport mode? Questions of this sort concern, not the frequencies of different responses in the respondent sample, but the **multiple response profiles** of different categories of commuter.

When a questionnaire includes a single question allowing the respondent to tick one or more modes of transport, one cannot transcribe the responses into one variable of an SPSS data set, since we must have one response for each category in a qualitative variable. The solution is to create several variables (e.g. *Do you walk? Do you cycle?*), one for each form of transport. (Special software is available for this purpose.) The researcher can then enter a value for each variable depending on the responses to the transport question. Two different systems of coding are possible here. In one system (which we shall call Format 1), 1 means Yes for every variable. In the other (which we shall call Format 2), 1 can mean Walk for the first variable, Cycle for the second, and so on. Unselected modes of transport are treated as missing values, i.e., they are assigned dots in Data View. With the special kind of data we have been discussing, procedures such as **Frequencies** will simply yield the frequencies with which different forms of transport are used in the respondent sample; whereas the researcher's question requires the comparison of multiple response profiles in different categories of commuter.

How SPSS produces multiple response profiles

In SPSS, there is a special procedure for obtaining multiple response profiles. It is called the **Multiple Response** procedure and we shall illustrate its use with a data set consisting of details of age, age group, sex and how the responders travel to work. The details of how they travel to work have been coded into seven binary variables: Travel_walk, Travel_cycle, …, Travel –train (Figure 9).

Travel_walk	Numeric	8	0	Do you walk?	{1, Yes}...
Travel_cycle	Numeric	8	0	Do you cycle?	{1, Yes}...
Travel_bus	Numeric	8	0	Do you take the bus?	{1, Yes}...
Travel_drivecar	Numeric	8	0	Do you drive a car?	{1, Yes}...
Travel_motorbike	Numeric	8	0	Do you drive a motorbike?	{1, Yes}...
Travel_sharecar	Numeric	8	0	Do you come by car with others	{1, Yes}...
Travel_train	Numeric	8	0	Do you come by train?	{1, Yes}...

Figure 9. Part of the data set showing the variables related to mode of travel

13.5.1   Multiple response set analysis with SPSS

Creating the data file

The first task is to create a **Multiple Response Set** for the type of transport used to get to work. To do this, select **Analyze➔Tables➔Multiple Response Sets...** (Figure 10) to access the **Define Multiple Response Sets** dialog box.

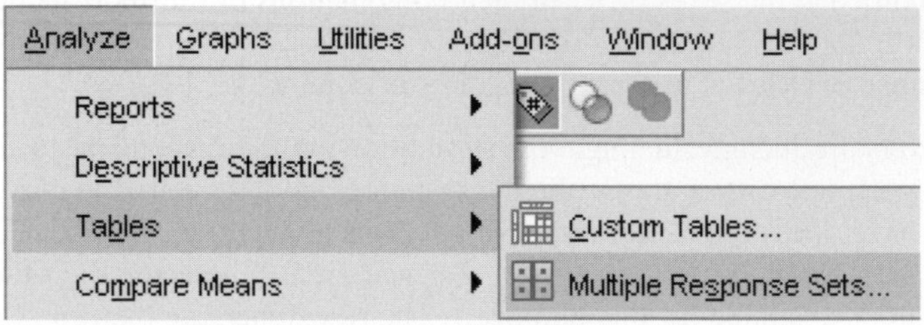

Figure 10. The **Multiple Response Sets** item in the **Analyze** menu

Complete the dialog box as shown in Figure 11 (assuming Format 1) and click **OK**. Confirmation of the creation of a new *Response Set* named *Travel_Mode* with a label *Travel to work* will appear in **SPSS Viewer** (Output 20).

If the travel variables are in Format 2 (1 = Walk for the first variable, 1 = Cycle for the second variable), then the radio button for **Labels of counted value** should be clicked instead of the default **Variable labels** (Figure 11).

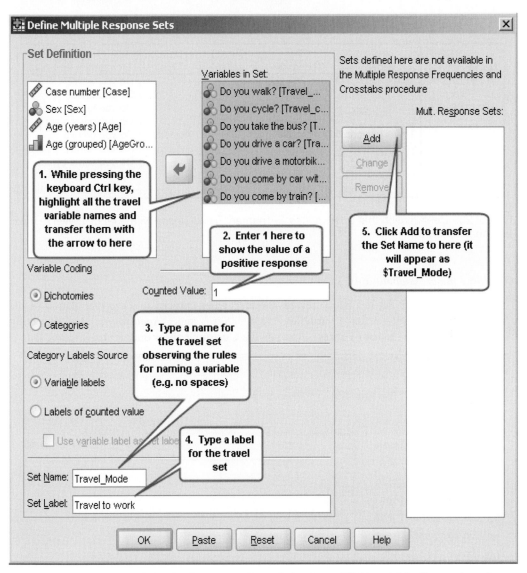

Figure 11. The **Define Multiple Response Sets** dialog box. Clicking **Add** will complete the dialog by transferring the Set Name to the right-hand panel

Multiple Response Sets

Name	Label	Coded As	Counted Value	Data Type	Elementary Variables
$Travel_Mode	Travel to work	Dichotomies	1	Numeric	Do you walk? Do you cycle? Do you take the bus? Do you drive a car? Do you drive a motorbike? Do you come by car with others? Do you come by train?

Output 20. Confirmation that a *Response Set* named *Travel_Mode* with a label *Travel to work* has been created

Obtaining the crosstabulations

Now that a *Response Set* has been created, the researcher can create a crosstabulation of the *Response Set* with other variables (e.g. *Sex* and *AgeGroup*) by selecting **Analyze➔Tables➔Custom Tables…** to open the **Custom Tables** dialog box (Figure 12).

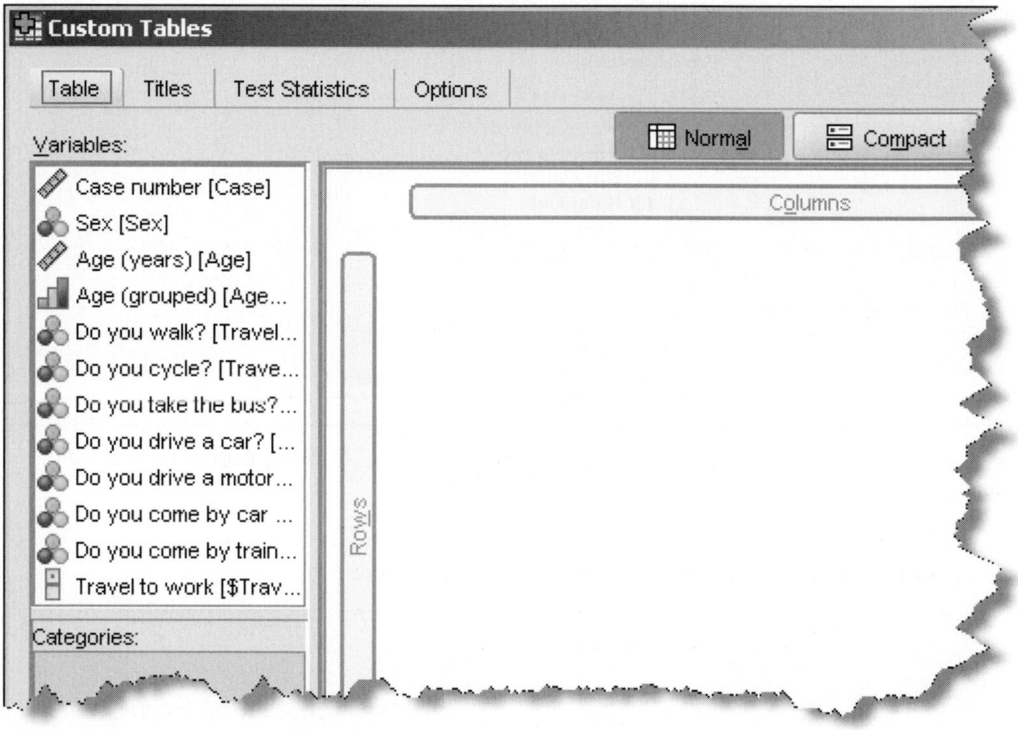

Figure 12. Part of the **Custom Tables** dialog box

Complete the dialog box as shown in Figure 13 and click **OK**.

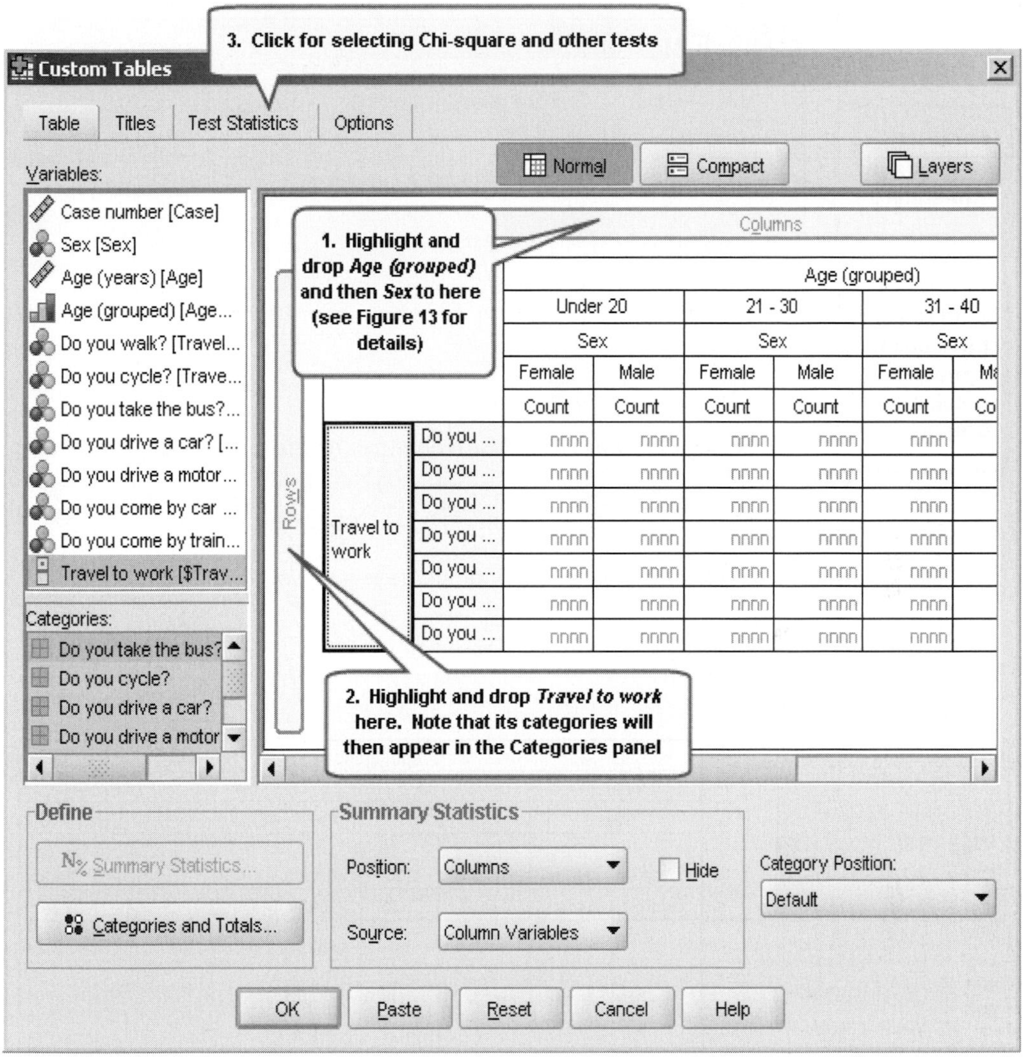

Figure 13. The completed **Custom Tables** dialog box for the contingency table of *Travel to work*

As each variable name is dragged into either the **Columns** or the **Rows** panels, the display changes to show the constituent levels of the variables (Figure 14).

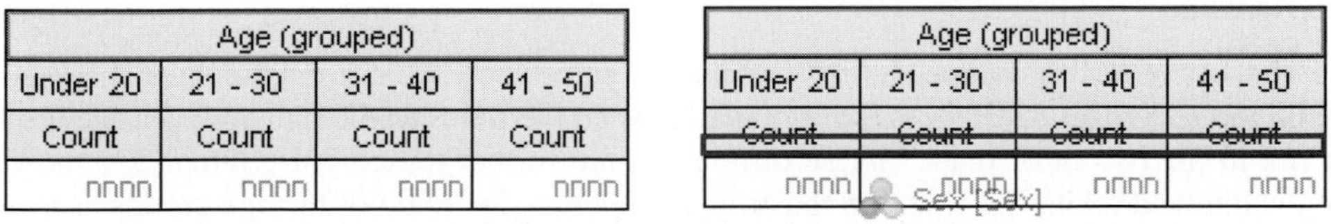

Figure 14. Hover *Age(grouped)* over the Columns box (left). Then hover *Sex* until horizontal coloured lines appear (right). Release the mouse button.

Various statistical tests can also be selected as shown in Figure 15.

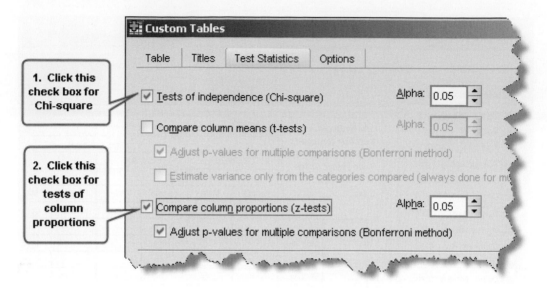

Figure 15. Click the check boxes for the appropriate test statistics, then click **OK**

The output is shown in Output 21.

		Age (grouped)							
		Under 20		21 - 30		31 - 40		41 - 50	
		Sex		Sex		Sex		Sex	
		Female	Male	Female	Male	Female	Male	Female	Male
		Count	Count	Count	Count	Count	Count	Count	Count
How to get to work	Do you walk?	153	76	207	167	26	17	10	7
	Do you cycle?	5	13	22	33	7	8	5	5
	Do you take the bus?	69	39	72	41	14	6	8	2
	Do you drive a car?	46	28	67	57	44	34	41	16
	Do you drive a motorbike?	0	0	3	2	0	0	1	0
	Do you come by car with others?	8	5	8	4	2	1	3	1
	Do you come by train?	0	4	1	7	1	2	2	1

Output 21. The contingency table of the various ways of getting to work categorised by *Sex* and *AgeGroup*

The chi-square test of independence (Output 22) shows that there are significant differences among the responses for *How to get to work* between the sexes in the two younger age groups but not in the two older ones. These differences are further teased out (Output 23) showing that cycling and taking the train are the critical responses for some of the age groups as shown by the letter A.

Pearson Chi-Square Tests

		Age (grouped)			
		Under 20	21 - 30	31 - 40	41 - 50
		Sex	Sex	Sex	Sex
Travel to work	Chi-square	21.258	17.581	3.675	5.456
	df	6	7	6	7
	Sig.	.002' a	.014' a	.720a	.605a.b

Results are based on nonempty rows and columns in each innermost subtable.

*. The Chi-square statistic is significant at the 0.05 level.

a. More than 20% of cells in this subtable have expected cell counts less than 5. Chi-square results may be invalid.

b. The minimum expected cell count in this subtable is less than one. Chi-square results may be invalid.

Output 22. The chi-square tests showing sex differences for *Travel to work* for the Under 20 and 21-30 Age Groups only

Comparisons of Column Proportions[b]

		Age (grouped)							
		Under 20		21 - 30		31 - 40		41 - 50	
		Sex		Sex		Sex		Sex	
		Female	Male	Female	Male	Female	Male	Female	Male
		(A)	(B)	(A)	(B)	(A)	(B)	(A)	(B)
Travel to work	Do you walk?								
	Do you cycle?		A		A				
	Do you take the bus?								
	Do you drive a car?								
	Do you drive a motorbike?	a	a			a	a		a
	Do you come by car with others?								
	Do you come by train?	a			A				

Results are based on two-sided tests with significance level 0.05. For each significant pair, the key of the category with the smaller column proportion appears under the category with the larger column proportion.

a. This category is not used in comparisons because its column proportion is equal to zero or one.

b. Tests are adjusted for all pairwise comparisons within a row of each innermost subtable using the Bonferroni correction.

Output 23. The column proportions tests. The letter A shows which proportions are significantly different

Other statistics such as percentages can be selected by highlighting sections of the table (e.g. *Sex*) in the dialog box (Figure 13), clicking **N% Summary Statistics** in the **Define** panel to open the **Summary Statistics** dialog box (see Section 4.3.1), selecting one (or more) of the options within the **Statistics** panel (e.g. *Row Valid N %*), clicking the arrow to transfer the chosen statistic to the next available row (or rows) in the **Display** panel, and clicking the **Apply to Selection** button. You will then be returned to the **Custom Tables** dialog box, where newly selected statistics are shown in the display. Finally click **OK** to obtain the contingency table. Care needs to be taken in selecting the appropriate percentage: there is a bewildering choice of options.

The *Response Set* can also be used as one of the variables in a graph such as a clustered bar chart. This is illustrated in Output 24, which shows the *Response Set* plotted with *Sex* and *AgeGroup*.

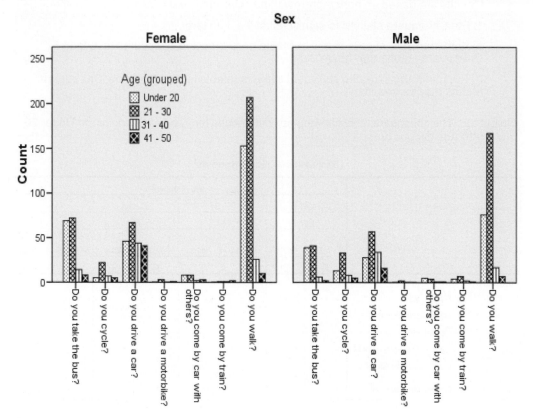

Output 24. Edited clustered bar chart showing the transport profiles for *Sex* and *AgeGroup*

Several respondents selected more than one mode of transport for getting to work because they have to walk to catch a bus or a train and perhaps walk at the work end to get from the bus or station to their workplace. They may also vary their mode of transport depending on the weather or the season of the year. One way of quantifying this would be to use the **Compute Variable** procedure to create a variable *Travel-Combo* but this only works if there are no missing values for travel variables that are not selected. This is easily remedied by using the **Recode into the Same Variables...** procedure in the **Transform** drop-down menu. Transfer the variable names of the seven travel variables into the **Numerical Variables** panel and click the **Old and New Values...** button to open the **Recode into Same Variables: Old and New**

Values dialog box. Click the **System-missing** radio in the **Old Value** panel, enter 0 in the **Value** box in the **New Value** panel and click **Add** to result in SYSMIS--> 0 appearing alongside. Click **Continue** to return to the original dialog box and then **OK**.

It is then possible to proceed with the **Compute Variable Numerical Expression** shown in Figure 16.

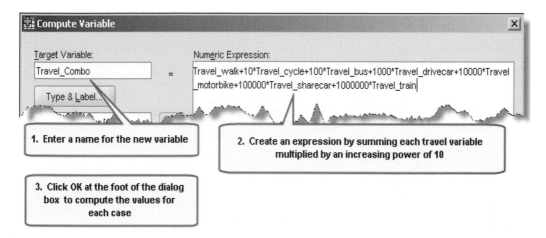

Figure 16. Using **Compute Variable** to calculate values of the new variable *Travel_Combo*

This expression would have a value of 1 for someone who only walks, 10 for someone who only cycles, 100 for someone who only takes the bus and so on. Someone who walks and takes the bus, however, would have a value of 101. The number of combinations is large but with perseverance it is possible to enter a value label (e.g. Walk, Bus for 101) for every travel mode in **Variable View** for the variable *Travel_Combo*. The frequencies of each combination can then be tabulated using **Analyze➔Tables➔Tables of Frequencies...** menu with *Sex* as a subgroup.

13.6   A FINAL WORD

In this chapter, we have looked at two types of frequency data, the first being multiway contingency tables, the second multiple response sets. For multiway contingency tables we have demonstrated the power of loglinear analysis to test specific hypotheses in a way that was impossible with the traditional Pearsonian test of the null hypothesis.

For multiple response sets, we have shown how SPSS can be used to discern patterns of multiple responses among the variables, especially by comparing the patterns of responses across the levels of one or more of the other variables.

Recommended reading

Howell (2007) has a lucid introductory chapter on the theory of loglinear analysis. Tabachnick & Fidell (2007) have an extensive chapter on loglinear analysis with various computing packages, including SPSS. Todman and Dugard (2007) take a more informal, hands-on approach.

Howell, D. C. (2007). *Statistical methods for psychology (6th ed.)*. Belmont, CA: Thomson/Wadsworth.

Tabachnick, B. G., & Fidell, L. S. (2007). *Using multivariate statistics (5th ed.)*. Boston: Allyn & Bacon (Pearson International Edition).

Todman, J., & Dugard, P. (2007). *Approaching multivariate analysis: An introduction for psychology*. London: Psychology Press.

Exercise

Exercise 22 *Loglinear analysis* is available in www.psypress.com/spss-made-simple and click on Exercises.

CHAPTER 14

Discriminant analysis and logistic regression

14.1   Introduction

14.2   Discriminant analysis with SPSS

14.3   Binary logistic regression

14.4   Multinomial logistic regression

14.5   A final word

14.1   INTRODUCTION

In Chapter 12, it was shown how the methods of regression could be used to predict scores on one dependent or **criterion** variable from knowledge of scores on dependent variables or **regressors**. In the situations we discussed, both the dependent variable and the independent variables were always scale or continuous data. There are circumstances, however, in which one might wish to predict, not scores on a quantitative dependent variable, but category membership: that is, the DV is qualitative, rather than quantitative.

Suppose that a premorbid blood condition has been discovered, which is suspected to arise in middle age partly because of smoking and drinking. A hundred people are tested for the presence of the condition and a record made of their smoking and alcohol consumption. Can people's levels of smoking and drinking be used to predict whether they have the blood condition?

Here, although the independent variables (smoking and alcohol consumption) are continuous variables, the dependent variable is qualitative, consisting merely of the categories Yes (condition present) and No (condition absent). Could we assign arbitrary code numbers to the categories (dummy coding: 0 = No; 1= Yes) and carry out a regression in the usual way? Well, yes, we could; but there are many problems with that approach, and it is not recommended.

In this Chapter, we shall discuss two regression techniques that have been specially designed to predict category membership:
    1.   Discriminant analysis.
    2.   Logistic regression.

14.1.1   Discriminant analysis

The topic of discriminant analysis was alluded to in Chapter 10, in the context of multivariate analysis of variance (MANOVA). Mathematically, MANOVA and discriminant analysis are equivalent and the outputs from the two techniques contain a common core of key statistics. The difference is one of perspective: in the MANOVA, the focus is on the making of comparisons; whereas in discriminant analysis, the researcher is more interested in the prediction of category membership than in the comparison of levels of performance among different groups.   At the same time, however, it must be said that, although discriminant analysis seems more at home in the context of correlational, rather than experimental, research, discriminant analysis can also be used as an effective follow-up to the MANOVA.

Discriminant functions

In discriminant analysis, the IVs are combined into a new variable known as a **discriminant function D** which, like the estimate of the DV in multiple regression, is a linear function of the IVs.

Let Y be the dependent variable which, we shall assume, consists of two number-coded categories: 1 = Condition Present; 0 = Condition Absent. Let X_1, X_2, ..., X_p be p independent variables from which we hope to predict category membership. The purpose of discriminant analysis is to find a linear function D of the independent variables, that is, a function of the form

$$D = b_0 + b_1 X_1 + b_2 X_2 + ... + b_p X_p \text{ - - - (1)} \textbf{ Discriminant function}$$

where the values of the coefficients and intercept of the discriminant function are chosen so that to the greatest possible extent, the group means on D (which are known as the **group centroids**) are as far apart as possible. If the discriminant function D separates the group means, we can imagine two overlapping, bell-shaped distributions (normality is an assumption in discriminant analysis) centred on the values of the group centroids.

In discriminant analysis, the value of the discriminant function D is used to classify the individuals in the study by assigning them to the Condition Present group ($Y = 1$) if their score on D exceeds a criterion cut-off value and to the Condition Absent group ($Y = 0$) if their score fails to reach the cut-off. If the group centroids (means on D) are sufficiently different, the number of correct assignments will exceed chance. The more widely separated the distributions of D in the two groups, the more successful we shall be in predicting group membership from a particular value of D.

Returning briefly to the MANOVA, in which discriminant functions also play a central role, the formula for a discriminant function was there expressed in terms of *dependent*, rather than *independent* variables. This difference in terminology reflects the different contexts in which the techniques are used: exactly the same function is being described in either case. In the present context, the variables X are termed IVs because they are regressors from which category membership is to be predicted.

The difference between discriminant analysis and MANOVA is one of supposed direction of causation. In the medical, correlational context, the assumption is that the categorical variable, i.e. the presence or absence of the antibody, is caused or influenced by the continuous variables. In the experimental context, in contrast, it is assumed that group membership (the treatment factor) causes or influences the continuous variables, which in MANOVA are thus seen as DVs, not IVs. In this chapter, since the emphasis is upon prediction of category membership rather than testing differences among means for significance, the continuous variables will be regarded as IVs, not DVs, as in the MANOVA.

Given that a discriminant function can be constructed, tests are available to ascertain which of the independent variables are significant contributors to the function and hence to the power of the function to discriminate among the target groups and so predict group membership. There are many other parallels between multiple regression and discriminant analysis; indeed, with discriminant analysis, there are all the ambiguities and other difficulties that one finds with multiple regression.

Measuring the predictive power of discriminant functions

Two statistics serve as measures of the power of discriminant functions to discriminate among the groups. The **canonical correlation** (see Section 15.4) is the correlation between scores on a discriminant function and scores on coding variables defining group membership. The **eigenvalue** (see Section 10.4.2) is another measure of the separation achieved by a discriminant function: it can readily be converted to the percentage of the between groups variance that is accounted for by a discriminant function.

14.1.2 Types of discriminant analysis

There are three types of discriminant analysis (DA): **direct**, **hierarchical**, and **stepwise**, where these terms have exactly the same meaning as they do in multiple regression. **Direct DA** is the equivalent of simultaneous multiple regression: all the variables are entered into the regression equation at once. In **hierarchical DA**, they are entered according to a schedule set by the researcher on the basis of theory or collateral evidence. In **stepwise DA**, statistical criteria alone determine the order of entry. Since in most analyses, the researcher has no reason for giving some predictors higher priority than others, the third (**stepwise**) method is the most generally used. On the other hand, the same uncertainties arise with stepwise discriminant analysis as with the use of stepwise methods in multiple regression. A *statistical* model alone is insufficient to resolve some issues: the researcher must also have recourse to a *substantive* model. On those grounds, it might be argued that the direct approach, in which all the independent variables are entered simultaneously, is more appropriate. The direct approach is also the one consistent with the MANOVA, in which the DVs (here they are the IVs) are entered simultaneously. Here, nevertheless, we shall opt for the stepwise approach, in order to illustrate some of the criteria for inclusion and exclusion of variables. Were we to use discriminant analysis as a follow-up to a MANOVA, we should take the direct approach.

14.1.3 Stepwise discriminant analysis

The statistical procedure for stepwise discriminant analysis is similar to multiple regression, in that the effect of the addition or removal of an IV is monitored by a statistical test and the result is used as a basis for the inclusion of that IV in the final analysis. When there are only two groups, there is just one discriminant function. With more than two groups, however, there can be several functions (one fewer than the number of groups), although it is unusual for more than the first two or three discriminant functions to be statistically robust.

Variables are added or removed from the analysis according to changes in the value of **Wilks' Lambda (Λ)**. When a new variable is added, the value of Wilks' lambda will decrease: that is, the discriminant function will be more effective in separating the groups. At the same time, when any variable is removed, lambda will generally increase; though sometimes this increase will be minimal, in which case the variable is a candidate for removal from the discriminant function. The significance of the change in Λ when a variable is entered or removed is obtained from an approximate F test. A criterion is set for values of F deemed to be sufficiently large to justify adding a variable to the function: this criterion is known as **F to Enter**. Similarly, a small value of F is set, below which a variable will be removed. At each step of adding a variable to the analysis, the variable with the largest F that exceeds **F to Enter** is included. This process is repeated until there are no further variables with an F value greater than **F to Enter**. Sometimes a variable, having been included at one point, is removed later when its F value falls below **F to Remove**. (This can happen with the stepwise multiple regression procedure as well – see Section 12.4.2.)

Eventually, the process of adding and subtracting variables is completed, and a summary table is shown indicating which variables were added or subtracted at each step. The variables remaining in the analysis are those used in the discriminant function(s). The next table shows which functions are statistically reliable. The first function provides the best means of predicting group membership. Later functions may or may not contribute reliably to the prediction process. Additional tables displaying the functions and their success rates for correct prediction can (and should) be requested. Plots can also be specified.

14.1.4   Restrictive assumptions of discriminant analysis

The use of discriminant analysis, however, carries several restrictive assumptions, as does the MANOVA, to which discriminant analysis is mathematically equivalent. It is assumed, for example, that the data are **multivariate normal** (i.e., for any fixed set of values for $p - 1$ variables, the remaining variable is normally distributed). The discriminant analysis tests are sufficiently robust to cope with some skewness, provided the samples are not too small. The problem of outliers, however, is potentially more serious. It is best to remove extreme values if that can be justified. As in the MANOVA, there is the assumption of **homogeneity of variance-covariance matrices**. Heterogeneity of variance-covariance matrices is most serious when the sample sizes are unequal. It is also important to avoid **multicollinearity** (high correlations among the independent variables). In particular, no variable must be an exact linear function of any of the others, a condition known as **singularity**.

While it is assumed that the independent variables will usually be quantitative, it is also possible to include the occasional qualitative independent variable (e.g. sex, marital status), just as it is in multiple regression.

14.2   DISCRIMINANT ANALYSIS WITH SPSS

A school's vocational guidance officer would like to be able to help senior pupils to choose which subjects to study at university. Fortunately, some data are available from a project on the background interests and school-leaving examination results of architectural, engineering and psychology students. The students also filled in a questionnaire about their extra-curricular interests, including outdoor pursuits, drawing, painting, computing, and kit construction. The problem is this: can knowledge of the pupils' scores on a number of variables be used to predict their subject category at university? In this study, subject category at university (psychologists, architects or engineers) is the dependent variable, and all the others are independent variables. Since the dependent variable is not continuous but a set of categories and the independent variables are continuous, discriminant analysis is an obvious approach to the analysis.

14.2.1 Preparing the data set

Since the data for this example are the scores of 118 participants on ten variables, it would be extremely tedious for readers to type the data into **Data View**. The data are available at: www.psypress.com/spss-made-simple. Select *Ch14 Vocational guidance data* and save it to the hard disk (or your stick) for easier access.

A section of the data set in **Data View** is shown in Figure 1.

Case	StudySubject	Sex	ConKit	ModelKit	Drawing	Painting	Outdoor	Computing	VisModel	Quals
32	Architect	Male	4	2	7	4	2	2	4	9
33	Architect	Female	4	10	7	3	5	1	6	7
34	Psychologist	Male	2	2	0	0	1	1	2	9
35	Psychologist	Female	2	4	3	1	1	1	6	9

Figure 1. Some cases in the Vocational Guidance data set

14.2.2 Exploring the data

Before embarking on the discriminant analysis, the user should probe the data for possible violations of the underlying assumptions. A full treatment of this topic is beyond the scope of this book, but the interested reader should consult a statistical text such as Tabachnick & Fidell (2007) for more details.

Here we suggest you check for extreme scores and outliers by using the **Explore** command (see Chapter 4, Section 4.3.2) to examine the distributions of the variables within the different categories of the grouping factor (*Study Subject*).

See Section 4.3.2

- In the **Explore** dialog box, click the **Plots** radio button in the **Display** options, and transfer the variable names of all the predictors except *Sex* into the **Dependent List** box. Transfer the variable name *Study Subject* into the **Factor List** box, and the variable name *Case Number* into the **Label Cases by** box.
- Click **OK** to plot all the boxplots and stem-and-leaf displays.

Most of the boxplots are satisfactory except for *Interest in Painting* (see Output 1). Here one box is much larger than the others; moreover, in the Engineers' box, the median line is positioned close to the lower side of the box, rather than centrally. There are also two outliers. (See Table 2 in Section 4.3.2 for a reminder of the layout of a boxplot.) The corresponding **stem-and-leaf**

See Section 4.3.2

displays also show discrepancies among the distributions and marked skewness of the distribution in the engineers. Should the first run of the discriminant procedure indicate that there are problems with the data, it might be advisable to omit the independent variable *Interest in Painting*.

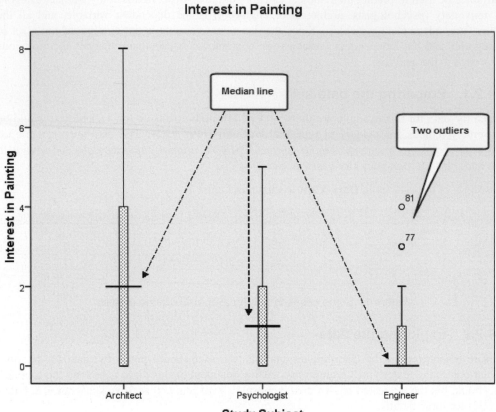

Output 1. The boxplots of *Interest in Painting* for the three subject categories

14.2.3   Running discriminant analysis

- Choose **Analyze→Classify** (see Figure 2)**→Discriminant...** to open the **Discriminant Analysis** dialog box, the completed version of which is shown in Figure 3.
- Transfer the dependent variable name (here it is *StudySubject*, the subject of study) to the **Grouping Variable** box. Click **Define Range** and type 1 into the **Minimum** box and 3 into the **Maximum** box.

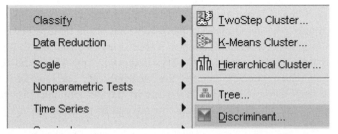

Figure 2. Finding the **Discriminant** procedure in the **Analyze** menu

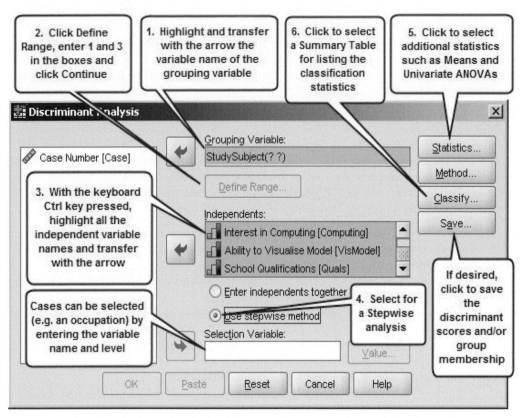

Figure 3. The **Discriminant Analysis** dialog box for the grouping variable *StudySubject* (with three levels) and several independent variables, using the **stepwise method**

On the upper right of the **Discriminant Analysis** dialog box are buttons labelled **Statistics...** and **Classify....** Clicking them will open further dialogs offering a variety of useful extra items for the output.

We shall certainly want descriptive statistics. Should we find, for instance, that the means on a variable are very similar across the three groups, this would indicate that the groups are not well differentiated by that variable. We can expect our best discriminating variables to show differences between the groups. For exploratory purposes, it will also be useful to have the univariate ANOVAs for the variables considered separately. Since the IVs are likely to be correlated, we can take the p-values of the ANOVAs with a pinch of salt: this is essentially the same problem that we discussed in Chapter 10, in the context of experiments with more than one DV. Nevertheless, the statistics of the univariate tests will highlight those variables that are playing the most important roles.

The **Discriminant Analysis: Statistics** dialog box (not shown) offers means, univariate ANOVAs and Box's M. (Box's test is for homogeneity of the variance-covariance matrices across groups.) These should all be selected, together with the unstandardised function coefficients. We shall also want the total covariance matrix, which will give us the variances and covariances of the independent variables in the data as a whole, ignoring the grouping factor. The separate-groups covariance will be useful as well.

Clicking the **Classify…** button will open the **Discriminant Analysis: Classification** dialog box (not shown). The most important item here is the summary table, which shows how successfully the discriminant functions have assigned the participants to the categories of the dependent variable.

If you click the **Method…** button, you will obtain the **Discriminant Analysis: Stepwise Method** dialog box (not shown). You will see that Wilks's lambda has been selected by default as the statistic that will be used for the addition and subtraction of variables to and from the discriminant functions. You will also see that the criteria for entry and removal have been set at 3.84 and 2.71, respectively. Here, you have the option of checking the lower radio button labelled Use probability of F, which will set the p-values for entry and removal at 0.05 and 0.01, respectively. Since we have plenty of data, we shall stay with the default criteria.

If you click the **Save…** button, you will open the **Discriminant Analysis: Save** dialog box, which offers discriminant scores and predicted group membership. It will be useful to have these values in **Data View** for further consideration and experiment.

- Drag the cursor down the names of the independent variables to highlight them and transfer them all to the **Independents** box.
- Since a stepwise analysis is going to be used, click the radio button for **Use stepwise method**.
- To obtain the means and one-way ANOVAs for each of the variables across the three levels of the independent variable, click **Statistics…** and select **Means** and **Univariate ANOVAs**. Click **Continue** to return to the original dialog box.
- To obtain a final summary table showing the success or failure of the discriminant functions to assign participants to their subject categories, click **Classify…** and select **Summary table**. Click **Continue** to return to the original dialog box.
- In some analyses there may be a grouping variable of which just one level is of interest. For example, we could have excluded *Sex* from the list of **Independents** and then carried out the analysis on males only by entering the variable name *Sex* in the **Selection Variable** box and then 1 for males in the **Value** box which would have appeared as soon as *Sex* was entered.
- Click **OK** to run the **Discriminant Analysis**.

14.2.4   Output for discriminant analysis

The output, as listed in the left-hand pane of the **SPSS Viewer** (Output 2), is rather daunting. Fortunately, as with the regression output, not all of it is required.

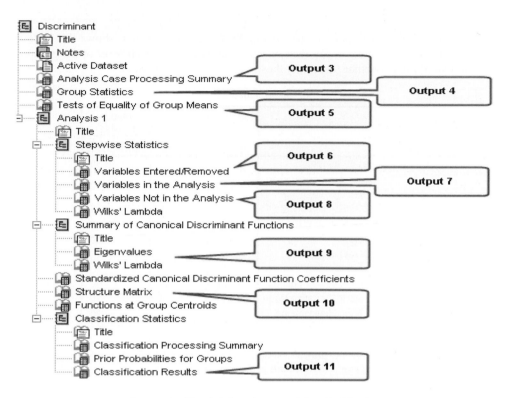

Output 2. The left-hand pane of the **SPSS Viewer**

Information about the data and the number of cases in each category of the grouping variable

Output 3 shows how many valid cases were used in the analysis. Ten cases, which were missing a score on one or more of the independent variables, have been excluded.

Analysis Case Processing Summary

Unweighted Cases		N	Percent
Valid		108	91.5
Excluded	Missing or out-of-range group codes	0	.0
	At least one missing discriminating variable	10	8.5
	Both missing or out-of-range group codes and at least one missing discriminating variable	0	.0
	Total	10	8.5
Total		118	100.0

Output 3. Information about the number of valid cases

Statistics

The next table (Output 4) is part of the **Group Statistics** table, which shows the optional statistics and the number of cases for each independent variable at each level of the grouping variable and all of them together (here only those for *Architect* are shown).

Group Statistics

Study Subject		Mean	Std. Deviation	Valid N (listwise) Unweighted
Architect	Sex of Student	1.27	.45	30
	Interest in Construction Kits	3.33	1.58	30
	Interest in Modelling Kits	3.97	2.68	30
	Interest in Drawing	5.10	2.29	30
	Interest in Painting	2.50	2.18	30
	Interest in Outdoor Pursuits	2.30	2.07	30
	Interest in Computing	1.77	1.45	30
	Ability to Visualise Model	5.53	1.25	30
	School Qualifications	6.63	2.86	30

Output 4. An edited table showing part of the optional statistics and the number of cases for each independent variable at each level of the grouping variable Study Subject

The **Univariate ANOVAs** (Output 5) show whether there is a statistically significant difference among the three grouping variable (*Study Subject*) means for each independent variable. All these differences are significant (as shown in the column **Sig.**), except for the variables *Interest in Computing* and *Interest in Modelling Kits*. We can therefore expect that neither of those two variables is likely to play an important role in the discriminant functions.

Tests of Equality of Group Means

	Wilks' Lambda	F	df1	df2	Sig.
Sex of Student	.77	15.99	2	105	.00
Interest in Construction Kits	.84	9.71	2	105	.00
Interest in Modelling Kits	.96	2.11	2	105	.13
Interest in Drawing	.90	6.09	2	105	.00
Interest in Painting	.83	10.41	2	105	.00
Interest in Outdoor Pursuits	.94	3.24	2	105	.04
Interest in Computing	1.00	.00	2	105	1.00
Ability to Visualise Model	.84	9.74	2	105	.00
School Qualifications	.88	7.38	2	105	.00

All ANOVAs are significant except those with p-value > 0.05

Output 5. Univariate **ANOVA**s

Returning to the point we made at the end of Chapter 10, when we were discussing the MANOVA, the p-values of F tests on each of a set of correlated DVs must be viewed with scepticism. This is also true of the tests reported in Output 5; although in the present context, the DVs have become IVs. The very small p-values of some of the tests, however, indicate that at least some of the differences are robust.

The summary table

The **Stepwise Statistics** section begins with a summary table (Output 6) showing which variables were entered and removed (though in this analysis none was removed), along with values of **Wilks' Lambda** and the associated probability levels. Notice the values of **F to Enter** and **F to Remove** in footnotes b and c. These are the default criteria, which can be changed in the **Stepwise Method** dialog box.

Variables Entered/Removed [a,b,c,d]

		Wilks' Lambda							
						Exact F			
Step	Entered	Stat-istic	df1	df2	df3	Stat-istic	df1	df2	Sig.
1	Sex of Student	.77	1	2	105	16.0	2	105	.00
2	Interest in Painting	.64	2	2	105	16.0	4	208	.00
3	School Qualifications	.54	3	2	105	12.4	6	206	.00
4	Ability to Visualise Model	.48	4	2	105	11.3	8	204	.00
5	Interest in Outdoor Pursuits	.44	5	2	105	10.3	10	202	.00
6	Interest in Construction Kits	.40	6	2	105	9.59	12	200	.00
7	Interest in Computing	.37	7	2	105	8.99	14	198	.00

At each step, the variable that minimizes the overall Wilks' Lambda is entered.

   a. Maximum number of steps is 18.

   b. Minimum partial F to enter is 3.84.

   c. Maximum partial F to remove is 2.71.

   d. F level, tolerance, or VIN insufficient for further computation.

Output 6. Summary table of variables entered and removed

Note the increments in Wilks' lambda are tested using *three* parameters: df1, df2 and df3. The value of *df1* is the number of predictors that have so far been added to the function, including the potential predictor. You can see that, as we move down through steps 1 to 7, the value of *df1* increases in value from 1 to 7. The value of *df2* is (number of groups − 1) = 2. The parameter *df3* is the degrees of freedom of the within groups mean square. Had the groups been of equal size, the value of *df3* would have been $3(n-1)$, where n was the number in each group. In this case, however, the groups are not of equal size, so the value of *df3* is

$$(n_1 - 1) + (n_2 - 1) + (n_3 - 1) = 29 + 36 + 40 = 105$$

which is the value given in Output 6. The value of the approximate F statistic is calculated from those of *df1*, *df2* and *df3* by using the formula shown in Tabachnick & Fidell (2007; p385).

Entering and removing variables step by step

The next table, **Variables in the Analysis**, lists the variables in the analysis at each step. Output 7 shows only Steps 1-3 and the final stage, Step 7.

Variables in the Analysis

Step		Toler- ance	F to Remove	Wilks' Lambda
1	Sex of Student	1.00	15.99	
2	Sex of Student	.88	15.71	.83
	Interest in Painting	.88	10.19	.77
3	Sex of Student	.88	15.26	.70
	Interest in Painting	.85	12.34	.67
	School Qualifications	.95	9.78	.64
7	Sex of Student	.59	7.47	.43
	Interest in Painting	.73	10.92	.46
	School Qualifications	.91	10.83	.46
	Ability to Visualise Model	.90	7.96	.43
	Interest in Outdoor Pursuits	.84	3.96	.40
	Interest in Construction Kits	.80	4.33	.41
	Interest in Computing	.70	3.85	.40

Output 7. Variables in the analysis at Steps 1 to 3, and finally at Step 7

In Output 7, the column labelled **Tolerance** is one minus the square of the multiple correlation coefficient between each candidate variable and all the other variables already entered. (It's value is 1 for Sex, because no other variable has yet been entered.) Very small values of the Tolerance suggest that a variable can contribute little to the analysis. The column **F to Remove** tests the significance of the decrease in discrimination should that variable be removed. Since, however, no F-ratio is less than the criterion value of 2.71 (the default criterion), all the variables have been retained.

The table **Variables not in the Analysis** (Output 8) shows the variables not in the analysis at the start and at each step thereafter until the final step (Output 8 shows only Steps 0 & 1, then Step 7). It can be seen that *Sex of Student* had the highest **F to Enter** value initially (and the lowest **Wilks' Lambda**) and is, therefore, selected as the first variable to enter at Step 1 (Output 7).

At Step 1, the variable with the next highest **F to Enter** value is *Interest in Painting*, which is then entered at Step 2 as shown in Output 7. Finally at Step 7, the variables *Interest in Modelling Kits* and *Interest in Drawing* are never entered because their **F to Enter** values are smaller than the default criterion of 3.84.

Variables Not in the Analysis

Step		Toler-ance	Min. Toler-ance	F to Enter	Wilks' Lambda
0	Sex of Student	1.00	1.00	15.99	0.77
	Interest in Construction Kits	1.00	1.00	9.71	0.84
	Interest in Modelling Kits	1.00	1.00	2.11	0.96
	Interest in Drawing	1.00	1.00	6.09	0.90
	Interest in Painting	1.00	1.00	10.41	0.83
	Interest in Outdoor Pursuits	1.00	1.00	3.24	0.94
	Interest in Computing	1.00	1.00	0.00	1.00
	Ability to Visualise Model	1.00	1.00	9.74	0.84
	School Qualifications	1.00	1.00	7.38	0.88
1	Interest in Construction Kits	0.93	0.93	3.43	0.72
	Interest in Modelling Kits	0.94	0.94	2.20	0.74
	Interest in Drawing	1.00	1.00	6.04	0.69
	Interest in Painting	0.88	0.88	10.19	0.04
	Interest in Outdoor Pursuits	0.98	0.98	1.49	0.75
	Interest in Computing	0.75	0.75	4.20	0.71
	Ability to Visualise Model	1.00	1.00	8.83	0.66
	School Qualifications	0.98	0.98	7.69	0.67
7	Interest in Modelling Kits	0.72	0.57	0.36	0.37
	Interest in Drawing	0.63	0.52	0.91	0.37

> This variable is entered at Step 1 (Output 7) with the largest F to Enter value

> This variable is entered at Step 2 (Output 7) with the largest F to Enter value

> These variables at Step 7 are excluded because their F to Enter values are <3.84

Output 8. Part of the table of variables not in the analysis at Steps 0, 1 and 7

The next table in the output, **Wilks' Lambda**, is a repeat of the table given in Output 5 and is not reproduced.

Statistics of the discriminant functions

Output 9 shows the percentage (**% of Variance**) of the between groups variance accounted for by each discriminant function and how many of them (if any) are significant (see the **Sig.** column in the **Wilks' Lambda** table). Here we see that both functions are highly significant. The **Canonical Correlation** for a discriminant function is the square root of the ratio of the between-groups sum of squares to the total sum of squares. The square of the canonical correlation is the proportion of the total variability explained by differences between groups. The canonical correlation is essentially **eta** (see Chapter 7), as applied to the one-way ANOVA of participants' scores on the discriminant function.

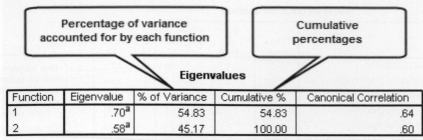

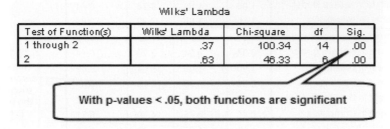

a. First 2 canonical discriminant functions were used in the analysis.

Wilks' Lambda

Test of Function(s)	Wilks' Lambda	Chi-square	df	Sig.
1 through 2	.37	100.34	14	.00
2	.63	46.33	6	.00

With p-values < .05, both functions are significant

Output 9. Statistics of the discriminant functions

In Output 9, note also that the eigenvalues (and hence the values of the percentage of between groups variance accounted for by each discriminant function) are smaller in the second function to be extracted. The canonical correlation (i.e. eta) is also smaller in the second function. The value of Wilks's lambda is higher for the second function, again reflecting that this function accounts for less of the variance: the Wilks's statistic is the error variance expressed as a proportion of the total, so the smaller its value, the greater the proportion of between groups variance accounted for.

Standardised coefficients and within groups correlations with discriminants

Two tables follow in the listing, the first (not reproduced here) being the **Standardized Canonical Discriminant Function Coefficients**, and the second (Output 10) the **Structure Matrix**, which is a table of pooled within groups correlations between the independent variables and the discriminant functions.

Structure Matrix

	Function	
	1	2
Ability to Visualise Model	-.51*	-.10
School Qualifications	.43*	-.16
Interest in Painting	-.42*	.36
Interest in Drawing a	-.22*	.12
Interest in Modelling Kits a	-.12*	.07
Interest in Computing	.01*	.00
Sex of Student	.19	.70*
Interest in Construction Kits	-.15	-.54*
Interest in Outdoor Pursuits	.19	.25*

Pooled within-groups correlations between discriminating
variables and standardized canonical discriminant functions
Variables ordered by absolute size of correlation within function.

*. Largest absolute correlation between each variable and
  any discriminant function

a. This variable not used in the analysis.

Output 10. The **Structure Matrix**

It is clear from the information in Output 10 that the first function is contributed to positively by School Qualifications and their interest in painting, and negatively by their ability to visualise models. The second function is contributed to positively by *Sex* and negatively by *Interest in Modelling Kits* and *Interest in Outdoor Pursuits*. The asterisks mark the correlations with the higher value for each variable (row).

The next table in the output (not reproduced), **Functions at Group Centroids**, lists the group means (for Architect, Psychologist, Engineer) for each discriminant function.

Success of predictions of group membership

The optional selection of **Summary table** from the **Classify** options in the **Discriminant Analysis** dialog box provides an indication of the success rate for predictions of group membership using the discriminant functions developed in the analysis (see Output 11). The footnote to the table indicates that the overall success rate is 72.2%.

Classification Results[a]

	Study Subject	Predicted Group Membership			Total
		Architect	Psychologist	Engineer	
Count	Architect	22	2	6	30
	Psychologist	4	25	8	37
	Engineer	5	5	31	41
%	Architect	73.3	6.7	20.0	100.0
	Psychologist	10.8	67.6	21.6	100.0
	Engineer	12.2	12.2	75.6	100.0

a. 72.2% of original grouped cases correctly classified.

Output 11. **Classification Results** table showing the predicted group membership

Output 11 also shows that the *Engineers* were the most accurately classified, with 75.6% of the cases correct. The *Architects* were next with 73.3%. The *Psychologists* were the least accurately classed, with a success rate of 67.6%. Notice also that incorrectly classified *Architects* were more likely to be classified as *Engineers* than as *Psychologists*, and that incorrectly classified *Psychologists* are more likely to be classified as *Engineers* than as *Architects*!

14.2.5   Predicting group membership

Section 14.2 posed the question of whether knowledge of pupils' scores on a number of variables could be used to predict their subjects of study at university. The analysis has demonstrated that two discriminant functions can be generated using all the variables except *Interest in Modelling Kits* and *Interest in Drawing*, and that these functions can predict 72.2% of the cases correctly, with some variation in levels across subjects. So far, however, we have not seen what the predicted subject of study was for any particular individual. The vocational guidance officer in our example wants to make predictions of the subjects that future students will eventually take on an individual basis, given knowledge of their scores on the same independent variables. It is easy to do either or both of these things with the **Discriminant** procedure.

To compare the actual subject of study with the predicted subject of study, proceed as follows:
- Complete the **Discriminant Analysis** dialog box as before but, in addition, click **Save…** and then click the radio button for **Predicted group membership**. Click **Continue** and **OK**.
- The predicted group membership will appear in a new column labelled **Dis_1** in **Data View**, along with the predictions for all the other cases.
- We suggest that you actually try this and, once **Dis_1** appears in **Data View**, switch to **Variable View** and rename the variable *PredictDiscrim*. Figure 4 is a section from **Data View** showing some of the predictions of choice of subject from the discriminant analysis.

To predict the subject of study for a future student, proceed as follows:
- Enter the data for the potential students at the end of the data in **Data View**. Leave the grouping variable (*StudySubject*) blank or enter an out-of-range number so that the analysis does not include these cases when it is computing the discriminant functions.
- Then after completing the steps described above, the predicted group membership will appear in a new column labelled *PredictDiscrim* in **Data View**, along with the predictions for all the other cases.

Case	StudySubject	Sex	ConKit	ModelKit	Drawing	Painting	Outdoor	Computing	VisModel	Quals	PredictDiscrim
96	Engineer	Male	4	2	4	0	2	1	4	7	Engineer
97	Engineer	Male	3	2	2	0	0	2	4	0	Architect
98	Engineer	Male	4	1	5	1	0	2	7	7	Architect
99	Engineer	Female	1	0	0	0	6	0	2	6	Psychologist
100	Engineer	Male	6	2	2	0	4	2	4	7	Engineer
101	Engineer	Female	4	2	5	1	4	1	4	9	Psychologist

Figure 4. Section of **Data View** showing the predictions from discriminant analysis of choice of main university subject

Before leaving the topic of discriminant analysis, some further consideration of the consequences of violation of the assumptions is in order. The procedure is vulnerable to the presence of extreme scores and outliers. In our preliminary exploratory analysis of the data, we found that the distribution of the scores on *Interest in Painting* was markedly skewed, with several outliers. It would be a worthwhile exercise to repeat the analysis with the outliers removed, and perhaps even with this variable omitted altogether.

With samples this size, departures from multivariate normality are unlikely to have serious consequences for the **Type I error rate**. Discriminant analysis, however, also requires that the variance-covariance matrices should be homogeneous across groups. If **Box's Test** is requested (as it should be), the result will be as shown in Output 12.

Box's Test of Equality of Covariance Matrices

Log Determinants

Study Subject	Rank	Log Determinant
Architect	7	4.518
Psychologist	7	3.419
Engineer	7	2.768
Pooled within-groups	7	4.432

The ranks and natural logarithms of determinants printed are those of the group covariance matrices.

Test Results

Box's M		100.520
F	Approx.	1.620
	df1	56.000
	df2	27655.091
	Sig.	.002

Tests null hypothesis of equal population covariance matrices.

Output 12. Result of **Box's Test** for homogeneity of variance-covariance matrices

We can see from Output 12 that the Box test has indicated that the variance-covariance matrices are not homogeneous across the groups. The Box test, however, is notoriously sensitive and, provided the researcher has large samples of equal size, a significant result can be ignored with impunity (Tabachnick & Fidell, 2007; p. 252). This robustness, however, does not necessarily extend to situations in which, although the samples are large, they are not of equal size. If the smaller samples have larger variances and covariances, there will be too many significant results; if, on the other hand, the larger samples have larger variances and covariances, the tests are conservative (Tabachnick & Fidell, *op. cit.*). In the present data set, we can see from Output 12 that the variance-covariance matrix for the data from the Engineers has the largest determinant. Since this is also the largest sample ($n = 41$), we can be more confident that the p-values of the test statistics do not overstate the case against the null hypothesis.

In the next section, we shall consider an alternative approach to regression with a categorical DV. The methods we shall describe carry fewer assumptions than does discriminant analysis: they do not require multivariate normality; nor need there be homogeneity of the variance-covariance matrices.

14.3   BINARY LOGISTIC REGRESSION

The method we shall describe in this section is applicable to situations in which the dependent variable consists of two categories only. It is not, therefore, applicable to the data set we have just analysed with discriminant analysis, in which the dependent variable consisted of three categories. Those data on subject choices at university, however, can be analysed by a more general method of logistic regression known as **multinomial logistic regression**, which we shall touch upon in the final section of this chapter.

14.3.1 Logistic regression

Logistic regression is another approach to category prediction. This method carries fewer assumptions than does discriminant analysis: neither multivariate normality nor homogeneity of variance-covariance matrices are required. Discriminant analysis, moreover, is also sensitive to the inclusion of qualitative IVs such as sex, blood group or nationality; logistic regression, on the other hand, can cope with any number of qualitative regressors: in fact, *all* the predictors can be categorical. For these reasons, logistic regression is fast overtaking discriminant analysis as the preferred technique for this kind of research problem.

Returning to the example of the premorbid blood condition mentioned at the start of this Chapter, suppose that of the hundred people studied, forty-four people have the condition and fifty-six do not. We shall assign code numbers to the two categories: to those who have the condition, we assign 1; and to those who do not, we assign 0. In this section, we shall outline the use of logistic regression to predict category membership.

On the basis of the foregoing information about the patients, a prediction of category membership can be made without running any regression at all. Since the probability that a person selected at random will have the condition is $44/100 = 0.44$ (44%) and the probability that they will not have the condition is $56/100 = 0.56$ (56%), our best a priori prediction of category membership for any particular person selected at random is to assign them to the 'condition absent' category. If we do that, we shall be right in 100% of the cases in which the condition was absent, but wrong in the 44% of cases in which the condition was present, giving us a net success rate of 56% over the hundred assignments. This prediction, which does not require any regression model, is the equivalent, in logistic regression, of 'intercept-only' prediction in multiple regression, in which we assign the mean value of the criterion variable, irrespective of the values of the regressors. The purpose of logistic regression is to improve upon this baseline success rate by exploiting any association between the dependent and independent variables to predict category membership (the dependent variable) with the greatest possible accuracy.

In what follows, it is assumed that, although the condition can only be present or absent, variables such as number of cigarettes smoked and amount of alcohol consumed actually increase the probability of developing the condition **continuously** throughout the range of consumption. This probability, however, cannot be expected to be a linear function of the independent variables: it is likely to rise with increasing rapidity as scores on the independent variable increase from zero and decelerate at a later stage, so that the probability graph would be rather like a flattened S (See Figure 5).

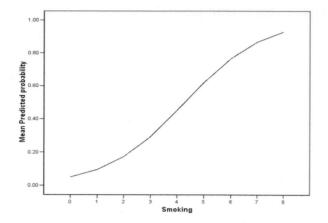

Figure 5. A logistic regression function, giving the estimated probability of a person smoking a certain number of cigarettes having the premorbid blood condition

This theoretical curve expressing the probability of the blood condition as a function of the number of cigarettes smoked is known as the **logistic regression function**. The purpose of logistic regression is to estimate this curve from the data. On the basis of the number of cigarettes that a person smokes, the estimate of the logistic regression function assigns a probability of belonging to the condition-present category. As in multiple regression with a continuous DV, further IVs, such as alcohol intake, can be added to improve predictive accuracy.

Probability estimates from the logistic regression function can be used to assign individuals to either of the two categories of the dependent variable. This is achieved by fixing a criterion probability (most commonly 0.5) and, should the probability estimate for a participant exceed the criterion, that person is assigned to the 'condition present' category. A value less than 0.05 will result in assignment to the 'condition absent' category (see Figure 6).

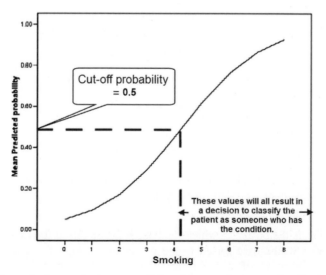

Figure 6. Decision rule for assigning a participant to a category using the logistic regression function

14.3.2 How logistic regression works

The following explanation assumes a knowledge of logarithms. Should the reader be rusty on logs, a brief review of the principles will be found in the Appendix.

We have seen that in the context of an experiment of chance, such as tossing a coin, or rolling a die, the **odds** in favour of an event is the number of ways in which the event could occur divided by the number of ways in which it could fail to occur. If a die is rolled, the odds in favour of a six are 1/5 and the odds in favour of an even number are 3/3 = 1. If we know that among 100 patients, 40 have the antibody in their blood and a patient is selected at random, the odds in favour of the patient selected having the antibody are 44/56 = 11/14.

Another measure of likelihood applicable in the same situation is the **probability**. The probability of an event is the number of ways in which the event could occur divided by the total number of possible outcomes. If a die is rolled, the probability of a six is 1/6 and the probability of an even number is 3/6 = ½ . The two measures of likelihood, the odds and the probability, are closely related:

$$p = \frac{odds}{1 + odds} \quad \text{- - - (2)}$$

Relation between probability and the odds

If we substitute the odds in favour of a six (1/5) into (2), we have p = (1/5)/(6/5) = 1/6. If we substitute the odds in favour of the antibody (11/14) into (2), we have p = (11/14)/(25/14) = 11/25 = 0.44 .

The logit

As a measure of likelihood, the odds has the disadvantage of asymmetry of range. If we start at fifty-fifty (i.e. odds = 1) and regard events with odds greater than 1 as 'likely' and those with odds less than 1 as 'unlikely', there is, in principle, no limit to how great the odds in favour of a 'likely' event could be; whereas those of an 'unlikely' event – however unlikely that event might be – are confined within the interval including zero but excluding 1.

The **logit** is the natural logarithm (log to the base *e*) of the odds:

$$logit = ln(odds) = log_e(odds) \quad \text{- - - (3)}$$

The logit or log odds

When the logit of an event is zero, the odds themselves are 50/50, because the log of 1 is 0 (if necessary, see the Appendix). We have seen that the odds in favour of the antibody are 11/14. The logit, therefore, is ln(11/14) = – 0.24. Had the number of patients with the antibody been 56 instead of 44, the odds would have been 14/11, but the logit would have been ln(14/11) = + 0.24, which is the same distance from zero, but in the opposite direction. In contrast with the odds, the logit has symmetry of range.

The log of a number is the power to which the base must be raised to equal the number itself (see the Appendix). So the base raised to the power of the log of a number is the number itself. From the definition of a logarithm, therefore, we can express the odds as an **antilogarithm**, that is, as the base *e* raised to the power of the log of the odds (i.e. the logit).

So if x and y are odds, they can be expressed as $x = e^{ln(x)} = e^{logit(x)}$ and $y = e^{ln(y)} = e^{logit(y)}$, respectively.

The logistic regression function

Recall that in **multiple regression**, the dependent variable Y is predicted from p independent variables $X_1, X_2, ..., X_p$ by means of the regression equation

$$Y' = b_0 + b_1 X_1 + b_2 X_2 + ... + b_p X_p \quad \text{- - - (4)}$$

Multiple regression equation

where b_0 is the regression constant and $b_1, b_2, ..., b_p$ are the regression coefficients.

The logistic regression function is, as we have seen, nonlinear. Expressing the probability in terms of the odds as in (2) and expressing the adds as an antilog, we have:

$$p = \frac{odds}{1 + odds} = \frac{e^{logit}}{1 + e^{logit}} \quad \text{- - - (5)}$$

Probability as a function of the logit

In the present context, p is the probability of a patient having the antibody and the logit is the natural log of the odds in favour of having the antibody.

In logistic regression, it is assumed that the logit is a linear function of the independent variables thus:

$$logit = b_0 + b_1 X_1 + b_2 X_2 + ... + b_p X_p \quad \text{- - - (6)}$$

The logit equation

If so, we can estimate the probability p of the antibody with $\hat{p}$, where

$$\hat{p} = \frac{e^{logit}}{1 + e^{logit}} = \frac{e^{b_0 + b_1 X_1 + b_2 X_2 + ... + b_p X_p}}{1 + e^{b_0 + b_1 X_1 + b_2 X_2 + ... + b_p X_p}} \quad \text{- - - (7)}$$

The logistic regression equation

Estimating the regression parameters

In logistic regression, as in ordinary multiple regression, the values of the parameters b_0, b_1, ..., b_p in the logit equation (6) are chosen so that the logistic regression equation predicts the independent variable (in this case category membership) as accurately as possible.

We should note that, in contradistinction to ordinary least squares (OLS) regression, there is no mathematical solution to the problem of determining the values of the parameter estimates in the logit equation. Instead, a highly computing-intensive algorithm is used to arrive at the estimates by a series of repetitions or **iterations**. If all goes well, the estimates of the parameters from successive iterations approximate ever more closely to, or **converge** upon, stable values for the parameter estimates. It is essential, however, when running logistic regression, that the user check the iteration history to make sure that convergence really has been achieved; otherwise the output may contain bizarre and self-contradictory information!

Centring the independent variables

As with OLS regression, it is often a good idea to centre continuous IVs by subtracting the mean from each score. While this transformation does not affect the correlations among the variables, it can sometimes enable the logistic regression algorithm to converge upon stable estimates that it would not achieve with the raw data. Centring the variables is particularly important if the researcher is testing a model with interaction terms.

The meaning of a logistic regression coefficient

A logistic regression coefficient b is the increase in the *logit* produced by an increase of one unit in the independent variable. The logit, however, is the log of the odds, so if the logit increases by b units, the raw odds are *multiplied* by the antilog of b, that is by e^b. Suppose, for instance, that we were to find that for the IV Smoking, $b = 1.1$. This means that if the amount of smoking were to increase by one unit, the odds in favour of having the antibody would increase by a factor of $e^b = e^{1.1} = 3.0$. In other words, an increase of one unit in Smoking multiplies the odds in favour of having the antibody by three.

14.3.3   An example of a binary logistic regression with quantitative independent variables

For our first example, we return to the data set on the premorbid blood condition, smoking and drinking. Table 1 shows the data on the first eight cases only - the complete data set is available at www.psypress.com/spss-made-simple. We shall assume that at the point when the data were being transcribed, convenient units for smoking and alcohol were decided upon: one smoking unit might have been ten cigarettes; one drinking unit might have been the equivalent of a large glass of wine or a half-pint of beer.

Table 1. The first eight cases in a hypothetical set of data showing the presence or absence of a blood condition, together with levels of smoking and alcohol consumption

Case	Blood	Smoke	Alcohol	Case	Blood	Smoke	Alcohol
1	Yes	7	18	5	Yes	5	11
2	Yes	6	15	6	Yes	2	18
3	Yes	1	10	7	Yes	0	0
4	Yes	7	16	8	No	6	12

Exploring the data

As usual, we recommend that you explore the data first before embarking upon any formal analysis. For example, an examination of the correlations among the three variables (see Output 13) shows that *Presence* of the antibody correlates substantially and significantly with the *Smoking* variable ($r = +0.586$). and with *Alcohol* intake ($r = +0.267$). The independent variables of *Alcohol* intake and *Smoking* level are also correlated ($r = + 0.443$).

See Section 11.2

Correlations

		Blood Condition	Number Smoked	Alcohol consumption
Blood Condition	Pearson Correlation	1.000	.586**	.267**
	Sig. (2-tailed)		.000	.007
	N	100.000	100	100
Number Smoked	Pearson Correlation	.586**	1.000	.443**
	Sig. (2-tailed)	.000		.000
	N	100	100.000	100
Alcohol consumption	Pearson Correlation	.267**	.443**	1.000
	Sig. (2-tailed)	.007	.000	
	N	100	100	100.000

**. Correlation is significant at the 0.01 level (2-tailed).

Output 13. Correlations among category membership (presence or absence of the premorbid blood condition), amount of smoking and level of alcohol consumption

Centring the independent variables

You will find from running **Descriptives** that the means for the smoking and alcohol variables are 1.38 and 3.87, respectively, with standard deviations 2.461 and 4.907. To centre the smoking and alcohol scores, use **Compute** to subtract their means from the raw values of their respective variables. The new smoking and alcohol means will now be zero. Check that the standard deviations are still 2.461 and 4.907, respectively, and that the correlations among the three variables are still exactly as in Output 13.

Running binary logistic regression

In its logistic regression dialog box, SPSS uses the term **covariate** for continuous independent variables. In this example, both IVs are continuous, so they are both covariates.
- Choose **Analyze➡Regression➡Binary Logistic ...** to open the **Logistic Regression** dialog box (Figure 7).
- Follow the steps in Figure 7.
- Click **Options...** to obtain the **Options** dialog box (Figure 8). Select **Hosmer-Lemeshow goodness-of-fit** and **Iteration history**. (The iteration history is essential.) Click **Continue** to return to the **Logistic Regression** dialog box.
- Click **OK** to run the logistic regression.

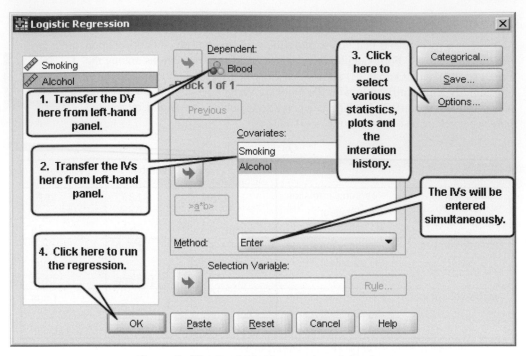

Figure 7. The **Logistic Regression** dialog box

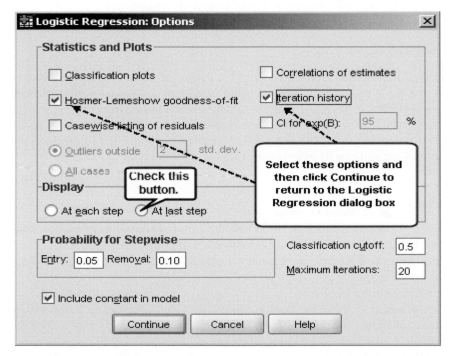

Figure 8. The **Options** dialog box with **Hosmer-Lemeshow goodness-of-fit** and **Iteration history** selected

We have seen that the logistic regression procedure maximises its predictions of category membership by a highly computer-intensive process which generates successive approximations called **iterations**. If all goes well, the estimates should converge upon (i.e. become progressively closer to) stable values, which are taken to be the best estimates. By choosing the item **Iteration history** in the **Options**, you can check that the successive iterations really have converged. (It may sometimes be necessary to increase the number specified in the Maximum Iterations slot to, say, 100 to achieve convergence.)

The analysis of a data set with many variables may take some time to complete. If some of the IVs are highly inter-correlated, the logistic regression algorithm may fail to converge upon stable estimates (the **multicollinearity** problem, which can occur with any regression method). The solution is to delete one or more redundant variables from the analysis.

In the **Logistic Regression** dialog box, there is another button labelled **Save…** which accesses the **Save New Variables** dialog box (not shown). Selecting items from this box will add several new variables to those already in **Data View**, including **Probabilities** and **Group membership** from the **Predicted Values** selection section, and **Standardized** and **Studentized** from the **Residuals** selection section. We suggest that, for the present, the reader might focus on the basic regression only and experiment with the **Save…** button options later.

Output for binary logistic regression

The output for logistic regression is extensive (see Output 14), even if no options are selected. Notice that the output, after the preliminaries, essentially consists of two Blocks. The first, **Block 0: Beginning Block**, gives the statistics of the baseline, intercept-only or guessing approach to prediction of category membership. The second, **Block 1: Method = Enter**, gives the statistics of prediction from the regression model with both IVs present in the regression equation.

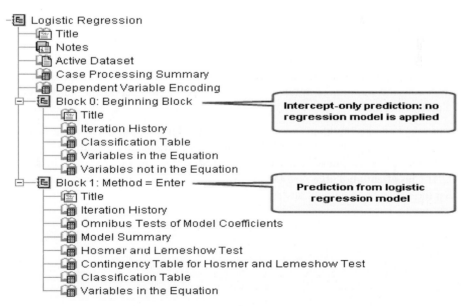

Output 14. The left-hand pane of **SPSS Viewer** showing the details of the output

In logistic regression, pivotal use is made of a statistic termed the **likelihood ratio**, which, in the output for logistic regression, is written as **– 2 Log likelihood**. This statistic behaves as chi-square: it has a large value when a model fits poorly, and a small value when the model fits well. The log likelihood statistic is analogous to the residual sum of squares in multiple regression: the larger its value, the more the variance that remains to be accounted for; a small, insignificant value indicates that the regression model fits the data well.

The first two tables in the output (not shown here) are a **Case Processing Summary** table specifying how many cases were selected and a **Dependent Variable Encoding** table tabulating the numerical values and value labels of the dependent variable. Examine both tables to make sure that the logistic regression procedure has processed all the data and that the value labels have been correctly assigned to the numerical values of the categorical dependent variable.

Next there is a block of tables under the heading **Block 0: Beginning Block** in which the logistic regression procedure begins with a model containing neither of the independent variables (i.e. the 'intercept only' model). Block 0 begins with the **Iteration History** (Output 15).

Iteration History[a,b,c]

Iteration		-2 Log likelihood	Coefficients
			Constant
Step 0	1	137.186	-.240
	2	137.186	-.241
	3	137.186	-.241

a. Constant is included in the model.

b. Initial -2 Log Likelihood: 137.186

c. Estimation terminated at iteration number 3 because parameter estimates changed by less than .001.

Output 15. Iteration history for Step 0 (the intercept-only model)

Notice that the convergence to stable values for the likelihood ratio and the estimate of the regression constant was almost instantaneous: the values in the second and third rows agree to three places of decimals.

In the introduction, we saw that, in the absence of any information about regression, the best bet of a person's category membership is the more frequently occurring category (i.e. condition absent). This 'guessing stage' is called **Step 0** by SPSS. Included in this block is the Step 0 **Classification Table** (see Output 16). There are no surprises here: we have already seen that the success rate without any regression is 56%.

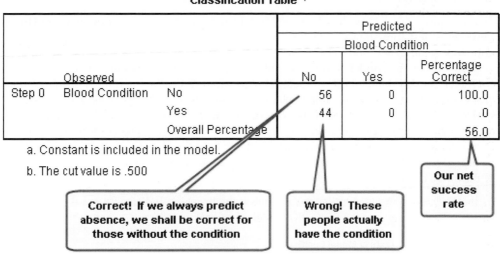

Output 16. The 'no regression' or 'intercept only' **Classification Table**

Two other tables in Block 0 (not shown here) are **Variables in the Equation** and the **Variables not in the equation**. The first table gives the statistics of the intercept, which are not generally of interest. The second table tells us that neither of the independent variables is in the regression equation.

The next block of tables of output is headed **Block 1: Method = Enter**. The first item in the block is the **Iteration History** (Output 17).

Iteration History[a,b,c,d]

Iteration		-2 Log likelihood	Coefficients		
			Constant	Smoking	Alcohol
Step 1	1	98.522	-.906	.472	.004
	2	88.269	-1.030	.875	-.029
	3	80.474	-1.202	1.530	-.061
	4	78.107	-1.355	2.108	-.078
	5	77.999	-1.392	2.256	-.079
	6	77.999	-1.394	2.264	-.078
	7	77.999	-1.394	2.264	-.078

a. Method: Enter

b. Constant is included in the model.

c. Initial -2 Log Likelihood: 137.186

d. Estimation terminated at iteration number 7 because parameter estimates changed by less than .001.

Output 17. The **Iteration History** for Step 1, the simultaneous regression of presence of the antibody upon smoking and alcohol intake

In the last three rows of entries in the iteration history table, the entries agree to three places of decimals, indicating that convergence to stable estimates has been achieved.

The next three items, **Omnibus Tests of Model Coefficients**, **Model Summary** and **Hosmer-Lemeshow test**, are shown in Output 18. The first table shows that the regression model improves significantly upon chance in predicting category membership: all the p-values are very small. In the **Model Summary** table, the **Nagelkerke R Square** statistic imitates the coefficient of determination R^2 in multiple regression: it can be interpreted as the proportion of variance of the dependent variable that is accounted for by the regression model. The other statistic in the table, **Cox & Snell R Square**, compares the log likelihood for the model with the log likelihood for the baseline, intercept-only model. The Nagelkerke R Square, unlike the Cox & Snell R^2, can take values over the full range from 0 to 1. The size of R^2 (60% after Step 2) indicates that the model contributes powerfully to the prediction of the presence or absence of the blood condition.

In the Hosmer-Lemeshow table, the p-value is high, which indicates that all the systematic variance has been accounted for by the model: the rest is error.

Omnibus Tests of Model Coefficients

		Chi-square	df	Sig.
Step 1	Step	59.187	2	.000
	Block	59.187	2	.000
	Model	59.187	2	.000

Model Summary

Step	-2 Log likelihood	Cox & Snell R Square	Nagelkerke R Square
1	77.999ª	.447	.599

a. Estimation terminated at iteration number 7 because parameter estimates changed by less than .001.

Hosmer and Lemeshow Test

Step	Chi-square	df	Sig.
1	6.155	7	.522

Output 18. Some output statistics indicating that regression accounts significantly for presence of the antibody

Output 19 shows the **Contingency Table for the Hosmer and Lemeshow Test**. The first column categorises, in order of increasing magnitude, the probabilities assigned by the regression model into divisions known as **deciles** (deciles divide the distribution into ten parts): the lowest probabilities are in deciles 1 and 2; the highest are in deciles 8 and 9. The table shows the association between assigned probability and presence or absence of the antibody. Notice that, in general, there is close agreement between the **Expected** frequencies (the assignments by the regression model and category assignment on the basis of the cut-off point of 0.05 for probability) and the **Observed** or actual frequencies of patients in those categories. In particular, notice that in deciles 1 and 2 (the first two rows of entries), both Observed and Expected frequencies are very low; whereas in deciles 8 and 9 (the last two rows of entries), both the Observed and Expected frequencies are considerably higher – and in complete agreement.

Contingency Table for Hosmer and Lemeshow Test

		Blood Condition = No		Blood Condition = Yes		
		Observed	Expected	Observed	Expected	Total
Step 1	1	13	11.254	0	1.746	13
	2	12	11.004	1	1.996	13
	3	4	3.311	0	.689	4
	4	17	19.523	7	4.477	24
	5	5	6.087	3	1.913	8
	6	4	4.134	10	9.866	14
	7	1	.687	9	9.313	10
	8	0	.000	9	9.000	9
	9	0	.000	5	5.000	5

Output 19. Contingency table showing the association between the size of the probability assigned by the regression model and presence or absence of the antibody.

Output 20 is the Classification Table showing the proportion of correct assignments when the regression model has been applied to the data. The new success rate of 85% is a spectacular improvement upon the baseline, intercept-only rate of 56%.

Classification Table[a]

			Predicted		
			Blood Condition		
	Observed		No	Yes	Percentage Correct
Step 1	Blood Condition	No	51	5	91.1
		Yes	10	34	77.3
		Overall Percentage			85.0

a. The cut value is .500

Output 20. The **Classification Table** with the regression model applied

Output 21 tabulates the variables that are included in the regression equation. Since we chose the **Enter** method, both DVs will be entered in the equation, even if one does not make a significant contribution when added to the other. It can be seen from the p-values that *Alcohol*, although correlating substantially with the incidence of the antibody, does not make a significant contribution when the *Smoking* variable is also present in the equation.

Variables in the Equation

		B	S.E.	Wald	df	Sig.	Exp(B)
Step 1	Smoking	2.264	.513	19.490	1	.000	9.623
	Alcohol	-.078	.085	.846	1	.358	.925
	Constant	-1.394	.373	13.979	1	.000	.248

Output 21. The table of variables in the equation

The **Wald statistic** tests a regression coefficient (or the constant) for significance. As with OLS regression, the null hypothesis is that, in the population, the value of the parameter is zero. The Wald statistic is defined as follows:

$$Wald = \frac{b^2}{s_b^2} \quad \text{- - - (8)}$$

The Wald statistic

and is distributed approximately as chi-square on one degree of freedom.

The first column of entries in Output 21 contains the estimates of the regression parameters: the constant and the two regression coefficients. We see that $b_0 = -1.394$, $b_{Smoking} = 2.264$ and $b_{Alcohol} = -0.078$. Substituting these values in (7), the logistic regression equation is

$$\hat{p} = \frac{e^{logit}}{1 + e^{logit}} = \frac{e^{-1.394 + 2.264\,Smoking - 0.078\,Alchohol}}{1 + e^{-1.394 + 2.264\,Smoking - 0.078\,Alchohol}}$$

In Output 21, the entries in the rightmost column, under Exp(B), are the factors by which the raw odds in favour of the occurrence of the antibody are *multiplied* by increasing the independent variable by one unit. The term Exp(B) is e^B , the **exponential function** of B. It is the antilog of the regression coefficient. For example, In the first row of entries in Output 21, the value of B for Smoking is given as 2.264. This means that an increase in smoking level of one unit produces, on average, an increase of 2.264 units in the logit (i.e. the natural log of the odds) in favour of having the antibody. But an increase of 2.264 units in the logarithm corresponds to *multiplication* of the raw odds by $Exp(2.264) = e^{2.264} = 9.623$. In words, an increase of one unit in Smoking, multiplies the likelihood of having the antibody by ten.

It is clear from Output 21 that *Smoking* makes both a significant and a substantial contribution to the regression: $p < 0.01$; Exp(B) = 9.623. *Alcohol*, on the other hand, makes neither a significant (p = 0.358) nor a substantial (Exp(B) = 0.925) contribution. That suggests that, in our regression exercise, we might dispense with the services of the *Alcohol* variable altogether.

We have been describing the output resulting from **simultaneous** regression, that is, regression with both the IVs entered into the regression equation in a single step. Returning to the **Logistic Regression** dialog box, the drop-down menu for **Method** gives us several other possible approaches. If we select, say, **Backward LR** (i.e. Backward Likelihood Ratio), we shall find that the regression will eliminate the *Alcohol* variable from the regression and still achieve a hit rate of 85% of accurate classifications. (As a matter of fact, you will obtain the same result if you select any of the other methods.) We suggest that, as an analytic strategy, it is often helpful to begin with simultaneous regression, whose output is easier to understand, and then proceed to the sequential methods in order to clarify the results of the simultaneous regression.

14.3.4 Binary logistic regression with categorical independent variables

Neither binary nor multinomial regression has any problems with the inclusion of categorical independent variables: in fact, all the independent variables can be qualitative, as the following example will illustrate.

In Chapter 13, we described an experiment on gender and professed helpfulness, in which participants were asked by a male or female interviewer whether they would be prepared to help in a certain situation. The research hypothesis was the opposite-sex dyadic hypothesis, which holds that one is more inclined to help someone of the opposite sex than someone of one's own sex. The results are reproduced in Table 2.

Table 2. Three-way contingency table showing the results of the Gender and professed helpfulness experiment

Incidence of helping by male and female participants with male and female interviewers

Count

Sex of Interviewer			Would you help?		Total
			Yes	No	
Male	Sex of Participant	Male	4	21	25
		Female	16	9	25
	Total		20	30	50
Female	Sex of Participant	Male	11	14	25
		Female	11	14	25
	Total		22	28	50

Here the implicit dependent variable was *Help*, a categorical, dichotomous variable with two values: 1 = Yes; 2 = No. The independent variables were *Sex of Interviewer* and *Sex of Participant*. As we saw in Chapter 13, however, the loglinear analysis does not frame the problem in regression terms. Instead, the analysis models the expected cell frequencies in the multiway contingency table. Confirmation of the opposite-sex dyadic hypothesis would take the form of a three-way interaction among the factors: in participants of either sex, there would be a higher helping rate when the interviewer was of opposite sex to that of the participant.

We have here a data set that meets all the requirements for logistic regression : there is a categorical dependent variable *Help*; and there are two categorical IVs, *Sex of Participant* and *Sex of Interviewer*. In the present regression context, however, confirmation of the opposite-sex dyadic hypothesis would take the form of a *two-way* interaction between *Sex of Participant* and *Sex of Interviewer*.

The running of logistic regression with these data involves two new moves: 1. an interaction term must be introduced; 2. SPSS must be informed that the IVs are categorical, not continuous.

The data are available at www.psypress.com/spss-made-simple. The file is *Ch13 Helping(3WayInteractionOnly).sav*. With this file in the **Data Editor**, proceed as follows:

- Choose **Analyze➔Regression➔Binary Logistic …** to open the **Logistic Regression** dialog box (Figure 9).
- Transfer the name of the DV to the **Dependent** slot and the names of the two IVs to the **Covariates** panel.
- Add the interaction term by selecting both IVs. The button marked **>a*b>** will come live. Click to transfer the interaction term *Interviewer*Participant* to the Covariates panel.

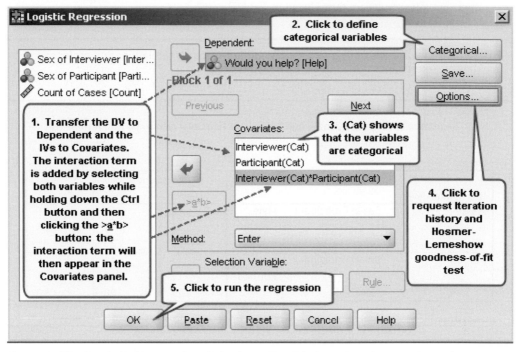

Figure 9. The **Logistic Regression** dialog box. The IVs (covariates) are registered as categorical by clicking the **Categorical** button and completing the **Define Categorical Variables** dialog box (see Figure 10)

- Click the **Categorical…** button to obtain the **Define Categorical Variables** dialog box (see Figure 10). Transfer the names *Participant* and *Interviewer* to the **Categorical Covariates:** box. The default type of **Contrast** is **Indicator**, which registers the presence or absence of the target category. Click **Continue** to return to the **Logistic Regression** dialog box, where you will now see the variable names marked with **(Cat).**

- Click the **Options** button and select **Iteration history** and the **Hosmer-Lemeshow goodness-of-fit test** from the **Options** dialog box. Click **Continue** to return to the **Logistic Regression** dialog box.
- Click **OK** to run the regression.

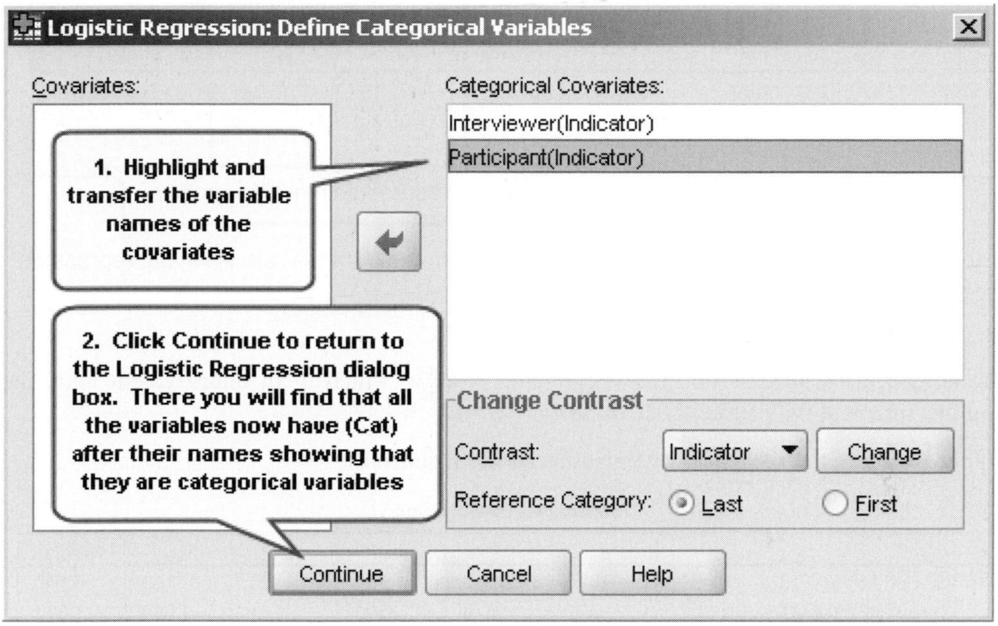

Logistic Regression: Define Categorical Variables

Covariates:

1. Highlight and transfer the variable names of the covariates

2. Click Continue to return to the Logistic Regression dialog box. There you will find that all the variables now have (Cat) after their names showing that they are categorical variables

Categorical Covariates:

Interviewer(Indicator)
Participant(Indicator)

Change Contrast

Co_ntrast: Indicator ▼   Change

Reference Category: ⦿ _Last   ○ _First

Continue   Cancel   Help

Figure 10. The completed dialog box for **Define Categorical Variables**

Output of binary logistic regression with categorical independent variables

As usual, following the preliminaries, the output is presented under the headings Step 0 (intercept-only prediction) and Step 1 (prediction from the regression model).

Output 22 shows the classification table at Step 0. The baseline success rate is 58%.

Classification Table[a,b]

			Predicted		
			Would you help?		
	Observed		Yes	No	Percentage Correct
Step 0	Would you help?	Yes	0	42	.0
		No	0	58	100.0
	Overall Percentage				58.0

a. Constant is included in the model.

b. The cut value is .500

Baseline, 'intercept-only' success rate

Output 22. The baseline classification success rate with 'intercept-only' prediction

Output 23 shows the classification success rate when the regression model is applied.

Classification Table^a

			Predicted		
			Would you help?		
Observed			Yes	No	Percentage Correct
Step 1	Would you help?	Yes	16	26	38.1
		No	9	49	84.5
		Overall Percentage			65.0

a. The cut value is .500   **Success rate when regression model is applied**

Output 23. Classification Table showing an increase in the success rate when the regression model is applied

The classification success rate from regression is 65%, which is an improvement upon the baseline, intercept-only success rate of 58%.

Output 24 shows the final table of **Variables in the Equation**.

Variables in the Equation

		B	S.E.	Wald	df	Sig.	Exp(B)
Step 1	Interviewer(1)	-.817	.580	1.985	1	.159	.442
	Participant(1)	.000	.570	.000	1	1.000	1.000
	Interviewer(1) by Participant(1)	2.234	.892	6.268	1	.012	9.333
	Constant	.241	.403	.358	1	.549	1.273

Output 24. Final table of Variables in the Equation

It can be seen from Output 24 that the only significant term in the regression is the **Interviewer × Participant** interaction. Notice that the value of Exp(B), the multiplier of the raw odds, is much greater than it is for the other terms in the regression equation. This result is the equivalent, in logistic regression, of the significant three-way interaction that we obtained when we used loglinear analysis to model the cell frequencies of the same contingency table. The outcome of the logistic regression is in complete agreement with that of the loglinear analysis of the same data.

14.4   MULTINOMIAL LOGISTIC REGRESSION

In Section 14.2, **discriminant analysis** was used to predict the university subject chosen by students on the basis of several independent variables. In Section 14.3, we introduced you to **logistic regression**, which carries fewer assumptions than does **discriminant analysis**. SPSS's **binary logistic regression** can only be used for predicting a dichotomous (two-category) dependent variable. If there are more than two categories, we must use **multinomial logistic regression**. The purpose of the following exercise is to see whether **multinomial**

logistic regression can predict choice of Subject at University with the same level of accuracy as can **discriminant analysis**. In multinomial logistic regression, the independent variables can be either **factors** or **covariates**. Factors are categorical variables (e.g. *Sex of Student*) and covariates are continuous variables (as are all the remaining variables in our example).

14.4.1 Running multinomial logistic regression

To run the multinomial logistic regression procedure with the choice of subject data:

- Choose **Analyze➜Regression➜Multinomial Logistic...** to open the **Multinomial Logistic Regression** dialog box (Figure 11).
- Transfer *StudySubject* to the **Dependent** box, *Sex of Student* to the **Factor(s)** box and the remaining quantitative independent variables into the **Covariate(s)** box.
- Click **Model...** at the side of the **Multinomial Logistic Regression** dialog box to open the **Model** dialog box (Figure 12). Follow the steps shown in Figure 12. Click **Continue** to return to the main dialog box.

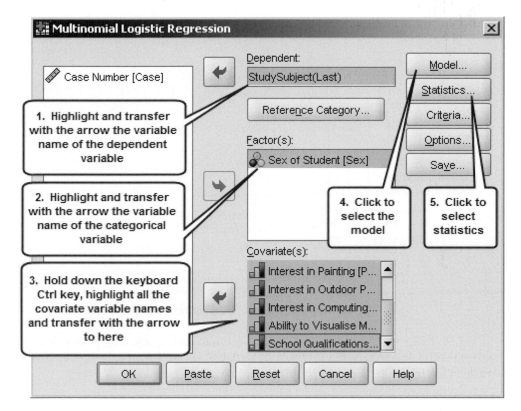

Figure 11. The **Multinomial Logistic Regression** dialog box

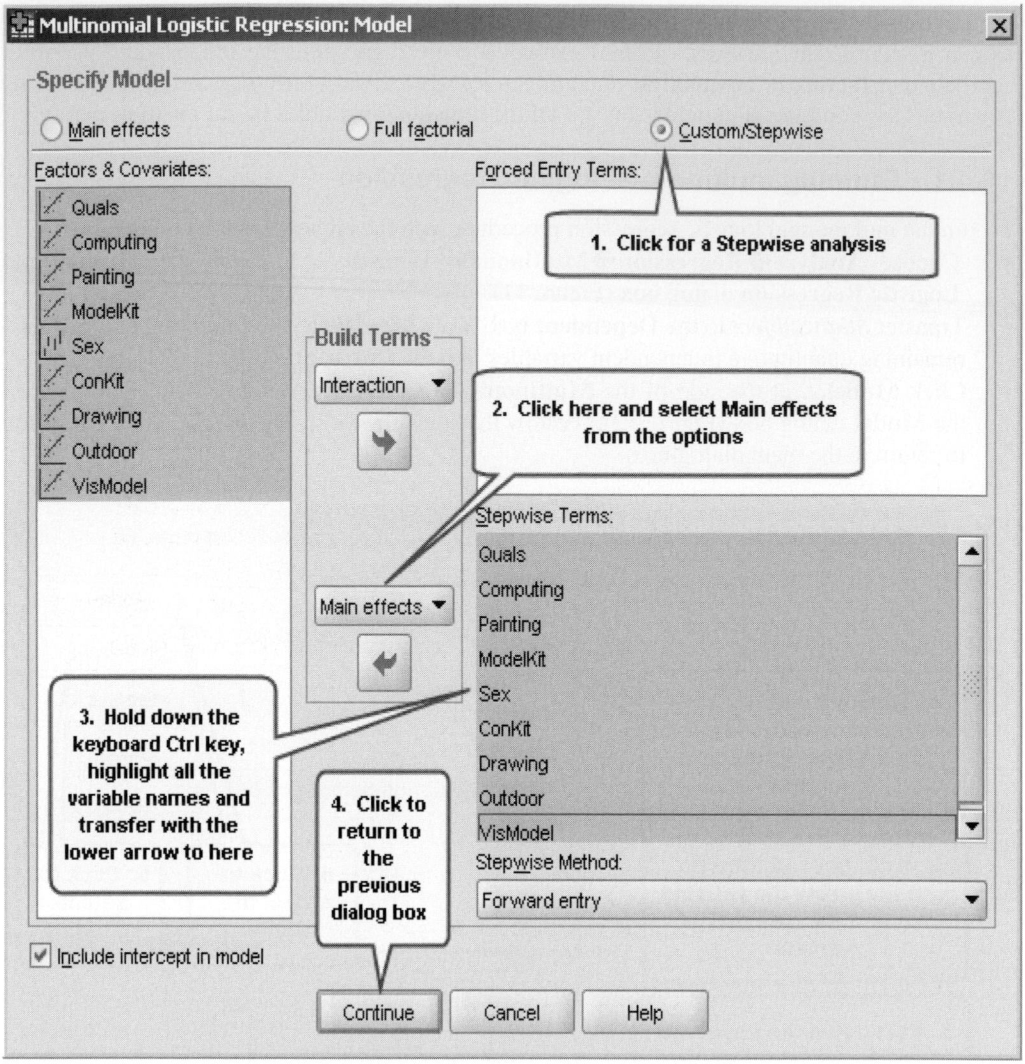

Figure 12. The **Model** dialog box with **Forward entry** selected

- Click **Statistics** to see a dialog box labelled **Multinomial Logistic Regression: Statistics** (Figure 13). Check the boxes as shown in the figure.
- Click **Continue** to return to the **Multinomial Logistic Regression** dialog box.
- Click **OK** to run the multinomial logistic regression.

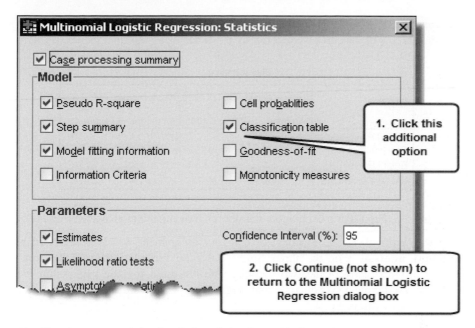

Figure 13. The upper part of the **Statistics** dialog box with **Classification table** selected in addition to those already highlighted when the dialog box is opened

Output of multinomial logistic regression

The output consists of several tables. First there is a **Case Summary Table** (not shown here) listing the levels of the dependent variable (*Study Subject*) and the numbers of each, and also the levels of the factor *Sex* and the numbers of males and females.

Next there is a **Step Summary** table (Output 25) showing which covariates were entered and in which order. Note that the variables *Drawing* and *Model Kit* were never entered, the same two that were omitted from the **discriminant analysis** model.

Step Summary

Model	Action	Effect(s)	-2 Log Likelihood	Chi-Square	df	Sig.
0	Entered	Intercept	235.548			
1	Entered	Sex	208.820	26.727	2	.000
2	Entered	Painting	191.144	17.677	2	.000
3	Entered	Quals	171.760	19.384	2	.000
4	Entered	VisModel	159.182	12.578	2	.002
5	Entered	Computing	146.761	12.422	2	.002
6	Entered	Outdoor	140.055	6.705	2	.035
7	Entered	ConKit	133.221	6.834	2	.033

Stepwise Method: Forward Entry

Output 25. The **Step Summary** table showing which IVs were entered in the model

Finally after several other tables not shown here, there is the **Classification** table (Output 26) showing that 72.2% of the cases were correctly predicted using the final model.

Classification

Observed	Predicted			
	Architect	Psychologist	Engineer	Percent Correct
Architect	20	2	8	66.7%
Psychologist	2	28	7	75.7%
Engineer	5	6	30	73.2%
Overall Percentage	25.0%	33.3%	41.7%	72.2%

Output 26. Predictions of category membership by multinomial logistic regression

Recall that a level of 72.2% accuracy of category assignment was also achieved by using **discriminant analysis**. For the three Study Subjects, however, the numbers of correct predictions differ slightly in the two outputs. **Multinomial logistic regression** was more successful at predicting Psychologists and slightly less successful at predicting Architects. Engineers differ by just one case.

Although the general level of accuracy of assignment is the same with the two procedures, you will find that, if you use the **Save** button to obtain the assignments by both techniques in **Data View**, there is some disagreement between the category assignments by the two procedures in individual cases. We should bear in mind that this data set failed to meet one of the criteria for discriminant analysis, namely, homogeneity of the variance-covariance matrices. Since that property is not a requirement for multinomial logistic regression, perhaps we should place more reliance upon the multinomial logistic regression.

14.5   A FINAL WORD

In this chapter, we have described some regression methods that have been specially designed for data sets in which the DV is a set of categories, rather than a continuous variable. We began with discriminant analysis, which assumes multivariate normality and homogeneity of variance-covariance matrices across the categories of the DV. We then described binary logistic regression, which assumes neither multivariate normality nor homogeneity of variance-covariance matrices. Finally, we touched upon multinomial logistic regression which is applicable when the DV consists of more than two categories. We found that, with the same data set on choices of subjects at university, discriminant analysis and multnomial logistic regression gave very similar results.

The use of logistic regression encounters many of the problems of interpretation that arise with multiple regression. In particular, when independent variables are correlated, there is always doubt about which IV makes the greatest contribution to the variance of the dependent variable. The design of any multiple regression project and the interpretation of the output require the guidance of a *causal* model: a *statistical* model is insufficient.

Recommended reading

Howell (2007) and Todman & Dugard (2006) have lively and helpful chapters on logistic regression. Tabachnick & Fidell (2007) go into the technicalities in most detail. We suggest you might begin with David Howell's chapter, which sets the scene very nicely.

Howell, D. (2007). *Statistical methods for psychology (6th ed.)*. Belmont, CA: Thomson/Wadsworth.

Tabachnick, B. G., & Fidell, L. S. (2007). *Using multivariate statistics (5th ed.)* Boston: Allyn & Bacon (Pearson International Edition).

Todman, J., & Dugard, P. (2006). *Approaching multivariate analysis: An introduction for psychology*. London: Psychology Press.

Exercise

Exercise 23 *Predicting category membership: Discriminant analysis and binary logistic regression* is available in www.psypress.com/spss-made-simple and click on Exercises.

CHAPTER 15

Latent variables: exploratory factor analysis & canonical correlation

15.1   Introduction

15.2   A factor analysis of data on six variables

15.3   Using SPSS syntax to run a factor analysis

15.4   Canonical correlation

15.5   A final word

15.1   INTRODUCTION

Suppose that some schoolchildren are tested on several variables, perhaps an assortment of school subjects such as foreign languages, music, mathematics and related activities such as mapwork. The correlations of performance on each test with every other test in the battery can be arranged in a rectangular array known as a **correlation matrix**, or **R-matrix** (Table 1).

Table 1. A correlation matrix (as output by SPSS) showing, in the off-diagonal elements of each row or column, the correlations of one test with each of the other tests. In each cell along the principal diagonal from top left to bottom right is the correlation of a test with itself.

Correlation Matrix

		French	German	Latin	Music	Maths	Mapwork
Correlation	French	1.000	.836	.742	.032	.083	.312
	German	.836	1.000	.715	-.081	.008	.118
	Latin	.742	.715	1.000	.022	.222	.131
	Music	.032	-.081	.022	1.000	.713	.783
	Maths	.083	.008	.222	.713	1.000	.735
	Mapwork	.312	.118	.131	.783	.735	1.000

In its basic form, a correlation matrix is **square**, that is, there are as many rows as there are columns. The diagonal of cells running from top left to bottom right is known as the **principal diagonal** of the matrix. The values in the off-diagonal cells are the same above and below the principal diagonal: e.g., the correlation of *French* with *German* is the same as that of *German* with *French*. Each row (or column) of the R-matrix contains all the correlations involving one particular test in the battery. Since the variables are labelled in the same order in the rows and columns of the R-matrix, each of the cells along the principal diagonal contains the correlation of one of the variables with itself (i.e. 1). The R-matrix can be the starting point for a variety of multivariate statistical procedures, but in this chapter we shall consider just one technique: **factor analysis.**

Factor analysis is one of several statistical techniques which were designed to enable the researcher to classify data on several variables with reference to a much smaller number of supposed underlying dimensions. Is it possible, for example, to account for the patterns shown by the correlations in Table 1 in terms of fewer dimensions (or **factors**) than there were tests in the battery?

Since the entries below the principal diagonal of the R-matrix in Table 1 are identical with those above it, we shall concentrate on the upper half of the table only. In Figure 1, we see that there are two groups of subjects showing high correlations with one another: 1. German, French and Latin; 2. Music, Maths and Mapwork.

Correlation Matrix

		French	German	Latin	Music	Maths	Mapwork
Correlation	French	1.000	.836	.742	.032	.083	.312
	German	.836	1.000	.715	-.081	.008	.118
	Latin	.742	.715	1.000	.022	.222	.131
	Music	.032	-.081	.022	1.000	.713	.783
	Maths	.083	.008	.222	.713	1.000	.735
	Mapwork	.312	.118	.131	.783	.735	1.000

Group 1: French, German and Latin show high intercorrelations, but each shows low correlations with the subjects in Group 2

Group 2: Maths, Mapwork and Music show high intercorrelations, but each shows low correlations with the subjects in Group 1

Figure 1. Exploring the R-matrix

While the members of each group correlate strongly with the other group members, they show much lower correlations with the members of the other group. For example, German (Group 1) correlates 0.008 with Maths and 0.118 with Mapwork. And Maths (Group 2) correlates 0.083 with French and 0.222 with Latin.

It is tempting to surmise that the clustering among the tests in the R-matrix arises because, although the tests in each group are measuring the same underlying ability (or very similar abilities), the groups are tapping different abilities or ability sets. The tests in Group 1 might be tapping general linguistic ability; whereas those in Group 2 might be tapping nonverbal, visuo-spatial abilities.

It would appear, therefore, that the 15 correlations among the six tests in the R-matrix can be accounted for in terms of just two underlying abilities or ability clusters. If the traditional British theories of the psychology of intelligence are correct, there should be fewer (indeed, far fewer) dimensions than there are tests in the battery. The purpose of factor analysis is to identify and to quantify the dimensions supposedly underlying performance on a variety of tasks.

The **factors** produced by factor analysis are mathematical entities, which can be thought of as classificatory axes for plotting the tests as points on a graph. The greater the value of a test's co-ordinate, or **loading**, on a factor axis, the more important that factor is in accounting for the variance of scores on that test. Theoretically, a loading can vary throughout the range from -1 to $+1$, inclusive. In practice, however, errors in measurement restrict this theoretical range considerably.

The term **factor** has also an equivalent algebraic interpretation as a linear function of the observed scores that people achieve on the tests in a battery. If a battery contains six tests (as in the present example), and each person tested were also to be assigned a seventh score consisting of the sum of the six test scores, that seventh (summative) score would be a **factor score**, and it would make sense to speak of correlations between the factor scores and the real test scores. Factor scores, in fact, can be used as representative variables for input into subsequent analyses.

We have seen that the loading of a test on a factor is, geometrically speaking, the co-ordinate of the test point on the factor axis. But that axis also represents a 'factor' in the second, algebraic sense, and the loading is the correlation between the original test scores and those on the factor. Ultimately, however, a factor (a mathematical entity) is assumed to represent an underlying or latent psychological or other variable, in terms of which the correlations in the R-matix are accounted for or explained.

In **exploratory factor analysis**, the aim is to determine the number and nature of the factors necessary to account adequately for the correlations in the R-matrix. It is hoped that the correlations among the observed variables can be accounted for in terms of comparatively few factors. In **confirmatory factor analysis**, on the other hand, the user hypothesises that there should be a predetermined number of factors, on which the tests in the battery should show specified patterns of loadings. Such a model can then be put to the test by gathering data and testing it against other models of the same data, positing different number of factors and other specifications. Recent years have seen dramatic developments in what is known as **structural equation modelling (SEM)**, of which confirmatory factor analysis is one aspect. (See, for example, Tabachnick & Fidell, 2007, Chapter 14.)

At present, SPSS itself offers exploratory factor analysis only. Under the aegis of SPSS, however, is also AMOS, a structural equation modelling package. Structural equation modelling, particularly confirmatory factor analysis, is an excellent follow-up to the exploratory procedures we shall describe in this chapter.

15.1.1 Stages in an exploratory factor analysis

An exploratory factor analysis usually takes place in three stages:
1. A **matrix of correlation coefficients** is generated for all possible pairings of the variables (i.e. the tests).

2. From the correlation matrix, **factors** are **extracted.** The most common method of extraction is called **principal factors** or **principal components**.

3. The factors (axes) are **rotated** to facilitate the interpretation of the results of the factor analysis.

Before you proceed with a factor analysis, it is advisable to inspect the **R-matrix** first. Since the purpose of factor analysis is to account for associations among the tests, the exercise is pointless if no substantial associations exist. By convention, all variables should show at least one correlation of the order of 0.3 before it is worth proceeding with a full factor analysis. Should any variables show no substantial correlation with any of the others, they should be removed from the R-matrix. It is also advisable to check that the correlation matrix does not possess the highly undesirable property of **multicollinearity**, that is, the presence of very high correlations arising from the inclusion of very similar tests in the battery. Should the R-matrix show multicollinearity, some of the variables must be omitted from the analysis; otherwise the factor analysis will not run.

15.1.2 The extraction of factors

The factors (or axes) in a factor analysis are **extracted** one at a time, leaving after each extraction a residual data set of scores that do not correlate with the extracted factor. The process is repeated with the residual data set until it is possible, from the loadings of the tests on the factors so far extracted, to generate good approximations to the correlations in the original **R-matrix**. Factor analysis tells us how many factors (or axes) are necessary to achieve an adequate reconstruction of R.

15.1.3 The rationale of rotation

We can think of the tests in the battery and the origin of the classificatory axes or factors as stationary points and rotate the axes around the origin to produce a new pattern of loadings known as a **rotated factor matrix**. We can do this because, although rotation will cause the values of all the loadings to change, the new set of loadings on the axes, *whatever the new position of the axes*, can still be used to produce exactly the same estimates of the correlations in the R-matrix. In this sense, the position of the axes is arbitrary: the factor matrix (or **F-matrix**) only tells us *how many* axes are necessary to classify the data adequately: it does not thereby establish that the initial position of the axes is the best position. There is, in fact, no unique position for the axes that is 'best' in every possible respect.

The factors or axes are rotated in order to make the results of the factor analysis easier to interpret. In general, it is easier to endow mathematical factors with substantive meaning if the tests in the R-matrix are loaded substantially on comparatively few factors, than if they have small loadings on many factors. The position of the axes (or rotated factor matrix) that best achieves this economy is said to have the property of **simple structure**. That term, however, is open to different interpretations and there exists no method of achieving all the desirable properties implied. Modern computing packages such as SPSS offer a selection of rotation methods, each based upon a different (but reasonable) interpretation of simple structure.

15.1.4 Some issues in factor analysis

So far, we have considered the use of factor analysis to ascertain the minimum number of classificatory variables (or axes) we need to account for the shared variance among a battery of tests. While the researcher will almost certainly have expectations about how many factors are likely to emerge (indeed, these expectations will determine the selection of the tests in the battery), the process of factor extraction proceeds automatically until a criterion for termination is reached. In several fields, such as human abilities and intelligence, 'factor invariance' has been found: that is, those factors accounting for the greatest amounts of variance, such as the general intelligence (g) factor and the major group factors, have emerged again and again in analyses with different data sets.

There are, nevertheless, several problems and issues with factor analysis. Some aspects of factor structure, such as the prevalence of a general factor as opposed to group factors, depend very much upon the composition of the test battery. Even when the same battery of tests has been used in different projects, the precise number of factors extracted has been found to vary from study to study. Moreover, the pattern shown by the loadings in the final rotated factor matrix depends upon the method of rotation used. The most commonly used method of rotation is **varimax**, which maintains independence among the mathematical factors. Geometrically, this means that during rotation, the axes remain **orthogonal** (i.e. they are kept at right angles). Orthogonal axes represent uncorrelated factors. There are other methods of rotation, however, which allow the axes to be non-orthogonal or **oblique**, so that they represent correlated factors. There has been much argument about which method of rotation is best, and the preferred method tends to reflect the theoretical views of the user. In view of the multiplicity of considerations that can influence the outcome of a factor analysis, it has often been argued that traditional factor analytic methods are ill-suited to the testing of specific hypotheses and are appropriate only in the early, exploratory stages of research. Confirmatory factor analysis, however, in contrast with exploratory factor analysis, allows the formulation of hypotheses that are sufficiently specific to be put to the empirical test.

15.1.5 Some key technical terms

An understanding of the SPSS output requires at least an intuitive grasp of the meaning of several technical terms.

- The **loading** of a test on a factor, as we have seen, is the correlation between the test and the factor.
- The **communality** of a test is the total proportion of its variance that is accounted for by the extracted factors. The communality is the **squared multiple correlation R^2** between the test and the factors emerging from the factor analysis. If the factors are orthogonal or independent (as they will be in the example we shall consider), the communality is given by the sum of the squares of the loadings of the test on the extracted factors. The communality of a test is a measure of its reliability.
- The **eigenvalue** (or **latent root**) of a factor is a measure of the variance of all the tests accounted for by the factor. If the total variance of each test is unity, the eigenvalue of the first factor extracted has a theoretical maximum equal to the number of tests in the battery. (In practice, of course, this cannot be achieved with variables having an element of measurement error.) The eigenvalue can be converted to a measure of the proportion of the total variance by dividing its value by the total number of tests in the battery. The first factor extracted has the largest eigenvalue, the second the next largest, and so on. The process of extraction continues until the factors extracted account for negligible proportions of the total variance.
- If the eigenvalues of successive factors are plotted against the ordinal numbers of the factors, the curve eventually flattens out and its appearance thereafter has been likened to

the rubble or scree on a mountainside. The eigenvalue plot is therefore known as a **scree plot** (see Figure 7). There is general agreement that the factorial litter begins when the eigenvalues fall below one.

- The process of **rotation** changes the eigenvalues of the factors that have been extracted, so that the common factor variance accounted for by the extraction is more evenly distributed among the rotated factors. The communalities, on the other hand, are unchanged by rotation, because their values depend only upon the number of factors and the correlations among the tests.

15.2   A FACTOR ANALYSIS OF DATA ON SIX VARIABLES

Table 2 contains the raw data from which the correlations in Table 1 were calculated.

Table 2. Marks of 10 children in six examinations						
Case	**French**	**German**	**Latin**	**Music**	**Maths**	**Mapwork**
1	56	66	53	47	50	48
2	46	48	43	53	69	55
3	56	51	43	40	49	45
4	29	42	39	53	56	48
5	71	67	84	66	67	60
6	56	47	58	59	67	74
7	62	69	48	59	58	66
8	46	42	38	46	38	42
9	66	73	85	34	49	42
10	36	42	48	53	59	48

From these raw data, we can run a factor analysis by choosing from menus and completing dialogs. Were we, however, to start from a correlation matrix such as that shown in Table 1, rather than the raw data, we should have to use SPSS syntax. We shall describe how that is done in a later section.

15.2.1   Entering the data for a factor analysis

Enter the data using the procedures described in Section 2.3. In **Variable View**, name the six variables for the factor analysis. Include an extra variable for the case number. Ensure that there are no decimals by changing the value in the **Decimals** to 0. Click the **Data View** tab at the foot of **Variable View** and enter the data in **Data View**.

15.2.2   Running a factor analysis on SPSS

To run the factor analysis, proceed as follows:
- Choose **Analyze**➔**Data Reduction**➔**Factor…** (Figure 2) to open the **Factor Analysis** dialog box (Figure 3).
- Transfer all the variable names except *Case Number* to the **Variables** box.

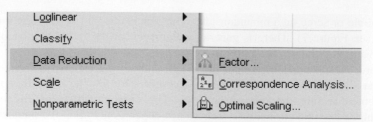

Figure 2. Finding the **Factor** dialog box in the **Analyze** menu

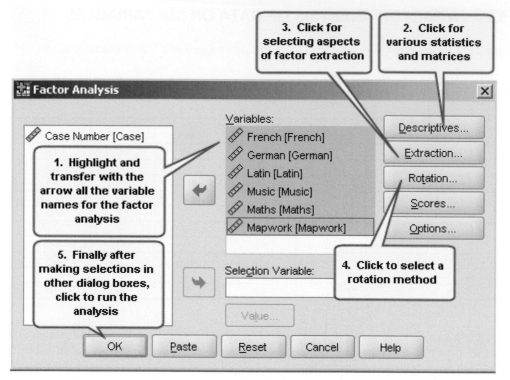

Figure 3. The **Factor Analysis** dialog box

Before running the analysis, you should select some options to control the analysis and add some useful extra items to the output.

- Click **Descriptives…** to open the **Descriptives** dialog box (Figure 4). Click the following check boxes: **Univariate descriptives**, to tabulate descriptive statistics; **Initial solution**, to display the original communalities, eigenvalues and the percentage of variance explained; **Coefficients**, to tabulate the R-matrix; and **Reproduced**, to obtain an approximation of the R-matrix from the loadings of the factors extracted by the analysis. The **Reproduced** option will also obtain communalities and the residual differences between the observed and reproduced correlations.
- Click **Continue** to return to the **Factor Analysis** dialog box.

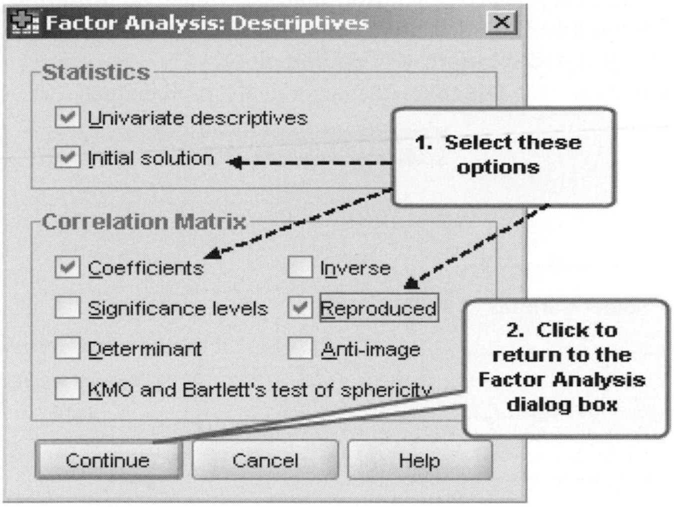

Figure 4. The **Descriptives** dialog box with **Univariate descriptives**, **Initial solution**, **Coefficients** and **Reproduced** selected

- Click **Extraction...** to open the **Extraction** dialog box (Figure 5). Click the **Scree plot** check box. The scree plot is a useful display showing the relative importance of the factors extracted.

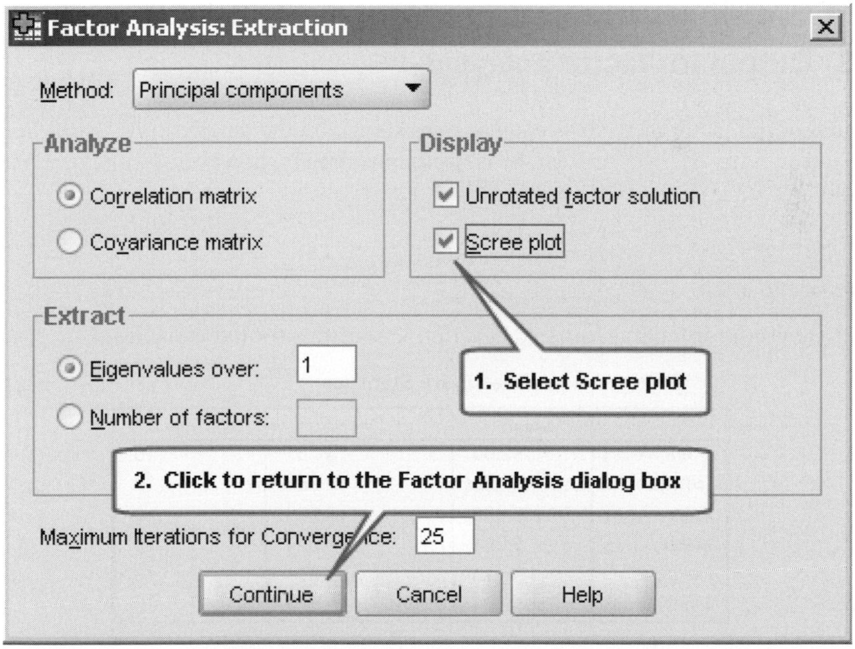

Figure 5. The **Extraction** dialog box with **Scree plot** selected

- Click **Continue** to return to the **Factor Analysis** dialog box.

- To obtain the rotated F-matrix, click **Rotation…** to obtain the **Rotation** dialog box (Figure 6). In the **Method** box, click the **Varimax** radio button. In the Display panel, check the boxes labelled **Rotated solution** and **Loading plots**.
- Click **Continue** and then **OK** to run the factor analysis procedure.

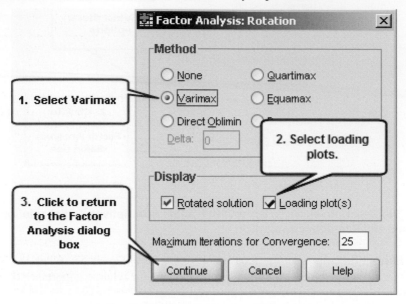

Figure 6. The **Rotation** dialog box with **Varimax** selected

15.2.3 Output for factor analysis

The output of the factor analysis is extensive, as shown by the length of the list of items in the **SPSS Viewer**. Any desired item can be viewed immediately, however, by clicking on its name in the list.

Descriptive statistics

Output 1 shows the specially requested descriptive statistics for the variables.

Descriptive Statistics

	Mean	Std. Deviation	Analysis N
French	52.00	13.167	10
German	55.00	12.561	10
Latin	54.00	17.233	10
Music	51.04	9.524	10
Maths	56.18	9.854	10
Mapwork	52.74	10.854	10

Output 1. Descriptive statistics for the variables

The correlation matrix (R-matrix)

The correlation matrix (edited by adding additional shading) is shown in Output 2. This is exactly the same R-matrix that we discussed in Section 15.1.

		French	German	Latin	Music	Maths	Mapwork
Correlation	French	1.000	.836	.742	.032	.083	.312
	German	.836	1.000	.715	-.081	.008	.118
	Latin	.742	.715	1.000	.022	.222	.131
	Music	.032	-.081	.022	1.000	.713	.783
	Maths	.083	.008	.222	.713	1.000	.735
	Mapwork	.312	.118	.131	.783	.735	1.000

Output 2. The correlation matrix (**R-matrix**) with additional shading

(The shaded groups in Output 2 look larger than the ringed groups in Figure 1; but note the duplication of correlations with the inclusion of elements on both sides of the principal diagonal.)

We saw in Section 15.1 that we can account for the pattern of correlations in terms of two independent dimensions of ability. The important question now is whether this view is confirmed by the results of the formal factor analysis. Are two factors sufficient to account for the correlations among the tests? Are the results of the factor analysis consistent with the simple interpretation we have arrived at through inspection of the R-matrix?

Communalities

Output 3 is a table of communalities assigned to the variables by the factor analysis. The communality of a test is, as we have seen, the proportion of the variance of the test that has been accounted for by the factors extracted. For example, we see that 89% of the variance of the scores on *French* is accounted for by the common factors extracted by the analysis.

Communalities

	Initial	Extraction
French	1.000	.888
German	1.000	.870
Latin	1.000	.783
Music	1.000	.852
Maths	1.000	.801
Mapwork	1.000	.862

Extraction Method: Principal Component Analysis.

Output 3. Table of variable communalities

The next table (Output 4) displays information about the factors (SPSS calls them 'components') that have been extracted. Technically, a 'component' is not identical with a 'factor'. In principal components analysis (as opposed to factor analysis), the analysis produces as many components as there are tests in the battery. You can see that this is so in Output 4, where 6 components are listed. A principal components analysis accounts for *all* the variance of the test scores, including error. In contradistinction, a factor represents only that portion of the variance that is common factor variance, that is, variance that is shared among the tests in the battery and accounted for by the factor analytic model. The common factor variance is the *reliable* part of the total variance.

A principal components analysis begins with the R-matrix and proceeds until the entries in R can be produced exactly. This includes the unit entries along the principal diagonal, each of which represents 100% of the variance of the test in the row or column of R. Exact reproduction of the unit entries will require as many components as there are tests. In a true factor analysis, an initial estimate of the communality of each test is made and that value is substituted for the initial unit value in the cell of the principal diagonal. The amended R-matrix (known as the **reduced R-matrix**) is sometimes denoted by R*. A factor analysis attempts to reproduce this reduced R-matrix, rather than the original R-matrix with 1's along the diagonal. We can see the results of a true factor analysis in the last six columns on the right of Output 4, each of which contains only two entries.

Earlier, we saw that the **eigenvalue** of a factor is a measure of the total test variance that is accounted for by that factor alone. The eigenvalue is an aggregate of the proportions of the variances of the individual tests that are accounted for by the factor and is the sum of the squares of the loadings of the tests on the factor. Since each loading is the correlation between a test and the factor, the square of the loading gives the proportion of test variance that is accounted for by regression of the test scores upon the factor scores. The squared loading is the **coefficient of determination**. Since the maximum value of each component of the eigenvalue is 1, the theoretical total value of an eigenvalue is the number of tests in the battery. If, therefore, we divide the eigenvalue by the number of tests and multiply by 100, we shall have the percentage of the total test variance that is accounted for by each factor.

In Output 4, the first block of three columns, labelled **Initial Eigenvalues**, contains the eigenvalues and the contributions they make to the total variance. The eigenvalues determine which factors (components) remain in the analysis: following Kaiser's criterion, factors with an eigenvalue of less than 1 (i.e. factors 3-6) are excluded. From the eigenvalues, the proportions of the total test variance accounted for by the factors are readily obtained. For example, the eigenvalue of the first factor is 2.81. Since the total test variance that could possibly be accounted for by a factor is 6 (the total number of tests), the proportion of the total test variance accounted for by the first factor is $2.81 \div 6 = 46.82\%$, the figure given in the **% of Variance** column. In this analysis, the two factors that meet the Kaiser criterion account for over 84% of the variance (see the column labelled **Cumulative %**).

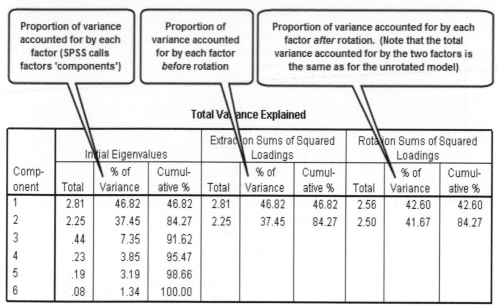

Output 4. Edited table of statistics relating to the two components extracted

The second block of three columns (**Extraction Sums of Squared Loadings**) repeats the output of the first block only for the two factors that have met Kaiser's criterion.

The third block (**Rotation Sums of Squared Loadings**) tabulates the output for the rotated factor solution. Notice that the proportions of variance explained by the two factors are more similar in the rotated solution than they are in the unrotated solution, in which the first factor accounts for a much greater percentage of the variance. Notice also that the accumulated proportion of variance from the two components/factors is the same for the unrotated and rotated solutions.

Scree plot

Figure 7 shows the **scree plot**, which was specially requested in the **Factor Analysis: Extraction** dialog box. The eigenvalues are plotted against the ordinal numbers of the factors extracted. The amount of variance accounted for (the eigenvalue) by successive components initially plunges sharply as successive factors (components) are extracted.

The point of interest is where the curve begins to flatten out. It can be seen that the 'scree' begins to appear between the second and third factors. Notice also that Component 3 has an eigenvalue of less than 1, so only the first two components have been retained.

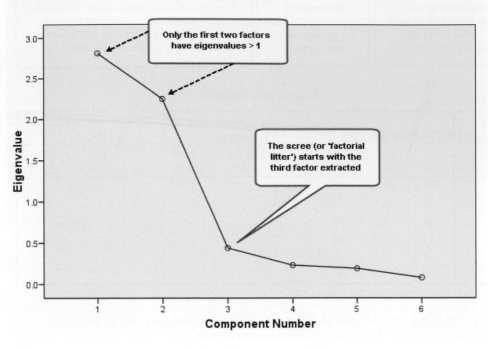

Figure 7. The scree plot

The component matrix (unrotated factor matrix)

Output 5 shows the component (factor) matrix containing the loadings of the six tests on the two factors extracted.

Component Matrix[a]

	Component	
	1	2
French	.764	-.551
German	.661	-.659
Latin	.714	-.523
Music	.566	.729
Maths	.647	.618
Mapwork	.735	.568

Extraction Method: Principal Component Analysis.

a. 2 components extracted.

Output 5. The component matrix (correlations between the variables and the unrotated components)

for the reproduced correlation between *French* and *German* in Output 7. The diagonal values labelled b are the communalities listed in Output 3. Each communality is the sum of the squares of the loadings of a test on the two factors extracted: so the sum of the squares of the entries in the first row of Output 5 is 0.888, the value given as the communality for French in Output 7. Notice that all the communalities are very large – at least 78%.

The **residuals** are the differences between the actual and reproduced correlations. For example, the original correlation between *French* and *German* was 0.836 (Output 2) and the reproduced correlation is 0.868, so the difference is –0.032, which is the residual shown in the lower half of Output 7. Footnote *a* states the number and proportion of residuals (i.e. the differences) that are greater than 0.05. Over 8 residuals (53%) are greater than 0.05; but none is greater than 0.10.

Matrix algebraic interpretation of factor analysis

(If you are unfamiliar with matrix algebra, we suggest that you skip this section. Should you wish to make progress with factor analysis, however, a working knowledge of matrix algebra is absolutely essential. Tabachnick & Fidell, 2007, have a helpful appendix introducing the principles).

$$\underbrace{\begin{pmatrix} l_{11} & l_{12} \\ l_{21} & l_{22} \\ l_{31} & l_{32} \\ l_{41} & l_{42} \\ l_{51} & l_{52} \\ l_{61} & l_{62} \end{pmatrix}}_{\mathbf{F}} \underbrace{\begin{pmatrix} l_{11} & l_{21} & l_{31} & l_{41} & l_{51} & l_{61} \\ l_{12} & l_{22} & l_{32} & l_{42} & l_{52} & l_{62} \end{pmatrix}}_{\mathbf{F'}}$$

$$= \begin{pmatrix}
h_1^2 & l_{11}l_{21}+l_{12}l_{22} & l_{11}l_{31}+l_{12}l_{32} & l_{11}l_{41}+l_{12}l_{42} & l_{11}l_{51}+l_{12}l_{52} & l_{11}l_{61}+l_{12}l_{62} \\
l_{11}l_{21}+l_{12}l_{22} & h_2^2 & l_{21}l_{31}+l_{22}l_{32} & l_{21}l_{41}+l_{22}l_{42} & l_{21}l_{51}+l_{22}l_{52} & l_{21}l_{61}+l_{22}l_{62} \\
l_{11}l_{31}+l_{12}l_{32} & l_{21}l_{31}+l_{22}l_{32} & h_3^2 & l_{31}l_{41}+l_{32}l_{42} & l_{31}l_{51}+l_{32}l_{52} & l_{31}l_{61}+l_{32}l_{62} \\
l_{11}l_{41}+l_{12}l_{42} & l_{21}l_{41}+l_{22}l_{42} & l_{31}l_{41}+l_{32}l_{42} & h_4^2 & l_{41}l_{51}+l_{42}l_{52} & l_{41}l_{61}+l_{42}l_{62} \\
l_{11}l_{51}+l_{12}l_{52} & l_{21}l_{51}+l_{22}l_{52} & l_{31}l_{51}+l_{32}l_{52} & l_{41}l_{51}+l_{42}l_{52} & h_5^2 & l_{51}l_{61}+l_{52}l_{62} \\
l_{11}l_{61}+l_{12}l_{62} & l_{21}l_{61}+l_{22}l_{62} & l_{31}l_{61}+l_{32}l_{62} & l_{41}l_{61}+l_{42}l_{62} & l_{51}l_{61}+l_{52}l_{62} & h_6^2
\end{pmatrix}$$

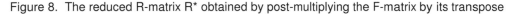

$$\mathbf{FF'} = \mathbf{R}^{*}$$

Figure 8. The reduced R-matrix R* obtained by post-multiplying the F-matrix by its transpose

In the previous section, we noted that good approximations to the original values of the correlations in the R-matrix could be obtained by taking the sum of the products of the loadings of any two tests on the two factors extracted by the factor analysis. The reader familiar with matrix algebra will have noticed that the sum of the products of the loadings on the two factors is an element in the product of the factor matrix and its transpose as in Figure 8, where the entries *l* are loadings. The subscripts *i* and *j* are, respectively, the number of the test and the number of the factor: for example, l_{51} is the loading of test 5 on Factor 1. The entries h^2 in the cells of the principal diagonal are the **communalities**, that is, the sums of the squares of the loadings of a test on the two factors: e.g. $h_1^2 = l_{11}^2 + l_{12}^2$; $h_5^2 = l_{51}^2 + l_{52}^2$. The product matrix R^* is known as the **reduced R-matrix** because the cells of its principal diagonal contain the communalities, rather than the unit values in the corresponding cells in the original R-matrix.

We have arrived at the **fundamental equation of factor analysis**, namely,

$$R^* = FF' \quad \text{- - - (1)}$$

Fundamental equation of factor analysis

where the terms in (1) are matrices, as opposed to scalar variables (i.e. those with point values).

The process of factor extraction continues until the addition of further factors would result in little improvement in the prediction of the actual values of the correlations in R, the original correlation matrix. Were the process to continue until there were as many factors as there were tests in the battery, however, it would be found that the product matrix would be identical with the R-matrix: the reproduced correlations would be identical with those in the R-matrix and the values in the cells of the principal diagonal would all be unity. The fact that we can achieve good approximations of the original correlations with just two factors is, from an explanatory point of view, a considerable economy.

The matrix multiplication shown in Figure 8 is easily run with SPSS syntax (Figure 9).

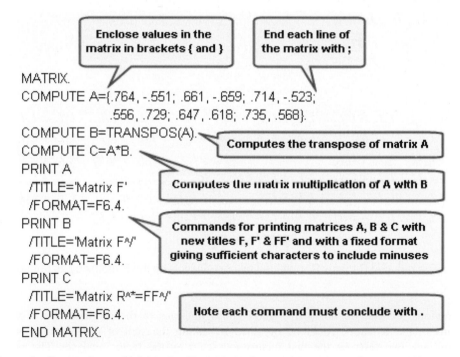

Figure 9. Syntax for multiplying the F matrix by its transpose to produce an estimate of the R-matrix with communalities in the cells of the principal diagonal

Output 8 (an edited version) shows the values in the reduced R-matrix R^* (see Output 5), the transpose, and the product of the factor matrix and its transpose (see Output 7).

Matrix F ⟶ **The factor matrix F**

```
.7640 -.5510
.6610 -.6590
.7140 -.5230
.5560  .7290
.6470  .6180
.7350  .5680
```

Matrix F^/ ⟶ **The matrix F', the transpose of F**

```
.7640  .6610  .7140  .5560  .6470  .7350
-.5510 -.6590 -.5230  .7290  .6180  .5680
```

Matrix R^*=FF^/ ⟶ **The matrix product R* = F F'**

```
.8873  .8681  .8337  .0231  .1538  .2486
.8681  .8712  .8166 -.1129  .0204  .1115
.8337  .8166  .7833  .0157  .1387  .2277
.0231 -.1129  .0157  .8406  .8103  .8227
.1538  .0204  .1387  .8103  .8005  .8266
.2486  .1115  .2277  .8227  .8266  .8628
```

Output 8. The reduced R-matrix obtained from multiplying the factor matrix by its transpose. The marked entries in the product matrix are the communalities of the tests

The rotated factor (component) matrix

Output 9 shows the rotated factor (component) matrix, which should be compared with the unrotated matrix in Output 5.

Rotated Component Matrix [a]

	Component	
	1	2
French	.936	.105
German	.932	-.045
Latin	.880	.092
Music	-.070	.920
Maths	.065	.892
Mapwork	.163	.914

Extraction Method: Principal Component Analysis.
Rotation Method: Varimax with Kaiser Normalization.

a. Rotation converged in 3 iterations.

Output 9. The rotated component matrix

Output 10 is a graph of the rotated F-matrix, in which each of the six tests is plotted as a point in space with its new loadings on the rotated axes as coordinates.

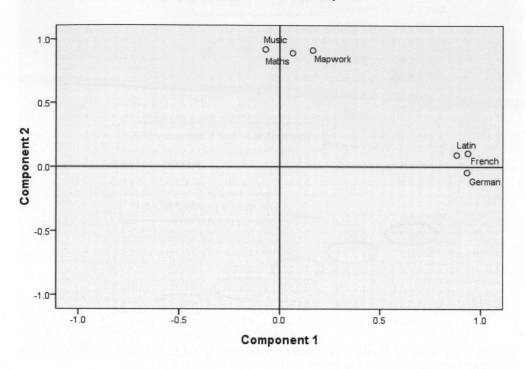

Output 10. Graph of the rotated R-matrix.

The purpose of rotation is not to change the number of components extracted, but to try to arrive at a new position for the axes (components) that is easier to interpret in substantive terms. You may wish to confirm, using the syntax in Figure 9 but substituting the values in the rotated F-matrix for those in the unrotated F-matrix, that you will obtain exactly the same reduced R-matrix $R^\ast$.

It can be seen from the graph in Output 10 that the rotated component/factor matrix is much easier to interpret than the unrotated matrix in Output 5. The three language tests now have high loadings on one factor only (Component 1); whereas *Mapwork*, *Mathematics* and *Music* have high loadings on the other factor only (Component 2). Since the rotation was orthogonal, that is, the axes were kept at right angles, the two factors are uncorrelated. This is quite consistent with what we concluded from our inspection of the original R-matrix, namely, that the correlations among the six tests in our battery could be accounted for in terms of two independent psychological dimensions of ability and that each group of tests measured a separate dimension of ability.

15.3   USING SPSS SYNTAX TO RUN A FACTOR ANALYSIS

Initially, the Windows graphical interface with its dialog boxes is the easiest way of running a factor analysis with SPSS. When the user is more familiar with the procedure, however, the syntax approach has much to recommend it. If you have several factor analyses to run, for example, it is much quicker to edit the syntax file and click the **Run** button, rather than complete the dialogs with every new data set.

15.3.1 Running a factor analysis with SPSS syntax

With the scores from Table 1 in **Data View**, access the **Factor Analysis** dialog box in the usual way. Make the selections as before, remembering to select the buttons at the bottom of the dialog box to specify the rotation, order a scree test, request a correlation matrix and so on. Now click **Paste**. When this is done, a window with the title **Syntax1 – SPSS Syntax Editor** (or the name of the syntax file followed by **SPSS Syntax Editor**) will appear on the screen. This is the **syntax window**, which will contain the commands written in SPSS syntax that have just been specified by your choices from the dialog boxes (see Figure 10).

Now select the whole of the written FACTOR command by emboldening the entire contents of the syntax window. Click **Run** in the toolbar above the syntax window and select **All** to re-run the entire factor analysis. Inspect the contents of the output window to confirm that the output is the same as before.

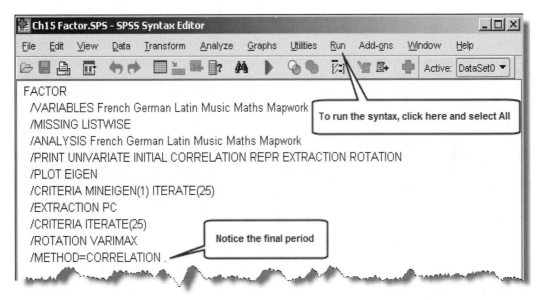

Figure 10. The syntax window and the **FACTOR** command

It is easy to see that with another data set, consisting of scores on a different battery of tests, it would be easy to edit the **FACTOR** command by changing the variable names and other specifications to match the active data set in **Data View**. Inevitably, the experienced user of SPSS will have built up a library of written commands, because it is quicker to carry out the analysis by editing the display in the **SPSS Syntax Editor** than to go through all the dialog and subdialog boxes again.

15.3.2   Using a correlation matrix as input for factor analysis

The Windows graphical interface with its dialog boxes is a comparatively recent development. SPSS (like several other major statistical packages) was originally designed to be run with syntax exclusively. The translation of all the SPSS procedures to dialog boxes is as yet incomplete: there are some procedures that cannot yet be accessed through the graphical interface. We have seen, for example, that in order to test for simple effects following the ANOVA, the user must run a syntax command: simple effects are not an option in the dialogs. Another hiatus in the procedures offered by the SPSS graphical interface is the running of a factor analysis with the R-matrix, rather than the raw data, as the starting point.

Running a factor analysis from a correlation matrix

Suppose that you already have an **R-matrix** and wish to start at that point, rather than going back to the raw data. The procedure has two stages, each of which requires a separate syntax command:

    1.   Entry of the correlation matrix into **Data View**.
    2.   The running of the factor analysis syntax.

Preparation of the correlation matrix
- Choose **File➔New➔Syntax** to open the **SPSS Syntax Editor** window.

The syntax must be in the correct format, but help with the syntax of the MATRIX DATA command can be obtained by entering the command keywords **MATRIX DATA** in the **Syntax Editor** and clicking 🔲 in the toolbar to open a window showing the structure of the syntax. Figure 11 shows the correct syntax for the commands needed for the entry of the R-matrix shown in Output 2. Note that it is immaterial whether upper or lower case text is used.

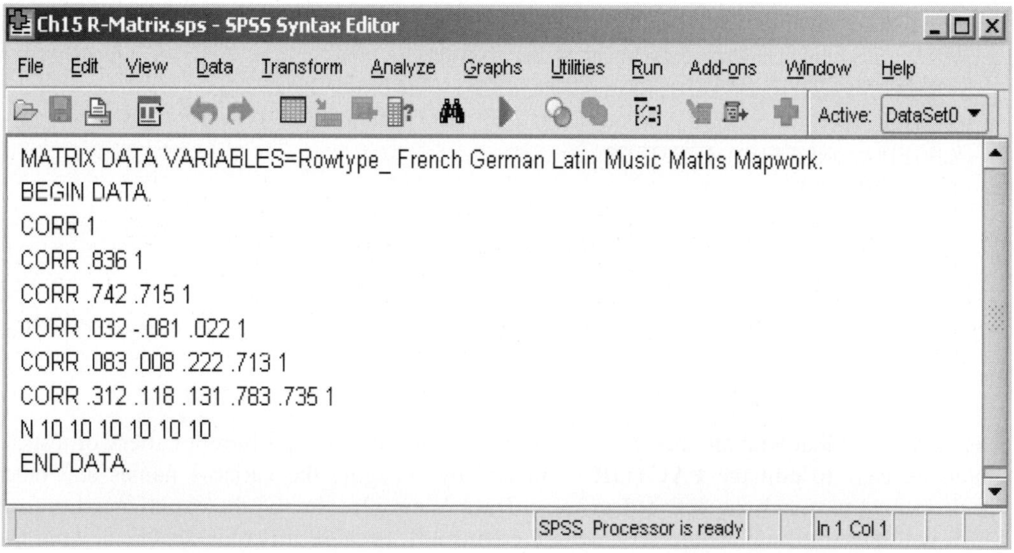

Figure 11. The commands for entering the **R-matrix** shown in Output 2

The first command is **MATRIX DATA** followed by **VARIABLES=** and a list of variable names. (The equals sign must come immediately after the word VARIABLES without a space in between. There must not be a space between the equals sign and Rowtype_either.) This command warns SPSS to prepare to receive data in the form of a matrix whose dimensions are specified by the number of variables in the list. Like all commands, MATRIX DATA must end with a full stop. Note the compulsory variable name **Rowtype_** , which is a special string variable used to identify the type of data for each record (row). By 'type of data', we mean the contents of the row, which might be correlations (CORR) or numbers of observations (N).

Next come the data commands. First there is **BEGIN DATA**, then the data themselves and finally the **END DATA** command. *Note the compulsory full stops after BEGIN DATA and END DATA*: each of these is a command in its own right.

The first six rows of the data begin with the word **CORR** (one of the strings making up the Rowtype variable), which tells SPSS that the data in those rows are correlation coefficients. The final (7th) row begins with **N** (another of the strings making up the Rowtype variable), which is a count of the number of data points in each column. The terms **CORR** and **N**, then, are instances of the generic term **Rowtype_** which appeared in the matrix data command.

By default, SPSS syntax expects a **lower triangular matrix**, which is a square matrix with all entries above the principal diagonal omitted. If an upper triangular or a square matrix were to be input instead, an additional **/FORMAT** subcommand would be required. The value of **N** is not needed for a basic factor analysis, but it is required for tests of significance and for assessing the sampling adequacy of the data. The correlation matrix and value of **N** are then entered (preceded in each row with **CORR** or **N**, as appropriate) between the usual **BEGIN DATA** and **END DATA** commands.

To execute the MATRIX DATA command, proceed as follows:
- Click **Run** in the toolbar above the syntax window and select **All**.
- The matrix will appear in **Data View** (Figure 12), not in the **SPSS Viewer**.
- If there are any errors in the syntax, however, they will be flagged in the **SPSS Viewer**.

ROWTYPE	VARNAME_	French	German	Latin	Music	Maths	Mapwork
N		10.000	10.000	10.000	10.000	10.000	10.000
CORR	French	1.000	.836	.742	.032	.083	.312
CORR	German	.836	1.000	.715	-.081	.008	.118
CORR	Latin	.742	.715	1.000	.022	.222	.131
CORR	Music	.032	-.081	.022	1.000	.713	.783
CORR	Maths	.083	.008	.222	.713	1.000	.735
CORR	Mapwork	.312	.118	.131	.783	.735	1.000

Figure 12. The data set after running the **MATRIX DATA** command

Syntax of the FACTOR command

• Return to the syntax window and type the **FACTOR** command below the previous syntax, as shown in Figure 13.

```
┌─────────────────────────────────────────────────────────────────────────┐
│ 🔲 Ch15 Factor from matrix.sps - SPSS Syntax Editor          _ □ ×        │
├─────────────────────────────────────────────────────────────────────────┤
│  File  Edit  View  Data  Transform  Analyze  Graphs  Utilities  Run  Add-ons  Window  Help │
├─────────────────────────────────────────────────────────────────────────┤
│  🗁 🔲 🔳  🖳  ↶ ↷  🔲 📇 📑 📄  🔍  ▶  🔵 🔴  🔢  🗑 📤  ➕   Active: Unnamed ▼ │
├─────────────────────────────────────────────────────────────────────────┤
│ FACTOR                                                                  ▲ │
│   /MATRIX=IN (CORR=*)                                                     │
│   /PRINT INITIAL EXTRACTION ROTATION CORRELATION REPRO                    │
│   /PLOT EIGEN                                                             │
│   /ROTATION VARIMAX.                                                      │
│                                                                         ▼ │
├─────────────────────────────────────────────────────────────────────────┤
│                                   SPSS Processor is ready    │ In 1 Col 1 │ │
└─────────────────────────────────────────────────────────────────────────┘
```

Figure 13. The **FACTOR** command for running a factor analysis from a correlation matrix in **Data View** with various options as chosen in Section 15.2.2

• Notice that the identification of the matrix in the **/MATRIX =IN** subcommand is given as **(CORR=*)**. This informs SPSS that the input will be a correlation matrix (and not, say, a factor matrix), and that it is in the current data file (represented by *), which can be seen in the **Data View** window. The **/PRINT** options are those selected in the **Descriptives** dialog box and the **/PLOT** option is that selected in the **Extraction** dialog box. It is not necessary to enter **/ROTATION VARIMAX**, because this is the default rotation method. *Again note the full stop at the end of the command: it is absolutely essential.*

• Run the **FACTOR** command by clicking **Run** in the toolbar at the top of the syntax window and selecting **All**. The output for the factor analysis will be identical with that previously described in Section 15.2.3.

15.3.3   Progressing with SPSS syntax

As we said earlier, we believe that the best way of learning SPSS syntax is by pasting the minimal basic commands into the **syntax window** from the appropriate dialog boxes in the usual way, and observing how the syntax becomes more elaborate when extra options are chosen from the subdialog boxes.

The more experienced user will find it helpful, when writing a command in SPSS syntax, to access the **Syntax Help** window by writing the command keyword in the syntax window and clicking [🔢] in the toolbar to open a window showing the structure of the syntax, as mentioned in the previous Section. Optional subcommands are shown in square brackets. Relevant parts can be typed in the syntax window. Alternatively, the whole block of syntax can be copied over for editing from the **Syntax Help** window to the **Syntax** window by using **Copy** and **Paste** in the usual way. (These moves are in the **Options** menu of the **Syntax Help** window.) We do not recommend that you follow this procedure until you have already acquired some experience with SPSS syntax.

15.4   CANONICAL CORRELATION

In multiple regression, the researcher is trying to predict the values of one **target**, **criterion** or **dependent** variable (on the left of the equation) from several **regressors** or **independent variables** (on the right of the equation).   Such research is invariably motivated by a causal model: the assumption is that one or more of the variables on the right of the equation have a causal influence upon (or, at least, are associated in some way with) the target variable on the left.

Now suppose that instead of having just one criterion variable, we were to have a whole set of criterion variables, all in the same domain. It is well known, for example, that among the many possible complications of diabetes is visual impairment. A researcher decides to investigate the effects of certain medical and lifestyle variables upon vision in diabetic patients. Four measures of visual functioning (the DVs in this study) are investigated:
1.   Colour discrimination.
2.   Detection of the velocity of a moving dot.
3.   The ability to see patterns in pseudo-isochromatic plates such as the Ishihara Test.
4.   Visual acuity.

The independent variables (IVs) are a set of four medical and lifestyle variables known to be risk factors for visual problems in diabetes:
1.   Age.
2.   Duration of the condition.
3.   Control of blood-sugar level.
4.   Blood pressure.

We could, of course, run several multiple regressions, one for each of the four visual variables. In doing so, however, we should run into the same problems as the researcher who runs an experiment in which there are several measures or dependent variables, among which there may be strong correlations and then proceeds to run a univariate analysis on each variable. Techniques such as discriminant function analysis and MANOVA were designed to overcome this difficulty. In those techniques, linear functions of the dependent variables (discriminant functions) are constructed from the observed variables and used as representatives of the set as a whole.

The purpose of the present exercise is to construct what is known as a **root pair** of representative or **canonical variates** (the term **variate** means 'random variable'), one from the visual set of DVs, the other from the medical/lifestyle set, in such a way that the two variables correlate to the greatest possible extent. This maximised correlation between the two constructed variables is known as a **canonical correlation**. After the construction of this root pair, the process can be continued to produce a second root pair with their own canonical correlation, a third pair with another canonical correlation and so on.

Once we have constructed several pairs of canonical variates, we shall want to determine the visual (DV) and medical (IV) variables that make the greatest contribution to each member of every pair. The purpose of the exercise, of course, is to identify any causal links there may be between the variables in the two domains and the key variables involved in those relationships. It should be noted that, although the representative canonical variates are not principal components or factors of the variables in their respective domains, they can, nevertheless, be thought of as 'latent' (that is, 'hidden' or 'underlying') substantive variables in terms of which the variance shared among the measured variables can be explained. The correlations between the observed DVs and IVs with their respective canonical variates are known as **loadings**.

Before embarking upon any multivariate analysis, including canonical correlation, the researcher must ensure that the data meet certain requirements. High correlations among the variables in either domain, for instance, can create **multicollinearity** in the key matrices involved in the calculations, and the canonical correlation procedure may not run as a result. If so, the presence of outliers must be detected and the appropriate action taken. SPSS offers collinearity diagnostics and the identification of outliers in its **Regression** procedure – see Chapter 4 of Tabachnick & Fidell (2007) for details.

15.4.1   Running canonical correlation on SPSS

Suppose twenty diabetic patients have been assessed with four tests of visual function (as described in the previous section) and their data on the medical and lifestyle variables have also been recorded (see Table 3). The visual function variables are the DVs; the medical variables are the IVs. (Only the first 5 cases are shown in Table 3: the complete data set is available at www.psypress.com/spss-made-simple.)

Case	ColDiscr	VelDet	Plates	Acuity	Age	Control	Duration	BloodPre
\multicolumn{9}{c}{Table 3. Visual function and diabetic variables}								
1	360	50	7	15	24	40	3	120
2	344	54	10	15	26	39	8	122
3	220	45	15	16	27	37	15	120
4	310	59	30	16	32	12	22	125
5	280	60	29	16	33	4	9	128
6	300	53	10	33	34	36		120

SPSS has two ways of carrying out a canonical correlation analysis, both of which require the use of **SPSS Syntax**. One method uses a macro called **CANCORR**; the other uses an option called **DISCRIM**, which is only available within the syntax for **MANOVA**. Since we have already been using the MANOVA command for other purposes, we shall use the MANOVA/DISCRIM procedure.

- Prepare the data file in the **Data Editor** in the usual way.
- Choose **File→New→Syntax** to open the **Syntax Editor**.
- Type in the commands shown in Figure 14, listing the visual DVs on the left of WITH and the medical IVs on the right. Note especially the forward slash preceding each subcommand and the final full stop signalling the end of the command. The **COR** option for **DISCRIM** selects the correlations between the scores on the measured variables and the canonical variates in each root pair. The **EIGEN** and **DIMENR** options in the **PRINT** command produce canonical correlations, eigenvalues and a dimension reduction analysis table showing how many of the pairs of canonical variates are significant.
- Click **Run** in the toolbar above and select **All** to run the analysis.

```
┌──────────────────────────────────────────────────────────────────────────────┐
│ ▓ *Syntax1 - SPSS Syntax Editor                                    _ □ ×       │
├──────────────────────────────────────────────────────────────────────────────┤
│  File   Edit   View   Data   Transform   Analyze   Graphs   Utilities   Run   Add-ons   Window   Help │
├──────────────────────────────────────────────────────────────────────────────┤
│  ▭ 🖫 🖨 ▭  ↰ ↱  ▭ ▭ ▭ ▭  ▰▰  ▶  ◐ ◑  ▭  ▭ ▭  ➕  Active: │Unnamed ▼│         │
├──────────────────────────────────────────────────────────────────────────────┤
│  MANOVA ColDiscr VelDet Plates Acuity WITH Age Control Duration BloodPress      │
│  /DISCRIM = COR                                                                │
│  /PRINT = SIGNIF(EIGEN DIMENR).                                                │
│                                                                                │
│                                                                                │
├──────────────────────────────────────────────────────────────────────────────┤
│                                   SPSS Processor is ready    │ In 3 Col 31 │    │
└──────────────────────────────────────────────────────────────────────────────┘
```

Figure 14. The completed syntax for canonical correlation

15.4.2 Output for canonical correlation

The output begins with a summary (not reproduced) of the number of cases processed.

As a measure of the importance of a root pair of canonical variates, SPSS uses a variance measure it terms the **eigenvalue** λ, which is given by

$$\lambda = \frac{r^2}{1-r^2} \quad \text{--- (2)}$$

The eigenvalue as a function of the canonical correlation

where r is the canonical correlation. (Other authors, such as Tabachnick & Fidell, 2007 (p.73), define the eigenvalue as the square of the canonical correlation, which is technically correct.)

```
Eigenvalues and Canonical Correlations

Root No.      Eigenvalue        Pct.     Cum. Pct.    Canon Cor.     Sq. Cor
     1           4.213        60.134       60.134        .899          .808
     2           2.278        32.515       92.649        .834          .695
     3            .471         6.721       99.370        .566          .320
     4            .044          .630      100.000        .206          .042
```

Output 11. Eigenvalues, percentages of variance and canonical correlations

The first relevant table in the output, **Eigenvalues and Canonical Correlations** (Output 11) lists the eigenvalues and canonical correlations between the first four root pairs of canonical variates. The canonical correlations, the first two of which are 0.899 and 0.834, diminish with successive root pairs. You can see that the value of the eigenvalue for the first root pair is $.899^2/(1 -.899^2) = 4.213$; for the second root pair, the eigenvalue is $.834^2/(1 - .834^2) = 2.28$. As usual in multivariate statistics, the first composite variable constructed accounts for the greatest proportion of the variance we are trying to account for and the second and subsequent 'extractions' account for progressively less of the variance. The table shows clearly that only the first two canonical pairs have eigenvalues > 1 and between them they account for 93% of the total variance shared by all the root pairs (**Cum. Pct**. Column). We can therefore ignore the remaining two root pairs.

The next table, the **Dimension Reduction Analysis** (Output 12), confirms that only the first two pairs of canonical variates are significant.

```
Dimension Reduction Analysis


Roots          Wilks L.          F Hypoth. DF    Error DF   Sig. of F
1 TO 4          .03811     4.46139      16.00      37.30       .000
2 TO 4          .19865     3.32972       9.00      31.79       .006
3 TO 4          .65115     1.67473       4.00      28.00       .104
4 TO 4          .95776      .66162       1.00      15.00       .429
```

Output 12. The dimension reduction analysis table showing how many pairs of canonical variates are significant: only two are significant

Note that the values of **Wilks' lambda** *increase* as we move down the table because the *smaller* the value this statistic, the more important the source and the most important sources are extracted first.

The next table **Correlations between DEPENDENT and canonical variables** (Output 13) shows the correlations or **loadings** of the DVs (i.e. the visual set) on the first two canonical variates, and the amount of variance accounted for by each root pair. Loadings of less than 0.3 are ignored. The loadings clearly show that, on the DV side, *ColDiscr* and *Plates* predominate in the first canonical variate and all the variables (*ColDiscr*, *VelDet*, *Plates* and *Acuity*) contribute to the second canonical variate. *VelDet* with a loading of 0.298 does not contribute significantly to the first canonical variate.

```
Correlations between DEPENDENT and canonical variables
          Function No.


Variable               1              2

ColDiscr             .686           .681
VelDet               .298           .555
Plates               .775          -.503
Acuity               .477          -.585


Variance in dependent variables explained by canonical variables

CAN. VAR.   Pct Var DE Cum Pct DE Pct Var CO Cum Pct CO

     1        34.712      34.712     28.053     28.053
     2        34.176      68.887     23.749     51.802
```

Output 13. Statistics of the dependent variables

In any regression technique, a focal point of interest is the extent to which the IVs account for variance in the DVs. In canonical correlation, the **redundancy index** is the proportion of variance in either the DV or the IV set that is accounted for by the opposite canonical variate.

The value of the redundancy index is given by the square of the canonical correlation multiplied by the proportion of the variance that a canonical variate extracts from the set of variables that it represents. Since this proportion is based upon the canonical correlation, it reflects the influence of the *opposite* set of variables.

In some regression procedures, such as logistic regression and canonical correlation, SPSS refers to the IVs as **covariates**. At the foot of the table in Output 13, notice the columns headed **Pct Var DE** and **Pct Var CO**. Here Pct Var DE stands for 'Percentage Variance of the DEpendent variables' and Pct Var CO stands for 'Percentage Variance of the COvariates'. The value 34.712 is the proportion of the variance of the DVs accounted for by the first representative canonical variate. The value 28.053 in the Pct Var CO column is the redundancy index calculated by squaring the canonical correlation ($.899^2$) and multiplying it by the proportion of the variance of the DVs ($.34712$). For the second root pair of canonical covariates, the variance of the DVs accounted for and the redundancy are 34.176% and 23.749%, respectively. These results show considerable overlap of explained variance between the canonical variates. Canonical variates cannot be equated with the factors in factor analysis.

Output 14 shows the same statistics for the independent variables or covariates. Here the loadings show that blood pressure *BloodPre*, *Control* and *Age* predominate in the first canonical variate and all the variables (*Age*, *Control*, *Duration* and *BloodPre*), contribute to the second canonical variate. *Duration* does not contribute to the first canonical variate. In Output 13, the columns headed **Pct Var DE** and **Pct Var CO** contained the variance of the DVs accounted for by the representative canonical variate and the redundancy, respectively. In Output 14, it is the other way round: the Pct Var DE column contains the redundancies and the Pct Var CO column contains the variance of the IVs accounted for by the representative canonical variate. Thus for the first canonical variate, the variance of the IVs accounted for is 25.967% and the redundancy is 20.985% (i.e. $0.899^2 \times 0.25967$). The corresponding values for the second canonical variate are 43.926% and 30.525%. Once again, there is considerable overlap of explained variance between the canonical variates.

```
Correlations between COVARIATES and canonical variables
             CAN. VAR.

Covariate              1            2

Age                 -.485        -.851
Control              .577        -.599
Duration             .104        -.545
BloodPre            -.678        -.615


Variance in covariates explained by canonical variables

CAN. VAR.   Pct Var DE Cum Pct DE Pct Var CO Cum Pct CO

      1        20.985     20.985    25.967     25.967
      2        30.525     51.510    43.926     69.893
```

Output 14. Statistics of the independent variables (covariates)

The remainder of the output can be ignored. The data are summarised in Table 4.

Table 4. Canonical correlation and correlations between variables relating to visual variables and diabetic variables

	First Canonical Variate	Second Canonical Variate
Canonical Correlation	.90	.83
VISUAL VARIABLES		
Colour Discrimination	.69	-.68
Velocity Detection	.30	-.56
Plates	.78	.50
Visual Acuity	.48	.59
Percentage of Variance	35%	34%
Redundancy	28%	24%
DIABETIC VARIABLES		
Age	-.49	.85
Control of Blood-Sugar Level	.58	.60
Duration of Diabetes	.10	.55
Systolic Blood Pressure	-.68	.62
Percentage of Variance	26%	44%
Redundancy	21%	31%

A pair of flow charts (Figure 15) displays these conclusions graphically.

The conclusion from this research is that there is a very high correlation between the canonical variates for both root pairs (canonical correlation coefficients = 0.90 and 0.83). The first canonical pair shows that colour discrimination, plates and to a lesser extent acuity are indexed by blood pressure, age and diabetic control, which may well be causal influences. The second canonical pair shows that colour discrimination, velocity detection, acuity and plates are indexed by age, blood pressure, control and duration.

In several respects, canonical correlation resembles factor analysis. Like factor analysis, canonical correlation aims to extract latent variables and the extent to which the observed variables correlate with, or load upon, these latent variables is taken to be the extent to which the latent variables account for the observed variables. Similarly, different data sets will result in varying numbers of root pairs, just as different R-matrices yield varying numbers of common factors.

There are also, however, important differences between canonical correlation and factor analysis. The canonical variates are not principal components or factors of the variables they represent. Unlike orthogonal factors, canonical variates are not independent and account for overlapping proportions of the variance. Unlike factor analysis, moreover, there is no equivalent of rotation to facilitate the interpretation of the loadings of the variables on the canonical variates.

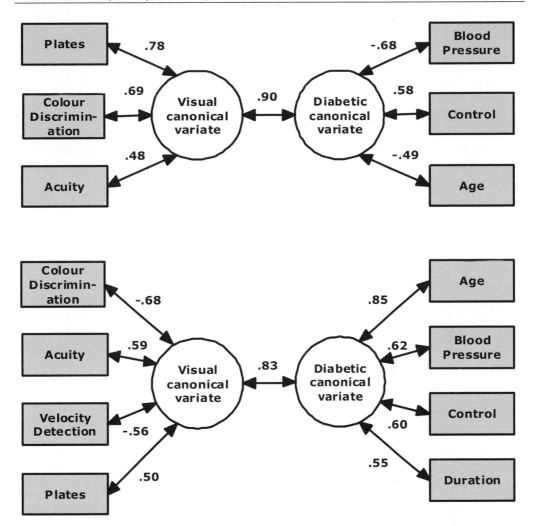

Figure 15. The first and second pair of canonical variates showing variable loadings for each canonical variate and the canonical correlations for the two pairs of canonical variates

15.5   A FINAL WORD

In this chapter, we have described some methods for classifying variables with respect to relatively few reference variables, which are taken to represent underlying substantive (medical, social or psychological) characteristics. Factor analysis and canonical correlation are just two of several ways of identifying such underlying or 'latent' variables: there are other methods, such as multidimensional scaling, which we do not consider in this book.

We have concentrated on factor analysis because that is the most widely used of the classificatory methods. SPSS provides exploratory factor analysis, the purpose of which is to determine the minimum number of latent variables or factors that can account adequately for or reproduce the correlation matrix. These factors can serve as reference axes, rather like longitude and latitude, with reference to which patterns among the correlations in the R-matrix can be displayed graphically in a most effective way.

Confirmatory factor analysis makes it possible to test different factor analytic models to determine which interpretation of the data is the most convincing. Confirmatory factor analysis is implemented by a set of methods known as structural equation modelling, for which several packages are available, including AMOS and LISREL.

In this book, we have concentrated on running SPSS by completing dialogs provided by a graphical interface. In this and other chapters, however, we have had recourse to SPSS syntax to run procedures that are not yet available as options in the graphical interface. To run a factor analysis with an R-matrix as the input, for example, there is no option but to use syntax. On the other hand, even where graphical dialogs are available, syntax provides a powerful, flexible and very fast way of running similar analyses on many different data sets without having to complete a series of dialog boxes each time. We believe that syntax is an absolute 'must' for those wishing to make further progress with SPSS.

Syntax offers much more than an alternative way of running statistical tests: it can also be an invaluable aid to the study of the basis principles of statistics and the properties of the most important distributions. A simple command or two can enable the user to obtain large samples from specified populations, such as F, t and other test statistics and examine their characteristics. Monte Carlo experiments are quite feasible with syntax. Einspruch (2004), in his book *Next steps with SPSS*, describes how to use looping functions and other devices to carry out operations that would be difficult or impossible to achieve without a knowledge of SPSS control language. We strongly recommend his book to anyone who wants to make progress with SPSS syntax.

Recommended reading

If you are unfamiliar with factor analysis, we suggest you read the lucid texts by Kim and Mueller (1978a, 1978b), before proceeding to more difficult books, such as Tabachnick and Fidell (2007). (Tabachnick and Fidell also have a chapter on canonical correlation.)

A strong feature of the books by Kim and Mueller is that they present factor analysis as an aspect of the analysis of covariance structures, which makes these texts an admirable preparation for books such as *Structural Equation Modeling with AMOS* (Byrne, 2001), which lucidly describes confirmatory factor analysis.

Byrne, B. M. (2001). *Structural equation modeling with AMOS: Basic concepts, applications and programming*. Mahwah, NJ: Lawrence Erlbaum Associates.

Einspruch, E. L. (2004). *Next steps with SPSS*. London: Sage.

Kim, J., & Mueller, C. W. (1978a). *Factor analysis: Statistical methods and practical issues*. Newbury Park, CA: Sage.

Kim, J., & Mueller, C. W. (1978b). *Introduction to factor analysis: What it is and how to do it*. Newbury Park, CA: Sage.

Tabachnick, B. G., & Fidell, L. S. (2007). *Using multivariate statistics (5th ed.)*. Boston: Allyn & Bacon (Pearson International Edition).

Exercise

Exercise 24 *Factor analysis* is available in www.psypress.com/spss-made-simple and click on Exercises.

APPENDIX

Logarithms

Indices

An **index** is a numerical superscript indicating repeated multiplication of a number by itself. For example, $x^2 = x \times x$; $x^4 = x \times x \times x \times x$. Such a product of repeated self-multiplication is known as a **power** of the number x.

The laws of indices

There are three laws of indices:

1. When powers of x are multiplied, their indices are summed: $x^k \times x^l = x^{k+l}$

2. When powers of x are divided, the index of the divisor is subtracted from that of the numerator: $x^k \div x^l = x^{k-l}$

3. When powers of x are themselves powered, the indices are multiplied: $\left(x^k\right)^l = x^{kl}$

Fractional, negative and zero indices

a. Roots are denoted by indices in the form of fractions: $\sqrt[3]{x} = x^{\frac{1}{3}}$; $\sqrt[5]{x} = x^{\frac{1}{5}}$. In general, $\sqrt[p]{x^q} = x^{\frac{q}{p}}$

b. If the index is negative, the product is the reciprocal of the product with the positive index value: $x^{-k} = \dfrac{1}{x^k}$

c. If the index is zero, the value of the power is 1: $x^0 = 1$

The conventions in a, b and c are best understood as ensuring that such expressions conform to the basic laws: e.g. when $x^{\frac{1}{3}}$ is raised to the power of three, we have $\left[x^{\frac{1}{3}}\right]^3 = x$, in conformance with law 3. Property c is necessary if $x^p \div x^p = 1$, as required by law 2.

Logarithms

In a logarithmic system, numbers are expressed as powers of a constant known as the **base** of the system. The **logarithm** of a number is the power to which the base must be raised to equal the number itself:

596

$$number = base^{logarithm}$$

The two most common bases are (in the system of **common logarithms**) 10 and (in the system of **natural logarithms**) the mathematical constant e (2.7182 …)*.

The numbers 10, 100, 1000, 10,000 100,000 and 1,000,000 can all be expressed as powers of 10 thus: $10 = 10^1$; $100 = 10^2$; $1000 = 10^3$; $10,000 = 10^4$; $100,000 = 10^5$; $1,000,000 = 10^6$. In the system of common logarithms, the powers 1, 2, 3, 4, 5 and 6 are termed the **logarithms** of the numbers 10, 100, … to the base 10. The common logarithmic function is written as

$$y = log_{10} x \quad \text{- - - (1)}$$

The common logarithmic function

where y is the common logarithm, the subscript is the value of the base of the system (10) and x, the **argument** of the function, is the number itself. Logarithms, then, are *powers* of the base. The **antilogarithm** is the inverse of the log function: if we raise the base to the power of the logarithm, we shall obtain the original number thus:

$$x = 10^y \quad \text{- - - (2)}$$

The antilogarithm

where $y = log_{10} x$.

The following table illustrates the definitions of the common logarithmic function and its inverse, the antilogarithmic function.

Number	Logarithm	Antilogarithm
x	$y = log_{10} x$	$10^y = x$
10	1	$10^1 = 10$
100	2	$10^2 = 100$
1000	3	$10^3 = 1000$
10,000	4	$10^4 = 10,000$

The same definitions apply to the system of natural logarithms, but the notation is somewhat different.

$$y = ln(x) = log_e x \quad \text{- - - (3)}$$

The natural logarithmic function

The antilogarithmic function reverses the natural logarithmic function and delivers the number itself. The power function of e, however, is known as the **exponential function** and is written as Exp(y).

$$x = e^y = Exp(y) \quad ---(4)$$

The natural antilogarithmic (exponential) function

The following table illustrates the notation for natural logs and antilogs.

Number	Logarithm	Antilogarithm
x	$y = \ln x = \log_e x$	$Exp(y) = e^y = x$
10	2.30	$Exp(2.30) = e^{2.30} = 10$
100	4.61	$Exp(4.61) = e^{4.61} = 100$
1000	6.91	$Exp(6.91) = e^{6.91} = 1000$
10,000	9.21	$Exp(9.21) = e^{9.21} = 10,000$

Domain of the log functions

Only positive numbers have finite logarithms. The log of zero is minus infinity. The log of a negative number is not defined.

Two noteworthy logarithms

The log (or ln) of 1 is zero, because $Exp(0) = e^0 = 10^0 = 1$.

The log of the base of either system is unity: $\ln(e) = \log_{10} 10 = 1$. This is because $Exp[\ln(e)] = e; \ 10^{\log_{10} 10} = 10$

The laws of logarithms

1. The log of the product is the sum of the logs: $\log(xy) = \log x + \log y$

2. The log of the quotient is the log of the numerator minus the log of the denominator:

$$log\left(\frac{x}{y}\right) = log\ x - log\ y$$

3. The log of the power is the index times the log: $log\left(x^k\right) = k\ log\ x$

These laws all follow very easily from the definition of an antilog and the laws of indices: for example, $10^{log_{10} xy} = xy$ (definition of an antilog). But $xy = 10^{log\ x} \times 10^{log\ y} = 10^{log\ x + log\ y}$ (first law of indices).   Therefore $10^{log\ xy} = 10^{log\ x + log\ y}$ Equating indices on both sides, we have $log\ xy = log\ x + log\ y$.

---

* $e = \lim\limits_{n \to \infty}\left(1 + \frac{1}{n}\right)^n = 1 + \frac{1}{1!^{**}} + \frac{1}{2!} + \frac{1}{3!} + ... = 2.71828...$

**   The exclamation mark ! indicates a **factorial**, that is, the number obtained by multiplying an integer (whole number) by all lesser integers: e.g., 4! ('factorial four') = $4 \times 3 \times 2 \times 1 = 24$. By convention, factorial zero 0! is taken to be unity.

Glossary

Adjusted R squared A measure of effect size in **Regression** and **Analysis of Variance (ANOVA)**. The adjustment corrects for positive bias.

Alternative hypothesis (H_1) In **hypothesis-testing,** the proposition that the **null hypothesis** is false.

Analysis of covariance (ANCOVA) In the context of **analysis of variance (ANOVA)**, an ancillary technique which corrects for the association between the dependent variable and another measured variable known as a **covariate**. A covariate is a potential nuisance variable, which may inflate the error term of the F-ratio and result in an incorrect decision about the null hypothesis.

Analysis of variance (ANOVA) A set of **univariate** statistical techniques for comparing means from experiments with three or more treatment conditions or groups. In ANOVA, the total variance is divided into components associated with treatment and error variance, which are compared by means of an **F ratio**.

Behrens-Fisher problem A problem with making an independent samples t test when the population variances are heterogeneous. Underlying the t test for independent samples is the assumption of homogeneity of variance. If that assumption is true, the t statistic is distributed as t on $n_1 + n_2 - 2$ degrees of freedom. With heterogeneity of variance, particularly when the sample sizes are unequal, the ordinary t statistic, in which there is a pooled estimate of the supposedly constant population variance, does not have this distribution. In such cases, the sample variances are no longer pooled for the calculation of the test statistic and the df is adjusted downwards by means of the Welch-Satterthwaite formula or an equivalent.

Between groups See **Between subjects designs**.

Between subjects designs Comparative experimental designs yielding independent samples of data, in which each participant is tested under only one condition and there is no basis for pairing the scores from one group with those in another. The term **between groups** is also used to describe this kind of design. (Compare with **Repeated measures**.)

Bivariate normality Two variables are said to have a bivariate normal distribution if, given a value of one variable, the distribution of the other variable at that value is normal. More technically, the conditional distributions must be normal. The correct application of the **Pearson correlation** assumes bivariate normality, which is indicated by an elliptical (or circular) scatterplot.

Bonferroni correction A procedure, based on the Bonferroni inequality in probability theory, for controlling the **experimentwise** or **familywise** Type I error rate. One can set a more stringent criterion for significance by dividing the ordinary (per comparison) significance level either by the number of planned comparisons or (with unplanned or **post hoc** comparisons) by the number of pairwise comparisons possible from an array of means of specified size. An equivalent procedure is to multiply the p-value by the same factor.

Canonical Correlation Applicable to a research situation in which one group of variables can be viewed as consequent upon or causally influenced by the variables in a second group, the former being viewed as dependent variables (DVs) and the latter as independent variables (IVs). A pair of linear functions, one for the DVs, the other for the IVs, is constructed so that the correlation between them is maximised. The functions make a canonical variate pair and the correlation between them is the canonical correlation.

Centring In **multiple regression**, problems arise when the correlations among the independent variables of regressors are too high, in which case we have multicollinearity. The risk of multicollinearity is particularly high if interaction terms or powers are included in the regression model. The risk is reduced if the raw scores on a variable are first transformed into deviations by subtracting the mean, an operation known as centring. (It is not necessary to standardise the scores by dividing by the standard deviation as well: deviations are sufficient.)

Chi-square distribution The sum of the squares of n independent squared standard normal variables has a chi-square distribution with n degrees of freedom. A chi-square variable has a continuous distribution. The familiar chi-square statistic used in the analysis of nominal data is only an approximation to a true chi-square variable, and the approximation becomes poor when expected cell frequencies are low. The (controversial) **correction for continuity** (Yates' correction) is an attempt to improve the approximation.

Cluster analysis A set of multivariate statistical techniques designed to account for (or classify) a multivariate data set in terms of relatively few reference groups or clusters, each cluster being interpreted as representing an underlying characteristic or property. The purpose of cluster analysis is thus similar to that of **factor analysis**, which is another set of techniques for classifying multivariate data.

Coefficient alpha (Cronbach's alpha) A measure of the reliability of a psychological test. Many psychological tests yield scores that are aggregates of the participant's responses to several items. Psychometric theory shows that the reliability of such a test increases with the number of items it contains, according to the following formula:

$$alpha = \frac{i}{i-1}\left(\frac{\sigma_Y^2 - \sum_{items}\sigma_{item}^2}{\sigma_Y^2}\right)$$

where i is the number of items in the test and σ_y^2 is the variance of the complete test. The relationship between number of items and reliability obtains because the items in a test constitute a sample from the domain of possible items and, other things being equal, the statistics of large samples are less subject to variability than are those of small samples. (See **Spearman-Brown formula**.)

Coefficient of determination (CD) In simple regression, the proportion of the variance of the target, criterion or dependent variable that is accounted for by regression upon another variable (the regressor or independent variable). Its value is given by the square of the Pearson correlation: thus if $r = 0.60$, $r^2 = .36$, which means that 36% of the variance of the criterion variable is accounted for by regression upon the other variable. In multiple regression, the CD is the square of the multiple correlation coefficient: $CD = R^2$.

Cohen's d A measure of effect size. In the two-sample case, Cohen's d is the difference between the two treatment means divided by a pooled estimate of the standard deviation.

Cohen's kappa A measure of agreement between raters who are assigning cases to the same set of mutually exclusive categories. Cohen's statistic provides a way of measuring the reliability of psychiatric diagnosis or the use of any other standard classificatory system.

Comparison   In **analysis of variance (ANOVA)**, the difference between two treatment means, either of which may itself be the mean of other treatment means. (See **Contrast**.)

Confidence interval An interval constructed around the value of a statistic such as the mean which would 'cover' or include the population value in a specified proportion of samples. A confidence interval is not a **sample space**: one cannot claim that there is a probability of .95 that the population mean lies within the limits of the 95% confidence interval obtained from a particular set of data. What the researcher can say is that, because the confidence interval has been constructed in such a way that it would include the population value in 95% of samples, one can be 95% 'confident' that the mean lies within the interval. Such a 'confidence', however, is not a probability.

Confirmatory factor analysis A set of techniques designed to account for an R-matrix in terms of a model in which the number of factors is pre-specified. (The model may make other specifications as well, such as the correlation between the factors.) Confirmatory factor analysis is an aspect of **structural equation modelling**.

Contingency table   A table classifying individuals with respect to two or more sets of categories (see **Qualitative variables**). The entries in the cells of a contingency table are the frequencies of individuals with the various combinations of attributes. For example, if patients are classified with respect to gender and blood group, the contingency table would show the numbers of females in group A, the numbers of males in group O and so on. A contingency table is the starting point for various statistical analyses. For example, a chi-squared test can be used to test for an association between two attributes. Complex multi-attribute contingency tables can be analysed with **loglinear analysis**.

Continuous variable   A quantitative variable that can have an infinite number of values within a specified interval. Height and weight are examples. SPSS uses the term **scale** to denote measurements of continuous variables.

Contrast   The comparison between two of an array of k treatment means can be written as a **linear contrast**, which is a weighted sum of the treatment means, such that the coefficients (weights) add up to zero. Suppose we have three treatment means and that we want to compare M_1 with M_2. The difference $M_1 - M_2$ can be expressed as the linear contrast L_1, where $L_1 = (+1)M_1 + (-1)M_2 + (0)M_3$. Similarly, if we wish to compare M_1 with the mean of M_2 and M_3, the difference $M_1 - (M_2 + M_3)/2$ can be expressed as the linear contrast L_2, where $L_2 = (+1)M_1 + (-\frac{1}{2})M_2 + (-\frac{1}{2})M_3$. In general, for a set of k treatment means M_j, the contrast L is given by $L = \Sigma c_j M_j$, where c_j is the coefficient of the treatment mean M_j. (See **Orthogonal contrasts**.)

Correction for continuity   When a continuous variable is used as an approximation to a discrete one or vice versa (as when using the normal distribution as an approximation to a binomial distribution or an approximate chi-square statistic with frequency data) the value 0.5 is first subtracted from the difference between the observed and expected values before the test statistic is calculated. The usual chi-square approximation formula, for example, becomes

$$\chi^2 = \Sigma \frac{(|O - E| - 0.5)^2}{E}$$

This is known as **Yates' correction**.

The normal approximation to the binomial becomes

$$z = \frac{X - np - 0.5}{\sqrt{npq}}$$

where p is the probability of a 'success', q is the probability of a 'failure' and n is the number of Bernoulli trials.

Correlation   A measure of a supposed linear relationship between two variables X and Y, one of the many formulae for which is

$$r_{XY} = \frac{\Sigma(X - M_X)(Y - M_Y)}{\sqrt{\Sigma(X - M_X)^2 \, \Sigma(Y - M_Y)^2}}$$

The value of r varies within the range from -1 to $+1$, inclusive.

Multiplying or dividing each raw score on one of the variables by a constant leaves the absolute value of r unchanged; but if the value of the constant is negative, the sign of the correlation is reversed. A nonlinear transformation, such as the logarithm or the square root, changes the absolute value of the correlation.

Correlation ratio CR   See **eta**.

Correlational research   A strategy whereby variables are measured as they occur in the individuals studied. Correlational research contrasts with **experimental** research, in which the supposedly causal variable is manipulated by the experimenter, independently of the characteristics of the participants.

Covariance   A measure of a supposed linear association between two variables. In a univariate data set, the variance is the average squared deviation of scores from their mean (though we divide by one less than the number of scores). In a bivariate data set, the covariance is the average of the cross-products of the deviations of pairs of scores on the two variables from their respective means. (We divide by one less than the number of pairs of scores.) If the scores on both variables are standardised, the covariance becomes the **Pearson correlation**.

Covariate[1]   In the context of an experiment, a variable that may be associated with the measure or dependent variable and therefore must be taken into consideration in the analysis. In some SPSS dialog boxes, such as those for logistic regression, the term covariate denotes the predictors, regressors or independent variables, provided they are continuous.

Covariate[2]   In some SPSS procedures, such as **logistic regression** and **canonical correlation**, a **covariate** is a continuous independent variable.

Cross-validation   A procedure for attempting to generalise the results of a multiple regression. One approach is to divide the original data set into two sub-samples, fit a regression model to the first sub-sample and then assess the predictive value of the model when applied to the second sub-sample. Applying a regression model to a fresh sample is likely to show a weakening of predictive power known as **shrinkage**. Shrinkage will be minimised with sufficiently large samples: Howell (2007, p506) reviews various recommendations, including the stipulation that in multiple regression we should have at least 40 or 50 more participants than there are predictors in the regression equation. The guiding principle is that, with multiple regression (as with many other techniques), the more data one has, the better.

Cumulative probability The probability of a value less than or equal to a specified value. Cumulative probabilities are given by **distribution functions**.

Degrees of freedom A term borrowed from physical science, in which the degrees of freedom of a system is the number of constraints needed to determine its state completely at any point. In statistics, the degrees of freedom df is given by the number of independent observations minus the number of parameters estimated. For example, for the variance estimate based upon n observations, there are n deviations from the mean. One parameter (the mean) has been estimated, however, so $df = n - 1$. In simpler terms, once we have specified the values of $n - 1$ deviations from the sample mean, the value of the remaining deviation is fully determined, because deviations about the mean sum to zero.

Deleted residual In **regression diagnostics**, it is often important to determine the influence of one particular case upon the regression statistics. Two regressions are run: the first with the entire data set; the second with the case omitted. The deleted residual for the target case is $Y - \hat{Y}_{i(i)}$, where $\hat{Y}_{i(i)}$ is the estimate of the true score Y from the model calculated from the reduced data set. The difference in magnitude between the *raw residual* $Y - \hat{Y}_i$ and the deleted residual $Y - \hat{Y}_{i(i)}$ can reveal the influence of the data for one particular case upon the regression statistics.

Dependent or outcome variable In the context of a true experiment, the variable (such as performance) that is measured during the course of the study, as opposed to the variable that is manipulated by the experimenter (the independent variable or IV). The purpose of an experiment is to determine whether the IV has a causal effect upon the DV.

Discriminant analysis (DA) A **multivariate** statistical technique which is mathematically equivalent to the one-way **multivariate analysis of variance (MANOVA)**. Here, however, the purpose is to predict group membership from two or more measured variables, which are therefore regarded as independent (rather than dependent) variables. Linear discriminant functions of the independent variables which maximise inter-group differences are found and used to predict group membership.

Distribution Any table, display or formula that pairs each of the values that a variable can take with a frequency or a probability. With continuous variables, the **distribution function** gives the cumulative probability of specific values; the **density function** gives the **probability density** of a particular value, that is, the derivative of the distribution function at that point. (Note that with a continuous variable, the probability of any particular value is zero.)

Distribution function See **Distribution**.

Dummy variables Variables consisting of the values 0 and 1 only are known as dummy variables. In SPSS, in order to compare the mean scores of three groups of participants, we can use a grouping variable with 3 different numerical values, say 1, 2 and 3, to code the conditions under which the scores were obtained and run a one-way ANOVA. We could, however, also code group membership by means of two dummy variables, the values of each being either 1 or 0, as in the two columns of the matrix below:

$$\begin{pmatrix} 1 & 0 \\ 0 & 1 \\ 0 & 0 \end{pmatrix}$$

In general, if there are g groups, we shall need $(g - 1)$ such dummy variables to identify each group uniquely. As explained in Chapter 12, the equivalent of a one-way ANOVA can be run as a regression of the participants' scores upon the dummy variables. If the number 0 is assigned to the control group on each dummy variable, the intercept will be the mean for that group and the regression coefficients will be the differences between the means of the treatment groups and the mean for the control group.

Eta The **correlation ratio**, a measure of effect size in **analysis of variance (ANOVA)**. **Eta squared** or $\mathbf{R}^2$ is a measure of the proportion of the total variance that is accounted for by differences among the treatment means. In the one-way ANOVA, eta squared is the ratio of the between groups sum of squares to the total sum of squares. As an estimator, eta squared is positively biased and statistics such as **adjusted R squared** and **omega squared** are preferred as estimators.

Event An outcome of an **experiment of chance**.

Event space In an **experiment of chance**, the subset of the sample space containing those elementary outcomes that qualify as instances of a defined event.

Experiment A research technique in which the independent variable (IV) is manipulated to ascertain its effects upon the dependent variable (DV). Such direct manipulation is the hallmark of a true experiment, as opposed to a **correlational** study or a **quasi-experiment**.

Experiment of chance In probability theory, a procedure with an uncertain outcome, such as tossing a coin or rolling a die. The entire set of possible **elementary outcomes** (an elementary outcome is one of the simplest possible ways in which the experiment can turn out) is termed the **sample space**. An **event space** is a subset of the sample space.

Experimentwise Type I error rate Following the analysis of variance of data from an experiment with three or more conditions, the researcher will often wish to make planned or unplanned comparisons among the means for specified groups or conditions. If the null hypothesis is true, the probability of at least one comparison showing significance is known as the experimentwise Type I error rate. The experimentwise Type I error rate may be considerably higher than the significance level set for any one comparison (the Type I error rate **per comparison**) and increases with the size of the array of treatment means. With large sets of comparisons, the experimentwise error rate greatly exceeds the significance level for each comparison, that is, the error rate per comparison, which is usually set at .05: for example, if we have a set of 5 treatment means and make all 10 possible pairwise comparisons, the probability that at least one comparison will show significance (the familywise error rate) is approximately $1 - .95^{10} = .40$. (This is an approximation, because the comparisons are not independent.) Conservative tests such as the **Bonferroni** and **Tukey** methods are designed to control the experimentwise Type I error rate.

Exploratory factor analysis A set of techniques designed to account for an **R-matrix** in terms of the minimum number of classificatory axes or dimensions, the latter being known as **factors** (See **Confirmatory factor analysis**.)

F distribution   The distribution of the ratio of two chi-square variables, each of which has been divided by its degrees of freedom.   An F distribution has two parameters, namely, df_1 and df_2, the degrees of freedom of the chi-square variables.   The mean of the distribution is $df_1/(df_2 - 2)$, provided that $df_2 > 2$.   It can be shown that the ratio of two independent estimates of the variance of a normal population is distributed as $F(df_1, df_2)$.   The F test in **analysis of variance (ANOVA)** is an application of this result.

F ratio   The ratio of two chi-square variables, each of which has been divided by its degrees of freedom.   (See **F distribution**.)

Factor[1]   In **Analysis of Variance (ANOVA),** a set of related categories, treatments or conditions.   A factor is thus a qualitative or categorical **independent variable**.

Factor[2]   See **Factor analysis**.

Factor analysis (FA)   A set of techniques enabling the researcher to account for the correlations among a battery of tests in terms of a relatively small number of classificatory axes or **factors**, which are assumed to represent theoretical dimensions, **latent variables** or hypothetical constructs.   Since a factor is also a function of the observed variables, individuals receive, in addition to scores on the tests in the battery, **factor scores** locating them on the dimension concerned.   (See **R-matrix**.)

Factor score   An individual's aggregate score on a combination of the scores on the tests in a battery.

Factorial experiments   Experiments in which there are two or more independent variables or factors.   If each level of one factor is found in combination with every level of another factor, the two factors are said to 'cross' and the factors are independent or orthogonal.   In nested or hierarchical factorial designs, on the other hand, the levels of some factors are distributed among the levels of other factors, so that not every combination of conditions can be found in the experimental design.

Familywise Type I error rate   This term, which we owe to Tukey, has largely replaced the older term: **experimentwise**. The problem with basing the experimentwise Type I error rate on the entire experiment is that the criteria for the significance of comparisons can become extremely stringent.   There may be grounds for defining the reference set of means as those making up only part of the experiment and thus working with a smaller 'family' of comparisons: hence the term **familywise**.   Such redefinition of the comparison 'family' must be justified by a procedure such as testing first for **simple effects**.

Greenhouse-Geisser correction   In **within subjects** or **repeated measures** experiments, the data may not have the property of **sphericity**, or **homogeneity of covariance**.   If so, the ordinary F test may be positively biased, that is, it may give too many significant results when the null hypothesis is true.   The correction adjusts the numerator and denominator degrees of freedom of the F ratio downwards by multiplying them by a constant epsilon, whose maximum value is 1.   Another corrective procedure is the Huynh-Feldt method, which is less conservative than the Greenhouse-Geisser correction.   SPSS offers several different corrections.

Grouping variable   In SPSS, a set of code numbers indicating group membership.   In Variable View, the numbers, or values, should always be assigned meaningful value labels.

Homogeneity of covariance (sphericity)   A property of the **variance-covariance matrix**, which is calculated from the data obtained from an experiment with a repeated measures factor.

Hypothesis   A supposition about the state of nature. In statistics, a hypothesis is a statement about a population, such as the value of a parameter or the nature of the distribution. (See **Null hypothesis**; **Alternative hypothesis**; **Hypothesis testing**.)

Hypothesis testing   A statistical procedure for testing the null hypothesis (H_0) against the alternative hypothesis (H_1). On the basis of the null hypothesis, the range of possible values of the test statistic (e.g., t, F, χ^2) is divided into an acceptance region and a critical region. The critical region contains values of the test statistic that are unlikely under H_0: that is, under H_0, there is a low probability α that the value of the test statistic will fall within the critical region. The value of α is known as the significance level and is conventionally set at .05, .01 (or sometimes .001), depending on the research area. Should the value of the test statistic fall within the critical region, the statistic is said to be significant beyond (or at) the level of α. Such a significant result is regarded as evidence against the null hypothesis and therefore, indirectly, as evidence for the alternative hypothesis. The location of the critical region depends upon the alternative hypothesis. In a t test, for example, if H_1 is the two-sided assertion that the population mean is not that specified by H_0 (i.e. μ_0), the critical region is located symmetrically in both tails of the distribution, that is, above the $(1 - \alpha/2)^{th}$ percentile and below the $\alpha/2^{th}$ percentile. If, on the other hand, H_1 states that the mean is greater than μ_0, that is, H_1 is a one-sided alternative, the critical region is located entirely in the upper tail of the t distribution, above the $(1 - \alpha)^{th}$ percentile. This is known as a **one-tailed test**.

Independent samples   Two samples are said to be independent if there is no basis for pairing the data they contain and the values in each have been drawn at random from the population.

Independent variable   In a true experiment, a variable manipulated by the experimenter, to determine whether it has a causal effect upon the dependent variable.   In **correlational research**, the term is used to denote a predictor variable or regressor, a variable that is being investigated as possibly having a causal effect upon a target, criterion or independent variable. In that context, the 'independent variable' is not manipulated by an experimenter, but is measured as a characteristic of the participant during the course of the investigation. The investigator attempts to neutralise the influence of possible confounds by statistical, rather than experimental means, by following a sampling strategy.

Interaction   In **analysis of variance (ANOVA),** two factors are said to interact when the effects of one factor are not the same at all levels of the other factor. In other words, the **simple main effects** of one factor are not homogeneous across all levels of the other factor.

Interval data   Data yielded by the measurement on a scale whose units are equally spaced on the property concerned. There has been much debate about whether data in the form of ratings (and other psychological measures) have the interval property. Arguably, therefore, not all continuous or scale data are interval data. Those who argue that ratings do not have the interval property tend to eschew the use of parametric tests and favour nonparametric or distribution-free tests. Others, however, believe that this issue is irrelevant to the choice of a statistical test.

Latent variable   A variable supposedly underlying associations among the variables in a multivariate data set. In several multivariate methods, such as **factor analysis, structural**

equation modelling (of which factor analysis is an aspect) and **canonical correlation**, linear functions are constructed which serve as reference variables or axes with reference to which the observed variables can be classified. Such linear functions are taken to represent latent variables.

Level In Analysis of Variance, one of the conditions or categories that make up an qualitative independent variable or **factor**[1]. Since, in the general case, a **factor** is a set of qualitatively different categories rather than a continuous independent variable, the term 'level' does not here carry its usual comparative meaning.

Levene's test Tests for homogeneity of variance, a requirement for the independent samples t test. A significant result on Levene's test indicates that the homogeneity assumption is untenable, a contraindication against the use of the traditional t test, which uses a pooled estimate of the supposedly uniform population variance.

Leverage In regression, the values of the statistics can be unduly influenced by atypical cases or outliers. Statistics are available for measuring the influence or leverage that such cases exert upon the regression model yielded by the analysis. If there is only one IV, the leverage exerted by the value X is measured by h, the formula for which is

$$h = \frac{1}{n} + \frac{(X - M_X)^2}{\Sigma(X - M_X)^2}$$

where n is the number of cases. The further from the mean X is, the greater the leverage it can exert, up to a maximum of 1. If there are k IVs in the regression, the average leverage exerted by the n cases is $(k + 1)/n$.

Linear Of the nature of a straight line. The straight line function $y = b_0 + b_1 x$ is the simplest in the family of linear equations $y = b_0 + b_1 x_1 + b_2 x_2 + ... + b_p x_p$. The analogues of the straight line when there are two or more IVs are, respectively, the plane (two IVs) and the hyperplane (three or more IVs). (See **Regression**.)

Loading In **factor analysis,** the loading of a test on a factor is the correlation between scores on the test and the **factor scores** of the participants in the study and is thus a measure of the extent to which performance on the test can be accounted for in terms of the factor concerned. The square of the loading is the proportion of the common factor variance of the test that is accounted for by the factor.

Logarithms or **logs** See Appendix.

Loglinear analysis A set of techniques for modelling the expected frequencies of observations in the cells of a multi-way contingency table. The expected raw cell frequencies can be estimated by multiplicative functions of the relevant marginal frequencies, in which the factors are estimates of main effects and interactions. Since, however, the logarithm of a product is the sum of the logarithms of its factors, the logarithm of the expected cell frequency can be modelled by a linear function of the various effect terms, which are estimated from the **logarithms** of the marginal frequencies.

Main effect In factorial analysis of variance, a factor is said to have a main effect if, in the population, the means on the dependent variable do not have the same value at all levels of the factor (ignoring all other factors in the design).

Mann-Whitney test The nonparametric equivalent of an independent samples *t-test*. It tests the null hypothesis that the two populations have the same median. Wilcoxon's rank-sum test another nonparametric test, is the exact equivalent of the Mann-Whitney.

MANOVA See **Multivariate analysis of variance**.

Model An interpretation of data, usually in the form of an equation or a path diagram, in which an observed score is presented as the sum of systematic and error components. The use of any standard statistical test requires that the assumptions of a specific model are applicable to the researcher's own data.

Multiple correlation coefficient R In **regression**, the Pearson correlation between the target or criterion variable and the estimates of its values from the regression equation. The value of R, however, unlike the Pearson correlation, cannot be negative, because the slope of the regression line, plane or hyperplane is always consistent with the orientation of the cloud of points in the scatterplot.

Multiple responses The compiler of a questionnaire may be interested in the mode of transport used by the respondents to get to their work. A single question inviting respondents to tick those modes of transport they use is likely to receive two, three or more responses, which would create problems for entry of the data into SPSS. Another approach, however, is to have a Yes/No question for each mode of transport and have the response to each question as a separate variable. SPSS offers a Multiple Response procedure which shows the frequencies with which different modes of transport are used by the respondents.

Multivariate analysis of variance (MANOVA) A generalisation of the analysis of variance (ANOVA) from the univariate to the multivariate situation, where there are two or more dependent variables.

Multivariate data A data set containing observations on three or more variables.

Multivariate normality A set of k variables is said to have a multivariate normal distribution if, given any set of values of $k - 1$ of them, the remaining variable is normally distributed. More technically, not only is the distribution of each variable considered separately (its marginal distribution) normal, but also the conditional distributions are normal. Techniques such as **Multivariate analysis of variance (MANOVA)** and **Discriminant Analysis (DA)** assume multivariate normality.

Multivariate statistics Statistical analyses in which there two or more dependent variables. Examples are **Multivariate analysis of variance (MANOVA)**, **Factor analysis (FA)** and **Principal components analysis (PCA)**. (See **Univariate statistics**.)

Nagelkerke's R^2 In **logistic regression**, a statistic which mimics the **coefficient of determination** (R^2) in ordinary least squares (OLS) regression. Nagelkerke's statistic was designed to overcome the inability of another measure, Cox and Snell's R^2, to achieve its maximum value.

Nominal data Numerical data consisting of records of category membership. Nominal data result from observations of qualitative variables.

Non-parametric or distribution-free test A test, such as the Mann-Whitney test or the Friedman test, which does not make assumptions about the population distribution such as normality or homogeneity of variance.

Normal (or Gaussian) distribution The famous 'bell curve', upon which much of classical statistical theory is based. A normal distribution has two parameters, the mean and the variance. Some naturally occurring variables, such as height and weight, have an approximately normal distribution. Since a linear function of two normal variables has itself a normal distribution, the mean of a sample of fixed size n drawn from a normal distribution is normally distributed. Moreover, the mean of a large sample of fixed size n from a non-normal distribution has an approximately normal distribution, provided n is sufficiently large. The sampling distribution of the mean can approximate a normal distribution to any degree of closeness, provided the sample is suffciently large (central limit theorem).

Null hypothesis In statistical hypothesis-testing, the null hypothesis (H_0) is the supposition of 'no effect': e.g., in the population, there is no difference between the means; in a bivariate population, there is no association between two variables; the sample we have selected has not been drawn from a population with a different mean, and so on. The null hypothesis, therefore, is usually the negation of the scientific hypothesis. The null hypothesis cannot be proved. This truth reflects the logical fact that it is easier to falsify than to verify. If I assert that all swans are white, you can continue to question my assertion no matter how many white swans I produce; whereas the production of a single black swan would refute my claim; moreover, you do not actually have to produce a black swan to maintain your scepticism. For this reason, should a statistical test fail to show significance, the null hypothesis is not said to be true, but is 'retained' or 'accepted'. In Neyman-Pearson hypothesis testing (as opposed to the traditional significance testing approach introduced by R. A. Fisher), the alternative hypothesis (H_1) is the supposition that the null hypothesis is false and that, in the population, the mean, variance, correlation or whatever measure we are studying has a value other than that specified by the null hypothesis. The alternative hypothesis is usually the statistical equivalent of the scientific hypothesis.

Omega squared A measure of effect size in analysis of variance which partially corrects for the positive bias of **eta squared**.

One-tailed test In hypothesis testing, a **critical region** of values for the test statistic is set up such that, under the null hypothesis, the probability of a value in the region is the significance level (usually .05). Some argue that the location of the critical region should depend upon the scientific or alternative hypothesis. There are situations in which it makes sense to look for a difference in one direction only: e.g. since brain injury is unlikely to improve test performance, the critical region for a suspiciously low performance on a diagnostic test should, arguably, be located entirely in the lower tail of the t-distribution. Since the null and alternative hypotheses are complementary (i.e. they exhaust the possibilities), the null hypothesis becomes 'equal to or greater than', rather than 'equal to'. An unexpected result in the 'wrong' direction, therefore, cannot be declared to be significant.

Ordinal data Data containing only information about order or sequencing. Examples of ordinal data are sets of ranks and sequences of outcomes over a set of trials.

Ordinary least squares (OLS) regression A set of techniques designed to predict value of a target, criterion or dependent variable from values of one, two or more predictors, regressors or independent variables. The regression line, plane or hyperplane is positioned so that it minimises the sum of the squares of the residuals $Y - Y'$, where Y and Y' are the target variable and the estimate from the regression equation, respectively. This is known as the **least-squares** criterion.

Orthogonal contrasts Two contrasts are said to be orthogonal (independent) if the products of their corresponding coefficients sum to zero. In the one-way ANOVA of data from an experiment with k treatment groups, a set of k − 1 orthogonal contrasts can be constructed, each member of which accounts for a portion of the between groups sum of squares, so that the total of the sums of squares of the contrasts is the between groups sum of squares itself.

Orthogonal polynomial coefficients A matrix of orthogonal contrast coefficients, each row of which contains different values of a polynomial of the same order, the order increasing with the 2nd and subsequent rows. For example, suppose we have three treatment means summarising the results of an experiment in which the three treatment conditions were different values of a continuous variable X, where $X_1 = 1$, $X_2 = 2$ and $X_3 = 3$. Since there are 3 means, a set of two orthogonal contrasts can be constructed. We want the first row of coefficients to be different values of a linear (1st order) polynomial and the second row to be values of a quadratic (2nd order) polynomial. The two desired polynomials are of the forms $a_1 + X$ and $a_2 + b_1 X + X^2$. Substituting $X = 1, 2, 3$ into these expressions gives us

$$\begin{pmatrix} a_1 + 1 & a_1 + 2 & a_1 + 3 \\ a_2 + b_2 + 1 & a_2 + 2b_2 + 4 & a_2 + 3b_2 + 9 \end{pmatrix}$$

Using the constraints that the elements of each row must sum to zero, as must the products of the corresponding elements of each row, we solve for a_1, a_2 and b_2 to obtain the desired orthogonal set

$$\begin{pmatrix} -1 & 0 & +1 \\ +1 & -2 & +1 \end{pmatrix}$$

The upper row of contrast coefficients has an associated sum of squares whose value reflects any linear trend present in the data; the lower row reflects any quadratic trend. Each SS can be tested against the error mean square in the usual way, confirming that component of trend in the data. In practice, we need never actually solve any equations: tables of orthogonal polynomial coefficients are available in standard statistics textbooks for arrays of means of any reasonable size.

Orthogonal rotation In factor analysis, the classificatory axes (factors) can be rotated around the origin in relation to the test points in order to produce a pattern of loadings that is easier to interpret than the original pattern. If the axes are kept at right angles during rotation, the process is known as **orthogonal rotation**. Axes at right angles represent uncorrelated factors. In oblique rotation, however, the axes are not maintained at right angles: that is, the axes represent correlated factors.

Outcome variable See **Dependent variable**.

p-value In statistical testing, the probability, under the null hypothesis, of obtaining a value of the test statistic at least as unlikely as the value that has been calculated from the data. If the p-value is smaller than 0.05 or 0.01, the test has shown significance beyond the 0.05 or the 0.01 level, respectively. If the alternative hypothesis is one-sided, the p-value must refer to values of the test statistic in one tail only of the distribution: extreme values in the opposite direction must result in acceptance of H_0.

Part correlation   See **Semipartial correlation**.

Partial correlation   What remains of the correlation between two variables when their relationships with a third variable have been neutralised or 'partialled out'.   A partial correlation is a correlation between the residuals of two variables that have been regressed upon a third variable.

Pearson correlation   A measure of the strength of a supposed linear (straight line) association between two quantitative variables, each measured on a continuous scale with units, which is so constructed that it can take values only within the range from -1 to $+1$, inclusive.   (See **Coefficient of determination**.)   The supposition of linearity must always be checked by examining the scatterplot.

Percentile   A score or value below which a specified proportion of the distribution lies: the 95th percentile is the score below which 95% of the distribution lies; the 5th percentile is the value below which 5% of the distribution lies.   The median (or middle score) is the 50th percentile.

Point-biserial correlation $r_{pt\text{-}bis}$ The Pearson correlation between a dichotomous qualitative variable (such as gender) and a continuous or scale variable.   The sign of the point-biserial correlation is of no importance, because it reflects only the ordinal relation between the arbitrary code numbers used to denote the two categories.   If the t-test between the group means on the scale variable is significant, then so will be the point-biserial correlation, because the two statistics are related according to:

$$r^2_{pt-bis} = \frac{t^2}{t^2 + df}$$

where $df = n_1 + n_2 - 2$.   In this book, we stress the difference between comparing average scores on the same variable under different conditions and investigating possible associations between measured variables.   The point-biserial correlation, however, expresses a comparison as an association between two variables; one of them being a set of arbitrary code numbers.

Polynomial   A sum of terms, each of which is a product of a constant and a power of the same variable thus

$$y = a_0 + a_1 x + a_2 x^2 + ... + a_n x^n$$

The highest power n is the degree or order of the polynomial.

Post hoc comparisons   Unplanned comparisons of the sort one inevitably makes after the data have been gathered.   Planned or *a priori* comparisons are decided upon before the data are gathered.   Since the family of possible post hoc comparisons is usually considerably larger than a set of planned comparisons, the familywise error rate associated with post hoc comparisons may also be much higher than the nominal per comparison error rate.   In either case, the per family error rate can be controlled by the **Bonferroni correction**, whereby the p-value for each comparison is multiplied by the number of comparisons in the family.

Power   The probability, assuming that the null hypothesis is false, that when a statistical test is made, the null hypothesis will be rejected.   The power P of a statistical test is related to the

Type II error rate (β) according to $P = 1 - \beta$. Power is affected by several factors, including the significance or alpha-level, the minimum effect size that the researcher considers worth reporting, the number of participants in the experiment, the design of the experiment (between subjects or within subjects) and the reliability of measurement.

Principal components (PC) A set of techniques enabling the researcher to account for the correlations among a battery of tests in terms of classificatory dimensions or components. In contrast with **factor analysis (FA)**, principal components is designed to account for 100% of the variance of each of the tests in the battery, rather than the variance it shares with the other tests.

Probability A measure of likelihood so constructed that it can have values only within the range from 0 (for an impossible event) to 1 (a certainty.) Probabilities arise in the context of **experiments of chance**, in which an event is viewed as a subset of the entire set of possible elementary outcomes. The results of an experiment can be viewed as an experiment of chance: the researcher's observations are usually a sample from a reference set or **population** of possible observations. On that basis, we can assign probabilities to ranges of values within which the sample mean might fall, assuming one of the competing hypotheses.

Probability density function (frequency function) A continuous random variable X assigns an infinite number of possible values within any specified interval in its range. The probability of any particular value of X, therefore, is zero. A probability density function, however, assigns a **probability density** to values of X. A probability density can be regarded as the probability of a value in the neighbourhood of a specified value. More technically, a probability density is the rate of change (i.e., the derivative) of the cumulative probability at that point.

Qualitative variables Characteristics or properties, such as nationality, gender and blood group, which can be possessed only in kind (not in degree) and comprise sets of categories, rather than numerical values.

Quantitative variables Characteristics or properties, such as height, weight or intelligence, that are possessed in degree, so that one individual can have more or less of the property than another. A quantitative variable consists of a set of values. The term **continuous variable** is often used for variables of this kind.

Quasi-experiment A hybrid of a true experiment and correlational research, in which sampling strategy is used in the attempt to create control groups for the purposes of comparison. In studies of the effects of smoking upon health and longevity, for example, sampling strategies are used in the attempt to equalise possible confounding variables such as education level and lifestyle. The quasi-experiment, however, has the same fundamental weakness as *correlational research*, namely, that the supposedly causal variable (e.g. smoking) is observed in the participants studied, rather than being manipulated by an experimenter, with the result that other characteristics of the participants are varying at the same time. As a consequence, however much the researcher attempts to make the samples comparable, it can never be claimed that all possible confounds have been controlled.

Random variable (variate) In probability theory, a rule for assigning a numerical value to outcomes in the **sample space**: 'Let X be the number of spots on the upper face when a die is rolled'; 'When a coin is tossed, Let Y be 1 for a head and 0 for a tail'.

Regression The prediction of a target, criterion or dependent variable from other variables known as regressors or independent variables. The prediction is made by constructing a **regression equation**, the subject of which is the estimate of the criterion from the regressors.

Reliability The extent to which a measuring instrument produces consistent results, in the sense that participants achieve scores at similar percentile levels with different testers or from occasion to occasion of testing. The various approaches to the determination of reliability include test-retest, parallel (or equivalent) forms and split-half. (See **Validity**.)

Repeated measures (or within subjects) design Experimental designs in which observations are made on the same participants on two or more occasions. The repeated measures design is a special case of the randomised blocks design, a block being a set of observations that are linked in some way, as when fertilizer is applied to plants in the same flowerbed. Such experiments yield sets of observations that can be paired or matched across samples: these four observations are John's scores; those four are Mary's. Repeated measures designs yield correlated data, as do experiments with different groups of participants who are matched in some way. (Compare **Between subjects design**.)

R-matrix A square array, or matrix, displaying the correlation of each of the tests in a battery with every other test. An R-matrix can be the starting point for **factor analysis**, which is a set of techniques for accounting for the correlations among the tests in terms of relatively few underlying variables or **factors**.

Rotation In **factor analysis**, the factors can be regarded as classificatory axes with respect to which the tests in the battery can be plotted as points. When the axes are orthogonal (at right angles to one another), the co-ordinates of each test point are the correlations between the test and the factors emerging from the analysis. Such a correlation is known as the **loading** of a test on the factor concerned. Should the axes be rotated around the origin in relation to the test points, all the loadings will change. The sum of the products of the loadings of any two tests on all the axes, however, will remain constant and affords the same estimate of the observed correlation between the two tests. Rotation makes it easier to interpret the results of a factor analysis because, in relation to the original pattern of loadings, each test tends after rotation to have higher loadings on fewer factors. (See **Orthogonal rotation**.)

Sample space In an **experiment of chance**, the set of all elementary outcomes, each of which is assumed to be equally likely.

Scale data A term in SPSS denoting data consisting of independent measurements on a scale with units. Examples are height, weight, intelligence, scores on questionnaires and ratings. Equivalent terms are **continuous data** and **interval data**.

Scatterplot A graphical display depicting a bivariate distribution, in which the axes represent the scales on the two variables and the individual is represented as a point whose coordinates are his or her scores on the variables. An elliptical cloud of points indicates a linear association between the two variables: the narrower the ellipse, the stronger the association. A circular cloud of points indicates independence of the distributions. The **Pearson correlation** is a measure of a supposedly linear association between two variables and, wherever possible, the supposition of linearity should be checked by inspecting the scatterplot.

Semipartial correlation In multiple regression, what remains of the correlation between a target or criterion variable and one of a set of predictor variables (regressors, independent variables) when the variance shared by the predictor with the other predictors has been partialled out of the predictor (but not the DV) by regression.

Shrinkage   The tendency for the predictive power of a regression model to weaken with resampling.

Simple effects   In factorial analysis of variance, the effect of one factor at one particular level of another. Simple effects analysis provides a way of analysing significant interactions. A two-way interaction can be explored by testing for the **simple main effects** of one factor at different levels of the other. Heterogeneity of simple effects, as when they act in opposite directions, helps to explain a significant interaction. A significant three-way interaction can be further explored by testing the simple two-way interactions between two of the factors at specific levels of the third.   In unplanned (post hoc) multiple pairwise comparisons, a significant simple effect is used as a justification for defining a smaller comparison family, rather than one based upon all the cell means involved in the interaction.

Simple main effect   See **Simple Effects**.

Spearman-Brown formula   A formula, equivalent to **coefficient alpha,** which expresses the reliability of a test in terms of mean of the correlations between every possible pair of items thus:

$$reliability = \frac{i\bar{r}}{1 + (i-1)\bar{r}}$$

where i is the number of items in the test and $\bar{r}$ is the mean of the correlations between pairs of items. It is clear from the formula that even if the average inter-item correlation is low, the total score on a test with many items can achieve a very high level of reliability.

Standard deviation   The positive square root of the variance, often written as s, where

$$s = +\sqrt{\frac{\sum(X-M)^2}{n-1}}$$

Unlike the variance, the standard deviation measures spread or dispersion in the original units of measurement. The square root operation, however, does not negate the distorting effects of extreme scores or outliers on the value of the standard deviation. Adding a constant k to each score leaves the standard deviation unaltered. If each score is multiplied by a constant k, the standard deviation is multiplied by k. (Compare **Variance**.)

Standard normal variable   See z.

Structural equation modelling   A structural equation model (SEM) is a statistical model of causal relationships among the variables in a set of multivariate data. Such a model takes the dual form of a set of regression equations and a pictorial representation showing the causal relationships among the variables. Different models can be compared in the extent to which they account for the data. In contrast to such techniques as exploratory factor analysis, SEM is **confirmatory** in nature. SEM is one of several multivariate methods whose purpose is to identify hypothetical constructs, **latent variables** or **factors** to account for the measured variables in the data set. Such latent variables or factors start life as linear functions of the observed variables; but later, they are given substantive meaning on the basis of the content of the tests in the battery. The observed, manifest or measured variables are assumed to be indicators of the underlying constructs. In correlational (as opposed to experimental) research, direction of causality is difficult to establish. Most research, however, is driven, at least implicitly, by some causal model. In a full SEM, some (endogenous) latent variables are supposed to be at least partially influenced by causally prior (or exogenous) latent variables. The terms exogenous and endogenous correspond to the terms independent variable and dependent variable in experimental research.

One important aspect of SEM is **confirmatory factor analysis**. In **exploratory factor analysis** (EFA), the researcher tries to identify the minimum number of latent variables or factors that underlie the covariation among a set of variables and to measure the extent to which the observed variables are loaded on these factors. In confirmatory factor analysis (CFA), more specific models can be tested: for example it might be hypothesised in advance that some measured variables will be loaded on some specific factors but not upon others. In both EFA and CFA, the focus is on the relationship between the latent factors and the observed variables. In SEM parlance, a model of this kind is known as a measurement model.

Latent variable (LV) models specify the regression structure among the latent variables. A complete or full LV model comprises both a measurement model (CFA) and a structural model of the links among the latent variables.

Sum of squares (SS) The sum of the squares of the deviations of scores X from their mean M, which is given by the formula: $SS = \Sigma(X - M)^2$. The sum of squares is the numerator of the variance estimate s^2.

t-**distribution** In the one-sample case, the distribution of the statistic t, where

$$t = \frac{M - \mu}{s/\sqrt{n}}$$

and M is the mean of a sample of size n drawn from a normal population. The distribution of t has one parameter, the **degrees of freedom** df, the value of which is given by $df = n - 1$. A t distribution resembles the standard normal distribution with mean zero and standard deviation 1; but it has thicker tails and its variance is $df/(df - 2)$. As n increases, the t distribution approximates the standard normal distribution ever more closely.

Trend analysis In **analysis of variance (ANOVA)**, the independent variable, rather than merely being a set of related treatments, groups or experimental conditions, may be quantitative and continuous, as when different groups of patients ingest different quantities of a drug. If so, the question arises as to the nature of the functional relationship between the dependent variable and the independent variable. In trend analysis, the treatment sum of squares is divided into orthogonal (independent) components accounted for by linear, quadratic and more complex polynomial functions. Each component of trend can be tested for significance. (See **Orthogonal polynomial coefficients**.)

Type I error The rejection of the null hypothesis when it is actually true. The probability of a Type I error is the significance level α and is also known as the alpha-level, or the alpha-rate.

Type II error The acceptance of the null hypothesis when it is actually false. Its probability β is known as the beta-level or beta-rate. The beta-level is determined by several factors, including the sample size and the significance level. (See **Power**.)

Univariate statistics Analyses in which there is only one dependent variable. Examples are the t-tests and **analysis of variance (ANOVA)**. (Compare **Multivariate statistics**.)

Unrelated samples See **Independent Samples**.

Validity[1] In psychological testing (psychometrics), a test is said to be valid if it measures what it is supposed to measure. This beguilingly simple definition is open to many interpretations, which is why, in Reber's Dictionary of Psychology (1985), there are more than 25 definitions of validity. In personnel selection, the predictive or criterion validity is the Pearson correlation between scores on a psychological test and a target or criterion variable (job efficiency, academic grade). In order to be valid in this sense, a psychological test must also be reliable. Reliability, however, does not ensure validity. A vocabulary test may be highly reliable; but it may be a very poor predictor of success on an IT course.

Validity[2] An experiment is said to have ecological validity when the dependent variable is a characteristic actually seen in everyday life. Is the result of a scenario study of bystander intervention generalisable to a real situation in which the protagonist is asked for (or should offer) help?

Validity[3] An experiment is said to be internally valid if the independent variable has been shown unequivocally to have had a causal effect upon the dependent variable. The internal validity of an experiment is threatened by such influences as placebo effects, extraneous variables, demand characteristics and experimenter effects.

Variable A property or characteristic consisting of a set of values or categories. (See **Qualitative variables**, **Quantitative variables**.)

Variance A measure of the extent to which scores are spread (or dispersed) around their mean. The variance estimate s^2 of a set of n scores is the sum of the squares of their deviations from the mean, divided by $n - 1$: that is, $s^2 = SS/(n - 1)$. The denominator of the variance estimate is also known as the degrees of freedom df, and the variance estimate can be expressed as SS/df. The variance is of great theoretical importance but, as a descriptive measure, its value is limited by the fact that it expresses the spread of a set of scores in squares of the original units of measurement. The positive square root of the variance estimate is known as the **standard deviation** s, which expresses spread in the original units of measurement. In the population, the variance is the mean squared deviation and the standard deviation is the root mean square. The df appears in the denominator of the sample variance to remove negative bias: that is, the expected value of the sample mean squared deviation is less than the value of the population variance. Adding a constant k to each score leaves the variance unaltered. Multiplying by k multiplies the variance by k^2.

Wald-Wolfowitz runs test There are situations, as when a participant makes a series of choices over a series of trials, in which the investigator is concerned with whether sequences of the same choice indicate a lack of randomness in the participant's strategy. The Wald-Wolfowitz tests for non-randomness.

Welch's F test A variation of the F test which is applicable when the assumption of homogeneity of variance has been violated.

Welch-Satterthwaite formula A formula used to adjust the degrees of freedom for a variant of the t statistic in which separate variance estimates are retained. See **Behrens-Fisher problem**.

Wilks' Lambda (Λ) In the univariate one-way ANOVA, variance estimates or mean squares (MS) are made by dividing the sums of squares SS by their degrees of freedom and using the F statistic to compare the between groups and within groups estimates $MS_{between}$ and MS_{within}. In **multivariate analysis of variance (MANOVA)**, where there are several DVs, the analogue of the variance estimate is the determinant of a matrix of cross-products of deviations. There is a between groups cross-product matrix $S_{between}$ and a within groups matrix S_{within} , which are analogous to the between groups and within groups sums of squares in the one-way ANOVA. There is also a total cross-product matrix S_{total} which, in a manner similar to the univariate ANOVA total sum of squares, can be partitioned by expressing it as the sum of the between groups and within groups matrices:

$$S_{total} = S_{between} + S_{within}$$

Wilks' lambda Λ is defined as a ratio of determinants:

$$\Lambda = \frac{|S_{error}|}{|S_{between} + S_{error}|}$$

In the univariate one-way ANOVA, where there is only one DV, the formula for Λ simplifies to:

$$\Lambda = \frac{SS_{within}}{SS_{within} + SS_{between}} = \frac{SS_{within}}{SS_{total}} = 1 - \eta^2$$

where η^2 is the **correlation ratio**. It is therefore clear that while Λ, like η^2, can take values in the range from 0 to 1, inclusive, small values of Λ indicate large differences among the group means, while large values of Λ indicate small differences. An approximate F statistic can be used to test a value of Λ for significance.

Within subjects designs See **Repeated measures**.

Yates' correction A modification of the approximate chi-square formula. See **Correction for continuity**.

z The **standard normal variable**, with a mean of zero and a standard deviation of 1. Any normally distributed variable X can be transformed to z by subtracting the mean and dividing by the standard deviation. A z-score expresses a value in units of standard deviation, not the original units. A positive sign for z indicates that the value is so-many standard deviations above the mean; a negative sign indicates that the value is so-many standard deviations below the mean. Standardising a variable does NOT normalise its distribution: if the raw scores have a skewed distribution, so will the standardised scores.

References

Agresti, A. (1990). *Categorical data analysis.* New York: Wiley.

American Psychological Association. (2001). *Publication manual of the American Psychological Association (5th ed.).* Washington, DC: American Psychological Association.

Anscombe, F. J. (1973). Graphs in statistical analysis. *American Statistician, 27,* 17-21.

Brown, M.B., & Forsythe, A.B. (1974). The ANOVA and multiple comparisons for data with heterogeneous variances. *Biometrics, 30,* 719-724.

Byrne, B. M. (2001). *Structural equation modeling with AMOS: Basic concepts, applications and programming.* Mahwah, NJ: Lawrence Erlbaum Associates.

Clark-Carter, D. (2004). *Quantitative psychological research: A student's handbook.* Hove and New York: Psychology Press.

Cohen, J. (1960). A coefficient of agreement for nominal scales. *Educational and Psychological Measurement, 10,* 37-46.

Cohen, J. (1962). The statistical power of abnormal-social psychological research: A review. *Journal of Abnormal and Social Psychology, 65,* 145 - 153.

Cohen, J. (1988). *Statistical power analysis for the behavioral sciences (2nd ed.).* Hillsdale, NJ: Lawrence Erlbaum Associates.

Cohen, J., Cohen, P., West, S. G., & Aiken, L. S. (2003). *Applied multiple regression/correlation analysis for the behavioral sciences (3rd ed.).* Mahwah, NJ: Lawrence Erlbaum Associates.

Darlington, R. B. (1968). Multiple regression in psychological research and practice. *Psychological Bulletin, 69,* 161-182.

Darlington, R. B. (1990). *Regression and linear models.* New York: McGraw-Hill.

Dodd, D.H., & Schultz, R.F. (1973). Computational procedures for estimating magnitude of effect for some analysis of variance designs. *Psychological Bulletin, 79,* 391-395.

Einspruch, E. L. (2004). *Next steps with SPSS.* London: Sage.

Erdfelder, E., Faul, F., & Buchner, A. (1996). GPOWER: A general power analysis program. *Behavior Research Methods, Instruments, and Computers, 28,* 1-11.

Faul, F., Erdfelder, E., Lang, A.-G., & Buchner, A. (2007). G*Power 3: A flexible statistical power analysis for the social, behavioral and biomedical sciences. *Behavior Research Methods, 39,* 175-191.

Field, A. (2005). *Discovering Statistics Using SPSS (2nd ed.).* London: Sage.

Field, A., & Hole, G. (2003). *How to design and report experiments.* London: Sage.

Howell, D. C. (2007). *Statistical methods for psychology (6th ed.).* Belmont, CA: Thomson/Wadsworth.

Keppel, G., & Wickens, T. D. (2004). *Design and analysis: A researcher's handbook (4th ed.).* Upper Saddle River, New Jersey: Pearson Prentice Hall.

Kim, J., & Mueller, C. W. (1978a). *Factor analysis: Statistical methods and practical issues.* Newbury Park, CA: Sage.

Kim, J., & Mueller, C. W. (1978b). *Introduction to factor analysis: What it is and how to do it.* Newbury Park, CA: Sage.

Nelson, D. (2004). *The Penguin dictionary of statistics.* London: Penguin Books.

Rasbash, J., Steele, F., Browne, W., & Prosser, B. (2004). *A user's guide to MLwiN (Version 2.0).* London: Centre for Multivel Modelling, Institute of Education, University of London.

Reber, A. S. (1985). *The Penguin dictionary of psychology.* Harmondsworth, Middlesex, England: Penguin Books.

Sani, F., & Todman, J. (2006). *Experimental design and statistics for psychology: A first course.* Oxford: Blackwell.

Siegel, S., & Castellan, N. J. (1988). *Nonparametric statistics for the behavioral sciences (2nd ed.).* New York: McGraw-Hill.

Tabachnick, B. G., & Fidell, L. S. (2007). *Using multivariate statistics (5th ed.).* Boston: Allyn & Bacon (Pearson International Edition).

Todman, J., & Dugard, P. (2007). *Approaching multivariate analysis: An introduction for psychology.* London: Psychology Press.

Welch, B.L. (1951). On the comparison of several mean values: An alternative approach. *Biometrika, 38*, 330-336.

Winer, B. J. (1962). *Statistical principles in experimental design.* New York: McGraw-Hill.

Winer, B. J., Brown, D. R., & Michels, K. M. (1991). *Statistical principles in experimental design (3rd ed.).* New York: McGraw-Hill.

Index